"Ideal as a reference for the bookshelf and as a book to curl up and get lost in, this volume will be turned to time and again for definitive instruction on just about any food-related matter."
PUBLISHERS WEEKLY ON *THE SCIENCE OF GOOD COOKING*

"A one-volume kitchen seminar, addressing in one smart chapter after another the sometimes surprising whys behind a cook's best practices. . . . You get the myth, the theory, the science and the proof, all rigorously interrogated as only America's Test Kitchen can do."
NPR ON *THE SCIENCE OF GOOD COOKING*

"The perfect kitchen home companion. The practical side of things is very much on display . . . cook-friendly and kitchen-oriented, illuminating the process of preparing food instead of mystifying it."
THE WALL STREET JOURNAL ON *THE COOK'S ILLUSTRATED COOKBOOK*

"A wonderfully comprehensive guide for budding chefs. . . . Throughout are the helpful tips and exacting illustrations that make ATK a peerless source for culinary wisdom."
PUBLISHERS WEEKLY ON *THE COOK'S ILLUSTRATED COOKBOOK*

"If this were the only cookbook you owned, you would cook well, be everyone's favorite host, have a well-run kitchen, and eat happily every day."
THECITYCOOK.COM ON *THE AMERICA'S TEST KITCHEN MENU COOKBOOK*

"This book upgrades slow cooking for discriminating, 21st-century palates—that is indeed revolutionary."
THE DALLAS MORNING NEWS ON *SLOW COOKER REVOLUTION*

"There are pasta books . . . and then there's this pasta book. Flip your carbohydrate dreams upside down and strain them through this sieve of revolutionary, creative, and also traditional recipes."
SAN FRANCISCO BOOK REVIEW ON *PASTA REVOLUTION*

"Forget about marketing hype, designer labels, and pretentious entrées: This is an unblinking, unbedazzled guide to the Beardian good-cooking ideal."
THE WALL STREET JOURNAL ON *THE BEST OF AMERICA'S TEST KITCHEN 2009*

"Expert bakers and novices scared of baking's requisite exactitude can all learn something from this hefty, all-purpose home baking volume."
PUBLISHERS WEEKLY ON *THE AMERICA'S TEST KITCHEN FAMILY BAKING BOOK*

"This tome definitely raises the bar for all-in-one, basic, must-have cookbooks. . . . Kimball and his company have scored another hit."
THE OREGONIAN ON *THE AMERICA'S TEST KITCHEN FAMILY COOKBOOK*

"A foolproof, go-to resource for everyday cooking."
PUBLISHERS WEEKLY ON *THE AMERICA'S TEST KITCHEN FAMILY COOKBOOK*

"Further proof that practice makes perfect, if not transcendent. . . . If an intermediate cook follows the directions exactly, the results will be better than takeout or Mom's."
THE NEW YORK TIMES ON *THE NEW BEST RECIPE*

"The best instructional book on baking this reviewer has seen."
THE LIBRARY JOURNAL (STARRED REVIEW) ON *BAKING ILLUSTRATED*

THE BEST OF

America's
TEST KITCHEN

**THE YEAR'S BEST RECIPES,
EQUIPMENT REVIEWS, AND TASTINGS**

2014

BY THE EDITORS AT
AMERICA'S TEST KITCHEN

AMERICA'S TEST KITCHEN
17 Station Street, Brookline, MA 02445

THE BEST OF AMERICA'S TEST KITCHEN 2014
The Year's Best Recipes, Equipment Reviews, and Tastings

1st Edition

Hardcover: $35 US
ISBN-13: 978-1-936493-54-8 ISBN-10: 1-936493-54-3
ISSN: 1940-3925

Manufactured in the United States of America

10 9 8 7 6 5 4 3 2 1

Distributed by America's Test Kitchen
17 Station Street, Brookline, MA 02445

EDITORIAL DIRECTOR: Jack Bishop
EDITORIAL DIRECTOR, BOOKS: Elizabeth Carduff
EXECUTIVE EDITOR: Lori Galvin
ASSOCIATE EDITOR: Alyssa King
DESIGN DIRECTOR: Amy Klee
ART DIRECTOR: Greg Galvan
ASSOCIATE ART DIRECTOR: Beverly Hsu
DESIGNER: Allison Pfiffner
FRONT COVER PHOTOGRAPH: Carl Tremblay
STAFF PHOTOGRAPHER: Daniel J. van Ackere
ADDITIONAL PHOTOGRAPHY BY: Keller + Keller, Carl Tremblay, and Steve Klise
FOOD STYLING: Marie Piraino and Mary Jane Sawyer
PHOTOSHOOT KITCHEN TEAM:
    ASSOCIATE EDITOR: Chris O'Connor
    TEST COOK: Daniel Cellucci
    ASSISTANT TEST COOK: Cecelia Jenkins
ILLUSTRATOR: John Burgoyne
PRODUCTION DIRECTOR: Guy Rochford
SENIOR PRODUCTION MANAGER: Jessica Quirk
SENIOR PROJECT MANAGER: Alice Carpenter
PRODUCTION AND TRAFFIC COORDINATOR: Brittany Allen
WORKFLOW AND DIGITAL ASSET MANAGER: Andrew Mannone
SENIOR COLOR AND IMAGING SPECIALIST: Lauren Pettapiece
PRODUCTION AND IMAGING SPECIALISTS: Heather Dube and Lauren Robbins
PROOFREADER: Barbara Wood
INDEXER: Elizabeth Parson

PICTURED ON THE FRONT COVER: Best Chocolate Tart (page 261)

CONTENTS

STARTERS & SALADS

CLASSIC SHRIMP COCKTAIL

CLASSIC SHRIMP COCKTAIL

✓ **WHY THIS RECIPE WORKS** Shrimp cocktail is a party classic, but it rarely does justice to the occasion: The shrimp are overcooked, rubbery, and flavorless and served with a sugary-sweet cocktail sauce. To ensure perfectly cooked shrimp, we favored a gentle poaching method. We start them in cool water flavored with thyme, peppercorns, bay leaves, and celery seeds. We bring the water to a gentle simmer, then kill the heat and cover the pot. When the shrimp are pink and tender, we add ice to stop the cooking process. Finally, we developed a traditional cocktail sauce of ketchup and horseradish flavored with lemon juice, Worcestershire, and Old Bay that perfectly complements the sweet shrimp.

Every year for Christmas Eve dinner, my uncle buys a big plastic tray of shrimp cocktail from his local seafood shop. You know the setup: Cooked shrimp are arranged in concentric circles around a tub of cocktail sauce. It looks festive, sure, but the positive impression dissipates at the first bite of a rubbery, watery shrimp and the ho-hum, oversweetened cocktail sauce. I knew I could do better.

I started at the supermarket. As soon as shrimp are harvested, their bodies are immediately flash-frozen. So (with few exceptions) the "fresh" shrimp I was seeing at the seafood counter were actually frozen shrimp that the grocer had thawed. If I couldn't get truly fresh shrimp, I thought it would be better to start with frozen shrimp so I could control the thawing myself, and so the shrimp wouldn't sit in a pool of liquid for days. Frozen shrimp come three ways: peeled and deveined; "EZ peel," with the shell cut down the back, the vein removed, and the shell left on; and whole, with the shell intact. Peeled and deveined shrimp curled up too tightly when cooked, and the EZ peel shrimp I tested had often been mangled during processing. I decided that I would use whole, shell-on shrimp and make them EZ peel myself by snipping the shells and deveining them. Shrimp prepared this way didn't curl when cooked, plus cooking them with the shells added flavor.

With my shrimp ready for cooking, I moved on to the method, which for shrimp cocktail is traditionally poaching. Poaching shrimp doesn't seem complicated,

so I was surprised when the recipes I'd gathered produced shrimp almost as bland and overcooked as the ones from the plastic tray. It was easy to see where the recipes went wrong: They called for boiling the shrimp, the culinary equivalent of flying down the interstate at 100 miles an hour and hoping you don't miss your exit. The delicate shrimp needed a gentler method.

Since boiling was out, what about bringing water to a boil, turning off the heat, and then adding the shrimp? To infuse the shrimp with flavor, I made a flavorful poaching liquid, adding thyme, peppercorns, bay leaves, and celery seeds to the water. A hefty amount of salt helped to season the shrimp throughout. I brought this liquid to a boil, turned off the burner, and added the prepared shrimp. By the time the water had cooled to room temperature, the shrimp were perfect on the outside—but unfortunately, not quite cooked through. I decided to switch my approach and try the opposite method, adding the shrimp to cold water, which I would then bring just to a boil.

These shrimp were a tad overcooked, but I knew I was on the right track. After much trial and error, I landed on the following method: Add the shrimp and seasonings to cold water in a large pot, turn the burner on, bring the liquid to 170 degrees (hot, but still a good 42 degrees away from boiling), and then pull the pot off the heat and let it sit, covered, for about 5 minutes. I refined the technique further by adding lemon juice and zest after turning off the heat (due to its high acidity, adding the lemon juice at the beginning of cooking made the shrimp too tough). Finally, I stirred in some ice at the end to cool the shrimp and prevent them from overcooking. Now my method consistently produced tender, juicy, and flavorful shrimp.

As for the cocktail sauce, I started with the standard mix of ketchup and prepared horseradish, and I added Worcestershire sauce for depth, lemon for brightness, Old Bay for seasoning, and a pinch of cayenne to wake things up. This sauce was robust and balanced but didn't overpower the shrimp. With my perfectly tender shrimp on ice surrounding my cocktail sauce, I called my tasters and watched the shrimp vanish. Uncle Mark, this year the shrimp are my treat.

—NICK IVERSON, *Cook's Country*

Shrimp Cocktail

SERVES 6 TO 8

We prefer to buy frozen shrimp and thaw them just before cooking; to thaw shrimp, place them in a colander under cold running water. The shrimp and sauce may be made up to 24 hours in advance and refrigerated.

SHRIMP

- 2 pounds shell-on jumbo shrimp (16 to 20 per pound)
- 2½ tablespoons salt
- 10 sprigs fresh thyme
- 2 teaspoons peppercorns
- 3 bay leaves
- ½ teaspoon celery seeds
- 8 (2-inch) strips lemon zest plus ¼ cup juice, spent halves reserved (2 lemons)
- 8 cups ice

COCKTAIL SAUCE

- 1 cup ketchup
- ¼ cup prepared horseradish
- 1 teaspoon lemon juice
- 1 teaspoon Worcestershire sauce
- ½ teaspoon Old Bay seasoning
- ⅛ teaspoon cayenne pepper

NOTES FROM THE TEST KITCHEN

PREPPING SHRIMP FOR POACHING

We cook the shrimp in their shells to prevent the shrimp from curling and to add flavor to the poaching liquid. You still need to do a little advance prep, though.

1. Use kitchen shears to cut through meat and top shell of each shrimp along vein line.

2. Pull out, then discard, vein from each shrimp. Now you're ready to poach.

1. FOR THE SHRIMP: Using kitchen shears, cut through top shell of shrimp along vein line. Leave shell on and remove and discard vein. Combine shrimp, 4 cups cold water, salt, thyme, peppercorns, bay leaves, and celery seeds in Dutch oven. Set pot over medium-high heat and cook, stirring occasionally, until water registers 170 degrees and shrimp are just beginning to turn pink, 5 to 7 minutes.

2. Remove from heat and add lemon zest and juice and spent halves. Cover and let sit until shrimp are completely pink and firm, 5 to 7 minutes. Stir ice into pot and let shrimp cool completely, about 5 minutes. Drain shrimp in colander and peel, leaving tails intact. Refrigerate shrimp until ready to serve.

3. FOR THE COCKTAIL SAUCE: Whisk all ingredients together in bowl until combined. Serve sauce with shrimp.

SAUSAGE BALLS

✓ **WHY THIS RECIPE WORKS** Sausage balls are a popular Southern party snack made by mixing sausage and cheese with biscuit mix. Most recipes are addictive, but overly salty and greasy. We wanted to balance the sausage and cheese flavor without losing sight of the biscuit. First we cut down the grease by cutting back on sausage, cheese, and butter. To keep the balls tender and help them to hold together, we added tangy, low-fat buttermilk. Sharp cheddar cheese plus a pinch of cayenne and black pepper was all we needed to give these crispy, meaty, buttery treats bold flavor.

Sausage balls, sometimes called sausage biscuits, are a fast, easy, habit-forming Southern party treat. The simplest recipe is nothing more than Bisquick, butter, raw bulk breakfast sausage, and a bag of preshredded cheese mixed together, formed into balls about the size of Ping-Pong balls, and baked on a sheet pan until golden brown. They are—that is, they should be—robustly flavored and deliciously rich.

I spent a morning preparing sausage ball recipes that I'd found in Southern and community cookbooks as well as online. Then I summoned tasters. The consensus? These sausage balls were too much of a good thing: too salty, too greasy, too much stuff packed into them. It was "overkill," as one taster put it. On the positive side, my task was clear: I needed to cut the salt, cut the grease, and reconsider the more-is-more philosophy of the recipes I had tried.

First, I'd lose the Bisquick. In combination with the sausage, it added too much salt. More important, I could make a cheaper, fresher-tasting facsimile in seconds. To do so, I combined 1½ cups of flour with ¾ teaspoon of baking powder and a mere ¼ teaspoon of salt (to yield three dozen balls). Next I inserted my flour-leavener mix into the recipe that we liked best from my initial test.

In round one, the sausage balls had left oily slicks on our fingers, napkins, and plates—just reading the recipes made me want to wash my hands. There was no mystery about why: My working recipe called for a very generous 3 cups of cheese, ¾ pound of sausage meat, and 4 tablespoons of butter. Cutting back gradually in a series of tests, I ultimately reduced the cheese to a single cup, cut the sausage to ½ pound, and halved the butter to 2 tablespoons. Now the biscuits were no longer greasy and had balanced amounts of cheese, meat, and butter—all nicely distributed, thanks to a quick whirl in the food processor.

Unfortunately, by cutting back, I'd inadvertently caused a new problem: There simply wasn't enough fat to hold the sausage balls together. Forming the now-dry dough into balls was challenging, and when I managed it, the baked balls were tough and crumbly. Since sausage balls are a cross between biscuits and meatballs, why not add buttermilk, which is often used to moisten and tenderize biscuit dough and is low fat to boot? After a few batches, I found that ¾ cup of buttermilk—plus a little extra baking powder to keep the sausage balls from turning dense—added to the dough ensured that the sausage balls came together. It also reinforced the delicate balance between biscuit and meatball, keeping one from overwhelming the other.

I put together a new batch to see how much headway I'd made. The sausage balls held together nicely, but their flavor was flat—more collateral damage from reducing the amounts of cheese, sausage, and butter. Switching to sharp cheddar cheese, rather than the mild cheddar I had been using, went a long way toward solving that problem, and hits of cayenne and black pepper reinvigorated the flavor.

I tallied my changes and made a new batch. I baked the sausage balls for about 20 minutes, fended off tasters for a further 5 minutes to let the balls cool, then watched in satisfaction as these crispy, cheesy, meaty,

peppery treats disappeared. Part meatball, part cheese biscuit, and part sausage breakfast sandwich, these sausage balls were entirely delicious.

—CAROLYNN PURPURA MACKAY, *Cook's Country*

Sausage Balls

MAKES 3 DOZEN BALLS

The test kitchen's favorite sharp cheddar is Cabot Sharp Vermont Cheddar Cheese. Do not overmix the dough or the sausage balls will be tough.

- 1½ cups (7½ ounces) all-purpose flour
- 1 teaspoon baking powder
- ¼ teaspoon salt
- ¼ teaspoon pepper
- ⅛ teaspoon cayenne pepper
- 2 tablespoons unsalted butter, cut into ½-inch pieces
- 8 ounces bulk breakfast sausage
- 4 ounces sharp cheddar cheese, shredded (1 cup)
- ¾ cup buttermilk

1. Adjust oven rack to middle position and heat oven to 400 degrees. Line rimmed baking sheet with parchment paper. Pulse flour, baking powder, salt, pepper, and cayenne in food processor until combined, about 3 pulses. Add butter and pulse until mixture resembles coarse meal, about 12 pulses. Add sausage and cheddar and pulse until combined, about 8 pulses. Transfer mixture to bowl and stir in buttermilk until just combined.

2. Working with wet hands, roll 1 tablespoon dough at a time into 1¼-inch balls and place, evenly spaced, on baking sheet. Bake until golden brown, 20 to 22 minutes, rotating baking sheet halfway through baking. Transfer baking sheet to wire rack and let balls cool for 5 minutes. Serve warm.

NOTES FROM THE TEST KITCHEN

DON'T MAKE THIS MISTAKE: TOO MUCH FAT

To make our Sausage Balls less greasy, we cut back on sausage, cheese, and butter. But don't worry—they still have plenty of flavor.

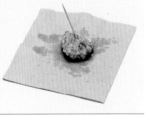

REDUCED-FAT BUFFALO WINGS

✔ **WHY THIS RECIPE WORKS** Fried to a golden brown and tossed in a buttery hot sauce, Buffalo wings are a once-in-a-while treat. To enjoy this American classic on any game day, not just the big one, we set out to lighten them up. We started by ditching the fryer in favor of baked wings. Tossing the wings with baking powder helped to dry out the skin so it became crisp when roasted in a super-hot oven; setting the wings on a wire rack let the rendered fat drip away for even more crispness. A quick stint under the broiler crisped the skin further and ensured a flavorful char. To lighten the fiery Buffalo sauce, we cut back on the butter. A single tablespoon was enough to temper the hot sauce and give it a glossy sheen. A spoonful of molasses added depth and richness to our made-over yet still finger-licking-good Buffalo wings.

While there is some fuzziness around the origin of Buffalo wings, the barroom sensation of crispy fried chicken wings tossed in a buttery hot sauce is generally traced back to the Anchor Bar in Buffalo, NY, circa 1964. The pub staple quickly transcended its local roots, becoming a mainstay on bar menus across the country. Given their widespread appeal, I knew that facing a kitchen full of wing lovers with anything less than an authentic recreation would be disastrous.

First, I did some research to see just how conventional Buffalo wings measure up. At Buffalo Wild Wings, a national chain specializing in chicken wings, a serving of just six pieces with their traditional Buffalo sauce clocks in at 670 calories and a whopping 55 grams of fat. I heard a collective thud as my colleagues' jaws hit the floor. Could I find a way to trim the fat, or would Buffalo wings be off the menu for good?

Even before I looked at cooking methods and high-fat sauces, I had to face facts: Chicken wings are the fattiest part of the chicken. Consider their meat-to-skin ratio; since chickens don't use their wings to fly, the paltry amount of muscle mass on a chicken wing pales in comparison to the surface area of the skin that surrounds it. Much of the wing is tendon, bone, and cartilage, so the real attraction in chicken wings is the skin. If I removed the skin, I would cut the fat of the dish exponentially, but would it still be worth eating?

I went into the kitchen, ready to do battle with chicken skin. But while skin peels away from cooked chicken easily, the skin on the raw wings was annoyingly stubborn. The skin on the drumettes (the parts that look like miniature drumsticks) yielded more easily, but the skin on the flats was all but impossible to remove. I wondered if partially cooking the wings would make things easier, so I tried blanching them for a few minutes before skinning. This method proved a nonstarter. While some of the skin gave way, I still had to deal with the interconnectedness of the joints, muscle, and tendons. In many places, it was impossible to remove the skin without severing the tendons that held the meat to the bone. What was the use of going to the trouble of making skinless chicken wings if the resulting wings were meatless as well?

Clearly I would have to leave the skin intact and find another way to slash fat and calories from the dish. That left only the cooking method and the sauce. First I turned my attention to the cooking method. Finding an alternative to deep-fat frying was a no-brainer. But there was no point in going to the trouble of trimming this recipe if it meant losing its hallmark crispy skin.

Roasting seemed the natural alternative to frying, since it would not require additional fat. To get the crispiest skin and the most flavor, I would need to focus on achieving good browning. Since the Maillard effect of browning cannot occur in the presence of moisture, getting the skin completely dry before roasting and using a high oven temperature seemed my best bet. I patted the wings dry with paper towels and spread them on a sheet pan in a super-hot oven. This method did render some of the wings' fat, but the skin didn't become crisp before the meat reached 175 degrees.

I remembered a test kitchen recipe for crispy roast chicken that used baking powder in the rub to achieve super-crisp skin. Since baking powder contributes to the skin's dehydration, it helps crisp the skin during roasting. This time, after patting the wings dry, I tossed them with a tablespoon of baking powder. The resulting wings were noticeably crisper, although the skin remained flabby in places, and I noticed that the rendered fat was pooling under the wings on the sheet pan.

For my next test, I put the wings on a rack to allow the rendered fat to drip onto the sheet pan below, as in a rotisserie. These wings were the crispest yet. Elevating the wings above the pan had also exposed more surface area to the heat, so even more fat rendered from the wings, leaving them both leaner and crisper. In fact, tasters were generally pleased with this batch. The only

REDUCED-FAT BUFFALO WINGS

MAKING OVER BUFFALO WINGS

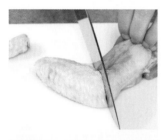

1. To prep wings, use kitchen shears or sharp chef's knife to cut through wing at two joints and discard wingtip.

2. We toss our wings with baking powder to help draw moisture from the skin so that it gets super-crisp when baked.

3. We roast the wings in a hot oven on a wire rack set in a rimmed baking sheet so the rendered fat drains away, then we run them under the broiler for skin as crispy as deep-fried.

4. Finally, we toss our super-crisp, browned wings in our lightened yet full-flavored sauce.

THE BEST HOT SAUCE

A great hot sauce is essential for great Buffalo wings, and the hot-sauce industry has never been, well, hotter. A stroll down the condiment aisle reveals a dizzying array of bottles. To find the best one for flavoring our Buffalo wings, we tasted eight top sellers. The winner would have to pack more than just a fiery punch; we wanted something that balanced heat, bright tanginess, and all-around good chile flavor. While a few samples delivered only sharp, vinegary shots of heat, **Frank's RedHot Original Cayenne Pepper Sauce** revealed more complex, nuanced flavors with hints of sweetness and smokiness and a heat that added to the chicken rather than overpowering it.

complaint was a lack of browning. Finishing the wings under the broiler solved that problem, giving them beautifully golden-brown skin. Reducing the roasting time slightly ensured that the wings didn't overcook while they broiled. Finally, my wings were crisp and browned enough to please my wing-loving tasters—and to withstand a toss in Buffalo sauce without becoming soggy.

With my cooking method perfected, it was time to examine the sauce. The test kitchen's recipe for Buffalo sauce is simple and classic: Frank's RedHot Sauce (our sauce of choice for authentic Buffalo wings), dark brown sugar, cider vinegar, and 4 tablespoons of butter. After all the work I had done to reduce the fat in my wings, the last thing I wanted was to dunk them in a buttery sauce. Since the hot sauce was the key to the classic Buffalo flavor, I added just enough butter to balance its vinegary heat. One tablespoon of butter provided sufficient richness. Then, to balance the heat with some sweetness, I swapped the brown sugar for molasses, which contributed body and a deep, caramelized note to the sauce.

No one would mistake my reduced-fat Buffalo wings for bland health food, but at 380 calories and 25 grams of fat per serving, I had slashed over half the fat and over 45 percent of the calories from a typical serving of fried wings without losing the classic flavor or the crispy skin. Tasters agreed that we could handle that kind of indulgence from time to time.

—CHRISTIE MORRISON, America's Test Kitchen Books

Reduced-Fat Buffalo Wings

SERVES 4

The mild flavor of Frank's RedHot Original Cayenne Pepper Sauce is crucial to the flavor of this dish; we don't suggest substituting other brands of hot sauce here.

> 3 **pounds chicken wings, halved at joint and wingtips removed, trimmed**
> 1 **tablespoon baking powder**
> ½ **teaspoon salt**
> ⅔ **cup Frank's RedHot Original Cayenne Pepper Sauce**
> 1 **tablespoon unsalted butter, melted**
> 1 **tablespoon molasses**

1. Adjust oven rack to middle position and heat oven to 475 degrees. Line rimmed baking sheet with aluminum foil and top with wire rack. Pat wings dry with paper towels, then toss with baking powder and salt in bowl. Arrange wings in single layer on wire rack. Roast wings until golden on both sides, about 40 minutes, flipping wings over and rotating sheet halfway through roasting.

2. Meanwhile, whisk hot sauce, butter, and molasses together in large bowl.

3. Remove wings from oven. Adjust oven rack 6 inches from broiler element and heat broiler. Broil wings until golden brown on both sides, 6 to 8 minutes, flipping wings over halfway through broiling. Add wings to sauce and toss to coat. Serve.

SPINACH SQUARES

☑ **WHY THIS RECIPE WORKS** Spinach squares are a warm, cheesy hors d'oeuvre that's convenient to make with a simple dump-and-stir method, but we found many versions were overly greasy, pale, and one-dimensional in flavor. We cut the grease by cutting back on the cheese and nixing the heavily buttered pan in favor of a light spritz of vegetable oil spray. We banished boring flavor by swapping the cheddar for a combination of nutty Gruyère and Parmesan and exchanging the milk for savory chicken broth. Squeezing the spinach dry prevented our squares from turning soggy. Increasing the oven temperature, cooking the squares on the upper-middle rack, and sprinkling more Parmesan over the squares gave us a deeply browned, crisp top.

A simple stir-and-bake technique, loads of cheese flavor, and finger-food ease have made this spinach hors d'oeuvre a harried host's helper for decades. I found recipes for spinach squares in dozens of Junior League and church recipe booklets, and like many easy, cheesy, crowd-pleasing recipes, this one is an Internet sensation.

The most basic spinach squares are made with cheddar cheese, chopped spinach, eggs, milk, baking powder, minced onion, and flour. Stir everything together, add the mixture to a baking dish slathered with melted butter, and bake it at 350 degrees for about a half-hour. Over the years, cooks have added their own touches: trading cheddar for different cheeses, using fresh instead of frozen spinach, and adding red pepper flakes or cayenne for a little heat.

I made a few batches, starting with one basic recipe plus a few variations. The simplest recipe wasn't bad; it sliced up neatly, like brownies, and had decent cheese flavor. But it left us with greasy fingers, and beyond the cheese flavor there wasn't much going on. Tasters found Monterey Jack versions too tame but praised Parmesan for its salty, nutty punch. Surprisingly, fresh spinach didn't perform any better than frozen (which I defrosted and squeezed dry), and we agreed that the convenience of prechopped frozen spinach was a holiday-season must. Crusty brown edges were a plus; pale centers and greasy bottoms, major problems.

Most recipes called for melting several tablespoons of butter in the baking dish before stirring in the spinach mixture. To fix the recurring grease problem, I traded in the butter for a light coating of vegetable oil spray. That got rid of the grease on the bottom of the squares, but tasters still found the whole assembly slightly oily. Decreasing the cheese from 4 cups to 3½ cups cut down on the oiliness and left the squares amply rich, but the missing cheese compounded the blandness problem. I'd have to find a way to add flavor while keeping the grease under control.

I experimented with a variety of cheeses, and while most worked fine, a combination of Gruyère and Parmesan was the favorite with tasters, so I went with that. We liked the heat of a little cayenne, and doubling the amount of onion and adding garlic provided an aromatic background. But something was still missing. My squares were cheesy, sure, but they lacked a robust, savory flavor. I scanned my ingredient list, searching for places to pack in more flavor. The cup of milk caught my eye. I needed liquid to help bind the squares together, but milk is hardly a flavor powerhouse. What if I tried exchanging it for something savory? Chicken broth seemed like an odd choice for this recipe, but I gave it a shot—and it proved perfect. Tasters loved the subtle savoriness and depth of flavor it contributed.

But it wasn't time to hang up my apron yet. The tops of my spinach squares were still pale. To produce the crusty, brown top I was after, first I raised both the oven rack and the oven temperature. Second, I baked the squares for 50 percent longer than most other recipes called for. Luckily, the eggs were sufficiently diluted and stabilized by the flour, broth, cheese, and spinach, so they didn't overcook. Now the edges were crusty, brown, and very flavorful, but the centers were still pale. Instead of mixing the Parmesan into the batter, I tried sprinkling it on top after adding the spinach mixture to the pan.

SPINACH SQUARES

This final change gave me deep, even browning from edge to edge. Mouths full, tasters nodded their approval.

"So you just stir it up and press it into the pan?" they asked incredulously. "No sautéing the onions? No blooming spices? No white sauce base?" Nope. For this holiday party classic, getting big, complex flavor didn't require more work—just a little ingenuity.

—SARAH GABRIEL, *Cook's Country*

Spinach Squares

MAKES 32 SQUARES

You can thaw the spinach in the microwave or overnight in the refrigerator. To squeeze the spinach dry, place it in a clean dish towel, gather the edges, and wring it out. Cooled spinach squares can be refrigerated for up to 24 hours and reheated, covered with foil, in a 375-degree oven.

- 1 **cup (5 ounces) plus 2 tablespoons all-purpose flour**
- 1 **teaspoon baking powder**
- ¾ **teaspoon salt**
- ½ **teaspoon pepper**
- ¼ **teaspoon cayenne pepper**
- 1 **cup chicken broth**
- 3 **large eggs**
- 1¼ **pounds frozen chopped spinach, thawed and squeezed dry**
- 12 **ounces Gruyère cheese, shredded (3 cups)**
- 1 **onion, chopped fine**
- 2 **garlic cloves, minced**
- 1 **ounce Parmesan cheese, grated (½ cup)**

1. Adjust oven rack to upper-middle position and heat oven to 375 degrees. Spray 13 by 9-inch baking dish with vegetable oil spray. Whisk flour, baking powder, salt, pepper, and cayenne together in large bowl. Add broth and eggs and whisk until smooth. Stir in spinach, Gruyère, onion, and garlic until combined.

2. Transfer mixture to prepared baking dish and sprinkle evenly with Parmesan. Bake until browned on top and bubbling around edges, 40 to 45 minutes. Let cool in pan for 20 minutes. Cut into 32 equal-size squares. Serve warm.

VARIATION

Bacon-Cheddar Spinach Squares

Cook 6 slices bacon in 12-inch nonstick skillet over medium heat until crisp, 5 to 7 minutes; transfer to paper towel–lined plate. When bacon is cool enough to handle, finely chop and set aside. In step 2, substitute cheddar for Gruyère and stir in chopped bacon along with spinach, cheddar, onion, and garlic.

BASIC VINAIGRETTE

✓ **WHY THIS RECIPE WORKS** Making a simple vinaigrette for a fresh green salad should be a snap, but there's one big hitch: To make it, you have to force oil and vinegar to combine. To get the two to emulsify, traditionally you slowly whisk the oil into the vinegar, but even if the dressing comes together at first, it often separates. To solve this problem, we came up with an easy trick. We combine the ingredients in a lidded jar and simply shake until they're well blended. A little mayonnaise and honey provide further emulsifying power to keep the dressing stable and smooth. For the seasonings, we preferred milder shallot to harsh onion and found that soaking the shallot in the vinegar for a few minutes tames its oniony bite. A little mustard along with some salt and pepper, and this vinaigrette is easy, tasty, and versatile.

Classically, vinaigrette is made by mixing together vinegar, seasonings, and sometimes mustard and onion and then ever so slowly whisking in oil (usually three times as much as the amount of vinegar) to emulsify. Whatever you do, take your time, because if you add the oil too quickly, either the dressing will never come together or it will do so for a few brief shining moments and then (oh, the heartbreak) separate.

Fortunately, the test kitchen knows an easier way: We dispense with the whisks, bowls, and towels (for keeping

NOTES FROM THE TEST KITCHEN

SQUEEZING SPINACH DRY

To prevent soggy spinach squares, squeeze the spinach dry before you stir it into the batter. We place the spinach on a clean dish towel, gather the edges, and wring.

BASIC VINAIGRETTE

the bowl from slipping), as well as the slow, exacting drizzle and the long minutes of whisking. Instead, we measure all the ingredients straight into a jar and shake. *Voilà*, vinaigrette. Over the years, we've made countless salads and numerous vinaigrettes, and along the way we've made a few additional discoveries to foolproof and perfect our version. I wanted to pull together all of our accumulated knowledge into one flawless basic vinaigrette recipe.

To begin, we prefer milder shallot to more sulfuric onion. To tame the shallot further, we macerate it in the vinegar. We've found that in just 5 minutes, the acid in the vinegar begins to break down and soften the minced shallot's texture and flavor. Since I knew I'd be using our easy jar method to emulsify my vinaigrette, I simply added the shallot and vinegar right to the jar. Then, when the 5 minutes were up, I added the rest of the ingredients, screwed on the lid, and gave the jar a vigorous shake.

Our easy trick gave me a beautifully blended vinaigrette, but the real test of vinaigrette is whether it stays emulsified. I knew that I'd need to include some emulsifying ingredients to keep the vinaigrette from separating. Mustard has emulsifying qualities, but not in the small quantity I was using (½ teaspoon for 1 tablespoon of vinegar and 3 tablespoons of oil, enough to dress about 8 cups of greens). Any more than that would turn my basic vinaigrette into a mustard vinaigrette, so I needed to find another solution. We've previously used mayonnaise as an emulsifier, so I added just enough to help stabilize the dressing without making it too heavy. I also had another (unlikely) trick up my sleeve: honey. Honey has stabilizing properties, and I hoped that together with the mayonnaise, it would ensure that my dressing emulsified with a 30-second shake—and stayed that way. It worked beautifully, and the sweet honey also nicely rounded out the vinaigrette's flavor. And because a simple vinaigrette offers endless options for easy variations, I came up with a few easy ways to change up the flavors.

My recipe was now foolproof and as easy as could be, plus it's tailor-made for transport. Simply mix the ingredients in a jar, screw the lid on, and carry it to your potluck, picnic, or cookout.

—NICK IVERSON, *Cook's Country*

MINCING SHALLOTS

1. Make several closely spaced parallel cuts through peeled shallot, leaving root end intact.

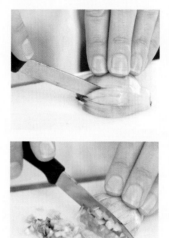

2. Next, make several cuts lengthwise through shallot.

3. Finally, thinly slice shallot crosswise, creating fine mince.

THE BEST SALAD SPINNER

All salad spinners share a basic design: a perforated basket that balances on a point in the center of a larger bowl. The lid houses a mechanism that spins the basket, and the resulting centrifugal force propels the contents of the spinner away from the center; greens are trapped while water passes through the perforations and collects in the outer bowl. But even slight differences in design affect how well salad spinners work.

We tested eight spinners with a variety of mechanisms. Our favorite method was the pump: The up-and-down motion takes little effort and doesn't make the spinner dance around on the counter. To test capacity, we recorded how many batches it took each spinner to dry 2 pounds of lettuce. The best performers did it in two, and the worst took four batches. To test drying ability, we weighed the greens before and after washing and spinning. When cleaning the baskets, green baskets obscured any trapped greens; we preferred clear or white baskets. Complicated lids were also harder to clean; our favorite model comes apart for thorough washing and drying. The **OXO Good Grips Salad Spinner**, $29.99, was our all-around favorite. (See page 305 for more information on our testing results.)

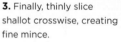

Basic Vinaigrette

MAKES ¼ CUP; ENOUGH FOR 8 TO 10 CUPS GREENS

The vinaigrette will keep for three days in the refrigerator. Shake well before using.

- 1 tablespoon cider vinegar
- 1 teaspoon minced shallot
- 3 tablespoons extra-virgin olive oil
- 1 teaspoon honey
- ½ teaspoon regular or light mayonnaise
- ½ teaspoon Dijon mustard
- ⅛ teaspoon salt
- ⅛ teaspoon pepper

Combine vinegar and shallot in small jar; let sit for 5 minutes. Add oil, honey, mayonnaise, mustard, salt, and pepper to jar, secure lid, and shake vigorously until emulsified, about 30 seconds.

VARIATIONS

Ginger-Sesame Vinaigrette

Substitute rice vinegar for cider vinegar, 1 tablespoon toasted sesame oil for 1 tablespoon olive oil, and Asian chili-garlic sauce for mustard. Add ½ teaspoon grated fresh ginger before shaking.

Lemon-Herb Vinaigrette

Substitute lemon juice for cider vinegar. Add 1½ teaspoons minced fresh thyme, 1 teaspoon chopped fresh mint, and ¼ teaspoon lemon zest before shaking.

Spicy Anchovy-Garlic Vinaigrette

Substitute balsamic vinegar for cider vinegar. Add 1 rinsed, dried, and minced anchovy fillet; ¼ teaspoon minced garlic; and ¼ teaspoon red pepper flakes before shaking.

Tarragon-Caper Vinaigrette

Substitute red wine vinegar for cider vinegar. Add 1½ teaspoons minced fresh parsley, 1½ teaspoons minced fresh tarragon, and ½ teaspoon minced rinsed capers before shaking.

GRILLED CAESAR SALAD

✔ WHY THIS RECIPE WORKS Grilled salad may seem like an oxymoron, but we were intrigued by the idea of the flavors of a classic Caesar salad enriched with the smoky char of the grill. To make the theory work in practice, we found that compact romaine hearts held their shape better than whole heads. We halved them lengthwise to increase their surface area, making sure to keep the core intact so the leaves didn't fall apart on the grill. Just 1 to 2 minutes over a hot grill gave us a smoky, charred exterior without wilting the whole heart. Brushing some of the dressing on the romaine before grilling kept the leaves from sticking to the grill and gave the dressing deeper flavor. To keep things simple, we replaced the croutons (which required us to heat the oven) with slices of crusty bread grilled alongside the lettuce.

Grill Caesar salad? Introduce delicate lettuce to a bed of hot coals? It sounded like a terrible idea. But as I paged through recipes, the universally enthusiastic descriptions piqued my interest. The smoky char of the grill, I read, brings a whole new dimension to Caesar salad.

Curious, I gave a few recipes a try—and my doubts returned. On the grill, the lettuce quickly scorched and wilted. At least that made the challenge clear: maintaining crispness while developing smokiness and char. Also, several recipes called for baking the croutons in the oven, which seemed crazy. Since the grill was already going, obviously I should grill them alongside the lettuce to let them develop some smoke flavor and char of their own.

I did pick up a few good ideas, though. To begin, I'd use romaine hearts, not heads. The hearts were sturdier and more compact, making them better able to withstand the heat. Also, before grilling, I'd halve them lengthwise, keeping the core attached. This gave them plenty of surface area to develop char while preventing the leaves from falling into the fire. To improve the odds of getting softness and char, as opposed to limpness, I'd grill the hearts on just one side.

I started again, brushing the halved romaine hearts with oil to encourage char and minimize sticking and then grilling them over a medium-hot fire. In 5 minutes, I had smokiness and char. Unfortunately, I also had wilted, slimy lettuce. I needed to get the surface to char faster so that the heat wouldn't have time to penetrate (read: wilt) the inner leaves. Well, then how about a hot fire? This worked much better; within a minute or two, the romaine had both distinct char and a crunchy interior.

For the dressing, I started with a test kitchen recipe that keeps things simple by using mayonnaise in place of the classic raw egg. Into the blender with the mayo went Parmesan, garlic (which I macerated in lemon juice to tame its flavor slightly), vinegar, Worcestershire sauce, and anchovies. The dressing was bold, well seasoned, and delicious—in fact, it was so good that I got the idea to brush it on the uncooked lettuce in place of the olive oil I'd been using. I brushed it on the cut side of the romaine and set the hearts on the grill. Happily, the emulsion held, and in just 1 minute over the heat the dressing picked up a mildly smoky, toasty flavor.

Next I needed to find a way to incorporate the croutons. Of course grilling small cubes of bread wasn't an option; they'd simply fall through the grill grates. What if I replaced the traditional croutons with slices of grilled bread, served with a romaine heart on top? I cut a baguette into slices on the bias, brushed them with olive oil, and toasted them over the coals. Borrowing a common technique for bruschetta, I added subtle flavor to the grilled bread by rubbing the slices with a cut raw garlic clove.

I combined the grilled romaine with the grilled bread, drizzled on extra dressing, dusted everything with more Parmesan, and called my tasters. The salad disappeared and so did my skepticism. With apologies to Shakespeare: It's not that I love Caesar less, but that I love grilled Caesar more.

—CRISTIN WALSH, *Cook's Country*

NOTES FROM THE TEST KITCHEN

DRESSING GRILLED CAESAR SALAD

1. Brush Caesar dressing onto the halved romaine hearts before grilling.

2. Grill the dressed romaine halves on just one side, to keep the lettuce from wilting.

3. Once the lettuce comes off the grill, finish with more dressing.

Grilled Caesar Salad

SERVES 6

Leave the core of the romaine intact to keep the leaves from falling apart on the grill.

DRESSING

- 1 tablespoon lemon juice
- 1 garlic clove, minced
- ½ cup mayonnaise
- ½ ounce Parmesan cheese, grated (¼ cup)
- 1 tablespoon white wine vinegar
- 1 tablespoon Worcestershire sauce
- 1 tablespoon Dijon mustard
- 2 anchovy fillets, rinsed
- ½ teaspoon salt
- ½ teaspoon pepper
- ¼ cup extra-virgin olive oil

SALAD

- 1 (12-inch) baguette, cut on bias into 5-inch-long, ½-inch-thick slices
- 3 tablespoons extra-virgin olive oil
- 1 garlic clove, peeled
- 3 romaine lettuce hearts (18 ounces), halved lengthwise through core
- ½ ounce Parmesan cheese, grated (¼ cup)

1. FOR THE DRESSING: Combine lemon juice and garlic in small bowl and let stand for 10 minutes. Process lemon-garlic mixture, mayonnaise, Parmesan, vinegar, Worcestershire, mustard, anchovies, salt, and pepper in blender until smooth, about 30 seconds. With blender running, slowly add oil until incorporated. Reserve 6 tablespoons dressing for brushing romaine.

2A. FOR A CHARCOAL GRILL: Open bottom vent completely. Light large chimney starter filled with charcoal briquettes (6 quarts). When top coals are partially covered with ash, pour evenly over half of grill. Set cooking grate in place, cover, and open lid vent completely. Heat grill until hot, about 5 minutes.

2B. FOR A GAS GRILL: Turn all burners to high, cover, and heat grill until hot, about 15 minutes. Leave all burners on high.

3. FOR THE SALAD: Clean and oil cooking grate. Brush bread all over with oil. Grill bread (directly over coals if using charcoal), uncovered, until well browned on both sides, about 1 minute per side. Transfer to platter. Lightly rub 1 side of grilled bread with garlic clove.

4. Brush cut sides of romaine with reserved dressing. Place half of romaine, cut side down, on grill (directly over coals if using charcoal). Grill, uncovered, until lightly charred, 1 to 2 minutes. Transfer to platter with grilled bread. Repeat with remaining romaine. Drizzle romaine evenly with remaining dressing to taste. Sprinkle with Parmesan and serve.

FENNEL SALAD

✓ **WHY THIS RECIPE WORKS** The sweet anise flavor of a sliced fennel salad makes a refreshing and elegant change from more familiar vegetable salads such as slaws. We quickly learned that, much like meat, fennel needs to be sliced against the grain to prevent tough, fibrous strands. We made a simple vinaigrette livened up with honey, lemon, and Dijon; mixed it with the fennel, sliced red onion, golden raisins, and capers; and let it sit to mellow the onion's bite and allow the flavors to meld. Right before serving, we tossed in whole parsley leaves and crunchy sliced almonds.

If you don't know fresh fennel—with its mild licorice flavor and celery-like crunch—you're in for a treat. A great way to get to know this underused (at least

PREPARING FENNEL

1. Cut off tops and feathery fronds, then trim very thin slice from base.

2. Cut bulb in half through base. Use small sharp knife to remove pyramid-shaped core.

3. Slice fennel against grain to shorten fibers so fennel won't be stringy in salad.

in the United States) vegetable is thinly sliced in salad. Since fennel is a classic Mediterranean ingredient, I decided I'd look there for inspiration. I rounded up and tested five fennel salad recipes, each with somewhat different ingredients and methods. After tasting them, I knew I wanted an assertive salad with a balance of sweet, salty, slightly sour, and bitter flavors.

For sweetness, I threw a handful of raisins into a salad bowl, and for the salty component, capers. Thinly sliced red onion added pungency, and Italian flat-leaf parsley added an herbal note. Tasters so liked the addition of the parsley that I decided to treat it more like a green, tossing in whole leaves instead of mincing it, so it would make even more of an impact.

My salad was coming together nicely, but I found myself wondering why the fennel was fibrous and stringy in some tests and pleasantly crunchy in others. It turns out that there's a right way and a wrong way to cut fennel. As with meat, cutting fennel against the

FENNEL SALAD

grain—or, in this case, fibers—shortens the fibers, which makes the slices less stringy.

For the vinaigrette, olive oil was a given, and I liked fresh lemon juice for its bright, cheery flavor; I balanced the lemon with a little honey. Dijon mustard helped emulsify the vinaigrette and added bite that nicely balanced the sweetness of the honey and raisins. I mixed the fennel slices with the other salad ingredients and poured on the dressing. The onion came on way too strong. For my next batch, I'd try letting the onion slices macerate briefly in some of the vinaigrette to tame their flavor—a method we often use with vinaigrettes in the test kitchen. I tossed the vinaigrette with the raisins and capers, then, as I was about to stir in the onion, it occurred to me to add the fennel as well. I let both vegetables sit in the vinaigrette for 30 minutes, which served to soften the onion's raw bite and to season the fennel. Just before serving, I stirred in the parsley and some sliced almonds for crunch. My salad, a mix of bright colors, lively flavors, and contrasting textures, was an edible advertisement for fennel.

—DIANE UNGER, *Cook's Country*

Fennel Salad
SERVES 4 TO 6

- ¼ cup extra-virgin olive oil
- 3 tablespoons lemon juice
- 2 teaspoons Dijon mustard
- 2 teaspoons honey
  Salt and pepper
- 2 fennel bulbs, stalks discarded, bulbs halved, cored, and sliced thin crosswise
- ½ red onion, halved through root end and sliced thin crosswise
- ½ cup golden raisins, chopped
- 3 tablespoons capers, rinsed and minced
- ½ cup fresh parsley leaves
- ½ cup sliced almonds, toasted

1. Whisk oil, lemon juice, mustard, honey, 1 teaspoon salt, and 1 teaspoon pepper together in large bowl. Add fennel, onion, raisins, and capers and toss to combine. Cover and refrigerate for 30 minutes to allow flavors to blend.

2. Stir in parsley and almonds. Season with salt and pepper to taste and serve.

CITRUS SALADS

✔ **WHY THIS RECIPE WORKS** Savory salads made with oranges and grapefruit are an impressive way to showcase colorful winter fruit—but only if you can tame the bitterness of the grapefruit and prevent the fruit's ample juice from drowning the other components. We started by treating the fruit with salt to counter its bitter notes (a technique we've used in the past with coffee and eggplant). Draining the seasoned fruit enabled us to preemptively remove the excess juice, and reserving some to use in the dressing for the salad greens helped to make the salad more cohesive. Toasted, salted nuts added richness that contrasted nicely with the fruit and the assertively flavored greens, and dried fruit added texture and sweetness.

Call it fate: Smack in the middle of the coldest part of the year, just as the hefty braises of winter begin to pall on us, citrus season begins, swooping in with brilliant hues and bracing flavors. But we rarely take full advantage, usually limiting ourselves to eating oranges out of hand and grapefruits only at breakfast. A more impressive setting for these seasonal fruits is a salad, and savory versions—augmented with crisp greens, crunchy nuts, and dried fruit—provide a particularly nice contrast.

For bold color, I decided to use both red grapefruits and navel oranges (the latter easily could be switched out for other varieties like blood oranges or tangelos). Painstakingly trimming the citrus into slim, membrane-free segments (or supremes) was too time-consuming, and simply dicing the flesh into chunks left diners contending with large, chewy pieces of membrane. I compromised and sliced the halved, peeled fruits into delicate half-moons that were easy on the eye and free of big chunks of membrane.

To complement the bright citrus, I mixed together peppery watercress, chopped pecans (toasted in butter for extra richness), and sweet dried cranberries. But when I dressed the citrus with a simple vinaigrette of olive oil, vinegar, mustard, and shallot and tossed it with the other components, the results were disheartening. The assertive grapefruits overpowered even these hearty flavors, and the heavier ingredients sank to the bottom of the bowl while the dressed greens sat blandly on top.

To temper the grapefruits' sourness, I seasoned them with a bit of sugar and also salt—a trick we use to tone down bitterness in foods like eggplant and coffee.

Rather than attempt to defy gravity's influence on the weighty fruit and nuts, I embraced it by composing the salad instead of tossing it: I arranged the citrus slices on a platter, dressed the watercress, and set the greens on top of the fruit. Finally, I scattered the nuts and dried cranberries over the top.

This attempt was better, but now the citrus juice pooled so heavily at the bottom of the salad that it threatened to overflow the platter. That's because the salt I had sprinkled on the fruit was pulling out much of its liquid. And there were other problems: The fruit and greens seemed like two distinct salads connected only by proximity, the oil in the vinaigrette had caused the watercress to wilt, and the vinegar combined with the grapefruit made the salad way too sour.

To remove excess liquid, I treated both the sliced grapefruits and oranges with salt, let their tangy juices drain off, and reserved them before plating the citrus. Since the olive oil had caused the watercress to droop, I drizzled it over the citrus instead, tossing the greens only with mustard, shallot, and some reserved juice instead of the vinegar. I mixed half of the nuts and cranberries into the greens and sprinkled the remainder on top.

This salad was pleasantly juicy but not swimming in liquid, and the flavors and textures were well integrated and complementary. As a last step, I devised a few variations, trading the watercress for arugula, radicchio, or napa cabbage; the cranberries for golden raisins, dates, or dried cherries; and the pecans for walnuts, rich smoked almonds, or cashews. Now citrus salads can light up my table all winter long.

—ANDREA GEARY, *Cook's Illustrated*

Citrus Salad with Watercress, Dried Cranberries, and Pecans

SERVES 4 TO 6

You may substitute tangelos or Cara Caras for the navel oranges. Valencia and blood oranges can also be used, but because they are smaller, increase the number of fruits to four.

- 2 **red grapefruits**
- 3 **navel oranges**
- 1 **teaspoon sugar**
  Salt and pepper
- 1 **teaspoon unsalted butter**
- ½ **cup pecans, chopped coarse**
- 3 **tablespoons extra-virgin olive oil**
- 1 **small shallot, minced**
- 1 **teaspoon Dijon mustard**
- 4 **ounces (4 cups) watercress, torn into bite-size pieces**
- ⅔ **cup dried cranberries**

1. Cut away peel and pith from grapefruits and oranges. Cut each fruit in half from pole to pole, then slice crosswise into ¼-inch-thick pieces. Transfer fruit to bowl and toss with sugar and ½ teaspoon salt. Set aside for 15 minutes.

2. Melt butter in 8-inch skillet over medium heat. Add pecans and ½ teaspoon salt and cook, stirring often, until lightly browned and fragrant, 2 to 4 minutes. Transfer pecans to paper towel–lined plate and set aside.

3. Drain fruit in colander, reserving 2 tablespoons juice. Transfer fruit to platter, arrange in even layer, and drizzle with oil. Whisk reserved juice, shallot, and mustard together in medium bowl. Add watercress, ⅓ cup cranberries, and ¼ cup reserved pecans and toss to coat. Arrange watercress mixture over fruit, leaving 1-inch border around edges. Sprinkle with remaining ⅓ cup cranberries and remaining ¼ cup reserved pecans. Season with salt and pepper to taste. Serve immediately.

VARIATIONS

Citrus Salad with Arugula, Golden Raisins, and Walnuts

Substitute coarsely chopped walnuts for pecans, arugula for watercress, and ½ cup golden raisins for cranberries.

Citrus Salad with Radicchio, Dates, and Smoked Almonds

Substitute coarsely chopped smoked almonds for pecans, omitting butter and step 2. Substitute 1 small head radicchio, halved, cored, and sliced ¼ inch thick, for watercress and chopped pitted dates for cranberries.

Citrus Salad with Napa Cabbage, Dried Cherries, and Cashews

Substitute coarsely chopped salted roasted cashews for pecans, omitting butter and step 2. Substitute 1 small head napa cabbage, cored and sliced thin, for watercress and dried cherries for cranberries.

AVOCADO SALAD WITH TOMATO AND RADISH

AVOCADO SALADS

✔ WHY THIS RECIPE WORKS In salad, buttery avocados demand an acidic dressing to cut their richness. Using a little mayonnaise as an emulsifier allowed us to make a creamy dressing with equal parts vinegar and olive oil. To add flavor and textural contrast, we steered clear of leafy greens and relied on crunchier vegetables like fennel and radishes and sweet juicy fruits like cherry tomatoes and mango. A garnish of salty cheese was the perfect finishing touch to complement the creamy avocado. Arranging the dressed avocado chunks below the other ingredients maximized visual appeal by preventing the avocado from turning the salad a murky army green.

Once exotic and rare, buttery avocado has become as common a salad ingredient as croutons. And yet your standard leafy salad doesn't really do this fruit justice. Since salad greens and avocado both have mild flavors and delicate textures (not to mention similar colors), the effect is often uninspiring. Worse, tossing ripe avocado with other salad ingredients tends to make it disintegrate, leading to a swampy mess.

But I'm a big avocado fan, and rather than banish it from my salad course altogether, I was determined to find a way to highlight its velvety-smooth texture and subtly rich flavor. First, I turned my attention to the primary problem with salads that include avocados: the dressing, which never seems tailored for the job. Creamy dressings are too rich and often so flavorful that they overwhelm the avocado's mild taste. But I found that a standard vinaigrette of 3 parts olive oil to 1 part vinegar was also too rich; tasters asked for more tartness to balance and brighten the buttery avocado. I tried dressing the salad with only vinegar, but surprisingly tasters found that this version was even less acidic. After some head-scratching, I realized that the vinegar, when not emulsified with oil, couldn't cling to the ingredients and was left pooling at the bottom of the bowl.

I needed an emulsified dressing made with minimal oil, so I started with our Basic Vinaigrette recipe (page 16), which uses ½ teaspoon of mayonnaise to stabilize the emulsion, and pushed it to its limits, decreasing the oil to 2 parts and finally 1 part. I found that the same amount of mayo was able to keep even a 1:1 mixture of oil and vinegar from separating. Tasters agreed that

this uniquely acidic vinaigrette worked perfectly with the avocado. For even more brightness, I swapped the more mellow cider vinegar for tart red wine vinegar.

With my dressing formulated, the flavor was there, and I was able to turn to assembling the complementary ingredients. Since avocados do very well in chunky salsas, I wondered if ditching the fluttery greens of a tossed salad and seeking out the bulkier ingredients of a chopped salad would be a better bet. Radishes were a definite: Their crisp, cool texture and sharp, peppery bite would be a good foil for the soft, rich avocado. Next, I singled out savory, aromatic shallot, which I would slice thinly. For balance, I needed something a little sweet and not very crunchy. The sweet-tart brightness of cherry tomatoes proved just the ticket. To round out their juiciness and to add complexity, I finished the salad with the bold, salty pop of some thinly shaved ricotta salata cheese and the herbal notes of chopped fresh basil.

My job was almost done but not quite: I hadn't addressed presentation. When I tossed the salad, it didn't look very appealing: As expected, the avocado coated the other ingredients with an army-green film. But when I put avocado slices in the shape of a fan atop everything else already tossed in the dressing, it seemed like a garnish or an afterthought. Furthermore, each diner still faced the challenge of mixing the fruit into the rest of the salad in order to coat it with dressing but without it leaving its visually off-putting mark.

Then I had two brainstorms: Why not toss the avocado separately in dressing as well, and why not flip the usual arrangement by placing the avocado underneath the other ingredients instead of on top? This approach not only eliminated any chance of the avocado getting all over the other ingredients but also allowed the fruit to soak up any additional dressing dripping down from the rest of the salad's components. Now my salad didn't just have the perfect flavor combination: It looked great, too.

I came up with three variations on this winning formula. Each included a cool, crunchy element (fennel, endive, or jícama); a sweet-tart component (orange, apple, or mango); and a bold, savory touch (green olives, pungent blue cheese, or salty feta).

And in each of these salads, avocado finally gets the treatment it deserves.

—CELESTE ROGERS, *Cook's Illustrated*

Avocado Salad with Tomato and Radish

SERVES 6

Crumbled feta cheese can be substituted for the ricotta salata. Don't skip the step of soaking the shallot—the ice water helps tame its oniony bite.

- 1 large shallot, sliced thin
- 3 tablespoons red wine vinegar
- 1 garlic clove, minced
- ½ teaspoon mayonnaise
  Salt and pepper
- 3 tablespoons extra-virgin olive oil
- 3 avocados, halved, pitted, and cut into ¾-inch pieces
- 12 ounces cherry tomatoes, quartered
- 3 radishes, sliced thin
- ½ cup chopped fresh basil
- 3 ounces ricotta salata, shaved thin

NOTES FROM THE TEST KITCHEN

PREPPING AVOCADOS

1. After slicing avocado in half around pit, lodge edge of knife blade into pit and twist to remove. Use large wooden spoon to pry pit safely off knife.

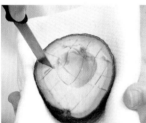

2. Use dish towel to hold avocado steady. Make ¾-inch crosshatch incisions in flesh of each avocado half with knife, cutting down to but not through skin.

3. Separate diced flesh from skin with soupspoon inserted between skin and flesh, gently scooping out avocado cubes.

1. Place shallot in 2 cups ice water and let stand for 30 minutes. Drain and pat dry with paper towels.

2. Whisk vinegar, garlic, mayonnaise, ¼ teaspoon salt, and ¼ teaspoon pepper together in nonreactive bowl until mixture appears milky and no lumps remain. Whisking constantly, slowly drizzle in oil. (Dressing should appear homogeneous, glossy, and slightly thickened, without pools of oil on surface.)

3. Gently toss avocados, 2 tablespoons dressing, and ½ teaspoon salt together in bowl. Transfer avocados to large platter or individual plates.

4. Toss shallot, tomatoes, radishes, and basil with remaining dressing. Spoon tomato mixture over avocados and sprinkle with ricotta salata. Serve immediately.

VARIATIONS

Avocado Salad with Orange and Fennel

Substitute sherry vinegar for red wine vinegar and ½ teaspoon hot paprika for garlic. Omit pepper. Starting with 3 oranges, remove 1 teaspoon finely grated zest from 1 orange and add to dressing in step 2. Peel, quarter, and cut oranges into ¼-inch pieces and add to vegetable mixture in step 4. Substitute 1 thinly sliced, cored fennel bulb for tomatoes, ⅓ cup toasted slivered almonds for radishes, ¼ cup chopped fresh parsley for basil, and ¼ cup sliced green olives for ricotta salata.

Avocado Salad with Apple and Endive

Reduce shallot to 1 tablespoon, minced, and skip step 1. Substitute minced shallot and 1 teaspoon honey for garlic and substitute cider vinegar for red wine vinegar. Substitute 1 Fuji apple cut into 1-inch-long matchsticks for tomatoes, 1 thinly sliced head Belgian endive for radishes, ¼ cup minced chives for basil, and blue cheese for ricotta salata.

Avocado Salad with Mango and Jícama

Reduce shallot to 1 tablespoon, minced, and skip step 1. Substitute shallot and pinch cayenne for garlic and substitute ½ teaspoon lemon zest and 3 tablespoons lemon juice for red wine vinegar. Substitute 2 peeled mangos cut into ½-inch pieces for tomatoes, 2 cups peeled jícama cut into 2-inch-long matchsticks for radishes, and feta cheese for ricotta salata. Reduce basil to ¼ cup and add ¼ cup chopped mint to salad.

TEXAS POTATO SALAD

🗸 WHY THIS RECIPE WORKS Texans take their potato salad up a notch with a hefty dose of mustard and spicy chopped jalapeños. We started creating our own version with classic potato salad, using firm Yukon Gold potatoes, which have a rich earthy flavor and hold their shape after cooking, and a mayonnaise-based dressing seasoned with onion, celery seeds, and dill pickles. To this we added plenty of bold yellow mustard and spicy jalapeños. We tempered the jalapeños' raw bite by quick-pickling them in a mixture of vinegar, sugar, and mustard seeds. We used the leftover pickling solution to flavor the hot potatoes and added a pinch of cayenne for extra kick.

Crank up the flavor of classic potato salad with yellow mustard and chopped jalapeños, and you've got "Texas potato salad." I liked the sound of it. And since we've already perfected potato salad in the test kitchen, I'd have a head start—I'd just need to Tex it up.

I started by boiling Yukon Gold potatoes, then tossed the hot potatoes with dill pickle juice to season them. After waiting 30 minutes for the flavors to meld (and the potatoes to cool), I mixed in mayonnaise, onions, celery, pickles, and hard-boiled eggs. Then I lavished the potato salad with 6 tablespoons of mustard and stirred in chopped fresh jalapeños. *Violà*—Texas Potato Salad.

Or so I thought. The punchy mustard flavor was great, but as for the jalapeños—ouch. They were raw and hot. I needed to find a way to tame their heat without losing the flavor. I tried replacing them with pickled jalapeños. But supermarket pickled jalapeños, it turns out, have little zip. Could I make a quick jalapeño pickle of my own? I heated vinegar, sugar, and lots of mustard seeds—to reinforce the potato salad's mustardy flavor—then I stirred in fresh jalapeños and onion slices and waited 20 minutes.

I mixed up another batch, replacing the dill pickles and raw jalapeños with my quick-pickled jalapeños and onion. As I was swapping out the dill pickles, I realized I could also replace the dill pickle juice in the original recipe with my homemade pickling solution. My next batch of potato salad was ready—and was awfully good. For extra kick, I added ¼ teaspoon of cayenne.

My Texas Potato Salad is spicy, bold, and bright no matter where you eat it—Brownsville or Jacksonville, Austin or Boston.

—CRISTIN WALSH, *Cook's Country*

Texas Potato Salad

SERVES 8

Annie's Naturals Organic Yellow Mustard is our favorite brand of yellow mustard.

- ½ cup red wine vinegar
- 1½ tablespoons sugar
-   Salt and pepper
- 1 teaspoon yellow mustard seeds
- ½ small red onion, sliced thin
- 2 jalapeño chiles, 1 sliced into thin rings; 1 stemmed, seeded, and minced
- 3 pounds Yukon Gold potatoes, peeled and cut into ¾-inch pieces
- 6 tablespoons mayonnaise
- 6 tablespoons yellow mustard
- ¼ teaspoon cayenne pepper
- 2 large hard-cooked eggs, peeled and cut into ¼-inch pieces
- 1 celery rib, chopped fine

1. Combine vinegar, sugar, 1½ teaspoons salt, and mustard seeds in bowl and microwave until steaming, about 2 minutes. Whisk until sugar and salt are dissolved. Add onion and jalapeños and set aside until cool, 15 to 20 minutes. Strain onion and jalapeños through fine-mesh strainer set over bowl. Reserve pickled vegetables and vinegar mixture separately.

2. Meanwhile, combine potatoes, 8 cups water, and 1 tablespoon salt in Dutch oven and bring to boil over high heat. Reduce heat to medium and simmer until potatoes are just tender, 10 to 15 minutes.

3. Drain potatoes thoroughly, then transfer to large bowl. Drizzle 2 tablespoons reserved vinegar mixture over hot potatoes and toss gently until evenly coated. (Reserve remaining vinegar mixture for another use.) Refrigerate until cool, about 30 minutes, stirring once halfway through chilling.

4. Whisk mayonnaise, mustard, ½ teaspoon pepper, and cayenne together in bowl until combined. Add mayonnaise mixture, reserved pickled vegetables, eggs, and celery to potatoes and stir gently to combine. Season with salt and pepper to taste. Cover and refrigerate to let flavors blend, about 30 minutes. Serve. (Salad can be refrigerated for up to 2 days.)

SOUPS & STEWS

CHILLED TOMATO SOUP

☑ **WHY THIS RECIPE WORKS** For a chilled tomato soup with complex flavor, we used a combination of fresh and roasted tomatoes. This gave us a dish with bright, tangy notes as well as a deep, sweet flavor. For savory depth, we roasted garlic and shallot along with the tomatoes. A little smoked paprika and cayenne lent smoky warmth to our soup. For a silky-smooth texture, we skipped flavor-dulling cream in favor of fruity olive oil; slowly blending it into the soup created a velvety emulsion.

On a sweltering day, an icy bowl of chilled soup is one of life's great pleasures. Gazpacho has its place, but ripe, peak-season tomatoes deserve a soup in which they don't have to share the spotlight. An ideal cold tomato soup would capture the essence of the fruit in silky-smooth liquid form: light yet satisfying, savory yet sweet, deeply flavorful yet simple. But my many failed attempts at attaining tomato soup perfection proved that exemplary fruit alone doesn't guarantee success. My results ranged from the thin, mealy mess that resulted from simply blending raw tomatoes with a couple of ice cubes to an overthickened, ketchuplike sludge that was the upshot of simmering tomatoes with tomato juice for half an hour before chilling. Determined to get it right, I loaded up on tomatoes at the farmers' market and headed into the kitchen.

But before I started cooking, I studied my past recipe flops for clues. It occurred to me that in order to get the best of both worlds—fresh yet potent flavor—a hybrid half-raw, half-cooked approach might be the answer. Oven roasting is an easy and effective way to concentrate flavor, so I halved the fruits crosswise, spread them on a baking sheet cut side up (to help excess moisture escape), and experimented until I determined that roasting the tomatoes for about 25 minutes at 375 degrees was enough to intensify their taste. I pureed the roasted tomatoes with an equal amount of uncooked fruit and strained out the skins and seeds. Happily, I found that this approach produced both deep, sweet flavor and bright, tangy freshness.

But pureed tomatoes alone do not a soup make, so next I looked for ways to round out the flavor.

Red bell pepper is a common addition, but it overwhelmed the tomatoes, as did fresh herbs, even when used in tiny amounts. Garlic and mild shallot seemed like natural additions—but only if I found a way to tame their raw pungency. I roasted two garlic cloves and one sliced shallot together with the tomatoes for the first 15 minutes, removing them from the oven as soon as they had softened. When I pureed the raw and roasted tomatoes with the gently roasted aromatics, the soup's flavor improved, but it was still missing some tomatoey backbone.

It made sense to turn to the test kitchen's secret weapon for tomato-based recipes: tomato paste. I blended some into my next batch, and sure enough, a small dose of the sweet, potent paste dramatically upped the flavor quotient. Smoked paprika and cayenne pepper added even more layers of subtle complexity. Finally, I found the soup benefited greatly from a touch of acid. Just a teaspoon of sherry vinegar perked up all of the flavors.

With the flavor profile complete, I now had to focus on texture. As it stood, my soup was delicious but dismally thin and runny. Cream added body, but it also dulled the fresh tomato flavor, and even worse, the acidic tomatoes made it curdle. Blending some bread along with the tomatoes thickened the mixture nicely, but its starchiness seemed heavy and out of place in the cool, fresh soup.

Inspiration struck one evening as I was making a batch of mayonnaise. I watched the slow drizzle of oil into eggs transform into creamy billows as the ingredients formed an emulsion. Lo and behold, 6 tablespoons of olive oil added gradually to the blender as I pureed the tomatoes took them from a thin liquid to a rich, spoon-coating consistency. The olive oil also added a satisfying richness, and its fruity, peppery notes were an ideal accent to the savory-sweet tomatoes. Strained and chilled for at least 2 hours to let the flavors blend, the soup was velvety and delicious.

Served with crostini or frico (thin, crisp cheese wafers) for textural contrast, my chilled tomato soup was summertime perfection in a bowl.

—DAWN YANAGIHARA, *Cook's Illustrated*

CHILLED FRESH TOMATO SOUP

CORING TOMATOES

Using tip of paring knife, cut around stem, angling top of knife slightly inward. Remove cone-shaped piece of stem and hard core.

THE BEST BLENDER

We set out to find a blender that could easily do it all: crush ice, make frozen drinks, and blend lump-free smoothies, milkshakes, and hummus. We corralled nine models—everything from an affordable $40 appliance to our luxe benchmark, the Vitamix 5200, $449, which has gone unmatched in the test kitchen for years. Hummus, crushed ice, margarita, and milkshake tests were givens, but to separate the workhorses from the wimps, we also made smoothies with fibrous frozen pineapple and mango and stringy raw kale in each one every day for a month. The losers were easy to pick out. Some blenders failed at ice crushing. Others sputtered their way through milkshakes and fruit smoothies. The task of demolishing kale proved the downfall of a number of machines. Only two models plowed through this and every other task without flinching.

Not unexpectedly, one of those was the **Vitamix** (left). This test kitchen stalwart proved that there's virtually nothing it can't handle, thanks to its long-armed, well-configured blades and souped-up 1,380-watt motor. Its performance comes at a steep price, but its exceptional durability (not to mention seven-year warranty) makes it cheaper in the long run than a less expensive blender that needs frequent replacing. But we also have a Best Buy: the **Breville Hemisphere Control** (right). It sports long blades, each set at a different position and angle; a bowl-shaped jar that keeps food moving; and a relatively powerful 750-watt motor that helped it sail through every test. To test the Breville's long-term durability (something we have found lacking in many blenders), we made 400 smoothies in a single model without a hitch. We also used several models daily in the test kitchen, and we did have an issue on some models with the blender's safety device getting stuck and preventing the motor from working. But our blenders experience heavy use and at $199.99, it's less than half the price of the Vitamix, so we still recommend it as our Best Buy. However, if you plan to use your blender daily for heavy-duty chopping and blending, you should consider investing in the Vitamix. (See page 313 for more information on our testing results.)

Chilled Fresh Tomato Soup

SERVES 4

In-season, locally grown tomatoes and good-quality extra-virgin olive oil are ideal for this recipe. Serve the soup with crostini topped with cheese or frico.

- 2 **pounds tomatoes, cored**
- 1 **shallot, sliced thin**
- 2 **garlic cloves, unpeeled**
- 2 **teaspoons tomato paste**
- ⅛ **teaspoon smoked paprika (optional)**
- **Pinch cayenne pepper**
- **Salt**
- 6 **tablespoons extra-virgin olive oil, plus extra for drizzling**
- 1 **teaspoon sherry vinegar, plus extra as needed**
- **Pepper (optional)**

1. Adjust oven rack to middle position and heat oven to 375 degrees. Line rimmed baking sheet with aluminum foil and lightly spray with vegetable oil spray.

2. Cut 1 pound tomatoes in half horizontally and arrange cut side up in prepared baking sheet. Arrange shallot and garlic cloves in single layer over 1 area of baking sheet. Roast for 15 minutes, then remove shallot and garlic cloves. Return baking sheet to oven and continue to roast tomatoes until softened but not browned, 10 to 15 minutes longer. Let cool to room temperature, about 30 minutes.

3. Peel garlic cloves and place in blender with roasted shallot and roasted tomatoes. Cut remaining 1 pound tomatoes into eighths and add to blender along with tomato paste; paprika, if using; cayenne; and ½ teaspoon salt. Puree until smooth, about 30 seconds. With motor running, drizzle in olive oil in slow, steady stream (puree will turn orange in color).

4. Pour puree through fine-mesh strainer into nonreactive bowl, pressing on solids in strainer to extract as much liquid as possible. Discard solids. Stir in vinegar. Cover and refrigerate until well chilled and flavors have blended, at least 2 hours or up to 24 hours.

5. To serve, stir soup to recombine (liquid separates on standing). Season to taste with salt and vinegar, as needed. Ladle soup into chilled bowls, drizzle sparingly with extra oil, and grind pepper over each, if using. Serve immediately.

SPANISH-STYLE LENTIL SOUP

☑ **WHY THIS RECIPE WORKS** For our own version of Spain's thick and smoky lentil soup, we started with the lentils. Soaking them in a warm brine for 30 minutes before cooking prevented blowouts and ensured they were well seasoned. Browning links of Spanish chorizo then simmering them in the soup ensured a juicy texture. Slowly sweating finely chopped aromatics in the chorizo's fat gave our soup incredible depth of flavor. For smoky flavor, we finished the soup with an Indian garnish called a *tarka*, a sautéed mixture of onion, garlic, black pepper, and—in this case, smoked—paprika. Adding a little flour helped thicken the soup and some sherry vinegar brightened its flavors.

Spaniards have a long tradition of taking *la comida*, their largest meal of the day, in the early afternoon. Hearty, sustaining soups and stews, many of which pair economical dried beans with a form of flavor-packed pork such as ham, bacon, or sausage, are typically on the table. A particularly intriguing example is *sopa de lentejas con chorizo* (lentil and chorizo soup). It's a standout not just for its robust taste—provided by rich, garlicky chorizo, heady smoked paprika (*pimentón*), and the bright depth of sherry vinegar—but also for its unique texture: Neither entirely brothy nor creamy, the soup features whole lentils suspended in a thick broth.

To come up with my own recipe, I started by evaluating different types of lentils. Spaniards are fond of *lentejas pardinas* (*pardo* means "brownish" or "darkish") from Castilla y León. I mail-ordered a bag and found that they cooked up with a nutty, buttery flavor. But since pardinas are difficult to locate, I also simmered a few more common varieties. They were all similar, though not without unique subtleties. French green *lentilles du Puy* were earthy; black beluga lentils, meaty; and standard brown lentils, vegetal. The du Puy type had the best tender-firm texture, so I stuck with them.

There was just one problem: keeping them intact. The "meat" of a lentil swells as it cooks, slipping out of its shell (which is called a blow out) and creating a mushy, split pea soup–like texture. Over the years, we have found two ways to address this issue. Both use salt and/or acid to weaken the pectin and soften the shell so it is more flexible and less likely to blowout. The first approach involves cooking the lentils with salt and vinegar before adding liquid and fully cooking them; the second requires soaking the beans in a warm saltwater brine for an hour prior to cooking.

I tried the salt and acid method first, sautéing some chopped onion in olive oil, then adding the lentils along with salt and sherry vinegar. I let the lentils cook, covered, for a few minutes before adding water, bay leaves, smoked paprika, and cloves and simmering until the beans were fully cooked. These lentils retained their shape somewhat, but many were still blown out. I got better results when I combined the methods by quick-brining the lentils in boiling water for 30 minutes before sweating them with the salt and vinegar. Now each and every bean emerged fully intact and beautifully creamy.

With the lentils settled, I focused on the chorizo. The word *chorizo* covers many versions of pork sausage made in Spain. The kind typically available in the United States is a cured sausage with a strong garlicky flavor, colored a distinctive red by pimentón. It is important not to confuse it with Mexican chorizo, which combines fresh ground pork or beef with chili powder and vinegar. To keep the links as moist as possible, I left them whole and browned them in olive oil, transferred them to a plate while I sweated the lentils, and then plopped them back into the pot along with the water to simmer (I would cut them into bite-size pieces toward the end of cooking). Prepared this way, the chorizo cooked up with a dense, juicy texture. But as good as the sausage was, the flavor of the soup itself wasn't nearly complex enough.

My first idea for creating depth was to swap chicken broth for some of the water, but that only seemed to cloud the soup's overall flavor. Next, I tried caramelizing the aromatics, but the profound sweetness that developed only obscured the smoky chorizo and tart vinegar. But the failed caramelized vegetable test got me thinking about an entirely different technique for enhancing the flavor of aromatics: sweating. This approach, used by cooks around the world, involves slowly cooking aromatics in a small amount of fat in a covered pot. The vegetables are kept just this side of browning, and during the process they develop a distinctive yet subtle flavor that is said to improve almost any dish.

It was certainly worth a try. I prepared another batch of soup, first browning the chorizo, then slowly cooking the onion (plus carrots and parsley for a vegetal boost) in the rendered fat on low heat, all while the lentils brined. After 30 minutes, I dipped my spoon in for a sample and discovered that a real transformation had occurred:

The sweated vegetables boasted a clean, pure, sweet flavor altogether different from the sweet, roasted taste produced via caramelization. In the finished soup, the effect was equally impressive: The slow-cooked aromatics turned out to be an extremely well-balanced base that highlighted the main flavors of the dish.

I was really getting somewhere, but the soup still didn't have that elusive "wow factor." As I mulled over ideas, a rather unorthodox thought came to mind: Since lentils are a staple not only of Mediterranean cooking but also of Indian cuisine, why not consult Indian cookbooks? Thumbing through classic sources, I found a technique that Indian cooks use to bolster flavor in all sorts of dishes: stirring in a so-called tarka, a mixture of spices and finely minced aromatics quickly bloomed in oil. Since the test kitchen recently discovered that a brief exposure to hot oil can boost the flavor of spices tenfold, I knew that the technique held a lot of promise.

Inspired, I whipped up a Spanish tarka for my next batch of soup. Instead of adding the smoked paprika to the simmering lentils, I sizzled it in olive oil along with black pepper, minced garlic, and finely grated onion (the small pieces ensured that it would soften quickly). This was potent stuff. Thinking that it might overwhelm the soup as a garnish, I decided to drizzle it into the broth for a few more minutes of simmering. While I was at it, I addressed the thickness of my soup (or, more accurately, the lack thereof) by stirring some flour into the oil in the tarka to make a sort of roux. Just 1 tablespoon was enough to develop the signature spoon-coating consistency.

With my first taste, I knew I'd hit the jackpot with my multicultural approach. The soup had a lush consistency, not to mention tons of flavor: sweet, savory, and smoky, with a hint of acidity.

—DAVID PAZMIÑO, *Cook's Illustrated*

Hearty Spanish-Style Lentil and Chorizo Soup
SERVES 6 TO 8

We prefer French green lentils, or lentilles du Puy, for this recipe, but it will work with any type of lentil except red or yellow, which disintegrate when cooked. Grate the onion on the large holes of a box grater. If Spanish-style chorizo is not available, kielbasa sausage can be substituted. Red wine vinegar can be substituted for the sherry vinegar. We prefer sweet (*dulce*) smoked paprika in this recipe.

1   **pound (2¼ cups) lentils, picked over and rinsed**
    Salt and pepper
1   **large onion**
5   **tablespoons extra-virgin olive oil**
1½ **pounds Spanish-style chorizo sausage, pricked with fork several times**
3   **carrots, peeled and cut into ¼-inch pieces**
3   **tablespoons minced fresh parsley**
7   **cups water, plus extra as needed**
3   **tablespoons sherry vinegar, plus extra for seasoning**
2   **bay leaves**
⅛   **teaspoon ground cloves**
2   **tablespoons sweet smoked paprika**
3   **garlic cloves, minced**
1   **tablespoon all-purpose flour**

1. Place lentils and 2 teaspoons salt in heatproof container. Cover with 4 cups boiling water and let soak for 30 minutes. Drain well.

2. Meanwhile, finely chop three-quarters of onion (you should have about 1 cup) and grate remaining quarter (you should have about 3 tablespoons). Heat 2 tablespoons oil in Dutch oven over medium heat until shimmering. Add chorizo and cook until browned on all sides, 6 to 8 minutes. Transfer chorizo to large plate. Reduce heat to low and add chopped onion, carrots, 1 tablespoon parsley, and 1 teaspoon salt. Cover and cook, stirring occasionally, until vegetables are very soft but not brown, 25 to 30 minutes. If vegetables begin to brown, add 1 tablespoon water to pot.

3. Add lentils and sherry vinegar to vegetables, increase heat to medium-high, and cook, stirring frequently, until vinegar starts to evaporate, 3 to 4 minutes. Add 7 cups water, chorizo, bay leaves, and cloves; bring to simmer. Reduce heat to low, cover, and cook until lentils are tender, about 30 minutes.

4. Heat remaining 3 tablespoons oil in small saucepan over medium heat until shimmering. Add paprika, grated onion, garlic, and ½ teaspoon pepper; cook, stirring constantly, until fragrant, 2 minutes. Add flour and cook, stirring constantly, 1 minute longer. Remove chorizo and bay leaves from lentils. Stir paprika mixture into lentils and continue to cook until flavors have blended and soup has thickened, 10 to 15 minutes. When chorizo is cool enough to handle, cut in half lengthwise, then cut each half into ¼-inch-thick slices. Return chorizo to soup along with remaining 2 tablespoons

HEARTY SPANISH–STYLE LENTIL AND CHORIZO SOUP

parsley and heat through, about 1 minute. Season with salt, pepper, and up to 2 teaspoons sherry vinegar to taste. Serve. (Soup can be made up to 3 days in advance.)

VARIATION

Hearty Spanish-Style Lentil and Chorizo Soup with Kale

Add 12 ounces kale, stemmed and cut into ½-inch pieces, to simmering soup after 15 minutes in step 3. Continue to simmer until lentils and kale are tender, about 15 minutes.

NOTES FROM THE TEST KITCHEN

WHAT MAKES IT SPANISH?

Three quintessential ingredients provide our soup with authentic Spanish flavor.

SMOKED PAPRIKA
Pimentón, made by drying red peppers over an oak fire, offers a distinctive rich and smoky taste.

SHERRY VINEGAR
Lightly sweet sherry vinegar boasts assertive yet balanced acidity.

SPANISH CHORIZO
This heady sausage combines coarsely ground, dry-cured pork with a hit of pimentón.

SWEATING IT OUT FOR A SWEET, VEGETAL TASTE

Caramelized vegetables are prized for a sweet, deeply roasted flavor—and the darker they get, the richer they taste. But what about the opposite approach, called sweating, which keeps vegetables entirely pale by cooking them ever so slowly in a covered pot? We knew that long cooking would develop a certain amount of sweetness in the chopped onion, carrot, and parsley we were using, as well as remove any trace of unpleasant sulfuric compounds in the onion. What we didn't know was that their flavor would be a revelation: The sweated aromatics offered a pure, sweet background taste that not only allowed our soup's primary ingredients (smoked paprika, chorizo, lentils, and sherry vinegar) to come to the fore but also seemed to fortify their individual flavors.

WILD RICE AND MUSHROOM SOUP

✓ **WHY THIS RECIPE WORKS** To keep the focus on the wild rice and mushrooms in this classic soup, we selected ingredients—such as tomato paste and soy sauce—that amplified their nutty, earthy, umami-rich flavor profile. Simmering the wild rice with baking soda decreased the cooking time and brought out its complex flavor. Cooking the rice in the oven, instead of on the stovetop, made it tender with a pleasant chew. We also used the leftover simmering liquid as a bouillon, infusing the entire soup with wild rice flavor. Fresh cremini mushrooms and ground dried shiitakes provided a winning combination of meaty texture and richness. A final addition of cornstarch helped suspend the rice in the broth to give our soup a velvety texture.

Wild rice has made numerous appearances at my dinner table over the years, but it's almost always been in the form of a salad or stuffing for the Thanksgiving bird. The grains have a remarkably nutty, savory depth, not to mention a distinct chew that makes them an ideal base for hearty side dishes, but hearty wild rice is also a natural choice for soups. I've come across a few intriguing recipes, and often they pair the grain with mushrooms. The combination makes sense: Together, they should produce a soup that's substantial but not heavy and full of earthy depth. Just the kind of food I want to tuck into in the dead of winter.

Having said that, I've never had a wild rice and mushroom soup that actually fit this description. All the soups I've made shared a common flaw: The namesake ingredients didn't play a starring role. I knew I could do better, so I decided to develop this soup with a clear objective in mind: Keep the focus on the nutty wild rice and meaty mushrooms.

I knew that getting perfectly cooked wild rice would be challenging. To establish a working recipe, I tabled testing wild rice cooking methods and simply boiled the grains separately until they were firm-tender, which took a good hour. In the meantime, I built my soup base from an entire pound of sliced cremini mushrooms (a test kitchen favorite for their meaty flavor and texture and wide availability) sautéed in a Dutch oven with onion, garlic, and tomato paste. By the time the mushrooms had taken on color, I was left with a dark fond at the bottom of the pot. I deglazed the pot with a generous pour of sherry, reduced the liquid to a fortified mushroom concentrate, added chicken stock (for savory depth) and water, then stirred in the cooked rice.

This soup was several steps in the right direction, but I still had a ways to go. The most glaring issue was the mushroom flavor, which was subtler than I'd hoped. Adding some soy sauce boosted savoriness, but the earthy quality I was after was still missing. Yet the soup was already brimming with mushrooms. I opted to supplement the cremini with dried shiitakes, which have the intense mushroom flavor I wanted without the bulk. Just ¼ ounce, pulverized to a powder in a spice grinder, infused the soup with full-bodied mushroom flavor.

I was making strides flavorwise, but so far my soup lacked body. Without it, the broth was unsatisfying and too thin to support the mushrooms and rice. I hoped that a flour-based roux might be an easy way to thicken the pot. It worked well, but it took a full ½ cup to get the right thickness, which dulled the earthy flavor I'd worked so hard to build. In search of alternatives, I considered cornstarch. Unlike flour, cornstarch is a pure starch and a more powerful thickener, which meant I could get away with using just ¼ cup. Robust mushroom flavor? Check. Hearty body? Check. Now my soup just needed to earn the other half of its title.

It would be simplest to dump the boiled rice into the soup and call it a day, but marrying the liquid and rice at the last minute wouldn't allow for much flavor transfer. As it was, the rice needed an hour of cooking time on its own, so simply simmering it in the soup base would drag out the overall cooking time. In search of a better way, I read up on wild rice cookery and ran some tests.

Each grain of wild rice has a thick, pectin-rich coat that hardens when the rice is dried during processing. Wild rice is properly cooked when this black seed coat splits and the grains are tender yet still chewy. But stovetop simmering using the pasta method (cooking the rice in an excess of water, then draining it) was not only a long process but an inconsistent one as well; I had to fiddle with the heat constantly to make sure the pot wasn't bubbling too slowly or too quickly. And using this method meant that I was discarding the cooking liquid—literally pouring some of the flavor from the wild rice down the drain. In an attempt to keep all that flavorful liquid in the pot, I tried the absorption method—cooking the rice in a measured amount of water that the grains completely soak up—but that method required even more babysitting to prevent the liquid from evaporating too quickly. No thanks.

Instead, I abandoned stovetop simmering altogether and turned to a more even heat source: the oven. After setting the dial to 375, I switched back to the pasta method and brought the water to a boil on the burner, added the rice, covered the pot, and transferred the vessel to the oven. Just as I'd hoped, the rice cooked—babysitter-free—at an even simmer and emerged firm with a tender and pleasant chew. Then, rather than pitching the leftover cooking liquid, I strained some of the flavorful liquid and substituted it for some of the water in the soup. One test proved that this method was an easy way to ensure that the flavor of the wild rice permeated the broth.

The good news: I finally had a foolproof cooking method and rich wild rice flavor throughout my soup. But it was still costing me an hour. Then a colleague reminded me that we had solved a similar dilemma in our recipe for polenta by adding a pinch of baking soda to the pot. The baking soda raised the pH in the pot, facilitating the breakdown of the pectin and shaving 15 minutes off the cooking time. This approach worked beautifully with the rice, too. When I added ¼ teaspoon of baking soda, the seed coat broke down faster, cutting down the rice's cooking time to about 45 minutes.

There was also another benefit to my baking soda trick that I didn't realize until I took a closer look at the strained cooking liquid. Unlike prior batches, which were straw-colored, this wild rice stock was deep brown. A spoonful surprised me with its savory nuttiness—it was far richer and more complex than the previous baking soda–free batches.

Our science editor explained that baking soda not only helps break down the pectin but also lowers the temperature necessary for Maillard reaction–induced browning to occur. Though most commonly associated with the browning of meat or baked goods, Maillard reactions occur when heated proteins and sugars undergo chemical changes, resulting in entirely new flavors. Typically these reactions require temperatures of at least 300 degrees, but alkaline baking soda effectively lowers this temperature barrier and allows the reactions to occur below the boiling point of water (212 degrees). Also working in my favor: Wild rice is especially well suited for the Maillard reaction, as it contains high concentrations of amino acids (lysine and glycine) that are particularly reactive.

Deeper, more complex flavor as a result of a faster cooking method? I'd take it. In fact, this soup was so full of earthy depth that my tasters suggested I balance it out with some fresher flavors. Chives and lemon zest brightened things up nicely. I also stirred in ½ cup of cream, which enriched the earthy broth.

Robustly flavored with its namesake ingredients, this soup had finally earned its title—not to mention a permanent spot in my collection of staple soups.

—CELESTE ROGERS, *Cook's Illustrated*

NOTES FROM THE TEST KITCHEN

MAKING WILD RICE ACT LIKE STEAK

We brown meat, baked goods, and many other foods as a matter of course, since the deeper color is an indication of the Maillard reaction, the process triggered by heat that causes a food's proteins and sugars to recombine into hundreds of new flavor compounds that boost complexity. To achieve richer browned flavor in ordinary rice, we often toast the raw grains in the pan before adding liquid. But toasting doesn't work as well with wild rice, since it is technically a grass with a hard pectin-rich coating that must break down before the proteins and sugars on the inside can brown. However, we stumbled upon another way to achieve browning: adding baking soda to the cooking water. Baking soda not only breaks down the pectin seed coat to speed cooking (our original goal) but also lowers the temperature necessary for browning to occur—from at least 300 degrees to below water's boiling point of 212. Another factor in our favor: Wild rice is high in the amino acids lysine and glycine, proteins that are particularly sensitive to browning. Baking soda added to the pot led to nuttier-tasting wild rice and a savory, deep-brown stock that enriched the soup.

THE BEST WILD RICE

Wild rice is not rice at all, but an aquatic grass that grows naturally in lakes and is cultivated in man-made paddies. When we tasted five brands both plain and in our Wild Rice and Mushroom Soup, textural differences stood out the most. The top three, including our winner from **Goose Valley**, cooked up springy and firm, while the other two blew out. The difference was processing. To create a shelf-stable product, manufacturers heat the grains, which gelatinizes their starches and drives out moisture by parching (the traditional approach) or parboiling. To parch, manufacturers load the rice into cylinders that spin over a fire—an inexact process that produces "crumbly" results. Parboiling, a newer method, steams the grains in a controlled pressurized environment for more uniform and complete gelatinization, which translates into rice that cooks more evenly.

Wild Rice and Mushroom Soup

SERVES 6 TO 8

White mushrooms can be substituted for the cremini mushrooms. We use a spice grinder to process the dried shiitake mushrooms, but a blender also works.

¼	ounce dried shiitake mushrooms, rinsed
4¼	cups water
1	sprig fresh thyme
1	bay leaf
1	garlic clove, peeled, plus 4 cloves, minced
	Salt and pepper
¼	teaspoon baking soda
1	cup wild rice
4	tablespoons unsalted butter
1	pound cremini mushrooms, trimmed and sliced ¼ inch thick
1	onion, chopped fine
1	teaspoon tomato paste
⅔	cup dry sherry
4	cups chicken broth
1	tablespoon soy sauce
¼	cup cornstarch
½	cup heavy cream
¼	cup minced fresh chives
¼	teaspoon finely grated lemon zest

1. Adjust oven rack to middle position and heat oven to 375 degrees. Grind shiitake mushrooms in spice grinder until finely ground (you should have about 3 tablespoons).

2. Bring 4 cups water, thyme, bay leaf, peeled garlic clove, ¾ teaspoon salt, and baking soda to boil in medium saucepan over high heat. Add rice and return to boil. Cover saucepan, transfer to oven, and bake until rice is tender, 35 to 50 minutes. Strain rice through fine-mesh strainer set in 4-cup liquid measuring cup; discard thyme, bay leaf, and garlic. Add enough water to reserved cooking liquid to measure 3 cups.

3. Melt butter in Dutch oven over high heat. Add cremini mushrooms, onion, minced garlic, tomato paste, ¾ teaspoon salt, and 1 teaspoon pepper. Cook, stirring occasionally, until vegetables are browned and dark fond develops on bottom of pot, 15 minutes. Add sherry, scraping up any browned bits, and cook until liquid is reduced and pot is almost dry, about 2 minutes. Add ground shiitake mushrooms, reserved rice cooking liquid, broth, and soy sauce and bring to boil.

Reduce heat to low and simmer, covered, until onion and mushrooms are tender, about 20 minutes.

4. Whisk cornstarch and remaining ¼ cup water together in small bowl. Stir cornstarch slurry into soup, return to simmer, and cook until thickened, about 2 minutes. Remove pot from heat and stir in cooked rice, cream, chives, and lemon zest. Cover and let stand for 20 minutes. Season with salt and pepper to taste and serve.

PRESSURE-COOKER BROTH

✔ **WHY THIS RECIPE WORKS** To make homemade broth faster and easier, we turned to an often-overlooked appliance: the pressure cooker. The intense heat inside a pressure cooker extracts flavor compounds from bones, skin, and vegetables far more quickly than conventional simmering. For our chicken broth, we browned chicken pieces and sautéed aromatics right in the pressure-cooker pot, added water, and in just 1 hour, we had the richest chicken broth we'd ever made. For an incredibly savory beef broth, we microwaved beef bones, sautéed aromatics, and added tomato paste, soy sauce, and mushrooms to build rich, meaty flavor in just 90 minutes.

Most of us think homemade broth is out of reach. After all, it typically takes hours of simmering to get really deep, rich flavor. We wanted to turn to an appliance that's been enjoying a resurgence lately—the pressure cooker—to develop faster, easier, richer-tasting versions of homemade broth.

Pressure cookers function based on a simple principle: In a tightly sealed pot, the boiling point of liquid is higher. As the pot heats up, pressure begins to build, raising the boiling point of water. The intense heat promotes a faster extraction of flavor compounds from bones, skin, and vegetables and encourages the breakdown of proteins into peptides, producing noticeably rich meatiness more potent than what you'd get from traditional simmering. Long story short: better broth, faster—a winning combination that I couldn't pass up.

I started testing with chicken broth. Most traditional chicken broth recipes will tell you that roasting the chicken parts first is essential for both color and flavor. While this is true, it's also a hassle. So to mimic the effect of roasting without tacking hours onto my recipe, I simply browned the chicken in the pressure cooker pot. I also hacked the chicken backs and necks into small pieces, which exposed more surface area, making it easier for the chicken's flavor to seep into the water in a short period of time. Three pounds of chicken pieces gave me plenty of meaty flavor.

Next I browned the onion and added the vegetables and water. The amount of water I used and the cooking time were the other two major variables, and I quickly learned that getting both right was crucial. Using more than 3 quarts of water resulted in a watery broth, but any less meant a skimpy yield that wasn't worth the effort.

As for the timing, while traditionally simmering stock takes 3 or 4 hours, I found that on high pressure it took only an hour to extract all the flavor from the bones and meat; additional cooking time produced little difference. I tested both quick release and natural release but found there was no benefit to using natural release, so I opted to quick-release the pressure, saving me another 15 minutes.

With my chicken broth close to the finish line, I made a version with onion and one with onion, celery, and carrot. The onion added a complexity tasters liked, but the celery and carrot didn't add to the final broth, so I left them out. Finally, in less than 2 hours (including preparation time), I had the fastest, richest chicken broth I'd ever made. Satisfied, I turned my attention to beef.

Beef broth should taste like beef—almost as intense and rich as pot roast jus—but often store-bought versions are watery and vegetal. To make a broth with rich body that tasted really meaty, I knew I would need to use beef bones. As with chicken broth, most recipes I found recommended roasting the beef bones in the oven to lend color and deep meaty flavor to the broth, but this took hours. Instead, I turned to my microwave, where they browned in just 10 minutes.

Up next were the aromatics. I found that onion, carrot, and celery were necessary; they reinforced the hearty flavor of the broth without tasting overly vegetal. Tomato paste added color and acidity. Deglazing the pot with red wine fortified the broth even further.

Though not perfect, this broth was well on its way. Unfortunately, it was still lacking some of the richness found in long-simmered broths. Looking for additional ingredients that might add flavor and body, I hit upon mushrooms and soy sauce; both are high in glutamates, naturally occurring compounds that make food taste richer and meatier. I decided to include them both.

Next I sought to determine the optimal pressurized cooking time and the right amount of beef bones to use. As in my chicken broth, 3 pounds of bones was enough to flavor 3 quarts of broth. However, I found a longer cooking time was beneficial since it gave the bones more time to release their flavor into the pot. Ultimately, tasters preferred a broth that had simmered for 1½ hours, noting that it had the cleanest, beefiest flavor.

Thanks to the unique environment of the pressure cooker, I now had recipes for the fastest, easiest, and richest chicken and beef broths I had ever made.

—DAN ZUCCARELLO, America's Test Kitchen Books

Pressure-Cooker Chicken Broth

MAKES 3 QUARTS

If you prefer a less cloudy broth, you can strain the finished broth a second time. This recipe can be made in an electric pressure cooker without any alterations.

- 1 tablespoon vegetable oil
- 3 pounds bone-in chicken pieces (leg quarters, backs, and/or wings), hacked into 2-inch pieces
- 1 onion, chopped
- 3 garlic cloves, lightly crushed, skins discarded
- 3 quarts water
- 1 teaspoon salt
- 3 bay leaves

1. Heat oil in pressure-cooker pot over medium-high heat until smoking. Brown half of chicken on all sides, about 6 minutes; transfer to bowl. Repeat with remaining chicken; transfer to bowl.

2. Pour off all but 1 tablespoon fat left in pot, add onion, and cook over medium heat until softened and well browned, 8 to 10 minutes. Stir in garlic and cook until fragrant, about 30 seconds. Stir in 1 cup water and scrape up all browned bits from bottom of pot using wooden spoon. Stir in remaining 11 cups water, salt, bay leaves, and browned chicken with any accumulated juices.

3. Lock pressure-cooker lid in place and bring to high pressure over medium-high heat. As soon as pot reaches high pressure, reduce heat to medium-low and cook for 1 hour, adjusting heat as needed to maintain high pressure.

4. Remove pot from heat. Quick-release pressure, then carefully remove lid, allowing steam to escape away from you.

5. Strain broth through fine-mesh strainer into clean container, pressing on solids to extract as much liquid as possible; discard solids. Using large spoon, skim excess fat from surface of broth. (Broth can be refrigerated for up to 2 days or frozen for several months.)

Pressure-Cooker Beef Broth

MAKES 3 QUARTS

Our favorite pressure cooker holds 8½ quarts; to make this recipe in a 6-quart pressure cooker or an electric pressure cooker, reduce all ingredients by half.

- 3 pounds beef bones
- 1 tablespoon vegetable oil
- 1 onion, chopped
- 1 carrot, peeled and chopped
- 1 celery rib, chopped
- 3 tablespoons tomato paste
- ¾ cup dry red wine
- 3 quarts water
- 1 pound white mushrooms, trimmed and halved
- 2 tablespoons soy sauce
- 1 teaspoon salt
- 3 bay leaves

1. Arrange beef bones on paper towel–lined plate and microwave until well browned, 8 to 10 minutes.

2. Heat oil in pressure-cooker pot over medium heat until shimmering. Stir in onion, carrot, and celery and cook until softened and well browned, 8 to 10 minutes. Stir in tomato paste and cook until fragrant, about 30 seconds. Stir in wine, scraping up any browned bits from bottom of pot using wooden spoon. Stir in water, mushrooms, soy sauce, salt, bay leaves, and microwaved beef bones.

3. Lock pressure-cooker lid in place and bring to high pressure over medium-high heat. As soon as pot reaches high pressure, reduce heat to medium-low and cook for 1½ hours, adjusting heat as needed to maintain high pressure.

4. Remove pot from heat. Quick-release pressure, then carefully remove lid, allowing steam to escape away from you.

5. Remove bones, letting excess broth drain back into pot; discard bones. Strain broth through fine-mesh strainer into clean container, pressing on solids to extract as much liquid as possible; discard solids. Using large spoon, skim excess fat from surface of broth. (Broth can be refrigerated for up to 2 days or frozen for several months.)

NOTES FROM THE TEST KITCHEN

THE BEST PRESSURE COOKER

Pressure cookers are simple to use and in less than an hour can produce food that tastes as if you spent all day at the stove. They function based on a simple principle: As the tightly sealed pot heats up, pressure builds, making it more difficult for water to turn to vapor and raising its boiling point from 212 to 250 degrees. This generates superheated steam that cooks food faster. And because the pot is sealed, cooking requires much less liquid than usual and flavors concentrate.

Today's pressure cookers are quieter, simpler, and safer than your grandmother's cooker. But that didn't necessarily mean that all models would work equally well. We selected eight sturdy, nonreactive stainless steel stovetop cookers and prepared risotto, chicken stock, beef stew, Boston baked beans, and meaty tomato sauce with pork ribs. We checked evenness of browning by cooking crêpes in the pan bottoms.

We preferred pots with at least an 8-quart capacity for big batches of stocks and sauces. Low, wide cookers provided a generous cooking surface that let us brown meat in fewer batches, and they were easier to see and reach into while working. We also found that steady heating was important. Once the cooker reaches high pressure, you turn down the heat as low as possible while maintaining pressure. In some models the pressure tended to drop when we turned down the heat, forcing us to constantly adjust the temperature. The top two performers were the thickest and they retained heat well, quickly reaching then maintaining pressure for steady, hands-off cooking. They also had brightly colored pressure indicators that were easy to read at a glance from several feet away.

After testing was complete, we had a clear winner: the **Fissler Vitaquick 8½-Quart Pressure Cooker**, $279.95. Sturdily built with a low, wide profile, steady heating, a clear pressure indicator, a convenient automatically locking lid, and low evaporation, this cooker was a pleasure to use and produced perfect finished dishes. But at that price, it's an investment.

Our Best Buy is the Fagor Duo 8-Quart Stainless Steel Pressure Cooker, $109.95, which performed nearly as well at a fraction of the price. (See page 312 for more information on our testing results, including the results of our testing of electric pressure cookers.)

PRESSURE-COOKER CHICKEN NOODLE SOUP

WHY THIS RECIPE WORKS To make a quick and easy chicken noodle soup with velvety broth and rich flavor, we turned to the pressure cooker, which can extract intense flavor from a chicken's skin and bones in far less time than traditional simmering. We started with a whole chicken, some aromatics, carrots, celery, and water. Placing the chicken in the pot breast side up, so the thighs were in contact with the bottom of the pot, helped the thighs and more delicate breast meat to cook though evenly. After 20 minutes, the vegetables were tender and the chicken was falling off the bones, making it easy to shred the meat into pieces. We simply simmered the noodles in the broth while shredding the chicken and added some fresh parsley.

After our success using a pressure cooker to make short work of chicken broth, a full-flavored chicken noodle soup was the natural next step. I wanted a classic soup with big flavor, a simple approach, and minimal prep. Could I do it, or was I counting my chickens before they hatched?

I started with the basics: a whole chicken and some water. Since I was looking for clean chicken flavor—and lots of it—I wanted most of the soup's flavor to come from the chicken. So I sealed the lid of my pressure cooker and counted down the minutes to my minimalist soup. Once the cooker had reached high pressure, it took just 20 minutes until the chicken was fully cooked. When we tasted the soup, we found that the pressure cooker had extracted deep flavor from the chicken's meat, skin, and bones to transform the water into an impressive broth.

What's more, I was pleased to find that I could skip butchering my bird. In many soup recipes, the chicken is cut into pieces to increase its surface area and lend the broth more flavor, but in the pressure cooker, simmering a whole 4-pound chicken yielded a richly flavored broth. Plus, when I opened up the pot, the meat was so tender that it practically fell off the bones, making it easy to shred into pieces and stir back into the soup later.

There was just one problem: The lean breast meat was cooking through faster than the darker thigh meat, giving me either dry, overcooked breast meat or underdone thighs. Luckily, the solution turned out to be simple.

PRESSURE–COOKER FARMHOUSE CHICKEN NOODLE SOUP

I found that placing the chicken in the pot breast side up so that the thighs were in direct contact with the pot ensured that the thighs and delicate breast meat would cook through in the same amount of time. Finally, the chicken in my chicken soup was perfectly cooked.

Next I focused on the vegetables and aromatics. Onion and a few garlic cloves provided a savory base, and I opted to stick with the classic combination of carrots and celery. I was concerned that the high pressure might prove too much for delicate bite-size vegetables in the soup, but my first test showed that the vegetables were sturdy enough to withstand the time under pressure without overcooking or losing their shape.

The resulting soup was deeply flavored and nicely balanced by the sweet and savory flavors of the carrots and celery. A splash of soy sauce enriched the flavor even more, drawing out the rich, meaty flavor of the chicken.

Last, I had to figure out how to cook the noodles. First I tried cooking the noodles separately, then adding them to the finished soup. But since it took almost 20 minutes just to boil the water, the chicken was finished before the noodles started cooking. Then it occurred to me that I could add the noodles to the hot soup and cook them right in the broth while I shredded the chicken. Plus, as they cooked, the noodles both absorbed the broth's rich flavor and released some of their starch, thickening the broth nicely. The resulting soup had even more chicken flavor than I expected, and it couldn't have been easier. All it took was a little pressure.

—CHRISTIE MORRISON,
America's Test Kitchen Books

NOTES FROM THE TEST KITCHEN

MAKING PRESSURE-COOKER CHICKEN NOODLE SOUP

1. When cooking a whole chicken in the pressure cooker, we found it best to keep the delicate breast meat facing up to give it some protection from the direct heat and to promote even cooking.

2. Once cooked, the chicken will be very tender and nearly falling apart. To remove the chicken from the pot to shred it, lift it out in one piece using tongs along with a large spoon for support.

3. Let chicken cool slightly, then discard skin and pull meat off bones. Shred meat using two forks, gently pulling meat apart and into bite-size strands.

4. The last step is adding the noodles. Simmering them in the soup ensures they absorb flavor. Be sure to do this just before serving or else the noodles can become bloated and mushy.

Pressure-Cooker Farmhouse Chicken Noodle Soup

SERVES 8

If you have at least an 8-quart pressure cooker, you can use up to a 5-pound chicken in this recipe; extend the pressurized cooking time to 30 minutes. To make this soup in an electric pressure cooker, quick-release the pressure immediately after the pressurized cooking time (do not let the cooker switch to the warm setting) and use the browning (not the simmer) setting to cook the noodles in step 4.

 1 **tablespoon vegetable oil**
 1 **onion, chopped fine**
 3 **garlic cloves, minced**
 1 **teaspoon minced fresh thyme or ¼ teaspoon dried**
 8 **cups water**
 4 **carrots, peeled and sliced ½ inch thick**
 2 **celery ribs, sliced ½ inch thick**
 2 **tablespoons soy sauce**
 1 **(4-pound) whole chicken, giblets discarded**
    Salt and pepper
 4 **ounces (2⅔ cups) wide egg noodles**
 ¼ **cup minced fresh parsley**

1. Heat oil in pressure-cooker pot over medium heat until shimmering. Add onion and cook until softened, about 5 minutes. Stir in garlic and thyme and cook until fragrant, about 30 seconds. Stir in water, carrots, celery, and soy sauce, scraping up any browned bits. Season chicken with salt and pepper and place, breast side up, in pot.

2. Lock pressure-cooker lid in place and bring to high pressure over medium-high heat. As soon as pot reaches high pressure, reduce heat to medium-low and cook for 20 minutes, adjusting heat as needed to maintain high pressure.

3. Remove pot from heat. Quick-release pressure, then carefully remove lid, allowing steam to escape away from you.

4. Transfer chicken to cutting board, let cool slightly, then shred meat into bite-size pieces, discarding skin and bones. Meanwhile, using large spoon, skim excess fat from surface of soup. Bring soup to boil, stir in noodles, and cook until tender, about 5 minutes. Stir in shredded chicken and parsley and season with salt and pepper to taste. Serve.

VARIATION

Pressure-Cooker Farmhouse Chicken and Rice Soup
Substitute 1 cup long-grain white rice for egg noodles and cook until tender, 15 to 18 minutes.

KNOEPHLA

✔ **WHY THIS RECIPE WORKS** Brought to the Midwest by German immigrants, *knoephla* soup is a hearty version of chicken and dumplings with a creamy base, tender potatoes, and chewy "knoephla" dumplings. To infuse our soup with flavor, we started by searing chicken thighs and simmering them in chicken broth to make a fortified base. We lightened up the leaden dumplings with baking soda and, instead of tediously spooning them into the simmering soup as most recipes instruct, we used a piping bag and snipped off the dumplings with kitchen shears. Half-and-half added richness to the dumplings and finished the soup for a creamy, satisfying dish.

Despite the funny name, *knoephla* (pronounced NEF-la) soup is really just a Midwestern take on chicken and dumplings. Hearty, creamy, and chock-full of chicken, potatoes, and bite-size dumplings, the soup is designed to get Minnesotans and North Dakotans through long, bitter winters. German settlers brought knoephla to the Midwest, handily turning sparse winter resources into a nourishing, comforting, and delicious meal.

"You can't live in Bismarck—or North Dakota, for that matter—for 10 minutes without running into that soup," said my friend John, who went to school in Bismarck. "It's good stuff." With his blessing, I gathered some recipes. Unfortunately, most were more like vague tips than detailed directions. With scant guidance, my attempts in the kitchen suffered. My soups were bland and my dumplings heavy and gummy. ("Soup is greasy. It looks like prison fare," one taster wrote on her tasting notes.)

Most of the recipes I did find called for simply boiling chopped onion in store-bought chicken broth to make the soup's base. One exception gave more explicit instructions, essentially describing how to make a quick chicken broth: Boil chicken parts in water with onion, celery, carrots, and herbs; remove the parts; shred the meat; and add it back to the soup. The bone-in chicken parts gave the soup far more body and flavor than the onion and store-bought broth combination. What if I combined these two methods? I took bone-in, skin-on thighs (their dark meat is more flavorful than white breast meat) and boiled them in store-bought chicken broth instead of water to make what chefs call a double chicken stock. I browned the thighs first to render their fat, removed them from the pot, then sautéed the onion in the fat. This method gave the onion great flavor, and the tasty fond at the bottom of my pot enriched my soup. I poured in 2 quarts of chicken broth, removed the skin from the chicken thighs, and returned them to the pot to simmer. Once the chicken was tender, I took it out, shredded the meat, and added potatoes to the pot to cook until tender. So far, so delicious.

Next, I turned to the dumplings, or knoephla (from a German dialect, meaning "little knob"). Made from flour, eggs, and water, they are usually dropped from a spoon into the simmering soup. For richer dumplings, I replaced some of the water with half-and-half. To fix the gummy, dense texture that had ruined my initial attempts, I tried adding baking powder to the batter for lift. I spooned these dumplings into my simmering broth and let them cook for about 15 minutes, until they floated to the surface. Just ¼ teaspoon of baking powder aerated the dumplings, giving them the correct chew, and as they puffed, bits sloughed off and dissolved in the broth, making the soup rich and creamy.

But somewhere after spooning up the 80th or so dumpling (each batch yields more than 100), I lost patience. That's when I noticed a fellow test cook using a pastry bag to ice a cake. Bingo: Instead of tediously spooning each dumpling, I'd simply pipe the dumpling batter into the hot broth. I loaded the batter into a zipper-lock bag, clipped off a corner, and tried to pipe out the dough. My first attempt was a failure; the soft mixture oozed out haphazardly. I found the trick was to chill the batter to firm it, then to snip off bite-size dumplings with kitchen shears as I squeezed out the batter. With this method, I could quickly produce shapely dumplings. After my dumplings had simmered for 10 minutes, I returned the shredded chicken to the pot and stirred in ½ cup of half-and-half for a hearty, savory, and deeply satisfying soup.

—NICK IVERSON, *Cook's Country*

Knoephla (Dakota Chicken-and-Dumpling) Soup

SERVES 6

Let the batter chill for at least 30 minutes before forming the dumplings. The chicken and broth can be made through step 2 and refrigerated; reheat before proceeding with step 3.

- 4 (5- to 7-ounce) bone-in chicken thighs, trimmed
  Salt and pepper
- 1 teaspoon vegetable oil
- 1 onion, chopped fine
- 8 cups chicken broth
- 2½ cups (12½ ounces) all-purpose flour
- ¼ teaspoon baking powder
- 3 large eggs, lightly beaten
- 1 cup half-and-half
- ½ cup water
- 2 pounds Yukon Gold potatoes, peeled and cut into ½-inch pieces

1. Pat chicken dry with paper towels and season with salt and pepper. Heat oil in Dutch oven over medium heat until just smoking. Cook chicken, skin side down, until well browned, 6 to 8 minutes; transfer chicken to plate. Remove and discard skin.

2. Pour off all but 1 teaspoon fat and return pot to medium heat. Add onion and cook until just beginning to brown, 3 to 5 minutes. Add broth, chicken, and

1¼ teaspoons salt and bring to boil. Reduce heat to medium-low, cover, and simmer until chicken is tender, about 30 minutes.

3. Meanwhile, whisk flour, 1 teaspoon salt, ½ teaspoon pepper, and baking powder together in large bowl. Whisk eggs, ½ cup half-and-half, and water into flour mixture until thick batter forms. Transfer batter to gallon-size zipper-lock bag and refrigerate until ready to use.

4. Remove chicken from pot and set aside. Add potatoes to broth and simmer for 10 minutes. Cut ¼ inch off corner of batter bag. Pipe batter into simmering broth, snipping dumplings with moistened kitchen shears every ½ to ¾ inch as extruded. Simmer until dumplings float to surface, 10 to 15 minutes, stirring occasionally.

5. Shred chicken meat into bite-size pieces and add to soup. Remove soup from heat and stir in remaining ½ cup half-and-half. Season with salt and pepper to taste and serve.

GUINNESS BEEF STEW

✓ **WHY THIS RECIPE WORKS** Guinness beef stew, a staple of Irish pubs and St. Patrick's Day, often falls short. The dark, malty Irish beer should be the perfect match for beef stew, but its bitterness often throws the flavors off balance. We added dark brown sugar, which offset some of the bitterness with sweetness and bolstered flavor with its molasses-y notes. Cooked beer can be especially bitter; adding some of the beer at the end gave us robust stout flavor that wasn't one-dimensional. For a simpler method, we found we could bypass the messy step of searing the meat by cooking the stew uncovered in the oven. This easy trick not only allowed the exposed meat to brown but also let the sauce reduce, concentrating its flavor.

As a lover of both beef stew and dark beers, it would stand to reason that I'd go nuts over Guinness beef stew. Unfortunately, I always find that this staple of Irish pubs and St. Paddy's Day get-togethers is somehow less than the sum of its parts. Guinness beef stew rarely tastes much of beer, and when it does, it captures only the bitterness and none of the deep, roasted flavors of the brew. In theory, toasty, malty flavor with a hint of bitterness should improve beef stew. Could I make that theory a reality?

I cooked half a dozen batches of stew from existing recipes, and while none was what I had in mind, I established some ground rules: I'd keep the vegetable selection simple (carrots and potatoes), use a combination of beer and chicken broth (beer alone yielded bitter sauce), and cut the meat myself from a chuck roast (precut stew chunks were inconsistent).

Most recipes followed a standard stew method: searing the meat in batches, browning the onions, sprinkling in flour, whisking in beer and broth, adding the vegetables, and then cooking it all, covered, either in the oven or on the stove. But one recipe called for just tossing everything in a Dutch oven, covering, and cooking until the meat was tender. The sauce came out thin in terms of both flavor and consistency, but the prospect of skipping the sear (and the resulting splatter) was enticing.

I remembered a test kitchen recipe for Spanish-style beef stew that didn't call for searing the meat; rather, it required browning the onions, tomato paste, and garlic and then cooking the stew uncovered. I gave this method a try, browning the onions, garlic, and paste and cooking my stew uncovered in a 325-degree oven.

Uncovered, the sauce reduced and concentrated as it cooked, making up for the lack of fond. The sauce and meat took on a more robust, roasted flavor, and the meat that was elevated above the liquid even browned—but the vegetables were practically baby food. To fix that, I let the meat cook for 90 minutes before stirring the vegetables into the pot. Tasters were impressed with my simple method but weren't entirely ready to sign off: "Where's the beer flavor?" Back to the kitchen.

I thought more beer would give me more potent beer flavor, so I upped the Guinness from 1 cup to 1½ cups. Bad move—50 percent more beer just made the stew 50 percent more bitter. Trying to amp up the stew's toasty flavors in other ways, I tested batches with molasses, brown sugar, espresso powder, ground-up toasted barley (it's an ingredient in the beer so I figured it might help; it didn't), various spices, and even bittersweet chocolate. Most additions didn't make a difference—or gave the stew strange flavors—but tasters liked brown sugar's toasty complexity and extra sweetness, which helped balance the bitterness of the beer. So far, it was a good, easy-to-put-together stew, but it still didn't exactly scream Guinness.

Most beef stew recipes called for adding all of the beer at the beginning, but a few called for adding most or all at the end. Maybe the key wasn't quantity but timing. I made several more batches, adding beer at the start, at the end, and splitting the difference. Eventually, I determined that ¾ cup of Guinness poured in along with the broth and ½ cup more added after cooking yielded the best balance of bitterness, hefty roasted taste, and bold beer flavor. With good timing and a streamlined method, I'd harnessed the roasty, complex flavor of Guinness beef stew.

—SARAH GABRIEL, *Cook's Country*

NOTES FROM THE TEST KITCHEN

COOK IT UNCOVERED

Most stew recipes start by searing meat in batches on the stovetop. We avoid that messy task by cooking the stew uncovered in the oven; the open pot allows the meat on top to take on flavorful browning. In addition, the liquid reduces, concentrating its flavor and texture, while the meat cooks.

GUINNESS BEEF STEW

SERVES 6 TO 8

Use Guinness Draught, not Guinness Extra Stout, which is too bitter.

- 1 (3½- to 4-pound) boneless beef chuck-eye roast, pulled apart at seams, trimmed, and cut into 1½-inch pieces
  Salt and pepper
- 3 tablespoons vegetable oil
- 2 onions, chopped fine
- 1 tablespoon tomato paste
- 2 garlic cloves, minced
- ¼ cup all-purpose flour
- 3 cups chicken broth
- 1¼ cups Guinness Draught
- 1½ tablespoons packed dark brown sugar
- 1 teaspoon minced fresh thyme
- 1½ pounds Yukon Gold potatoes, unpeeled, cut into 1-inch pieces
- 1 pound carrots, peeled and cut into 1-inch pieces
- 2 tablespoons minced fresh parsley

1. Adjust oven rack to lower-middle position and heat oven to 325 degrees. Season beef with salt and pepper. Heat oil in Dutch oven over medium-high heat until shimmering. Add onions and ¼ teaspoon salt and cook, stirring occasionally, until well browned, 8 to 10 minutes.

2. Add tomato paste and garlic and cook until rust-colored and fragrant, about 2 minutes. Stir in flour and cook for 1 minute. Whisk in broth, ¾ cup Guinness, sugar, and thyme, scraping up any browned bits. Bring to simmer and cook until slightly thickened, about 3 minutes. Stir in beef and return to simmer. Transfer to oven and cook, uncovered, for 90 minutes, stirring halfway through cooking.

3. Stir in potatoes and carrots and continue cooking until beef and vegetables are tender, about 1 hour, stirring halfway through cooking. Stir in remaining ½ cup Guinness and parsley. Season with salt and pepper to taste and serve.

FIVE-ALARM CHILI

✔ **WHY THIS RECIPE WORKS** As the name implies, five-alarm chili should be spicy enough to make you break a sweat, but it has to have rich, complex chile flavor as well. We used a combination of dried anchos, smoky chipotle chiles in adobo sauce, fresh jalapeños, cayenne, and chili powder to create layers of flavor. Ground beef added meaty bulk, and pureeing the chiles along with canned tomatoes and corn chips added extra body and another layer of flavor. Although unusual, some light-bodied beer added an intriguing hint of bitterness. Mellowed with a bit of sugar, and enriched with creamy pinto beans, this chili is well balanced and intensely spicy without being harsh.

"Five-alarm chili" is cute shorthand to remind diners that what they're about to eat is HOT. And on that count, there was little question that the recipes I tested for five-alarm beef-and-bean chili lived up to their name. But judged on any other grounds, they were a harsh and bitter disappointment, or, as one taster put it, "one-note firebombs." On the plus side, my goal was plain as day: Simply loading up on chili powder and cayenne was a dead end. For multilayered heat, I'd need to combine different types of chiles.

First, the recipe mechanics: Brown and then drain ground beef. Soften chopped onion, garlic, and spices in the drippings. Return the browned beef to the pot along with tomatoes, water, and beans (we liked creamy pintos, canned for ease) and simmer. Next I picked and chose the chiles, limiting myself to what I could easily find at an average supermarket. Cayenne gave a good initial blast of heat. Chili powder—typically made from ground chiles plus cumin and oregano—was a strong supporting player, though I still needed more heat and flavor. I tested jalapeños in two guises: chopped fresh jalapeños and canned chipotle chiles in adobo sauce for smoky flavor. (Chipotles in adobo are ripe jalapeños that have been dried, smoked, and canned in vinegar-tomato sauce.) We liked both, so both went into my recipe. Now I was almost there, but I wanted a little more depth and a touch of sweetness. Dried ancho chiles (called poblanos when fresh) seemed like they might be the answer. Since they are tough and papery, the anchos required rehydrating. Just 3 minutes in the microwave was enough to soften them. To break them down, I'd also need to puree them, so as long as I had the blender out, I tossed in the canned chipotle chiles and canned whole tomatoes as well. Less chopping meant less work, which was OK by me.

With the chiles selected and mechanics set, I thought I might be finished. I made a batch of my recipe to prove it and . . . was forced to admit that, although the chili had multiple levels of flavor and heat, it tasted a little flat. How could that be? I studied my recipe looking for places to cram in more flavor. Substituting chicken broth for some of the water I had been using helped, but what really invigorated the chili was a bottle of beer. It may sound strange, but the beer introduced malty, mellow depth and a hint of bitterness.

Serious chili recipes for serious chiliheads often rely on masa (ground dried corn) to add subtle corn flavor. Few of us keep masa around, but I loved the concept of another flavor booster, so I substituted more convenient corn tortilla chips. By adding them to the blender with the tomatoes, chiles, and water, I made a smooth paste that contributed body along with the flavor of corn. As the chili simmered, the flavors melded, the broth thickened, and complexity met raw heat. After an hour, I cautiously dipped in a spoon. My eyes teared, my face

flushed, and I had to mop my brow. Yes, this chili built to a thrilling tingle, but the other flavors came through loud and clear as well.

—DIANE UNGER, *Cook's Country*

Five-Alarm Chili
SERVES 8 TO 10

Look for ancho chiles in the international aisle at the supermarket. Light-bodied American lagers, such as Budweiser, work best here. Serve chili with lime, sour cream, scallions, and cornbread.

 2 **ounces dried ancho chiles (4 to 6 chiles), stemmed, seeded, and flesh torn into 1-inch pieces**
3½ **cups water**
 1 **(28-ounce) can whole peeled tomatoes**
 ¾ **cup crushed corn tortilla chips**
 ¼ **cup canned chipotle chile in adobo sauce plus 2 teaspoons adobo sauce**
 2 **tablespoons vegetable oil**
 2 **pounds 85 percent lean ground beef**
    Salt and pepper
 2 **pounds onions, chopped fine**
 2 **jalapeño chiles, stemmed, seeds reserved, and minced**
 6 **garlic cloves, minced**
 2 **tablespoons ground cumin**
 2 **tablespoons chili powder**
 1 **tablespoon dried oregano**
 2 **teaspoons ground coriander**
 2 **teaspoons sugar**
 1 **teaspoon cayenne pepper**
1½ **cups beer**
 3 **(15-ounce) cans pinto beans, rinsed**

1. Combine anchos and 1½ cups water in bowl and microwave until softened, about 3 minutes. Drain and discard liquid. Process anchos, tomatoes and their juice, remaining 2 cups water, tortilla chips, chipotle, and adobo sauce in blender until smooth, about 1 minute; set aside.

2. Heat 2 teaspoons oil in Dutch oven over medium-high heat until just smoking. Add beef, 1 teaspoon salt, and ½ teaspoon pepper and cook, breaking up pieces with spoon, until all liquid has evaporated and meat begins to sizzle, 10 to 15 minutes. Drain in colander; set aside.

3. Heat remaining 4 teaspoons oil in now-empty Dutch oven over medium-high heat until simmering. Add onions and jalapeños and seeds and cook until

---

NOTES FROM THE TEST KITCHEN

FIVE HITS FOR FIVE ALARMS

CHILI POWDER
Wouldn't be chili without it.

CAYENNE
Adds raw heat.

JALAPEÑO
Brings fresh vegetable flavor.

CHIPOTLE IN ADOBO
Easy shortcut to smokiness.

ANCHO
Adds depth, complexity, and mild heat.

onions are lightly browned, about 5 minutes. Stir in garlic, cumin, chili powder, oregano, coriander, sugar, and cayenne and cook until fragrant, about 30 seconds. Pour in beer and bring to simmer. Stir in beans, reserved ancho-tomato mixture, and reserved cooked beef and bring to simmer. Cover, reduce heat to low, and cook, stirring occasionally, until thickened, 50 to 60 minutes. Season with salt to taste and serve.

BEST VEGETARIAN CHILI

✔ **WHY THIS RECIPE WORKS** Vegetarian chilis are often little more than a thin mishmash of beans and vegetables. To create a true chili—not just a bean and vegetable stew—we knew we'd need to find replacements for the different ways that meat adds depth and flavor to chili. Along with two kinds of beans, bulgur bulked up the chili, giving it a substantial texture. An unusual combination of umami-rich walnuts, soy sauce, dried shiitake mushrooms, and tomatoes added deep savory flavor. Using a generous amount of oil to sauté the onion and spices helped to bloom the chili's flavors, lending a rich, lingering flavor. A final vigorous stir released starch from the beans and bulgur and emulsified the oil for a thick, velvety texture.

I love chili, but I have to admit that vegetarian versions are usually the last kind I'd think to make. Most lack depth and complexity; while they may taste lively and bright initially, their flavor fades. They rely on beans and chunky veggies for heartiness—but in truth that heartiness often falls short. Neither ingredient is a real replacement for the flavor, texture, and richness that meat provides. It doesn't help matters that such chilis are typically made with canned beans and one-dimensional commercial chili powder.

But do vegetarian chilis really have to be this way? I set out to build a version as rich, savory, and deeply satisfying as any meat chili out there—one that even meat lovers would make on its own merits, not just to serve to vegetarian friends.

The first ingredient to tackle was the seasoning that gives the dish its name. Though we often use store-bought chili powder in our recipes, even the best brands can't compete with a powder that you grind yourself from dried chiles. For my homemade blend, I opted for two widely available dried chiles: mild, sweet ancho and earthy New Mexican. I toasted them to bring out their flavor and then, after removing the stems and seeds, I pulverized the peppers to a fine powder in a spice grinder along with some dried oregano.

Next up: the beans. For greater complexity, I wanted to use a mix of different beans, singling out sweet, nutty cannellinis and meaty, earthy pintos. Canned beans are certainly convenient, but their texture and flavor are never quite as good as dried. Since the beans would be the star of the show, I opted for dried, calling on our quick-brining method. This entails bringing the beans to a boil in a pot of salted water and then letting them sit, covered, for an hour. The brine ensures soft, creamy beans (sodium ions from salt weaken the pectin in the bean skins for a softer texture) that are well seasoned and evenly cooked.

Meanwhile, the beans' hour-long rest gave me plenty of time to prep the remaining ingredients. I started out with my dried chile and oregano powder, plus some cumin for earthy depth and finely chopped onions for sweetness. I sautéed the onions just until they began to brown, then added the spices to bloom in the hot oil. In went my brined, rinsed beans and the water; then I covered the pot and placed it in a 300-degree oven. On the stovetop, I'd have to stir the beans to prevent scorching, but in the more even, gentle heat of the oven they could simmer unattended. I simply checked the beans periodically as they cooked. After 45 minutes, they were just tender.

Next I added a can of diced tomatoes, which I whizzed in a food processor with lots of garlic and some fresh jalapeños to kick up the heat. The tomatoes would keep the beans from falling apart during the remainder of cooking, since the basic building blocks of legumes—polysaccharides—do not readily dissolve in acidic conditions. Another 2 hours and the beans were perfectly cooked: creamy and tender but not blown out.

But I still had just a pot of flavored beans. Now to turn it into a real chili . . .

Along with the beans, most vegetarian chilis replace the bulk that meat contributes with some combination of diced vegetables. But these recipes miss a major point: In addition to adding volume and flavor, meat gives chili its distinctive texture. Properly made meat chili is a homogeneous mixture of ground or diced meat napped with a thick, spicy sauce. No matter how you slice or dice them, cut vegetables can't deliver that same sturdy texture. They also tend to water down the dish.

In my research I'd come across vegetarian chilis that called for nuts, seeds, or grains, and with nothing to lose I decided to try a few of these more unusual add-ins. Chopped pumpkin seeds were a failure: They didn't break down during cooking, leaving sharp, crunchy bits in the chili. Long-grain rice, meanwhile, turned to mush by the time the beans were cooked through, and large, round grains of pearl barley were too chewy and gummy. Finally, I hit the jackpot: I stirred in some nutty granules of bulgur when I added the tomatoes to the pot. Even after the long simmer, these precooked wheat kernels (which are normally plumped up by a quick soak in water) retained their shape, giving the chili the textural dimension that it had been missing.

My recipe was progressing nicely, but it still didn't have the rich depth of flavor that turns a good chili into something great. The canned tomatoes were contributing some savory flavor, but I needed a more potent source, so I added a few dollops of umami-packed tomato paste as well as a few tablespoons of soy sauce.

But even with these additions, the flavor was still too one-dimensional. Recently, while developing a vegetable soup, I'd learned that umami boosters like tomato paste and soy sauce fall into two categories—glutamates and nucleotides—and that the two types have a synergistic effect when used together. To amplify the effect of the glutamate-rich soy sauce and tomatoes, I needed something rich in nucleotides. What about dried mushrooms? Since I was already grinding my chile peppers, I simply tossed in some chopped, dried shiitake mushrooms at the same time. This way, I could take advantage of their flavor-boosting qualities without adding distinct chunks of mushroom to the chili.

Sure enough, this batch was the meatiest yet. But could I take things even further? I reviewed a list of umami-rich foods and was surprised to see that walnuts contain more than twice as many glutamates as do tomatoes. From the failed pumpkin seed test I knew that I didn't want a crunchy chili, so for my next batch I toasted some walnuts, ground them in a food processor, and then stirred them into the chili along with the tomatoes and bulgur. In terms of savory depth, tasters unanimously deemed this batch the winner to date, and there were added bonuses: The fat from the nuts offered

some richness, and the tannins in the skins contributed a slightly bitter note that balanced the other flavors nicely.

Now my chili had complexity, but it still didn't have the lingering depth of a meat chili. I took a step back and thought about what else meat brings to chili. Its fat not only contributes flavor but also boosts the flavors of the other ingredients and affects how you taste them. The flavor compounds in spices (chile peppers and cumin, in particular) are far more soluble in fat than in water, so a watery sauce dulls their flavor, whereas oils and fats allow them to bloom. What's more, fat coats

NOTES FROM THE TEST KITCHEN

GIVE IT A STIR (AND A REST)

To capitalize on the ability of the fat in the chili to create body in the sauce, we gave the chili a vigorous stir and a 20-minute rest after we took it out of the oven. Stirring helped to release starch from the beans and the bulgur. The starch then clustered around the fat droplets in the chili, preventing them from coalescing and helping to create a thick, velvety emulsion that never left a slick of oil on top of the chili, no matter how many times we reheated it.

MEET THE MEATY ALTERNATIVES

We got all the texture, savory flavor, and richness of classic chili in our meatless chili with the help of some surprising add-ins.

BULGUR
Small grains of tender, chewy wheat add a hearty textural element.

WALNUTS
Ground toasted walnuts add richness and body as well as tons of flavor-boosting glutamates.

SHIITAKES
These nucleotide-rich dried mushrooms have a synergistic effect when combined with glutamates, cranking up savory umami flavor even more.

BEST VEGETARIAN CHILI

the surface of your mouth, giving flavors staying power on the palate. I began slowly increasing the amount of vegetable oil that I was using to sauté the aromatics. Ultimately, I found that ¼ cup brought the chile's flavors into focus and allowed them to linger pleasantly instead of disappearing after a few seconds.

Now everything was perfect but for one issue: When I took the chili out of the oven, I found that some of the fat had separated out, leaving an oil slick on top. A quick stir helped some, but at the suggestion of our science editor, I tried a more vigorous stir followed by a 20-minute rest. This led to a thick, velvety chili that you could stand a spoon in. Here's why: Stirring released starches from the beans and bulgur, which absorbed the water in the sauce, allowing the sauce to stabilize around the fat droplets and prevent the oil from separating out again—in a sense creating a kind of emulsion.

There was nothing left to do but stir in some cilantro for a touch of freshness and then let my tasters loose on the toppings. Whether garnished with a little of everything or just a dollop of sour cream, each bite of chili was hearty and full-flavored—and no one missed the meat.

—LAN LAM, *Cook's Illustrated*

Best Vegetarian Chili

SERVES 6 TO 8

We prefer to make this chili with whole dried chiles, but it can be prepared with jarred chili powder. If using chili powder, grind the shiitakes and oregano and add them to the pot with ¼ cup of chili powder in step 4. We also recommend a mix of at least two types of beans, one creamy (such as cannellini or navy) and one earthy (such as pinto, black, or red kidney). For a spicier chili, use both jalapeños. Serve the chili with lime wedges, sour cream, diced avocado, chopped red onion, and shredded Monterey Jack or cheddar cheese, if desired.

  Salt
1 pound (2½ cups) dried beans, picked over and rinsed
2 dried ancho chiles
2 dried New Mexican chiles
½ ounce dried shiitake mushrooms, chopped coarse
4 teaspoons dried oregano
½ cup walnuts, toasted

1 (28-ounce) can diced tomatoes, drained with juice reserved
3 tablespoons tomato paste
1-2 jalapeño chiles, stemmed and coarsely chopped
6 garlic cloves, minced
3 tablespoons soy sauce
¼ cup vegetable oil
2 pounds onions, chopped fine
1 tablespoon ground cumin
7 cups water
⅔ cup medium-grind bulgur
¼ cup chopped fresh cilantro

1. Bring 4 quarts water, 3 tablespoons salt, and beans to boil in large Dutch oven over high heat. Remove pot from heat, cover, and let stand for 1 hour. Drain beans and rinse well. Wipe out pot.

2. Adjust oven rack to middle position and heat oven to 300 degrees. Arrange anchos and New Mexican chiles on rimmed baking sheet and toast until fragrant and puffed, about 8 minutes. Transfer to plate and let cool, about 5 minutes. Stem and seed anchos and New Mexican chiles. Working in batches, grind toasted chiles, mushrooms, and oregano in spice grinder or with mortar and pestle until finely ground.

3. Process walnuts in food processor until finely ground, about 30 seconds. Transfer to bowl. Process drained tomatoes, tomato paste, jalapeño(s), garlic, and soy sauce in food processor until tomatoes are finely chopped, about 45 seconds, scraping down bowl as needed.

4. Heat oil in now-empty Dutch oven over medium-high heat until shimmering. Add onions and 1¼ teaspoons salt and cook, stirring occasionally, until onions begin to brown, 8 to 10 minutes. Lower heat to medium and add ground chile mixture and cumin; cook, stirring constantly, until fragrant, about 1 minute. Add rinsed beans and water and bring to boil. Cover pot, transfer to oven, and cook for 45 minutes.

5. Remove pot from oven. Stir in bulgur, ground walnuts, tomato mixture, and reserved tomato juice. Cover pot and return to oven. Cook until beans are fully tender, about 2 hours.

6. Remove pot from oven, stir chili well, and let stand, uncovered, for 20 minutes. Stir in cilantro and serve. (Chili can be made up to 3 days in advance.)

CHAPTER 3

VEGETABLES & SIDES

MEDITERRANEAN BRAISED GREEN BEANS

✓ **WHY THIS RECIPE WORKS** Unlike crisp-tender green beans that have been steamed or sautéed, braised green beans boast a uniquely soft, velvety texture without being mushy. Unfortunately, achieving this usually takes as much as 2 hours of simmering. To get ultratender braised green beans in half the time, we first simmered them with a pinch of baking soda to partially dissolve the pectin in their cell walls. Once the beans were partially softened, we added tomatoes to add sweet flavor and neutralize the soda. This allowed the beans to turn meltingly tender after a gentle simmer in a low oven. To infuse the beans with bright Mediterranean flavors, we added sautéed garlic and onion plus some piquant red wine vinegar and chopped fresh parsley.

Quickly steamed or sautéed, lightly crisp green beans are commonplace. But there's a lesser-known approach that turns them into something altogether different: braising. Southern-style green beans are slowly braised in broth with ham hocks or bacon until they pick up smoky flavor. The time-honored Mediterranean take on this method (my personal favorite) calls for sautéing garlic and onions in olive oil, adding tomatoes and green beans along with water, then simmering until the sauce is thickened and the beans are infused with tomato and garlic flavor. The best part is the texture of the beans: The slow cooking renders them so meltingly tender that they're almost creamy.

There are just two problems: First, it takes at least 2 hours of cooking to turn the beans ultratender. (Some recipes call for shorter cooking times, but they don't produce the truly silky texture that makes this dish so special.) Second, I often find that by the time the skins have fully softened, the interiors have practically disintegrated. I wanted the beans to turn velvety soft but remain intact. I also wanted a reasonable cooking time—no more than an hour.

Before I started cooking, I brushed up on the makeup of green beans. Their pods are composed primarily of cellulose and pectin, polysaccharides that are the main building blocks of most plant cell walls. The tough fibers of cellulose are impossible to dissolve, but when pectin breaks down during cooking, water is able to enter the fibers, swelling and softening them over time. The key

to speedier cooking, then, would be to focus on the pectin. Pectin is affected by pH and will break down more slowly in an acidic environment. That meant that one of the key components of my dish—the acidic tomatoes—was lengthening the cooking time. To confirm my hunch, I made one batch of beans with tomatoes and another without. Sure enough, the tomato-free beans needed far less time to soften.

Tomatoes are integral to the dish, and ditching them wasn't an option. But could I come up with another way to speed up the breakdown of the pectin in the beans? I decided to try a technique we developed while searching for a way to get the pectin in broccoli to rapidly disintegrate for quick broccoli-cheese soup: We added baking soda to the pot to create an alkaline cooking environment.

To test whether this technique would work here, I sautéed onion and garlic and added the green beans, water, and ½ teaspoon of baking soda. I held off on incorporating the tomatoes so they wouldn't neutralize the baking soda. This method worked perfectly; just 10 minutes of simmering was enough to soften the beans significantly.

Now I could use the acidity of the tomatoes to my advantage. Once added to the pot, they would slow any further breakdown of pectin while the beans continued to simmer, giving the cellulose time to swell with water and fully soften. I mixed in diced tomatoes and some tomato paste for sweetness and depth and continued simmering. When I lifted the lid about 45 minutes later, the beans were soft and creamy but not at all mushy.

One minor outstanding issue: The beans were a bit raggedy around the edges. So for the next batch, after incorporating the tomatoes, I moved the pot from the

---

NOTES FROM THE TEST KITCHEN

TRIMMING GREEN BEANS

Instead of trimming green beans one at a time, line up beans on cutting board and trim all ends with just 1 slice.

stove to a low oven so the beans could finish cooking in the more gentle heat. This batch was perfect, with tender skins, intact interiors, and rich flavor. To brighten the flavors, I stirred in a pinch of cayenne and a little red wine vinegar, plus chopped parsley for freshness.

Crisp-tender green beans have their place, but it's nice to have the option to put this entirely different, satisfyingly rich side dish on the table.

—ANDREW JANJIGIAN, *Cook's Illustrated*

Mediterranean Braised Green Beans
SERVES 4 TO 6 AS A SIDE DISH

A dollop of yogurt spooned over the beans adds nice tang. To make a light entrée, serve the beans with rice or crusty bread.

- 5 tablespoons extra-virgin olive oil
- 1 onion, chopped fine
- 4 garlic cloves, minced
  Pinch cayenne pepper
- 1½ cups water
- ½ teaspoon baking soda
- 1½ pounds green beans, trimmed and cut into 2- to 3-inch lengths
- 1 (14.5-ounce) can diced tomatoes, drained with juice reserved, chopped coarse
- 1 tablespoon tomato paste
- 1 teaspoon salt
- ¼ teaspoon pepper
- ¼ cup chopped fresh parsley
  Red wine vinegar

1. Adjust oven rack to lower-middle position and heat oven to 275 degrees. Heat 3 tablespoons oil in Dutch oven over medium heat until shimmering. Add onion and cook, stirring occasionally, until softened, 3 to 5 minutes. Add garlic and cayenne and cook until fragrant, about 30 seconds. Add water, baking soda, and green beans and bring to simmer. Reduce heat to medium-low and cook, stirring occasionally, for 10 minutes. Stir in tomatoes and their juice, tomato paste, salt, and pepper.

2. Cover pot, transfer to oven, and cook until sauce is slightly thickened and green beans can be easily cut with side of fork, 40 to 50 minutes. Stir in parsley and season with vinegar to taste. Drizzle with remaining 2 table-spoons oil and serve warm or at room temperature.

ROASTED CAULIFLOWER

✔ **WHY THIS RECIPE WORKS** Roasting vegetables is all about caramelizing sugars to produce big flavor. Since browning takes place only where the vegetables are in contact with the hot pan, we sliced a head of cauliflower into eight wedges, creating more flat surface area than you'd get with florets. To keep the cauliflower from drying out, we first cooked it covered in a hot oven, letting it steam for a few minutes until barely soft, then we uncovered it so it could brown. Flipping each slice halfway through roasting ensured even cooking and color.

Until recently, cauliflower, at least for me, either lived on a crudités tray or in the freezer section, paired with broccoli and carrots and sold as a "vegetable medley." Both were equally bad, which explains why I never liked cauliflower. When I first tried roasted cauliflower, though, I began to see it in a whole new light. Roasting is a great technique for coaxing big flavor from vegetables, and the dry heat gives cauliflower a creamy texture and a sweet, caramelized flavor. But there are still problems with this technique. Most recipes call for simply tossing the florets with oil and roasting them on a baking sheet. But the oddly shaped florets don't brown evenly, and the high heat dehydrates the florets before they can brown—and browning equals flavor.

To fix these problems, I started by ditching the florets and cutting the cauliflower into eight wedges, which were flatter and had more surface area for browning (and were much easier to flip partway through). The wedges browned much more quickly and evenly, but their edges were still drying out before their centers were tender.

What if I covered the cauliflower for part of the cooking time? For my next test, I covered the baking sheet tightly with foil so the cauliflower would gently steam in its own moisture as it cooked. After 10 minutes, I removed the foil to let the cauliflower brown and caramelize. This method worked perfectly, giving me intensely sweet, tender cauliflower without dried edges.

With my roasting method perfected, I got to work on some interesting flavor variations. Paired with smoked paprika and chorizo in one, and bacon and scallions in another, the cauliflower tastes so substantial it could almost be a meal. Curry, cilantro, and cashews give it an exotic edge. Finally, it takes a detour to the Mediterranean with briny capers and bright lemon.

—NICK IVERSON, *Cook's Country*

Roasted Cauliflower

SERVES 4 TO 6

Wedges are easy to flip and have a lot of surface area in contact with the pan, which leads to great browning.

- 1 head cauliflower (2 pounds)
- ¼ cup extra-virgin olive oil
  Kosher salt and pepper

1. Adjust oven rack to lowest position and heat oven to 475 degrees. Trim outer leaves of cauliflower and cut stem flush with bottom of head. Cut head into 8 equal wedges, keeping core and florets intact. Place wedges cut side down in parchment paper–lined rimmed baking sheet. Drizzle with 2 tablespoons oil and season with salt and pepper to taste; rub gently to distribute oil and seasonings.

2. Cover sheet tightly with aluminum foil and cook for 10 minutes. Remove foil and continue to roast until bottoms of cauliflower wedges are golden, about 15 minutes. Remove sheet from oven and, using spatula, carefully flip wedges. Return sheet to oven and continue to roast until cauliflower is golden all over, about 15 minutes longer. Season with salt and pepper to taste, transfer to platter, and drizzle with remaining 2 tablespoons oil. Serve.

VARIATIONS

Roasted Cauliflower with Bacon and Scallions

In step 1, combine 2 tablespoons oil and 4 minced garlic cloves in small bowl before drizzling over cauliflower. Distribute 6 slices bacon, cut into ½-inch pieces, and ½ onion, cut into ½-inch-thick slices, on baking sheet around cauliflower before roasting. In step 2, whisk remaining 2 tablespoons oil with 2 teaspoons cider vinegar in large bowl. Toss roasted cauliflower mixture with oil-vinegar mixture. Season with salt and pepper to taste, transfer to platter, and sprinkle with 2 thinly sliced scallions.

Roasted Cauliflower with Curry and Lime

In step 1, combine 2 tablespoons oil and 1½ teaspoons curry powder in small bowl before drizzling over cauliflower. Distribute ½ onion, cut into ½-inch-thick slices, on baking sheet around cauliflower before roasting.

In step 2, whisk remaining 2 tablespoons oil with 2 teaspoons lime juice in large bowl. Toss roasted cauliflower with oil–lime juice mixture. Season with salt and pepper to taste; transfer to platter; and sprinkle with ¼ cup cashews, toasted and chopped, and 2 tablespoons chopped fresh cilantro.

Roasted Cauliflower with Lemon and Capers

In step 1, combine 2 tablespoons oil and 1½ teaspoons chopped fresh thyme in small bowl before drizzling over cauliflower. Distribute 2 shallots, cut into ¼-inch-thick rings, on baking sheet around cauliflower before roasting. In step 2, whisk remaining 2 tablespoons oil with ¼ teaspoon grated lemon zest and 2 teaspoons lemon juice in large bowl. Toss roasted cauliflower mixture with oil-lemon mixture. Season with salt and pepper to taste; transfer to platter; and sprinkle with 2 tablespoons rinsed, chopped capers.

Roasted Cauliflower with Paprika and Chorizo

In step 1, combine 2 tablespoons oil and 1½ teaspoons smoked paprika in small bowl before drizzling over cauliflower. Distribute ½ red onion, cut into ½-inch-thick slices, on baking sheet around cauliflower before roasting. In step 2, when removing aluminum foil, distribute 6 ounces chorizo sausage, halved lengthwise and sliced ½ inch thick, on sheet. In step 2, whisk remaining 2 tablespoons oil with 2 teaspoons sherry vinegar in large bowl. Toss roasted cauliflower mixture with oil-vinegar mixture. Season with salt and pepper to taste, transfer to platter, and sprinkle with 2 tablespoons chopped fresh parsley.

NOTES FROM THE TEST KITCHEN

CUTTING CAULIFLOWER INTO WEDGES

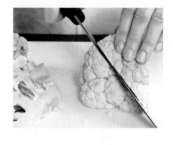

For better browning, we cut the cauliflower into wedges. First trim outer leaves and cut stem flush with bottom of head. Next cut head into wedges, keeping florets attached to core of each wedge.

ROASTED CAULIFLOWER WITH PAPRIKA AND CHORIZO

FRESH CORN SALSA WITH JÍCAMA AND PINEAPPLE

FRESH CORN SALSA

✔ **WHY THIS RECIPE WORKS** Sweet summer corn is the perfect starting point for a fresh, spicy salsa to accompany simple grilled chicken or fish or even as a dip for tortilla chips. To cook the corn just enough to soften the hulls and the starchy insides, we steeped the kernels in boiling water. Adding a touch of baking soda worked like magic to soften the raw corn and loosen the hulls without losing the corn's fresh crispness. To complement the corn without overwhelming its delicate flavor and texture, we chose sweet yet acidic tomato. Some lime juice added tartness, and mixing it with vegetable oil and honey helped it cling to the vegetables. A minced fresh jalapeño and some scallion added heat and complexity.

I love the ease, flavor, and brightness of fresh salsas served alongside a grilled chicken breast or a fish fillet. And of all of summer's produce, corn just might be my favorite as a central ingredient for these vibrant dishes: Its juicy, crisp texture lights up a simple dinner and is equally terrific with chips. Plus, corn's natural sweetness makes it a great foil for spicy chiles and tart citrus juice.

Many salsa recipes call for grilling the corn, but that approach isn't always convenient. It makes sense when I have additional foods to throw on the fire, but I wanted a less complicated version—one that I could whip up without striking a match. Plus, without bitter char from the grill, the sweet flavor and crisp texture of fresh-picked corn could really shine.

My first thought was to simply use raw corn, since I wanted fresh, clean flavor. But I quickly learned that although uncooked kernels taste perfectly sweet, their interiors can be somewhat starchy and their hulls chewy. I tried using the microwave to cook the corn just slightly, but the results were inconsistent. Even with frequent stirring, the kernels cooked unevenly: Some boasted the plump tenderness I wanted, but others emerged still raw and chewy.

I traded the microwave for pots of salted water and tried cooking both whole cobs and stripped kernels for times ranging from 2 to 7 minutes. These samples were more consistently cooked—but they were also overcooked. Even just 2 minutes of boiling destroyed the freshness that I was trying to retain. For a gentler approach, I tried pouring some boiling water onto a bowlful of kernels, but the water cooled too quickly and the corn remained virtually raw. To hold on to a little more heat, I reversed the process, putting the kernels directly into the pot of boiling water, removing the pan from the stove, and letting the corn steep for 10 minutes. This was closer to what I was looking for: The inside of the kernel had lost any trace of starchiness, but the hull was still too chewy.

Softening the hull without overcooking the center seemed impossible—until I considered salsa's natural partner, the tortilla chip. Corn tortillas are formed out of masa, a dough made with ground hominy, which is dried corn that has been soaked in alkaline limewater. This ancient process, called nixtamalization, was first used by Mesoamerican cultures thousands of years ago to soften corn and loosen the hulls. Could I get a similar effect by introducing an alkali to the cooking water for my corn? Just a quarter-teaspoon of baking soda added to the boiling water worked like magic: As the corn steeped, its hulls softened just enough that they weren't leathery, but the kernels still burst with crisp sweetness.

With the corn texture just where I wanted it, I turned to the other ingredients. So far my fresh corn salsa was relatively one-dimensional. I tried a host of fruit and vegetable add-ins but soon learned that it was all too easy to overwhelm the corn's delicate flavor and texture. Fruits that were sweet but with a hint of acidity like tomato and pineapple worked best; very sweet choices like red bell peppers were overwhelming. As for texture, extra-crunchy ingredients like fennel masked the delicate crispness of the corn; elements that were either softer (like avocado) or similarly crisp-tender (like cucumber) worked better. Herbs and chiles were essential additions, as was finely minced shallot. Alongside a simple version with corn, tomato, and jalapeño, I made flavorful variations using avocado and cumin, jícama and pineapple, peach and radishes, and mango and cucumber.

Now I just needed to tie everything together. To bolster the slightly acidic fruit with even more tartness, I tried a variety of vinegars and citrus juices. Tasters found lemon juice and all types of vinegar too brassy and harsh; their preference was mildly acidic lime juice. On its own, though, lime juice pooled at the bottom of the bowl. A tablespoon of vegetable oil and a tiny bit of honey whisked into the lime juice helped give the dressing body so that it could cling to the solids.

Fresh-tasting and a cinch to prepare, these corn salsas will be making regular appearances on my warm-weather menus.

—KEITH DRESSER, *Cook's Illustrated*

Fresh Corn Salsa with Tomato

MAKES 3 CUPS

Do not substitute frozen corn for fresh. For a spicier salsa, add some or all of the jalapeño seeds and ribs. This salsa can be served on chicken or fish or with corn chips.

- 3 ears corn, kernels cut from cobs (2¼ cups)
- ¼ teaspoon baking soda
- Salt and pepper
- 2 tablespoons lime juice
- 1 tablespoon vegetable oil
- ½ teaspoon honey
- 1 tomato, cored, seeded, and cut into ¼-inch pieces
- 1 shallot, minced
- 1 jalapeño chile, stemmed, seeded, and minced
- ¼ cup chopped fresh cilantro

1. Bring 2 cups water to boil in small saucepan over high heat. Stir in corn, baking soda, and ¼ teaspoon salt; remove pan from heat and let stand for 10 minutes. Drain corn and let cool slightly, about 10 minutes.

2. Whisk lime juice, oil, honey, and ⅛ teaspoon salt together in bowl. Add corn, tomato, shallot, jalapeño, and cilantro to lime juice mixture and toss to combine. Let stand for 10 minutes. Season with salt and pepper to taste and serve.

VARIATIONS

Fresh Corn Salsa with Avocado and Toasted Cumin

Add ½ teaspoon toasted cumin seeds and ⅛ teaspoon cayenne pepper to lime juice mixture in step 2. Substitute 1 avocado cut into ¼-inch pieces and 3 thinly sliced scallions for tomato.

Fresh Corn Salsa with Jícama and Pineapple

Substitute ¾ cup pineapple cut into ¼-inch pieces and ½ cup jícama cut into ¼-inch pieces for tomato. Substitute 1 minced serrano chile for jalapeño.

Fresh Corn Salsa with Peach and Radishes

Substitute 1 peeled peach cut into ¼-inch pieces and 4 thinly sliced radishes for tomato. Substitute 1 minced habanero chile for jalapeño and basil for cilantro.

Fresh Corn Salsa with Mango and Cucumber

Add ¼ teaspoon chipotle chile powder to lime juice mixture in step 2. Substitute half of peeled mango cut into ¼-inch pieces and 1 small peeled and seeded cucumber cut into ¼-inch pieces for tomato. Omit jalapeño and substitute mint for cilantro.

EASY BAKED POLENTA

✓ WHY THIS RECIPE WORKS Creamy polenta, cornmeal simmered in water until softened, is a classic Italian side dish, but cooking it on the stove requires up to a half-hour of nonstop stirring. We wanted to take advantage of the steady, even heat of the oven to adapt traditional polenta into a completely hands-off dish. We stuck with our standard 1:4 ratio of polenta to water and chose medium-grain polenta, which had the right balance of creaminess and chew. A shallow-sided baking dish increased evaporation, which sped up the cooking time, and a moderate oven temperature prevented the liquid from evaporating too quickly, causing dry pockets. Butter and Parmesan stirred in at the end added richness. To complement the simple side, we made a quick sautéed cherry tomato topping with shallot and garlic, and another with earthy mushrooms.

Polenta, at its most basic, is nothing more than cornmeal cooked in liquid until it softens and swells. Sure, you can dress it up—adding a sauce, ladling on a topping, forming it into cakes and then sautéing or frying it—but properly cooked polenta makes for a satisfying side dish flavored with nothing more than butter, Parmesan, salt, and pepper. Unfortunately, the traditional stovetop version has a major drawback: It requires 20 to 30 minutes of constant stirring. The accepted wisdom is that since the starchy mixture is prone to forming lumps during cooking, it requires almost constant churning. As a polenta lover who is always looking to avoid work, I hoped to use the oven to turn this labor of love into an easy, mostly hands-off affair.

An important first step was choosing the cornmeal. This was more complicated than you might think, as the labels on the supermarket products seem almost intended to confuse: Polenta may be labeled "polenta," or "cornmeal," or even "corn semolina." Add to that the fact that it comes in a range of grinds. And there are also "instant" or "quick-cooking" polentas, both of which are parcooked. I eliminated those last two because they produced mushy results. I also rejected coarser grinds, which seemed better suited to grits than to creamy polenta. After many tests, I landed on medium-grind polenta (which is the same as medium-grind cornmeal) because it yielded just the right balance of creaminess and grit.

With my main ingredient selected, I moved on to the actual cooking. I started with the same ratio of water to cornmeal (4:1) that we use on the stove; to my satisfaction, my initial tests proved that it worked in the oven, too. I simply dumped the polenta into a pot with salt and pepper, added water, and baked it until it was fully softened and creamy. The only problem was that it took as long as 2 hours to cook.

To speed things up, I tried swapping the pot for a baking dish with shallow sides to increase evaporation. This proved problematic, too. Now the liquid evaporated too quickly, leaving the polenta riddled with dry, undercooked pockets. Luckily, the solution was as simple as turning down the heat. With the oven temperature set to 375 degrees, I produced creamy, moist polenta in just 1 hands-off hour. The cornmeal was submerged the entire time it baked, so even, lump-free cooking happened automatically without my having to stir the polenta once.

With my method down, I turned to adding flavor. To keep the recipe classic, I stuck with the traditional butter and Parmesan—4 tablespoons and 2 cups, respectively, added plenty of richness and flavor.

The recipe was terrific on its own, but to add variety, I wanted to come up with a couple of quick toppings. To give the polenta some sweetness, I halved cherry tomatoes and sautéed them with garlic, white wine, and chicken broth, then spooned the flavorful mixture atop the creamy polenta. For the second twist, I topped the polenta with sautéed white mushrooms, shallot, and garlic.

With or without the toppings, the polenta proved to be every bit as good as the stovetop version. With all due respect to centuries of Italian grandmothers, I had proved that I could make tasty, creamy polenta—

without stirring. Sure, it took a little longer than stovetop recipes, but this hands-off method conserved something arguably more valuable than time: energy.

—SARAH WILSON WITH CHRIS DUDLEY,
Cook's Country

Easy Baked Polenta

SERVES 6 TO 8

You can use medium-grind cornmeal or polenta here; they are different names for the same thing. Do not use instant polenta, however. Serve with Cherry Tomato Topping or Mushroom Topping (page 62), if desired.

- 8 **cups water**
- 2 **cups medium-grind polenta**
- 2 **teaspoons salt**
- ⅛ **teaspoon pepper**
- 4 **ounces Parmesan cheese, grated (2 cups)**
- 4 **tablespoons unsalted butter, cut into 6 pieces**

1. Adjust oven rack to middle position and heat oven to 375 degrees. Combine water, polenta, salt, and pepper in 13 by 9-inch baking dish. Transfer dish to oven and bake, uncovered, until water is absorbed and polenta has thickened, about 60 minutes.

2. Remove baking dish from oven. Whisk in Parmesan and butter until polenta is smooth and creamy. Serve.

Cherry Tomato Topping

When polenta has cooked for 45 minutes, heat 2 tablespoons olive oil in 12-inch skillet over medium-high heat until shimmering. Add ¼ cup minced shallot and cook, stirring occasionally, until softened but not browned, about 3 minutes. Add 2 minced garlic cloves and cook, stirring, until fragrant, about 30 seconds. Add 1½ pounds halved cherry (or small grape) tomatoes and cook until softened, 4 to 6 minutes, adjusting heat to ensure that shallot and garlic don't burn. Add ¼ cup white wine and cook until reduced to syrup, about 1 minute. Add 1 cup chicken broth and cook until reduced to ⅓ cup, 3 to 5 minutes. Off heat, swirl in 2 tablespoons butter and ¼ cup chopped fresh parsley. Spoon over polenta just before serving.

Mushroom Topping

When polenta has cooked for 45 minutes, heat 2 tablespoons olive oil in 12-inch skillet over medium-high heat until shimmering. Add ¼ cup minced shallot and cook, stirring occasionally, until softened, about 3 minutes. Add 2 minced garlic cloves and cook, stirring, until fragrant, about 30 seconds. Add 1 pound sliced white mushrooms and cook until liquid is released and mushrooms begin to brown, 5 to 8 minutes, adjusting heat to ensure that shallot and garlic don't burn. Add ¼ cup white wine and cook until reduced to syrup, about 1 minute. Add 1 cup chicken broth and cook until reduced to ⅓ cup, 3 to 5 minutes. Off heat, swirl in 2 tablespoons butter and ¼ cup chopped fresh parsley. Spoon over polenta just before serving.

NOTES FROM THE TEST KITCHEN

SHOPPING FOR POLENTA

Buying polenta can be confusing. Not only are several different types of polenta widely available at the market—traditional, instant, and precooked—but they all are simply labeled "polenta." Here's how to tell them apart. The real deal (left) is labeled as either "polenta" or "traditional polenta," and it is simply medium-ground cornmeal with a very even grind and no small floury bits. It is often sold in clear bags so you can inspect it. Avoid coarse-grain cornmeal without the term "polenta" clearly listed on the package, as it often includes a portion of fine, floury bits that will make the polenta taste gluey. Instant polenta (center) and precooked tubes of polenta (right) are parcooked convenience products that have short cooking times (much like instant rice). Precooked polenta is easy to spot thanks to its tubelike packaging. Instant polenta, on the other hand, can look just like traditional polenta at the store and is identifiable only by the word "instant" in its title (which can be slightly hidden, in our experience).

PRESSURE-COOKER PARMESAN RISOTTO

WHY THIS RECIPE WORKS A dish that notoriously requires near-constant stirring, risotto is probably low on most people's lists of easy side dishes. But not for home cooks with a pressure cooker. After sautéing aromatics and briefly toasting the rice, we stirred in wine, then broth. Then, instead of the typical method of stirring for up to 30 minutes, we simply locked on the lid and let the magic happen. Six minutes under pressure delivered risotto that was nearly done. We finished cooking it uncovered, stirring for just 6 minutes more, until it was perfectly al dente and creamy.

There are many reasons people avoid making risotto: It can be time-consuming, laborious, and difficult to get just right. Accepted wisdom dictates near-constant stirring for as much as 30 minutes to achieve perfect tender grains with a slight bite in the center. But most of us have neither the time nor the patience to watch the pot, let alone keep stirring. So I decided to take advantage of a convenient but often underappreciated appliance—the pressure cooker—to reinvent risotto.

Pressure cookers work by raising the boiling point of water to around 250 degrees so that food cooks much faster than when boiled or steamed. I wanted to use the pressure cooker to make risotto faster, easier, and more hands-off. I started my recipe just as I would for traditional risotto. First I built up flavor by sautéing onion and garlic in butter in the bottom of the pressure-cooker pot. Next I added raw Arborio rice and toasted the grains for a few minutes. This step deepens the rice's flavor and improves the final texture of the risotto, keeping it from turning overly starchy and gluey. I deglazed the pot with some white wine, then added the broth, using a traditional liquid-to-rice ratio of 3:1.

Now it was time to put it all under pressure. I sealed the pot and brought it to high pressure over medium-high heat. For my first test, I cooked the rice for just 3 minutes under pressure, then quick-released the pressure (the natural-release method, which slowly releases the pressure over about 15 minutes, would undoubtedly overcook the rice to the point of being mush). When the steam cleared, I found that my rice was still undercooked and crunchy.

Clearly it would take a few trials to nail down the cooking time. I continued with this procedure, increasing the under-pressure cooking time by 1-minute increments.

PRESSURE–COOKER PARMESAN RISOTTO

MAKING RISOTTO IN A PRESSURE COOKER

1. After sautéing aromatics, briefly toast rice in pot to deepen its flavor and improve its final texture.

2. Slightly undercook rice under pressure, then finish it with just a few minutes of hands-on stirring to get texture just right.

3. Risotto will continue to thicken as it sits; loosen it with additional broth before serving as necessary.

THE BEST CHICKEN BROTH

We rarely go a day without using chicken broth in the test kitchen, putting it to work in everything from soups and stews to pilafs and risottos to braises, pan sauces, and gravies. And considering how time-consuming it can be to make homemade broth, we often reach for store-bought broth to save time. To find the best brand, we set about tasting 10 nationally available brands—including eight liquids and two concentrates—plain, in a simple risotto, and reduced in an all-purpose gravy.

Some had flavor that was so wan it was practically nonexistent; others were "beefy" or "vegetal" or had bizarre off-flavors. Only two stood apart: One was a traditional boxed liquid, Swanson Chicken Stock. The other was a concentrate. While tasters praised Swanson's "rich," "meaty" flavor, they were even more impressed by the "clean," "savory" taste of the chicken base. And at just 16 cents per cup, it was the cheapest by far because you aren't paying to transport water. It will last for two years in the refrigerator, whereas liquid broths keep for no more than two weeks once opened. However, it had the most sodium of all the brands and turned some dishes overly salty.

Ultimately, we decided that rich-tasting **Swanson Chicken Stock** will be our stand-in for homemade. But given its great flavor, long shelf life, and price, we're naming Better Than Bouillon Chicken Base our Best Buy.

After 6 minutes under pressure, the results were close to perfect, but the grains were still a little too chewy. But if I left the rice under pressure any longer, I risked overcooking the delicate grains. To do away with the guesswork, I settled on 6 minutes of cooking under pressure, releasing the pressure when the rice was still slightly undercooked, then finishing it with another few minutes of stirring over medium heat with the pot uncovered. This method gave me complete control over the doneness of the rice and accounted for slight variations among pressure cookers and rice grains.

A little Parmesan and salt and pepper were the only finishing touches needed for this simple recipe, or you can garnish it with a little parsley and shaved Parmesan.

—ASHLEY MOORE, America's Test Kitchen Books

Pressure-Cooker Parmesan Risotto

SERVES 4

For an electric pressure cooker, use your own timer and quick-release the pressure immediately after the pressurized cooking time; do not let the cooker switch to the warm setting. Use the browning (not the simmer) setting to finish cooking the risotto in step 4. Garnish with parsley if desired.

- 2 tablespoons unsalted butter
- 1 small onion, chopped fine
- 3 garlic cloves, minced
- 1½ cups Arborio rice
- ½ cup white wine
- 4 cups chicken broth, warmed
- 1 ounce Parmesan cheese, grated (½ cup), plus extra for serving
  Salt and pepper

1. Melt butter in pressure-cooker pot over medium-high heat. Add onion and cook until softened, about 5 minutes. Stir in garlic and cook until fragrant, about 30 seconds. Stir in rice and toast lightly, about 3 minutes. Stir in wine and cook until almost evaporated, about 1 minute. Stir in 3¼ cups broth. Using wooden spoon, scrape up any rice sticking to bottom of pot.

2. Lock pressure-cooker lid in place and bring to high pressure over medium-high heat. As soon as pot reaches high pressure, reduce heat to medium-low and cook for 6 minutes, adjusting heat as needed to maintain high pressure.

3. Remove pot from heat. Quick-release pressure, then carefully remove lid, allowing steam to escape away from you.

4. Continue to cook risotto over medium heat, stirring constantly, until rice is tender and liquid has thickened, about 6 minutes. Stir in Parmesan and season with salt and pepper to taste. Add remaining ¾ cup broth as needed to loosen risotto consistency before serving.

VARIATIONS

Butternut Squash and Sage Risotto

Add 8 ounces butternut squash, peeled and cut into ½-inch cubes (1⅓ cups), to pot with onion and cook until onion and squash are browned, about 10 minutes. Add 3 tablespoons chopped fresh sage to pot with garlic in step 1.

Mushroom Risotto

Add 8 ounces cremini mushrooms, trimmed and sliced thin, to pot with onion and cook until onion and mushrooms are browned, about 10 minutes. Stir in ½ ounce dried porcini mushrooms, rinsed and minced, with garlic in step 1.

BISCUIT DRESSING

✔ **WHY THIS RECIPE WORKS** The Appalachian tradition of substituting leftover biscuits for bread in holiday stuffing, or dressing, sounded very appealing to us. First we came up with a quick dump-and-stir method to make buttermilk biscuits without extra hassle. For crunchy biscuit "crumbs" that wouldn't get soggy in the finished dressing, we pinched off small pieces of biscuit dough and baked them for twice as long as usual biscuits to get extra browned, crispy pieces. To keep the dressing from being too rich, we cut way back on the butter. As for the flavors, we kept to the classic mix of sautéed onion, celery, thyme, and sage.

A century ago Appalachian women preparing for Thanksgiving often used biscuits as the base for their dressing. They didn't have the option of driving to the supermarket to pick up pre seasoned stuffing mix or hearty white sandwich bread. These thrifty home cooks used what they had around—typically leftover biscuits that they'd baked a day or two before. Tender, buttery biscuits as the basis for a homey turkey dressing? That doesn't sound like a hardship to me.

I immediately started searching for recipes, but finding them wasn't easy. When biscuits did appear in dressing recipes, it was to supplement cornbread, not to play the leading role. I turned to our food historian, who eventually uncovered a vague recipe for pure, 100 percent all-biscuit dressing. It called for "biscuits about two days old crumbled up," moistened with broth "off the hen," and combined with onions, celery, and herbs. It was just the kind of dish I hoped to bring to my table: simple enough to execute amid the frenzy of the holidays and enticing enough to persuade my clan of stuffing traditionalists to try something new.

With our food historian's help, I managed to dig up a few more recipes, mostly from Appalachia, and I began cooking. The older recipes simply called for "biscuit crumbs." I didn't have any on hand (no surprise there), so in their place I baked a few batches of a standard biscuit recipe, crumbled them up, and began to make dressings, following the vague recipes as well as I could. Clearly, these home cooks of a century ago cooked mostly by feel, smell, and years of experience—not by recipe. I was mostly on my own. And when we tasted the dressings I'd made, I could see that I hadn't hit the mark. As a group, they were soggy and extremely rich. With so much else to eat on the Thanksgiving table, that was the last thing I wanted. To top it off, the dressings didn't taste like biscuits, so really, what was the point?

The obvious starting point was figuring out the proper biscuit. It would need distinct flavor and enough heft to work in the dressing, plus it would have to be easy, since after baking the biscuits I'd still have to make the stuffing itself. I began working my way through the test kitchen's many biscuit recipes. Over a series of days, I determined the following: Buttermilk added nice, tangy flavor, the dump-and-stir method—using melted butter—trumped the more laborious method of cutting cold fat into flour, and "dropping" the biscuits from a spoon was easier than rolling out the dough and cutting individual biscuits.

With my working biscuit recipe in hand, I turned my attention to the rest of the dish. After much eating and appraising, we opted for classic flavors: onion (two chopped fine) and celery (three ribs minced) sautéed in butter and seasoned with fresh thyme and sage for a 13 by 9-inch pan of biscuit stuffing. I started with a stick of butter, which was an average amount (or even on

BISCUIT DRESSING

the low side) for this amount of dressing, but my dressing was still much too rich. Since I was replacing the usual bread with very rich, buttery biscuits, shouldn't I account for that by using less butter for sautéing? More testing showed that just 2 tablespoons was sufficient for rich—but not too rich—stuffing.

Now that I had made this stuffing a number of times, the liquid ratios had worked themselves out: Four eggs and 4 cups of broth were enough to moisten the casserole. But I still hadn't solved the sogginess. Biscuit interiors are so fluffy that they practically dissolve when moistened. But if I used any less liquid, the biscuits tasted cottony and dry. What I needed, I realized, was less fluffy interior and more crusty biscuit edge, which could soak up moisture without falling apart. The next time I mixed up a batch of dough, instead of making full-size biscuits I pinched off 1-inch pieces and scattered them over two baking sheets. Then I baked the biscuit pieces for twice as long as normal. The extra cooking time essentially staled the biscuits, duplicating the old recipes I'd started with that had called for stale biscuit crumbs.

I made my dressing recipe one more time, sautéing the vegetables and mixing them gently with the well-browned biscuit crumbles and the egg-broth mixture. I dumped everything into a casserole dish and then baked it. Some 40 minutes later, I pulled the dressing out of the oven. I knew I had a winner: The top was golden and crispy, the inside moist but not dense. Bite after bite, the dressing maintained recognizably buttery, biscuitlike qualities alongside traditional stuffing flavor. Biscuit dressing was born out of hard times, but good taste will ensure its survival.

—REBECCAH MARSTERS, *Cook's Country*

NOTES FROM THE TEST KITCHEN

BISCUIT BITS

To mimic stale biscuits, pinch biscuit dough into 1-inch bits to yield more firm edges, then "stale" them by baking them nearly twice as long as normal biscuits.

Biscuit Dressing

SERVES 10 TO 12

Flour your fingers to keep the biscuit dough from sticking in step 2. The biscuits can be baked and cooled a day ahead of time and stored at room temperature.

BISCUITS

- 3 cups (15 ounces) all-purpose flour
- 1 tablespoon baking powder
- ¾ teaspoon baking soda
- 1½ teaspoons sugar
- 1¼ teaspoons salt
- 1½ cups buttermilk, chilled
- 12 tablespoons unsalted butter, melted

DRESSING

- 2 tablespoons unsalted butter
- 2 onions, chopped fine
- 3 celery ribs, minced
- 2 tablespoons chopped fresh sage
- 2 tablespoons chopped fresh thyme
- 1½ teaspoons pepper
- 1 teaspoon salt
- 4 cups chicken broth
- 4 large eggs

1. FOR THE BISCUITS: Adjust oven racks to upper-middle and lower-middle positions and heat oven to 400 degrees. Line 2 rimmed baking sheets with parchment paper. Whisk flour, baking powder, baking soda, sugar, and salt together in large bowl. Combine buttermilk and melted butter in bowl and stir until butter forms clumps. Add buttermilk mixture to dry ingredients and stir with rubber spatula until just incorporated.

2. Using floured fingers, break off 1-inch pieces of dough and scatter evenly on baking sheets. Bake until tops are deep golden brown, about 25 minutes, switching and rotating baking sheets halfway through. Let biscuits cool on baking sheets. When biscuits are cool enough to handle, crumble into ½-inch pieces into large bowl.

3. FOR THE DRESSING: Grease 13 by 9-inch baking dish. Melt butter in 12-inch skillet over medium-low heat. Add onions and celery and cook, covered, until softened and lightly browned, 10 to 12 minutes, stirring occasionally. Stir in sage, thyme, pepper, and salt and cook until fragrant, about 30 seconds. Add vegetable mixture to bowl with biscuits.

4. Whisk broth and eggs together in bowl. Add broth mixture to biscuits and vegetables and stir gently to combine. Let sit until biscuits have softened slightly, about 3 minutes. Transfer to prepared baking dish and press gently into even layer. Bake dressing on lower-middle rack until top is golden brown and crisp, 35 to 40 minutes, rotating dish halfway through baking. Let cool for 20 minutes. Serve.

ROASTED ROOT VEGETABLES

✔ **WHY THIS RECIPE WORKS** Root vegetables develop complex flavors with just a quick toss in oil, salt, and pepper and a stint in a hot oven—until you try to roast different vegetables at once. We wanted a medley of vegetables that would cook through evenly. The trick was to carefully prep each vegetable according to how long it took to cook through. With each vegetable cut into the right size and shape, we could roast them together in one batch for uniformly tender results. To speed up the roasting, we briefly microwaved the vegetables, then placed them on a preheated baking sheet to jump-start the browning. A rich bacon topping, fruity salsa garnish, and an easy spice blend gave us some flavorful seasoning options.

Looking for a way to transform humble root vegetables into a side dish that's the star of the dinner? Simply stick them in the oven. Well, OK, it's not quite that easy. But roasting a root vegetable transforms it into something richly flavored and complex and takes almost no effort. Simply cut the root into equal-size pieces so they all cook evenly, toss them with some oil, and roast them until they're tender, browned, and caramelized.

Of course, that's if you're cooking just one vegetable. I wanted to roast an assortment for an appealing variety of textures and flavors. To see if this simple method would work with a variety of vegetables, I chose sweet carrots, parsnips, and shallots; earthy celery root; and peppery turnips and cut everything into uniform chunks (except the shallots, which I peeled and left whole).

This method was a complete failure. After roasting the vegetables in a 400-degree oven for 90 minutes, I found myself looking at every possible bad result, from raw and crunchy to charred and desiccated. Only the shallots came out tender with crisp, caramelized exteriors. Clearly I would need a new approach.

Maybe instead of simply cutting equal-size pieces, I should let the density and texture of the vegetable determine its shape. Since cutting the carrots into chunks had left them undercooked, this time I cut them into sticks, halving or quartering pieces so the diameter of each was no more than an inch. This increased the amount of surface area, which allowed the interiors to cook faster. After 90 minutes, I was pleased to find that the carrots were now tender and nicely browned.

Parsnips were up next. Since they have a similar shape to carrots, I cut them into the same sticks. But parsnips are more fibrous than carrots, and they came out a little stringy and chewy. It occurred to me that cutting them across the grain to shorten their fibers, a trick we use to make tough cuts of meat more tender, might help. I sliced the parsnips on the bias into 1-inch-wide oblong disks. After 90 minutes, my parsnips were perfect.

Next I peeled and cut celery root, which in my first test was the slowest-cooking. I cut the celery root into ¾-inch-thick slices, then cut them into planks to maximize the amount of surface area in direct contact with the baking sheet. Sure enough, when added to the next test with the carrots and parsnips, the celery root was as tender and well browned as its two compatriots.

Finally, I considered the turnips. In my initial tests, they had charred while the other roots remained too hard, so it made sense to take the opposite approach with them and minimize their surface area. After trying several different shapes, I found that the most effective was to cut them horizontally, then slice each half into four wedges. With their relatively small surface area, these pieces cooked through at just the right speed.

Now all of my vegetables were cooking at the same rate, but I wanted to speed things up. I realized that during the first hour of cooking, the veggies were merely warming up, not actually browning or even softening. I covered them with foil when they first went into the oven to speed up cooking. With the foil trapping the vegetables' moisture and creating steam, the veggies were piping hot after just 20 minutes, but they still took nearly an hour more to brown after I took off the foil.

After I removed the foil, the vegetables sat in a pool of juices that took at least 15 minutes to evaporate, hindering browning. So for my next test, instead of covering the raw vegetables with foil, I put all except the quick-cooking turnips in the microwave. A 10-minute zap in a bowl softened them enough that they released liquid, which I then drained off. After incorporating the turnips and

ROASTED ROOT VEGETABLES

SHAPING ROOTS FOR ROASTING

The trouble with roasting a medley of vegetables is that each type cooks at a different rate. For uniformly tender, caramelized results, cut each one into a specific shape and size.

CELERY ROOT PLANKS
Cut dense celery root into wide, flat shape to accelerate cooking and browning.

CARROT STICKS
Long, slender sticks have large surface area that browns quickly.

PARSNIP DISKS
Cut on bias across fibrous cores to create oblong disks that will become more tender.

WHOLE SHALLOTS
Left whole, small shallots cook at same rate as other vegetables.

TURNIP CHUNKS
Cut quick-cooking turnips into eighths to minimize surface area.

THE BEST VEGETABLE PEELER

We rounded up 10 vegetable peelers and put each peeler through produce boot camp, peeling potatoes and carrots as well as trickier vegetables like tough-skinned butternut squash and delicate ripe tomatoes. We also tested their precision by pulling each blade across pieces of Parmesan cheese and chocolate, noting whether the peelers chipped at the blocks or pulled off long, elegant curls. The **Original Swiss Peeler by Kuhn Rikon** was our all-around winner. The Y-shaped peeler is a featherweight, but it's surprisingly sturdy and its razor-sharp blade effortlessly skinned anything we threw at it— and at just $3.50, it's a steal. (See page 304 for more information on our testing results).

giving them all a quick toss in oil, I spread them on a preheated baking sheet for even faster cooking and better browning. Just 25 minutes later, their bottoms were golden brown. I stirred them so the unbrowned sides faced down and rotated the pan for even cooking. After 15 minutes more, I removed the pan from the oven. To my delight, all the veggies were moist on the inside and sported crisp, golden-brown crusts—and I'd done it in under an hour.

A simple garnish of chopped parsley was all these richly flavored vegetables really needed, but I couldn't resist the urge to create a few flavorful toppings. For deep savory flavor, I made a topping with crispy bacon, minced shallot, sherry vinegar, and chives. A bright salsa made of orange, parsley, almonds, and cumin highlighted their sweet caramelized notes. Finally, a Turkish spice blend brought thyme, sesame seeds, and orange and lemon zests to the mix.

—LAN LAM, *Cook's Illustrated*

Roasted Root Vegetables

SERVES 6

Use turnips that are roughly 2 to 3 inches in diameter. Try garnishing the vegetables with one of the toppings that follow instead of sprinkling the roasted vegetables with chopped parsley.

- 1 celery root (14 ounces), peeled
- 4 carrots, peeled and cut into 2½-inch lengths, halved or quartered lengthwise if necessary to create pieces ½ to 1 inch in diameter
- 12 ounces parsnips, peeled and sliced 1 inch thick on bias
- 5 ounces small shallots, peeled
  Kosher salt and pepper
- 12 ounces turnips, peeled, halved horizontally, and each half quartered
- 3 tablespoons vegetable oil
- 2 tablespoons chopped fresh parsley, tarragon, or chives

1. Adjust oven rack to middle position, place rimmed baking sheet on rack, and heat oven to 425 degrees. Cut celery root into ¾-inch-thick rounds. Cut each round into ¾-inch-thick planks about 2½ inches in length.

2. Toss celery root, carrots, parsnips, and shallots with 1 teaspoon salt and pepper to taste in large microwave-safe bowl. Cover bowl and microwave until small pieces of carrot are just pliable enough to bend, 8 to

10 minutes, stirring once halfway through microwaving. Drain vegetables well. Return vegetables to bowl, add turnips and oil, and toss to coat.

3. Working quickly, remove baking sheet from oven and carefully transfer vegetables to baking sheet; spread into even layer. Roast for 25 minutes.

4. Using thin metal spatula, stir vegetables and spread into even layer. Rotate pan and continue to roast until vegetables are golden brown and celery root is tender when pierced with tip of paring knife, 15 to 25 minutes longer. Transfer to platter and sprinkle with parsley. Serve.

Bacon-Shallot Topping
MAKES ABOUT ⅓ CUP

- 4 **slices bacon, cut into ¼-inch pieces**
- ¼ **cup water**
- 2 **tablespoons minced shallot**
- 1 **tablespoon sherry vinegar**
- 2 **tablespoons minced fresh chives**

Bring bacon and water to boil in 8-inch skillet over high heat. Reduce heat to medium and cook until water has evaporated and bacon is crisp, about 10 minutes. Transfer bacon to paper towel–lined plate and pour off all but ½ teaspoon fat from skillet. Add shallot and cook, stirring frequently, until softened, 2 to 4 minutes. Remove pan from heat and add vinegar. Transfer shallot mixture to bowl and stir in bacon and chives. Sprinkle over vegetables before serving.

Orange-Parsley Salsa
MAKES ABOUT ½ CUP

- ¼ **cup slivered almonds**
- ¼ **teaspoon ground cumin**
- ¼ **teaspoon ground coriander**
- 1 **orange**
- ½ **cup minced fresh parsley**
- 2 **garlic cloves, minced**
- 2 **teaspoons extra-virgin olive oil**
- 1 **teaspoon cider vinegar**
- ¼ **teaspoon kosher salt**

1. Toast almonds in 10-inch skillet over medium-high heat until fragrant and golden brown, 5 to 6 minutes.

Add cumin and coriander; continue to toast, stirring constantly, until fragrant, about 45 seconds. Immediately transfer to bowl.

2. Cut away peel and pith from orange. Use paring knife to slice between membranes to release segments. Cut segments into ¼-inch pieces. Stir orange pieces, parsley, garlic, oil, vinegar, and salt into almond mixture. Let stand for 30 minutes. Spoon over vegetables before serving.

Turkish Spice Blend
MAKES ABOUT ¼ CUP

- 2 **tablespoons sesame seeds, toasted**
- 4 **teaspoons minced fresh thyme**
- ¼ **teaspoon kosher salt**
- ¼ **teaspoon finely grated orange zest**
- ¼ **teaspoon finely grated lemon zest**

Combine all ingredients in bowl. Sprinkle over vegetables before serving.

SALT-AND-VINEGAR POTATOES

✓ **WHY THIS RECIPE WORKS** For roasted potatoes with classic salt-and-vinegar flavor, we started by boiling small red potatoes in heavily salted water. This gave them incredibly creamy, well-seasoned interiors and delicious salt-crusted skins. Once the potatoes were parcooked, we "smashed" them to expose some of their flesh, brushed them with slightly sweet and tangy malt vinegar, and roasted them on a baking sheet until golden brown and crispy. A final brush with vinegar when the potatoes came out of the oven reinforced the addictive salty-sour flavor of these spuds.

German potato salad, salt-and-vinegar potato chips, and English "chips" sprinkled with malt vinegar—potatoes seasoned with vinegar are perennial favorites in any form. I wanted to translate this classic salty-sour flavor combination into a crispy potato side dish.

I had more of a concept than a specific dish in mind, but I did discover a few recipes online. I followed two of the recipes I found to get an idea of where to start.

ROASTED SALT-AND-VINEGAR POTATOES

For one, I boiled potatoes in a mixture of vinegar and lightly salted water. But I couldn't taste the vinegar or the salt, and obviously the boiled spuds had no crunch or browning. For the other recipe, I roasted seasoned potato quarters and doused them in vinegar when they came out of the oven. The vinegar tasted raw and harsh and the salt was barely skin-deep.

I abandoned these half-baked efforts in favor of a technique we've used for Syracuse Salt Potatoes, boiling small red potatoes in very heavily salted water. The concentrated salt solution cooks the potato starch more completely than usual, resulting in extremely creamy flesh. These potatoes also develop an amazingly salt-encrusted exterior and a well-seasoned interior (the potato skin protects the interior from being inedibly salty). Salt solved, the vinegar challenge lay ahead.

So far, I knew that I'd need to roast the potatoes for crispness and that simply sprinkling vinegar on cooked potatoes was not the answer. So for my next batch, after boiling the potatoes in the super-saturated salt solution, I cut them into quarters, brushed them with vinegar, and roasted them in an extremely hot oven. This was a definite step forward.

But had I gone too far? The whole point of baking the vinegar into the roasting potatoes was to mellow it, but I found myself missing its brightness. So while the roasted potatoes were still very hot, I brushed them with extra vinegar. This time I got a nice jolt of pleasing sourness, with none of the harshness that had ruined earlier versions. Why? Our science editor explained that as the water molecules rising from the hot potatoes evaporate, they carry some acetic acid molecules from the vinegar along with them. This technique worked better when I replaced the neat wedges with a "smash": I pressed each potato with the bottom of a measuring cup to about a ½-inch thickness. This way, the interiors of the smashed potatoes stayed soft when roasted, so they could better absorb the vinegar brush.

So far I'd been using cider vinegar for my tests, but was it the best choice? I tried white vinegar, only to find it too harsh. Cider and red wine vinegars were good, but balsamic vinegar was better. Unfortunately, it turned the potatoes the color of mud. Hoping for the same sweetness but a more appealing color, I tried malt vinegar, a sweet, mild vinegar popular in Britain. The flavor of these potatoes was addictively salty and sour. Finally my salt-and-vinegar potatoes hit the mark.

—DIANE UNGER, *Cook's Country*

Roasted Salt-and-Vinegar Potatoes

SERVES 4

Use small red potatoes, measuring 1 to 2 inches in diameter. If you prefer to use kosher salt, you will need 1½ cups of Morton or 2½ cups of Diamond Crystal. Cider vinegar is a good substitute for the malt vinegar.

- **6 tablespoons olive oil**
- **2 pounds small red potatoes**
- **1¼ cups salt**
- **3 tablespoons malt vinegar**
- **Pepper**

1. Adjust oven rack to upper-middle position and heat oven to 500 degrees. Set wire rack inside rimmed baking sheet. Brush second rimmed baking sheet evenly with oil. Bring 2 quarts water to boil in Dutch oven over medium-high heat. Stir in potatoes and salt and cook until just tender and paring knife slips easily in and out of potatoes, 20 to 30 minutes. Drain potatoes and transfer to wire rack; let dry for 10 minutes.

2. Transfer potatoes to oiled baking sheet. Flatten each potato with underside of measuring cup until ½ inch thick. Brush potatoes with half of vinegar and season with pepper. Roast until potatoes are well browned, 25 to 30 minutes. Brush with remaining vinegar. Transfer potatoes to platter, smashed side up. Serve.

NOTES FROM THE TEST KITCHEN

SCRUB THE POTATOES

Because the skins will be in the finished dish, it's important to scrub the potatoes well before cooking.

MALT VINEGAR SUBSTITUTES

For our salt-and-vinegar potatoes, we raided the English larder for a beloved condiment: malt vinegar. The vinegar, which is made from sprouted barley grains, gives the potatoes a pleasantly malty, tangy taste. If you don't have it, cider or red wine vinegars are good substitutes. Balsamic vinegar tastes great in this dish but gives the potatoes a muddy color.

BRAISED RED POTATOES

✓ **WHY THIS RECIPE WORKS** What if you could get red potatoes with the creamy interiors of steaming and the crispy browned exteriors of roasting—without doing either? That's the result promised by recipes for braised red potatoes, but they rarely deliver. To make good on the promise, we combined halved small red potatoes, butter, and salted water (plus thyme for flavoring) in a 12-inch skillet and simmered the spuds until their interiors were perfectly creamy and the water was fully evaporated. Then we let the potatoes continue to cook in the now-dry skillet until their cut sides browned in the butter, developing the rich flavor and crisp edges of roasted potatoes. These crispy, creamy potatoes were so good they needed only a minimum of seasoning: We simply tossed them with some minced garlic (softened in the simmering water along with the potatoes), lemon juice, chives, and pepper.

I love the versatility of waxy potatoes like Red Bliss. Steamed whole, they turn tender and creamy—perfect canvases for tossing with butter and fresh herbs. They also take well to halving and roasting, taking on crispy, browned cut surfaces. So when I came across recipes for braised new potatoes, I wondered if this approach, which pairs dry heat for browning with moist heat for simmering, would yield the best of both worlds. I also thought there might be a third benefit to braising: Many recipes call for simmering the spuds in chicken broth, and I reasoned that the potatoes would soak up all that flavorful liquid like little savory sponges. All in all, it sounded like a promising—and convenient—alternative method for cooking waxy potatoes.

Except it wasn't that simple. To my surprise, every recipe I made was a failure. Any flavor that the potatoes picked up from the broth was barely discernible, even when I halved or thin-sliced the spuds to expose more interior to the broth. Worse, the typical brown-and-then-simmer approach to braising had been a bust, as all the flavorful browning that the potatoes developed during searing washed away by the time they had cooked through in the liquid.

Clearly this technique needed some revising. My first change would be ditching the chicken broth since there was no point in using broth if it wasn't improving the potatoes' flavor. Instead, I would use heavily salted water.

While most of the aromatic flavor molecules in chicken are fat-soluble and therefore won't penetrate water-filled potatoes, salt is water-soluble and will seep into the spuds' flesh. I halved 1½ pounds of small red potatoes—enough to feed at least four—placed them cut side down in an oiled 12-inch skillet, and turned the dial to medium-high. Once they'd browned, I reexamined the steaming step by adding 2 cups of seasoned water (to evenly cover the surface of the pan), covering the pan, and leaving the potatoes to braise until tender. Removing the lid revealed potatoes with smooth and creamy interiors. But as expected, their cut sides were wan in appearance and flavor.

That's when I realized I needed to reverse the order of operations and brown the potatoes after simmering them. For my next test, once the potatoes were tender, I carefully drained off the water, added some oil to the dry pan, and let the pieces brown over high heat. This time my colleagues assured me that I was getting somewhere, as the salt had thoroughly seasoned the spuds, and searing after simmering had produced the rich, deeply flavorful browning that I'd hoped for.

The downside was that straining off simmering water from a large skillet was cumbersome, and rearranging each of the hot potato halves cut side down to ensure that they browned properly was fussy—too fussy for a simple side dish. When a colleague suggested that I simply simmer the potatoes uncovered so that the water would evaporate, I was skeptical: The time it would take to simmer off a full 2 cups of liquid would certainly mean overcooking the spuds. But at that point, I didn't have any better ideas, so I decided to give it a shot.

It did, in fact, take about 35 minutes for the water to cook off, at which point I expected to find a mushy, overcooked mess. Imagine my surprise, then, when I stuck a fork into a few of the potatoes and found that they were holding together just fine. More than that, these potatoes were remarkably silky and smooth—by far the best texture I'd produced to date. Pleased by the results, I researched an explanation and learned that if low-starch potatoes like Red Bliss are cooked long enough, they exude a fluid gel that keeps the potatoes "glued" together and also gives them an exceptionally creamy texture. Still, my newfound cooking method for waxy potatoes had one big problem: Their undersides, now in contact with a dry, hot skillet, were stuck fast to the pan and scorched.

The more I thought about it, the more I realized that my method paralleled that of classic Chinese potstickers. To make them, you first brown the flat-sided dumplings in an oil-coated skillet, then you add water and simmer them until the water evaporates and the dumplings once again make contact with the skillet and crisp in the oil. The main difference was that with potstickers, the oil goes in at the beginning. I wondered if adding the oil earlier in the potato-cooking process might coat the potatoes and prevent them from sticking after the water evaporated.

So I combined everything—water, salt, potatoes, and a few tablespoons of oil—in the skillet and brought it to a simmer. After a few minutes of covered cooking (to ensure that any unsubmerged potato would steam), I removed the lid and upped the burner to medium-high. My hope was that, just as with potstickers, the water would evaporate and leave the oil and potatoes alone in the pan to brown.

About 15 minutes later, I got my wish: As the last few wisps of steam escaped, the oil sizzled and the potatoes developed rich color. To get even more browning, I switched from oil to butter; the protein in the butter's milk solids magnified the effects of browning (known as the Maillard reaction) and left the potatoes significantly richer and more complex-tasting.

Even better, as I poked a fork into the velvety pieces, every bit of their deeply browned surface pulled away cleanly from the pan's surface. My tasters were thrilled with the results of this unlikely approach to potato cookery. All I had left to do was jazz up the potatoes' earthy flavor.

Tossing a few sprigs of thyme into the pan during the covered simmering step was an easy way to add some herbal depth (thyme is soluble in both water and fat). Garlic was trickier; when added to the pan while the spuds browned, the garlic burned, and simply stirring in raw minced garlic at the end left a flavor that was unpalatably sharp. Instead, I simmered whole cloves with the potatoes to mellow their bite before mincing them into a paste and stirring it into the finished potatoes.

Tasters loved the now-mellow garlic's flavor, not to mention the body that it lent to the sauce. With a few grinds of black pepper, a squeeze of fresh lemon juice, and a sprinkling of minced chives, these spuds had it all: creamy, well-seasoned interiors, flavorful browned exteriors, and a heady sauce. For a little variety, I also worked up a variation with Dijon mustard and tarragon and a super-savory version with miso and scallions. Best of all, I'd done little hands-on cooking and dirtied just one pan.

—DAN SOUZA, *Cook's Illustrated*

NOTES FROM THE TEST KITCHEN

THE BENEFITS OF OVERCOOKING WAXY POTATOES

The rules for cooking potatoes seem pretty straightforward: Undercook them and they'll stay intact; overcook them and they'll break down into crumbly bits. But while developing my recipe for braised red potatoes, I allowed a batch of halved red potatoes to simmer for an extra-long 35 minutes and noticed that they not only stayed intact but actually cooked up incredibly creamy and smooth. Had I been wrong about the effects of overcooking potatoes in general, or was there something different about the low-starch red kind?

To find out, I prepared two batches of my working recipe, one with low-starch red potatoes and another with high-starch russets (quartering these larger spuds), and simmered each for 35 minutes. Just as they had before, the red potatoes held their shape and boasted remarkably silky interiors. The russets, however, broke down and turned crumbly and mushy.

A little-known but key difference between waxy potatoes (such as red or new potatoes) and starchy potatoes (such as russets) is that they contain different ratios of two different starches: amylopectin and amylose. Waxy potatoes contain very little amylose; as they cook, the starch granules in waxy potatoes burst, releasing very sticky amylopectin, which in essence glues the potato structure together, giving the impression of creaminess. In a russet or other starchy potato, there is a higher ratio of the second starch—amylose—which is made up of smaller molecules that are less sticky. Despite the fact that, overall, russets contain more starch than do waxy potatoes (hence they are often described as being "high starch"), russets simply fall apart once overcooked because most of their starch is the less sticky amylose.

CRUMBLY
Overcooked starchy russets break apart.

CREAMY
Overcooked waxy red potatoes hold together.

Braised Red Potatoes with Lemon and Chives

SERVES 4 TO 6

Use small red potatoes measuring about 1½ inches in diameter.

- 1½ pounds small red potatoes, unpeeled, halved
- 2 cups water
- 3 tablespoons unsalted butter
- 3 sprigs fresh thyme
- 3 garlic cloves, peeled
- ¾ teaspoon salt
- 1 teaspoon lemon juice
- ¼ teaspoon pepper
- 2 tablespoons minced fresh chives

1. Arrange potatoes in single layer, cut side down, in 12-inch nonstick skillet. Add water, butter, thyme, garlic, and salt and bring to simmer over medium-high heat. Reduce heat to medium, cover, and simmer until potatoes are just tender, about 15 minutes.

2. Remove lid and use slotted spoon to transfer garlic to cutting board; discard thyme. Increase heat to medium-high and vigorously simmer, swirling pan occasionally, until water evaporates and butter starts to sizzle, 15 to 20 minutes. When cool enough to handle, mince garlic to paste. Transfer paste to bowl and stir in lemon juice and pepper.

3. Continue to cook potatoes, swirling pan frequently, until butter browns and cut sides of potatoes turn spotty brown, 4 to 6 minutes longer. Off heat, add garlic mixture and chives and toss to thoroughly coat. Serve immediately.

VARIATIONS

Braised Red Potatoes with Dijon and Tarragon
Substitute 2 teaspoons Dijon mustard for lemon juice and 1 tablespoon minced fresh tarragon for chives.

Braised Red Potatoes with Miso and Scallions
Reduce salt to ½ teaspoon. Substitute 1 tablespoon red miso paste for lemon juice and 3 thinly sliced scallions for chives.

POTATO LATKES

WHY THIS RECIPE WORKS We wanted latkes that were light, not greasy, with buttery-soft interiors and crisp outer crusts. We started with high-starch russets, shredded them, mixed them with some grated onion, then wrung the mixture out in a kitchen towel to rid it of excess moisture, which would prevent the latkes from crisping. To ensure that the latkes' centers were cooked before their crusts were too dark, we parcooked the potato-onion mixture in the microwave. This step also caused the starches in the potatoes to coalesce, further inhibiting the release of the potatoes' moisture when frying. We tossed the mixture with beaten egg to help bind the cakes and pan-fried them in just ¼ inch of oil. With the excess water taken care of, our latkes crisped up beautifully and absorbed minimal oil.

Latkes come in all shapes and sizes. But the goal is always the same: delicate and light potato cakes with a creamy, buttery-soft interior surrounded by a shatteringly crisp outer shell. Unfortunately, many recipes produce latkes that soak up oil like a sponge, leaving them greasy and soft inside and out. Others are crisp outside but gluey and starchy within. Still others are simply undercooked and tough, with the texture and flavor of raw potato. Determined to produce a crispy latke with real contrast between the crust and the center, I stockpiled potatoes and got to work.

Most latke recipes consist of the same core elements and a simple formula: Combine raw potatoes and onions and toss them with beaten egg, starch, salt, and pepper. Shallow-fry mounds of the thick batter until the disks are crisp and golden brown.

Trouble is, raw potatoes exude tons of moisture when their cells are broken, and excess water is the enemy of crispness. More moisture leads to a wetter interior, and water that seeps out of the pancake during frying drags down the temperature of the oil for soggier, greasier results. That meant both the variety of potato and how I processed it would greatly affect my latkes' texture.

A side-by-side test of several types of potato settled the first question: Russets, with their high concentration of moisture-absorbing starch, produced the driest and crispiest pancakes. As for the cutting method, shredded (versus ground or chopped) potatoes yielded superior texture, the fine threads forming a lacy, weblike matrix.

That said, even floury russets gave up a tremendous amount of water, so I'd still need to get rid of some of their moisture. I defaulted to the test kitchen's favorite method for drying vegetables: wringing out the shreds in a dry dish towel. I mixed the potato shreds with grated onion (a fine pulp gave the latkes good flavor without noticeably affecting the texture) and gave the mixture a few good squeezes. I mixed in a couple of eggs and some potato starch that I drained from the exuded potato liquid, then I fried up another batch. Without all that water, these pancakes were on the right track—they were crispier for sure but also a bit raw-tasting and oily.

The tricky thing was that these two problems presented something of a Catch-22: If I fried the latkes long enough to ensure a fully cooked interior, the crust became too dark. But if I lowered the oil temperature so that they cooked more slowly, they absorbed too much of the oil.

Precooking the potatoes seemed like a good way to solve my problem, but when I quickly blanched the spuds, they turned mushy and bland, the water literally washing away their flavor. Could the microwave do a better job? I placed the shredded, squeezed potatoes in a covered bowl and zapped them for a couple of minutes before mixing them with the other ingredients. Sure enough, this batch of latkes was the best yet: tender inside and shatteringly crisp outside. And the greasiness? Nowhere to be found.

Wondering if there was more to the microwave than I'd thought, I did some research and uncovered an interesting explanation. A potato's starch granules begin to absorb water at temperatures as low as 137 degrees. Briefly heating the shreds in the microwave causes the starches to corral the water they contain into a gel, preventing it from leaching into the batter and lowering the oil temperature. In other words, the microwave had solved the greasiness problem, too. Latke mission accomplished.

—ANDREW JANJIGIAN, *Cook's Illustrated*

Crispy Potato Latkes

SERVES 4 TO 6 AS A SIDE DISH

We prefer shredding the potatoes on the large holes of a box grater, but you can also use the large shredding disk of a food processor; cut the potatoes into 2-inch lengths first so you are left with short shreds. Serve with applesauce and sour cream.

2   **pounds russet potatoes, unpeeled, scrubbed, and shredded**
½   **cup grated onion**
    Salt and pepper
2   **large eggs, lightly beaten**
2   **teaspoons minced fresh parsley**
    Vegetable oil

1. Adjust oven rack to middle position, place rimmed baking sheet on rack, and heat oven to 200 degrees. Toss potatoes, onion, and 1 teaspoon salt together in bowl. Place half of potato mixture in center of dish towel. Gather ends together and twist tightly to drain as much liquid as possible, reserving liquid in liquid measuring cup. Transfer drained potato mixture to second bowl and repeat process with remaining potato mixture. Set potato liquid aside and let stand so starch settles to bottom, at least 5 minutes.

2. Cover potato mixture and microwave until just warmed through but not hot, 1 to 2 minutes, stirring mixture with fork every 30 seconds. Spread potato mixture evenly on second rimmed baking sheet and let cool for 10 minutes. Don't wash out bowl.

3. Pour off water from reserved potato liquid, leaving potato starch in measuring cup. Add eggs and stir until smooth. Return cooled potato mixture to bowl. Add parsley, ¼ teaspoon pepper, and potato starch mixture and toss until evenly combined.

4. Set wire rack in clean rimmed baking sheet and line with triple layer of paper towels. Heat ¼-inch depth of oil in 12-inch skillet over medium-high heat until shimmering but not smoking (350 degrees). Place ¼-cup mound of potato mixture in oil and press with nonstick spatula into ⅓-inch-thick disk. Repeat until 5 latkes are in pan. Cook, adjusting heat so fat bubbles around latke edges, until golden brown on bottom, about 3 minutes. Turn and continue cooking until golden brown on second side, about 3 minutes longer. Drain on paper towels, then transfer to baking sheet in oven. Repeat with remaining potato mixture, adding oil to maintain ¼-inch depth and returning oil to 350 degrees between batches. Season with salt and pepper to taste. Serve immediately.

TO MAKE AHEAD: Cooled latkes can be covered loosely with plastic wrap and held at room temperature for up to 4 hours. Alternatively, they can be frozen on baking sheet until firm, transferred to zipper-lock bag, and frozen for up to 1 month. Reheat latkes in 375-degree oven until crisp and hot, 3 minutes per side for room-temperature latkes and 6 minutes per side for frozen latkes.

FLUFFY OMELETS

✔ **WHY THIS RECIPE WORKS** A different breed from French-style rolled omelets or diner-style omelets folded into half-moons, fluffy omelets are made by baking whipped eggs in a skillet until they rise above the lip of the pan. But most recipes result in oozing soufflés or dry, bouncy Styrofoam rounds—or eggs that barely puff up at all. To give our omelet lofty height without making it tough, we folded butter-enriched yolks into stiffly whipped whites stabilized with cream of tartar. The whipped whites gave the omelet great lift, and the yolks and butter kept it tender and rich-tasting. We chose light but flavorful fillings that satisfied without weighing down the omelet.

I've worked a lot of restaurant brunch shifts over the years, so I've made my fair share of omelets. Most of those have been either the refined French roll with its pure yellow surface and creamy, sparingly filled center or the hearty diner version that's spottily browned, generously stuffed with cheese and fillings, and folded into a half-moon. But there's a third, less familiar style that's nothing like either of these. Often called a fluffy omelet, it is whipped, then baked so it rises tall, almost like a folded-over soufflé. Beyond the appeal of its lofty height and delicate, airy texture, cooking an omelet in the oven should be a more forgiving—and hands-off—approach.

With my expectations high, I tried several recipes—and got a motley crew of wet, oozing soufflés and dry, bouncy Styrofoam rounds. Where had these recipes gone wrong? To find out, I stocked up on eggs and got to work. The most promising recipe began with whipping whole eggs in a stand mixer until the mixture was foamy (aerating the eggs helps them rise), then pouring the eggs into a buttered nonstick skillet and baking them in a 375-degree oven for 7 minutes. The omelet's inside had set nicely, but its sides and bottom had toughened up. Adjusting the cooking times and oven temperature didn't improve the results. I tried covering the pan while it baked, but this kept only the top tender and moist; the bottom still formed a tough, scaly crust.

Putting the oven aside for now, I moved on to the other main variable: the eggs. My omelets were tough, so I needed to weaken the structure of the whipped egg foam. Adding dairy seemed logical since it contains the dual tenderizers water and fat. When the proteins in eggs are heated, they bond in a process known as coagulation. Fat coats the proteins and prevents the bonds from becoming so strong that the eggs toughen, and the dairy's water dilutes the proteins, making it more difficult for them to come into contact.

I tried 1 tablespoon each of milk, heavy cream, and melted butter. But each weakened the egg foam so much that it couldn't hold enough air to puff up. The only upside was that the melted butter added a nice richness my lean omelet was lacking, so I decided to stick with it. For my second attempt, I whipped the eggs before adding the butter, hoping that creating structure before adding the tenderizer would achieve the right balance of lift and tenderness. But the egg foam still wasn't strong enough to support the extra fat, and it collapsed.

I was several dozen tests (and many dozens of eggs) in at this point, but I had clarified a couple of points: I needed to tenderize the eggs and to start with the strongest possible egg foam. Maybe the problem was that the fat in the yolks was tenderizing the mixture from the start. I tried separating the eggs, whipping just the whites to form stiff peaks (like meringue), then whisking 1 tablespoon of melted butter with the yolks before folding them into the whites. This test was the turning point. Now that the whipped whites were stiff and stable, they were able to support the fat of the yolks and butter.

Well, for a few minutes at least. Then they separated and deflated again. I felt defeated, until I thought more about meringue. To ensure a stable meringue, you add a stabilizer such as cream of tartar, which slows the formation of sulfur bonds in egg whites. If too many bonds form, the white's protein structure becomes too rigid, and the network begins to collapse. I wondered if it would have the same effect in my omelet. This time, before beating the whites, I sprinkled ¼ teaspoon of cream of tartar evenly over their surface. This batch of whites didn't look any different as they whipped, but the results became clear as I folded in the yolk mixture and waited. Seven minutes later, they were still standing tall.

Buoyed by my success, I melted a pat of butter in the skillet, poured in the airy eggs, smoothed the top with a spatula, and slid the pan into a preheated oven. About 4 minutes later, I pulled a gorgeously puffed omelet out of the oven. It looked beautiful, held its shape, and was also perfectly tender, with just enough richness.

My only remaining task was to come up with a few fillings. The delicate nature of this omelet meant that I couldn't use a heavy filling or lots of it. Instead, I would need to use small amounts of bold ingredients. A light sprinkle of Parmesan made for a nice minimalist option, but I also worked up a few more substantial variations: one with mushrooms, one with asparagus and smoked salmon, and another with artichokes and bacon.

The final trick was figuring out when, exactly, to add the fillings. Sprinkling them on after the omelet had baked meant that the filling rested on—but did not mesh with—the puffy bed of eggs. Filling the omelets before they went into the oven was a better solution. To make sure that the eggs set but didn't brown too thoroughly, I poured them into the hot buttered skillet, then immediately removed the skillet from the heat to sprinkle on the fillings. Then into the oven it went. When I pulled the baked omelet from the oven, the eggs were beautifully puffed up and gently surrounded the fillings, ensuring that each bite contained a flavor and texture contrast: rich but delicate eggs, a hit of salty Parmesan, and savory filling.

It was safe to say that my puffy omelet was the most impressive-looking omelet I'd ever made—and now it was the most forgiving to pull off, too.

—LAN LAM, *Cook's Illustrated*

Fluffy Omelet

SERVES 2

A teaspoon of white vinegar or lemon juice can be used in place of the cream of tartar, and a hand-held mixer or a whisk can be used in place of a stand mixer. The fillings that accompany this recipe are designed not to interfere with the cooking of the omelet.

- 4 large eggs, separated
- 1 tablespoon unsalted butter, melted, plus
  1 tablespoon unsalted butter
- ¼ teaspoon salt
- ¼ teaspoon cream of tartar
- 1 recipe filling (optional; recipes follow)
- 1 ounce Parmesan cheese, grated (½ cup)

1. Adjust oven rack to middle position and heat oven to 375 degrees. Whisk egg yolks, melted butter, and salt together in bowl. Place egg whites in bowl of stand mixer and sprinkle cream of tartar over surface. Fit stand mixer with whisk and whip egg whites on medium-low speed until foamy, 2 to 2½ minutes. Increase speed to medium-high and whip until stiff peaks just start to form, 2 to 3 minutes. Fold egg yolk mixture into egg whites until no white streaks remain.

2. Heat remaining 1 tablespoon butter in 12-inch ovensafe nonstick skillet over medium-high heat, swirling to coat bottom of pan. When butter foams, quickly add egg mixture, spreading into even layer with spatula. Remove pan from heat and gently sprinkle filling, if using, and Parmesan evenly over top of omelet. Transfer to oven and cook until center of omelet springs back when lightly pressed, 4½ minutes for slightly wet omelet or 5 minutes for dry omelet.

3. Run spatula around edges of omelet to loosen, shaking gently to release. Slide omelet onto cutting board and let stand for 30 seconds. Using spatula, fold omelet in half. Cut omelet in half crosswise. Serve immediately.

Mushroom Filling

MAKES ¾ CUP

- 1 teaspoon olive oil
- 1 shallot, sliced thin
- 4 ounces white or cremini mushrooms,
  trimmed and chopped
  Salt and pepper
- 1 teaspoon balsamic vinegar

Heat oil in 12-inch nonstick skillet over medium-high heat until shimmering. Add shallot and cook until softened and starting to brown, about 2 minutes. Add mushrooms and ⅛ teaspoon salt and season with pepper to taste. Cook until liquid has evaporated and mushrooms begin to brown, 6 to 8 minutes. Transfer mixture to bowl and stir in vinegar.

Asparagus and Smoked Salmon Filling

MAKES ¾ CUP

- 1 teaspoon olive oil
- 1 shallot, sliced thin
- 5 ounces asparagus, trimmed and cut
  on bias into ¼-inch lengths
  Salt and pepper
- 1 ounce smoked salmon, chopped
- ½ teaspoon lemon juice

Heat oil in 12-inch nonstick skillet over medium-high heat until shimmering. Add shallot and cook until softened and starting to brown, about 2 minutes. Add asparagus, pinch salt, and pepper to taste and cook, stirring frequently, until crisp-tender, 5 to 7 minutes. Transfer asparagus mixture to bowl and stir in salmon and lemon juice.

Artichoke and Bacon Filling

MAKES ¾ CUP

- **2 slices bacon, cut into ¼-inch pieces**
- **1 shallot, sliced thin**
- **5 ounces frozen artichoke hearts, thawed, patted dry, and chopped**
- **Salt and pepper**
- **½ teaspoon lemon juice**

Cook bacon in 12-inch nonstick skillet over medium-high heat until crisp, 3 to 6 minutes. Using slotted spoon, transfer bacon to paper towel–lined plate. Pour off all but 1 teaspoon fat from skillet. Add shallot and cook until softened and starting to brown, about 2 minutes. Add artichokes, ⅛ teaspoon salt, and pepper to taste. Cook, stirring frequently, until artichokes begin to brown, 6 to 8 minutes. Transfer artichoke mixture to bowl and stir in bacon and lemon juice.

NOTES FROM THE TEST KITCHEN

GOING THEIR SEPARATE WAYS

To create an omelet that was fluffy but didn't taste like Styrofoam, we needed to separate the whites from the yolks and treat them separately. This is because they contribute different—and competing—qualities: Whites build structure, but the fat in yolks weakens it. Our next steps: We whipped the whites with cream of tartar to add stability and stirred a little melted butter into the yolks to enhance their rich taste. We then gently recombined the two components. The extra fat kept the omelet tender and prevented it from tasting too lean, and the cream of tartar allowed the omelet to stand tall and sturdy, despite the weakening effects of butter and yolks.

THE BEST BUTTER KEEPER

The high fat content of butter means it quickly picks up off-flavors in the fridge. Butter keepers promise to keep sticks fresh-tasting. We tried out seven models from $5 to $35. Our winner, the **Lock & Lock Rectangular Food Container with Tray**, $4.99, has markings for easy measurement, a removable tray for table service, and a shape that fits a range of stick sizes. Most important, it kept butter fresher the longest.

BAKED EGGS FLORENTINE

✔ WHY THIS RECIPE WORKS Individual baked eggs make an elegant alternative to the usual breakfast strata or casserole. But baked eggs worth serving pose a challenge: namely, achieving set, tender whites and buttery, runny yolks in the same ramekin. We started with a blazing-hot oven. To give the longer-cooking whites a head start on the yolks, we added the raw eggs to preheated ramekins so that the heat transfer was rapid and the egg whites cooked before the yolks turned dry and chalky. But to protect the egg whites from scorching and to give our simple dish more substance (and style), we lined each ramekin with spinach mixed with a creamy roux-based sauce—flavored with Parmesan, nutmeg, and dry mustard—before adding the eggs. For perfectly cooked eggs every time, we pulled the eggs from the oven when the whites had just turned opaque but were still jiggly and allowed gentle carryover cooking to finish the job.

Scrambled, hard-boiled, or over-easy eggs are fine for everyday breakfast, but when I'm hosting brunch, I want an egg dish with a little more substance and style. On those occasions, I'm tempted to turn to baked eggs. The preparation might be a bit old-school, but when done well, it's undeniably elegant: individual ramekins (often lined with a dairy-enriched base or enhanced with savory add-ins), each filled with a gently set white surrounding a rich, runny yolk. And it's a great dish for entertaining since there's no à la minute cooking at the stove.

But the reality is that most recipes fail in one of two predictable ways. I've enjoyed perfectly runny, creamy yolks and firm yet tender whites—but rarely both in the same ramekin. It turns out that there's concrete science behind the problem: For the yolks to stay liquid, their temperature needs to hover around 150 degrees—and no higher. But maddeningly, the whites are just starting to turn opaque at that temperature and need to reach about 165 degrees to be properly cooked. That means that to achieve the set-white, runny-yolk ideal, the cook needs to work some magic, manipulating the cooking process so that the white firms up before the yolk, not the other way around. It was a tall order, so I stockpiled eggs, rounded up some ramekins, and got crackin'.

Most of the methods I came across fell into one of two categories: low and slow or high and fast. The gentlest cooked the eggs (often set in a water bath to temper the heat transfer) for 40 minutes in a 200-degree oven.

The speediest called for less than 10 minutes of baking with the oven cranked to its maximum temperature. I even came across a more direct (and rather drastic) solution in legendary French chef Auguste Escoffier's *Larousse Gastronomique*, in which he suggested separating the eggs, baking the whites alone until they begin to set, and then adding the yolks to the ramekins. I decided not to go there; though logical, it was hardly the fuss-free approach I was looking for.

Instead, I played it safe and decided to start by experimenting with gentle-heat methods. In addition to trying a water bath, I even tested nestling the ramekins in salt (a weaker heat conductor and therefore a better insulator than water). These approaches proved highly effective at preventing overcooked extremes—tough, rubbery whites and dry, chalky yolks—but the yolk still invariably thickened and turned pasty before the white was fully set.

Maybe increasing the heat would help create the large temperature difference I needed between the edge of the ramekin (where the whites were) and the center (where the yolks sat). For that I turned to the broiler. But my first attempt was a disaster. Just a few minutes under the blazing heat was too much: At the surface, the whites were blistered and the yolks dry, and digging a spoon underneath revealed a loose, watery mess. I knocked the temperature down to 500 degrees and tried preheating the empty ramekins for a couple of minutes in hopes of giving the whites a head start. When the ramekins were hot, I slid an egg into each one and then returned them to the oven to finish. The results? Overkill. The yolks were fine, but direct contact with the scorching ramekin walls browned the edges of the whites and turned them rubbery.

I took a step back and reviewed my results thus far. Maybe I just needed a buffer between the ramekin and the egg. With that in mind, I decided to line the ramekin with a rich base made from one of my favorite omelet fillings: spinach. I simply defrosted frozen spinach, wrung it dry, briefly sautéed it, and mixed in some heavy cream to make a more cohesive cushion for the eggs.

The result wasn't disastrous, but it wasn't perfect either, mostly because the creamed spinach was still loose enough that the egg white could swim under and around it, again coming into direct contact with the bottom and sides of the hot ramekin, where it seized up and browned. Plus the minimal spinach–heavy cream mixture tasted a bit too rich and dull. My next order of business: Thicken up the spinach barrier so that the egg could no longer leak through and, while I was at it, work some supporting flavors into the mix.

I decided to use a roux to thicken the filling. I melted some butter, added a minced shallot for depth, then whisked in some flour. I swapped the heavy cream for half-and-half and added grated Parmesan cheese, then stirred the spinach into the cheesy sauce with pinches of ground nutmeg, dry mustard, salt, and pepper. I spooned about ¼ cup of the creamy mixture into each ramekin. I pushed some halfway up the sides (leaving an indented mound in the middle to help keep the yolk in the center of the dish), loaded the ramekins into a baking dish, and popped the whole thing into the oven to preheat for a few minutes before adding an egg to each cup.

After about 10 minutes, when the whites registered 165 degrees, I pulled the baking dish out of the oven and saw that I was finally on the right track. The surfaces of the eggs looked a bit scathed from the blast of heat (nothing a spritz of vegetable oil before baking couldn't fix), but the hot creamed spinach barrier had effectively cradled the whites so that they were tender throughout and the yolks were still jiggly. But as I waited a few minutes for the piping-hot eggs to cool down enough to taste, I noticed the yolks firming up. And by the time I could comfortably eat a spoonful, carryover cooking had ruined my breakfast, leaving me with rubbery whites and chalky yolks.

To compensate for the residual heat, I would have to remove the eggs from the oven shy of their ideal final temperature and allow them to finish cooking on the counter. After several more tests, I found that the eggs had to be pulled out when they looked quite underdone—at roughly the 7-minute mark, when the whites registered only 145 to 150 degrees, were just barely opaque, and trembled like Jell-O. But what a difference a 10-minute rest made. When I nicked the rested eggs with my fork, the whites were fully set, and the yolks gushed out their rich, golden sauce. Since taking the individual temperature of six eggs was a hassle, I was happy to find during subsequent tests that I could abandon the thermometer—the jiggly appearance of the whites was a consistent indicator of when to remove the eggs from the oven.

Knowing that I had solved the baked egg conundrum tasted almost as good as that first bite of tender egg coated in Parmesan-laced creamed spinach. The only thing missing was some toast—and perhaps a mimosa.

—CELESTE ROGERS, *Cook's Illustrated*

BAKED EGGS FLORENTINE

Baked Eggs Florentine

SERVES 6

In order for the eggs to cook properly, it is critical to add them to the ramekins quickly. Use 6-ounce ramekins with 3¼-inch diameters, measured from the inner lip. Remove the eggs from the oven just after the whites have turned opaque but are still jiggly—carryover cooking will finish the job. If using a metal baking pan, reduce the oven temperature to 425 degrees. To double this recipe, bake the ramekins in two 13 by 9-inch dishes and increase the baking times in steps 3 and 4 by 1 minute.

> 2 tablespoons unsalted butter
>
> 1 large shallot, minced
>
> 1 tablespoon all-purpose flour
>
> ¾ cup half-and-half
>
> 10 ounces frozen spinach, thawed and squeezed dry
>
> 2 ounces Parmesan cheese, grated (1 cup)
>
> Salt and pepper
>
> ⅛ teaspoon dry mustard
>
> ⅛ teaspoon ground nutmeg
>
> Pinch cayenne pepper
>
> Vegetable oil spray
>
> 6 large eggs

1. Adjust oven rack to middle position and heat oven to 500 degrees.

2. Melt butter in medium saucepan over medium heat. Add shallot and cook, stirring occasionally, until softened, about 3 minutes. Stir in flour and cook, stirring constantly, for 1 minute. Gradually whisk in half-and-half; bring mixture to boil, whisking constantly. Simmer, whisking frequently, until thickened, 2 to 3 minutes. Remove pan from heat and stir in spinach, Parmesan, ¾ teaspoon salt, ½ teaspoon pepper, mustard, nutmeg, and cayenne.

3. Lightly spray six 6-ounce ramekins with oil spray. Evenly divide spinach filling among ramekins. Using back of spoon, push filling 1 inch up sides of ramekins to create ⅛-inch-thick layer. Shape remaining filling in bottom of ramekin into 1½-inch-diameter mound, making shallow indentation in center of mound large enough to hold yolk. Place filled ramekins in 13 by 9-inch glass baking dish. Bake until filling just starts to brown, about 7 minutes, rotating dish halfway through baking.

4. While filling is heating, crack eggs (taking care not to break yolks) into individual cups or bowls.

Remove baking dish with ramekins from oven and place on wire rack. Gently pour eggs from cups into hot ramekins, centering yolk in filling. Lightly spray surface of each egg with oil spray and sprinkle each evenly with pinch salt. Return baking dish to oven and bake until whites are just opaque but still tremble (carryover heat will cook whites through), 6 to 8 minutes, rotating dish halfway through baking.

5. Remove dish from oven and, using tongs, transfer ramekins to wire rack. Let stand until whites are firm and set (yolks should still be runny), about 10 minutes. Serve immediately.

TO MAKE AHEAD: Follow recipe through step 3, skipping baking of spinach mixture–lined ramekins. Wrap ramekins with plastic wrap and refrigerate for up to 3 days. To serve, remove plastic and heat ramekins, directly from refrigerator, for additional 3 to 4 minutes (10 to 11 minutes total) before proceeding with recipe.

HAM-AND-CHEESE PIE

WHY THIS RECIPE WORKS "Impossible" pie is a 1970s phenomenon that promises a pie "crust" without rolling out finicky dough. Traditionally, a simple Bisquick batter was whisked with eggs and poured over vegetables, meat, and cheese and baked. To give our "crust" good color and flavor, we buttered the pie dish and coated it with Parmesan cheese, which made for a crispy, browned exterior. We replaced the Bisquick with a simple batter of flour, baking powder, eggs, and creamy half-and-half. Doubling the number of eggs made for a richer, custardy pie. For the filling, we chose ingredients that required a minimum of prep work: scallions, diced deli ham, and Gruyère cheese.

What do you remember about the 1970s? Watergate? The Bicentennial? Call us kitchen geeks, but we remember "impossible" pies. A Bisquick-and-egg-based batter is poured over ingredients (diced vegetables, diced cooked meats, grated cheese, fruit, etc.) that are scattered over a pie plate. The selling point? A pie without the bother of a pie shell: no mixing dough, no rolling, no shaping, no chilling, and no parbaking. General Mills popularized these pies by printing recipes on the Bisquick box throughout the 1970s, transforming simple ingredients into easy pies for dinner or dessert. Impossible? Impossibly great, said the pies' many fans.

These recipes have been printed in many newspapers and community cookbooks, and they're all more or less the same. I knew I wanted to make a savory version, so I grabbed a classic recipe that called for crumbled bacon, sautéed onions, and cheese. Then I baked a pie and called the tasting team. We were underwhelmed. The "pie" was very bland. Its pale, soft bottom didn't even remotely suggest pie crust, and most of it stuck to the pie plate anyhow. We didn't see the need for the Bisquick (it merely combines flour, shortening, leavener, and sugar). I preferred to make my own mix so I'd have control over each ingredient. Also, we were expecting something with a custardy center, like quiche, but this recipe produced a pie that was cakey and not very rich.

To fix it, I'd start with the (so-called) crust. I buttered three pie plates to keep the batter from sticking. Then I mulled over ingredients that could give the crust texture and color without added work. I sprinkled one pie plate generously with Parmesan cheese, the second with crunchy panko bread crumbs, and a third with ordinary bread crumbs. I filled the shells with bacon, onion, Gruyère cheese, and, for now, the classic Bisquick batter. To give the crusts a better shot at browning, I baked the pies on the lowest oven rack, nearest the heating element, for about 30 minutes, until they were golden brown. All three pies released without a hitch and were much improved from my first attempts, but the attractively browned, slightly crispy, nutty-flavored Parmesan crust was our undisputed favorite. Admittedly, it wasn't indistinguishable from a pastry pie crust, but it was crisp and brown on the bottom and had a distinct textural contrast from the filling.

Now for the filling: Impossible pies are meant to be easy, but my working filling required a fair amount of prep work. To simplify it, I replaced the sautéed onions with mince-and-go scallions. Likewise, I skipped the bacon and opted for diced deli ham instead. To replace the Bisquick, I made a homemade mix using our usual proportions of flour, baking powder, and shortening, then scaled it down to make enough for one impossible pie. I assembled and baked a new pie incorporating all my changes. The improvement was marked, but my pie was still bland and cakey. To make it creamier, I doubled the number of eggs to four, and I switched from milk to half-and-half. To improve the flavor of the pie, I swapped out the shortening for richer-tasting butter, and I experimented with adding hot sauce (nope), white wine (nope), and mustard (yes, indeed) to the batter. Specifically, Dijon mustard gave the pie a nice, tangy shot in the arm. After more testing, I also added a little nutmeg (a classic quiche ingredient), and I learned to scatter the cheese, ham, and scallions evenly on the pie plate bottom and pour the custard over them gently so they didn't get piled up in one spot.

I baked one last pie, cut it into wedges, and called the tasters to the table. We all agreed that the name was a bit of a gimmick: This wasn't exactly a pie. Maybe more like a frittata or a quiche? Whatever we called it, we all agreed that our impossible pie was incredibly easy and totally delicious.

—DIANE UNGER, *Cook's Country*

"Impossible" Ham-and-Cheese Pie

SERVES 8

Use a rasp-style grater or the smallest holes on a box grater for the Parmesan.

- 1 tablespoon unsalted butter, softened, plus 2 tablespoons melted
- 3 tablespoons finely grated Parmesan cheese
- 8 ounces Gruyère cheese, shredded (2 cups)
- 4 ounces thickly sliced deli ham, chopped
- 4 scallions, minced
- ½ cup (2½ ounces) all-purpose flour
- ¾ teaspoon baking powder
- ½ teaspoon pepper
- ¼ teaspoon salt
- 1 cup half-and-half
- 4 large eggs, lightly beaten
- 2 teaspoons Dijon mustard
- ⅛ teaspoon ground nutmeg

1. Adjust oven rack to lowest position and heat oven to 350 degrees. Grease 9-inch pie plate with softened butter, then coat plate evenly with Parmesan.

NOTES FROM THE TEST KITCHEN

FINGER FOOD

To serve our "Impossible" Ham-and-Cheese Pie as an hors d'oeuvre at your next party, forgo the pie plate and instead bake it in an 8-inch square baking dish. Slice it into 1-inch squares and serve warm or at room temperature.

2. Combine Gruyère, ham, and scallions in bowl. Sprinkle cheese-and-ham mixture evenly in bottom of prepared pie dish. Combine flour, baking powder, pepper, and salt in now-empty bowl. Whisk in half-and-half, eggs, melted butter, mustard, and nutmeg until smooth. Slowly pour batter over cheese-and-ham mixture in pie dish.

3. Bake until pie is light golden brown and filling is set, 30 to 35 minutes. Let cool on wire rack for 15 minutes. Slice into wedges. Serve warm.

TEN-MINUTE STEEL-CUT OATMEAL

✔ **WHY THIS RECIPE WORKS** Most oatmeal fanatics agree that steel-cut oats offer the best flavor and texture, but many balk at the 40-minute cooking time. We were determined to find a way to make really good oatmeal that would take just 10 minutes before serving. The solution was to jump-start the oats' cooking by stirring them into boiling water the night before so they gently hydrated and softened overnight. In the morning, we simply added more watered then simmered the oats for just 4 to 6 minutes, until they were thick and creamy. Then we briefly rested the oatmeal off the heat so that it could thicken to the perfect consistency: creamy with a subtle chew and nutty flavor.

"Nemo me impune lacessit" was the motto of the kings of ancient Scotland. It means "No one attacks me with impunity" or, more plainly, "Don't mess with me." I resided in Scotland for several years, and I can confirm that, though the kings are long gone, that fiercely proud spirit lives on. It takes a brave (or perhaps foolish) person to criticize any aspect of Scottish identity, but as it happens I have a serious problem with one of the country's most iconic dishes: oatmeal.

I would eat traditional Scottish oat porridge every day if I could. It's delicious and sustaining, and preparing it couldn't be simpler: Steel-cut oats, which are dried oat kernels cut crosswise into coarse bits, are gently simmered in lightly salted water until the hard oats swell and soften and release some of their starch molecules into the surrounding liquid. Those freed starches bond with the liquid, thickening it until the oatmeal forms a substantial yet fluid mass of plump, tender grains. So, what's the problem? That transformation from gravelly oats to creamy, thick porridge takes a minimum of 30 minutes; closer to 40 minutes is preferable. There's just no way I can squeeze that into a busy weekday morning.

To reduce the prebreakfast rush, some cooks allow steel-cut oats to just barely bubble in a slow cooker overnight, but I've never had luck with that approach. After 8 hours the oats are mushy and blown out and lack the subtle chew of traditionally prepared oatmeal. If I was going to work my favorite kind of oatmeal into my regular breakfast rotation, I'd have to find a quicker way to cook it. My goal: perfect porridge that required less than 10 minutes of active engagement.

Oat cookery has changed little over the centuries; the only Scot-sanctioned shortcut I knew was one I'd learned working as a breakfast cook at a small hotel in Scotland: soaking the steel-cut oats in tap water overnight to initiate the hydration of the grain. Thinking that I'd give this approach some further scrutiny, I prepared two batches of oatmeal using a fairly standard ratio of 1 cup oats to 4 cups water. I soaked one measure of the grains overnight in room-temperature water and cooked the other straight from the package and then compared their respective cook times. As it turned out, presoaking saved some time, but not enough. Almost 25 minutes passed before the soaked oats morphed into the loose yet viscous result I was after—only about 15 minutes faster than the unsoaked batch. I wasn't quite convinced that some sort of presoak treatment wouldn't help, but for now I went back to the drawing board.

As a matter of fact, I had a trick in mind. When developing a streamlined recipe for polenta, we'd had the same timesaving goal, and we'd discovered an unlikely addition that sped things up considerably: baking soda. Introducing just a pinch of the alkali to the pot raised the pH of the cooking liquid, causing the corn's cell walls to break down more quickly, thereby allowing water to enter and gelatinize its starch molecules in half the time. I thought that the baking soda might have a similarly expediting effect on my steel-cut oats, so I dropped a pinch into the pot and waited. And waited. Twenty minutes later, I had the creamy porridge I was after, but a mere 5-minute savings wasn't going to do it. I decided to ditch the baking soda idea.

At a dead end, I reconsidered the notion of jumpstarting the hydration process with a presoak. Obviously I needed a more aggressive method than simply resting the oats in a bowl of room-temperature water. That's when my thoughts turned from presoaking to parcooking. Surely boiling water would hasten the softening of the oats faster than room-temperature water, right? To find out, I brought the oats and the water to a boil together, cut the heat, covered the pot, and left it to sit overnight. When I uncovered the pot the next morning, I knew I was getting somewhere. Thanks to this head start, the coarse, gravelly oats I'd started with had swelled and fully softened. Encouraged, I turned the burner to medium to see how long it would take before the cereal turned creamy and thickened. About 10 minutes of simmering later, the porridge was heated through and viscous—but was also mushy and pasty like the slow-cooker oats. Simmering the oats for less time wasn't the answer: It left the liquid in the pot thin and watery. I could only conclude that parcooking by bringing the oats up to a boil with the water was too aggressive, causing too many starch molecules to burst, which turned the oats to mush and caused the surrounding liquid to become pasty.

Still, things were looking up. A 10-minute cook time was a major step in the right direction. In my next test, I decided to split the difference between the Scottish room-temperature soak and the mushy boiled-water method. Instead of bringing the oats to a boil with the water, I boiled the water by itself, poured in the oats, covered the pot, and then left them to hydrate overnight. The next morning I got the pot going again. With this slightly more gentle method, 10 minutes later the oatmeal was perfectly creamy and not at all blown out or sticky.

I had just one other problem to solve—though the finished oatmeal looked appropriately creamy in the pot, the mixture continued to thicken after I poured it into the bowl as the starches continued to absorb the water. By the time I dug in, the result was so thick and pasty that I could stand my spoon in it.

That's when I seized on my last adjustment: I would cut the heat before the oatmeal had achieved its ideal thickness and then let it sit for a few minutes, until it thickened up just enough. I gave it a whirl, simmering the oatmeal for a mere 5 minutes and then moving the pot off the heat to rest. Five minutes later my tasters and I dug into bowls of perfect porridge: creamy and viscous and not the least bit pasty. Goal achieved.

My tasters' only criticism: Though a bowl of unadulterated oatmeal might be traditional in Scotland, on this side of the Atlantic we like ours loaded up with toppings. Of course I could easily serve my cereal with the usual fixings (brown sugar, maple syrup, dried fruit, etc.), but I wondered if I could change the flavor of the porridge more fundamentally by swapping out some of the water for more flavorful liquids and by adding some punchier ingredients.

Our science editor informed me that letting milk or juice sit out overnight might be pushing food-safety limits (water was fine), so I came up with an alternative approach that worked brilliantly: rehydrating the oats in just 3 cups of boiling water and withholding the last cup of liquid until the following morning, when it could be replaced with milk or juice right before simmering. This way, I could adjust the ingredients to make enough varieties of oatmeal to please even the most jaded palate. I came up with apple-cinnamon made with cider, a spin on carrot cake made with carrot juice, and a cardamom-scented cranberry-orange variation made with orange juice.

As much as the Scots are known for being proud and stubborn, they are also known for their inventiveness and imagination. It is, after all, Scots whom we have to thank for penicillin, Sherlock Holmes, and television. I'm confident that my 10-minute steel-cut oatmeal will appeal to the innovative side of the national character.

—ANDREA GEARY, *Cook's Illustrated*

Ten-Minute Steel-Cut Oatmeal

SERVES 4

The oatmeal will continue to thicken as it cools. If you prefer a looser consistency, thin the oatmeal with boiling water. Customize your oatmeal with toppings such as brown sugar, toasted nuts, maple syrup, or dried fruit.

- **4 cups water**
- **1 cup steel-cut oats**
- **¼ teaspoon salt**

1. Bring 3 cups water to boil in large saucepan over high heat. Remove pan from heat; stir in oats and salt. Cover pan and let stand overnight.

2. Stir remaining 1 cup water into oats and bring to boil over medium-high heat. Reduce heat to medium and cook, stirring occasionally, until oats are softened but still retain some chew and mixture thickens and resembles warm pudding, 4 to 6 minutes. Remove pan from heat and let stand for 5 minutes. Stir and serve, passing desired toppings separately.

NOTES FROM THE TEST KITCHEN

KNOW YOUR OATS

The cereal aisle stocks a variety of oat products—but not all of them make for a good bowl of oatmeal.

GROATS
Whole oats that have been hulled and cleaned. They are the least processed oat product, but we find them too coarse for oatmeal.

STEEL-CUT OATS
Groats cut crosswise into coarse bits. We strongly prefer them in oatmeal; they cook up creamy yet chewy with rich, nutty flavor.

ROLLED OATS
Groats steamed and pressed into flat flakes. They cook faster than steel-cut but make for a gummy, lackluster bowl of oatmeal.

VARIATIONS

Apple-Cinnamon Steel-Cut Oatmeal

Increase salt to ½ teaspoon. Substitute ½ cup apple cider and ½ cup whole milk for water in step 2. Stir ½ cup peeled, grated sweet apple, 2 tablespoons packed dark brown sugar, and ½ teaspoon ground cinnamon into oatmeal with cider and milk. Sprinkle each serving with 2 tablespoons coarsely chopped toasted walnuts.

Carrot Spice Steel-Cut Oatmeal

Increase salt to ¾ teaspoon. Substitute ½ cup carrot juice and ½ cup whole milk for water in step 2. Stir ½ cup finely grated carrot, ¼ cup packed dark brown sugar, ⅓ cup dried currants, and ½ teaspoon ground cinnamon into oatmeal with carrot juice and milk.

Sprinkle each serving with 2 tablespoons coarsely chopped toasted pecans.

Cranberry-Orange Steel-Cut Oatmeal

Increase salt to ½ teaspoon. Substitute ½ cup orange juice and ½ cup whole milk for water in step 2. Stir ½ cup dried cranberries, 3 tablespoons packed dark brown sugar, and ⅛ teaspoon ground cardamom into oatmeal with orange juice and milk. Sprinkle each serving with 2 tablespoons toasted sliced almonds.

CRUNCHY FRENCH TOAST

✓ **WHY THIS RECIPE WORKS** Unlike your usual French toast, crunchy French toast is coated in crushed cornflakes to give it a crispy fried exterior and a moist, custardy center. We used thick slices of challah in our French toast because they stay moist and custardy in the middle when cooked. Making a thick, fortified custard mixture with half-and-half instead of milk helped the coating to adhere. Ultimately we found the flavor of a cornflake crust was bland; Cap'n Crunch cereal gave our toast the best flavor and (no surprise here) crunch. To simulate the crunchy fried texture of French toast without the mess and bother of actually frying, we baked our French toast in the oven on a preheated baking sheet with a generous amount of oil.

The very first thing I can remember cooking on my own without parental supervision, French toast holds a special place in my heart. It probably wasn't very good, but I did get the basics down: Give stale bread a quick soak in eggs beaten with milk, cinnamon, and vanilla; put the slices in a skillet to brown; flip them to brown more; and breakfast is served. It's still my favorite breakfast, but recently at a diner I encountered something new to me, and even better: crunchy French toast, which combined the soft, slightly sweet, custardy interior of classic French toast with a satisfyingly crunchy exterior. As soon as I took a bite, I knew I had to learn how to make it.

Back in the test kitchen, I did some research and found a few recipes. The egg-and-dairy mixtures (basically simple custards) varied slightly in ingredients and proportions; crushed cornflakes was the usual coating; and some of the recipes called for sautéing the French toast, while others required shallow-frying it in a few inches of oil. I set out the ingredients and got down to work.

Unfortunately, many of these toasts had flaws that even a gallon of maple syrup couldn't cover up. The questions they raised were many and perplexing: How do you get the coating to stick? (I quickly learned that it has a tendency to slough off in the frying pan.) How do you keep the coating from getting soggy when it meets the wet custard? How do you keep the coating from burning yet ensure that the inside cooks through? And I also wondered just what would make for the tastiest coating—my tasters were lukewarm about the cornflakes.

This first round of testing did lead to a few helpful discoveries, though. First, fat 1-inch-thick slices produced the best ratio of soft inside to crunchy outside. Next, shallow-fried French toast produced hyper-crunchy slices that beat the pants off slices that were merely sautéed. But I definitely didn't want the bother and mess of frying first thing in the morning (and in multiple batches); I'd have to figure out an easier way.

Cherry-picking these winning features from the sample recipes, I started again: I used a custard made from milk, eggs, and the standard flavorings, mixing up enough to yield eight slices. For now I used cornflakes to coat the toast. A problem immediately presented itself: In order to saturate the thick slices, I needed extra custard. Doubling the amounts was more successful. My next concern was getting the cornflakes to stick. I figured that if the custard were thicker, it would have better adhesive powers. I replaced the 2½ cups of milk with an equal amount of half-and-half. Problem solved. Along the way, as I adjusted here and tweaked there, I found that dipping the slices in the custard mixture for just 15 seconds per side let the custard saturate the slices without producing wet, squishy toast.

Now it was time to deal with the bland cornflake coating, which we'd never liked much. One taster had compared it (kindly, I thought) to cardboard. So I rounded up some other candidates: Frosted Flakes, Cap'n Crunch, Honey Bunches of Oats, and panko, a Japanese-style bread crumb that the test kitchen often uses for its extreme crunch. Cap'n Crunch won the day by a long shot. Ground down to a coarse crumb, it adhered well to the moistened bread without soaking up too much liquid, and tasters deemed it crunchy, satisfyingly sweet, and kid-friendly, too, as one mom in the group added.

Up until now I had been shallow-frying the toast in batches in a skillet. That meant that, in order to make eight pieces of this Texas-size toast, I had to do four separate batches, which was tedious to say the least.

CRUNCHY FRENCH TOAST

I wondered if I could move my recipe to the oven without sacrificing the pan-fried crunch. Taking inspiration from a recipe that we'd developed a few years ago for oven-baked French toast, I baked almost 20 batches over six days, making a series of discoveries as I went along: It was important to set each piece to rest on a wire cooling rack after I dredged it in the cereal so that the bottoms wouldn't get soggy before I'd even started cooking. I didn't merely grease the baking sheet; I simulated pan-frying by pouring in a generous ½ cup of oil (tasters liked butter, but unfortunately it burned). To guarantee great crunch, first I let the baking sheet

get good and hot; then I let the oil heat up; and only at that point did I carefully slide in the custard-soaked, cereal-coated French toast pieces. The loud sizzling boded well.

Twenty minutes (and one flip) later, I took a batch out of the oven, poured on the maple syrup, and called my tasters. Their smiles, their empty plates, and the sound of crunching told me all I needed to know.

—NICK IVERSON, *Cook's Country*

NOTES FROM THE TEST KITCHEN

MAKING CRUNCHY FRENCH TOAST

1. Dip thick slices of bread in custard mixture for just 15 seconds per side to give finished toast custardy (but not soggy) center.

2. Dredge each custard-soaked slice in coarsely crushed Cap'n Crunch for best crunchy coating.

3. Cook on preheated baking sheet in generous amount of oil to simulate shallow frying and guarantee crunchy crust.

SECRET INGREDIENT: CAP'N CRUNCH

Most recipes call for coating French toast with cornflakes to make crunchy French toast. We found a cereal that stood up better to the custard without getting soggy. With Cap'n Crunch, we had our golden-brown, crunchy exterior locked up.

Crunchy French Toast

SERVES 6 TO 8

Day-old challah works best. To crush the cereal, pour it into a 1-gallon zipper-lock bag, seal, and use a rolling pin to roll over it several times.

6   cups Cap'n Crunch cereal, crushed coarse
2½ cups half-and-half
3   large eggs
3   tablespoons sugar
1   tablespoon vanilla extract
1½ teaspoons ground cinnamon
½   teaspoon salt
1   (12 by 5-inch) loaf challah, cut into
     eight 1-inch-thick slices
½   cup vegetable oil

1. Adjust oven rack to middle position, place rimmed baking sheet on rack, and heat oven to 450 degrees. Set wire cooling rack inside second rimmed baking sheet. Place cereal in 13 by 9-inch baking dish. Whisk half-and-half, eggs, sugar, vanilla, cinnamon, and salt together in large bowl until combined.

2. Working with 2 slices of bread at a time, soak in half-and-half mixture until just saturated, about 15 seconds per side. Transfer soaked bread to cereal and press lightly to adhere; transfer to prepared wire rack. Repeat with remaining bread.

3. Add oil to preheated sheet, tilting to coat evenly. Return sheet to oven and heat until oil is just smoking, about 4 minutes. Carefully remove sheet from oven and arrange bread in even layer on sheet. Bake until exterior is golden brown and crunchy, about 20 minutes, flipping once and rotating sheet halfway through baking. Transfer toast to clean wire cooling rack and let cool for 5 minutes. Serve.

OATMEAL MUFFINS

✔ **WHY THIS RECIPE WORKS** For an oatmeal muffin with plenty of oat flavor and a fine, tender texture, we processed old-fashioned rolled oats into a meal. To boost the oat flavor even more, we first toasted the oats in butter. To ensure that the oat flour was fully hydrated, so that our muffins were moist, not dry, we let the batter rest for 20 minutes before baking. Finally, we made a tasty apple crisp-inspired topping with oats, nuts, and brown sugar.

I've always been interested in the idea of a breakfast that boasts the best qualities of a great bowl of oatmeal—lightly sweet, oaty flavor and satisfying heartiness—in the convenient, portable form of a muffin. But I've yet to find a decent example of the confection. I suppose it isn't all that surprising: Oats are dry and tough, making them difficult to incorporate into a tender crumb. And what chance does their mild, nutty flavor have of shining through when it is clouded by loads of spices and sugar? Determined to bake my way to a richly flavored, moist, and tender oatmeal muffin, I headed into the kitchen and got to work.

Aside from a barrage of sugar and spice, the real problem with most of the initial recipes I tested was the oats themselves. The most common approach was to toss a few handfuls of the old-fashioned rolled type (our usual choice for baking) into a quick bread–style muffin batter. This calls for separately combining the wet ingredients (melted butter, milk, light brown sugar, and eggs) and dry ingredients (all-purpose flour, baking powder, baking soda, and salt) and then blending the two mixtures together. The result of this dead-simple style? Muffins speckled with dry, chewy oats featuring raw white centers.

It was clear that simply stirring raw oats into the batter wasn't enough to sufficiently hydrate and cook them. A few recipes sought to avoid the problem by calling for quick oats, which are precooked and rolled into thin flakes before packaging, but these muffins presented their own issues. Gone were the dry, uncooked bits flecking the crumb, but with them went any trace of oat taste.

Sticking with the more robust old-fashioned rolled oats, I set out to find the best way to ensure that they would cook through. When a soak in cold milk (the primary liquid for my muffin batter) failed to soften the sturdy flakes, I tried heating the milk first. I poured 2 cups of boiling milk over an equal amount of oats, and after allowing the mixture to cool to room temperature, I incorporated the oatmeal mush into my batter. Still no luck: The muffins were now riddled with gummy pockets. I produced similar results in a batch in which I simmered the oats and milk on the stovetop as I would for a bowl of oatmeal. What had gone wrong?

Well, it turns out that when oats are hydrated and heated, they release lots of starch. This is good news if you're trying to make a creamy bowl of porridge, but it spells disaster when it comes to baking muffins. The oat starch ends up trapping some of the moisture in the batter, thus preventing the flour from evenly hydrating. The result: those ruinous thick, gummy patches.

Frustrated, I scratched soaking the oats from my method and took a step back to reflect. When I used quick oats, the texture of the muffins had been perfect. Because they are broken down and precooked, quick oats absorb liquid more readily than do thicker rolled oats and thus fully soften during baking. What if I processed my rolled oats so that they would drink up liquid more easily?

I broke out my food processor and whizzed 2 cups of chunky rolled oats into a pile of fine oat flour—just 30 seconds did the trick. Exactly as I'd hoped, the finely ground meal readily absorbed milk (heating it was now unnecessary) and fully softened once incorporated into the batter and baked. There was just one caveat: My home-ground oat flour absorbed liquid much more slowly than wheat flour did. I found that if I mixed up the batter and immediately portioned it into a muffin tin, its consistency was too thin and my muffins spread and ran into one another during baking. This was an easy problem to fix: After mixing the batter, I gave it a 20-minute rest to fully hydrate, thereby ensuring that the batter would be thick enough to scoop.

I was finally making progress on the texture, but there was one issue that I had yet to address: When mixed with the wet ingredients, the oat flour occasionally developed a few large clumps that stubbornly refused to hydrate and dissolve into the batter during baking, leaving dry, floury pockets in the finished muffins. To find a route to a consistently hydrated batter, I tried vigorously folding with a spatula, whisking energetically, and even processing the mixture in a blender. But manhandling the batter to smooth it out only resulted in a crumb with a tough texture—a repercussion of overworking the oat starch and gluten.

GETTING MOIST, FLAVORFUL OATMEAL MUFFINS

Old-fashioned rolled oats have a subtle taste and don't easily absorb the liquid in a batter. Here are the steps we took to transform their flavor and texture.

1. Brown oats in butter to develop rich, complex flavor and aroma.

2. Process oats into fine meal so that they will absorb liquid.

3. Let rest for 20 minutes to give oat flour time to hydrate in batter.

MUFFIN MISHAPS

Developing a great oatmeal muffin required a lot of trial and error, particularly when it came to deciding which type of oats to use and how to incorporate them. Here are a few of our not-so-successful attempts.

PRETTY BUT BLAND
Highly processed quick oats produced an attractive muffin—with dull flavor.

DRY AND CRUMBLY
Raw rolled oats never fully hydrated, leading to a dry, chewy crumb.

SQUAT AND GUMMY
Cooked rolled oats were too wet, yielding a muffin with gummy patches.

Seeing my predicament, a colleague suggested that I try a lesser-known technique called whisk folding. In this method, a whisk is gently drawn down and then up through the batter before being tapped lightly against the side of the bowl to knock any clumps back into the mixture. The wires of the whisk exert very little drag and thus develop minimal gluten, and the tapping action helps rupture pockets of dry ingredients. Sure enough, whisk folding made all the difference, ridding the batter of large clumps and preserving a tender, moist texture.

With my muffins' texture perfected, I switched my attention to flavor. With a ratio of 2 cups oats to 1¾ cups flour, my muffins boasted a prominent oat flavor. Still, I wanted their nutty taste to be even more noticeable, so I turned to a technique that we've used to intensify oat flavor when making granola: toasting. I tried two options: tossing the whole oats in a dry skillet over medium heat until they turned golden versus sautéing them in a couple of tablespoons of butter. It was no contest: The muffins made with butter-toasted oats won hands down for their richer, more complex taste and aroma. Next, I experimented with adding spices and seasonings. I incorporated varying amounts of ground nutmeg, ground ginger, cinnamon, and vanilla extract, yet time and again tasters singled out the muffins without any extras. With great buttery, toasted-oat flavor in the mix, spices seemed to only muddy the waters.

Happy with my tender, jam-packed-with-oats muffins, I needed to come up with a topping. Just as one might garnish a bowl of oatmeal with crunchy nuts or chewy, sweet raisins, I wanted a contrasting adornment on my muffin that featured crunch and a bit of sweetness. I played around with toasted nuts, a cinnamon-sugar mixture, and even an unconventional broiled icing, but nothing tasted quite right. While pondering my next move, I watched a colleague pull a bubbling-hot apple crisp from the oven and it hit me: A crisplike topping would be just right.

I stirred together some more oats, finely chopped pecans, brown sugar, flour, melted butter, salt, and a hint of cinnamon in a medium bowl, and then I crumbled my crisp-inspired topping evenly over the muffin batter before baking. Twenty minutes later, my muffins emerged with a tasty crown of crunchy, chewy, sweet, and salty oats and nuts—the perfect accent to the rich crumb. Finally, I'd succeeded in turning the best traits of a humble bowl of oatmeal into a satisfying breakfast on the go.

—DAN SOUZA, *Cook's Illustrated*

Oatmeal Muffins

MAKES 12 MUFFINS

Do not use quick or instant oats in this recipe. Walnuts may be substituted for the pecans. The easiest way to grease and flour the muffin tin is with a baking spray with flour.

TOPPING

- ½ cup (1½ ounces) old-fashioned rolled oats
- ⅓ cup (1⅔ ounces) all-purpose flour
- ⅓ cup packed (2⅓ ounces) light brown sugar
- ⅓ cup pecans, chopped fine
- 1¼ teaspoons ground cinnamon
- ⅛ teaspoon salt
- 4 tablespoons unsalted butter, melted

MUFFINS

- 2 tablespoons unsalted butter, plus 6 tablespoons melted
- 2 cups (6 ounces) old-fashioned rolled oats
- 1¾ cups (8¾ ounces) all-purpose flour
- 1½ teaspoons salt
- ¾ teaspoon baking powder
- ¼ teaspoon baking soda
- 1⅓ cups packed (9⅓ ounces) light brown sugar
- 1¾ cups milk
- 2 large eggs, beaten

1. FOR THE TOPPING: Combine oats, flour, sugar, pecans, cinnamon, and salt in medium bowl. Drizzle melted butter over mixture and stir to thoroughly combine; set aside.

2. FOR THE MUFFINS: Grease and flour 12-cup muffin tin. Melt 2 tablespoons butter in 10-inch skillet over medium heat. Add oats and cook, stirring frequently, until oats turn golden brown and smell of cooking popcorn, 6 to 8 minutes. Transfer oats to food processor and process into fine meal, about 30 seconds. Add flour, salt, baking powder, and baking soda to oats and pulse until combined, about 3 pulses.

3. Stir 6 tablespoons melted butter and sugar together in large bowl until smooth. Add milk and eggs and whisk until smooth. Using whisk, gently fold half of oat mixture into wet ingredients, tapping whisk against side of bowl to release clumps. Add remaining oat mixture and continue to fold with whisk until no streaks of flour remain. Set aside batter for 20 minutes to thicken. Meanwhile, adjust oven rack to middle position and heat oven to 375 degrees.

4. Using ice cream scoop or large spoon, divide batter equally among prepared muffin cups (about ½ cup batter per cup; cups will be filled to rim). Evenly sprinkle topping over muffins (about 2 tablespoons per muffin). Bake until toothpick inserted in center comes out clean, 18 to 25 minutes, rotating muffin tin halfway through baking.

5. Let muffins cool in muffin tin on wire rack for 10 minutes. Remove muffins from muffin tin and serve or let cool completely before serving.

MUFFIN TIN DOUGHNUTS

☑ **WHY THIS RECIPE WORKS** Muffin tin doughnuts promise the flavor and texture of cake doughnuts with the simplicity of a dump, stir, and bake muffin recipe. To get the compact and tender crumb of a cake doughnut, we added more butter and an extra egg yolk and cut the flour with some cornstarch. A pinch of nutmeg in the batter and a coating of cinnamon sugar gave our doughnut convincing flavor. To get the sugar to stick, we used a pastry brush to brush on melted butter, then rolled each doughnut in the sugar. A hotter-than-usual 400-degree oven gave our muffin tin doughnuts a subtle just-fried crunch.

As a doughnut devotee, I took notice when something called a doughnut muffin appeared at my local coffee shop. Could a baked item possibly achieve the sugary, fried deliciousness that has me hooked on doughnuts? The doughnut muffin was more cousin than twin to a fried doughnut; the crumb was unevenly bubbly, unlike the compact, tender, almost crumbly texture of a true doughnut. But the cinnamon-sugar coating and the nutmeg inside were undeniably reminiscent of a classic cake doughnut. This particular fauxnut was imperfect, but judging from the preponderance of recipes (some called doughnut muffins, others muffin doughnuts), perfection just might be achievable.

I baked up six batches of muffin tin doughnuts from popular recipes, and while none was bad, none captured both the essence of a doughnut and the ease of a muffin. I collated our tasting notes and jotted down all the characteristics that this muffin would need to persuade eaters that it was a cake doughnut in disguise: a very tender crumb, a crisp exterior, nutmeg and cinnamon flavors, and a buttery spiced coating.

What I wanted were great doughnuts without rolling, cutting, or a pot of hot oil.

I picked the best of the lot: a recipe that had yielded doughnut muffins with good flavor and crumb structure. But they were a little tough and dry, the coating method was problematic, and they required that I cream butter and sugar in a stand mixer. I hoped for a simpler method. I started by nixing the mixer; instead, I simply melted the butter, then whisked the wet ingredients (butter, eggs, and buttermilk) into the dry (flour, sugar, baking powder, salt, and ground nutmeg).

To fix the tough, dry texture, I first tried an extra egg yolk. That tenderized the crumb slightly and made my doughnut muffins a little moister and richer. Next I tried replacing the all-purpose flour with cake flour, which is lower in gluten, the protein network that gives baked goods their structure. Now the doughnuts were too tender: They disintegrated when I tried to take a bite. I considered using half cake flour and half all-purpose, but that seemed too fussy. However, we've found that you can cut all-purpose flour with cornstarch as an emergency substitute for cake flour, so I tested varying proportions of each. Ultimately, 2¾ cups of flour and ¼ cup of cornstarch gave me just the right crumb.

Now that I had my batter, I moved on to the method. To replicate frying, I tried scooping the batter into a hot, heavily buttered muffin tin and then rolling the finished doughnuts in cinnamon sugar. Fail. The edges of the doughnuts were cracked, and without any moisture, the sugar didn't adhere. The solution to the cracking came from simply increasing the oven temperature from 325 to 400 degrees, which crisped the crust nicely.

Time to figure out the mechanics of the coating, which had frustrated me from the start. Brushing the muffin tops with melted butter and then sprinkling on cinnamon sugar, as some recipes suggest, was easy, but it didn't produce a crisp, rich, sugary layer on the tops and it left the bottoms naked. Rolling the baked muffins in melted butter and then cinnamon sugar, as other recipes required, yielded the rich exterior of a real fried doughnut, but as the butter level dropped, it was hard to coat the last few. Exasperated, I tried applying the butter with a pastry brush. This worked perfectly. Tender and consistently coated, these treats "really do taste like doughnuts," one taster said, dusting the cinnamon sugar from her fingers.

—SARAH GABRIEL, *Cook's Country*

Muffin Tin Doughnuts
MAKES 12 DOUGHNUTS

In step 3, brush the doughnuts generously, using up all the melted butter. Use your hand to press the cinnamon sugar onto the doughnuts to coat them completely.

DOUGHNUTS
- 2¾ cups (13¾ ounces) all-purpose flour
- 1 cup (7 ounces) sugar
- ¼ cup cornstarch
- 1 tablespoon baking powder
- 1 teaspoon salt
- ½ teaspoon ground nutmeg
- 1 cup buttermilk
- 8 tablespoons unsalted butter, melted
- 2 large eggs plus 1 large yolk

COATING
- 1 cup (7 ounces) sugar
- 2 teaspoons ground cinnamon
- 8 tablespoons unsalted butter, melted

1. FOR THE DOUGHNUTS: Adjust oven rack to middle position and heat oven to 400 degrees. Spray 12-cup muffin tin with vegetable oil spray. Whisk flour, sugar, cornstarch, baking powder, salt, and nutmeg together in bowl. Whisk buttermilk, melted butter, and eggs and yolk together in separate bowl. Add wet ingredients to dry ingredients and stir with rubber spatula until just combined.

2. Divide batter evenly among prepared muffin cups. Bake until doughnuts are lightly browned and toothpick inserted in center comes out clean, 19 to 22 minutes. Let doughnuts cool in tin for 5 minutes.

NOTES FROM THE TEST KITCHEN

BRUSH WITH BUTTER

We liberally brush the warm doughnuts with melted butter before rolling them in cinnamon sugar. The butter helps the coating stick and makes the muffins taste more like fried doughnuts.

3. FOR THE COATING: Whisk sugar and cinnamon together in bowl. Remove doughnuts from tin. Working with 1 doughnut at a time, brush all over with melted butter, then roll in cinnamon sugar, pressing lightly to adhere. Transfer to wire rack and let cool for 15 minutes. Serve.

BEIGNETS

✔ **WHY THIS RECIPE WORKS** To replicate the airy, crisp texture and tangy yeast flavor of these classic New Orleans doughnuts, we began by using plenty of yeast and proofing it with warm water and sugar to develop lots of flavor fast. Replacing the milk with water gave the beignets more structure for just the right amount of chew. To give them their trademark honeycombed texture, we made a super-hydrated dough; when the dough hit the hot oil, it created steam pockets within the doughnuts for an open, airy interior. Since wet dough is tricky to roll out, we let it rise in the refrigerator to firm it up. After a few minutes of frying and a shower of powdered sugar, our beignets were ready to be enjoyed, Big Easy–style.

European cooks have been frying bits of sweet dough since the Middle Ages, and naturally the French were in on it. Beignets (ben-YEYS), as the French call these fritters, reached Louisiana in the 18th century with French settlers, or French Canadians, or then again it could have been the nuns; culinary historians can't say for sure. What is certain is that once these golden doughnuts came, they conquered. Today, beignets are the object of desire of every tourist in New Orleans and even the barometer of the city's recovery from Hurricane Katrina—it began when the city's fabled beignet cafés reopened. I can state for a fact that when my beignet order at the Morning Call café reached my table, things were definitely looking up.

They didn't taste like ordinary doughnuts. They were delicate, lightly sweet, and yeasty—almost tangy. Their structure, a gossamer honeycomb of holes, reminded me of ciabatta bread. And the "chew" was good, with the slightest of tugs to the bite. Although the café's recipe is an old and closely guarded secret (make that really old; the café opened in 1870), Morning Call's manager kindly let me watch the dough get mixed, rolled, cut into squares, and deep-fried. The really interesting part? The baker incorporated dough scraps from the previous day

into this new batch. I was beginning to understand where these beignets got their fabulous and complex flavor.

Some travelers to New Orleans bring home T-shirts; others carry Mardi Gras masks. I wanted a memento of a different sort: a recipe for beignets like these.

I had plenty of recipes to choose from, with plenty of variables—although I didn't find any calling for old dough scraps. All beignets are made from flour, eggs, fat, liquid, and leavener; sugar is a common addition. The leavener is traditionally yeast but occasionally baking powder; the fat may be butter, shortening, or oil; and the liquid options are water, fresh or evaporated milk, or a combination. The techniques vary, too. Sometimes, the ingredients are stirred together to form a soft dough that rises for up to 2 hours, after which it's rolled out and cut. Other recipes produce a batter, which is simply dropped into the hot oil to form fritters.

Following a selection of these recipes, I produced cakey, sweet, dense beignets; squishy, gummy beignets; and beignets that disintegrated into flakes before I could get them off the plate and into my mouth. None matched the Morning Call beignets.

This test had clarified a few points, though: My dough would have to be easy enough for a home cook to make, and without the dough scraps at my disposal, I'd have to find a way to replicate their complex flavor. I'd use yeast, and to streamline, I would limit myself to 1 hour of rising time. The recipe that had come nearest the mark called for yeast, fresh milk, and oil (along with flour, sugar, and egg). I let this dough rise for just 1 hour, rolled it out, cut beignets, and fried them.

But my fast rise meant I'd given the dough less time than ever to develop flavor. To compensate, first I went up on yeast (from 2¼ teaspoons to 1 tablespoon); the flavor of the beignets improved somewhat. Next, I tried warming the milk before combining it with the yeast and a little sugar, which yeast converts into flavor molecules. I let this mixture sit for a few minutes. Although instant yeast doesn't require warm liquid to proof, heat does jump-start the fermentation process. I hoped that it would jump-start the flavors, too. With these two fixes in place, I fried a new batch of beignets. Amazingly, this batch was full-flavored, with that slightly sour yeastiness.

My beignets still lacked the right chew, though. Chewiness in baked goods comes from gluten development, which occurs both when flour gets wet and when it is kneaded vigorously. To keep my recipe simple, I ruled out kneading. I scanned my recipe looking for

BEIGNETS

other ideas and noticed the milk. Milk contains fat and a gluten-weakening peptide called glutathione, both of which make for tender baked goods—the opposite of what I wanted. I replaced the milk with water and, easy as that, got chewier beignets. No one even noticed the swap.

But the crumb was still even and cakey instead of airy. A coworker who is a whiz at bread baking advised me to build a wetter dough. More water means more steam, he explained. As bread bakes, the carbon dioxide in yeast creates holes, the steam enlarges these holes, and the holes set. Although beignets are fried, not baked, he thought the same principle might apply. I gradually added water, until I had a very sticky dough—which made the best beignets to date. Since wet dough is tricky to roll and chilled dough easier, I stuck it in the refrigerator to rise. Luckily, 1 hour's chilling time curbed the stickiness without slowing down the yeast.

These beignets—light and delicately chewy, with a simultaneously sweet yet slightly tangy yeast flavor—disappeared faster than a Sazerac on Mardi Gras. But now that I could make them, I'd need a new excuse to visit New Orleans. So . . . how about some jambalaya?
—REBECCAH MARSTERS, *Cook's Country*

Beignets

MAKES ABOUT 2 DOZEN BEIGNETS

This dough is very wet and sticky, so flour the counter and baking sheet generously. You will need at least a 6-quart Dutch oven for this recipe.

- 1 cup warm water (110 degrees)
- 3 tablespoons granulated sugar
- 1 tablespoon instant or rapid-rise yeast
- 3 cups (15 ounces) all-purpose flour
- ¾ teaspoon salt
- 2 large eggs
- 2 tablespoons plus 2 quarts vegetable oil
  Confectioners' sugar

1. Combine water, 1 tablespoon granulated sugar, and yeast in large bowl and let sit until foamy, about 5 minutes. Combine flour, remaining 2 tablespoons granulated sugar, and salt in second bowl. Whisk eggs and 2 tablespoons oil into yeast mixture. Add flour mixture and stir vigorously with rubber spatula until dough comes together. Cover bowl with plastic wrap and refrigerate until nearly doubled in size, about 1 hour.

2. Set wire rack inside rimmed baking sheet. Line second sheet with parchment paper and dust heavily with flour. Place half of dough on well-floured counter and pat into rough rectangle with floured hands, flipping to coat with flour. Roll dough into ¼-inch-thick rectangle (roughly 12 by 9 inches). Using pizza wheel, cut dough into twelve 3-inch squares and transfer to floured sheet. Repeat with remaining dough.

3. Add enough of remaining 2 quarts oil to large Dutch oven to measure about 1½ inches deep and heat over medium-high heat to 350 degrees. Place 6 beignets

NOTES FROM THE TEST KITCHEN

FORMING BEIGNETS
Our dough is very wet to allow a network of delicate holes to develop in the beignets. However, wet dough can be tricky to work with. Here's how to easily shape and cut the beignets.

1. Dust counter and rolling pin heavily with flour before you roll out chilled beignet dough.

2. Use pizza wheel to cut 3-inch squares. (Traditionally, beignets are measured by the size of the cook's hands: four fingers by four fingers.)

THE BEST DRIP COFFEE MAKER
Although they're convenient and easy to use, the vast majority of automatic drip coffee makers don't brew coffee to industry standards. We have found only two worth recommending. Our favorite, the **Technivorm Moccamaster 10-Cup Coffee Maker**, $299, uses a copper heating element that keeps water at just the right temperature to brew smooth, velvety coffee. It consistently makes excellent coffee and is intuitive to use—but it's also pricey. The Bonita 8-Cup Coffee Maker, $149, is our Best Buy. It makes coffee that has bright, full flavor, though it is a bit more acidic than the Technivorm's, and it lacks a brew-through lid. (See page 311 for more information on our testing results.)

in oil and fry until golden brown, about 3 minutes, flipping halfway through frying. Adjust burner, if necessary, to maintain oil temperature between 325 and 350 degrees. Using slotted spoon or tongs, transfer beignets to prepared wire rack. Return oil to 350 degrees and repeat with remaining beignets. Dust beignets with confectioners' sugar. Serve immediately.

BRIOCHE

✔ **WHY THIS RECIPE WORKS** For rich, tender brioche without the hassle of painstakingly adding softened butter to the dough little by little as it is kneaded, we melted the butter and added it directly to the eggs. Then we dispensed with the stand mixer and opted for an equally effective no-knead approach that lets time do most of the work: An overnight rest in the fridge developed both structure and flavor. We ditched the specialty brioche pan in favor of a simple loaf pan, then, to build structure and ensure an even, fine crumb, we shaped the dough into tight balls before placing them in the pans.

Well-made brioche is something of a miracle: Despite being laden with butter and eggs, it manages to avoid the density of a pound cake and turn out incredibly light and airy. Yet this gossamer-wing texture still provides brioche with enough structure to serve as a base for a sandwich, a slice of toast slathered with jam, or even the foundation for bread pudding. But achieving these results is a balancing act—and a tricky one at that.

Most butter-enriched doughs, like those for sandwich bread or dinner rolls, contain between 10 and 20 percent butter. The average brioche recipe has up to 50 percent (or 5 parts butter to 10 parts flour). Fat lubricates the wheat proteins in the flour, inhibiting their ability to form gluten, the network of cross-linked proteins that gives bread its structure. The more fat, the greater the interference. This can make brioche incredibly tender—or it can cause the dough to separate into a greasy mess.

The typical brioche method goes as follows: A sponge of flour, yeast, and water sits overnight to ferment and build flavor; additional flour, yeast, and water, plus salt, sugar, and several eggs, are added; and the mixture is kneaded in a stand mixer until a strong gluten network begins to form. Then butter, softened to just the right temperature, is added a few tablespoons at a time. Only after one portion is fully incorporated into the dough is the next added. This painstaking process, which can take more than 20 minutes, is necessary to ensure that the butter is completely and evenly combined without causing the dough to separate. Next, the dough is left to rise at room temperature for a few hours, then chilled in the refrigerator for anywhere from an hour to overnight to firm up the butter—an essential step when shaping a sticky, wet dough. Finally the dough is shaped into loaves, left to rise yet again, and—at long last—baked. Phew.

My goal: to make tender, plush brioche with butter-rich flavor but no butter-induced headache.

Though tempting, I knew that dumping everything (butter included) together at the start and letting the stand mixer knead it all into submission wouldn't work. All that softened butter would coat the wheat proteins so thoroughly that no amount of kneading would develop sufficient structure. But what about cold butter? Cut into the flour before adding other ingredients, the solid little chunks surely wouldn't coat the proteins as readily as softened fat, making it possible to develop at least some gluten before the butter coated the wheat proteins—or so I hoped.

I also cut back on the butter slightly. Using a respectable 45 percent fat-to-flour ratio and simplifying things by leaving out the overnight sponge, I began by cutting cold butter into flour in a food processor. After transferring the mixture to the bowl of a stand mixer, I threw in the yeast, sugar, and salt. With the dough hook turning, I gradually added some water and a few beaten eggs. The dough was quite wet but still had a surprising amount of structure. After putting the dough through the usual steps—proof, chill, proof—I baked it, fingers crossed.

The results? Not great, but not half bad either. The interior crumb was far too open, with large, irregular holes, and the bread had a cottony, crumbly texture, both of which suggested that it needed more gluten development. But the fact that it had any structure at all meant that I was onto something.

But though my method was simpler than the usual method, it still felt too fussy and hands-on. A familiar approach popped to mind: the "no-knead" bread technique first popularized by Mark Bittman and Jim Lahey in *The New York Times,* which we adapted for our Almost No-Knead Bread recipe. Basically, you combine all your ingredients and let the mixture sit for hours. During this long rest, enzymes naturally present in wheat help untangle the wheat proteins that eventually come together to form an organized gluten network. This allows the dough to stitch itself together into a loaf containing plenty of structure with only a bit of stirring and a couple of folds—no actual kneading required. The key to this technique is a very wet dough (the more water, the more efficient the enzymes). And happily, brioche dough is normally highly hydrated.

I gave the no-knead approach a whirl, cutting the butter into the flour in the food processor as before, then simply mixing the liquid ingredients into the dry ones and stirring them together with a wooden spoon. This produced a dough that was soupy—exactly what I wanted. I covered it and let it sit at room temperature while it proofed, folding it at 30-minute intervals to encourage the gluten to form. As I'd hoped, after several hours, the dough had just as much strength as the machine-kneaded one. Even better: After being chilled, shaped, and proofed a second time, it baked up just as nicely. I wondered if I could eliminate the food processor step as well. So this time, I simply melted the butter, let it cool, and then whisked it into the egg-and-milk mixture before adding the liquid to the dry ingredients. Happily, this simplification produced a loaf just as good as the one in which I'd cut the butter into the flour first.

Still, my loaves remained cottony and open-crumbed—a sure sign that they needed more gluten than my hand-mixed method could provide on its own. But I had a few tricks up my sleeve. First, the flour: Since its protein content is directly related to its ability to form gluten (the more protein it has, the more structure it can provide to the dough), a higher-protein flour should give me more structure. I swapped out the all-purpose flour I had been using for higher-protein bread flour. This brioche was the clear winner.

Next, I'd let the dough sit even longer, to not only increase gluten development but also add more flavor, since it would give the starches in the dough more time to ferment, replacing the complex, yeasty flavor I'd lost when I scrapped the sponge. Gluten development and fermentation are slowed but not halted by cold temperatures, so I'd also extend the dough's second rest (in the fridge, where it wouldn't run the risk of overproofing and collapsing), letting it rest overnight to give it even more strength. Sure enough, this brioche

was much improved: It had a more finely textured and resilient crumb than any previous versions, as well as a more complex flavor.

Last, I gave some consideration to my shaping method. Until now, I'd been forming the dough into a single long loaf. I realized that I could add even more strength and structure to the dough by dividing it in two and shaping each half into two tight, round balls instead. Placed side by side in the pan, the two balls merged during rising and baking to form a single loaf. Even this little bit of extra manipulation made the crumb a bit finer and more uniform. And if shaping them once was good, I figured that twice might be even better. After letting the dough rounds rest, I patted them flat once more and then reshaped them into tight balls. This time, the interior crumb was fine-textured, uniform, and resilient but still delicate.

Finally, I had a reliable and relatively hands-off brioche recipe that could hold its own against those from the best bakeries in town.

—ANDREW JANJIGIAN, *Cook's Illustrated*

NOTES FROM THE TEST KITCHEN

NO KNEADING NECESSARY

Folding the dough as it proofs is the only active work you'll have to do. Gently lift edge of dough and fold it over itself, turning bowl 45 degrees and repeating until you've made full circle (total of 8 folds).

MELTED BUTTER EASES THE WAY

Traditionally, making a rich dough like brioche means kneading all of the ingredients to develop gluten—except butter. Butter (softened to 68 degrees) is added tablespoon by tablespoon only after the mixture begins to develop into dough. This is a long and painstaking process. It's an important one, too: If the butter isn't added slowly, the dough can break into a greasy mess. When we decided to ditch tradition and use a "no-knead" technique, we realized that this would also solve our tricky butter problem. In a no-knead approach, the dough (which must be very wet) sits for a long time, stitching itself together to form gluten—all without any help from a mixer. With kneading out of the equation, we were able to melt the butter and add it all at once—a faster and far less demanding approach.

No-Knead Brioche

MAKES 2 LOAVES

High-protein King Arthur Bread Flour works best with this recipe, though other bread flours will work. If you don't have a baking stone, bake the bread on a preheated rimmed baking sheet.

- 3¼ cups (17¾ ounces) bread flour
- 2¼ teaspoons instant or rapid-rise yeast
- 1½ teaspoons salt
- 7 large eggs, 1 lightly beaten with pinch salt
- ½ cup water, room temperature
- ⅓ cup (2⅓ ounces) sugar
- 16 tablespoons unsalted butter, melted and cooled slightly

1. Whisk flour, yeast, and salt together in large bowl. Whisk 6 eggs, water, and sugar together in medium bowl until sugar has dissolved. Whisk in butter until smooth. Add egg mixture to flour mixture and stir with wooden spoon until uniform mass forms and no dry flour remains, about 1 minute. Cover bowl with plastic wrap and let stand for 10 minutes.

2. Holding edge of dough with your fingertips, fold dough over itself by gently lifting and folding edge of dough toward middle. Turn bowl 45 degrees; fold again. Turn bowl and fold dough 6 more times (for total of 8 folds). Cover with plastic and let rise for 30 minutes. Repeat folding and rising every 30 minutes, 3 more times. After fourth set of folds, cover bowl tightly with plastic and refrigerate for at least 16 hours or up to 48 hours.

3. Transfer dough to well-floured counter and divide into 4 pieces. Working with 1 piece of dough at a time, pat dough into 4-inch disk. Working around circumference of dough, fold edges of dough toward center until ball forms. Flip dough over and, without applying pressure, move your hand in small circular motions to form dough into smooth, taut round. (If dough sticks to your hands, lightly dust top of dough with flour.) Repeat with remaining dough. Cover dough rounds loosely with plastic and let rest for 5 minutes.

4. Grease two 8½ by 4½-inch loaf pans. After 5 minutes, flip each dough ball so seam side is facing up, pat into 4-inch disk, and repeat rounding step. Place 2 rounds, seam side down, side by side in prepared pans and press gently into corners. Cover loaves loosely with plastic and let rise at room temperature until almost doubled in size (dough should rise to about ½ inch below top edge of pan), 1½ to 2 hours. Thirty minutes before baking, adjust oven rack to middle position, place baking stone on rack, and heat oven to 350 degrees.

5. Remove plastic and brush loaves gently with remaining 1 egg beaten with salt. Set loaf pans on stone and bake until golden brown and internal temperature registers 190 degrees, 35 to 45 minutes, rotating pans halfway through baking. Transfer pans to wire rack and let cool for 5 minutes. Remove loaves from pans, return to wire rack, and let cool completely before slicing and serving, about 2 hours.

KOLACHES

✔ **WHY THIS RECIPE WORKS** Originally brought to the States by Czech immigrants and now popular in Texas hill country, kolaches are sweet Danish-like pastries heaped with a fruit or cheese filling and topped with streusel. Many recipes call for mixing the dough gently, but we found that lengthy kneading yielded a more supple dough, giving our kolaches a lighter crumb. We also increased the amount of egg yolks and butter for more tender, flavorful pastries. Next, we traded in traditional dried fruit for juicy, pie-like fruit fillings and came up with an easy, sweet cheese option. A greased and floured measuring cup made even indentations in the pastries to securely cradle the filling.

Sibling to a Danish and a brioche, a kolache is a palm-size round of sweetened bread with a streusel topping and a dollop of sweet cheese or fruit filling in the center. Czech immigrants brought kolaches to Texas in the late 19th century, and over time Texans have added variations, from sausage and jalapeño to barbecued beef. Today, these pastries are so popular in parts of the Lone Star State that multiple towns claim the title "kolache capital," and there are annual kolache festivals and even kolache chain restaurants. Just as New Yorkers lay claim to the only real bagels, the kolache cognoscenti with whom I spoke insisted that their own favorite bakery was the only place to get a real kolache. To sort this out, I was going to need a plane ticket.

But first I headed to our cookbook library to check out recipes. In general, the ingredient lists (consisting of flour, milk, eggs, butter, sugar, salt, and yeast) indicated that kolaches are basically enriched white bread, not unlike brioche, but I was puzzled by two common deviations. First, some recipes called for oil or shortening in place of butter. Why skip the delicious butter? Second, while a few recipes called for kneading the dough like bread dough (either by hand or with a machine), many others required mixing the dough as if it were a batter, combining the wet ingredients in one bowl and the dry in a second, then gently stirring one into the other. Why forgo the long mixing that develops stretchy gluten, helping the dough to hold air and bake up light?

I had some time before my trip, so I headed to the kitchen and baked a few dozen kolaches, some with butter, others with oil and shortening. I tried long- and short-mixed recipes, machine- and hand-mixed recipes. After mixing, proofing, shaping, and baking, I lined up five batches of kolaches on the counter. They looked impressive, but the taste and texture seriously underwhelmed us. Those that were kneaded had the better texture but were dismayingly lean. As for the treated-like-batter type, the worst of the lot (dry, crumbly, bland, and tough) prompted one taster to liken them to a "cheap hamburger bun." Neither approach produced the rich, tender, and briochelike pastries I'd pictured. What was I missing?

A few weeks later, I landed in Dallas and set out on a kolache hunt through central Texas. Many of the beloved kolache meccas that people had recommended to me weren't bakeries at all, but gas stations and doughnut shops. That fact might have charmed me had the kolaches been good. I tried a decent one in a town called West, which gave me enough encouragement to keep searching. Still, a few days later, having driven for two days and 250 miles, sampling every kolache I could find between Dallas and San Antonio, while I'd eaten a few that I liked, I hadn't found the one. I had one more stop scheduled in Boerne, northwest of San Antonio. I figured I'd enjoy the scenery, dutifully eat a few last kolaches, and fly home. Suddenly, my luck changed.

I pulled up to Little Gretel restaurant (no gas pumps) and met Denise Mazal, a classically trained chef and Czech expat. Little Gretel's host sat me down at a sunny table with a plate of tidy, round, shining, golden kolaches with broad wells of cheese, prune, and apricot fillings. I hesitated for fear of being disappointed. Maybe I was the problem—a cynical Northerner who just didn't get it. And then . . . one bite of Denise's cheese kolache, and boy, did I get it. It was exactly what I had imagined: subtly sweet, tender, buttery, and . . . gone. I had polished

off the prune and was reaching for the apricot by the time Denise got to the table. She generously agreed to show me her secrets.

In the kitchen at Little Gretel, Denise mixed together the flour, sugar, and salt in the big bowl of her commercial Hobart mixer, then put on the dough hook; added milk, yeast, eggs, some extra yolks, and melted butter; and mixed until it all came together. Then she turned up the mixer and let it spin for several minutes, until the dough was smooth, shiny, and elastic—mixing it, I noted, just like bread.

She let it rise, punched it down, divided it into balls, let those rise, then, by pressing slowly with a special cylindrical wooden tool, transformed each ball into a disk with a puffy perimeter and a deep well. She filled the broad divots with heaping spoonfuls of cheese or fruit filling, and after about 20 minutes in the oven, they were just as gorgeous as the ones I'd eaten earlier. (As she worked, Denise described a Czech wedding tradition in which the bride-to-be bakes 1,000 kolaches for the wedding to prove to her betrothed that she will keep him well fed.) Denise packed up a box of kolaches for me and hugged me goodbye, and I headed to the airport. I felt ready to have a go at my own recipe.

With the inside scoop from a pro, I was sure I could handily transform the best from my first round of testing into something special. I added extra yolks and nearly doubled the butter. The added fat tenderized, moisturized, and flavored the dough—no more dry, tough kolaches. Long mixing with the dough hook developed plenty of stretchy gluten so the dough held air, making the finished pastries light and pleasantly chewy. Along with the added fat, increasing the salt by 50 percent took care of the blandness. The shaping method that Denise showed me made my kolaches picture-perfect (I used the bottom of a measuring cup to create the well).

Now for the fillings. First I made a simple sweetened cheese filling. A combination of tangy cream cheese and milkier, slightly salty ricotta was a perfect base; a little sugar and lemon zest balanced the flavor, and 1 tablespoon of flour bound it nicely.

Next I wanted something fruity. I loved Denise's Czech-style dried fruit fillings, but there was also something very appealing about the Texan approach: Pie-filling-like concoctions of pineapple, blueberry, or cherry were especially popular with tasters. I started with a test kitchen fruit cobbler recipe that calls for microwaving frozen fruit with sugar and cornstarch.

KOLACHES

After a little fiddling to get the yield and thickness right, I arrived at a simple formula that worked for pineapple, blueberry, or cherry. I filled the kolaches and sprinkled them with streusel.

I had just one more order of business. I e-mailed my recipe to Denise to get her opinion. When she e-mailed the following week with her approval, I was ecstatic. Kolaches were out of the gas station and back in the kitchen.

—SARAH GABRIEL, *Cook's Country*

Kolaches

MAKES 16 KOLACHES

Do not use nonfat ricotta cheese in this recipe. In step 1, if the dough hasn't cleared the sides of the bowl after 12 minutes, add more flour, 1 tablespoon at a time, up to 2 tablespoons. In step 6, to prevent sticking, reflour the bottom of the measuring cup (or drinking glass) after making each indentation.

DOUGH

- 1 **cup whole milk**
- 10 **tablespoons unsalted butter, melted**
- 1 **large egg plus 2 large yolks**
- 3½ **cups (17½ ounces) all-purpose flour**
- ⅓ **cup (2⅓ ounces) sugar**
- 2¼ **teaspoons instant or rapid-rise yeast**
- 1½ **teaspoons salt**

CHEESE FILLING

- 6 **ounces cream cheese, softened**
- 3 **tablespoons sugar**
- 1 **tablespoon all-purpose flour**
- ½ **teaspoon grated lemon zest**
- 6 **ounces (¾ cup) whole-milk or part-skim ricotta cheese**

STREUSEL

- 2 **tablespoons plus 2 teaspoons all-purpose flour**
- 2 **tablespoons plus 2 teaspoons sugar**
- 1 **tablespoon unsalted butter, cut into 8 pieces and chilled**

- 1 **large egg beaten with 1 tablespoon milk**

1. FOR THE DOUGH: Grease large bowl. Whisk milk, melted butter, and egg and yolks together in 2-cup

FILLING KOLACHES

1. Divide dough into 16 balls, let each ball double in size, then shape and fill them. Using greased and floured measuring cup, press indentation into each ball of dough. Dough will deflate slightly.

2. Spoon filling into each indentation. Brush kolaches with egg wash, sprinkle with streusel, and bake.

liquid measuring cup (butter will form clumps). Whisk flour, sugar, yeast, and salt together in bowl of stand mixer. Fit stand mixer with dough hook, add milk mixture to flour mixture, and knead on low speed until no dry flour remains, about 2 minutes. Increase speed to medium and knead until dough clears sides of bowl but still sticks to bottom, 8 to 12 minutes.

2. Transfer dough to greased bowl and cover with plastic wrap. Adjust oven racks to upper-middle and lower-middle positions. Place dough on lower-middle rack and place loaf pan on bottom of oven. Pour 3 cups boiling water into loaf pan, close oven door, and let dough rise until doubled, about 1 hour.

3. FOR THE CHEESE FILLING: Using stand mixer fitted with paddle, beat cream cheese, sugar, flour, and lemon zest together on low speed until smooth, about 1 minute. Add ricotta and beat until just combined, about 30 seconds. Transfer to bowl, cover with plastic, and refrigerate until ready to use.

4. FOR THE STREUSEL: Combine flour, sugar, and butter in bowl and rub between fingers until mixture resembles wet sand. Cover with plastic and refrigerate until ready to use.

5. Line 2 rimmed baking sheets with parchment paper. Punch down dough and place on lightly floured counter. Divide into quarters and cut each quarter into 4 equal pieces. Form each piece into rough ball by pulling dough edges underneath so top is smooth.

On unfloured counter, cup each ball in your palm and roll into smooth, tight ball. Arrange 8 balls on each prepared sheet and cover loosely with plastic. Place sheets on oven racks. Replace water in loaf pan with 3 cups boiling water, close oven door, and let dough rise until doubled, about 90 minutes.

6. Remove sheets and loaf pan from oven. Heat oven to 350 degrees. Grease and flour bottom of ⅓-cup measure (or 2¼-inch-diameter drinking glass). Make deep indentation in center of each dough ball by slowly pressing until cup touches sheet. (Perimeter of balls may deflate slightly.)

7. Gently brush kolaches all over with egg-milk mixture. Divide filling evenly among kolaches (about 1½ tablespoons per kolache) and smooth with back of spoon. Sprinkle streusel over kolaches, avoiding filling. Bake until golden brown, about 25 minutes, switching and rotating sheets halfway through baking. Let kolaches cool on pans for 20 minutes. Serve warm.

VARIATION

Fruit-Filled Kolaches

Combine 10 ounces frozen pineapple, blueberries, or cherries; 5 tablespoons sugar; and 4 teaspoons cornstarch in bowl. Microwave, covered, until bubbling and thickened, about 6 minutes, stirring once halfway through cooking. Mash with potato masher. Let cool completely and fill kolaches as directed in step 7.

PUMPKIN BREAD

🗸 **WHY THIS RECIPE WORKS** For pumpkin bread to be quick and easy, canned pumpkin puree is a must, but it has a raw, metallic flavor. To get rid of the canned taste and highlight the sweet flavor of the pumpkin, we cooked the puree until just caramelized. Then we mixed the bread batter right in the pot, adding cream cheese and buttermilk for tangy flavor and moisture. Toasted walnuts lent a nice crunch, and a quick streusel topping added texture and a subtle sweetness.

After testing a half-dozen different recipes for pumpkin bread, I found myself thinking of it as the John Doe of quick breads: No loaf was remarkably bad—and none was remarkably good. They were all just fine.

But if I'm going to devote time to making something, even a quick bread, I want it to be more than just OK; I want it to be great. For that, I knew I'd need a bread that had just the right texture—neither too dense nor too cakey—and a rich pumpkin flavor that was properly tempered with sweetness and lightly enhanced—rather than obscured—by spices.

I reasoned that the best pumpkin bread needed to begin with the best pumpkin puree, which, of course, would mean made from scratch rather than canned. Unfortunately, after spending 2 hours seeding, roasting, scraping, and pureeing (and then washing all the dishes), I'd changed my recipe from "quick bread" to "what-a-pain bread." And after all that, the loaf made with the from-scratch puree was only marginally better than the one made from canned. From-scratch puree was out.

But I was definitely going to have to do something to improve the canned puree, since it had noticeable off-flavors, described by my tasters as "metallic" and "raw." First I attempted to mask the canned flavor by using more spices or adding molasses or prune puree, but these tests all flopped (the spices overwhelmed the pumpkin's flavor, and the other two just tasted slightly odd). I wondered if I was overthinking the problem: The puree tasted raw, so why not just cook it? I dumped a can of the puree into a saucepan and stirred it over medium heat until it just barely began to caramelize. Then I cooled it down and quickly stirred together another batch of bread using this cooked-down puree. When I pulled the loaves from the oven and sliced them, tasters marveled at the way the bread had changed: The pumpkin flavor was full and rich, no longer raw-tasting or metallic.

Unfortunately, though, the texture of these loaves was a little dense and dry. By cooking down the pumpkin I had driven off some of the moisture. This problem was easily solved by adding a bit of buttermilk. But caramelizing the puree had also increased its sweetness, throwing off the balance of flavors. I needed to add a bit of tanginess to the mix. It occurred to me that since gently tangy cream cheese is often slathered onto slices of pumpkin bread, I might try directly incorporating it into the batter. The only downside was that doing so would require dirtying a stand mixer. But as I was cooking my pumpkin puree, I had an epiphany. What if I simply added the cream cheese straight to the hot puree so that the cheese melted, cooling the puree at the same time? I cut a block of cream cheese into small chunks, tossed them into the pan with the hot puree, and stirred—the lumps became streaks that melted away with a few swirls of the spatula.

Now that I'd gone this far, could I put the mixing bowl away and combine everything in the saucepan? I cracked my eggs into the measuring cup with the buttermilk, gave them a quick whisk, then stirred them into the puree. Next came the dry ingredients. I divided the batter between the prepared pans and put them into the oven. After an anxious wait, I took out loaves that had perfectly balanced flavor plus just the texture I was after: moist but not greasy, with a crumb that was neither cakey nor dense and rubbery.

The only thing missing was some textural contrast. Toasted walnuts were a nice addition, but I still wanted something more crunchy and flavorful to complement the bread's crumb and flavor. Why not add something to the top? Sprinkled on just before baking, a simple streusel gave the perfect amount of sweet crunch to each slice. As a bonus, the topping prevented the surface of the loaf from getting soggy when stored overnight, so my bread was just as delicious the next day. Now this was a pumpkin bread to make you sit up and take notice.

—LAN LAM, *Cook's Illustrated*

Pumpkin Bread

MAKES 2 LOAVES

The test kitchen's preferred loaf pan measures 8½ by 4½ inches; if using a 9 by 5-inch loaf pan, start checking for doneness 5 minutes early.

TOPPING

5 tablespoons packed (2¼ ounces) light brown sugar
1 tablespoon all-purpose flour
1 tablespoon unsalted butter, softened
1 teaspoon ground cinnamon
⅛ teaspoon salt

BREAD

2 cups (10 ounces) all-purpose flour
1½ teaspoons baking powder
½ teaspoon baking soda

1 (15-ounce) can unsweetened pumpkin puree
1½ teaspoons ground cinnamon
1 teaspoon salt
¼ teaspoon ground nutmeg
⅛ teaspoon ground cloves
1 cup (7 ounces) granulated sugar
1 cup packed (7 ounces) light brown sugar
½ cup vegetable oil
4 ounces cream cheese, cut into 12 pieces
4 large eggs
¼ cup buttermilk
1 cup walnuts, toasted and chopped fine

1. FOR THE TOPPING: Using fingers, mix all ingredients together in bowl until well combined and topping resembles wet sand; set aside.

2. FOR THE BREAD: Adjust oven rack to middle position and heat oven to 350 degrees. Grease two 8½ by 4½-inch loaf pans. Whisk flour, baking powder, and baking soda together in bowl.

3. Combine pumpkin puree, cinnamon, salt, nutmeg, and cloves in large saucepan over medium heat. Cook mixture, stirring constantly, until reduced to 1½ cups, 6 to 8 minutes. Remove pot from heat; add granulated sugar, brown sugar, oil, and cream cheese and stir until combined. Let mixture stand for 5 minutes. Whisk until no visible pieces of cream cheese remain and mixture is homogeneous.

4. Whisk together eggs and buttermilk. Add egg mixture to pumpkin mixture and whisk to combine. Fold flour mixture into pumpkin mixture until combined (some small lumps of flour are OK). Fold walnuts into batter. Scrape batter into prepared pans. Sprinkle topping evenly over top of each loaf. Bake until skewer inserted in center of loaf comes out clean, 45 to 50 minutes. Let breads cool in pans on wire rack for 20 minutes. Remove breads from pans and let cool for at least 1½ hours. Serve warm or at room temperature.

VARIATION

Pumpkin Bread with Candied Ginger
Substitute ½ teaspoon ground ginger for cinnamon in topping. Fold ⅓ cup minced crystallized ginger into batter after flour mixture has been added in step 4.

POTATO ROLLS

✔ **WHY THIS RECIPE WORKS** Potato roll recipes abound, but they're inconsistent. Almost none specify what type of potato to use, and some use so much potato that the bread gets weighed down by the load. We wanted to figure out how to use starchy potatoes to make exceptionally soft, tender, moist dinner rolls or burger buns. For the lightest rolls, we found a combination of 1 cup of mashed russet potatoes and high-protein bread flour worked best. This gave our rolls a stable structure that supported the greatest amount of potatoes for rolls that rose quickly (thanks to potato's yeast-activating potassium) and emerged from the oven moist, light, and airy.

Maybe it's absurdly retro, but sometimes I long for a homemade bread with a soft, moist, light crumb and a delicate crust. I'm not talking about the decadently buttery rolls associated with holiday dinners (though I do love those) but something a bit leaner and more versatile—a bread that can be shaped into sandwich buns or formed into small dinner rolls. My hankering, I realized, was for good old-fashioned potato rolls. This bread delivers the same soft tenderness of a classic American dinner roll but without its richness. What's more, the dough should work equally well for burger buns—something I've always wanted a great recipe for.

A roundup of recipes showed that potato bread could include virtually any amount of potato, from 2 tablespoons to 2 cups. There was also no consensus on what form the potatoes should take. Some called for freshly mashed spuds (and often a bit of the cooking water), others for cold leftovers, still others for the instant kind. Almost none of the recipes specified what type of potato to use, and even peeling them wasn't a given.

To my surprise, all of the recipes I tried produced loaves that were remarkably tender and moist—even the ones made with instant potatoes and potato starch. But I did notice a few trends. First, the more potato in the mix, the softer and more airy the bread—but only up to a point. Too much potato and the bread began to be weighed down. Second, doughs made with warm, freshly mashed spuds seemed to rise more quickly, and doughs that included the cooking water from the potatoes rose fastest of all.

Before I went further, I had to answer a fundamental question: How is it that mashed potato has the ability to bestow such a light, soft character on bread in the first place? Our science editor enlightened me: When potatoes are boiled, their starch granules swell with water. When those swollen starches are mixed into bread dough, they interfere with the flour proteins' ability to bond and form gluten, weakening the dough's structure so that it bakes up softer and more tender. What's more, potato starch granules are four to five times larger than wheat starch granules and thus can hold much more water than the wheat starches can, making potato bread moister than straight wheat bread and contributing to our perception of the crumb as soft and light.

I just needed to figure out how much potato was optimal and what form would achieve the fluffy texture I wanted. I don't normally keep instant spuds or potato starch in my pantry. I also vetoed cold leftover mash, since I'm not likely to have it on hand. I would start with freshly boiled peeled potatoes and keep the amount on the lower end of the spectrum, with just ¼ cup (2 ounces) replacing 2 ounces of all-purpose flour. I also opted for russet potatoes, thinking that their floury texture would serve me best. After mashing the potatoes with butter, I kneaded them in a stand mixer with the flour, whole egg, milk (which some recipes added for a subtle dairy sweetness), salt, sugar, and yeast and then left the dough to rise for an hour before shaping it into sandwich rolls. After another rise—45 minutes this time—I baked the batch in a 425-degree oven.

I was on the right track: These rolls had a tenderness approaching that of richer breads, even though they contained just 2 tablespoons of butter. And I ended up with the same results whether I created a feathery mash using a ricer or pounded the potatoes into glueyness with a potato masher. Excited by this effect, I wondered just how far I could push the potato's magical properties. I increased the mash by another ¼ cup, decreasing the flour by the same 2 ounces, and the rolls got even lighter and fluffier.

The more I upped the potato, the less time the dough needed to rise. I chalked that up to the dispersal of more warm potato throughout the dough, since yeast thrives in a warm environment. But when I did a little research, I learned that there was a more specific reason behind the faster rise: The potassium in potatoes activates yeast, and the more of it there is, the quicker and more vigorous the rise. Furthermore, when potatoes are boiled, they leach almost half of their potassium into the cooking water—helping to explain why so many recipes include it in the dough. I found that when I switched

POTATO ROLLS

from using 5 tablespoons of milk to the same amount of potato water, the proofing times dropped still more.

Encouraged by these successes, I increased the potatoes from ½ cup to a full packed cup, reducing the flour by a corresponding 4 ounces. However, this time the dough fell flat, making coarse-crumbed rolls with a compromised rise. Could it be that a full cup of potato was just too much to cram into my bread? But before failing so dramatically, this batch had risen in record time, and I was reluctant to give that up. But maybe the problem was not with the potatoes; maybe I had chosen the wrong flour for the job.

Clearly, the protein in the 2-odd cups of all-purpose flour in my recipe wasn't providing enough muscle to support ½ pound of freeloading potato starch. But what if I switched to higher-protein bread flour? This simple swap did the trick: The increased protein provided just enough stable yet tender structure to support the potatoes, yielding rolls that were not only perfectly risen but also the lightest, airiest yet. And I could use my dough for sandwich rolls or dinner rolls, depending on how large I made the pieces.

Now that I know how and why adding potatoes to bread improves its texture (not to mention how potatoes speed up bread preparation), I'm ready to start a potato bread renaissance.

—ANDREA GEARY, *Cook's Illustrated*

NOTES FROM THE TEST KITCHEN

POTATO ROLL HIGHS (AND LOWS)

The more mashed potato we added to our dough, the better the results—until we hit 1 full cup, at which point the rolls started to collapse under the weight of the spuds. But switching from all-purpose flour to higher-protein bread flour gave the dough the strength it needed to support the mash, so the rolls baked up tall, light, and fluffy.

LOW RISE
Avoid all-purpose flour.

HIGH RISE
Use high-protein bread flour.

WHY POTATO?

Here are four good reasons why we crammed a full packed cup of mashed potatoes into our rolls.

QUICKER RISE The potassium in potatoes has a positive effect on yeast, causing it to rise faster and more vigorously than it would in wheat-only breads, which also leads to lighter texture.

SUPER-SOFT CRUMB When boiled, potato starch molecules swell and interfere with the ability of flour proteins to form gluten, ensuring tender bread.

MOIST TEXTURE Potato starch granules are about five times larger than wheat starch granules and are therefore capable of absorbing at least five times more water, resulting in a moister crumb.

LONGER SHELF LIFE Potato starch molecules hinder wheat starches from staling, thereby keeping the bread's crumb soft for days.

Potato Burger Buns
MAKES 9 ROLLS

These rolls are ideal for both burgers and sandwiches. Don't salt the cooking water for the potatoes. A pound of russet potatoes should yield just over 1 very firmly packed cup (½ pound) of mash. To ensure optimum rise, your dough should be warm; if your potatoes or potato water is too hot to touch, let cool before proceeding with the recipe. This dough looks very dry when mixing begins but will soften as mixing progresses. You may portion the rolls by weight in step 5 (2.75 ounces of dough per roll).

- 1 **pound russet potatoes, peeled and cut into 1-inch pieces**
- 2 **tablespoons unsalted butter, cut into 4 pieces**
- 2¼ **cups (12⅓ ounces) bread flour**
- 1 **tablespoon sugar**
- 2 **teaspoons instant or rapid-rise yeast**
- 1 **teaspoon salt**
- 2 **large eggs, 1 lightly beaten with 1 teaspoon water and pinch salt**
- 1 **tablespoon sesame seeds (optional)**

1. Place potatoes in medium saucepan and add water to just cover. Bring to boil over high heat; reduce heat to medium-low and simmer until potatoes are cooked through, 8 to 10 minutes.

2. Transfer 5 tablespoons potato water to bowl to cool; drain potatoes. Return potatoes to saucepan and place over low heat. Cook, shaking pot occasionally, until any surface moisture has evaporated, about 1 minute. Remove from heat. Process potatoes through ricer or food mill or mash well with potato masher. Measure 1 very firmly packed cup potatoes and transfer to bowl. Reserve any remaining potatoes for another use. Stir in butter until melted.

3. Combine flour, sugar, yeast, and salt in bowl of stand mixer. Add warm potato mixture to flour mixture and mix with hands until combined (some large lumps are OK). Add 1 egg and reserved potato water; mix with dough hook on low speed until dough is soft and slightly sticky, 8 to 10 minutes.

4. Shape dough into ball and place in lightly greased container. Cover tightly with plastic wrap and allow to rise at room temperature until almost doubled in volume, 30 to 40 minutes.

5. Turn out dough onto counter, dusting with flour only if dough is too sticky to handle comfortably. Pat gently into 8-inch square of even thickness. Using bench knife or chef's knife, cut dough into 9 pieces (3 rows by 3 rows). Separate pieces and cover loosely with plastic.

6. Working with 1 piece of dough at a time and keeping remaining pieces covered, form dough pieces into smooth, taut rounds. To round, set piece of dough on unfloured counter. Loosely cup hand around dough and, without applying pressure to dough, move hand in small circular motions. (Tackiness of dough against counter and circular motion should work dough into smooth, even ball, but if dough sticks to hands, lightly dust fingers with flour.) Cover rounds with plastic and allow to rest for 15 minutes.

7. Line 2 rimmed baking sheets with parchment paper. On lightly floured counter, firmly press each dough round into 3½-inch disk of even thickness, expelling large pockets of air. Arrange on prepared baking sheets. Cover loosely with plastic and let rise at room temperature until almost doubled in size, 30 to 40 minutes. While rolls rise, adjust oven racks to middle and upper-middle positions and heat oven to 425 degrees.

8. Brush rolls gently with egg wash and sprinkle with sesame seeds, if using. Bake rolls until deep golden brown, 15 to 18 minutes, rotating and switching baking sheets halfway through baking. Transfer baking sheets to wire racks and let cool for 5 minutes. Transfer rolls from baking sheets to wire racks. Serve warm or at room temperature.

Potato Dinner Rolls
MAKES 12 ROLLS

Line rimmed baking sheet with parchment paper. In step 5, divide dough square into 12 pieces (3 rows by 4 rows). Shape pieces into smooth, taut rounds as directed in step 6. Transfer rounds to prepared baking sheet and let rise at room temperature until almost doubled in size, 30 to 40 minutes. Bake on upper-middle rack until rolls are deep golden brown, 12 to 14 minutes, rotating baking sheet halfway through baking.

DAKOTA BREAD

✔ **WHY THIS RECIPE WORKS** This hearty loaf from the breadbasket of America usually contains a daunting variety of flours and seeds. We shortened the ingredient list with a creative substitution: seven-grain cereal mix. This one easy addition gave our loaf hearty texture and complex flavor. To round it out, we stirred some seeds into the batter and sprinkled more on top of the loaf. Starting the bread in a hot oven created an initial "spring," giving the loaf lift for a lighter crumb, then lowering the temperature prevented the seeds from burning. High-protein bread flour gave us the gluten development necessary to make our loaf rise high, and a pan of water in the oven prevented the crust from setting before the bread was fully risen.

In 1989, North Dakota celebrated the 100th anniversary of its statehood in a manner that we here at *Cook's Country* heartily approve: with a recipe. Dakota bread—chock-full of whole-wheat and rye flours, barley, oats, sunflower seeds, and more—was created as a tribute to the state's bountiful harvest. It is also a rustic, hearty, and truly delicious loaf.

I rounded up some recipes. Even before I mixed, kneaded, shaped, and baked my way through them, I was taken aback by the lengthy lists of ingredients. Recipes called for so many types of flours, grains, and seeds that I'd need a granary instead of a pantry. But how could I streamline without losing the bread's complex, nutty taste and moist and chewy texture? As I made various versions, other questions arose: Which flours were best? How long to let the dough rise? Recipes ran the gamut. Naturally, these recipes produced quite different results, too. Some doughs yielded loaves that were closer to airy white sandwich bread than to multigrain bread.

DAKOTA BREAD

Other doughs made heavy, dense loaves. My version would meet in the middle, with a hearty yet light crumb and a pared-down ingredient list that still captured the many flavors and textures that made this bread so appealing in the first place.

I put together a working recipe that picked up the features we liked best from my initial test. My first order of business was to trim back the ingredients. Fortunately, I already had an idea: seven-grain cereal, which I figured could provide a multigrain fix in a single, easy package. I made a loaf using all-purpose flour (for now) in combination with the cereal, adding up the amounts of individual grains and non–white flours and replacing them all with an equal amount of cereal. I found that I needed to soften the cereal first, so I soaked it in warm water for 10 minutes before making the dough; while I was at it, I added the other wet ingredients—oil and honey—to the cereal.

I did a few more tests to work out the best ratio of cereal to flour. With 1½ cups of cereal combined with 3½ cups of the all-purpose flour (plus more seeds added at the end of kneading), this Dakota bread had a delicious, wholesome flavor and was pleasantly coarse. Alas, the loaf was somewhat flat and saggy; it got little to no gluten (which is what gives dough elasticity and structure) from the grains in the seven-grain cereal. I didn't want to cut back on the grains—that was the whole point, after all—so I hoped that using a different type of flour would help. I was pretty sure that whole-wheat flour would only make the problem worse, as the bran in the flour inhibits gluten development. That's why 100 percent whole-wheat flour breads are so often heavy and dense. But bread flour, a higher-protein white flour, is designed to maximize gluten development. Sure enough, bread flour combined with the seven-grain cereal made a strong, flexible dough and bread with a tender, light crumb.

Even with the bread flour, I knew that this dough would still need all the help it could get in order to rise and form a tall, domed loaf rather than a short, squat one. My first step was to bake it at a toasty 425 degrees. The nice, hot oven would aid "oven spring," a term for the fast expansion of bread dough in the first few minutes of baking, thanks to an initial blast of hot air and steam that encourages the gases inside dough to swell. I learned the hard way that it also encourages burning; the seeds on the top of the loaf were especially vulnerable. Things worked better when I preheated the oven to 425 and then dropped it to 375 as soon as I put in the dough to bake. But I still had a problem. The crust of the loaf set too quickly in the still-quite-hot oven, which meant that the dough couldn't take full advantage of oven spring. To address that, I put a loaf pan in the bottom of the oven and filled it with boiling water. The humidity from the water kept the dough moist, allowing it to rise impressively high before the crust set.

I baked a final loaf. The smell was heavenly, and the loaf emerged from the oven tall, round, and even, with a beautiful brown sheen. When I cut into it, I was pleased to see that the grain-speckled crumb was even and tight. Best of all, it tasted fantastic. This Dakota bread was definitely something to celebrate.

—CRISTIN WALSH, *Cook's Country*

Dakota Bread

MAKES ONE 10-INCH LOAF

In step 2, if the dough is still sticking to the sides of the mixing bowl after 2 minutes, add more flour 1 tablespoon at a time, up to 3 tablespoons. Be sure to use hot cereal mix, not boxed cold breakfast cereals, which may also be labeled "seven-grain."

- 2 **cups warm water (110 degrees)**
- 1½ **cups (7½ ounces) seven-grain hot cereal mix**
- 2 **tablespoons honey**
- 2 **tablespoons vegetable oil**
- 3½ **cups (19¼ ounces) bread flour**
- 1¾ **teaspoons salt**
- 1 **teaspoon instant or rapid-rise yeast**
- 3 **tablespoons raw, unsalted pepitas**
- 3 **tablespoons raw, unsalted sunflower seeds**
- 1 **teaspoon sesame seeds**
- 1 **teaspoon poppy seeds**
- 1 **large egg, lightly beaten**

1. Grease large bowl. Line rimmed baking sheet with parchment paper. In bowl of stand mixer, combine water, cereal, honey, and oil and let sit for 10 minutes.

2. Add flour, salt, and yeast to cereal mixture. Fit stand mixer with dough hook and knead on low speed until dough is smooth and elastic, 4 to 6 minutes. Add 2 tablespoons pepitas and 2 tablespoons sunflower seeds

MAKING A ROUND LOAF

On lightly floured counter, shape loaf by pulling and pinching dough and tucking it under until it forms smooth, taut ball. (In French, this shape is known as a boule.)

THE RIGHT MIX

Our Dakota Bread recipe calls for bread flour (for an appropriately chewy texture) supplemented with seven-grain hot cereal mix, which provides the bread with nutty depth. Don't confuse seven-grain hot cereal with seven-grain cold cereal; the latter will harm the texture of the loaf.

to dough and knead for 1 minute longer. Turn out dough onto lightly floured counter and knead until seeds are evenly distributed, about 2 minutes.

3. Transfer dough to greased bowl and cover with plastic wrap. Let dough rise at room temperature until almost doubled in size and fingertip depression in dough springs back slowly, 60 to 90 minutes.

4. Gently press down on center of dough to deflate. Transfer dough to lightly floured counter and shape into tight round ball. Place dough on prepared sheet. Cover dough loosely with plastic and let rise at room temperature until almost doubled in size, 60 to 90 minutes.

5. Adjust oven racks to upper-middle and lowest positions and heat oven to 425 degrees. Combine remaining 1 tablespoon pepitas, remaining 1 tablespoon sunflower seeds, sesame seeds, and poppy seeds in small bowl. Using sharp knife, make ¼-inch-deep cross, 5 inches long, on top of loaf. Brush loaf with egg and sprinkle seed mixture evenly over top.

6. Place 8½ by 4½-inch loaf pan on lowest oven rack and fill with 1 cup boiling water. Place baking sheet with dough on upper-middle rack and reduce oven to 375 degrees. Bake until crust is dark brown and bread registers 200 degrees, 40 to 50 minutes. Transfer loaf to wire rack and let cool completely, about 2 hours. Serve.

BROWN IRISH SODA BREAD

✓ **WHY THIS RECIPE WORKS** For a brown soda bread with good wheaty flavor but without a gummy, dense texture, we started by finding the right ratio of whole wheat to all-purpose flour. Including toasted wheat germ played up the sweet, nutty flavor of the whole-wheat. To keep the texture light, we needed plenty of leavening; baking soda alone gave the bread a soapy taste, so we used a combination of baking soda and baking powder. Just a touch of sugar and a few tablespoons of butter kept our bread wholesome but not too lean, and brushing a portion of the melted butter on the loaf after baking gave it a rich crust.

Robust, moist, and permeated with a delicious wheaty sweetness, brown Irish soda bread is very easy to like, very easy to make, and—unlike yeast breads—doesn't require much waiting around. This bread adds coarse, whole-meal flour to the all-purpose flour used in the more familiar Irish soda bread. In the most basic versions, the flours are simply stirred together with baking soda and buttermilk, briefly kneaded, patted into a round, and baked. (Eggs, sugar, and butter are American additions.) It sounded great to me.

I rounded up recipes for brown soda bread. A few called for the traditional whole-meal flour, but that's hard to find in the United States. Most recipes simply substitute ordinary whole-wheat flour for the whole-meal flour. Other recipes skip the white flour altogether and combine whole-wheat flour with practically the entire contents of a natural foods store, from bran to ground oatmeal. Predictably, the former produced loaves with scarcely any wheat flavor, and the latter made loaves with great wheaty taste but heavy, gummy, crumbly textures.

To get the flavor right, I tried the most basic recipe from my first round of testing with varying ratios of all-purpose and whole-wheat flours. Eventually, I opted for 2 cups of white flour combined with 1½ cups of whole-wheat for a loaf with nice wheat flavor and mild sweetness. To round out that flavor and play up the toasty, nutty aspects, I added by turns wheat germ (the embryo of the wheat berry), wheat bran (the outer layer of the grain that's removed to make white flour), and oatmeal (which I toasted and ground to make oat flour). My tasters and I liked them all, but the bran required a trip to a specialty store, and the oats demanded both toasting and processing. Toasted wheat germ is sold in convenient jars at the supermarket, so that's what I'd use.

The wheaty taste was now spot-on, but just like many of the loaves in my initial test, my loaf was dense and crumbly. I knew why: The extra bran and germ in whole-wheat products mean less gluten formation, and gluten is what gives bread its chew and elastic structure. To fix that, I swapped out the all-purpose flour in my recipe for bread flour, which can form stronger gluten. But the loaf was denser and more compact than ever. What was going on? Our science editor explained that while bread flour is capable of developing more gluten than all-purpose is, it needs time to do so. With quick bread, it doesn't get that. I switched back to all-purpose flour and tried more baking soda. Instead of lightening the loaf, it imparted a chemical, soapy flavor. What about baking powder? Though it's not traditional in soda bread, I found that equal amounts of the two leaveners lightened the bread without changing its flavor.

I called over tasters to get their take. They approved of the earthy flavor and hearty texture, but they complained that I'd gone all-or-nothing on them: Just because it's healthier brown soda bread, they said, doesn't mean it can't have any butter or sugar. I added them in, tentatively and gradually. Ultimately, I decided that 3 tablespoons of sugar and 2 tablespoons of melted butter added sweetness, tenderness, and a delicate richness without crossing the line into scone territory.

NOTES FROM THE TEST KITCHEN

FASTEST. BREAD. EVER.
No yeast, no rise time, and almost no kneading or shaping.

Measure and whisk dry ingredients	5 minutes
Measure and combine wet ingredients	2 minutes
Stir wet into dry	1 minute
Knead briefly	1 minute
Shape simply	1 minute
Total work time	**10 minutes**

When the bread came out of the oven, I brushed it with extra melted butter. Wholesome and wholly delicious, this loaf was as good warm from the oven as it was sliced, toasted, and slathered with jam the next morning.

—REBECCAH MARSTERS, *Cook's Country*

Brown Soda Bread
MAKES 1 LOAF

  2 **cups (10 ounces) all-purpose flour**
1½ **cups (8¼ ounces) whole-wheat flour**
 ½ **cup toasted wheat germ**
  3 **tablespoons sugar**
1½ **teaspoons salt**
  1 **teaspoon baking powder**
  1 **teaspoon baking soda**
1¾ **cups buttermilk**
  3 **tablespoons unsalted butter, melted**

1. Adjust oven rack to lower-middle position and heat oven to 400 degrees. Line rimmed baking sheet with parchment paper. Whisk all-purpose flour, whole-wheat flour, wheat germ, sugar, salt, baking powder, and baking soda together in large bowl. Combine buttermilk and 2 tablespoons melted butter in liquid measuring cup.

2. Add wet ingredients to dry ingredients and stir with rubber spatula until dough just comes together. Turn out dough onto lightly floured counter and knead until cohesive mass forms, about 8 turns. Pat dough into 7-inch round and transfer to prepared sheet. Using sharp serrated knife, make ¼-inch-deep cross about 5 inches long on top of loaf. Bake until skewer inserted in center comes out clean and loaf registers 195 degrees, 45 to 50 minutes, rotating sheet halfway through baking.

3. Remove bread from oven. Brush with remaining 1 tablespoon melted butter. Transfer loaf to wire rack and let cool for at least 1 hour. Serve.

VARIATION
Brown Soda Bread with Currants and Caraway
Add 1 cup dried currants and 1 tablespoon caraway seeds to dry ingredients in step 1.

PASTA ALL'AMATRICIANA

PASTA ALL'AMATRICIANA

✔ **WHY THIS RECIPE WORKS** *Pasta all'amatriciana* is a boldly flavored pasta dish whose rich tomato sauce boasts tangy Pecorino Romano cheese and meaty but hard-to-find *guanciale*, or cured pork jowl. Humble salt pork seemed an unlikely solution, but it lent the sauce the rich meatiness we were after. To ensure tender bites of pork throughout, we first gently simmered the salt pork to render its fat, then allowed the water to evaporate so that the pork browned and developed deep flavor. Finally, to keep the grated cheese from clumping in the sauce, we mixed it with a little cooled rendered pork fat, which also added another layer of meaty flavor to this Italian classic.

If there's one thing Italians love more than eating, it's arguing about cooking. Case in point: *pasta all'amatriciana.* Residents of Amatrice (a mountain town northeast of Rome) claim to have originated the dish, and their official recipe calls for spaghetti, *guanciale* (salt-cured pork jowl), fresh or canned tomatoes, hot red peppers, freshly grated pecorino, and sometimes white wine. Romans, on the other hand, insist on bucatini (a long, thin, hollow pasta) and onions but don't usually add wine. On a recent trip, I sampled both and sided with the Amatricians, whose take elegantly balances the bold flavors of the dish, with no alliums to distract. Leaving the disagreement in the Italian countryside, I headed home to reproduce the Amatrician recipe.

I faced one problem right away. Guanciale, the star of the dish, can be difficult to find in the United States. Made by salting and drying hog jowls, it boasts unmatched pork flavor. My first idea for a substitute was pancetta, which is essentially spiced, unsmoked Italian bacon. I prepared two sauces: one with imported guanciale and one with pancetta. For each sauce, I sautéed the pork, bloomed red pepper flakes in the rendered fat, stirred in and cooked down wine and tomatoes, tossed the sauce with spaghetti, and finished the dish with grated Pecorino Romano. My colleagues' frowns said it all: Pancetta produced an oddly sour-tasting dish that lacked the heady porkiness of the guanciale version.

American bacon was another option, but I knew that its smoky flavor would be out of place. How about bacon's cousin, salt pork? It may have a humble American pedigree, but, like guanciale, it is simply salt-cured, not smoked. The only difference is that the meat for salt pork comes from the belly of the pig, not the jowl. Sure enough, tasters found that the clean, meaty flavor of salt pork closely mimicked that of guanciale. Now I just needed to weed through the conflicting advice to figure out how best to cook it.

Some recipes recommend lightly browning the pork before simmering it in the sauce, and others warn against doing so. In a side-by-side test, sauces made with lightly browned pork boasted a richer flavor. This method also rendered more fat from the pork, which boosted meaty flavor and led to a more voluptuous sauce. But one problem remained: The pork pieces had turned tough during browning.

I looked to a recent test kitchen discovery for a solution. We found that simmering bacon in water until the moisture evaporates and the strips brown and sizzle holds the temperature low enough to keep the bacon tender. I gave it a shot with the salt pork and was extremely pleased. It remained supple even after simmering and browning.

When it came to white versus red wine, I decided it made sense to depart from tradition: The heartier red wine provided a deeper, richer background flavor. And while the official recipe from Amatrice allows for fresh or canned tomatoes, we decisively preferred canned diced, which offered satisfying, sweet bites throughout any time of year. To help the sauce cling to the pasta, I also added a couple of spoonfuls of tomato paste.

I turned my attention to the cheese. Pecorino Romano is a sheep's-milk cheese with real funk and bite that pairs extremely well with the rich pork, tomato, and red pepper flakes. But I kept running into the perennial problem with stirring grated aged cheese into a hot pot of pasta: It clumps into unattractive globs. With most pastas, you can work around the problem by simply passing the cheese at the table. But all'amatriciana relies on the tang and saltiness of the Pecorino Romano throughout the dish. Another possible solution was to mix the grated cheese with cream and starch to provide stability while the cheese melted into the pasta. But this only resulted in muted flavors. What if instead of cream I mixed the cheese with some cooled pork fat? Success! The fat acted as a barrier to prevent the proteins in the cheese from bonding together as the cheese melted, and I now had a clump-free dish and extra pork flavor to boot.

By carefully considering each ingredient, I had finally developed an authentic-tasting version of this classic dish. Let the dining—and the disagreement—begin.

—DAN SOUZA, *Cook's Illustrated*

Pasta all'Amatriciana
SERVES 4 TO 6

Look for salt pork that is roughly 70 percent fat and 30 percent lean meat; leaner salt pork may not render enough fat. If it is difficult to slice, put the salt pork in the freezer for 15 minutes to firm up. High-quality imported Pecorino Romano will work best here—avoid the bland domestic cheese labeled "Romano."

8 ounces salt pork, rind removed, rinsed thoroughly, and patted dry

½ cup water

½ teaspoon red pepper flakes

2 tablespoons tomato paste

¼ cup red wine

1 (28-ounce) can diced tomatoes

2 ounces Pecorino Romano cheese, finely grated (1 cup)

1 pound spaghetti

1 tablespoon salt

1. Slice pork into ¼-inch-thick strips, then cut each strip crosswise into ¼-inch pieces. Bring pork and water to simmer in 10-inch nonstick skillet over medium heat; cook until water evaporates and pork begins to sizzle, 5 to 8 minutes. Reduce heat to medium-low and continue to cook, stirring frequently, until fat renders and pork turns golden, 5 to 8 minutes longer. Using slotted spoon, transfer pork to bowl. Pour off all but 1 tablespoon fat from skillet. Reserve remaining fat.

2. Return skillet to medium heat and add pepper flakes and tomato paste; cook, stirring constantly, for 20 seconds. Stir in wine and cook for 30 seconds. Stir in tomatoes and their juice and rendered pork and bring to simmer. Cook, stirring frequently, until thickened, 12 to 16 minutes. While sauce simmers, stir 2 tablespoons reserved fat and ½ cup Pecorino Romano together in bowl to form paste.

3. Meanwhile, bring 4 quarts water to boil in large Dutch oven. Add spaghetti and salt and cook, stirring often, until al dente. Reserve 1 cup cooking water, then drain spaghetti and return it to pot.

4. Add sauce, ⅓ cup cooking water, and Pecorino Romano–pork fat mixture to pasta and toss well to coat, adjusting consistency with remaining cooking water as needed. Serve, passing remaining ½ cup Pecorino Romano separately.

SPAGHETTI CARBONARA

✓ **WHY THIS RECIPE WORKS** Spaghetti carbonara is delicious, but also it's overwhelmingly rich and heavy. To keep the flavor but lighten things up, we swapped the cream, butter, and oil for a simple egg-based sauce. We whisked three whole eggs and one extra yolk with plenty of Pecorino Romano cheese. To give the sauce a smooth, silky consistency and ensure that it wouldn't get gluey after being tossed with the pasta, we thinned it with pasta cooking water. Boiling the pasta in half the usual amount of water gave us extra-starchy water to coat the proteins and fats in the cheese, preventing them from separating or clumping. Tossing the spaghetti with the sauce in a warm serving bowl allowed the warm pasta to gently "cook" the carbonara sauce without overcooking the eggs. Stirring crisp chopped bacon plus 1 tablespoon of bacon fat into the sauce gave it lots of meaty flavor throughout.

There's a reason that spaghetti alla carbonara is wildly popular not just in Rome but here in the United States, too. It's a minimalist Roman pasta dish made from a handful of pantry staples—pasta, eggs, some form of cured pork, Pecorino Romano cheese, garlic, and black pepper—that add up to something incredibly satisfying and delicious. But don't be fooled by its short ingredient list: The dish is devilishly hard to get right. The finicky egg-based sauce (made from either whole eggs or just yolks, plus finely grated cheese) relies on the heat of the warm pasta to become lush and glossy, but that rarely happens. Instead, the egg either scrambles from too much heat or, as the pasta cools, the sauce thickens

---

NOTES FROM THE TEST KITCHEN

PORK VERSUS PORK
Guanciale is made by salting and drying hog jowls and gives this dish a uniquely intense, clean pork flavor. For something similar but more readily available, we turned to salt pork, which is also salt-cured but is cut from the belly.

GUANCIALE
Salted jowl.

SALT PORK
Salted belly.

and turns gluey. Often the cheese clumps, too. The few recipes that do produce a creamy, velvety sauce succeed by adding tons of fat. Case in point: The silky-smooth carbonara recipe from British chef Jamie Oliver that's built on five egg yolks, nearly ½ cup of heavy cream, and a good amount of rendered bacon fat. Delicious as it was, I couldn't handle more than a couple of forkfuls.

That, I realized, was precisely the problem I had to solve as I set out to perfect my own version: how to make a classic carbonara that was foolproof but not so rich that eating a full serving was impossible.

The ingredient list for carbonara is already short, but to isolate what makes or (literally) breaks the sauce, I started my testing with an even more pared-down recipe: two whole eggs, a couple of ounces of finely grated Pecorino Romano, and 8 ounces of cooked bacon pieces drained of all their rendered fat (*guanciale*, or cured pork jowl, is a more typical choice, but I wanted to use a pantry staple). I boiled 1 pound of spaghetti, set it aside briefly, and made the sauce by thoroughly whisking the eggs and finely grated cheese in a serving bowl before tossing the mixture with the hot pasta and crisp bacon pieces. The final product? Dry, thin, and, thanks to the cheese, a little gritty. Things went even further downhill after just a few minutes. The longer the sauced pasta sat, the pastier it became. Also, my tasters complained that it lacked the eggy richness they were expecting and that the pork flavor was a little faint.

I figured that adding a third egg would help with the dryness and the thinness. (I'd circle back to boosting porkiness later.) And it did—at least for a couple of minutes. But just as with my first test, the light, glossy sauce quickly dried up and left the pasta coated with a thin, pasty residue; within minutes I was left with a bowl of dry, stuck-together spaghetti strands.

Since a sauce made with whole eggs didn't have rich flavor or much staying power, I decided to change course. I'd ditch the whites and revisit the idea of an entirely yolk-based sauce, minus all the extra fat in the Oliver recipe. I mixed up a new batch of sauce with six yolks and the same amount of cheese, and for a few moments things looked better: The fat and emulsifiers in the yolks made for a sauce with velvety body, not to mention superbly rich, eggy flavor. But once again my success was short-lived as the fat and emulsifiers (and the loss of the moisture contributed by the whites, which are about 90 percent water) quickly caused the sauce to tighten up into a tacky glue.

Lessons learned: Lots of yolks were a must for flavor and richness, but without enough water in the mix, there was no hope of producing a fluid sauce. The challenge would be making a sauce that was loose enough to gloss the pasta strands but still creamy and viscous enough to cling nicely—and to stay that way throughout the meal.

I was about to go back to testing whole eggs when I realized that I had another liquid I could put to use: the pasta cooking water. Reserving some of the starchy liquid when draining pasta and using it to loosen over-thickened sauces is a common Italian trick. I tried it here, thinning out my yolk mixture with ¾ cup of cooking water. Once again, I met with initial success, but, maddeningly, the sauced spaghetti turned gluey moments later and the sauce continued to tighten up no matter how much extra cooking liquid I added.

The only option I hadn't yet tried was making a sauce with whole eggs and adding the cooking water. I circled back to the sauce I'd made with three whole eggs and added the cheese and a little less of the starchy cooking liquid (to account for the extra water in the whites). This time something had changed: The sauce wasn't as velvety as I wanted, but it was surprisingly stable, holding creamy and fluid for a good 10 minutes without need for further adjustment. The gritty bits of cheese were gone, too.

I was pleased with my success, but I was also baffled. Why would a combination of whole eggs and pasta water create a smoother, more stable sauce than yolks and pasta water? Our science editor offered an answer: The key was the relationship between the starch and ovomucin, one of 148 different proteins in egg whites. When ovomucin and the starch from the cooking water interact, they form a network that not only contributes viscosity but is also fairly stable and less responsive to temperature decline than a sauce made with just egg yolks. The starch was also coating both the egg and the cheese proteins, preventing the eggs from curdling and the cheese from clumping.

This information was encouraging and also gave me an idea about how to further boost the viscosity of the sauce—I just needed to add more starch. I decided to try a trick we discovered when developing our recipe for *cacio e pepe,* another of those minimalist Roman pasta dishes. For this dish, we cooked the pasta in less water (just 2 quarts per pound of pasta rather than the typical 4) to produce a starchier liquid that in turn makes a "creamier" sauce when tossed with the pasta. I applied the technique here, halving the amount of water that I used to cook the spaghetti, then whisking ½ cup of this super-starchy liquid into the eggs and cheese before combining the sauce with the pasta. It was a huge success. This sauce was rich and glossy and, what's more, it held its consistency for a record 15 minutes. To ensure that the egg mixture thickened properly, I also made two small but critical tweaks to my technique. First, I warmed the empty serving bowl with the drained cooking water—another classic Italian pasta trick—to help "cook" the egg sauce. Second, I let the sauced pasta rest briefly and tossed it several times before serving; as the pasta cooled, the sauce reached just the right consistency.

This carbonara sauce was already the best I'd had to date—stable and creamy but not cloyingly rich. But it still lacked the rich egg flavor of the all-yolk sauce, so I made that my next goal. Since yolks were the key to eggy richness, I tried adding an extra yolk to my whole-egg sauce to test if it would give the pasta sauce sufficient richness without turning it gluey. I was pleasantly surprised to see that the sauce was just as glossy and loose as the batch without the extra yolk, and the flavor was custardy and rich but not heavy.

My tasters just had one last request: Could I please amp up the meaty pork flavor? I was sure the ½ pound of bacon I was using was plenty, but my tasters were right: Simply tossing bacon bits into the pasta didn't make for well-rounded pork flavor. The carbonara traditionalists among us also wished that the texture of the bacon could more closely mimic the satisfying chew of guanciale. I had ideas for addressing both issues. First, I cooked the bacon with a little water, which we've recently discovered produces tender and chewy—not crumbly—pieces. Second, I caved just a little on my resolution not to add extra fat. Whisking a mere tablespoon of bacon fat into the sauce before tossing it with the pasta brought meaty bacon flavor to every bite.

Finally, I'd nailed it: carbonara that was lush and rich with egg, bacon, and cheese but still light enough that my tasters didn't just eat a full bowl—they went back for seconds.

—CELESTE ROGERS, *Cook's Illustrated*

NOTES FROM THE TEST KITCHEN

WARM THE BOWL

To help the sauced pasta stay creamy longer, warm the mixing bowl (and the serving bowls).

Drain cooked spaghetti in colander set in large serving bowl. The water will heat the bowl, and some of it can be reserved for the sauce.

LESS FAT, MORE STABLE SAUCE

The hardest part about making carbonara isn't coming up with the right ratio of egg whites to yolks to make a creamy, rich sauce; it's figuring out how to make a sauce that doesn't curdle, turn gritty, or tighten up into a glue—the usual problems as the pasta cools down. Some recipes get around the issues by adding lots of fat, which boosts the viscosity of the sauce and makes it more stable. We came up with a better, less cloying alternative: starchy pasta cooking water. The starch performs two functions in this dish. First, it coats the proteins in the eggs and the cheese, preventing them from curdling in the heat and clumping, respectively. Second, it combines with ovomucin, a protein in the egg whites, to form a network that is relatively resistant to temperature change, which means the sauce does not tighten up as it cools.

To take full advantage of the starch's effect, we concentrate it by cooking the pasta in half the usual amount of water and then add up to 1 cup of the starchy water to the sauce. The dressed pasta stays silky for a good 15 minutes.

Foolproof Spaghetti Carbonara
SERVES 4

It's important to work quickly in steps 2 and 3. The heat from the cooking water and the hot spaghetti will "cook" the sauce only if used immediately. Warming the mixing and serving bowls helps the sauce stay creamy. Use a high-quality bacon for this dish; our favorites are Farmland Hickory Smoked Bacon and Vande Rose Farms Artisan Dry Cured Bacon, Applewood Smoked.

- 8 slices bacon, cut into ½-inch pieces
- ½ cup water
- 3 garlic cloves, minced
- 2½ ounces Pecorino Romano cheese, grated (1¼ cups)
- 3 large eggs plus 1 large yolk
- 1 teaspoon pepper
- 1 pound spaghetti
- 1 teaspoon salt

1. Bring bacon and water to simmer in 10-inch nonstick skillet over medium heat; cook until water evaporates and bacon begins to sizzle, about 8 minutes. Reduce heat to medium-low and continue to cook until fat renders and bacon browns, 5 to 8 minutes longer. Add garlic and cook, stirring constantly, until fragrant, about 30 seconds. Strain bacon mixture through fine-mesh strainer set in bowl. Set aside bacon mixture. Measure out 1 tablespoon fat and place in medium bowl. Whisk Pecorino, eggs and yolk, and pepper into fat until combined.

2. Meanwhile, bring 2 quarts water to boil in Dutch oven. Set colander in large bowl. Add spaghetti and salt to pot; cook, stirring frequently, until al dente. Drain spaghetti in colander set in bowl, reserving cooking water. Pour 1 cup cooking water into liquid measuring cup and discard remainder. Return spaghetti to now-empty bowl.

3. Slowly whisk ½ cup reserved cooking water into Pecorino mixture. Gradually pour Pecorino mixture over spaghetti, tossing to coat. Add bacon mixture and toss to combine. Let spaghetti rest, tossing frequently, until sauce has thickened slightly and coats spaghetti, 2 to 4 minutes, adjusting consistency with remaining reserved cooking water if needed. Serve immediately.

LIGHTER FETTUCCINE ALFREDO

✔ **WHY THIS RECIPE WORKS** Most folks reserve indulgent fettuccine Alfredo for a rare splurge when dining out, but this easy, à-la-minute sauce is perfect for making at home—if you can keep the fat and calories within reason. We wanted to cut back on the cream and butter in this classic dish but keep its rich flavor. We found that a combination of whole milk and half-and-half worked best to replace the heavy cream without compromising richness. We turned to a roux, a cooked mixture of butter and flour, to give the sauce just enough body. As for the cheese, a full cup of grated Parmesan added nutty, complex flavor but minimal fat. For a subtle savory note, we added a pinch of nutmeg and simmered a crushed garlic clove in the sauce. Finally, we found that serving the pasta immediately in warmed bowls was crucial to ensure that it stayed hot, rich, and creamy all the way to the table.

Ready in just 20 minutes, fettuccine Alfredo is perfect for weeknight cooking. But with standard recipes containing as much as 1½ cups of heavy cream, a whole stick of butter, and 2 cups of cheese, most home cooks consign this dish to the occasional restaurant indulgence. That's a shame, because fettuccine Alfredo is actually better suited to home preparation; the creamy sauce turns cold and stiff if it sits for even a few minutes, as invariably happens in restaurants. Could I develop a recipe that would drastically cut the fat while retaining the rich flavor of traditional Alfredo?

Many low-fat Alfredo recipes cut calories simply by switching out the cream for lower-fat dairy products such as half-and-half, whole milk, or evaporated milk. I tried each one, adding a cornstarch slurry (cornstarch dissolved in liquid) to replicate the thickening effect of heavy cream. Tasters preferred the product with the most fat, the half-and-half, praising its rich flavor. But they also commented that the half-and-half and cornstarch combination wasn't producing a properly thickened sauce. I scrapped that idea and went back to the drawing board.

Then it occurred to me to try another classic thickener: a roux. Commonly used to thicken soups and sauces, a roux is a simple mixture of butter and flour that is cooked over low heat. This method worked beautifully with my sauce. With very little roux—just 1½ tablespoons of butter and 1 tablespoon of flour—I was able to thicken the sauce nicely.

With an effective thickener in place, I wondered if I could use a less fattening dairy than half-and-half. After several tests, I settled on 1 cup of whole milk and just ⅓ cup of half-and-half for a nice balance between creamy texture, rich taste, and a reasonable amount of fat. As for the cheese, a generous 1 cup of Parmesan contributed just 4 grams of fat per serving but added nutty, complex flavor.

My sauce was getting pretty good, but my tasters rightfully complained that it was still one-dimensional; it seemed "too sweet" and "too milky." A pinch of nutmeg and a good amount of black pepper added some welcome savory notes, but simmering a crushed garlic clove in the sauce was the key to giving my sauce full, balanced, complex flavor. The sharpness of the garlic worked perfectly to cut any hint of sweetness and added another dimension of flavor to the sauce.

So far I had made tremendous progress, cutting nearly three-quarters of the fat from the original recipe.

LIGHTER FETTUCCINE ALFREDO

But while my Alfredo sauce was silky and rich, it still clumped and clotted if not served right away. I found that tossing the pasta and sauce with some of the starchy pasta cooking water thinned the sauce just enough to keep it from over thickening as it cooled. And I had one last trick up my sleeve: By heating my serving bowls with hot water before filling them with pasta, I was able to keep my rich Alfredo piping hot and at just the right consistency long enough for my tasters to scrape their bowls clean.

—CALI RICH, *Cook's Country*

Lighter Fettuccine Alfredo
SERVES 4

1½ tablespoons unsalted butter
1 tablespoon all-purpose flour
1 cup whole milk
⅓ cup half-and-half
1 garlic clove, peeled and lightly crushed
 Salt and pepper
 Pinch nutmeg
2 ounces Parmesan cheese, grated (1 cup)
1 pound fresh fettuccine

1. Bring 4 quarts water to boil in large pot. Using ladle, fill 4 individual serving bowls with about ½ cup boiling water; set aside.

2. Melt butter in large saucepan over medium heat. Whisk in flour until smooth and cook until golden, 1 to 2 minutes. Whisk in milk, half-and-half, garlic, ½ teaspoon salt, ½ teaspoon pepper, and nutmeg and bring to simmer. Reduce heat to medium-low and simmer gently until sauce is slightly thickened, 1 to 2 minutes. Off heat, remove garlic and stir in Parmesan; cover and set aside.

3. Return water to boil, add pasta and 1 tablespoon salt, and cook, stirring often, until al dente. Reserve 1 cup cooking water, then drain pasta. Return sauce to low heat and stir in cooked pasta and ⅓ cup reserved cooking water. Cook gently, tossing pasta with tongs, until everything is heated through and sauce nicely coats pasta, about 1 minute. Season with salt and pepper to taste and add remaining cooking water as needed to adjust consistency. Working quickly, empty water from serving bowls and fill with pasta. Serve immediately.

SKILLET PENNE WITH CHICKEN AND BROCCOLI

✔ **WHY THIS RECIPE WORKS** For a weeknight-friendly version of this Italian-American restaurant classic, we were determined to re-create it in a single skillet. We browned the chicken to build flavor, then set it aside and sautéed onion, garlic, red pepper flakes, and oregano. We deglazed the pot with white wine and added enough chicken broth and water both to cook the pasta right in the skillet and to make the sauce. Stirring the pasta frequently helped it cook evenly, and leaving the skillet uncovered allowed the flavors to intensify as the sauce reduced. For perfectly crisp-tender broccoli, we added it to the pan for just the last few minutes of cooking, then we returned the chicken to the pan to heat through. Finally, we stirred in lots of Parmesan cheese for creaminess and rich, savory flavor.

You'll usually find it listed between the shrimp scampi and the three-cheese ravioli: Penne (or ziti) with chicken and broccoli is one of the heavy hitters of the Italian-American restaurant menu. I wanted to figure out how to turn this simple but satisfying restaurant classic into a one-skillet weeknight meal.

We've developed recipes for skillet pasta dishes in the test kitchen before. Instead of boiling pasta in a large pot and making the sauce separately, our approach is to combine the two from the get-go, cooking the pasta right in the sauce. We've found that not only does this technique save on dirty dishes, but it also allows the noodles to absorb the flavor of the sauce as they cook. The first time I tried this approach for penne with chicken and broccoli, however, I got—literally and figuratively—a hot mess.

I started by following the traditional recipe, using boneless, skinless chicken breasts, which I sliced thin. I sautéed the usual onion, lots of garlic, red pepper flakes, and oregano in olive oil in a large nonstick skillet. Once they'd softened, I added water, wine, and chicken broth as both the cooking liquid and the sauce. Next I tossed in raw chicken slices and bite-size broccoli florets and brought everything to a boil. Finally, I added the pasta. Fifteen minutes later, when the pasta seemed soft and the sauce mostly absorbed, I dished it up, sprinkled it with Parmesan cheese, and watched as tasters tried it—and politely put down their forks. The problems? Where to begin? The chicken was rubbery and tasteless.

The broccoli was mushy and army green. The noodles were simultaneously overcooked and undercooked depending on where your fork happened to land. And the sauce was acidic and unbalanced.

Clearly, timing was everything, and I'd need to give it more consideration. For my next batch, I added the broccoli florets for just the last few minutes of cooking. They brightened and tenderized as the noodles finished cooking, and this time they didn't turn into vegetable mush. Next I turned to the chicken. I tried adding it at different points in the cooking process, but after a few tries, I was ending up with either rubbery and dry or undercooked chicken. I decided that I'd be better off cooking the delicate chicken slices ahead of time, removing them from the skillet, then adding them back in at the end to warm through and finish cooking. This allowed me to control their cooking much better. Plus, it made it possible to brown the chicken initially, boosting the flavor of the dish.

To bring all the flavors of the sauce into harmony, I added the wine to the skillet on its own once the onion and garlic were soft. I let it cook off before pouring in the broth and water. It contributed flavor without the off-kilter acidity of my first attempt. To cook the pasta evenly, I simply needed to stir the pasta frequently as it cooked. Once the pasta was done, I stirred in a whole cup of Parmesan cheese for lots of nutty flavor and creaminess.

With each of my individual problems solved, I simply combined all of my changes into a single recipe. In less than a half-hour, I had dinner ready. I called my tasters to the table again. This time, they asked for seconds.

—NICK IVERSON, *Cook's Country*

NOTES FROM THE TEST KITCHEN

THE BEST NONSTICK SKILLET

No matter how gently you treat your nonstick skillet, its slickness will inevitably wear away, and food will start sticking. It's hard to beat nonstick pans for cooking fragile foods like eggs and thin fish fillets, but if we have to keep replacing them, we'd prefer to spend less each time. To find the best inexpensive nonstick pan, we put seven pans from $17 to $49.95 to the test.

Slickness wasn't our only criterion for a nonstick skillet. It should also cook food evenly, have good size and heft but be easy to maneuver, and hold up to kitchen abuse. To see how the pans would cope, we began by frying eggs without fat in each one. One pan stuck on the third egg. We also stir-fried beef and vegetables, made crêpes, and cooked frittatas, serving them with a metal spatula to see how easily the pans scratched.

Although a loose handle from our abuse testing was a sign that it's not high-end cookware, at $34.99, the **T-fal Professional Non-Stick 12-Inch Fry Pan** is a bargain. Its proprietary five-layer nonstick (most pans have two or three layers) never gave up during our testing, remaining slick and intact to the very end. It was the only pan in the lineup to give us the best of both worlds: an exceptionally slick, durable nonstick coating and top performance in cooking.

Skillet Penne with Chicken and Broccoli
SERVES 4

Use a dry white wine, such as Sauvignon Blanc, for this recipe.

- 1 pound boneless, skinless chicken breasts, trimmed and sliced thin
  Salt and pepper
- ¼ cup olive oil
- 1 onion, chopped fine
- 6 garlic cloves, minced
- ¼ teaspoon red pepper flakes
- ¼ teaspoon dried oregano
- ½ cup dry white wine
- 2½ cups water
- 2 cups chicken broth
- 8 ounces (2½ cups) penne
- 8 ounces broccoli florets, cut into 1-inch pieces
- 2 ounces Parmesan cheese, grated (1 cup), plus extra for serving

1. Pat chicken dry with paper towels and season with salt and pepper. Heat 1 tablespoon oil in 12-inch nonstick skillet over medium-high heat until just smoking. Add chicken in single layer and cook, without stirring, until chicken begins to brown, about 1 minute. Stir chicken and continue to cook until nearly cooked through, about 2 minutes; transfer to bowl and cover to keep warm.

2. Add 1 tablespoon oil to now-empty skillet and heat over medium heat until shimmering. Add onion and ½ teaspoon salt and cook until softened, 5 to 7 minutes. Stir in garlic, pepper flakes, and oregano and cook until fragrant, about 30 seconds. Stir in wine and simmer until nearly evaporated, 1 to 2 minutes. Stir in water, broth,

SKILLET PENNE WITH CHICKEN AND BROCCOLI

and penne. Increase heat to medium-high and cook at vigorous simmer, stirring often, until penne is nearly tender, about 12 minutes.

3. Stir in broccoli and cook until penne and broccoli are tender and sauce has thickened, 3 to 5 minutes. Stir in chicken, along with any accumulated juice, and cook until warmed through, about 1 minute. Off heat, stir in remaining 2 tablespoons oil and Parmesan and season with salt and pepper to taste. Serve, passing extra Parmesan separately.

SPANISH-STYLE PASTA WITH SHRIMP

WHY THIS RECIPE WORKS *Fideuà*, a rich Spanish seafood dish similar to *paella* but made with noodles instead of rice, traditionally takes hours to prepare. We wanted to streamline the recipe—without losing its signature flavor. We started by ditching slow-cooked fish stock for a quick microwaved stock made with shrimp shells, chicken broth, water, and a bay leaf. We sped up the *sofrito*, the sautéed base of aromatics, with finely minced onion and canned diced tomatoes, which softened and browned quickly. For bold savory flavor, we also added smoked paprika and some anchovy paste. We swapped the hard-to-find *fideo* noodles for spaghettini broken into short pieces and toasted them in a skillet for a rich nutty flavor. The noodles absorbed the flavors of the sofrito and shrimp broth as they simmered. To boost the shrimp's flavor, we marinated them briefly in olive oil, garlic, salt, and pepper, then we stirred them into the pasta and broiled the dish until the shrimp were done and the top of the pasta was crisp and browned.

The biggest star of traditional Spanish cooking is arguably *paella*, but there's another closely related dish equally deserving of fame: *fideuà*. This richly flavored dish swaps the rice for thin noodles that are toasted until nut-brown before being cooked in a garlicky, tomatoey stock loaded with seafood and sometimes chorizo sausage. As with the rice in paella, the noodles (called *fideos*) should be tender but not mushy. But whereas paella tends to be moist but not soupy, fideuà is often a little brothy.

One thing that paella and fideuà have in common: a lengthy and involved cooking process. Almost all of the recipes we tried called for the same series of steps: Simmer fish and shellfish scraps to create stock. Toast the fideos and put together a flavorful base (called the *sofrito*) by slowly reducing fresh tomatoes with aromatics and seasonings. Combine the sofrito with the stock, then simmer the toasted noodles and seafood in the rich-tasting liquid until cooked. Finally, put the whole thing in a hot oven to create a crunchy layer of pasta on top.

Our crash course in the dish taught us that the results were often well worth the effort. But just as with paella, tinkering with fideuà is part of the art. We decided that our efforts would be aimed at streamlining the recipe while keeping it every bit as deeply flavorful as the more time-consuming versions.

Our first decision was to keep things simple in the seafood department and use shrimp alone. Our next step was to make a stock so simple it didn't even dirty a pot. We knew that shrimp shells can build a surprisingly flavorful seafood broth, so we combined the shells from 1½ pounds of shrimp in a bowl with some water and a bay leaf and microwaved them until the shells turned pink and the water was hot. The resulting broth wasn't bad for something that took such little effort, but it was still lacking some depth. Its taste improved when we replaced a portion of the water with chicken broth and added a splash of white wine for brightness. Now we had a full-flavored shrimp broth that was ready in less than 10 minutes.

Next we turned our attention to the noodles. Traditional fideos come in varying thicknesses and shapes, including short, straight strands and coiled nests of thin, vermicelli-like noodles. We found that snapping spaghettini (which is more widely available than fideos) into pieces gave us a fine approximation of the short type of fideos. Not all fideuà recipes call for toasting the pasta, but skipping that step led to a dish that tasted weak and washed out. So what was the simplest way to toast them? The oven provided controlled heat but required a baking sheet—which added another item to the dirty-dish pile—and repeatedly stirring the noodles. Toasting on the stovetop in a skillet also required stirring, but it was much easier to monitor, and it saved us a dirty dish since we could use the same skillet to cook the dish.

Next we examined the sofrito. This flavor base shows up in a variety of forms in Spanish dishes, but it always features some combination of aromatics—onion, garlic, celery, and bell pepper are common—slow-cooked in oil to soften and concentrate their flavors. In fideuà, onion and garlic are typical, along with tomato. In the interest of efficiency, we ruled out preparing the sofrito separately in another skillet. We also chopped our onion finely so that it would cook more quickly, and we added ¼ teaspoon of salt to help draw out its moisture so that the onion softened and browned even faster.

Fresh tomatoes can take a long time to cook down, so we opted for canned diced tomatoes that we drained well and chopped fine. Added to the skillet with the softened onion, they reduced to a thick paste in a matter of minutes. Then we introduced minced garlic and cooked the mixture for a minute to bloom the flavors. When we pitted fideuà made with our speedy sofrito against a traditional slow-cooked version, tasters were hard pressed to taste any difference.

Our next task: getting just the right proportions of liquid and pasta. After testing several different ratios, we found that for 8 ounces of pasta, 3¾ cups of liquid was the perfect amount. It allowed the pasta to soak up enough liquid to become tender while leaving just a little sauce behind in the skillet.

It was time to fine-tune the flavors. A mixture of both sweet and Spanish smoked paprikas won praise for its balance of smokiness and earthy sweetness. While we liked the distinctly Spanish flavor of saffron, we decided the subtle flavor it lent wasn't worth the exorbitant cost in this dish, so we left it out. Half a teaspoon of anchovy paste, a go-to flavor booster in the test kitchen, added to the sofrito along with the garlic and paprika, offered depth, and its briny flavor blended well with the shrimp.

Now for the shrimp. We tried simply adding them to the skillet with the pasta, but they came out rubbery. Adding them during the last 5 minutes of cooking and covering the skillet while they cooked improved their texture but not their wan flavor. Soaking them in olive oil flavored with garlic, salt, and pepper while we prepared the rest of the dish took care of that problem, infusing them with flavor.

Some recipes finish fideuà in the oven to get the surface of the pasta crisp and brown for a nice contrast with the tender noodles and seafood underneath. The broiler seemed ideal for achieving such a crust, but its intense heat toughened up the shrimp. Happily, the problem was solved with just a small change: After scattering the raw shrimp over the surface of the pasta,

we gently stirred them into the noodles to partially submerge them, protecting them from the intense heat.

Finally, we served our fideuà with two traditional condiments: lemon wedges and a spoonful of aïoli, a rich, garlic-spiked mayonnaise. So what had our tweaks accomplished? A recipe for Spanish-style fideuà that delivered terrific flavor in far less time and with far less effort.

—THE *COOK'S ILLUSTRATED* TEST KITCHEN

Spanish-Style Toasted Pasta with Shrimp
SERVES 4

In step 5, if your skillet is not broiler-safe, once the pasta is tender transfer the mixture to a broiler-safe 13 by 9-inch baking dish lightly coated with olive oil; scatter the shrimp over the pasta and stir them in to partially submerge. Broil and serve as directed. Serve this dish with lemon wedges and Aïoli, stirring it into individual portions at the table.

- 3 tablespoons plus 2 teaspoons extra-virgin olive oil
- 3 garlic cloves, minced (1 tablespoon)
  Salt and pepper
- 1½ pounds extra-large shrimp (21 to 25 per pound), peeled and deveined, shells reserved
- 2¾ cups water
- 1 cup chicken broth
- 1 bay leaf
- 8 ounces spaghettini or thin spaghetti, broken into 1- to 2-inch lengths
- 1 onion, chopped fine
- 1 (14.5-ounce) can diced tomatoes, drained and chopped fine
- 1 teaspoon paprika
- 1 teaspoon smoked paprika
- ½ teaspoon anchovy paste
- ¼ cup dry white wine
- 1 tablespoon chopped fresh parsley
  Lemon wedges
- 1 recipe Aïoli (optional; recipe follows)

1. Combine 1 tablespoon oil, 1 teaspoon garlic, ¼ teaspoon salt, and ⅛ teaspoon pepper in medium bowl. Add shrimp, toss to coat, and refrigerate until ready to use.

2. Place reserved shrimp shells, water, chicken broth, and bay leaf in medium bowl. Cover and microwave

SPANISH–STYLE TOASTED PASTA WITH SHRIMP

until liquid is hot and shells have turned pink, about 6 minutes. Set aside until ready to use.

3. Toss spaghettini and 2 teaspoons oil in broiler-safe 12-inch skillet until spaghettini is evenly coated. Toast spaghettini over medium-high heat, stirring frequently, until browned and nutty in aroma (spaghettini should be color of peanut butter), 6 to 10 minutes. Transfer spaghettini to bowl. Wipe out skillet with paper towel.

4. Heat remaining 2 tablespoons oil in now-empty skillet over medium-high heat until shimmering. Add onion and ¼ teaspoon salt; cook, stirring frequently, until onion is softened and beginning to brown around edges, 4 to 6 minutes. Add tomatoes and cook, stirring occasionally, until mixture is thick, dry, and slightly darkened in color, 4 to 6 minutes. Reduce heat to medium and add remaining garlic, paprika, smoked paprika, and anchovy paste. Cook until fragrant, about 1½ minutes. Add spaghettini and stir to combine. Adjust oven rack 5 to 6 inches from broiler element and heat broiler.

5. Pour shrimp broth through fine-mesh strainer into skillet. Add wine, ½ teaspoon pepper, and ¼ teaspoon salt and stir well. Increase heat to medium-high and bring to simmer. Cook, uncovered, stirring occasionally, until liquid is slightly thickened and spaghettini is just tender, 8 to 10 minutes. Scatter shrimp over spaghettini and stir into spaghettini to partially submerge. Transfer skillet to oven and broil until shrimp are opaque and surface of spaghettini is dry with crisped, browned spots, 5 to 7 minutes. Remove from oven and let stand, uncovered, for 5 minutes. Sprinkle with parsley and serve immediately, passing lemon wedges and Aïoli, if using, separately.

Aïoli

MAKES ¾ CUP

1	**garlic clove, finely grated**
2	**large egg yolks**
4	**teaspoons lemon juice**
¼	**teaspoon salt**
⅛	**teaspoon sugar**
	Ground white pepper
¾	**cup olive oil**

In large bowl, combine garlic, egg yolks, lemon juice, salt, sugar, and pepper to taste until combined.

NOTES FROM THE TEST KITCHEN

IT'S A SNAP

Traditional short *fideos* noodles are hard to find, so we came up with an easy way to break long-strand pasta into even lengths.

Loosely fold spaghettini in kitchen towel, keeping pasta flat, not bunched. Position with 1 to 2 inches of pasta resting on counter. Holding bundle against counter, press down on long end of towel to break strands into pieces. Slide up and continue breaking into 1- to 2- inch lengths.

SPEEDING UP SPANISH-STYLE PASTA

A series of shortcuts allowed us to create this traditionally labor-intensive dish in a single skillet in just an hour.

1. Marinate shrimp in olive oil, garlic, salt, and pepper to infuse them with flavor as you prepare other ingredients.

2. Microwave shrimp shells with diluted chicken broth and bay leaf to create quick, surprisingly rich-tasting stock.

3. Toast pasta pieces in skillet with olive oil until well browned to develop deep, nutty flavor, then simmer noodles in stock and sautéed onion, garlic, and tomatoes so they soak up flavor.

4. Partially submerge shrimp under pasta, then transfer skillet to broiler to crisp and brown crust.

Whisking constantly, very slowly drizzle oil into egg mixture until thick and creamy. Season with salt and pepper to taste.

VARIATION

Spanish-Style Toasted Pasta with Shrimp and Clams
Reduce amount of shrimp to 1 pound and water to 2½ cups. In step 5, cook pasta until almost tender, about 6 minutes. Scatter 1½ pounds scrubbed littleneck or cherrystone clams over pasta, cover skillet, and cook until clams begin to open, about 3 minutes. Scatter shrimp over pasta, stir to partially submerge shrimp and clams, and proceed with recipe as directed.

THAI-STYLE STIR-FRIED NOODLES

✓ **WHY THIS RECIPE WORKS** We wanted to create our own version of *pad see ew*, a traditional stir-fried Thai noodle dish with chicken, broccoli, moist egg, and a salty-sweet soy-based sauce. To keep the lean chicken breast moist, we used baking soda to raise its pH, which kept its proteins from bonding too tightly and turning the meat chewy. We easily swapped convenient supermarket ingredients for the fresh rice noodles, Chinese broccoli, and sweet Thai soy sauce, but simulating the high heat of a restaurant wok burner on a home stovetop proved challenging. A combination of high heat, a 12-inch skillet with plenty of surface area, cooking in batches, and eliminating much of the stirring in our stir-fry gave us restaurant-quality results with the all-important char that characterizes pad see ew.

The amazingly varied and inventive street food of Thailand is a big reason that Bangkok is at the top of my list of dream destinations. Until I get there, though, I'm happy to console myself with frequent visits to my local Thai restaurant, which specializes in the kinds of stir-fries that are offered on the streets of Bangkok. I usually order my favorite dish, *pad see ew*, which consists of chewy, lightly charred rice noodles studded with tender slices of meat (I always order chicken), crisp Chinese broccoli, and moist scrambled egg, all lightly coated with a beautifully balanced sweet and salty soy-based sauce. It's a simple dish, but that subtle browning of the noodles is like a secret ingredient that elevates pad see ew above other more elaborate stir-fries. Unlike a

lot of Thai dishes, it is not inherently fiery, though each serving is usually seasoned to taste with chile vinegar.

The delicious simplicity of pad see ew makes it a natural choice for weeknight dinners at home, so I decided to figure out how to add it to my repertoire. I'd have to find substitutions for some of the more exotic ingredients—fresh wide rice noodles, sweet Thai soy sauce, and leafy Chinese broccoli. And while I expected it would take a bit longer to make than it does at my local Thai place, to keep it weeknight-friendly, I wanted to get it on the table in less than 45 minutes.

Authentic pad see ew calls for fresh thick rice noodles, which require no precooking or soaking. However, since they have a shelf life of only a few days, they're difficult to find. For my home version, I'd stick with the dried rice noodles available at any supermarket: flat, ¼-inch-wide noodles called rice sticks that are used for Thailand's most famous dish, *pad thai*.

Unlike Italian pasta, rice sticks absorb a good bit of the sauce they're cooked with and when properly prepared are soft and delicately chewy throughout. To get them to this state, you soak them in water to make them pliable before cooking. Sounds easy enough, but I found that recommended soaking times and water temperatures vary. Many Thai cookbooks say that rice sticks should be covered with room-temperature water for about 30 minutes, but other sources advise hot tap water, reducing the soaking time to 20 minutes. Plus, given my time constraint, waiting 20 to 30 minutes before I could even start heating my pan was too long.

The advantage of the room-temperature water is that it gives the cook a little wiggle room—an extra 5 minutes will not harm your noodles, whereas in very hot water it can turn them soggy. But I was willing to be diligent if it meant a much shorter soaking time. With speed in mind, I devised the following method: I placed ½ pound of dried noodles in a bowl, poured in 6 cups of boiling water, and let them sit for exactly 8 minutes, stirring them well when the water went in and once again halfway through to prevent them from sticking together. Then I drained them thoroughly, rinsed them with cold water to remove the surface starch that would otherwise cause them to clump, and tossed them with a little bit of oil for some extra anti-stick insurance. With my noodles sorted out, I moved on to the dish's other components: chicken, broccoli, eggs, and sauce.

The boneless, skinless chicken breast I prefer for my pad see ew is notoriously tricky to cook properly in a fast-paced stir-fry scenario. I tend to worry that, given the brief time cooking in a crowded pan, my chicken will turn out undercooked, so I overcompensate, ending up with dry and fibrous meat. To ensure that my chicken came out moist and tender, I employed a technique that we developed for another stir-fry recipe: I raised the meat's pH by soaking it briefly in a baking soda and water solution. This prevented the proteins in the meat from bonding together as tightly, enabling me to cook the meat thoroughly without fear of its being chewy.

I went through the rest of the dish's components in quick succession. Chinese broccoli is rarely sold in supermarkets, so I swapped in broccolini (which is a hybrid of Chinese and conventional broccoli). After a few egg tests, I found that adding unbeaten eggs straight into the pan gave me the denser, variegated curds usually found in Asian stir-fries, rather than fluffy, American-style scrambled eggs. And I replicated the traditional sweet, salty sauce by mixing up ingredients I had on hand: oyster sauce, brown sugar, molasses, fish sauce, garlic (which I browned much more deeply than we typically do in American cooking), and—of course—soy sauce. With all the components in place, I was ready to refine my cooking technique. And that's where things started to go horribly wrong.

In developing previous stir-fry recipes, we'd found that the tapered shape of a wok doesn't absorb as much heat on a flat Western burner as a flat-bottomed skillet, which comes in more direct contact with the heat. So I reached for a 12-inch skillet. I chose stainless steel, figuring that a slick nonstick surface wouldn't deliver enough char. I poured in 2 tablespoons of oil and placed the skillet over high heat until it was smoking hot. Then I added my ingredients: chicken first, then eggs, followed by broccoli, and noodles last, with splashes of sauce introduced throughout the process.

But 2 tablespoons of oil were not enough to keep my stir-fry from sticking. Three tablespoons were not enough. In the end, it took nearly ½ cup of oil to keep my ingredients from fusing themselves to the surface of my skillet. As a result, my stir-fry was limp, greasy, and thoroughly unappetizing. I would have to use nonstick.

Now I could cut back oil without my ingredients sticking, but in the crowded nonstick skillet, my noodles achieved hardly any of the smoky char that makes this simple dish interesting. So rather than adding all the ingredients in turn, I tried cooking them in batches to maximize the heat, stirring frantically, adding a bit of sauce to everything, and transferring each batch to a bowl when it was cooked. But even with this method, the all-important char continued to elude me.

In the end, I stumbled on the key to proper browning quite by accident. I had transferred everything back to the skillet for a final warm-through when I realized I had forgotten to prepare a platter for serving. I rushed to grab a dish and returned to find the contents of the skillet just beginning to burn. I quickly flipped my stir-fry out onto the platter. And there, crowning my creation, was the burnished brown charring I had been after. All I had to do to get it was . . . nothing. I made my dish once more, letting the noodles cook without constant stirring. This time, it was perfect. Ultimately, the key to adapting pad see ew to the home kitchen was all about standing back and letting the magic happen. I call it "Zen and the Art of Stir-Frying."

—ANDREA GEARY, *Cook's Illustrated*

Thai-Style Stir-Fried Noodles with Chicken and Broccolini (Pad See Ew)

SERVES 4

The flat rice noodles in this recipe can be found in the Asian foods section of most supermarkets. If you can't find broccolini, you can substitute an equal amount of broccoli; be sure to trim and peel the stalks before cutting.

CHILE VINEGAR

⅓ cup white vinegar

1 serrano chile, stemmed and sliced into thin rings

STIR-FRY

2 (6-ounce) boneless, skinless chicken breasts, trimmed and cut against grain into ¼-inch-thick slices

1 teaspoon baking soda

8 ounces (¼-inch-wide) rice noodles

¼ cup vegetable oil

¼ cup oyster sauce

1 tablespoon plus 2 teaspoons soy sauce

2 tablespoons packed dark brown sugar

1 tablespoon white vinegar

1 teaspoon molasses

1 teaspoon fish sauce

3 garlic cloves, sliced thin

3 large eggs

10 ounces broccolini, florets cut into 1-inch pieces, stalks cut on bias into ½-inch pieces (5 cups)

1. **FOR THE CHILE VINEGAR:** Combine vinegar and serrano in bowl. Let stand at room temperature for at least 15 minutes.

2. **FOR THE STIR-FRY:** Combine chicken with 2 tablespoons water and baking soda in bowl. Let sit at room temperature for 15 minutes. Rinse chicken in cold water and drain well.

3. Bring 6 cups water to boil. Place noodles in large bowl. Pour boiling water over noodles. Stir, then soak until noodles are almost tender, about 8 minutes, stirring once halfway through soaking. Drain and rinse with cold water. Drain well and toss with 2 teaspoons oil.

4. Whisk oyster sauce, soy sauce, sugar, vinegar, molasses, and fish sauce together in bowl.

5. Heat 2 teaspoons oil and garlic in 12-inch nonstick skillet over high heat, stirring occasionally, until garlic is deep golden brown, 1 to 2 minutes. Add chicken and 2 tablespoons sauce mixture, toss to coat, and spread chicken into even layer. Cook, without stirring, until chicken begins to brown, 1 to 1½ minutes. Using tongs, flip chicken and cook, without stirring, until second side begins to brown, 1 to 1½ minutes. Push chicken to 1 side of skillet. Add 2 teaspoons oil to cleared side of skillet. Add eggs to clearing. Using rubber spatula, stir eggs gently and cook until set but still wet. Stir eggs into chicken and continue to cook, breaking up large pieces of egg, until eggs are fully cooked, 30 to 60 seconds. Transfer chicken mixture to bowl.

6. Heat 2 teaspoons oil in now-empty skillet until smoking. Add broccolini and 2 tablespoons sauce and toss to coat. Cover skillet and cook for 2 minutes, stirring once halfway through cooking. Remove lid and continue to cook until broccolini is crisp and very brown in spots, 2 to 3 minutes, stirring once halfway through cooking. Transfer broccolini to bowl with chicken mixture.

7. Heat 2 teaspoons oil in now-empty skillet until smoking. Add half of noodles and 2 tablespoons sauce and toss to coat. Cook until noodles are starting to brown in spots, about 2 minutes, stirring halfway through cooking. Transfer noodles to bowl with chicken mixture. Repeat with remaining 2 teaspoons oil, noodles, and sauce. When second batch of noodles is cooked, add contents of bowl back to skillet and toss to combine. Cook, without stirring, until everything is warmed through, 1 to 1½ minutes. Transfer to platter and serve immediately, passing chile vinegar separately.

NOTES FROM THE TEST KITCHEN

RETHINKING THE "STIR" IN STIR-FRYING
The constant flipping and turning of stir-fries made in restaurants is critical, since more than a few seconds over a commercial-grade wok setup would turn food from pleasantly charred to carbonized. But at home, with a flat-bottomed skillet over a relatively weak Western-style burner, does all that stirring make sense? We decided to let the food stay put, stirring each ingredient just once or twice during cooking. The upshot: a "stir"-fry almost as nicely browned as in a restaurant.

THE BEST DRIED RICE NOODLES
When cooked, a good dried rice noodle (made from ground rice and water) should taste like fresh rice with a tender but not mushy bite. We gathered three national brands, tasting them plain and in our Thai noodle stir-fry. Tasted plain, the brands were very similar, but in our stir-fry, one stood out: The broad, planklike strands of **A Taste of Thai Straight Cut Rice Noodles** were tender with a good chew, and they delivered far more of the char that is critical to the dish.

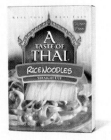

CLASSIC PAN PIZZA

✓ WHY THIS RECIPE WORKS Unlike its thin-crust cousin, pan pizza has a soft, chewy, thick crust that can stand up to substantial toppings. Since most of the allure of deep-dish pizza is in the crust, we knew it was important to get it right. After trying numerous ingredients and techniques, we took a cue from a similar Italian flatbread, focaccia, which is sometimes made with potato. Surprisingly, adding boiled potato to our pizza dough gave it exactly the right qualities. It was soft and moist, yet with a bit of chew and good structure. The potato even made the dough easier to work with. To keep the crust from toughening during baking, we added a generous amount of olive oil to the pan before putting in the dough. Topping the pizza before it went into the oven weighed down the crust and prevented it from rising, so we baked it untopped for a few minutes first. This pizza crust wasn't just a platform for the toppings; it had great flavor and texture of its own.

Deep-dish pizza (also known as Chicago-style or pan pizza) may have its roots in Italy, but this recipe is as American as apple pie. In fact, Italians would not recognize this creation—it has no counterpart in Italy.

Deep-dish pizza is about 75 percent crust, so the crust must be great. I wanted it to be rich, substantial, and moist, with a tender yet slightly chewy crumb and a well-developed flavor, like that of a good loaf of bread. I also thought the crust should be crisp and nicely browned without being dry or tough. Finally, knowing how time-consuming pizza making can be, I wanted a pizza dough that could be made in as little time as possible without sacrificing quality.

After scouring various cookbooks, I made five different pizza doughs and baked them in deep-dish pans. To my disappointment, none delivered the flavorful, crisp brown crust that I was after.

After my disappointing initial tests, I tried dozens of variations. I played around with the ratio of water to flour, the amount of oil, the type of flour, and just about every other variable I could think of. But none were great. Then, as I was searching for inspiration, I found a recipe for focaccia that used boiled, riced potatoes to add moisture and flavor to the dough. Curious if this trick would work for pizza dough, I gave it a try. This dough was just what I was hoping for: very wet and yet easy to handle, light, and smooth, and, when baked, it was soft and moist, with a bit of chew and a sturdiness and structure that were lacking in my previous attempts.

Now that I had a dough I liked, my next challenge was to come up with a rising and baking method suited to deep-dish pizza. I placed the pizza dough in a barely warmed oven for the first rise; this reduced the initial rising time from 1 hour to 35 minutes and produced a dough that tasted no different from dough that rose at room temperature for a full hour.

Next I tried reducing—and even eliminating—the amount of time allowed for the second rise. However, dough given a full 30 minutes for the second rise was vastly better than doughs given only 15 minutes or no second rise at all. The flavor was more complex, and the texture of the pizza crust was softer and lighter, making the second rise too important to pass up or shorten.

After some more testing, I found that a crust baked at 425 degrees on a baking stone was almost perfect—the bottom and sides of the pizza were well browned, and the interior crumb was moist, light, and evenly cooked through. The exterior of this crust was, however, slightly tough. To combat this, I tried coating the pizza pan with oil. After some experimentation, I found that the pizzas made with a generous amount of oil coating the pan had a far better crust than those made with little or no oil in the pan. Lightly "frying" the dough in the pan gave it a browned, caramelized exterior and added a good amount of flavor and a secondary texture to the crust without drying it out or making it tough.

Now it was time for the toppings. On most pizzas, the toppings can simply be placed on raw dough and baked, since the crust bakes in about the same amount of time as the toppings. But I found that the weight of the toppings prevented my crust from rising in the oven, resulting in a dense, heavy crust, especially in the center of the pie. So I tried prebaking the crust, testing times from 5 minutes up to 15 minutes, to develop some structure before adding the toppings. The pizza that I prebaked for 10 to 15 minutes was perfect. The crust had a chance to rise in the oven without the weight or moisture of the toppings, and the toppings had just enough time to melt and brown. Finally, I had a deep-dish pizza with all the flavor of Chicago.

—ANNE YAMANAKA, *Cook's Illustrated*

Classic Pan Pizza with Tomatoes, Mozzarella, and Basil

MAKES ONE 14-INCH PIZZA, SERVING 4 TO 6

Prepare the topping while the dough is rising so it will be ready at the same time the dough is ready. The amount of oil used to grease the pan may seem excessive, but it prevents sticking and helps the crust brown nicely.

DOUGH

   9 ounces russet potatoes, peeled and quartered
3½ cups (17½ ounces) all-purpose flour
   1 cup warm water (110 degrees)
1½ teaspoons instant or rapid-rise yeast
   6 tablespoons extra-virgin olive oil
1¾ teaspoons salt

TOPPING

   4 tomatoes, cored, seeded, and cut into 1-inch pieces
   2 garlic cloves, minced
      Salt and pepper
   6 ounces mozzarella cheese, shredded (1½ cups)
   1 ounce Parmesan cheese, grated (½ cup)
   3 tablespoons shredded fresh basil

1. FOR THE DOUGH: Bring 1 quart water and potato to boil in medium saucepan and cook until tender, 10 to 15 minutes. Drain potato and process through ricer or food mill onto plate. Measure out and reserve 1⅓ cups potato; discard remaining potato.

2. Adjust oven racks to upper-middle and lowest positions and heat oven to 200 degrees. Once oven temperature reaches 200 degrees, maintain heat for 10 minutes, then turn off oven.

3. Using stand mixer fitted with dough hook, mix ½ cup flour, ½ cup water, and yeast together on low speed until combined; cover bowl tightly with plastic wrap and let sit until bubbly, about 20 minutes.

4. Add 2 tablespoons oil, remaining 3 cups flour, remaining ½ cup water, salt, and potato to flour mixture and mix on low speed until dough comes together. Increase speed to medium and knead until dough comes together and is slightly tacky, about 5 minutes. Transfer dough to large, lightly greased bowl; cover tightly with plastic and let rise on lower rack in warm oven until doubled in size, 30 to 35 minutes.

5. Grease bottom of 14-inch cake pan with remaining 4 tablespoons oil. Remove dough from oven; transfer to clean counter and press into 12-inch round. Transfer round to pan, cover with plastic, and let rest until dough

no longer resists shaping, about 10 minutes. Uncover dough and pull up into edges and up sides of pan to form 1-inch-high lip. Cover with plastic; let rise at room temperature until doubled in size, about 30 minutes.

6. FOR THE TOPPING: Mix tomatoes and garlic together in bowl and season with salt and pepper to taste; set aside.

7. TO BAKE THE PIZZA: One hour before baking, set baking stone on lower rack and heat oven to 425 degrees. Uncover dough and prick generously with fork. Bake on baking stone until dry and lightly browned, about 15 minutes.

8. Remove pizza from oven. Spread partially baked crust with tomato mixture; sprinkle with mozzarella, then Parmesan. Return pizza to baking stone and continue baking until cheese melts, 10 to 15 minutes. Move pizza to upper rack and continue to bake until cheese is spotty brown, about 5 minutes longer. Remove pizza from oven, sprinkle with basil, and let rest for 10 minutes before slicing. Serve.

VARIATIONS

Classic Four-Cheese Pan Pizza with Pesto
Omit tomatoes, garlic, salt, pepper, and basil from topping. Process 2 cups basil leaves, 7 tablespoons extra-virgin olive oil, ¼ cup pine nuts, 3 minced garlic cloves, and ½ teaspoon salt in food processor until smooth, scraping down sides of bowl as needed, about 1 minute. Stir in ¼ cup finely grated Parmesan or Pecorino Romano cheese and season with salt and pepper to taste. Spread ½ cup pesto on partially baked crust in step 8, then sprinkle with mozzarella, followed by 1 cup shredded provolone cheese, ¼ cup crumbled blue cheese, and Parmesan. Continue baking as directed.

10-inch Classic Pan Pizza
If you don't own a 14-inch deep-dish pizza pan, divide dough between two 10-inch cake pans. Grease bottom of each cake pan with 2 tablespoons olive oil. Turn dough onto clean, dry counter and divide in half. Pat each half into 9-inch round; continue with recipe, reducing initial baking time on lowest rack to 5 to 10 minutes and dividing topping evenly between pizzas.

NOTES FROM THE TEST KITCHEN

SCIENCE: THE ROLE OF POTATOES IN PIZZA DOUGH
The boiled potatoes in our deep-dish pizza dough have a distinct effect on the flavor and texture of the final crust. The result: a moister, more tender, sweeter, and softer dough than one made with just wheat flour. We wanted to know why the boiled potatoes made such a difference.

Our food science editor explained that it's because potatoes contain more starch than wheat. Since starch traps moisture during baking, this creates a moister dough. Potatoes also contain less protein than flour. This results in less gluten being formed in the dough, which in turn produces a softer, more tender product. Finally, potatoes add another dimension of flavor in two ways. First, the free sugars in the potatoes cause faster fermentation, resulting in a more complex flavor in a shorter period of time. Second, the sugars that are not consumed by the yeast in the fermentation process add sweetness to the final dough.

THIN-CRUST WHOLE-WHEAT PIZZA

✔ **WHY THIS RECIPE WORKS** Whole-wheat pizza crust is often heavy and dense. For a crisp, parlor-style pie with the hearty flavor of whole wheat, we used a combination of 60 percent whole wheat flour and 40 percent bread flour. To ensure that our flavorful whole-wheat dough still produced a great crust, we increased its hydration to provide better gluten development and chew. To compensate for the added moisture, we preheated our baking stone for an hour, then heated it under the broiler for 10 minutes before baking the pizza. This ensured that the crust would cook quickly, guaranteeing a crisp exterior and moist, tender interior. Finally, we ditched the traditional tomato sauce, which clashed with the wheat flavor, instead opting for oil- and cream-based sauces with bold toppings like blue cheese, pesto, and wine-braised onions.

A quick survey of pizza parlor menus suggests that pies are going the way of rustic bread: They're no longer a white flour–only affair. Even most supermarkets offer a partial whole-wheat-flour dough alongside their standard white. In theory, this is good news, since whole wheat can lend rich, nutty flavor and satisfying depth to almost any kind of baked good. But in practice, I often find the marriage of whole wheat and pizza crust to be strained at best.

Most recipes seem to fear commitment to the style, casually throwing a scant amount of whole-wheat flour into a white-flour formula. The resulting pies may have decent texture, but if they don't have noticeable nuttiness or flavor complexity, what's the point? At the other end of the spectrum, I've tried following pizza dough recipes with a high percentage of whole-wheat flour (some with as much as 100 percent), and I've found that for the most part they produce dense crusts devoid of satisfying chew or crispness. Not to mention that these crusts have an overly wheaty flavor that competes for attention with the pizza toppings. I decided to rethink whole-wheat pizza, examining it through the lens of a bread baker in order to formulate a dough and a cooking technique that would give me a crust that had it all: good but not overwhelming wheat flavor; a crisp bottom; and a moist, chewy interior.

I started my journey by deciding exactly what style of crust I wanted. After all, whole-wheat pizza crusts run the same gamut as white-flour ones: from thin and crispy to thick, deep-dish-style pies. I wanted a crust that could withstand some full-flavored toppings, but not one that would overwhelm with wheaty heft. I decided to start with our recipe for Thin-Crust Pizza: Its crust is thin and crisp with perfect spots of char alongside a tender, chewy interior. I would start there, tailoring the ingredient ratio and baking techniques to withstand the challenges of whole wheat.

This pizza dough is made with high-protein bread flour and uses the food processor for fast kneading. I knew before I even began baking that the use of bread flour would be particularly important. Bread flour contains more of the proteins (glutenin and gliadin) that form gluten—the network of proteins that gives dough structure and chew—than all-purpose flour. I also would use King Arthur brand bread flour, which features a particularly high protein content of 12.7 percent. This would help compensate for the fact that, while high in protein, whole-wheat flour has less gluten potential than does white flour for two reasons. One is that whole-wheat flour has more of the types of protein that can't develop gluten than all-purpose flour does. The second is that whole-wheat flour, ground from the wheat berry, includes both the germ and the bran. They provide great flavor, but the sharp bran physically inhibits gluten development by cutting gluten strands. I would therefore need to punch up the gluten potential in other ways; bread flour would be a great start.

But the thin-crust pizza recipe also used an overnight rise in the refrigerator to allow for better flavor development and an easier-to-stretch dough. Since the nutty flavor of the whole wheat would cover up any flavor benefits of letting the dough sit overnight, I wondered if I could skip that step, simplifying my recipe and eliminating the need for so much forethought.

I started my testing by swapping in varying proportions of whole-wheat flour in our thin-crust pizza dough recipe. My goal for this initial round of testing was to determine the ideal amount of whole-wheat flour from a flavor perspective, then deal with textural issues as they arose. For each test, I pulsed the flours, water, yeast, and a sweetener (to promote browning;

THIN–CRUST WHOLE–WHEAT PIZZA WITH GARLIC OIL, THREE CHEESES, AND BASIL

I opted for honey to complement the wheat flavor) until they were just combined, then I allowed the dough to sit for 10 minutes. During this brief respite, called an autolyse, gluten formation gets a jump start. I then added salt and oil and processed the dough until it was smooth and satiny. After a final rise, I shaped, topped, and baked each pizza on a preheated 500-degree pizza stone. Ultimately, tasters preferred a dough with 60 percent whole-wheat and 40 percent white flour. This ratio provided a distinct, pleasant wheatiness that was recognizable but not too strong. I was pleased with the flavor of my pizza, but, unsurprisingly, the texture was lacking. To start improving it, I looked to the second key ingredient: water.

I knew that dough with more water produces chewier breads, as the added hydration allows for a stronger, more stretchable gluten network. This was of relevance to my dough because whole-wheat flour, thanks to its mix of starch, bran, and germ, absorbs more water than does white flour. With this in mind, I started increasing the water in batches and tracking the results.

At about 64 percent hydration (this number represents the weight of the water compared with that of the flour), my current formula sat in the midrange of white-flour doughs. Sure enough, adding more water led to a pizza with better chew and larger, slightly more irregular holes—something that bakers refer to as a more open crumb structure. It also made the dough easier to work with and to stretch thin—at least to a point. I found that dough with a hydration of 80 percent and up was too soft and sticky to reliably form into a 13-inch disk, and the resulting pies had a tendency to stick to the pizza peel when I attempted to slide them into the oven. In the end, I found my sweet spot with 10 ounces of water for 13¾ ounces of flour, or roughly 73 percent hydration.

But this ratio still caused trouble when it came to stretching my dough out nice and thin with ease. I found myself doubling back to the overnight rise. It may not be necessary for flavor development, but the long rest in the fridge also greatly improved the extensibility of our original thin-crust pizza. Would it do the same here? One test and I knew: This dough was a pleasure to handle and stretch, and it baked up with satisfying chew and a thin but airy interior.

But while the increased hydration had helped with gluten development and chew, it wasn't perfect. If I let my pizzas bake long enough for them to really crisp on the bottom, they overbaked and dried out. It turns out that browning and crisping the bottom of a pizza is much like trying to get a good sear on a steak. We all know that a wet steak takes much longer to sear than a dry one, so that by the time you achieve a good crust, much of the interior is overcooked. This holds true for pizza as well: A wetter dough will take longer to brown and crisp because the oven's heat has to drive off the extra moisture before it begins crisping the crust. Feeling as though I'd just shot myself in the foot, I scrambled for a solution.

Up to this point, I'd been following our thin-crust pizza baking protocol, cooking my pies in a 500-degree oven on a preheated pizza stone set on the oven rack's second-highest position. The thinking behind this method is that by keeping the pizza near the top of the oven, we create a smaller oven space where reflected heat is trapped around the pizza. This means the top and bottom of the pizza bake at a more even rate. This was good, but how could I speed up that rate?

If I were cooking a steak in a skillet, I'd simply turn up the heat, but my oven was already set to 500 degrees. I did have a super-hot broiler, but given that I was trying to get the bottom of the pizza to cook faster, I wasn't quite sure how to put it to use. After some failed experiments resulting in seriously burnt toppings, I hit on a winning solution. After preheating the stone in a 500-degree oven to ensure that it was fully heated, I turned on the broiler for 10 minutes. Then, when I slid in the pizza, I switched the oven back to bake. The brief blast from the broiler served two purposes: It increased the stone's exterior temperature by about 10 to 15 degrees, leading to better oven spring and faster evaporation of moisture from the bottom of the crust. It also boosted the air temperature above the stone. The upshot? I pulled a finished pizza out of the oven after just 8 minutes—an almost 50 percent reduction in baking time. And you could taste it: This pizza featured a crisp bottom and a super-moist interior.

One problem remained. I had a great crust, but it didn't quite fit with the flavor of the toppings, which so far were simply an easy uncooked tomato sauce and some shredded mozzarella cheese. The sweetly acidic tomato sauce wasn't a great match with the slightly sweet whole-wheat flavor of the crust. I wanted to

SECRETS TO WHOLE-WHEAT PIZZA WORTH MAKING

Our approach transforms whole-wheat flour into a crust that's wonderfully chewy and crisp, with an earthy complexity that distinguishes it from a traditional pizza crust.

1. Use both whole-wheat flour and white bread flour (which has more structure-building proteins than all-purpose flour does) to increase chewiness.

2. Make a highly hydrated dough to help strengthen the gluten network, and add ice water to keep the dough from overheating as it kneads in the food processor.

3. Rest the dough overnight to give enzymes in the dough time to slightly weaken gluten strands, increasing extensibility, and to allow more flavor-boosting fermentation.

4. Use the broiler; because our dough is so wet, preheating the pizza stone under the broiler's high heat (after an hour at 500 degrees) is key to a nicely browned crust.

5. The sweet-tart flavors of tomato sauce clash with earthy whole wheat. Instead, we top our pizza with three cheeses, garlicky oil, and basil.

find a combination of toppings that would perfectly complement the flavorful crust I had worked so hard to develop.

I experimented with a range of ingredients and found that garlicky oil, rich and nutty cheeses, and punchy ingredients like pesto and anchovies were a better match for the earthy flavor of the crust than the tomato sauce. Eventually I landed on a simple combination: I briefly heated garlic, anchovies, oregano, and red pepper flakes in extra-virgin olive oil, then brushed the mixture onto the dough. Next, I added a layer of fresh basil leaves, grated Pecorino Romano, and shredded mozzarella. After the pie emerged from the oven, I dotted it with small dollops of fresh ricotta. This mix of toppings added richness and complexity without overpowering the flavorful crust. To ensure that I could happily eat my whole-wheat pizza as often as possible, I also developed variations featuring braised onions and blue cheese and garlicky basil pesto and goat cheese.

As taster after taster gave my pizza rave reviews, I realized why the pies were such a success: They didn't represent mere tweaks to traditional pizza. I'd invented an entirely new concept: truly good whole-wheat pizza meant to be enjoyed on its own terms.

—DAN SOUZA, *Cook's Illustrated*

Thin-Crust Whole-Wheat Pizza with Garlic Oil, Three Cheeses, and Basil

MAKES TWO 13-INCH PIZZAS

We recommend King Arthur brand bread flour for this recipe. Some baking stones, especially thinner ones, can crack under the intense heat of the broiler. Our recommended stone, by Old Stone Oven, is fine if you're using this technique. If you have another stone, you might want to check the manufacturer's website.

DOUGH

1½ cups (8¼ ounces) whole-wheat flour

1 cup (5½ ounces) bread flour

2 teaspoons honey

¾ teaspoon instant or rapid-rise yeast

1¼ cups ice water

2 tablespoons extra-virgin olive oil

1¾ teaspoons salt

GARLIC OIL

- ¼ cup extra-virgin olive oil
- 2 garlic cloves, minced
- 2 anchovy fillets, rinsed, patted dry, and minced (optional)
- ½ teaspoon pepper
- ½ teaspoon dried oregano
- ⅛ teaspoon red pepper flakes
- ⅛ teaspoon salt

- 1 cup fresh basil leaves
- 1 ounce Pecorino Romano cheese, grated (½ cup)
- 8 ounces whole-milk mozzarella cheese, shredded (2 cups)
- 6 ounces (¾ cup) whole-milk ricotta cheese

1. FOR THE DOUGH: Process whole-wheat flour, bread flour, honey, and yeast in food processor until combined, about 2 seconds. With processor running, add water and process until dough is just combined and no dry flour remains, about 10 seconds. Let dough stand for 10 minutes.

2. Add oil and salt to dough and process until it forms satiny, sticky ball that clears sides of workbowl, 45 to 60 seconds. Remove from bowl and knead on oiled counter until smooth, about 1 minute. Shape dough into tight ball and place in large, lightly oiled bowl. Cover tightly with plastic wrap and refrigerate for at least 18 hours or up to 2 days.

3. FOR THE GARLIC OIL: Heat oil in 8-inch skillet over medium-low heat until shimmering. Add garlic; anchovies, if using; pepper; oregano; pepper flakes; and salt. Cook, stirring constantly, until fragrant, about 30 seconds. Transfer to bowl and let cool completely before using.

4. One hour before baking pizza, adjust oven rack 4½ inches from broiler element, set pizza stone on rack, and heat oven to 500 degrees. Remove dough from refrigerator and divide in half. Shape each half into smooth, tight ball. Place balls on lightly oiled baking sheet, spacing them at least 3 inches apart. Cover loosely with plastic coated with vegetable oil spray; let stand for 1 hour.

5. Heat broiler for 10 minutes. Meanwhile, coat 1 ball of dough generously with flour and place on well-floured counter. Using your fingertips, gently flatten into 8-inch disk, leaving 1 inch of outer edge slightly thicker than center. Lift edge of dough and, using back

of your hands and knuckles, gently stretch disk into 12-inch round, working along edges and giving disk quarter turns as you stretch. Transfer dough to well-floured peel and stretch into 13-inch round. Using back of spoon, spread half of garlic oil over surface of dough, leaving ¼-inch border. Layer ½ cup basil leaves over pizza. Sprinkle with ¼ cup Pecorino, followed by 1 cup mozzarella. Slide pizza carefully onto stone and return oven to 500 degrees. Bake until crust is well browned and cheese is bubbly and partially browned, 8 to 10 minutes, rotating pizza halfway through baking. Remove pizza and place on wire rack. Dollop half of ricotta over surface of pizza. Let pizza rest for 5 minutes before slicing. Serve.

6. Heat broiler for 10 minutes. Repeat process of stretching, topping, and baking with remaining dough and toppings, returning oven to 500 degrees when pizza is placed on stone.

VARIATIONS

Thin-Crust Whole-Wheat Pizza with Pesto and Goat Cheese

Process 2 cups basil leaves, 7 tablespoons extra-virgin olive oil, ¼ cup pine nuts, 3 minced garlic cloves, and ½ teaspoon salt in food processor until smooth, scraping down sides of bowl as needed, about 1 minute. Stir in ¼ cup finely grated Parmesan or Pecorino Romano cheese and season with salt and pepper to taste. Substitute pesto for garlic oil. In step 5, omit basil leaves, Pecorino Romano, mozzarella, and ricotta. Top each pizza with ½ cup crumbled goat cheese before baking.

Thin-Crust Whole-Wheat Pizza with Wine-Braised Onions and Blue Cheese

Bring 1 onion, halved through root end and sliced ⅛ inch thick; 1½ cups water; ¾ cup dry red wine; 3 tablespoons sugar; and ¼ teaspoon salt to simmer over medium-high heat in 10-inch skillet. Reduce heat to medium and simmer, stirring often, until liquid evaporates and onion is crisp-tender, about 30 minutes. Stir in 2 teaspoons red wine vinegar, transfer to bowl, and let cool completely. Substitute ⅔ cup crème fraîche for garlic oil. In step 5, omit basil leaves, Pecorino Romano, mozzarella, and ricotta. Top each pizza with half of onion mixture, ½ cup coarsely chopped walnuts, and ½ cup crumbled blue cheese before baking. Sprinkle each pizza with 2 tablespoons shredded fresh basil before serving.

CHAPTER 6

MEAT

GRILLED COWBOY RIB-EYE STEAKS

✓ **WHY THIS RECIPE WORKS** Beefy and tender, the cowboy rib-eye steak possesses another advantage—its hulking size, which means it can stay on the grill longer than smaller cuts and absorb great smoky flavor. But achieving a perfectly cooked interior and a beautifully charred crust isn't easy. We found the trick to even cooking was to build a two-level fire and slow-"roast" the steaks on the cool side of the grill until they were nearly done, then quickly sear them over the hot side. Layering unlit coals under lit ones kept the fire burning hotter longer. Letting the steaks come to room temperature before grilling made for faster, more even cooking. And salting the steaks before cooking perfectly seasoned the meat throughout.

When it comes to steak, you generally get what you pay for. High-quality premium cuts like rib eye, strip, and tenderloin will always cost you—and that's just fine with me. These steaks—especially the rib eye, the steak with the best balance of beefy flavor and tender texture—are worth it. And the king of steaks is the cowboy-cut rib eye. These 2-inch-thick, 1½-pound, bone-in behemoths can cost upward of $25 each at the supermarket. The advantage to buying these huge steaks—aside from impressing your guests—is that they can stay on the grill longer than smaller steaks, soaking up more smoke and grill flavor.

The challenge when grilling any piece of meat is cooking the inside to just the right temperature while getting a dark, flavorful sear on the outside. The larger the piece of meat, the harder it is to get these things to happen at the same rate. If you put a big steak over a hot fire, the inside won't cook through in the short time it takes to get a good sear. But if you put the steak over a cooler fire, when the inside is a perfect medium-rare, the outside still won't have enough char. To solve this problem, most grilling experts instruct the cook to build a fire with hotter and cooler zones: You first sear the steaks over a hot fire, then you move them to the cooler side of the grill to finish cooking. I gave this method a go and ended up with steaks that looked mouthwatering: The center registered a nice 125 degrees (exactly medium-rare) and the exterior had a nice, crusty char. But when I sliced into one, a serious problem emerged. Although pink in the center, the steak had a large gray band of overcooked meat around the exterior—a sure sign that it had been cooked too aggressively.

Luckily I had another idea. Instead of searing the steaks first and then finishing them gently, what if I reversed the order, cooking them gently most of the way (to about 100 degrees), then moving them to a hot fire to finish cooking and achieve that flavorful sear? I hoped that the low heat would fix my overcooking problem and eliminate the unappealing gray band. In preparation, I set up the grill with a layer of lit coals on one side and no coals on the other. I put the steaks on the cooler side and waited patiently. And waited some more, periodically checking the steaks' internal temperature. After almost an hour, the meat finally hit 100 degrees—but by that time, the coals had burned down so much that a good sear was impossible. How could I speed up the slower "roasting" portion of cooking so that I'd have enough fire to quickly sear the steaks at the end?

I headed inside and took the temperature of the eight steaks that still remained in the refrigerator. They registered an appropriately chilly 35 to 40 degrees—no wonder it was taking the low heat so long to warm the centers of the steaks. I needed to "acclimate" the steaks so that they weren't so cold when they hit the grill. I unwrapped the steaks and set them out on the counter. To increase air circulation for even warming, I put them on a wire rack. I came back after an hour and checked their temperature again. The steaks registered roughly 55 degrees, a difference of about 20 degrees. As it turned out, those 20 degrees shaved a good 30 minutes off the initial cooking time. But after moving the steaks to the hotter part of the grill, I still wasn't getting the solid sear that these hefty steaks deserve.

It was time to bust out my trump card: the Minion method. This is a charcoal setup (named for the guy who popularized it on the barbecue circuit) in which you put a pile of unlit charcoal in the grill, then pour lit charcoal on top; as the fire burns, the unlit fuel ignites, providing a longer-burning fire. It's a technique often used for long-cooking items like ribs and pork shoulder so you don't have to add more charcoal in the middle of grilling.

I scaled down the amounts to fit the time my steaks needed on the grill and gave it a try. By the time the steaks were done roasting, there was plenty of heat left to create a crusty sear on the outside of the rib eyes. (This took about 4 minutes per side.) Two other tricks ensured success: When searing, I bucked tradition and kept the grill covered to minimize flare-ups and to make sure the steaks cooked all the way through. Also, side-by-side tests proved that rubbing the steaks with oil before grilling helped them pick up a little color during the first part of cooking, leading to an improved sear at the end. Finally, I'd achieved success.

With my cooking method worked out, I considered flavoring the steaks. Most cooks, myself included, don't add much to rib eyes—why cover up that wonderful beefy flavor with spice rubs or pastes? So I would just use salt and pepper. But I wanted the seasoning to be more than superficial. Since I was pulling the steaks out of the refrigerator an hour before cooking anyway, I tried salting a batch before letting them warm to room temperature. The prolonged salting worked wonders, seasoning these hefty slabs throughout. I finally had steaks that were flavorful and juicy, without a gray band or a burned exterior; frankly, this was the best steak I'd ever eaten. These steaks are expensive, sure, but when cooked just right, they're worth every penny.

—NICK IVERSON, *Cook's Country*

Grilled Cowboy-Cut Rib Eyes

SERVES 4 TO 6

Don't start grilling until the steaks' internal temperatures have reached 55 degrees or the times and temperatures in this recipe will be inaccurate. You will need a wire rack and a rimmed baking sheet for this recipe.

- 2 (1¼- to 1½-pound) double-cut bone-in rib-eye steaks, 1¾ to 2 inches thick, trimmed
- 4 teaspoons kosher salt
- 2 teaspoons vegetable oil
- 2 teaspoons pepper

1. Set wire rack inside rimmed baking sheet. Pat steaks dry with paper towels and sprinkle all over with salt. Place steaks on prepared rack and let stand at room temperature until meat registers 55 degrees, about 1 hour. Rub steaks with oil and sprinkle with pepper.

2A. FOR A CHARCOAL GRILL: Open bottom vent halfway. Arrange 4 quarts unlit charcoal briquettes in even layer over half of grill. Light large chimney starter one-third filled with charcoal briquettes (2 quarts). When top coals are partially covered with ash, pour evenly over unlit coals. Set cooking grate in place, cover, and open lid vent halfway. Heat grill until hot, about 5 minutes.

NOTES FROM THE TEST KITCHEN

IN PRAISE OF COWBOY STEAKS
Rib-eye steaks are deeply marbled, tender, and beefy—they're from the same part of the steer that's used for prime rib. The bone contributes flavor and protects against overcooking. The exterior band of fat and meat on a rib eye is called the deckle; connoisseurs say it is the most flavorful part of the cow.

BIGGER IS BETTER
Cowboy-cut rib eyes are double-thick bone-in steaks. They take longer to cook than single-serving rib eyes, so they have more time to soak up smoky grill flavor.

GRILLING OVER A FORTIFIED FIRE
We slowly "roast" these huge steaks with indirect heat for about 30 minutes before moving them over the coals to brown and finish cooking. To be sure that we have enough heat left in the coals without the hassle of having to add extra charcoal partway through cooking, we borrow a technique from the barbecue circuit. Called the Minion method, it creates a longer-burning fire by pouring lit briquettes on top of unlit briquettes.

THE BEST STEAK SAUCE
A.1. reigns supreme in the United States, accounting for about 70 percent of steak sauce sold. But it's not the only steak sauce on the market. To find out which we liked best, we tasted seven brands on their own and with steak.

Some were too sweet, too vinegary, or so sour that we scarcely noticed the meat. Textures varied almost as much; tasters preferred smooth sauces with enough body to cling to the steak without being stiff and gluey. In the end, A.1. finished third; its sour acidity tended to overpower the meat. Our winner, **Heinz 57 Sauce**, had a mellow, fruity tomato base; tangy acidity; a peppery kick; and a hint of smokiness—but the flavor was still all about the meat. (See page 293 for more information on our testing results.)

2B. FOR A GAS GRILL: Turn all burners to high, cover, and heat grill until hot, about 15 minutes. Turn primary burner to medium-low and turn off other burner(s). Adjust primary burner as needed to maintain grill temperature of 300 degrees.

3. Clean and oil cooking grate. Place steaks on cooler side of grill with bones facing fire. Cover and cook until steaks register 75 degrees, 10 to 20 minutes.

Flip steaks, keeping bones facing fire. Cover and continue to cook until steaks register 95 degrees, 10 to 20 minutes.

4. If using charcoal, slide steaks to hotter part of grill. If using gas, remove steaks from grill, turn primary burner to high, and heat until hot, about 5 minutes; place steaks over primary burner. Cover and cook until well browned and steaks register 120 degrees (for medium-rare), about 4 minutes per side. Transfer steaks to clean wire rack set in rimmed baking sheet, tent loosely with foil, and let rest for 15 minutes. Transfer steaks to carving board, cut meat from bone, and slice into ½-inch-thick slices. Serve.

OKLAHOMA FRIED ONION BURGERS

✔ **WHY THIS RECIPE WORKS** This Oklahoma specialty features a thin patty of ground beef topped with a crispy crust of caramelized onion cooked on a griddle until well-done. Topped with a buttery grilled bun, yellow mustard, dill pickles, and a slice of American cheese, this exceptional burger is well worth a road trip. To make them at home, we sliced and salted the onions, then squeezed out their excess moisture so they'd brown quickly and stick to the burgers. We mashed the onions into the burgers on a spacious baking sheet, then added the burgers to a buttered skillet onion side down to brown the onions. Then we flipped the burgers and turned up the heat to finish cooking and get a nice sear.

If you should happen to drive to El Reno, a small Oklahoma town about 25 miles west of Oklahoma City, you'll find an unusual burger that's the object of much local adoration. The fried onion burger (or FOB, to locals) was born in the 1920s out of Depression-era necessity at the Hamburger Inn out on Route 66. By mashing thinly sliced onions into beef patties, cooks could use less meat without reducing the portion size. But the onions don't just sit on top of this burger: They are pressed into the meat so they cook together and the flavors meld. And since the onions are layered onto the outside of the meat rather than mixed into it, they get nicely caramelized by direct contact with the hot griddle, infusing the meat with their flavor. Every May, thousands attend the Fried Onion Burger Day festival to view the assembly of an 800-pound FOB. My quest was for something more modest. I wanted to be able to make four well-browned fried onion burgers in a stovetop skillet, with the proper integration of beef and onion.

I knew that slicing the onion very thin was key, so I used a mandoline set to about ⅛ inch. On a restaurant's heavy-duty griddle, the slices get hit instantly with an intense, even heat that dries them out and browns them in minutes. Not so on a home stove. My thin slices refused to adhere to the burgers; they oozed moisture, which practically repelled the meat. I borrowed a trick that we've used to remove moisture from cabbage for coleslaw: salting. I sprinkled the onions with a teaspoon of salt and let them sit for 30 minutes. The slices threw off lots of moisture, and squeezing them in a clean kitchen towel dried them further. Now my onions browned quickly and adhered to the meat.

A restaurant's large griddle also boasts plenty of surface area, making it easy to slap a patty on the hot griddle, heap sliced onions on top, and mash them together. But my attempts to replicate this process in a 12-inch skillet with four burgers at a time proved futile: There just wasn't enough room to maneuver a spatula on top of the burgers. To get around that, I set four piles of drained and dried onion slices on a baking sheet. Next I made four 3-ounce balls of ground beef, mashed the beef into the onions right on the sheet, and formed them into 4-inch patties. By pressing the onions into the meat outside the skillet, I could ensure that they were firmly embedded before I started cooking.

Classic El Reno onion burgers are usually quite thin. I wanted to make mine thicker (no more wartime shortages, after all), but when I tried cooking them in a super-hot skillet, their girth translated to onions that burned before the meat was cooked. I had better luck starting the burgers onion side down over medium heat so the onions could gently brown, then flipping the burgers and cranking up the heat to get a good, hard sear on the meat side. A nonstick skillet prevented the onions from sticking, and using butter (plus a little oil so the butter wouldn't burn) added extra richness.

Served on a buttered, griddled bun with classic yellow mustard, pickles, and American cheese (on the bottom, to keep the onion crust crisp), these burgers were wickedly delicious—salty and sweet, tangy and juicy, and very hard to stop eating.

—DIANE UNGER, *Cook's Country*

OKLAHOMA FRIED ONION BURGERS

Oklahoma Fried Onion Burgers

SERVES 4

A mandoline makes quick work of slicing the onion thinly. Squeeze the salted onion slices until they're as dry as possible, or they won't adhere to the patties. These burgers are traditionally served with yellow mustard and slices of dill pickle.

    1 large onion, halved and sliced ⅛ inch thick
       Salt and pepper
   12 ounces 85 percent lean ground beef
    1 tablespoon unsalted butter
    1 teaspoon vegetable oil
    4 slices American cheese (4 ounces)
    4 hamburger buns, buttered and toasted

1. Combine onion and 1 teaspoon salt in bowl and toss to combine. Transfer to colander and let sit for 30 minutes, tossing occasionally. Using tongs, transfer onion to clean dish towel, gather edges, and squeeze onion dry. Sprinkle with ½ teaspoon pepper.

2. Divide onion mixture into 4 separate mounds in rimmed baking sheet. Form beef into 4 lightly packed balls and season with salt and pepper. Place beef balls on top of onion mounds and flatten beef firmly so onion adheres and patties measure 4 inches in diameter.

NOTES FROM THE TEST KITCHEN

KEYS TO FRIED ONION BURGERS
A few tricks helped the onions adhere to the burgers and caramelize rather than burn.

1. After salting onions and squeezing them dry, divide into 4 piles, place beef balls on top, and press to adhere.

2. Brown burgers, onion side down, over gentler medium heat. Then flip burgers and increase heat to sear beef side.

3. Melt butter with oil in 12-inch nonstick skillet over medium heat. Using spatula, transfer patties to skillet, onion side down, and cook until onion is deep golden brown and beginning to crisp around edges, 6 to 8 minutes. Flip burgers, increase heat to high, and cook until well browned on second side, about 2 minutes. Place 1 slice cheese on each bottom bun. Place burgers on buns and add desired toppings. Serve.

ATLANTA BRISKET

✓ **WHY THIS RECIPE WORKS** Atlanta brisket is a regional braise featuring onion soup mix, ketchup, and Atlanta's own Coca-Cola. We wanted to keep the regional charm but update the convenience-product flavor. To season the brisket, we pierced it with a fork, salted it, and let it sit overnight. For a great crust and to prevent the large cut from curling, we seared the brisket weighed down with a heavy pot. Finally, for the characteristic braising liquid, we combined cola and ketchup and replaced the artificial-tasting soup mix with our own blend of sautéed onions, onion and garlic powders, brown sugar, and dried thyme. The mixture both flavored the meat and became a sweet, tangy sauce for serving.

Coca-Cola is such a global presence these days that few people realize it was once just a local specialty, created by an Atlanta pharmacist and sold for a nickel a drink. The company is still headquartered in Atlanta. Today, Southerners drink more soda than people in other parts of the country (so says the U.S. Department of Agriculture). And they don't just drink it—they cook with it, too. It could be that the kola nuts and essence of coca leaf rumored to be in Coke's secret formula give recipes a pleasing extra dimension. Recently, one recipe in particular caught my eye: Coca-Cola–braised brisket, also called Atlanta brisket. Truthfully, I doubted that it could be any good.

A colleague persuaded me to drop my skepticism and give it a try. Don't think warm soda pop, she insisted. Imagine brisket in a sweet-yet-savory sauce with the caramelized complexity of cola. Most of the recipes I found were dead simple: Sear the brisket on both sides in oil in a hot pan; put it in a baking dish; pour a combination of onion soup mix, cola, and ketchup over the meat; cover; and bake. I appreciated the simplicity of the recipes but not the results. The briskets were difficult to sear well, the meat was tough and dry, and the gravies were unpleasantly sweet. On the plus side, these were problems I knew I could fix.

I started by tackling the first problem: A 3½-pound brisket is a big, flat piece of meat that curls up in a hot skillet, which means it doesn't get a uniform sear—and a good sear not only adds flavor to the meat but also creates fond in the pan to enrich the sauce. To get that sear, I tried a technique we've used before to make panini sandwiches with really crispy edges. I placed a Dutch oven on top of the brisket to weigh it down and increase its contact with the hot pan (you can wrap the bottom of the Dutch oven in foil for easier cleanup). This technique yielded a nicely browned brisket and plenty of flavorful fond. Now my problems were down to two: the texture of the meat and the flavor of the sauce.

A few of the recipes I'd found called for marinating the brisket in cola before cooking, the idea being that the sweet, acidic soda tenderizes and flavors the brisket. This premise seemed worth testing. I got two briskets and marinated both in cola, one overnight and the other for 2 hours. Then I braised them, sliced them, and tasted them. The acidic, sugary cola definitely had an impact on the texture of the meat—but not in a good way. The briskets were spongy and dry. I tried adding salt to the cola marinade, hoping the salt would help keep the brisket juicy (as with a brine), but to no avail. I'd save the cola for braising.

Although adding salt to the cola marinade hadn't worked, I had one more salt test up my sleeve. Salting large cuts of meat is a favorite test kitchen technique for seasoning and improving the texture of meat. Would rubbing salt into the brisket and resting it overnight before braising yield moist, tender meat? Thankfully, this trick worked wonders. After a few more tests I found that I could salt for just 6 hours (although overnight is preferable) and that poking the meat with a fork before salting helped the salt penetrate more effectively.

I was ready to move on to the braising liquid. Several of the recipes I'd made at the beginning called for 2 cups of cola, 1½ cups of ketchup, and one packet of onion soup mix for one 3½-pound brisket. I'd start with those ratios, but the packet of hyper-salty, artificial-tasting onion soup mix would definitely have to go. I've overhauled recipes designed to use packaged onion soup

mix before, so I knew that onion and garlic powders, brown sugar, and a little dried thyme would provide a similar flavor with none of the unnecessary ingredients. I whisked this new spice mixture into the ketchup and cola and set it aside. I salted a brisket, let it rest, then seared it, poured the cola mixture over it, covered the pan with foil, and put it in the oven.

This brisket was much better, though it still lacked some depth and complexity. To add savor and reinforce the flavor of the onion powder, I sautéed chopped onions in the drippings left from searing the brisket. The sautéed-then-braised onions practically melted into the resulting gravy, supplying the missing balance and depth.

We gave this brisket a taste. It was moist and tender, and the sweet, caramelized flavor of the cola offset the oniony, savory meatiness. The formula for Coca-Cola may be famously top secret, but the formula for good Atlanta brisket is now yours.

—NICK IVERSON, *Cook's Country*

Atlanta Brisket

SERVES 6

Parchment paper provides a nonreactive barrier between the cola-based braising liquid and the aluminum foil.

- 1 (3½-pound) beef brisket, flat cut, fat trimmed to ¼ inch
  Salt and pepper
- 4 teaspoons vegetable oil
- 1 pound onions, halved and sliced ½ inch thick
- 2 cups cola
- 1½ cups ketchup
- 4 teaspoons onion powder
- 2 teaspoons packed dark brown sugar
- 1 teaspoon garlic powder
- 1 teaspoon dried thyme

1. Using fork, poke holes all over brisket. Rub entire surface of brisket with 1 tablespoon salt. Wrap brisket in plastic wrap and refrigerate for at least 6 or up to 24 hours.

2. Adjust oven rack to lower-middle position and heat oven to 325 degrees. Pat brisket dry with paper towels and season with pepper. Heat 2 teaspoons oil in 12-inch nonstick skillet over medium-high heat until just smoking. Place brisket fat side down in skillet; weigh down brisket with heavy Dutch oven or cast-iron skillet and cook until well browned, about 4 minutes. Remove Dutch oven, flip brisket, and replace Dutch oven on top of brisket; cook on second side until well browned, about 4 minutes longer. Transfer brisket to plate.

3. Heat remaining 2 teaspoons oil in now-empty skillet over medium heat until shimmering. Add onions and cook, stirring occasionally, until soft and golden brown, 10 to 12 minutes. Transfer onions to 13 by 9-inch baking dish and spread into even layer.

4. Combine cola, ketchup, onion powder, sugar, garlic powder, thyme, 1 teaspoon salt, and 1 teaspoon pepper in bowl. Place brisket fat side up on top of onions and pour cola mixture over brisket. Place parchment paper over brisket and cover dish tightly with aluminum foil. Bake until tender and fork easily slips in and out of meat, 3½ to 4 hours. Let brisket rest in liquid, uncovered, for 30 minutes.

5. Transfer brisket to carving board. Skim any fat from top of sauce with large spoon. Slice brisket against grain into ¼-inch-thick slices and return to baking dish. Serve brisket with sauce.

TO MAKE AHEAD: Follow recipe through step 4. Allow brisket to cool in sauce, cover, and refrigerate overnight or up to 24 hours. To serve, slice brisket, return to sauce, and cover with parchment paper. Cover baking dish with aluminum foil and cook in 350-degree oven until heated through, about 1 hour.

NOTES FROM THE TEST KITCHEN

GETTING A GREAT SEAR

Brisket is a flat cut of meat that curls up when you try to sear it. We fixed this problem with an unlikely tool: a Dutch oven. Weighing down the brisket with a heavy Dutch oven (the foil makes cleanup easier) ensures a more even, more thorough sear.

SHEPHERD'S PIE

✓ **WHY THIS RECIPE WORKS** Tender chunks of meat and rich gravy under a thick blanket of mashed potatoes is undeniably delicious—and labor intensive. We streamlined the dish by building the pie in a skillet and using convenient lean ground beef rather than cutting up a roast into chunks. To keep the beef tender, we simmered the meat in the gravy instead of searing it, and we used baking soda to raise its pH, keeping its proteins from bonding too tightly and turning tough. To replace the flavorful fond usually provided by searing, we sautéed onions, mushrooms, and tomato paste until quite dark, then deglazed the pan with fortified wine. To keep the dish from being too heavy, we lightened the mashed potatoes by swapping half-and-half for milk and cutting back on the butter; chopped fresh scallions added bright flavor.

I once made a fabulous shepherd's pie. It was the very antithesis of those watery, gray, flavorless pies pushed by frozen food companies and school cafeterias. But this story is not about that shepherd's pie, because I will never make that particular recipe again. The reason is simple: It took most of a day to produce. After boning, trimming, and cutting up lamb shoulder, I seared the meat in batches (making a greasy mess of the stovetop in the process), then braised it with vegetables and homemade stock for a couple of hours. From there, I reduced the cooking liquid to make a sauce, chopped the cooked meat, replaced the spent vegetables with fresh, and transferred the filling to a baking dish. Finally, I prepared the mashed potatoes (boiling, mashing, mixing) and piped them over the filling. While the top crisped in the oven, I cleaned up the kitchen—no small feat because I had used almost every piece of cooking equipment I owned. I loved that pie, but it was hardly comfort food.

Another thing: Though it made a very satisfying meal, the pie was very heavy. Shepherd's pie may be from a time when physical laborers needed robust sustenance, but I can't really justify eating like a preindustrial farmer. Still, the classic combination of meat, gravy, and potatoes is undeniably attractive on chilly winter nights. Maybe I could make a place in my life for a modernized shepherd's pie—a bit lighter, less messy, and a lot quicker to prepare. Now that would be comforting indeed.

I'm not the first to think shepherd's pie needs an overhaul, and the most common shortcut is to use ground meat. Ground lamb seemed the obvious choice until I learned in *Irish Traditional Cooking* by Darina Allen, godmother of the cuisine, that modern-day shepherd's pie in Ireland is almost always made with beef. Since beef is more popular in the United States, ground beef it would be. But it took me only one test to realize that I couldn't simply swap out chunks of meat for the ground kind; the two don't cook the same way. Searing chunks produces tender meat with a lovely brown crust. Ground beef, on the other hand, has so much surface area that it gives up considerably more moisture as it cooks. The result: nubbly, dry crumbles that don't brown well. No thanks. I skipped browning the meat and moved on to the vegetables.

I added onions and carrots and let them soften a bit, then I added flour to help thicken the cooking liquid into a sauce. I stirred in herbs along with some beef broth and let the whole thing simmer and reduce while I cooked and mashed the potatoes. I transferred the filling to a baking dish and—thinking I was simplifying things—ditched my piping bag. Instead, I spread the potatoes on top with a rubber spatula, which turned out to be both messy and difficult because the soupy filling conspired against me. Finally, I placed the pie in the oven to crisp the top.

Had my aim been to re-create the shepherd's pie served on budget airlines or in hospitals, I could have called this a success. The meat, even unbrowned, was chewy; the carrots were cooked to mush; and the "gravy" tasted pretty much like what it was: thickened canned beef broth.

Fortunately, I had an idea to improve the meat's texture. We recently discovered that treating pork with baking soda tenderizes the meat by raising its pH. Hoping to achieve the same effect here, I stirred ½ teaspoon of baking soda and 2 tablespoons of water (to help it distribute evenly) into the raw ground meat and let the mixture rest while I prepared the mashed potatoes. That did the trick, rendering the meat soft and tender.

On to beefing up the filling's lackluster flavor. Since my gravy wasn't benefiting from fond lent by browning the meat, I looked to other options. An approach to vegetarian gravy looked promising: Cook onions and mushrooms in a skillet with a little fat over fairly high heat until they're deep brown and a fond starts to form in the pan; then stir in tomato paste and garlic and allow the fond to get quite dark. I tried this method, deglazing the pan with some fortified wine (ordinary red wine required me to use so much it left the sauce boozy). Then I added flour and, when the mixture was very deeply browned, fresh thyme and a bay leaf, followed by beef broth and Worcestershire sauce. I was rewarded with a sauce that boasted rich color and savory depth.

With my sauce bubbling and thick, I added 1½ pounds of ground beef and let it simmer, covered, for roughly 10 minutes, lifting the lid once during cooking to stir. That's when I noticed the pools of grease exuded by the meat. One downside of not browning the meat was that I had no opportunity to pour off its fat. I wondered if switching from 85 percent lean ground beef (the test kitchen's usual choice) to 93 percent lean beef would help. Happily, the leaner beef stayed moist and tender, thanks to the baking soda treatment, and only a few tiny pools of fat remained. To get rid of these, I first tried adding more flour, but mixed in so late in the process, it tasted raw and starchy. Happily, stirring in a slurry of cornstarch and water took care of the problem nicely.

As for the spuds, the recipe I'd been using calls for a full stick of butter and 1 cup of half-and-half—not exactly the lighter approach I was going for. I halved the butter and subbed milk for the half-and-half. To ensure that the mashed potatoes would have enough structure to form a crust, I also decreased the dairy by 50 percent and added an egg yolk.

For convenience, I wanted to finish my pie right in the skillet. But I still had to figure out how to spread the solid potatoes over the soupy mixture. I decided to give piping another go, but I eschewed my fancy pastry bag and star tip for a simple zipper-lock bag with a corner cut off. Depositing the potatoes onto the filling from above was far easier than trying to spread them over a wet base. Once they were in place, I smoothed them with the back of a spoon and traced ridges in them with a fork so they'd get really crusty under the broiler.

One problem remained: The browned, crispy potato topping certainly looked appealing, but its flavor paled in comparison with the robust filling. Looking to add some pizzazz, I scoured some Irish cookbooks, and a recipe for champ, Ireland's simple mixture of mashed potatoes and chopped scallions, caught my attention. Stirring a handful of chopped scallion greens into my own mash freshened the whole dish without adding heft.

With its simmered lean ground beef, rich but not heavy gravy, and lighter, fresher mash, my updated shepherd's pie was not just faster to make than the traditional version but also less guilt-inducing—and still every bit as delicious. At last, comfort food that even the cook could enjoy.

—ANDREA GEARY, *Cook's Illustrated*

SHEPHERD'S PIE

Shepherd's Pie

SERVES 4 TO 6

Don't use ground beef that's fattier than 93 percent or the dish will be greasy.

- 1½ pounds 93 percent lean ground beef
- 2 tablespoons plus 2 teaspoons water
-   Salt and pepper
- ½ teaspoon baking soda
- 2½ pounds russet potatoes, peeled and cut into 1-inch chunks
- 4 tablespoons unsalted butter, melted
- ½ cup milk
- 1 large egg yolk
- 8 scallions, green parts only, sliced thin
- 2 teaspoons vegetable oil
- 1 onion, chopped
- 4 ounces white mushrooms, trimmed and chopped
- 1 tablespoon tomato paste
- 2 garlic cloves, minced
- 2 tablespoons Madeira or ruby port
- 2 tablespoons all-purpose flour
- 1¼ cups beef broth
- 2 teaspoons Worcestershire sauce
- 2 sprigs fresh thyme
- 1 bay leaf
- 2 carrots, peeled and chopped
- 2 teaspoons cornstarch

1. Toss beef with 2 tablespoons water, 1 teaspoon salt, ¼ teaspoon pepper, and baking soda in bowl until thoroughly combined. Set aside for 20 minutes.

2. Meanwhile, place potatoes in medium saucepan; add water to just cover and 1 tablespoon salt. Bring to boil over high heat. Reduce heat to medium-low and simmer until potatoes are soft and tip of paring knife inserted into potato meets no resistance, 8 to 10 minutes. Drain potatoes and return to saucepan. Return saucepan to low heat and cook, shaking pot occasionally, until any surface moisture on potatoes has evaporated, about 1 minute. Remove pan from heat and mash potatoes well or press through ricer set over pan. Stir in melted butter. Whisk together milk and egg yolk in small bowl, then stir into potatoes. Stir in scallion greens and season with salt and pepper to taste. Cover and set aside.

3. Heat oil in broiler-safe 10-inch skillet over medium heat until shimmering. Add onion, mushrooms, ½ teaspoon salt, and ¼ teaspoon pepper; cook, stirring occasionally,

NOTES FROM THE TEST KITCHEN

THE BEST POTATO RICER

For perfectly smooth and fluffy mashed potatoes, a ricer is a must-have tool. The best models require little muscle power and produce a uniform texture. Our favorite, the **RSVP International Potato Ricer**, $13.95, boasts a smart rectangular design with surprisingly sturdy handles, allowing us to process pounds of spuds neatly, easily, and efficiently. Its interchangeable disks deliver a range of fine to coarse textures, and its sturdy hook rests securely on a pot rim.

THE BEST BEEF BROTH

To find out if any supermarket beef broths could provide a suitable stand-in for homemade, we tasted 13 different broths, stocks, and bases plain and in French onion soup and gravy.

Two brands were voted beefiest of the bunch. College Inn Bold Stock Tender Beef Flavor offered "robust flavor" and tasted "nicely beefy," but a quick scan of the label revealed a list of nearly 20 ingredients, many of them processed additives. Our winner, **Rachael Ray Stock-in-a-Box All-Natural Beef Flavored Stock**, took a different approach, relying on a much shorter roster of ingredients. It includes concentrated beef stock, a pile of vegetables, and just one processed additive, yeast extract (which amplifies flavor like salt, but without the straight-up salty flavor). This stock elicited consistent praise from tasters, who found it to have "steak-y," "rich" flavor and "thick, gelatin-like body."

until vegetables are just starting to soften and dark bits form on bottom of skillet, 4 to 6 minutes. Stir in tomato paste and garlic; cook until bottom of skillet is dark brown, about 2 minutes. Add Madeira and cook, scraping up any browned bits, until evaporated, about 1 minute. Stir in flour and cook for 1 minute. Add broth, Worcestershire, thyme, bay leaf, and carrots; bring to boil, scraping up any browned bits. Reduce heat to medium-low, add beef in 2-inch chunks to broth, and bring to gentle simmer. Cover and cook until beef is cooked through, 10 to 12 minutes, stirring and breaking up meat chunks with 2 forks halfway through. Stir cornstarch and remaining 2 teaspoons water together in bowl. Stir cornstarch mixture into filling and continue to simmer for 30 seconds. Remove thyme and bay leaf. Season with salt and pepper to taste.

4. Adjust oven rack 5 inches from broiler element and heat broiler. Place mashed potatoes in large zipper-lock bag and snip off 1 corner to create 1-inch opening. Pipe potatoes in even layer over filling, making sure to cover entire surface. Smooth potatoes with back of spoon, then use tines of fork to make ridges over surface. Place skillet in rimmed baking sheet and broil until potatoes are golden brown and crusty and filling is bubbly, 10 to 15 minutes. Let cool for 10 minutes before serving.

NATCHITOCHES MEAT PIES

✅ **WHY THIS RECIPE WORKS** Similar to Latin American empanadas, these deep-fried hand pies from Louisiana are filled with savory ground meat and spices. For the filling, we used equal parts ground beef and pork along with the classic Creole combination of onions, green bell peppers, and a pinch of cayenne for heat. Chicken broth and flour made the filling cohesive, and scallions added freshness. Using chicken broth rather than milk in the dough gave the crust a subtle savory flavor. To assemble the pies, we simply rolled the dough out into circles, spooned on the filling, and folded the dough over into a half-moon shape, sealing the edges. After a few minutes in hot oil, they emerged with a crisp, flaky crust and piping-hot filling.

New Orleans is one of the best food towns in America, so why on a recent trip to the region did I find myself driving away from the city in search of a recipe? Three words: Natchitoches meat pies. Wrapped in dough with a texture sturdier than pie crust but flakier than pizza dough, these half-moon-shaped, hand-held, simply seasoned turnovers are filled with ground beef, pork, or both and then deep-fried. They are deeply delicious.

In search of Natchitoches ("NACK-uh-dish") meat pies, I had flown from Boston to New Orleans and then zipped along Louisiana highways and bayous, on a 250-mile drive to the city of Natchitoches, which sits near the Texas border. It's the oldest permanent settlement in Louisiana and the star of the 1980s movie *Steel Magnolias*. Nice, but I wasn't interested in stars; I was there to eat and evaluate, in order to engineer my own meat pies back in the test kitchen.

Culinary historians argue about the origins of these fried turnovers, but no one disputes that in the late 1960s, James Lasyone revived their popularity at Lasyone's Meat Pie Restaurant. Today his daughter Angela runs the place, so that's where I headed. Soon I

was sitting inside with a hot meat pie before me, Angela across the table, and James's original cast-iron frying pot on the sideboard. I paused to savor the moment and breathe in the pie's fragrant steam. Then I made quick work of it—but not without noting the meat pie's yellow-tinged, crackery crust; rich, stewlike filling; and whisper of heat. Angela told me enough to tantalize without giving away her secrets: The filling was 80 percent beef and 20 percent pork and included chopped onions and green peppers.

Natchitoches meat pies are also sold at gas stations all over town, I soon discovered. Don't bother. But if you run into the exceptionally generous Gay Melder, you're in luck. Every December, she makes hundreds of meat pies for the town's annual Christmas festival, and she was willing to show me how. In her kitchen, she eyeballed the measurements for both filling and dough and then organized her visiting friends and family (and me) into an assembly line to form the pies; in short order, we had a growing pile. Gay slipped the meat pies into shimmering oil to fry, and some 15 minutes later they were ready to taste. The crust was delicate and flaky, the filling moist and well seasoned. But that doesn't begin to do them justice; these pies were much more than the sum of their parts. Could I ever do as well?

Back in the test kitchen the following week, I had to quantify and foolproof what Gay did by instinct. For starters, I'd need to pin down her instructions to add "just enough" flour and to salt generously until I thought I'd "ruined it." Plus, I was willing to bet that no other home outside Louisiana had the customized meat-pie-crimping appliance that Gay owned, so instructions for forming the pies were in order. I'd bring to bear all my test kitchen expertise so that even meat pie novices (like me) could pull off the recipe.

Like Gay, I started with equal amounts of ground pork and beef—not too lean, she had warned. Following her instructions, I sautéed the meat with the onion, green pepper, garlic, and scallion whites (I reserved the greens to add at the end for a fresh, mild, oniony hit). I drained off and discarded most of the meat juices, as I'd seen her do. And finally I thickened the filling with flour and seasoned it with salt, pepper, and cayenne. To simplify the dough, I used the food processor, first mixing flour, salt, and baking powder; then cutting in the shortening; and finally adding eggs and milk. It was an unusual dough, like a cross between pastry and pasta dough. Gay's had been sturdy, smooth, and slightly glossy, so I aimed for the same. I rolled out balls of dough, filled and crimped meat pies by hand, and dropped them into hot oil. In 10 minutes they were golden brown.

But this first attempt missed the mark. The filling was crumbly, the meat pebbly and overcooked, and the flavor flat. To buttress the flavor, I relied on the test kitchen's full repertoire of techniques. I sautéed the cayenne in fat at the start to unlock its flavor. I added chicken broth to reinforce the filling's savory flavor. And I retained the meat juices and succulent fat to take advantage of their flavor, too. Finally, I discovered that the pies were better if I sautéed the meat and vegetables sequentially. This way, the vegetables browned in the meat drippings rather than steaming with the browning meat.

At this point, I ran into a piece of luck: The dry, pebbly meat situation resolved itself. Since I'd removed the browned meat from the pan, it couldn't overcook while waiting for the onion and green pepper to soften.

My changes also had an unfortunate side effect, though. The added broth and meat juices made the filling less cohesive than ever. To fix it, I simply added more flour. Bad move—unless you like the taste of raw flour. I needed more flour but less flour taste. For my next test, instead of adding it at the end, I sautéed it with the meat to cook out its raw taste. The pies were much better for it.

I was proud of my filling, so I got to work on the dough. There wasn't much room for improvement (though not for lack of testing). Even swapping the shortening for butter, which we *Cook's Country* natives normally can't live without, was a mistake in this dough; when I tried it, the meat pies' superlative tenderness vanished. In the end, I made just one small change, and it happened almost by chance: One afternoon, I had some chicken broth left over from making the filling. On a hunch, I used it in place of the milk in the dough. It made the most tender and flavorful crust yet.

I consolidated everything I'd learned into one last batch and then set out a platter of beautiful Natchitoches meat pies for my coworkers. The filling was thick, rich, and cohesive, they said, the dough tender and savory. Against all odds, these deep-fried, meat-stuffed pies tasted subtle, even delicate. A good cook's intuition, which Gay had in spades, is hard to capture on paper, and when I'd tasted her meat pies in Natchitoches, I'd feared I never would. Now I realized that I hadn't messed much with perfection. I'd just spread the news.

—REBECCAH MARSTERS, *Cook's Country*

Natchitoches Meat Pies
MAKES 16 PIES

You can make the dough and the filling up to 24 hours ahead and refrigerate them separately. You can also shape and fill the pies, then refrigerate them for up to 24 hours before frying. You will need at least a 6-quart Dutch oven for this recipe.

FILLING
- 5 teaspoons vegetable oil
- ¾ pound 85 percent lean ground beef
- ¾ pound ground pork
  Salt and pepper
- 1 onion, chopped fine
- 1 green bell pepper, stemmed, seeded, and minced
- 6 scallions, white parts minced, green parts sliced thin
- 3 garlic cloves, minced
- ¼ teaspoon cayenne pepper
- 2 tablespoons all-purpose flour
- 1 cup chicken broth

DOUGH
- 4 cups (20 ounces) all-purpose flour
- 2 teaspoons salt
- 1 teaspoon baking powder
- 8 tablespoons vegetable shortening, cut into ½-inch pieces
- 1 cup chicken broth
- 2 large eggs, lightly beaten

- 1 quart vegetable oil for frying

1. FOR THE FILLING: Heat 2 teaspoons oil in 12-inch skillet over medium-high heat until just smoking. Add beef, pork, 1 teaspoon salt, and ½ teaspoon pepper and cook, breaking up pieces with spoon, until no longer pink, 8 to 10 minutes. Transfer meat to bowl.

2. Add remaining 1 tablespoon oil to now-empty skillet and heat over medium-high heat until shimmering. Add onion, bell pepper, scallion whites, ½ teaspoon salt, and ½ teaspoon pepper and cook until vegetables are just starting to brown, 3 to 5 minutes. Stir in garlic and cayenne and cook until fragrant, about 30 seconds.

3. Return meat and any accumulated juices to skillet with vegetables. Sprinkle flour over meat and cook, stirring constantly, until evenly coated, about 1 minute. Add broth, bring to boil, and cook until slightly thickened, about 3 minutes. Transfer filling to bowl and stir in scallion greens. Refrigerate until completely cool, about 1 hour. (Filling can be refrigerated for up to 24 hours.)

4. FOR THE DOUGH: Process flour, salt, and baking powder in food processor until combined, about 3 seconds. Add shortening and pulse until mixture resembles coarse cornmeal, 6 to 8 pulses. Add broth and eggs and pulse until dough just comes together, about 5 pulses. Transfer dough to lightly floured counter and knead until dough forms smooth ball, about 20 seconds. Divide dough into 16 equal pieces. (Dough can be covered and refrigerated for up to 24 hours.)

5. Line rimmed baking sheet with parchment paper. Working with 1 piece of dough at a time, roll into 6-inch circle on lightly floured counter. Place ¼ cup filling in center of dough round. Brush edges of dough with water and fold dough over filling. Press to seal, trim any ragged edges, and crimp edges with tines of fork.

NOTES FROM THE TEST KITCHEN

SEALING MEAT PIES

1. Brush edges of each round with water and fold 1 side over filling to form half-moon. For tidy pies, trim edges with pastry wheel.

2. Use tines of fork to make decorative crimp that tightly seals pie.

DON'T OVERSTUFF THE PIES

Be sure to roll dough into 6-inch rounds and fill each meat pie using ¼-cup measure. If meat pies are overstuffed, they may rupture and leak filling out into hot frying oil.

Transfer to prepared sheet. (Filled pies can be covered and refrigerated for up to 24 hours.)

6. Adjust oven rack to middle position and heat oven to 200 degrees. Set wire rack in second rimmed baking sheet. Add up to 1 quart oil to large Dutch oven until it measures about ¾ inch deep and heat over medium-high heat to 350 degrees. Place 4 pies in oil and fry until golden brown, 3 to 5 minutes per side, using slotted spatula or spider to flip. Adjust burner, if necessary, to maintain oil temperature between 325 and 350 degrees. Transfer pies to prepared wire rack and place in oven to keep warm. Return oil to 350 degrees and repeat with remaining pies. Serve.

GRILL-ROASTED BEEF SHORT RIBS

WHY THIS RECIPE WORKS To transform beef short ribs from cold-weather fare to a summer staple, we wanted to use the grill to give them smoky flavor and good char. We first seasoned the ribs with a simple spice rub and some bright red wine vinegar. To ensure that the ribs cooked evenly, we jump-started them in the oven in a foil-covered baking dish. As they cooked, their fat rendered and their tough, chewy collagen was transformed into moisture-retaining gelatin. When they were nearly done, we headed out to the grill to finish our ribs over the fire, basting them with a flavorful glaze until they developed a dark, lacquered crust.

I usually reserve buying short ribs for the winter months. It's a great time of year to let the moist heat and long, slow cooking of a braise do what they do best: convert this cut's abundant collagen into gelatin, which coats the protein fibers and makes the ribs meltingly tender. But this summer, while casting around at the meat counter for something new and different to grill, my eyes landed on short ribs. I wondered why I shouldn't take this supremely flavorful cut, which happens to have more meat on it than almost any other rib around, to the grill instead of the same old steak or burger. I was envisioning tender ribs with a little bit of chew and a nicely browned, crusty exterior. And to distinguish my grilled short ribs from your typical slab of barbecued ribs, I'd skip the barbecue sauce in favor of a bold spice rub and a sweet-tart glaze that would balance their richness.

My first decision to make: bone-in or boneless ribs? I purchased some of each and, leaving the glaze aside for the moment, mixed up a fragrant spice rub of salt, pepper, cayenne, ground cumin, and ground fennel. For good measure, I also threw in two ingredients commonly used in pork-rib rubs: garlic powder and brown sugar.

To ensure that the ribs' collagen had sufficient time to melt, I built a low-temperature indirect fire, placing some unlit briquettes on the grill grid and covering them with hot coals to generate a fire that would burn steadily for several hours. I sprinkled both batches of ribs with my rub and arranged them on the cooler side of the grates to grill-roast, occasionally rotating and flipping them until both were tender, about 4 hours later. But when I brought in both platters of ribs for tasting, my colleagues frowned. Instead of being beautifully marbled slabs, the boneless ribs had shrunk and blackened to unappealing briquettes.

What had happened? Well, without a bone to insulate the meat from the heat of the grill, the boneless samples simply shriveled up and dried out. But if I'd pulled the ribs off the grill any sooner, the collagen wouldn't have broken down and they'd have been tough. Clearly boneless ribs were out. Though far from perfect, the bone-in ribs at least had a fighting chance at still having a juicy, tender interior by the time a crisp crust had formed.

Now I just needed to figure out how to improve the texture of the bone-in ribs, which, among other problems, weren't cooking evenly. Although I'd flipped them every 30 minutes or so during cooking, there were still small pockets of unrendered fat, and some ribs were definitely more tender than others. The problem was that in order to render its fat and become tender, meat needs to reach a temperature hot enough for the tough collagen to start to melt (140 to 165 degrees). But if the meat gets too hot, so much moisture burns off that it becomes dry and jerkylike. To make matters worse, even a carefully monitored grill inevitably produces hot and cold spots, so the results within a single batch of ribs can be dramatically different. Maintaining a steady, perfectly consistent grill temperature is a near-impossible feat, and let's face it: Even die-hard grillers don't want to fuss for hours on end, rearranging meat, opening and closing vents, and adding hot coals.

It was clear that to make this work, I was going to need a more controlled environment. I would have to bring the ribs indoors to cook partway in the oven, where even heating is effortless and temperature adjustment is as easy as turning a dial. I hoped that by finishing the ribs on the grill I'd get the substantial charred crust and the smoky flavor I was after.

For my first test in the oven, I rubbed three batches of ribs with my spice rub, sprinkled them with a little red wine vinegar to cut the richness, covered them with foil (so the ribs would cook more quickly and evenly), and slid the pans into 300-degree ovens until the ribs hit 140, 165, and 175 degrees, respectively (80, 105, and 120 minutes later). Then I moved the operation outside to slowly finish each batch on the grill. When the ribs were dark and crusty an hour and a half later, I called my tasters for lunch.

The results were clear: The ribs pulled from the oven at 140 degrees were rubbery—obviously still packed with collagen. On the other hand, so much collagen had broken down in the 175-degree batch that the meat had a shredded pot roast–like texture. In the middle, the 165-degree ribs boasted tender meat that sliced neatly.

To find a foolproof indicator of doneness, I made another batch of ribs, standing grillside after they had been on the fire for an hour while evaluating the meat's texture and taking its temperature at regular intervals. One hundred ninety-five degrees turned out to be the magic number for the finished meat: Intramuscular fat had completely melted and most of the collagen had broken down, turning the meat tender—but not so much so that it disintegrated at the touch of a fork.

With my ribs tender and evenly cooked, I moved on to create a few glazes. The red wine vinegar that I had added to the ribs before baking tempered their fattiness somewhat, but they would still benefit from some tangy flavors. I started with a classic Dijon mustard and brown sugar mixture, then came up with a fruity blackberry and bourbon variation. Finally, hoisin and tamarind took center stage in an Asian-inspired version.

To achieve a substantial lacquered crust, I brushed the ribs every time I rotated them on the grill. This allowed each layer of glaze to dry out and give the subsequent layer a base to which it could adhere. It was a bit of hands-on work, but any doubt I had that it was worth the trouble was erased when tasters devoured the latest batch before I could even get my hands on one rib.

With meaty, finger-licking results like these, I'd no longer wait for the dead of winter to make short ribs. In fact, they are now at the top of the list for my next summer cookout.

—LAN LAM, *Cook's Illustrated*

Grill-Roasted Beef Short Ribs

SERVES 4 TO 6

Make sure to choose ribs that are 4 to 6 inches in length and have at least 1 inch of meat on top of the bone.

SPICE RUB

- 2 tablespoons kosher salt
- 1 tablespoon packed brown sugar
- 2 teaspoons pepper
- 2 teaspoons ground cumin
- 2 teaspoons garlic powder
- 1¼ teaspoons paprika
- ¾ teaspoon ground fennel
- ⅛ teaspoon cayenne pepper

SHORT RIBS

- 5 pounds bone-in English-style beef short ribs, trimmed
- 2 tablespoons red wine vinegar
- 1 recipe glaze (recipes follow)

1. FOR THE SPICE RUB: Combine all ingredients in bowl. Measure out 1 teaspoon rub and set aside for glaze.

2. FOR THE SHORT RIBS: Adjust oven rack to middle position and heat oven to 300 degrees. Sprinkle ribs with spice rub, pressing into all sides of ribs. Arrange ribs, bone side down, in 13 by 9-inch baking dish, placing thicker ribs around perimeter of baking dish and thinner ribs in center. Sprinkle vinegar evenly over ribs. Cover baking dish tightly with aluminum foil. Bake until thickest ribs register 165 to 170 degrees, 1½ to 2 hours.

3A. FOR A CHARCOAL GRILL: Open bottom vent halfway. Arrange 2 quarts unlit charcoal into steeply banked pile against 1 side of grill. Light large chimney starter half filled with charcoal (3 quarts). When top coals are partially covered with ash, pour on top of unlit charcoal to cover one-third of grill with coals steeply banked against side of grill. Set cooking grate in place, cover, and open lid vent halfway. Heat grill until hot, about 5 minutes.

3B. FOR A GAS GRILL: Turn all burners to high, cover, and heat grill until hot, about 15 minutes. Leave primary burner on medium and turn off other burner(s). Adjust primary burner as needed to maintain grill temperature of 275 to 300 degrees.

4. Clean and oil cooking grate. Place short ribs, bone side down, on cooler side of grill about 2 inches from flames. Brush with ¼ cup glaze. Cover and cook until ribs register 195 degrees, 1¾ to 2¼ hours, rotating and brushing ribs with ¼ cup glaze every 30 minutes. Transfer ribs to large platter, tent loosely with foil, and let rest for 5 to 10 minutes before serving.

Mustard Glaze

MAKES ABOUT 1 CUP

- ½ cup Dijon mustard
- ½ cup red wine vinegar
- ¼ cup packed brown sugar
- 1 teaspoon reserved spice rub
- ⅛ teaspoon cayenne pepper

Whisk all ingredients together in bowl.

Blackberry Glaze

MAKES ABOUT 1 CUP

- 10 ounces (2 cups) fresh or frozen blackberries
- ½ cup ketchup
- ¼ cup bourbon
- 2 tablespoons packed brown sugar
- 1½ tablespoons soy sauce
- 1 teaspoon reserved spice rub
- ⅛ teaspoon cayenne pepper

Bring all ingredients to simmer in small saucepan over medium-high heat. Simmer, stirring frequently to break up blackberries, until reduced to 1¼ cups, about 10 minutes. Strain through fine-mesh strainer, pressing on solids to extract as much liquid as possible. Discard solids.

Hoisin-Tamarind Glaze

MAKES ABOUT 1 CUP

- 1 cup water
- ⅓ cup hoisin sauce
- ¼ cup tamarind paste
- 1 (2-inch) piece ginger, peeled and sliced into ½-inch-thick rounds
- 1 teaspoon reserved spice rub
- ⅛ teaspoon cayenne pepper

Bring all ingredients to simmer in small saucepan over medium-high heat. Simmer, stirring frequently, until reduced to 1¼ cups, about 10 minutes. Strain through fine-mesh strainer, pressing on solids to extract as much liquid as possible. Discard solids.

MODERN BEEF BURGUNDY

✔ **WHY THIS RECIPE WORKS** We wanted to update the French classic *boeuf bourguignon* to get tender braised beef napped in a silky sauce with bold red wine flavor—without all the work that traditional recipes require. To eliminate the time-consuming step of searing the beef, we cooked the stew uncovered in a roasting pan in the oven so that the exposed meat browned as it braised. This method worked so well that we used the oven, rather than the stovetop, to also render the salt pork and to caramelize the traditional mushroom and pearl onion garnish. Salting the beef before cooking and adding some anchovy paste and porcini mushrooms enhanced the meaty savoriness of the dish without making our recipe too fussy.

Julia Child once wrote that *boeuf bourguignon* "is the best beef stew known to man," and I'm inclined to agree. This hearty braise, arguably one of the most defining dishes in French cuisine, is the ultimate example of how rich, savory, and satisfying a beef stew can be. By gently simmering chunks of well-marbled meat in beef stock and a good amount of red wine, you end up with fork-tender beef and a braising liquid that's transformed into a silky, full-bodied sauce. The result is equally suitable for a Sunday-night supper or an elegant dinner party.

The problem is, boeuf bourguignon is a pain to make. Most recipes, Child's included, come with a serious time commitment: roughly 40 minutes of browning bacon lardons and batch-searing beef, in addition to the lengthy braising time. Then there's the "garnish"—in this case not a quick embellishment but an integral element—of pearl onions and button mushrooms, which are cooked separately and added to the stew toward the end of cooking. The combination of all three is enough to deter most of us busy home cooks from attempting the dish even on weekends, which is a shame. But what if there was a way to revise the old-school technique, eliminating some of the fuss while staying true to this stew's bold, sumptuous profile? I couldn't resist trying.

The classic bourguignon formula goes something like this: Crisp strips of salt pork in a Dutch oven, sear the beef in batches, sprinkle it with flour, and toss it over the heat to create a sauce-thickening roux.

Then add a few cups of beef stock, a bottle of wine, some tomato paste, and aromatics (onions, garlic, herbs, and peppercorns); bring the pot to a boil; cover it; and set it in a low (325-degree) oven to simmer until the meat is tender and the sauce is full-bodied and lush. That takes a good 3 hours, during which time you make the "garnish" by browning and braising the onions in one pan and lightly sautéing the mushrooms in another. When the meat is done, the sauce gets strained and reduced, and the vegetables join the pot just before serving.

I decided to start my testing with the original and see where I could pare down. I also incorporated a couple of tweaks from past test kitchen recipes for beef stew: salting the meat (well-marbled chuck-eye roast is our go-to for stews) for 30 minutes to season it and help it retain moisture during cooking, and beefing up the lackluster commercial broth with umami enhancers (I chose anchovy paste and porcini mushrooms). To build body, I added a couple of packets of powdered gelatin; when stirred into the braising liquid, it mimicked the rich, glossy consistency of from-scratch stock made from gelatin-rich beef bones.

I'd be lying if I said the stew didn't taste beefy and sumptuous. But, as predicted, I'd hovered at the stove for well over 30 minutes, and all that searing had produced a greasy mess. My knee-jerk reaction was to try something drastic, so I started another batch, this time ditching the browning step altogether. Unsurprisingly, it was a flop; sure, it cut the active work time way back, but without all those complex flavors that develop during browning (known as the Maillard reaction), the sauce was downright dull.

Fortunately, I had another idea to try, based on a discovery that we made a few years back: Given enough time, braised meat can develop color if the pieces are not fully submerged in liquid, because its exposed surface will eventually reach 300 degrees—the temperature at which meat begins to brown. To see if this technique would work here, I proceeded with another test, placing the raw meat chunks on top of the aromatics so that they rested above the liquid. After 3 hours in the oven, the meat looked almost seared, and my tasters attested to its savoriness. But they wanted even more flavorful browning. The liquid covered too much of the meat to generate sufficient browning.

Then it occurred to me to try moving my dish to a roasting pan; it would be deep enough to contain the stew, but thanks to its generous surface area, the braising liquid would pool less deeply, exposing more of the beef chunks for better browning. When I tried it, the result was better than I'd expected: The tops of the meat chunks took on lots of color, and that rich browning flavor seeped into the sauce. (Defatting and reducing the sauce on the stove were still necessary, but with the searing step gone it didn't seem too much to ask.)

I was so pleased with my roasting pan technique that I wondered if I could streamline my recipe even further by browning the salt pork in the roasting pan before I added the beef. This, too, turned out to be easy. By initially cranking up the oven to 500 degrees, I mimicked the stove's searing heat and got the pork pieces good and crispy. I also realized that the salt pork could serve as a platform for the beef chunks to sit on as they cooked, raising them even higher out of the liquid and encouraging more browning. And since I was going for the meatiest flavor I could get, I tossed in the trimmed beef scraps and browned them with the salt pork.

Now that the oven was doing most of the flavor development work for me, I wanted to pare down the time-consuming garnish steps, too. Cooking the mushrooms and pearl onions separately from the stew was already asking a lot, to say nothing of the good hour that I spent browning and braising the onions to get them good and caramelized. I tried simply tossing the vegetables into the stew, but the spongy, bland result was a nonstarter. Instead, I spread the onions and mushrooms on a baking sheet with a pat of butter and slid the sheet onto the lower oven rack while the salt pork and beef scraps cooked above in the roasting pan. Stirred once or twice, the vegetables were nicely glazed by the time the pork and beef scraps were rendered. Tossing the vegetables with a bit of sugar before roasting deepened their caramelized color and flavor.

The only matter left unattended? After cooking, the wine flavor was falling a little flat. Adding part of another bottle to the braising liquid seemed extravagant, and the flavor wasn't much better. A more successful— and economical—solution was to reserve part of the wine and add it just before the final reduction of the sauce, which left the flavor noticeably brighter.

I had no doubt that my mostly hands-off method was considerably less fussy than classic recipes, but just how much time had I trimmed? I went back to my notes to see how long it had taken me to make Julia Child's boeuf bourguignon recipe. Turns out that I'd saved a very respectable 45 minutes. What's more, the flavors of the stews were remarkably similar.

An almost entirely hands-off boeuf bourguignon that tasted just as rich and complex as the classic version? The thought was almost as satisfying as the stew itself.

—ANDREW JANJIGIAN, *Cook's Illustrated*

Modern Beef Burgundy

SERVES 6 TO 8

If the pearl onions have a papery outer coating, remove it by rinsing the onions in warm water and gently squeezing individual onions between your fingertips. Two minced anchovy fillets can be used in place of the anchovy paste. To save time, salt the meat and let it stand while you prep the remaining ingredients. Serve with mashed potatoes or buttered noodles.

- 1 (4-pound) boneless beef chuck-eye roast, trimmed and cut into 1½- to 2-inch pieces, scraps reserved
  Salt and pepper
- 6 ounces salt pork, cut into ¼-inch pieces
- 3 tablespoons unsalted butter
- 1 pound cremini mushrooms, trimmed, halved if medium or quartered if large
- 1½ cups frozen pearl onions, thawed
- 1 tablespoon sugar
- ⅓ cup all-purpose flour
- 4 cups beef broth
- 1 (750-ml) bottle red Burgundy or Pinot Noir
- 5 teaspoons unflavored gelatin
- 1 tablespoon tomato paste
- 1 teaspoon anchovy paste
- 2 onions, chopped coarse
- 2 carrots, peeled and cut into 2-inch lengths
- 1 garlic head, cloves separated, unpeeled, and crushed
- 2 bay leaves
- ½ teaspoon black peppercorns
- ½ ounce dried porcini mushrooms, rinsed
- 10 sprigs fresh parsley, plus 3 tablespoons minced
- 6 sprigs fresh thyme

1. Toss beef and 1½ teaspoons salt together in bowl and let stand at room temperature for 30 minutes.

2. Adjust oven racks to lower-middle and lowest positions and heat oven to 500 degrees. Place salt pork, beef scraps, and 2 tablespoons butter in large roasting pan. Roast on lower-middle rack until well browned and fat has rendered, 15 to 20 minutes.

3. While salt pork and beef scraps roast, toss cremini mushrooms, pearl onions, remaining 1 tablespoon butter, and sugar together in rimmed baking sheet. Roast on lowest rack, stirring occasionally, until moisture released by mushrooms evaporates and vegetables are lightly glazed, 15 to 20 minutes. Transfer vegetables to large bowl, cover, and refrigerate.

4. Remove roasting pan from oven and reduce temperature to 325 degrees. Sprinkle flour over rendered fat and whisk until no dry flour remains. Whisk in broth, 2 cups wine, gelatin, tomato paste, and anchovy paste until combined. Add onions, carrots, garlic, bay leaves, peppercorns, porcini mushrooms, parsley sprigs, and thyme to pan. Arrange beef in single layer on top of vegetables. Add water as needed to come three-quarters up side of beef (beef should not be submerged). Return roasting pan to oven and cook until meat is tender, 3 to 3½ hours, stirring after 90 minutes and adding water to keep meat at least half-submerged.

5. Using slotted spoon, transfer beef to bowl with cremini mushrooms and pearl onions; cover and set aside. Strain braising liquid through fine-mesh strainer set over large bowl, pressing on solids to extract as much liquid as possible; discard solids. Stir in remaining wine and let cooking liquid settle, 10 minutes. Using wide shallow spoon, skim fat off surface and discard.

6. Transfer liquid to Dutch oven and bring mixture to boil over medium-high heat. Simmer briskly, stirring occasionally, until sauce is thickened to consistency of heavy cream, 15 to 20 minutes. Reduce heat to medium-low, stir in beef and mushroom-onion garnish, cover, and cook until just heated through, 5 to 8 minutes. Season with salt and pepper to taste. Stir in minced parsley. Serve. (Stew can be made up to 3 days in advance.)

PEPPER-CRUSTED BEEF TENDERLOIN ROAST

✓ WHY THIS RECIPE WORKS For a tender, rosy roast with a crunchy, spicy peppercorn crust, we needed a few tricks. Rubbing the raw tenderloin with an abrasive mixture of kosher salt, sugar, and baking soda transformed its surface into a magnet for the pepper crust. In order to tame the heat of the pepper, we simmered cracked peppercorns in oil, then strained out the oil. To replace some of the subtle flavors we had simmered away, we added some orange zest and nutmeg. With the crust in place, we gently roasted the tenderloin in the oven until it was perfectly rosy, then served it with a tangy fruit juice–based sauce to complement the rich beef.

When it comes to special-occasion entrées, it's hard to beat beef tenderloin. It's easy to make—just oven-roast it until it's done—and, as the absolute tenderest cut of beef, it's luxurious to eat.

But that tenderness comes at a cost—and I'm not just talking about the high price it fetches at the butcher's counter. In addition to buttery texture, these roasts are renowned for the relative meekness of their beef flavor. To counter this, they are often dressed up with flavor-packed flourishes. One such enhancement is a pepper crust. In the past I've always used this technique on individual filets mignons, but pepper is such a great complement to beef that I was eager to give it a try on a whole roast.

I knew that the idea had merit as soon as I started digging for recipes: There were dozens. But when I prepared the most promising of the bunch, a number of problems unique to making a pepper-crusted roast revealed themselves. First, I had to tie the roast with kitchen twine to ensure that it cooked evenly from end to end, but when I removed the string, the surrounding peppercorns came with it. More cracked pepper rained down on the carving board as I sliced the roast—even when I used my sharpest carving knife and the gentlest strokes. Worst of all, the peppercorns' crunch was wimpy, but their heat was pungent and lingering. The only good part: the meat itself, which had been gently cooked and, as a result, was juicy and uniformly rosy.

My goal was clear: Create a crunchy crust that stayed put but was not punishingly spicy.

Initially, I drew on prior test kitchen solutions for crusting meat, coating the surface with various sticky substances before packing on the peppercorns. My edible "glues" included a mixture of mayonnaise and gelatin, another of finely grated Parmesan cheese and olive oil, and one that's named for a painter's trick: I "primed" the roast with a dusting of cornstarch before brushing it with foamed egg white.

I immediately dismissed the mayo-gelatin and the cornstarch–egg white combinations; both left an unattractive white residue on the meat. The Parmesan-oil paste fixed the crust beautifully and lent a rich, flavorful punch, but the cheesiness obscured the pepper and beef flavors that I wanted to highlight.

Clearly I needed another idea. I turned to the beef itself, wondering if I might be able to transform its surface into a pepper magnet through mechanical or chemical means. A colleague suggested that I try roughing up its surface with a sandpaper-like mixture of gritty kosher salt enhanced with some baking soda. The latter would raise the beef's pH, in turn triggering enzymes in the meat to dissolve some of the surface proteins, which I hoped would create a tacky exterior. Not wanting to turn the roast's exterior to mush, I kept the volume of baking soda small—only ¼ teaspoon—and skipped any resting time. Sure enough, the surface became sticky after a brief rubdown. I pressed on ½ cup of cracked peppercorns mixed with a few tablespoons of oil. I also sprayed the twine I would use to tie the roast with vegetable oil to keep it from sticking to the meat when I removed it. Finally, I transferred the roast to a 300-degree oven.

This time, the peppercorns held tight to the tenderloin even after slicing, and my tasters applauded the gorgeously crusted roast I served for lunch that day. Until they dug in, that is. Then they winced and reached for water, complaining that the heat was too aggressive now that every bite was loaded with peppercorns.

I needed to bring down the heat level to the point at which it was enhancing rather than overpowering the meat's flavor. To do so, I took a cue from a study funded by the National Institutes of Health that demonstrated that both sugar and citric acid can effectively temper the spiciness of black pepper. For now I tabled the addition of citric acid, imagining tart fruit juices as a good base for an accompanying sauce. Instead I tried mixing a little sugar into the salt rub, and I found that it not only lessened tasters' perception of heat but also enhanced the pepper's more subtle flavors, thus lending more complexity.

PEPPER–CRUSTED BEEF TENDERLOIN ROAST

The sugar hadn't tamed the heat enough, though, so I turned to an approach that the test kitchen has used in other such situations: simmering the cracked pepper in oil. We've found this is an effective way to mellow piperine, the flavor compound responsible for peppercorns' pungency. But as I did some further reading, I learned that piperine is also soluble in alcohol and acid, which inspired my next test. I simmered a batch of peppercorns in each of the three liquids (using neutral-flavored vodka for the alcohol test and white vinegar for the acid test), drained away the spicy liquids, then mixed the tamed pepper with fresh oil (to help the crust stick).

Tasters' universal verdict: All three methods were highly successful at mellowing the heat, but the vodka gave the meat a boozy taste and the vinegar turned it unappealingly gray. The oil-simmered peppercorns, on the other hand, lent a pleasant spiciness without generating any off-flavors or negatively affecting the meat's appearance.

That said, the toned-down heat came at a cost. Simmering the peppercorns in oil had diminished not only their spiciness but also the nuanced piney and floral flavors that contributed much to making this dish so good. Essentially, I'd been pitching the best part of the peppercorns into the trash.

Looking for a way to restore these flavors, I did more digging and discovered some interesting information. It turns out that three of the main flavor compounds in peppercorns—sabinene, pinene, and limonene—are also found in high concentrations in the oil in orange zest (95 percent limonene) and nutmeg (58 percent pinene and sabinene). Intrigued, I tried adding both to the rub. Sure enough, mixing a tablespoon of zest and ½ teaspoon of ground nutmeg with the simmered and drained peppercorns hit the mark, restoring a balance of flavors that made the crust taste more like, well, pepper. Now my crust was both boldly flavored and balanced.

At last I was ready for the final flourish: a tangy fruit juice–based sauce. Since I was already using orange zest, I figured I'd squeeze the juice as well and combine it with some red wine, beef broth, and other pantry staples for a complex-tasting finish. For a little variety, I also mixed up a version with pomegranate juice and port. Both sauces were hits with my tasters, their fruity tang complementing and slightly tempering the peppercorns' aromatic, toasty heat—not to mention they gussied up this luxe cut enough to qualify as holiday dinner-party fare.

—CELESTE ROGERS, *Cook's Illustrated*

Pepper-Crusted Beef Tenderloin Roast
SERVES 10 TO 12

If your pepper mill does not produce a coarse grind, place 2 tablespoons of peppercorns on a cutting board and rock the bottom edge of a skillet or pot over the peppercorns until they crack. Serve with Red Wine–Orange Sauce or Pomegranate-Port Sauce (recipes follow).

- 4½ teaspoons kosher salt
- 1½ teaspoons sugar
- ¼ teaspoon baking soda
- 9 tablespoons olive oil
- ½ cup coarsely cracked black peppercorns
- 1 tablespoon finely grated orange zest
- ½ teaspoon ground nutmeg
- 1 (6-pound) whole beef tenderloin, trimmed

1. Adjust oven rack to middle position and heat oven to 300 degrees. Combine salt, sugar, and baking soda in bowl; set aside. Heat 6 tablespoons oil and peppercorns in small saucepan over low heat until faint bubbles appear. Continue to cook at bare simmer, swirling pan occasionally, until pepper is fragrant, 7 to 10 minutes. Using fine-mesh strainer, drain cooking oil from peppercorns. Discard cooking oil and mix peppercorns with remaining 3 tablespoons oil, orange zest, and nutmeg.

2. Set tenderloin on sheet of plastic wrap. Sprinkle salt mixture evenly over surface of tenderloin and rub into tenderloin until surface is tacky. Tuck tail end of tenderloin under about 6 inches to create more even shape. Rub top and sides of tenderloin with peppercorn mixture, pressing to make sure peppercorns adhere. Spray three 12-inch lengths of kitchen twine with vegetable oil spray; tie head of tenderloin to maintain even shape, spacing twine at 2-inch intervals.

3. Transfer prepared tenderloin to wire rack set in rimmed baking sheet, keeping tail end tucked under. Roast until thickest part of meat registers about 120 degrees for rare and about 125 degrees for medium-rare (thinner parts of tenderloin will be slightly more done), 60 to 70 minutes. Transfer to carving board and let rest for 30 minutes.

4. Remove twine and slice meat into ½-inch-thick slices. Serve.

Red Wine–Orange Sauce
MAKES 1 CUP

- 2 tablespoons unsalted butter, plus 4 tablespoons cut into 4 pieces and chilled
- 2 shallots, minced
- 1 tablespoon tomato paste
- 2 teaspoons sugar
- 3 garlic cloves, minced
- 2 cups beef broth
- 1 cup red wine
- ¼ cup orange juice
- 2 tablespoons balsamic vinegar
- 1 tablespoon Worcestershire sauce
- 1 sprig fresh thyme
- Salt and pepper

1. Melt 2 tablespoons butter in medium saucepan over medium-high heat. Add shallots, tomato paste, and sugar; cook, stirring frequently, until deep brown, about 5 minutes. Add garlic and cook until fragrant, about 1 minute. Add broth, wine, orange juice, vinegar, Worcestershire, and thyme, scraping up any browned bits. Bring to simmer and cook until reduced to 1 cup, 35 to 40 minutes.

2. Strain sauce through fine-mesh strainer and return to saucepan. Return saucepan to medium heat and whisk in remaining 4 tablespoons butter, 1 piece at a time. Season with salt and pepper to taste.

Pomegranate-Port Sauce
MAKES 1 CUP

- 2 cups pomegranate juice
- 1½ cups ruby port
- 1 shallot, minced
- 1 tablespoon sugar
- 1 teaspoon balsamic vinegar
- 1 sprig thyme
- Salt and pepper
- 4 tablespoons cold butter, cut into 4 pieces

Bring juice, port, shallot, sugar, vinegar, thyme, and 1 teaspoon salt to simmer over medium-high heat. Cook until reduced to 1 cup, 30 to 35 minutes. Strain sauce through fine-mesh strainer and return to saucepan. Return saucepan to medium heat and whisk in butter, 1 piece at a time. Season with salt and pepper to taste.

NOTES FROM THE TEST KITCHEN

PREPARING—AND PACKING ON—A PEPPERCORN CRUST
Most peppercorn crusts either bring big crunch or grip the meat—but rarely both. Here's how we got it right.

1. For a crunchy crust that also sticks, coarsely crack—don't pulverize—peppercorns.

2. To remove dusty bits of ground pepper, sift cracked peppercorns in strainer.

3. Rub meat with salt, sugar, and baking soda to make surface tacky.

THE BEST PEPPER MILL
For our money, a pepper mill has one purpose: to swiftly crank out the desired size and amount of fresh ground pepper, without any guesswork in grind selection or extra strain on our wrists. Simple criteria, and yet many models fail to measure up. To find a pepper mill that would live up to our expectations, we rounded up nine contenders, both manual and battery-powered, priced from $27 to nearly $100, and got grinding.

At the end of testing, we had a clear winner. The carbon steel grind mechanism in the **Cole & Mason Derwent Gourmet Precision Pepper Mill**, $40, features seven large grooves on the nut (most have only five) that taper into finer grooves at the base. These allow it to swiftly channel peppercorns toward the deep, sharp serrations on its ring for fast, efficient grinding. Its spring provides just the right tension to bring the nut and the ring the appropriate distance together (or apart) to create a uniform grind in each of its six fixed, clearly marked grind sizes. We also appreciated its clear acrylic body, which allows you to track when you need a refill. (See page 310 for more information on our testing results.)

ROAST LEG OF LAMB

✔ **WHY THIS RECIPE WORKS** Roast leg of lamb is both delicious and daunting. The usual bone-in or boned, rolled, and tied legs cook evenly and are tricky to carve. Choosing a butterflied leg of lamb did away with these problems; we simply pounded it to an even thickness and salted it for an hour to encourage juicy, evenly cooked meat. To cook the lamb, we first roasted it gently in the oven until it was just medium-rare, then we passed it under the broiler to give it a crisp, browned crust. We tried a standard spice rub, but it scorched under the broiler, so we ditched it in favor of a spice-infused oil. The oil seasoned the lamb during cooking, then became a quick sauce for serving alongside the juicy, boldly spiced lamb.

Not many people cook lamb. Not in America, anyway. Not even I cook it, and it's not because I don't enjoy eating it. Lamb has a richness of flavor unmatched by beef or pork, with a meaty texture that can be as supple as that of tenderloin. It pairs well with a wide range of robust spices, and my favorite cut, the leg, can single-handedly elevate a holiday meal from ordinary to refined. The reason I avoid leg of lamb is that my past experiences cooking it were undermined by the many challenges it can pose.

Roasting a bone-in leg of lamb invariably results in meat of different degrees of doneness; the thin sections of muscle near the shank go beyond well-done while you wait for the meat closest to the bone to come up to temperature. And carving the meat off the bone into presentable pieces can prove humbling. Opting for a boneless, tied leg of lamb partly alleviates these issues—the meat cooks more evenly and carving is simplified. But this approach presents problems of its own, the biggest being the poor ratio of well-browned crust to tender meat and the unavoidable pockets of sinew and fat that hide between the muscles.

Still, I love a challenge. I wanted a roast leg of lamb with a good ratio of crispy crust to evenly cooked meat that was dead simple to carve and serve, all the while providing me with a ready-made sauce. I guess you could say I was after a lazy man's roast leg of lamb.

I immediately decided to forgo bone-in and tied boneless roasts in favor of a different preparation: a butterflied leg of lamb. Essentially a boneless leg in which the thicker portions have been sliced and opened up to yield a relatively even slab of meat, this cut is most often chopped up for kebabs or tossed onto a hot grill. But its uniformity and large expanse of exterior made me think it might do well as a roast, too. My first move was to ensure an even thickness by pounding any thicker areas to roughly 1 inch. Examining this large slab of lamb on my cutting board, I realized there was an unexpected benefit to this preparation: access to the pockets of intermuscular fat and connective tissue. These chewy bits, which aren't accessible even in boneless roasts, don't render or soften enough during cooking. Now I was able to carve out and remove them easily. Another benefit: seasoning this roast was far more efficient than seasoning either a bone-in or a boneless leg.

Though lamb is often brined, I realized that the profile of my butterflied leg resembled that of a very large, thick-cut steak, so I decided to treat it like one. I seasoned both sides with kosher salt and let it sit for an hour. This method provided many of the benefits of a brine: The lamb was better seasoned, juicier, and more tender than untreated samples. Unlike brining, however, salting left my lamb with a relatively dry surface—one that would brown and crisp far better during roasting. To ensure that the salt would reach more of the meat, I crosshatched the fat cap on the surface of the leg by scoring just down to the meat in ½-inch intervals. Roasted to 130 degrees on a baking sheet in a moderate oven, the lamb was well seasoned and featured a decent crust, but I was disappointed to find that the exterior portions were still overcooked by the time the center came up to temperature. I knew I could do better.

We have years of experience roasting meat in the test kitchen, and one thing we've learned is that roasting low and slow ensures good moisture retention and even cooking. With this in mind, I tried roasting my salted lamb at a range of relatively low oven temperatures, from 225 degrees on up to 325 degrees. Sure enough, going lower resulted in juicier, more evenly cooked meat. I struck a balance between time and temperature at 250 degrees. So far, so good: I was turning out a tender, juicy leg of lamb in only 40 minutes of roasting.

But there's also a second tenet of good roasting: High heat develops the rich, meaty flavors associated with the Maillard reaction. It's a paradox we commonly address by cooking at two different heat levels, searing in a skillet over high heat, then gently roasting. But my roast was too large for stovetop searing. It was clear that I'd need to sear it in the oven, either at the maximum

ROAST BUTTERFLIED LEG OF LAMB WITH CORIANDER, CUMIN, AND MUSTARD SEEDS

temperature of 500 degrees or under the broiler. I tested both options and found that even a 500-degree oven was too slow for my thin roast. By the time I had rendered and crisped the exterior, I'd overcooked the meat below the surface. Broiling was markedly better. I achieved the best results by slow-roasting the lamb first, then finishing it under the broiler, which dried the meat's surface further and promoted faster browning. Just 5 minutes under the broiler produced a burnished, crisped crust without overcooking the meat's interior. Now it was time to address the spices.

Because liberal amounts of bold spices complement, rather than overpower, lamb's unique flavor, I wanted to find the ideal way to incorporate a nice spice blend. My first thought was to include the spices from the outset to give their flavors plenty of time to mellow and deepen. I toasted equal parts cumin, coriander, and mustard seeds and rubbed the mixture over both sides of the lamb along with the salt. Things looked (and smelled) quite good while the lamb gently roasted, but they took a turn for the worse under the broiler. The broiler's intense heat turned the top layer of spices into a blackened, bitter mess in a matter of minutes.

But it wasn't all bad news—the spices on the bottom of the lamb had bloomed and softened in the oven, adding texture and flavor where they clung to the meat. What if I ditched the top layer of spices and focused on getting the most out of what was underneath? For my next attempt, I placed whole coriander, cumin, and mustard seeds plus some smashed garlic and sliced ginger on a baking sheet, stirred the mixture with some vegetable oil, and popped it into the oven. The steady, gentle heat of the oven bloomed the spices—a process by which, through the application of heat, fat-soluble flavor compounds in a spice or other aromatic are released, mixing together and physically interacting with one another, gaining more complexity. When the lamb was ready to be cooked, I simply removed the baking sheet, placed the lamb (fat side up) on top of the spice-oil mixture, and returned it to the oven to roast.

When I tasted this roast, it was clear that I had hit the roast-lamb jackpot. Without a layer of spices to absorb the heat, the top of the roast once again turned a handsome golden brown under the broiler, and the aromatics and infused oil clung to the bottom and provided rich flavor. Tasters were pleased but wanted more complexity, so I added shallots, strips of lemon zest, and bay leaves (which I removed before adding the

lamb) to the pan oil. This lamb was close to my ideal: a browned crust encasing medium-rare meat, perfumed with pockets of spice and caramelized alliums. The last step was to put all of that infused oil to good use.

While the lamb rested, I strained the infused oil and pan juices into a bowl and whisked in some lemon juice, shallot, and cilantro and mint. This vinaigrette was silky, aromatic, and fresh-tasting. The time had come to carve my lamb roast, and it proved as simple as slicing up a steak. I transferred the meat to a platter, dressed it with some of the sauce, and—in less than 2 hours—was ready to eat. Lazy man's leg of lamb, indeed.

—DAN SOUZA, *Cook's Illustrated*

Roast Butterflied Leg of Lamb with Coriander, Cumin, and Mustard Seeds

SERVES 8 TO 10

We prefer the subtler flavor and larger size of lamb labeled "domestic" or "American" for this recipe. The 2 tablespoons of salt in step 1 is for a 6-pound leg. If using a larger leg (7 to 8 pounds), add an additional teaspoon of salt for every pound.

LAMB

- 1 (6- to 8-pound) butterflied leg of lamb
  Kosher salt
- ⅓ cup vegetable oil
- 3 shallots, sliced thin
- 4 garlic cloves, peeled and smashed
- 1 (1-inch) piece ginger, sliced into ½-inch-thick rounds and smashed
- 1 tablespoon coriander seeds
- 1 tablespoon cumin seeds
- 1 tablespoon mustard seeds
- 3 bay leaves
- 2 (2-inch) strips lemon zest

SAUCE

- ⅓ cup chopped fresh mint
- ⅓ cup chopped fresh cilantro
- 1 shallot, minced
- 2 tablespoons lemon juice
  Salt and pepper

1. FOR THE LAMB: Place lamb on cutting board with fat cap facing down. Using sharp knife, trim any pockets of fat and connective tissue from underside of lamb.

Flip lamb over, trim fat cap so it's between ⅛ and ¼ inch thick, and pound roast to even 1-inch thickness. Cut slits, spaced ½ inch apart, in fat cap in crosshatch pattern, being careful to cut down to but not into meat. Rub 2 tablespoons salt over entire roast and into slits. Let stand, uncovered, at room temperature for 1 hour.

2. Meanwhile, adjust oven racks 4 to 5 inches from broiler element and to lower-middle position and heat oven to 250 degrees. Stir together oil, shallots, garlic, ginger, coriander seeds, cumin seeds, mustard seeds, bay leaves, and lemon zest in rimmed baking sheet and bake on lower-middle rack until spices are softened and fragrant and shallots and garlic turn golden, about 1 hour. Remove sheet from oven and discard bay leaves.

3. Thoroughly pat lamb dry with paper towels and transfer, fat side up, to sheet (directly on top of spices). Roast on lower-middle rack until lamb registers 120 degrees, 30 to 40 minutes. Remove sheet from oven and heat broiler. Broil lamb on upper rack until surface is well browned and charred in spots and lamb registers 125 degrees, 3 to 8 minutes for medium-rare.

4. Remove sheet from oven and, using 2 pairs of tongs, transfer lamb to carving board (some spices will cling to bottom of roast); tent loosely with aluminum foil and let rest for 20 minutes.

5. FOR THE SAUCE: Meanwhile, carefully pour pan juices through fine-mesh strainer into medium bowl, pressing on solids to extract as much liquid as possible; discard solids. Stir in mint, cilantro, shallot, and lemon juice. Add any accumulated lamb juices to sauce and season with salt and pepper to taste.

6. With long side facing you, slice lamb with grain into 3 equal pieces. Turn each piece and slice across grain into ¼-inch-thick slices. Serve with sauce. (Briefly warm sauce in microwave if it has cooled and thickened.)

NOTES FROM THE TEST KITCHEN

CONFIGURED FOR EASY CARVING

First position meat so that long side is facing you. Then slice lamb with grain into 3 equal pieces. Turn each piece so that you can now cut across grain, and cut into ¼-inch-thick slices.

VARIATIONS

Roast Butterflied Leg of Lamb with Coriander, Rosemary, and Red Pepper

Omit cumin and mustard seeds. Toss 6 sprigs fresh rosemary and ½ teaspoon red pepper flakes with oil mixture in step 2. Substitute parsley for cilantro in sauce.

Roast Butterflied Leg of Lamb with Coriander, Fennel, and Black Pepper

Substitute 1 tablespoon fennel seeds for cumin seeds and 1 tablespoon black peppercorns for mustard seeds in step 2. Substitute parsley for mint in sauce.

EASY GRILLED BONELESS PORK CHOPS

✓ **WHY THIS RECIPE WORKS** To get juicy yet well-charred boneless center-cut pork chops on the grill, we came up with a two-pronged approach. First we brined the chops to season them throughout and to help them hold on to their juices during cooking. Then, to get a substantial, flavorful browned crust before the lean chops overcooked, we looked for a coating that would brown quickly. We found our solution in umami-rich anchovy paste and thick, sweet honey. The anchovies' amino acids coupled with the fructose from the honey kick-started the flavorful Maillard browning reaction, giving our grilled pork chops a crisp, burnished crust in record time.

Grab a pack of thin, boneless, center-cut pork chops from the supermarket, fire up the grill, and you're moments away from an inexpensive, simple, and satisfying supper. Or you would have been, half a century ago when American pork was still well marbled and stayed juicy on the grill. Because today's pigs are bred for leanness rather than flavor, modern pork chops present a challenge: How do you get a flavorful browned crust without sapping the interior of its already meager juices?

Most recipes for grilled pork chops produce either beautifully charred slices of cardboard or juicy chops that are still pale and bland. Frustrated by these half measures, I wanted to develop a recipe that paid equal attention to juiciness and browning. At the same time, I aimed to retain the speed and ease that have always made grilled pork chops such an attractive weeknight dinner in the first place.

The most obvious way to guarantee juicy meat is to cook it at a gentle, low temperature and pull it off the heat just before it reaches the desired final temperature (to allow for a few degrees of carryover cooking). On a grill, low temperatures are usually achieved through indirect heat, by stacking the coals beneath one side of the grate and cooking the food on the opposite side. The meat is given a few minutes directly above the coals to brown and char before it's moved to the cooler side to finish cooking. But my thin pork chops needed every second they could get over the coals to have a fighting chance at browning before they were cooked through.

Luckily, we've done a lot of testing over the years to figure out how to keep meat juicy during cooking. Two of the most effective methods we've found are salting and brining. Both slightly alter muscle fibers so they are better able to hold on to moisture. Salting pulls moisture from the meat, then allows it to reabsorb, while brining actually increases the amount of moisture in the meat. I ran a quick side-by-side test, and the brined chops, with their added moisture, won hands down.

But despite the added moisture, I was fighting a losing battle. Even when I cooked my chops over an entire chimneyful of coals stacked in a thick layer, they refused to develop nicely browned grill marks and rich flavor in the 8 to 10 minutes it took them to cook. I needed help, so I turned to our science editor for some guidance. What I got was a new way of thinking about browning.

Browning is essentially a process of destruction. Heat breaks down proteins into their amino-acid building blocks and complex carbohydrates into simple sugars like fructose, glucose, and lactose (called reducing sugars). Then the Maillard—or browning—reaction can begin. Cooking temperature affects the speed of the reaction, but both the amount and type of amino acids released and the concentration of reducing sugars play big roles as well. Meat browns relatively slowly because its proteins break down gradually in the presence of so much moisture (meat is about 70 percent water) and it doesn't have many carbohydrates to transform into reducing sugars. This gave me two ideas for faster browning: I could either find a way to crank up the heat and overcome pork's inherent shortcomings or coat the chop in something designed for speedy browning.

My first move was to adjust the grill setup. So far, I'd been emptying a full chimney of coals onto half of the grill and cooking my chops over this relatively hot fire. What if I could bring the chops closer to the flames?

I tried raising the coals by stacking them on top of an inverted, perforated disposable roasting pan, but the glowing-hot coals melted right through the aluminum. A real roasting pan didn't have that problem, but it restricted airflow, choking the fire. After a few smoky afternoons grilling in the back alley, I gave up on this direction and turned to the second option.

To get my pork chops to brown faster, I'd need a coating that contained both protein and reducing sugars. I started working from a list of ingredients provided by our science editor. One of the most interesting options was dry milk powder, which is rich in both protein and lactose. I dusted a few chops with milk powder and popped them onto the grill. I got rapid browning, but the taste test was disappointing. The chops didn't taste like milk—but they didn't taste especially meaty either. Next I tried coating them with flour (which contains proteins as well as lots of carbohydrates that break down into reducing sugars), but again, while the chops browned more quickly, they didn't taste that meaty. Disheartened, I went back to our science editor.

I soon learned that not all browning is created equal. In reality, meat muscle proteins produce far more complex flavor and aroma than other types of proteins, due to their high levels of sulfur-containing amino acids. Milk protein contains only about half as many, and wheat flour protein even fewer. That explained why I was getting the appearance of browned meat while the flavor was falling short.

Frustrated by my lack of progress, I took a break from grilling and threw together a quick pasta dish for lunch. I softened some sliced garlic in olive oil, tossed in a few minced anchovies, and marveled at how quickly they turned a rich golden brown in the hot oil. Why were they browning so quickly? It turns out that not only are anchovies a particularly concentrated source of muscle proteins, but their protein has already been broken down through fermentation into many sulfur-containing amino acids. I suspected that I might have finally hit the browning jackpot. I dropped everything and excitedly brined another batch of chops, patted them dry, and applied a thin layer of anchovy paste to both sides. Back on the grill, these chops browned much faster than plain chops and emerged with a rich, meaty-tasting crust without a hint of fishiness, thanks to the flavor contributed by browning and the smoke from the grill.

With a solution within reach and my confidence regained, I wondered if I could get the chops to brown even better and faster. After all, I now had plenty of amino acids but little in the way of reducing sugars. But I had a convenient (and tasty) source of fructose right in the pantry: honey. This time I mixed up the anchovy paste with some honey and a little vegetable oil (which made the mixture easier to spread) and smeared the concoction over both sides of six chops. In just 4 minutes over the fire, the underside of the chops had turned a gorgeous burnished brown dotted with spots of real char. Another 4 to 6 minutes on the second side and they were done.

Juicy? Check. Well browned? Check. Meaty? Check. And these chops can be prepped for the grill in about the time it takes to ready the charcoal. Mission accomplished.

—DAN SOUZA, *Cook's Illustrated*

Easy Grilled Boneless Pork Chops

SERVES 4 TO 6

If your pork is enhanced, do not brine it in step 1. Very finely mashed anchovy fillets (rinsed and dried before mashing) can be used instead of anchovy paste.

- 6 (6- to 8-ounce) boneless pork chops, ¾ to 1 inch thick
- 3 tablespoons salt
- 1 tablespoon vegetable oil
- 1½ teaspoons honey
- 1 teaspoon anchovy paste
- ½ teaspoon pepper
- 1 recipe relish (optional; recipes follow)

1. Cut 2 slits about 1 inch apart through outer layer of fat and connective tissue on each chop to prevent buckling. Dissolve salt in 1½ quarts cold water in large container. Submerge chops in brine and let stand at room temperature for 30 minutes.

2. Whisk together oil, honey, anchovy paste, and pepper to form smooth paste. Remove pork from brine and pat dry with paper towels. Using spoon, spread half of oil mixture evenly over 1 side of each chop (about ¼ teaspoon per side).

3A. FOR A CHARCOAL GRILL: Open bottom vent completely. Light chimney starter filled with charcoal briquettes (6 quarts). When top coals are partially covered with ash, pour evenly over half of grill. Set cooking grate in place, cover, and open lid vent completely. Heat grill until hot, about 5 minutes.

NOTES FROM THE TEST KITCHEN

BETTER BROWNING IN A HURRY

For grilled pork chops with deeply seared crusts and juicy centers, speedy browning was crucial. But before browning can start, heat must break down proteins into amino acids and carbohydrates into so-called reducing sugars. We tried dredging the chops in flour (full of carbohydrates and some protein), as well as milk powder, which is loaded with not only protein but also the reducing sugar lactose. Both significantly sped up browning, but neither was particularly meaty-tasting.

Then we discovered a breakthrough combination: honey and anchovy paste. Honey is loaded with the reducing sugar fructose, and anchovy paste has the same concentration of meaty-tasting amino acids as pork—and its large proteins are already broken down into the fast-reacting amino acids. Those traits added up to faster browning and big, meaty flavor.

THE BEST CHARCOAL GRILL

In search of a well-engineered, user-friendly charcoal grill that's up to any outdoor cooking task—ribs, pork loin, fish, burgers, chicken—we set an upper price limit of $400 and lined up seven promising grills. Our battery of cooking tests included big batches of burgers, skewers of sticky glazed beef satay, thick salmon fillets, and barbecued ribs. We ran a height check by shutting each grill's lid over a whole turkey; we monitored temperature retention; and we kept track of how easy the grills were to set up and to clean. Most did a good job grilling, but some had design flaws that limited how easy they were to use. Some skimped on the space beneath their cooking grates; some grills lacked ample space between their grates and lids—a good 3 inches or more of headroom above food is ideal for proper air circulation and even cooking. Some grills' grates were flush with the cooker's top edge, allowing burgers to slip off.

While flawless cooking performance is essential, we found that convenience can make or break your charcoal grilling experience. The **Weber Performer Platinum 22.5-Inch Charcoal Grill with Touch-n-Go Gas Ignition**, $349, came with a roomy cart, a lid holder, a built-in thermometer, and a gas ignition button that eliminates the need for a chimney starter, essentially combining the convenience of gas grilling with the flavor of charcoal. We couldn't resist its perks and declared this model our new winner. That said, the more basic, budget-minded version of our winner, the Weber One-Touch Gold 22.5-Inch Charcoal Grill, $149, offers all the necessary cooking functions, plus the simplest assembly and cleanup, and is our Best Buy. (See page 315 for more information on our testing results.)

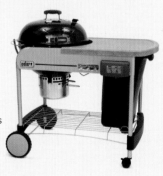

3B. FOR A GAS GRILL: Turn all burners to high, cover, and heat grill until hot, about 15 minutes. Leave primary burner on high and turn off other burner(s).

4. Clean and oil cooking grate. Place chops, oiled side down, over hot part of grill and cook, uncovered, until well browned on first side, 4 to 6 minutes. While chops are grilling, spread remaining oil mixture evenly over second side of chops. Flip chops and continue to cook until chops register 140 degrees, 4 to 6 minutes longer (if chops are well browned but register less than 140 degrees, move to cooler part of grill to finish cooking). Transfer chops to plate and let rest for 5 minutes. Serve with relish, if using.

Onion, Olive, and Caper Relish

MAKES ABOUT 2 CUPS

- ¼ cup olive oil
- 2 onions, cut into ¼-inch pieces
- 6 garlic cloves, sliced thin
- ½ cup pitted kalamata olives, chopped coarse
- ¼ cup capers, rinsed
- 3 tablespoons balsamic vinegar
- 2 tablespoons minced fresh parsley
- 1 teaspoon minced fresh marjoram
- 1 teaspoon sugar
- ½ teaspoon anchovy paste
- ½ teaspoon pepper
- ¼ teaspoon salt

Heat 2 tablespoons oil in 10-inch nonstick skillet over medium heat until shimmering. Add onions and cook until softened, about 5 minutes. Stir in garlic and cook until fragrant, about 30 seconds. Transfer onion mixture to medium bowl; stir in remaining 2 tablespoons oil, olives, capers, vinegar, parsley, marjoram, sugar, anchovy paste, pepper, and salt. Serve warm or at room temperature.

Orange, Jícama, and Pepita Relish

MAKES ABOUT 2 CUPS

- 1 orange
- ¼ cup olive oil
- 2 jalapeño chiles, stemmed, seeded, and sliced into thin rings
- 3 shallots, sliced thin
- 6 garlic cloves, sliced thin
- 2 cups jícama, peeled and cut into ¼-inch pieces
- ¼ cup pepitas, toasted
- 3 tablespoons chopped fresh cilantro
- 3 tablespoons lime juice (2 limes)
- 1 teaspoon sugar
- ¾ teaspoon salt
- ½ teaspoon pepper

Cut away peel and pith from orange. Quarter orange, then slice crosswise into ¼-inch-thick pieces. Heat 2 tablespoons oil in 10-inch skillet over medium heat until shimmering. Add jalapeños and shallots and cook until slightly softened, about 5 minutes. Stir in garlic and cook until fragrant, about 30 seconds. Transfer jalapeño-shallot mixture to medium bowl; stir in remaining 2 tablespoons oil, orange, jícama, pepitas, cilantro, lime juice, sugar, salt, and pepper. Serve warm or at room temperature.

Tomato, Fennel, and Almond Relish

MAKES ABOUT 2 CUPS

- ¼ cup olive oil
- 1 fennel bulb, stalks discarded, bulb halved, cored, and cut into ¼-inch pieces
- 6 garlic cloves, sliced thin
- 2 tomatoes, cored and cut into ½-inch pieces
- ¼ cup pitted green olives, chopped coarse
- ¼ cup slivered almonds, toasted
- 3 tablespoons sherry vinegar
- 3 tablespoons minced fresh parsley
- 1 teaspoon sugar
- ¾ teaspoon salt
- ½ teaspoon pepper

Heat 2 tablespoons oil in 10-inch skillet over medium heat until shimmering. Add fennel and cook until slightly softened, about 5 minutes. Stir in garlic and cook until fragrant, about 30 seconds. Stir in tomatoes and continue to cook until tomatoes break down slightly, about 5 minutes. Transfer fennel mixture to medium bowl; stir in remaining 2 tablespoons oil, olives, almonds, vinegar, parsley, sugar, salt, and pepper. Serve warm or at room temperature.

CRUMB-COATED HAM

✓ **WHY THIS RECIPE WORKS** This Swedish special-ty takes moist, meaty ham and adds a crispy, crunchy, toasted crumb coating. To prevent our spiral-cut ham from drying out, we baked it in a low oven and used an oven bag to trap steam. To make it easy to pull the bag off and apply the coating once the meat was warmed through, we put the ham under—not in—the bag. To en-sure that the crumb coating stayed put, we reduced the spicy-sweet mustard glaze on the stovetop until it was extra-thick and sticky. Crispy panko bread crumbs, sim-ply seasoned with salt, pepper, and fresh parsley, gave us the crunchiest coating. Finally, we topped our ham with a no-cook spicy mustard sauce.

During my years in the test kitchen, I've crumb-coated fish fillets, chicken, baked tomatoes, macaroni and cheese, pork chops, beef tenderloin . . . the list goes on. But it had never occurred to me to apply this technique to ham. Then I heard about crumb-coated baked ham from the mother of a friend of Scandinavian descent—apparently it's a common way to prepare the Christmas ham in Sweden. Curious, I checked our library for recipes. They called for both spiral-cut and uncut hams; the crust might be made of fresh bread crumbs, dried bread crumbs, or crushed gingersnaps; and the crumbs were adhered to the ham with everything from mustard to melted butter, beaten raw egg yolks, brown sugar, sweet glazes, or some combination of these. A few recipes required pressing the crumbs onto the ham at the start, but most called for warming the ham without the crumbs, which were then applied toward the end of cooking. Following along, I baked six hams.

The results were dismaying: The bread crumbs were uniformly soggy, although definitely better when applied toward the end of cooking. Obviously, they were absorbing moisture from the ham. Likewise, the gingersnaps had lost their snap. When I tried to carve the uncut hams, the crumb coatings simply fell off. The spiral-cut hams fared better, but since they were not only precooked (like the uncut hams) but also presliced, they were prone to drying out. As one taster summed it up, "These taste like wet bread wrapped around dried-out ham."

Although the problem rather than the promise was in evidence, I still hadn't lost confidence in the concept. I just needed to figure out how to keep the ham moist

and the crumbs dry. Meanwhile, I narrowed the scope of my recipe, deciding on bread crumbs and glaze (for now, a basic mix of brown sugar and mustard).

Also, since the test recipes were universal failures, I'd start with a test kitchen recipe for spiral-cut ham, then address the crumbs. Our recipe is simple: We enclose a sliced, room-temperature ham in an oven bag and bake it at a gentle 300 degrees. The room-temperature ham heats up faster, with less time to dry out, and the low temperature cooks the ham gently while the bag creates a humid environment that keeps the ham moist. Once the ham was warm, I figured I'd simply glaze and crumb-coat it and return it to the oven to brown the crumbs.

A couple of hours later, I rolled back the oven bag to expose the hot ham and apply the crumbs. With the bag scrunched up at the bottom of the roasting pan, it was awkward to reach in to try to press on the crumbs. The deep roasting pan compounded the prob-lem. After trying out several contortions with hams and bags, I realized that rather than put the ham in the bag, I should put the bag over the ham. I did so, tucking the bag under the edges of the meat. To "seal" the bag at the bottom to create the closed, moist environment, I set the ham on a square of aluminum foil. When it was time to remove the bag, it pulled off easily. As for pans, after trying out a few, I settled on a favorite test kitchen rig: a wire rack set inside a rimmed baking sheet. All parts of the ham were now easily accessible.

With the crumb-application mechanics worked out, I circled back to the coating itself. Since the bread crumbs I'd been using thus far turned mushy time after time, I tried panko, super-crunchy Japanese-style bread crumbs. I tossed them with a little oil and some seasonings. Once the ham was warm, the bag came off and the glaze and crumbs went on. With the oven cranked to 400 degrees, the crumbs browned in about 25 minutes. The panko was a rousing success, but the glaze still needed fine-tuning to hold the crumbs in place. Hoping to turn it into the Krazy Glue of glazes, I cooked it down for about 15 minutes, until it was thick and ultrasticky. While I was at it, I added balsamic vin-egar for mellow acidity and the classic ham flavorings of dry mustard, ginger, and cloves. Then I painted the glaze on the ham, pressed on the panko crumbs, and baked.

While the ham was in the oven, I took a few minutes to stir together ingredients for a slightly spicy, no-cook mustard sauce. Half an hour later, I put several slices of ham on my plate—and was thrilled to see that the crumb coating stayed put. I took a bite: The ham was moist, the crumbs were crunchy, and the combination was everything I'd hoped for.

—DIANE UNGER, *Cook's Country*

Crumb-Coated Baked Ham

SERVES 12 TO 14

Our favorite spiral-sliced ham is Cook's Spiral Sliced Hickory Smoked Bone-In Honey Ham. This recipe requires a turkey-size oven bag. Serve the ham with Hot Mustard Sauce.

 1 (8- to 9-pound) bone-in spiral-sliced ham
 1 cup packed brown sugar
 ½ cup spicy brown mustard
 ½ cup balsamic vinegar
 2 tablespoons dry mustard
 2 teaspoons ground ginger
 ¼ teaspoon ground cloves
 1½ cups panko bread crumbs
 ½ cup minced fresh parsley
 3 tablespoons vegetable oil
 ¼ teaspoon salt
 ¼ teaspoon pepper

1. Line rimmed baking sheet with aluminum foil; set wire rack inside sheet. Place 12-inch square of foil in center of rack. Set ham on foil, flat side down, and cover with oven bag, tucking bag under ham to secure it. Let ham sit at room temperature for 1½ hours.

2. Adjust oven rack to lowest position and heat oven to 325 degrees. Bake ham until it registers 100 degrees, about 2 hours. (Lift bag to take temperature; do not puncture.)

3. Meanwhile, combine sugar, brown mustard, vinegar, dry mustard, ginger, and cloves in medium saucepan and bring to boil over medium-high heat. Reduce heat to medium-low and simmer until reduced to ¾ cup, 15 to 20 minutes. Let cool while ham cooks.

4. Combine panko, parsley, oil, salt, and pepper in bowl. Remove ham from oven, remove and discard oven bag, and let ham cool for 5 minutes. Increase oven temperature to 400 degrees.

5. Brush ham all over with brown sugar–mustard glaze. Press panko mixture against sides of ham to coat evenly. Bake until crumbs are deep golden brown, 20 to

30 minutes. Transfer ham, flat side down, to carving board and let rest for 30 minutes. Carve and serve.

Hot Mustard Sauce

MAKES ABOUT 1 CUP

The longer this sauce sits, the milder it becomes.

 3 tablespoons cold water
 2 tablespoons dry mustard
 ½ teaspoon salt
 ½ cup Dijon mustard
 2 tablespoons honey

Whisk water, dry mustard, and salt together in bowl until smooth; let sit for 15 minutes. Whisk in Dijon mustard and honey. Cover and let sit at room temperature for at least 2 hours. Use immediately or transfer sauce to glass jar with tight-fitting lid and refrigerate for up to 2 months.

NOTES FROM THE TEST KITCHEN

PREPARING A CRUMB-COATED HAM

1. Cover ham with oven bag, tucking it under ham to prevent meat from drying out. Bake bagged ham for about 2 hours.

2. Remove ham from oven, lift off oven bag, and brush warm ham with brown sugar–mustard glaze.

3. Sprinkle seasoned crumbs on ham and press them on to coat. Bake until golden brown.

CRUMB–COATED BAKED HAM

MILK-CAN SUPPER

✔ **WHY THIS RECIPE WORKS** Invented to feed a crowd of cowboys, this hearty mix of vegetables and sausage was traditionally layered into a large milk can and cooked over an open fire. We swapped the milk can for a Dutch oven but kept the basic technique. We put the sturdy potatoes on the bottom closest to the heat, followed by cabbage, then more delicate onions, carrots, and corn. To prevent them from overcooking, we added bell peppers partway through. Browning bratwurst developed its meaty flavor and created a fond that gave savory backbone to the cooking liquid. American lager gave the dish complex toasty flavors, and garlic, bay leaves, and thyme rounded out the seasonings.

A milk-can supper is the cowboy equivalent of all-in-one meals like the New England clambake or the Low Country shrimp boil. In this case, enough meat (usually sausage) and vegetables to feed a crowd are cooked in a 10-gallon milk can over a campfire. The ingredients are layered in the pot according to their cooking times: Items that need more cooking go in toward the bottom, where the pot will be hotter, and more delicate ingredients get piled on top, where the heat is more gentle. If all goes according to plan, the flavors mingle, all the ingredients are done at the same time, and the meal is enjoyed with a minimum of fuss and ceremony. It's a quick, easy, and inexpensive crowd-pleaser.

Like many such folk dishes, milk-can supper derived from a combination of necessity and hospitality. Before the days of train cars and 18-wheelers, cowboys drove large herds of cattle by horseback north from Texas to the railroad lines in the northern plains. Cattle became big business in the plains, and with the boom came the need for more open range. Ranchers set their gaze toward the relatively untouched grasslands of Nebraska, South Dakota, and Wyoming to establish new ranches. Some of the busiest times on these ranches were branding days. Ranchers showed their appreciation to all who lent a hand by offering them supper—often cooked in the giant tin cans used for milk delivery to accommodate the huge amount of food. Local home cooks soon started cooking large meals in the cans, and a tradition was born.

I don't own a ranch, I have no cowhands to feed, and I don't live in the plains states. Still, a milk-can supper sounded like a fun way to make a simple meal for a crowd. I was excited to cook this dish for myself (on the stovetop, not an open fire). First, I'd need to get my hands on a milk can. Luckily, it was as simple as searching online. I found a company out of Nebraska that sells stainless steel milk cans for cooking. I ordered the modest 1-gallon can (which feeds about six people). When it arrived, I was happy to see that it came with a recipe for a traditional milk-can supper. I collected a few other recipes to try and got busy prepping ingredients.

In the old days, cooks would line the bottom of the can with rocks to keep the food from scorching; instead, the manufacturer of my shiny new can recommended using canning rings to elevate the food, so I loaded them in. Then came the long-cooking vegetables that were standard in all milk-can supper recipes: cabbage, corn, and potatoes. After that, recipes vary widely in terms of what other vegetables they call for. I settled on the most common, piling in onion, carrots, celery, summer squash, bell peppers, sweet potatoes, and broccoli. Following the procedure of most recipes, I placed a few pounds of bratwurst on top, poured in a can of Budweiser, and brought it all to a boil on the stovetop. At this point I turned down the heat, put on the lid, and let it all cook for 30 minutes. Then I poured the contents into a large roasting pan (I didn't have a serving platter big enough to corral all that food) and called over my tasters.

To be honest, I was expecting mushy, watery vegetables and gray, spent bratwurst. To our surprise, many of the vegetables were perfectly tender, and the savory juices from the cooking bratwurst had dripped down and infused the vegetables with meaty flavor and deep seasoning. Still, there were a few issues to work through. Even with the sausage seasoning the vegetables, my milk-can supper needed more flavor. And certain vegetables were problematic. The summer squash and green peppers had turned to mush—they cooked faster than the other vegetables and fell apart. I decided I'd omit the squash (it didn't add much flavor), but my tasters lobbied to keep the green bell peppers, so next time I'd add them partway through cooking. Also, all those vegetables created a mishmash of flavors. With input from my tasters, I nixed the celery, sweet potatoes, and broccoli.

And although the milk can was fun and authentic, I knew I'd have to find a substitute cooking vessel that didn't require mail-ordering. I started my next test in a Dutch oven, but I immediately realized the pot wouldn't be able to accommodate all the ingredients. I wondered if I could save some room by leaving out the canning rings and placing sturdy red potatoes on the bottom of the pot. This worked well; the potatoes held up to the heat and protected the other vegetables from burning.

To boost the dish's flavor, I added garlic, thyme, and a couple of bay leaves to the mix with good results. Next I considered the liquid that I was adding. I pitted traditional American lager against dark ale, chicken stock, water, and white wine (not very "cowboy," but hey, I went to culinary school). But the cowboys were right: The lager was the clear winner. It added a balanced, toasty depth that the other liquids didn't.

I was making progress, but the flavor still wasn't good enough. Could the sausages contribute a little more? Maybe I could coax more flavor out of them by browning them first. In fact, not only did browning boost the sausages' flavor, but it also created a tasty fond on the bottom of the Dutch oven that enhanced the cooking liquid to nice effect. Plus, the browned sausages looked much more appealing than when they were simply steamed.

I made one more batch. I browned the brats, removed them from the pot, and cut them in half (so they'd release more flavorful juices), then I layered in the potatoes, cabbage, and corn, then the carrots, onion, garlic, thyme sprigs, and bay leaves. I poured in the beer; put the browned brats on top of everything; and turned on the burner. After 15 minutes, I added the quick-cooking bell peppers. Another 15 minutes later, I emptied the Dutch oven into a roasting pan to serve, reserving some of the juices for passing at the table. I called over my tasters for what I hoped was my final tasting. Though we hadn't worked up a cowboy-size appetite rounding up cattle, we loved this milk-can supper: The vegetables were tender, the brats juicy, and the mix of flavors delicious. Altogether, this dinner was unfussy and just plain fun to eat—no milk can or campfire necessary.

—NICK IVERSON, *Cook's Country*

Milk-Can Supper

SERVES 6 TO 8

If your Dutch oven is slightly smaller than 8 quarts, the lid may not close all the way at first, but as the contents of the pot cook, they will decrease in volume. Use small red potatoes, measuring 1 to 2 inches in diameter. Light-bodied American lagers, such as Budweiser, work best in this recipe.

- 1 tablespoon vegetable oil
- 2½ pounds bratwurst (10 sausages)
- 2 pounds small red potatoes, unpeeled
- 1 head green cabbage (2 pounds), cored and cut into 8 wedges
- 3 ears corn, husks and silk removed, ears cut into thirds
- 6 carrots, peeled and cut into 2-inch pieces
- 1 onion, halved and cut through root end into 8 wedges
- 4 garlic cloves, peeled and smashed
- 10 sprigs fresh thyme
- 2 bay leaves
  Salt and pepper
- 1½ cups beer
- 2 green bell peppers, stemmed, seeded, and cut into 1-inch-wide strips

1. Heat oil in 8-quart Dutch oven over medium heat until shimmering. Add bratwurst and cook until browned all over, 6 to 8 minutes. Remove pot from heat. Transfer bratwurst to cutting board and halve crosswise.

2. Place potatoes in single layer in now-empty Dutch oven. Arrange cabbage wedges in single layer on top of potatoes. Layer corn, carrots, onion, garlic, thyme, bay leaves, 1 teaspoon salt, and ½ teaspoon pepper over cabbage. Pour beer over vegetables and arrange browned bratwurst on top.

3. Bring to boil over medium-high heat (wisps of steam will be visible). Cover, reduce heat to medium, and simmer for 15 minutes. Add bell peppers and continue to simmer, covered, until potatoes are tender, about 15 minutes. (Use long skewer to test potatoes for doneness.)

4. Transfer bratwurst and vegetables to large serving platter (or roasting pan, if your platter isn't large enough); discard thyme sprigs and bay leaves. Pour 1 cup cooking liquid over platter. Season with salt and pepper to taste. Serve, passing remaining cooking liquid separately.

IRON RANGE PORKETTA

✔ **WHY THIS RECIPE WORKS** Similar to Italian *porchetta*, Iron Range porketta is fennel-and-garlic-seasoned pulled pork hailing from Minnesota. Butterflying the pork butt sped up cooking, and cutting a crosshatch in the surface of the roast ensured that the seasoning—a bold mixture of granulated garlic, crushed fennel seeds, salt, and pepper—penetrated the meat. And, before roasting, we topped the meat with sliced fresh fennel for a second layer of bright flavor.

On a recent trip to Minnesota's Iron Range, I found that porketta sandwiches are as ubiquitous as burgers in that part of the country. These sandwiches are all about the meat: roasted, shredded pork seasoned with fennel, garlic, salt, and pepper and served on crusty rolls. They are a simplified take on Italian *porchetta,* which was brought to the area by Italian iron miners around the turn of the 20th century. Every restaurant and sandwich shop has it on the menu. It's served at parties and in schools. Grocery stores even sell seasoned roasts and premixed spice packets for the dish. In short, it's everywhere. But outside the region, the sandwich becomes a mystery.

It's much too good to remain unknown, so I set out to develop my own version. Recipes for porketta are few and far between, and the recipes I did track down were often no more than lists of ingredients (pork roast, garlic, fennel, salt, and pepper) with no quantities or cooking instructions. In the Iron Range you will see porketta made with pork loin, turkey (turketta), or beef (beefetta). But according to the porketta experts at two places that serve a ton of the stuff—Fraboni's and Cobb Cook Grocery in the town of Hibbing in the heart of the Iron Range—flavorful pork shoulder, or pork butt roast, is the best and most traditional choice. I hit the test kitchen determined to do this iconic regional recipe justice.

Using the guidelines I found in a tattered community cookbook generously lent to me by my Hibbing innkeeper, I butterflied a 5-pound boneless pork shoulder (I cut into it and opened it like a book); seasoned it with salt, pepper, fennel seeds, and garlic; rolled it up; tied it tightly with twine; wrapped it in foil; and cooked it in a 325-degree oven until the meat was tender, which took about 5½ hours. The result was a shreddable pork roast, a tad dry in parts, with decent fennel and garlic flavor that, unfortunately, was not present in every bite. I had some work ahead of me, but I was on my way to producing respectable porketta.

My tasters were clamoring for more seasoning. To get the seasoning to adhere and penetrate better, I tried a trick I had heard about in Minnesota: I cut a ¼-inch-deep crosshatch pattern into both sides of the butterflied meat. As for the seasonings themselves, most porketta I tried in Minnesota used fennel seeds; Fraboni's used the feathery fresh fronds, but those can be hard to find. But what about fennel bulbs? Fresh fennel is widely available in supermarkets, so I tried finely chopping a bulb (after cutting out the tough core) and adding it to the pork. Tasters loved the fresh, mild licorice flavor, so I kept it, supplementing it with fennel seeds for added depth and complexity.

Next, I tried several types of garlic—chopped fresh cloves, granulated, and garlic powder. Granulated garlic won out, in part because its coarse granules were easy to apply in a consistent layer across the butterflied roast, thus leading to more even seasoning. After a few additional tests, I found it best to spread the fennel seeds, salt, pepper, and granulated garlic on the roast, then let the roast sit for at least 6 hours (or up to a day) before cooking. Then I chopped the fresh fennel and added it right before cooking. This method gave the roast deep seasoning throughout and produced by far the most flavorful finished porketta.

I butterflied, stuffed, rolled, tied, and roasted another pork butt, and as I was cutting the twine I'd used to secure it, I wondered why the roasts were rolled in the first place. It's one thing to roll and tie an elegant stuffed roast that you're going to slice at the table, but porketta is served shredded. Skipping the rolling and tying was not only easier, but it shaved more than an hour off the cooking time, too. It also exposed more of the meat's surface area to crisp up in the oven.

I made one last important discovery when I noticed all the meat drippings left behind in the roasting pan. As any seasoned cook knows, pan drippings equal flavor. I ran the drippings through a fat separator and poured ½ cup of the savory juices over the warm shredded pork. This simple step both amplified the flavor of the pork and made the meat more moist.

I'll still go back and visit the Iron Range. But now I can have porketta whenever I want—and so can you.

—CAROLYNN PURPURA MACKAY, *Cook's Country*

IRON RANGE PORKETTA

SERVES 8

Pork butt roast is often labeled Boston butt in the supermarket. Granulated garlic has a well-rounded garlic flavor. It is golden and the texture of table salt. Garlic powder is paler, with the texture of flour, and can be acrid. Don't confuse the two or substitute garlic powder in this recipe. To crack the fennel seeds, spread them on a cutting board, place a skillet on top, and press down firmly with both hands. The porketta tastes best when the raw meat sits for a full 24 hours with the spices.

3 tablespoons fennel seeds, cracked
  Salt and pepper
2 teaspoons granulated garlic
1 (5-pound) boneless pork butt roast, trimmed
1 fennel bulb, stalks discarded, bulb halved, cored, and chopped
8 crusty sandwich rolls

1. Combine fennel seeds, 1 tablespoon salt, 2 teaspoons pepper, and garlic in bowl. Butterfly pork and cut 1-inch crosshatch pattern, ¼ inch deep, on both sides of roast. Rub pork all over with spice mixture, taking care to work spices into crosshatch. Wrap meat tightly with plastic wrap and refrigerate for at least 6 or up to 24 hours.

NOTES FROM THE TEST KITCHEN

PREPPING THE PORKETTA
We butterfly and crosshatch to expose maximum surface area to soak up seasoning.

1. Slice through pork parallel to counter, stopping ½ inch from edge. Then open meat flat like book.

2. Use chef's knife to cut 1-inch crosshatch pattern ¼ inch deep on both sides of meat.

2. Adjust oven rack to middle position and heat oven to 325 degrees. Unwrap meat and place in roasting pan, fat side down. Spread chopped fennel evenly over top of roast. Cover roasting pan tightly with aluminum foil. Roast pork until temperature registers 200 degrees and fork slips easily in and out of meat, 3 to 4 hours.

3. Transfer pork to carving board and let rest for 30 minutes. Strain liquid in roasting pan into fat separator. Shred pork into bite-size pieces, return to pan, and toss with ½ cup defatted cooking liquid. Season with salt and pepper to taste. Divide meat among rolls and serve.

PRESSURE-COOKER RIBS

✓ **WHY THIS RECIPE WORKS** We wanted to put our pressure cooker to work to get barbecued ribs with the same fall-off-the-bone texture as grill-roasted ribs—without the 4-hour cooking time. A dry rub of paprika, brown sugar, chili powder, cayenne, salt, and pepper gave the ribs bold spicy flavor. Cutting them into two-rib sections made them easy to arrange in the pot. For a cooking liquid that could double as our barbecue sauce, we sautéed onion and garlic, then stirred in ketchup, molasses, cider vinegar, and Dijon mustard. We poured some of the sauce over the ribs so that it basted and flavored the meat as it cooked. After just 30 minutes, the ribs were tender; to give them an authentic, lightly charred exterior, we finished them under the broiler, brushing them with barbecue sauce every few minutes, until they were sticky and caramelized.

Glazy, smoky, and fall-off-the-bone tender, barbecued baby back ribs are one of my favorite foods…as long as someone else is doing the cooking. I don't mind the sticky fingers or the piles of shredded paper napkins involved in eating them, but most recipes require grilling the ribs for at least 4 hours. A visit to a barbecue competition last summer gave me a deep appreciation for the time and work required to achieve the perfect rib: days for the meat to absorb the "rub" of salt, sugar, and spices; hours for the meat to tenderize in the smoker; and repeated brushings with the "mop" of sauce to develop a sticky glaze. I had resigned myself to being a fair-weather rib fan until I got to know my pressure cooker. After seeing that it made short work of pot roast, brisket, and pulled pork, I began to wonder if I could finally add barbecued ribs to my repertoire.

I started searching for indoor rib recipes. Slow-cooker recipes abounded; the long hours spent in a moist environment are ideal for melting the collagen in the meat and tenderizing the muscles. But while I liked the idea of hands-off cooking, these recipes wouldn't save me any time. The pressure cooker, with its sealed pot, seemed like the perfect compromise: Since moisture couldn't escape, the ribs would effectively braise in the moist environment. And thanks to the increased pressure in the pot, the meat would cook many times faster than on the grill or in the oven without drying out.

To start, I selected two 2-pound rib racks. The first problem? Fitting them into the pressure cooker without crowding the meat. Cutting the racks into two-rib portions streamlined the process. It also left me with more surface area on the ribs—which meant more nooks and crannies to coat with glaze later. I seasoned the ribs with a rub of paprika, brown sugar, chili powder, cayenne, salt, and pepper and placed them in the pressure cooker.

Now, what about the "mop," or sauce? In outdoor barbecue, the meat is first cooked dry, then the mop is added in stages to build a thick glaze. Since I couldn't open my pressure cooker halfway through cooking to glaze the ribs, I'd need to either cook the ribs in the sauce or add it at the end. Added at the end, it would taste like more of an afterthought than a part of the dish. But added at the beginning, it could serve as the cooking liquid and mix with the juices from the ribs to build even more flavor. I made one of the test kitchen's go-to barbecue sauces, poured it over the ribs, and brought the ribs up to high pressure (since I was in a hurry).

Getting the timing right was critical: Cooked too long, the rib meat would fall off the bone completely; cooked too little, I'd get chewy pork. I estimated that my ribs would need slightly less time than our pressure-cooker pulled pork (a 4-pound pork roast, cut into 4 sections, cooks for 45 minutes). I checked the ribs after 30 minutes, then, growing impatient, opted for an instant release (rather than a natural release, which slowly releases the pressure for about 15 minutes). The meat was just shy of perfectly tender. But I wasn't sure that it needed more time under pressure to tenderize. Wondering if my impatience had cost me the right texture, I tried again, this time allowing the pressure to release naturally. Sure enough, the pork continued to cook as the pot slowly depressurized. This time, the meat was perfect. And the spices in the rub fully penetrated the meat, giving each bite well-rounded flavor.

The sauce, on the other hand, had doubled in volume due to the fat and juices released by the pork. It was delicious, for sure, but fatty and far too thin. I removed the pork and defatted the sauce, then, to thicken it into a proper glaze, I reduced it on the stovetop until it had the proper clingy consistency.

Now I had my sauce, but I wanted a sticky glaze that would coat my ribs, not a dipping sauce. And while my ribs were tender, they lacked the char of ribs grilled over a fire. To give the ribs the proper barbecued finish, I spread them on a wire rack set inside a rimmed baking sheet, brushed them with the sauce, and turned on the broiler. The sugar in the sauce began to caramelize almost at once. I brushed the ribs with more sauce every few minutes until I had built a glaze that was a shiny burnished brown and tacky to the touch.

Maybe I wasn't quite ready for the barbecue circuit, but now I could make competition-worthy ribs in a fraction of the time.

—CHRISTIE MORRISON, America's Test Kitchen Books

NOTES FROM THE TEST KITCHEN

MAKING BARBECUED RIBS IN A PRESSURE COOKER

1. Cut each rack of ribs into 2-rib sections to ensure ribs easily fit inside pressure-cooker pot. This also makes things simpler when serving.

2. To help them cook evenly, arrange ribs upright around pot's perimeter, sitting in some of sauce, then pour more sauce over tops of ribs so that sauce will baste them as they cook.

3. To replicate char from grilling, run ribs under broiler, basting them with sauce every few minutes, until they are charred and sticky.

Pressure-Cooker Barbecued Baby Back Ribs

SERVES 4 TO 6

For an electric pressure cooker, use your own timer and turn the cooker off immediately after the pressurized cooking time, then let the pressure release naturally for 15 minutes; do not let the cooker switch to the warm setting. Use the browning (not the simmer) setting to simmer the sauce in step 5.

- 3 tablespoons paprika
- 2 tablespoons packed brown sugar
- 2 teaspoons chili powder
  Salt and pepper
- ¼ teaspoon cayenne pepper
- 2 (1½- to 2-pound) racks baby back ribs, cut into 2-rib sections
- 1 tablespoon vegetable oil
- 1 onion, chopped fine
- 2 garlic cloves, minced
- 1 cup ketchup
- ½ cup water
- ¼ cup molasses
- 2 tablespoons cider vinegar
- 2 tablespoons Dijon mustard

1. Combine paprika, sugar, chili powder, 1 teaspoon salt, 2 teaspoons pepper, and cayenne in bowl, then rub mixture evenly over ribs.

2. Heat oil in pressure-cooker pot over medium heat until shimmering. Add onion and cook until softened, about 5 minutes. Stir in garlic and cook until fragrant, about 30 seconds. Stir in ketchup, water, molasses, vinegar, and mustard. Measure out and reserve 1 cup sauce. Arrange ribs upright in pot with meaty sides facing outward, then pour reserved sauce over ribs.

3. Lock pressure-cooker lid in place and bring to high pressure over medium-high heat. As soon as pot reaches high pressure, reduce heat to medium-low and cook for 30 minutes, adjusting heat as needed to maintain high pressure.

4. Remove pot from heat and allow pressure to release naturally for 15 minutes. Quick-release any remaining pressure, then carefully remove lid, allowing steam to escape away from you.

5. Adjust oven rack 6 inches from broiler element and heat broiler. Place wire rack inside aluminum foil–lined rimmed baking sheet and spray with vegetable oil spray. Transfer ribs, meaty side up, to prepared baking sheet.

Using large spoon, skim excess fat from surface of sauce. Bring sauce to simmer and cook until sauce is thickened and measures 2 cups, about 10 minutes. Brush ribs with some of sauce, then broil until browned and sticky, 10 to 15 minutes, flipping and brushing with additional sauce every few minutes. Serve ribs with remaining sauce.

MEMPHIS-STYLE WET RIBS

✔ **WHY THIS RECIPE WORKS** For these saucy Memphis wet ribs, a potent spice rub performs double duty, seasoning the meat and creating the backbone for our barbecue sauce. Tying two racks together allowed us to double our yield and cook four hefty racks of ribs at once. To keep the ribs moist, we grilled them over indirect heat and basted them with a traditional "mop" of juice and vinegar. After a few hours of smoking on the grill, we brushed the ribs with our flavorful barbecue sauce and transferred them to the steady, even heat of the oven to finish tenderizing.

Wet or dry? You'd better be prepared to answer that question when ordering ribs in Memphis, a city that has the highest density of barbecue establishments in the country. Memphis dry ribs are spice-rubbed, slow-smoked ribs served dry, meaning without sauce, while wet ribs are sauced both during and after cooking with a tangy, tomato-based concoction that falls somewhere between the sharp, vinegary bite of North Carolina–style sauces and the heavy sweetness of Kansas City sauces.

While I appreciate the clean, minimalist approach of dry ribs, for me it's just not barbecue without sauce. My mission was to create a backyard recipe for wet ribs that a Memphis pit master would be proud to serve.

The test kitchen has a lot of experience grilling pork ribs, so I wasn't starting from scratch. I knew that I'd use St. Louis–cut ribs, which are spareribs with the bulky brisket bone and meat cut off. These ribs are easier to eat, cook faster, and fit better on a backyard kettle grill than full spareribs. With that in mind, I sorted through dozens of recipes and whittled them down to six that claimed to create the best, most "authentic" Memphis wet ribs. I prepped the recipes and stepped into the alley behind the test kitchen to do some serious smoking. About 6 hours later I hauled the ribs inside and called my colleagues to come taste. Their bright-eyed enthusiasm quickly faded. While none was downright awful, we were disappointed by ribs that were dry or tough and by rubs and sauces that were acrid and harsh or almost unnoticeable.

Clearly I would need to begin my testing with a clean slate. My first task was the rub. A good spice rub provides balanced flavor without dominating the pork; I threw together a basic barbecue mixture of paprika, brown sugar, salt, pepper, onion powder, and granulated garlic. As for the sauce, I mail-ordered several sauces from Memphis restaurants and put together a recipe based on our favorite, from Charlie Vergo's Rendezvous. I used some of the spice rub in the sauce, along with ketchup, yellow mustard, apple juice, cider vinegar, Worcestershire, and molasses. A 20-minute simmer thickened it and brought all the flavors together.

Ribs take at least 4 hours of low-and-slow cooking to become tender. Three-quarters of a chimney's worth of charcoal (our preferred amount for ribs) burns for about 2 hours. This means that on a charcoal kettle grill—the kind most of us have at home—you must refuel the grill at least once or the heat will go out before the ribs tenderize. Thankfully, the test kitchen has a better way: We smoke the ribs with indirect heat on the grill for 2 hours before bringing them inside to finish in the controlled heat of a 250-degree oven. It may not be traditional, but it creates reliably smoky, tender ribs. I basted the ribs with the sauce several times during the last 45 minutes in the oven and painted them with sauce again when they were done. Now my tasters were really smiling.

But I wasn't. Although the ribs were tender, saucy, and plenty tasty, this recipe (like all of our barbecued rib recipes) made two racks, which is all you can fit on a backyard grill when cooking with indirect heat, since the meat can never sit directly over the fire. But two racks feed just four people, which seemed like too few eaters for the hefty 4-hour time investment. I was determined to find a way to double the recipe to four racks without using a second grill.

I came up with several ideas. I tried smoking four racks in several configurations—in V-racks, stacked up in a tower with large onion rounds in between, and even in a wire file folder—but nothing worked. After days of trial and error, though, my perseverance finally paid off: I tied two racks together (bone sides facing each other) with kitchen twine and then positioned them as before on the cooler side. This arrangement let me cook twice as much meat in the same amount of space; I just needed to tweak the method a bit.

First, with twice the amount of meat, I needed more heat on the grill. The solution was something called the Minion method: You put unlit briquettes in the grill then cover them with lit coals for a longer-burning fire. Next, with more heat, I had to avoid drying out the meat. I added some water to a disposable roasting pan placed below the ribs on the grill to create steam that helped the ribs render and stay moist. A simple barbecue mop (or thin basting sauce) of apple juice, cider vinegar, and yellow mustard—ingredients that were already in my sauce—cooled the surface of the ribs (and prevented overcooking) while adding subtle flavor. I mopped the ribs twice during their time on the grill and once more before moving them to the oven.

It takes a bit of engineering, but if you want Memphis wet ribs—and a lot of them—that taste like they were born in Tennessee, what are you waiting for?

—DIANE UNGER, *Cook's Country*

Memphis-Style Wet Ribs for a Crowd

SERVES 8 TO 12

This recipe requires heavy-duty aluminum foil, a 13 by 9-inch disposable aluminum pan (or an 8½ by 4½-inch loaf pan for a gas grill), kitchen twine, and two rimmed baking sheets. You'll get the best results from a charcoal grill. If you're cooking with gas, you'll need a large grill with at least three burners. If you'd like to use wood chunks instead of wood chips when using a charcoal grill, substitute two medium wood chunks, soaked in water for 1 hour, for the wood chip packet.

SPICE RUB

- ¼ cup paprika
- 2 tablespoons packed brown sugar
- 2 tablespoons salt
- 2 teaspoons pepper
- 2 teaspoons onion powder
- 2 teaspoons granulated garlic

BARBECUE SAUCE

- 1½ cups ketchup
- ¾ cup apple juice
- ¼ cup molasses
- ¼ cup cider vinegar
- ¼ cup Worcestershire sauce
- 2 tablespoons yellow mustard
- 2 teaspoons pepper

MEMPHIS–STYLE WET RIBS FOR A CROWD

MOP

- ½ cup apple juice
- ¼ cup cider vinegar
- 1 tablespoon yellow mustard

RIBS

- 4 (2½- to 3-pound) racks St. Louis–style spareribs, trimmed, membrane removed
- 2 cups wood chips, soaked in water for 15 minutes and drained
- 1 (13 by 9-inch) disposable aluminum roasting pan (if using charcoal) or 1 (8½ by 4½-inch) disposable aluminum loaf pan (if using gas)

1. FOR THE SPICE RUB: Combine all ingredients in bowl.

2. FOR THE BARBECUE SAUCE: Combine ketchup, apple juice, molasses, vinegar, Worcestershire, mustard, and 2 tablespoons spice rub in medium saucepan and bring to boil over medium heat. Reduce heat to medium-low and simmer until thickened and reduced to 2 cups, about 20 minutes. Off heat, stir in pepper; set aside.

3. FOR THE MOP: Whisk apple juice, vinegar, mustard, and ¼ cup barbecue sauce together in bowl.

4. FOR THE RIBS: Pat ribs dry with paper towels and season all over with remaining spice rub. Place 1 rack of ribs, meaty side down, on cutting board. Place second rack of ribs, meaty side up, directly on top of first rack, arranging thick end over tapered end. Tie racks together at 2-inch intervals with kitchen twine. Repeat with remaining 2 racks of ribs. (You should have 2 bundles of ribs.) Using large piece of heavy-duty aluminum foil, wrap soaked chips in foil packet and cut several vent holes in top.

5A. FOR A CHARCOAL GRILL: Open bottom vent halfway and place disposable roasting pan on 1 side of grill. Add 2 quarts water to pan. Arrange 3 quarts unlit charcoal briquettes on other side of grill. Light large chimney starter half filled with charcoal briquettes (3 quarts). When top coals are partially covered with ash, pour evenly over unlit coals. Place wood chip packet on coals. Set cooking grate in place, cover, and open lid vent halfway. Heat grill until hot and wood chips are smoking, about 5 minutes.

5B. FOR A GAS GRILL: Place wood chip packet and disposable loaf pan over primary burner and add 2 cups

water to pan. Turn primary burner to high (leave other burners off), cover, and heat grill until hot and wood chips are smoking, about 15 minutes. (Adjust primary burner as needed to maintain grill temperature of 275 to 300 degrees.)

6. Clean and oil cooking grate. Place ribs on cooler side of grill and baste with one-third of mop. Cover (positioning lid vent over ribs for charcoal) and cook for 2 hours, flipping and switching positions of ribs and basting again with half of remaining mop halfway through cooking.

7. Adjust oven racks to upper-middle and lower-middle positions and heat oven to 300 degrees. Line 2 rimmed baking sheets with foil. Cut kitchen twine from racks. Transfer 2 racks, meaty side up, to each sheet. Baste with remaining mop and bake for 2 hours, switching and rotating sheets halfway through baking.

8. Remove ribs from oven and brush evenly with ½ cup barbecue sauce. Return to oven and continue to bake until tender, basting with ½ cup barbecue sauce and rotating and switching sheets twice during baking, about 45 minutes. (Ribs do not need to be flipped and should remain meaty side up during baking.)

9. Transfer ribs to carving board. Brush evenly with remaining ½ cup barbecue sauce, tent loosely with foil, and let rest for 20 minutes. Cut ribs between bones to separate. Serve.

NOTES FROM THE TEST KITCHEN

MAKING RIB BUNDLES
Most rib recipes for backyard grills make only one or two racks. Our ribs were so good that we wanted more. We tied racks of ribs together with kitchen twine (with the meaty sides facing out) to create two 2-rack bundles that'll feed a small party.

BUNDLE UP
With a little finessing, our two-rack bundles cook just as evenly as a single rack.

CHAPTER 7

POULTRY & SEAFOOD

BEST CHICKEN PARMESAN

✔ **WHY THIS RECIPE WORKS** Classic chicken Parmesan should feature juicy chicken cutlets with a crisp, pan-fried breaded coating complemented by creamy mozzarella and a bright, zesty marinara sauce. But more often it ends up dry and overcooked with a soggy crust and a chewy mass of cheese. To prevent the cutlets from overcooking, we halved them horizontally and pounded only the fatter sides thin. Then we salted them for 20 minutes to help them hold on to their moisture. To keep the crust crunchy, we replaced more than half of the sogginess-prone bread crumbs with flavorful grated Parmesan cheese. For a cheese topping that didn't turn chewy, we added some creamy fontina to the usual shredded mozzarella and ran it under the broiler for just 2 minutes to melt and brown. Melting the cheese directly on the fried cutlet also formed a barrier between the crispy crust and the tomato sauce.

It's surprising that chicken Parmesan ever became so popular. True, at its best it's a wonderful combination of juicy chicken, crisp breaded crust, and rich cheesy flavor offset by zippy tomato sauce, but the classic cooking method makes it difficult for the home cook to achieve such results with any regularity.

In traditional recipes, boneless, skinless chicken breasts are pounded until thin, then coated in breading and fried until crispy and golden—so far, so good. But then those fully cooked cutlets are blanketed with tomato sauce, mozzarella, and a token dusting of Parmesan and baked in the oven. During baking, the sauce saturates and softens the crust, the chicken overcooks, and the cheeses meld into a thick mass that turns tough soon after being removed from the oven. After all that work, what should be a delicious indulgence is usually a soupy, soggy, chewy disappointment. I wanted to buck tradition and create a version that delivered the best features every time. Only then would it earn a place in my collection of classic recipes.

First, I wondered if I could avoid the usual frying step by coating the chicken with precrisped crumbs and a bit of fat and baking it, simplifying the dish and making it a bit lighter at the same time. No such luck. The coating wasn't as crunchy or cohesive as I wanted, and it turned soggy the second it came in contact with the sauce. Clearly I'd need to stick with shallow frying.

Following the usual method, I pounded four boneless, skinless chicken breasts with a rubber mallet until they were ¼ inch thick. Their surface area increased almost threefold, making the breading process (flour, then beaten egg, then seasoned bread crumbs) unwieldy, but I consoled myself with the thought that more surface area would mean more crunch.

I shallow-fried the cutlets in batches in several table-spoons of oil until they were crispy, drained them on paper towels, shingled them in a baking dish covered with a simple tomato sauce, then topped it all with a layer of mozzarella and Parmesan. After 20 minutes in a 375-degree oven, the cheese was bubbly and starting to brown in spots.

This test turned out to be a successful demonstration of everything that can possibly go wrong. The cutlets were overcooked and tough, and the delicate crust that frying had wrought was soft and soggy. And the cheese? It quickly coagulated into an unyielding sheet.

I flirted with the idea of subbing chicken thighs for the usual breasts, thinking that they would stay moister, but when I tried it the flavor was all wrong. Chicken Parmesan relies on the clean, neutral flavor of white meat to balance the fried coating, zesty sauce, and creamy cheese—the slight gaminess of dark meat just didn't work. Breasts it would be, but I'd have to find a way to keep them moist and tender.

I realized that pounding the chicken very thin increased the likelihood of overcooking, but taking the breasts straight from the packaging to the breading didn't work either. The thick breasts didn't cook through in the quick frying time, so they had to spend more time in the oven, which gave the crust even more time to get soggy.

Eventually, I settled on slicing two large breasts horizontally and pounding only the thick end of each piece to achieve a consistent ½-inch thickness from end to end. Then I looked for a way to simplify the tedious and messy three-step breading procedure. For some recipes each step of the process is vital: The initial coat of flour helps the egg stick, and the egg helps the crumbs stick. Not in this case. I found that I could simply mix a bit of flour into the egg; coat the cutlets with the mixture; and proceed straight to crumbs with cleaner fingers, one less dish to wash, and no decrease in crumb adherence. Next I salted the cutlets for 20 minutes so the salt would penetrate the surface of the meat and alter the proteins in such a way as to help them hold on to more of their moisture. Now I had the moistest, most tender, most well-seasoned cutlets yet—but the crust still had no chance against the sauce.

There are three parts to the crust problem. The first and biggest issue is that bread crumbs are starch, and starch readily absorbs liquid and turns soft. Second, completely covering the crusted cutlets with a very wet sauce exposes the most crust to the most liquid. And third, waiting around for the cheese to melt in the oven gives the sauce plenty of time to saturate and soften the crust.

First I turned my attention to the sauce, cooking the canned tomatoes, garlic, and seasonings longer so that the sauce thickened. Then I brightened it with red pepper flakes and fresh basil. Rather than saucing the entire surface of the chicken, I put just a small amount on top of each cutlet, figuring I could pass more at the table. And I radically limited the time the two components spent together; because I needed to bake the dish only long enough to melt the cheese, I swapped the moderate oven for the fierce heat of the broiler and took the 20 minutes of baking time down to just 2 minutes.

A thicker sauce and less oven time helped the soggy situation, but they didn't fix it completely. The breading would still need to be reengineered. And how do you get around the problem that breading is, well, bread? I started thinking about what else I could use for a coating. I needed something that is mostly protein and fat and contains no starch to keep it from getting soggy . . . what about Parmesan cheese? Replacing more than half of the bread crumbs with grated Parmesan not only made the crust on my cutlets more moisture-proof but also meant that my chicken Parmesan was starting to earn its surname.

The soggy crust problem had lessened, but it was not completely solved—not until I began to play with the order in which the components of the dish were assembled. Instead of putting the cheese combo on top of the sauce, I placed it between the crust and the sauce so it melted to form a cheesy layer that protected the cutlet. Sogginess? Gone.

However, I still had one problem to solve. The mozzarella continued to mar the dish by forming a leathery layer on top of the chicken. Recalling a test kitchen recipe for macaroni and cheese in which the solution to a texture problem was using a combination of cheeses, I considered possible creamy, tenderizing companions for the rubbery mozzarella. Cream cheese and heavy cream were too liquid, and cheddar and Monterey Jack (the solution to the mac and cheese) had the wrong flavors. Mozzarella's ideal accomplice turned out to be creamy, nutty fontina. Used in equal parts, the two cheeses provided the perfect combination of authentic Italian flavor and tender, soft texture.

Every bite of my revamped chicken Parmesan offered crispy, juicy chicken; wispy strands of creamy mozzarella and fontina cheeses; fresh, bright tomato sauce; and nutty Parmesan flavor. Finally it was worth the indulgence.

—ANDREA GEARY, *Cook's Illustrated*

Best Chicken Parmesan

SERVES 4

Our preferred brands of crushed tomatoes are Tuttorosso and Muir Glen. This recipe makes enough sauce to top the cutlets as well as four servings of pasta. Serve with pasta and a simple green salad.

SAUCE

- 2 tablespoons extra-virgin olive oil
- 2 garlic cloves, minced
  Kosher salt and pepper
- ¼ teaspoon dried oregano
  Pinch red pepper flakes
- 1 (28-ounce) can crushed tomatoes
- ¼ teaspoon sugar
- 2 tablespoons coarsely chopped fresh basil

CHICKEN

- 2 (6- to 8-ounce) boneless, skinless chicken breasts, trimmed, halved horizontally, and pounded ½ inch thick
- 1 teaspoon kosher salt
- 2 ounces whole-milk mozzarella cheese, shredded (½ cup)
- 2 ounces fontina cheese, shredded (½ cup)
- 1 large egg
- 1 tablespoon all-purpose flour
- 1½ ounces Parmesan cheese, grated (¾ cup)
- ½ cup panko bread crumbs
- ½ teaspoon garlic powder
- ¼ teaspoon dried oregano
- ¼ teaspoon pepper
- ⅓ cup vegetable oil
- ¼ cup torn fresh basil

1. FOR THE SAUCE: Heat 1 tablespoon oil in medium saucepan over medium heat until just shimmering.

Add garlic, ¾ teaspoon salt, oregano, and pepper flakes; cook, stirring occasionally, until fragrant, about 30 seconds. Stir in tomatoes and sugar; increase heat to high and bring to simmer. Reduce heat to medium-low and simmer until thickened, about 20 minutes. Off heat, stir in basil and remaining 1 tablespoon oil; season with salt and pepper to taste. Cover and keep warm.

2. FOR THE CHICKEN: Sprinkle each side of each cutlet with ⅛ teaspoon salt and let stand at room temperature for 20 minutes. Combine mozzarella and fontina in bowl; set aside.

3. Adjust oven rack 4 inches from broiler element and heat broiler. Whisk egg and flour together in shallow dish or pie plate until smooth. Combine Parmesan, panko, garlic powder, oregano, and pepper in second shallow dish or pie plate. Pat chicken dry with paper towels. Working with 1 cutlet at a time, dredge cutlet in egg mixture, allowing excess to drip off. Coat all sides with Parmesan mixture, pressing gently so crumbs adhere. Transfer cutlet to large plate and repeat with remaining cutlets.

4. Heat oil in 10-inch nonstick skillet over medium-high heat until shimmering. Carefully place 2 cutlets in skillet and cook without moving them until bottoms are crisp and deep golden brown, 1½ to 2 minutes. Using tongs, carefully flip cutlets and cook on second side until deep golden brown, 1½ to 2 minutes. Transfer cutlets to paper towel–lined plate and repeat with remaining cutlets.

5. Place cutlets in rimmed baking sheet and sprinkle cheese mixture evenly over cutlets, covering as much surface area as possible. Broil until cheese is melted and beginning to brown, 2 to 4 minutes. Transfer chicken to serving platter and top each cutlet with 2 tablespoons sauce. Sprinkle with basil and serve immediately, passing remaining sauce separately.

NOTES FROM THE TEST KITCHEN

CREATING THIN, EVEN CUTLETS

Slice cutlets horizontally (freeze them first for 15 minutes to help with slicing), then pound only thicker ends to achieve even ½-inch thickness.

CHICKEN NOODLE CASSEROLE

✔ **WHY THIS RECIPE WORKS** To update this retro dish from a muddle of convenience products to a hearty homemade casserole, we started by ditching the condensed soup and canned ingredients. A simple flour-thickened sauce of chicken broth and half-and-half created a rich, savory base. A combination of cheeses—cheddar for flavor and American for smooth melting—was key. Precooked chicken turned rubbery after being baked into the casserole, so we simmered boneless, skinless chicken breasts in the sauce until they were nearly cooked through before shredding the meat and returning it to the casserole. To keep the noodles from turning mushy and overcooked while the casserole baked, we boiled them until just al dente, then ran them under cold water to stop the cooking. Buttery Ritz Crackers made a quick, crunchy, classic topping.

Chicken noodle casserole was first conceived and developed by the Campbell's company in the 1940s as a way to boost sales of its canned condensed soup. The simplest (and in my opinion, scariest) version I found of this classic casserole called for canned condensed soup, canned vegetables, and canned chicken. Gloppy, bland, and gross, it didn't justify even the minimal effort involved. But creamy, satisfying casseroles are our stock-in-trade at *Cook's Country;* I was confident we were the right folks for this job.

The test kitchen had already developed a recipe for tuna noodle casserole without condensed soup; since the two recipes are similar, I decided to start there. I swapped the tuna for store-bought rotisserie chicken instead of canned chicken (which is precooked, like canned tuna), then I loosely followed the instructions for tuna noodle casserole: I sautéed some diced onion and built a flour-thickened sauce from a little chicken broth (1½ cups) and a lot of half-and-half (3½ cups). I stirred in 1 cup each of cheddar and Monterey Jack cheeses; the diced rotisserie chicken; and boiled, cooled egg noodles (cooked to barely al dente, since they'd continue to cook while the casserole baked). I poured the mixture into a dish and stuck it in the oven for just 15 minutes.

This casserole was a big improvement over the all-canned version. That said, it hadn't translated perfectly from tuna. While the plentiful half-and-half balanced the fishy tuna, with milder chicken the sauce was bland. Meanwhile, the chicken itself was tough and rubbery.

CHICKEN NOODLE CASSEROLE

To lighten the sauce, I went down on the half-and-half and up on the chicken broth. But because fat helps keep a sauce from breaking, this sauce separated. I'd have to compensate for the loss of the fat from the half-and-half. I was able to stabilize the sauce by melting in cream cheese, which contains stabilizers that help prevent curdling, in place of the Monterey Jack. But its tangy flavor was jarring. Casting about for a mellower cheese that also has stabilizers, I landed on American cheese. Ultimately, a combination of American and cheddar cheeses, plus 2½ cups each of half-and-half and chicken broth, yielded a lighter, very tasty, but still cohesive sauce.

Now how to fix the rubbery chicken? When I tried adding raw chicken to the casserole, it didn't cook through. But the rotisserie chicken overcooked during its round in the oven. What if I abandoned the rotisserie chicken and instead cooked raw chicken on the stovetop, slightly undercooking it, before stirring it into the casserole to gently finish in the oven? Breast meat

was a given. All recipes for chicken noodle casserole use it, and it suits this old-fashioned dish. I settled on boneless, skinless chicken breasts and employed a method the test kitchen has used with success before: poaching the meat in the thickened cream sauce, stopping just before it was cooked through, then cubing it. It worked well here and, as a bonus, added more chicken flavor to the sauce. A few tests later, I opted to shred (not cube) the chicken so that it would meld better with the other ingredients. My method, which took just 10 minutes of hands-off poaching, was barely more work than if I had bought a rotisserie chicken.

I had two more elements of the dish to figure out: the vegetables and a crunchy topping. Recipes variously call for peas, carrots, peppers, celery, and mushrooms. All tasted fine, but our favorite was a combination of peas and red bell peppers. For the topping, after testing the usual (and some unusual) suspects, I landed on Ritz Crackers. Buttery, crunchy, and retro, they suited this creamy, cheesy comfort casserole perfectly.

—CAROLYNN PURPURA MACKAY, *Cook's Country*

NOTES FROM THE TEST KITCHEN

THE BEST ARTISANAL CHEDDAR CHEESE

Cheddar—which in 2010 accounted for more than 30 percent of the cheese produced in this country—is the variety you're most likely to see melted on a burger or oozing from a grilled cheese sandwich. And while your average American cheddar doesn't resemble the complex-tasting cheese produced in England for centuries, American cheddar is poised to climb out of this rut. Many stores now offer "artisanal" domestic cheddars that claim to rival the English stuff and fetch prices just as high. And not just from grassroots dairy farms; some of the biggest names in domestic cheddar production have debuted higher-end lines.

We sampled nine artisanal cheddars, setting benchmarks on either end of the spectrum, adding our supermarket favorite, Cabot Private Stock, to the mix, and pitting the domestic winners against Keen's Cheddar, long considered one of the gold standards of English farmhouse cheddars.

The first thing we noticed was that all of the cheddars tasted remarkably different. Texture also varied hugely. Some cheddars were so dry that they crumbled in our hands, and others were as moist and creamy as Monterey Jack. One thing was clear, though: Our top cheddars were worth every penny. Several wowed us with "intensely nutty," "buttery" tang and creamy-textured crumbliness. Our winning cheddar, **Milton Creamery Prairie Breeze**, had "buttery," caramel-like flavor with hints of "fruity" sweetness that had tasters raving, and it boasted a crumbly yet creamy texture. (See page 298 for more information on our testing results.)

Chicken Noodle Casserole

SERVES 8 TO 10

Cooking the egg noodles until just al dente, then shocking them in cold water prevents them from overcooking.

12	ounces (7¾ cups) wide egg noodles
	Salt and pepper
3	tablespoons unsalted butter
1	red bell pepper, stemmed, seeded, and chopped fine
1	onion, chopped fine
3	tablespoons all-purpose flour
2½	cups half-and-half
2½	cups chicken broth
1	pound boneless, skinless chicken breasts, halved lengthwise and trimmed
4	ounces deli American cheese, chopped coarse
4	ounces sharp cheddar cheese, shredded (1 cup)
1½	cups frozen peas
25	Ritz Crackers, crushed coarse

1. Bring 4 quarts water to boil in Dutch oven. Add noodles and 1 tablespoon salt and cook, stirring often, until just al dente, about 3 minutes. Drain noodles and rinse with cold water until cool, about 2 minutes. Drain again and set aside.

2. Melt 1 tablespoon butter in now-empty pot over medium-high heat. Add bell pepper and onion and cook, stirring occasionally, until softened, about 5 minutes. Transfer to bowl; set aside. In now-empty pot, melt remaining 2 tablespoons butter over medium heat. Add flour and cook, whisking constantly, for 1 minute. Slowly whisk in half-and-half and broth and bring to boil. Reduce heat to medium-low and simmer until slightly thickened, about 5 minutes. Add chicken and cook until no longer pink, 8 to 10 minutes.

3. Adjust oven rack to upper-middle position and heat oven to 425 degrees. Remove pot from heat, transfer chicken to plate, and shred into bite-size pieces once cool enough to handle. Whisk American and cheddar cheeses into sauce until smooth. Stir shredded chicken, noodles, bell pepper mixture, peas, 1½ teaspoons salt, and 1¼ teaspoons pepper into cheese sauce.

4. Transfer mixture to 13 by 9-inch baking dish and top with crackers. Bake until golden brown and bubbling, about 15 minutes. Let casserole cool on wire rack for 10 minutes. Serve.

HONEY FRIED CHICKEN

WHY THIS RECIPE WORKS Really good honey fried chicken is juicy and tender on the inside with a crispy, sticky, honey-flavored coating. To keep the meat moist, we brined the chicken first. For a crispy coating, we dusted the chicken with cornstarch and dipped it in a thin cornstarch-and-water batter. The hardest part was glazing the fried chicken in honey without making the crust soggy. We found that the key was to double-fry the chicken: We partially fried the chicken, let it rest to allow moisture from the skin to evaporate, then fried it again for an incredibly crunchy crust that stayed crispy when dunked in a glaze of warm honey and hot sauce.

Honey fried chicken seems to have gone the way of big band music and mambo dancing, but given how delicious it is, that's a real shame. The concept of drizzling fried chicken with honey was popularized in the 1930s by Oklahoma restaurateur Beverly Osborne and his franchise, Chicken in the Rough. By 1950, nearly 250 of the restaurants operated across the United States, serving up fried half chickens, hot buttered rolls, and jug honey. Over the years, there have been occasional copycats (Yogi Bear's Honey-Fried Chicken, for one), but the pairing has mostly vanished. Recently, though, I came across such a recipe. But with the honey soak, could the chicken possibly stay crispy? I had to find out.

I rounded up the few other recipes I could find, but when I took them into the kitchen, I was underwhelmed. The chicken was dry and the glaze, honey mixed with hot sauce, was poorly distributed. What's worse, though, was that while the chicken had emerged from the fryer crunchy, just as I'd feared, the subsequent honey bath had made it soggy. Fortunately, I'm hard to dissuade where fried chicken is concerned, so I persevered.

I knew exactly how to keep the chicken moist: I'd brine it. Instead of a standard test kitchen brine of water, salt, and sugar, I customized my brine by replacing the sugar with honey; I hoped to work some honey flavor into the chicken meat. But the flavor was too fleeting, so I reverted to sugar.

It was obvious that this particular fried chicken would require extra-crispy skin to withstand the honey glaze. The thick, flour-based coatings from my initial tests had soaked up the honey like sponges and ended up sodden. Clearly, the thinner the coating, the better. I decided to scratch the flour, which absorbed moisture too readily, and instead turned to a simple batter of cornstarch and water. Cornstarch helps make for particularly crispy skin. I dipped the raw, brined chicken into the batter and then fried it. The coating was tantalizingly crispy straight from the oil. But . . . the subsequent honey drizzle still drenched it. Frustrated, I stepped away from the kitchen to read and think.

I read about a craze for Korean fried chicken that has swept Los Angeles and New York. That chicken is made according to an unusual two-fry method, which is said to produce the crispiest skin imaginable. The chicken pieces are fried until the skin is just beginning to crisp, removed from the boiling oil, rested for several minutes, and then returned to the oil to finish cooking. Our science editor explained the theory behind this method: Essentially, the two-fry technique is more effective at evaporating the moisture in chicken skin, which allows the skin to crisp and brown before the chicken meat overcooks.

Idea and explanation in hand, I headed back into the kitchen, where I tested the two-fry method alongside the more usual method (chicken cooked through in a single, roughly 13-minute fry). The twice-fried method won hands down, resulting in an extremely crispy-skinned bird with a beautifully golden crust. A quick preliminary test of drizzling on plain honey showed that the chicken was finally able to maintain its crunch. Hallelujah!

This two-fry method created a new problem, though—the coating began to unstick after the first fry. Fortunately, solving that was a simple matter of dusting the raw chicken pieces lightly with cornstarch. The dusting dried the chicken skin, so the wet batter had something to stick to.

It was time to nail down the glaze. Straight out of the jar, honey is pretty thick, so it coated the chicken inconsistently. Since honey thins when heated, I heated ¾ cup of mild honey in the microwave until it was pourable. I stirred in 2 tablespoons of hot sauce and also circled back to the batter and seasoned it with lots of pepper to complement the sweetness. Now that the glaze was thinner, for the best coverage I'd dip rather than drizzle. Working with one piece at a time, I dunked the fried chicken and then set it on a baking rack to drip-dry. I called over my colleagues and distributed drumsticks, breasts, and thighs. Well? The coating was crisp, the chicken moist, and the honey glaze added balanced, sweet heat. Honey fried chicken is ready for its second act.

—DIANE UNGER, *Cook's Country*

Honey Fried Chicken

SERVES 4

You will need a 6-quart (or larger) Dutch oven to make this recipe.

BRINE

½ cup salt

½ cup sugar

3 pounds bone-in chicken pieces (split breasts cut in half, drumsticks, and/or thighs), trimmed

BATTER

1½ cups cornstarch

¾ cup cold water

2 teaspoons pepper

1 teaspoon salt

3 quarts peanut or vegetable oil

HONEY GLAZE

¾ cup honey

2 tablespoons hot sauce

NOTES FROM THE TEST KITCHEN

FRY TWICE

Chicken skin is mostly fat and water, roughly half of each. When chicken is fried, the moisture in the skin begins to evaporate. The skin can't get hot enough to brown until all the water has evaporated, but by that point the chicken meat may be overcooked. To get both moist meat and super-crispy skin, we fried our chicken twice, resting it between its dunks in hot oil. While the chicken cooled, additional water evaporated from its skin. When the chicken pieces went back into the oil, the last bit of water in the skin quickly evaporated, letting the skin brown and crisp fast, before the meat overcooked.

DON'T STOP YET
The chicken is pale after its first fry. It will brown and crisp during the second fry.

1. FOR THE BRINE: Dissolve salt and sugar in 2 quarts cold water in large container. Add chicken, cover, and refrigerate for 30 minutes or up to 1 hour.

2. FOR THE BATTER: Whisk 1 cup cornstarch, water, pepper, and salt together in bowl until smooth. Refrigerate batter while chicken is brining.

3. Set wire rack inside rimmed baking sheet. Sift remaining ½ cup cornstarch into medium bowl. Remove chicken from brine and dry thoroughly with paper towels. Working with 1 piece at a time, coat chicken thoroughly with cornstarch, shaking to remove excess; transfer to platter.

4. Add oil to large Dutch oven until it measures about 2 inches deep and heat over medium-high heat to 350 degrees. Whisk batter to recombine. Transfer half of chicken to batter and turn to coat. Remove chicken from batter, allowing excess to drip back into bowl, and add chicken to hot oil. Adjust burner, if necessary, to maintain oil temperature between 325 and 350 degrees. Fry chicken, stirring to prevent pieces from sticking together, until slightly golden and just beginning to crisp, 5 to 7 minutes. (Chicken will not be cooked through at this point.) Transfer parcooked chicken to platter. Return oil to 350 degrees and repeat with remaining raw chicken and batter. Let each batch of chicken rest for 5 to 7 minutes.

5. Return oil to 350 degrees. Return first batch of chicken to oil and fry until breasts register 160 degrees and thighs/drumsticks register 175 degrees, 5 to 7 minutes. Transfer to wire rack. Return oil to 350 degrees and repeat with remaining chicken.

6. FOR THE HONEY GLAZE: Combine honey and hot sauce in large bowl and microwave until hot, about 1½ minutes. Add chicken pieces 1 at a time to honey mixture and turn to coat; return to wire rack, skin side up, to drain. Serve.

JERK CHICKEN

✔ **WHY THIS RECIPE WORKS** Traditional Jamaican jerk recipes rely on island ingredients for both marinade and cooking technique. Fortunately, we were able to achieve the characteristic spicy-sweet-fresh-smoky balance with the right combination of stateside staples. Keeping the marinade pastelike and cooking the meat over indirect heat first prevented the jerk flavors from dripping or peeling off during grilling. Enhancing our hickory chip packet with allspice berries, thyme, and rosemary allowed our jerk chicken recipe to mimic the unique smoke of authentic pimento wood.

The roots of Jamaican jerk recipes date back more than 300 years, when Taino Indians inhabited the island's forests along with escaped African slaves brought over by the British when they colonized the country. The refugees used salt, pepper, and the fragrant berries of the pimento (aka allspice) tree to flavor and preserve strips of wild boar, then they used the tree's leaves and branches to slowly smoke the meat.

The technique has come a long way since then, but the flavors still reflect the Jamaican original. Rather than boar meat smoked in fire pits, most modern-day jerk recipes call for marinating the meat—chicken, pork, and goat are all common—with an intensely flavorful liquid paste of allspice berries, fiery Scotch bonnet chiles, thyme, a little sugar, and a dozen or so other herbs and spices and smoking it over pimento wood. When this is done well, the meat emerges aromatic, woodsy, spicy, and sweet, with a clean, lingering burn from the fresh chiles—an appealing flavor profile that inspired me to come up with a recipe of my own. Chicken was my meat of choice, and for the sake of even cooking, I'd stick with individual parts rather than a whole bird.

Little did I know that jerk recipes are rife with pitfalls. Dense, thick spice pastes were tricky to spread evenly over the meat and tended to stick to the hot grill grates and burn. Thinner, more liquid concoctions ran right off the chicken pieces and into the fire—but not before they saturated the skin, preventing it from rendering and browning. Drier, rublike mixtures tasted dull and dusty. Beyond that, none of the marinades hit on the ideal aromatic-sweet-spicy balance I was hoping for, and since pimento wood isn't easy to come by here in the Northeast, I was stuck with a more widely available option: hickory. Needless to say, I had a lot of work ahead of me.

Nailing down the flavor and consistency of the marinade seemed like the obvious first step, so I lined up a slew of potential ingredients, set up a basic indirect fire to cook the chicken (I'd revisit the grilling method later), and got busy. Allspice, thyme, and chiles (I chose habaneros in place of hard-to-find Scotch bonnets) were definites, as were scallions for their grassy freshness, plenty of garlic, and salt (which we've discovered is the most important element of any marinade). From there, I went about adding—and subtracting—herbs, spices, and condiments until I'd come up with a formula that got me close to the complex balance I was after: the aforementioned core elements, plus coriander seeds and peppercorns (coarsely ground in a spice grinder with the allspice berries) and a mixture of dried thyme, basil, and rosemary for woodsy depth; ground nutmeg and ginger plus a touch of brown sugar for warmth and sweetness, respectively; a good amount of grated lime zest and yellow mustard for brightness; and soy sauce for a savory boost.

At this point, the marinade's flavor was relatively full-bodied, but the consistency was a little too thick. So I scoured my pantry for liquid helpers and spotted vegetable oil. Sure enough, a few spoonfuls of that loosened things up just enough for the marinade to thoroughly coat and cling to the chicken pieces. Even better, between the salt and the soy sauce, the chicken tasted well seasoned after just 30 minutes of marinating. (I also tried testing longer marinating times—up to 24 hours—and happily discovered that the longer the chicken sat, the more flavorful the meat became, thanks to the water-soluble flavor compounds in the marinade ingredients penetrating even further. It's just a matter of how much time you have.)

Back to the grilling method. Cooking the chicken over the cool side of an indirect fire (where all the coals are banked to one side of the grill) was a close imitation of the traditional low-fire method, and it ensured that

JERK CHICKEN

the chicken stayed juicy. But while gentle heat made for succulent meat, it didn't do much for the skin, which was pale and rubbery. I modified my coal setup and made use of the hotter half of the grill as well, spreading the briquettes evenly over one side, which gave me the space I needed to sear the marinated chicken pieces in one batch before finishing them on the cooler half of the grill.

Unfortunately, there was a major snag in my plans to brown and render the skin: the marinade, which burned by the time the skin dried enough to get any color. I thought that switching the order of operations—from searing first to searing last—might solve the problem by allowing the marinade to dry out before I put it face-to-face with the hot grates, but at that point the fire had died down considerably and didn't offer enough heat for searing. My frustration was building, but my colleagues reminded me that I had one more trick to try: a barbecue technique that we devised for prolonging a grill's heat output. I placed a batch of unlit coals in the kettle, followed by a batch that I'd ignited as usual in a chimney starter, so that the lit briquettes would slowly ignite the unlit batch, prolonging the fire's burn. I gave it a whirl and was relieved to find that did it: The delayed fire setup accommodated both the meat and the skin.

I liked to think I was making progress, but the truth was that I'd put off the most challenging part of my jerk recipe—the elusive pimento wood smoke flavor—until the very end. There was no way I was shelling out for mail-order wood every time I wanted some Jamaican barbecue, but for the sake of comparing the real deal with hickory wood, I special-ordered some pimento chips and prepared a double batch of my recipe, one cooked over hickory and the other over my costly pimento.

The difference was clear: While the hickory wood infused the meat with an assertive smokiness, the pimento wood lent the chicken a fresher, sweeter, and more herbal smoke flavor that tasters preferred. How could I make hickory smoke taste like pimento?

That's where the science journals came in. To get a better understanding of smoke flavor, I decided to sift through some articles about wood and the types of flavor compounds they release when they smolder. The research made sense: Depending on the type of wood, some of these compounds (known as phenols and terpenes) can be robust and meaty (like hickory) or cleaner and more delicate (like pimento). That much I'd inferred from my taste test. What was enlightening, however, was an article that I came across in *Flavour & Fragrance Journal* detailing the flavor compounds of edible spices and herbs. It had never occurred to me that I could "smoke" herbs and spices, but the idea sounded promising. Allspice berries were an obvious source of pimento wood flavor compounds, so I added a couple of tablespoons to the packet with my hickory chips, whipped up another batch of the jerk marinade, and got grilling. This test was a real breakthrough: I hadn't quite nailed the complexity of the pimento wood flavor just yet, but the warm fragrance of the allspice berries had made a noticeable difference. This got me wondering what else my spice cabinet might have to offer. Two bottles jumped out at me: dried rosemary and dried thyme, which both happen to contain many of the flavor compounds in the leaves of the pimento tree. Two tablespoons of each helped even out the smoke flavor, save for one problem: The herbs and spices were smoldering too quickly, resulting in the same carbonized off-flavors you get when wood burns too hot. I tried soaking and draining the spice mixture along with the wood chips, but that simply washed out their flavor. So I opted for the halfway point: moistening the spices with just enough water (2 tablespoons) to dampen the smolder and still preserve their delicate flavor.

I may have been in Massachusetts when I took a bite of that final batch of jerk chicken, but thanks to the marinade's complexity and the delicate warmth of my faux pimento wood packet, I could just as easily have been standing in Jamaica's Boston Bay.

—CELESTE ROGERS, *Cook's Illustrated*

NOTES FROM THE TEST KITCHEN

WOOD CHIP PACKET WITH A JAMAICAN ACCENT
The delicately fragrant, herby smoke of pimento wood is a fundamental element of jerk flavor. We weren't about to mail-order the hard-to-find timber every time we got a craving, but with a little help from our spice cabinet, we came up with a good imitation.

HOMEGROWN APPROACH
To replicate that profile, we add allspice berries, dried thyme, and rosemary to hickory chips.

Jerk Chicken

SERVES 4

For a milder dish, use one seeded chile. If you prefer your food very hot, use up to all three chiles including their seeds and ribs. Scotch bonnet chiles can be used in place of the habaneros. Wear gloves when working with the chiles.

JERK MARINADE

- 1½ tablespoons whole coriander seeds
- 1 tablespoon whole allspice berries
- 1 tablespoon whole peppercorns
- 1–3 habanero chiles, stemmed, quartered, and seeds and ribs reserved, if using
- 8 scallions, chopped
- 6 garlic cloves, peeled
- 3 tablespoons vegetable oil
- 2 tablespoons soy sauce
- 2 tablespoons finely grated lime zest (3 limes), plus lime wedges for serving
- 2 tablespoons yellow mustard
- 1 tablespoon dried thyme
- 1 tablespoon ground ginger
- 1 tablespoon packed brown sugar
- 2¼ teaspoons salt
- 2 teaspoons dried basil
- ½ teaspoon dried rosemary
- ½ teaspoon ground nutmeg

CHICKEN

- 3 pounds bone-in chicken pieces (split breasts cut in half, drumsticks, and/or thighs)
- 2 tablespoons whole allspice berries
- 2 tablespoons dried thyme
- 2 tablespoons dried rosemary
- 2 tablespoons water
- 1 cup wood chips, soaked in water for 15 minutes and drained

1. FOR THE JERK MARINADE: Grind coriander seeds, allspice berries, and peppercorns in spice grinder or mortar and pestle until coarsely ground. Transfer spices to blender jar. Add habanero(s), scallions, garlic, oil, soy sauce, lime zest, mustard, thyme, ginger, sugar, salt, basil, rosemary, and nutmeg and process until smooth paste forms, 1 to 3 minutes, scraping down sides of blender jar as necessary. Transfer marinade to gallon-size zipper-lock bag.

2. FOR THE CHICKEN: Place chicken pieces in bag with marinade and toss to coat; press out as much air as possible and seal bag. Let stand at room temperature for 30 minutes while preparing grill, flipping bag after 15 minutes. (Marinated chicken can be refrigerated for up to 24 hours.)

3. Combine allspice berries, thyme, rosemary, and water in bowl and set aside to moisten for 15 minutes. Using large piece of heavy-duty aluminum foil, wrap soaked chips and moistened allspice mixture in foil packet and cut several vent holes in top.

4A. FOR A CHARCOAL GRILL: Open bottom vent halfway. Arrange 1 quart unlit charcoal briquettes in single layer over half of grill. Light large chimney starter one-third filled with charcoal briquettes (2 quarts). When top coals are partially covered with ash, pour evenly over unlit briquettes, keeping coals arranged over half of grill. Place wood chip packet on coals. Set cooking grate in place, cover, and open lid vent halfway. Heat grill until hot and wood chips are smoking, about 5 minutes.

4B. FOR A GAS GRILL: Place wood chip packet over primary burner. Turn all burners to high, cover, and heat grill until hot and wood chips begin to smoke, 15 to 25 minutes. Turn primary burner to medium and turn off other burner(s).

5. Clean and oil cooking grate. Place chicken, with marinade clinging and skin side up, as far away from fire as possible, with thighs closest to fire and breasts farthest away. Cover (positioning lid vent over chicken if using charcoal) and cook for 30 minutes.

6. Move chicken, skin side down, to hotter side of grill; cook until browned and skin renders, 3 to 6 minutes. Using tongs, flip chicken pieces and cook until browned on second side and breasts register 160 degrees and thighs/drumsticks register 175 degrees, 5 to 12 minutes longer.

7. Transfer chicken to serving platter, tent loosely with foil, and let rest for 5 to 10 minutes. Serve warm or at room temperature with lime wedges.

SKILLET CHICKEN FAJITAS

✔ **WHY THIS RECIPE WORKS** To create indoor chicken fajitas that didn't require a slew of garnishes to be tasty, we took a fresh look at the key ingredients. For well-charred, juicy chicken we marinated boneless, skinless breasts in a potent mix of smoked paprika, garlic, cumin, cayenne, and sugar before searing them on one side and finishing them gently in a low oven. We revamped the pedestrian mix of bell pepper and onion by charring poblano chiles and thinly sliced onion, then cooking them with cream and a squeeze of fresh lime juice. Finally, we finished the dish with just a few fresh-flavored garnishes: pickled radishes, *queso fresco*, cilantro, and lime wedges.

Fajitas originated in the 1930s when hungry ranch hands in the Rio Grande Valley of Texas filled up on grilled leftover beef trimmings wrapped in charred flour tortillas. In 1973, Houston restaurateur Ninfa Rodriguez Laurenzo picked up on the idea and started offering the dish in her restaurant, much to the delight of the locals. Fast-forward almost a decade to 1982, when enterprising chef George Weidmann of the Hyatt Regency's La Vista restaurant in Austin put "sizzling fajitas" on his menu. To say that his signature dish was a hit is putting it mildly: Surging sales made La Vista the most profitable restaurant in the Hyatt chain, and chefs across the country were quick to jump on the fajita bandwagon.

Today, fajitas are made with everything from steak to shrimp to chicken. But truth be told, it almost doesn't matter what the protein is, since it's usually buried under flavor-dulling gobs of sour cream and shredded cheese. I wanted to reinvigorate fajitas, using convenient boneless, skinless chicken breasts and finding a good way to cook them indoors for year-round appeal. My lighter, contemporary twist would abandon the stodgy Tex-Mex garnishes and put the spotlight where it belongs: on the chicken, peppers, and onions.

Boneless, skinless chicken breasts may be convenient, but the downside is that they're also lean and somewhat bland. My first inclination was to pump them up with a brinerade—a concentrated liquid with the salt content of a brine plus the acid and seasonings of a marinade. The salt seasons the meat and helps keep it moist during cooking, and the herbs, spices, and acid begin to penetrate the surface of the flesh with robust flavor.

I gave it a shot, mixing up a punchy concoction of salt, lime juice, garlic, cumin, and cayenne pepper—some

of the key flavors of Mexican cuisine. I also added oil—important because the flavor compounds in cayenne and cumin are largely fat soluble. I pounded the breasts to a ½-inch thickness so they would fit tidily into tortillas and then slipped them into the brinerade. After 30 minutes, I removed the chicken, wiped off the excess moisture, and seared it in a hot skillet. Unfortunately, by the time the meat was adequately charred, it was also dry as a bone.

I needed a way to get the chicken to brown faster—and even blacken slightly in spots. Would adding sugar to the brinerade do the trick? Since it caramelizes much more quickly (and at lower temperatures) than meat browns, I had high hopes. Sure enough, just 1 teaspoon of sugar made a huge difference, rapidly charring without contributing a noticeable sweetness. To further replicate the smoky heat of the grill, I stirred heady smoked paprika into the brinerade.

I now had some seriously flavorful chicken, but in spite of the brinerade it was difficult to keep it moist in the blazing-hot skillet. What if I compromised by searing just one side of the chicken over high heat and finishing the other side over low heat? I gave it a shot, and lo and behold, the chicken that I'd charred on only one side was indeed juicier. I had to wonder, though: If the low heat of a stove was good, would the indirect heat of the oven be even better? To find out, I seared a batch on one side over high heat, then flipped the breasts and transferred the skillet to a 200-degree oven for 10 minutes. After letting it rest, I sliced up my moistest chicken yet and tossed it back into the skillet to soak up the flavorful pan juices. Next up: vegetables.

Fajitas' ubiquitous peppers and onions have a firm footing in Mexican cuisine, where they are known as *rajas*, or strips. While most rajas we eat stateside seem like an afterthought, they frequently take center stage in Mexico. In fact, *rajas con crema*—strips of roasted pepper and onion cooked down with tangy Mexican cultured cream—are often served alone in a tortilla. Providing a rich counterpoint to the lean chicken seemed an ideal way to breathe new life into my fajitas.

I threw a final batch of chicken into its brinerade and followed a promising-looking rajas recipe using poblano chiles (they have a fruitier flavor than the usual bell peppers), which I broiled to blister the skins. After the broiled chiles steamed in a covered bowl for about 10 minutes, most of the skins slipped right off (though I did leave some charred bits behind for flavor). I sliced the chiles and sautéed them along with onion strips, then stirred in sour cream (my substitute for hard-to-find crema). That's where things started to fall apart. First, the sour cream curdled as it made contact with the hot pan. Then, as I stubbornly persevered, the roasted poblanos overcooked into green mush.

My first move was to swap heavy cream for the sour cream. The latter's high level of acidity and relatively low fat content make it a prime candidate for curdling, whereas fattier heavy cream is remarkably stable. To make up for the cream's lack of tang, I added a splash of lime juice toward the end of cooking. And to preserve my perfectly roasted poblanos, I added them to the onions and cream at the last minute to rewarm. Final touches of garlic, thyme, and oregano tied everything together.

After searing the chicken, finishing it in the oven, and charring some flour tortillas, I proudly laid out my modern fajita feast, offering crumbled *queso fresco*,

chopped cilantro, lime wedges, and spicy pickled radishes for garnishing. These skillet fajitas provide all of the easy-to-love flavor of their grilled forebears—no shredded cheddar or salsa required.

—DAN SOUZA, *Cook's Illustrated*

Skillet Chicken Fajitas

SERVES 4

We like to serve these fajitas with crumbled *queso fresco* or feta in addition to the other garnishes.

CHICKEN
- ¼ **cup vegetable oil**
- 2 **tablespoons lime juice**
- 4 **garlic cloves, peeled and smashed**
- 1½ **teaspoons smoked paprika**
- 1 **teaspoon sugar**
- 1 **teaspoon salt**
- ½ **teaspoon ground cumin**
- ½ **teaspoon pepper**
- ¼ **teaspoon cayenne pepper**
- 1½ **pounds boneless, skinless chicken breasts, trimmed and pounded to ½-inch thickness**

RAJAS CON CREMA
- 1 **pound (3 to 4) poblano chiles, stemmed, halved, and seeded**
- 1 **tablespoon vegetable oil**
- 1 **onion, halved and sliced ¼ inch thick**
- 2 **garlic cloves, minced**
- ¼ **teaspoon dried thyme**
- ¼ **teaspoon dried oregano**
- ½ **cup heavy cream**
- 1 **tablespoon lime juice**
- ½ **teaspoon salt**
- ¼ **teaspoon pepper**

- 8-12 **(6-inch) flour tortillas, warmed**
- ¼ **cup minced fresh cilantro**
  Spicy Pickled Radishes (recipe follows)
  Lime wedges

1. FOR THE CHICKEN: Whisk 3 tablespoons oil, lime juice, garlic, paprika, sugar, salt, cumin, pepper, and cayenne together in bowl. Add chicken and toss to coat. Cover and let stand at room temperature for at least 30 minutes or up to 1 hour.

2. FOR THE RAJAS CON CREMA: Meanwhile, adjust oven rack to highest position and heat broiler. Arrange poblanos, skin side up, in aluminum foil–lined rimmed baking sheet and press to flatten. Broil until skin is charred and puffed, 4 to 10 minutes, rotating baking sheet halfway through cooking. Transfer poblanos to bowl, cover, and let steam for 10 minutes. Rub majority of skin from poblanos and discard (preserve some skin for flavor); slice into ¼-inch-thick strips. Adjust oven racks to middle and lowest positions and heat oven to 200 degrees.

3. Heat oil in 12-inch nonstick skillet over high heat until just smoking. Add onion and cook until charred and just softened, about 3 minutes. Add garlic, thyme, and oregano and cook until fragrant, about 15 seconds. Add cream and cook, stirring frequently, until reduced and cream lightly coats onion, 1 to 2 minutes. Add poblano strips, lime juice, salt, and pepper and toss to coat. Transfer vegetables to bowl, cover with foil, and place on middle oven rack. Wipe out skillet with paper towels.

4. Remove chicken from marinade and wipe off excess. Heat remaining 1 tablespoon oil in now-empty skillet over high heat until just smoking. Add chicken and cook without moving it until bottom side is well charred, about 4 minutes. Flip chicken; transfer skillet to lower oven rack. Bake until chicken registers 160 degrees, 7 to 10 minutes. Transfer to cutting board and let rest for 5 minutes; do not wash out skillet.

5. Slice chicken crosswise into ¼-inch-thick strips. Return chicken strips to skillet and toss to coat with pan juices. To serve, spoon few pieces of chicken into center of warmed tortilla and top with spoonful of vegetable mixture, cilantro, and Spicy Pickled Radishes. Serve with lime wedges.

Spicy Pickled Radishes
MAKES ABOUT 1¾ CUPS

- 10 radishes, trimmed and sliced thin
- ½ cup lime juice (4 limes)
- ½ jalapeño chile, stemmed and sliced thin
- 1 teaspoon sugar
- ¼ teaspoon salt

Combine all ingredients in bowl. Cover and let stand at room temperature for 30 minutes (or refrigerate for up to 24 hours).

FRENCH-STYLE CHICKEN AND STUFFING IN A POT

✔ **WHY THIS RECIPE WORKS** The French have a curious take on stuffed chicken: Rather than roasting it, they braise the stuffed bird with vegetables in a Dutch oven to make a one-pot meal. The dish sounded delicious, but our first attempts gave us wan flavor and dry chicken. To ensure that the sausage-and-bread-crumb stuffing would cook through before the chicken was overdone, we skipped stuffing the bird and instead patted the stuffing into logs, wrapped the logs in parchment paper, and nestled them into the pot. To make room for the chicken and vegetables, we swapped out the whole bird for chicken parts and browned them first to give the broth rich flavor. To keep the chicken moist and juicy, we layered it on top of the vegetables with just enough broth to cover the veggies so the delicate breast meat could cook more gently raised above the simmering liquid. A simple herb sauce flavored with the traditional cornichons and mustard rounded out this rustic meal.

In America, we tend to roast whole chickens, but French cooks like to put them in a pot, add vegetables and a little broth, and simmer them until tender and juicy. There are countless takes on *poule au pot,* but the one that intrigues me the most hails from southwest France. For this traditional Sunday dinner, cooks stuff the bird with bread crumbs and some form of pork before cooking it in the pot with vegetables. To serve, the stuffing is removed from the cavity, the bird is carved, and both components are placed in bowls with the vegetables, a ladle of the rich broth, and accompaniments like crusty bread, cornichons, and mustard.

The dish's hearty profile appealed to me, but the handful of recipes I tried produced dismal results: Most of the birds were dry, the broths washed out, and the stuffings loose and damp. Still, the concept was interesting, so I decided to refine poule au pot, with the following goals: juicy chicken, tender vegetables, a hearty stuffing, and a clean, concentrated jus.

Throughout the next several days, I stuffed and stewed several birds according to various methods: simmered high, low, on the stove, and in the oven. But no matter what approach I took, the white meat cooked up dry and stringy by the time the stuffing was cooked through. Plus, cramming the stuffing inside the bird and then extracting it was a pain. I decided I would get better results by separating the two components.

The idea wasn't entirely mine. One recipe I'd tried from Linda Arnaud's *The Artful Chicken* skipped the stuffed-bird route and instead called for forming the bread-sausage mixture into cylinders, wrapping them in foil or parchment paper, and steaming the packages in the pot until the meat had cooked through. The stuffing cylinders came out lightly springy, sliceable, and much tidier than the usual inside-the-bird stuffing. This seemed promising.

The only problem was where to fit a pair of stuffing "logs" in a Dutch oven already crowded with a whole chicken and a pile of vegetables (for now, carrots, celery, and potatoes). But as I thought more about the space issue, an idea occurred to me: Since I no longer needed the chicken's cavity to house the stuffing, why not work with chicken parts instead? That way I could arrange the chicken pieces, vegetables, and stuffing logs as needed. Using parts would also speed up the cooking time for the meat, and it would save me the trouble of carving the chicken.

I gave it a try, seasoning two leg quarters and two breasts with salt and pepper and placing them in the pot, then nestling the vegetables and stuffing logs around the chicken. I poured in just enough chicken broth to partially submerge the meat and vegetables, brought the liquid to a simmer, and transferred the vessel to a low (300-degree) oven, hoping the gentle heat would help prevent the white meat from drying out.

Now the chicken and stuffing were done in about an hour, but the flavor of the dish was thin and the white meat was still dry. Brainstorming ways to prevent the lean meat from overcooking, I recalled solving a similar problem when I developed a recipe for Red Wine–Braised Pork Chops. For that recipe, I propped the chops above the cooking liquid on top of meat scraps and vegetables, which allowed them to cook more gently, since air conducts heat less efficiently than water. With that in mind, I rearranged the pot's contents and came up with the following stacking order (from the bottom up): vegetables, leg quarters, stuffing logs (on either side of the dark meat), and breasts. I added just enough broth to partially submerge the vegetables, making sure that the white meat sat above the liquid, then slid the pot into the oven.

After about an hour, I pulled the lid off the pot and sampled both the white and dark meat, which were, just as I'd hoped, equally tender and juicy. Now all I had to do was tune up the flavors.

My original stuffing was a little bread-heavy, so I upped the sausage from 12 ounces to a full pound to help build savory depth, and I mixed in whole-grain mustard, garlic, and shallot. This meatier batch was also juicier and firmer and thus easier to form into sturdy logs.

The broth, however, was still weak, so though it went against tradition, I browned the chicken pieces before adding the liquid. This step considerably boosted the savory flavor. (I removed the skin before serving, since it lost its appealing crispness as it simmered.) Some recipes called for adding a bouquet garni (herbs and aromatics tied together with twine) to flavor the pot, so I did the same, to great effect. And to add some fresh sweetness, I turned to a classic sausage mate: fennel. The quartered bulb went in with the other vegetables and the minced fronds went into the stuffing.

Serving the mustard and cornichons alongside the dish was fine, but the flavors came together nicely when I mixed those accoutrements (along with more aromatics) into an olive oil–based dressing, which I passed at the table along with bread.

As I set out my final batch of poule au pot, I found myself thinking that, although I'd strayed from the classic recipes, there was something timeless about this package of juicy meat, savory stuffing, tender vegetables, and rich-tasting jus.

—LAN LAM, *Cook's Illustrated*

French-Style Chicken and Stuffing in a Pot
SERVES 4 TO 6

A neutral bulk sausage is best, but breakfast or sweet Italian sausage can be used. You'll need a Dutch oven with at least a 7¼-quart capacity. Use small red potatoes, measuring 1 to 2 inches in diameter. Serve this dish with crusty bread and cornichons and Dijon mustard or Herb Sauce (recipe follows).

SAUSAGE STUFFING

- 2 slices hearty white sandwich bread, crusts removed, torn into quarters
- 1 large egg
- 1 shallot, minced
- 2 garlic cloves, minced
- 2 tablespoons minced fresh parsley
- 2 tablespoons minced fennel fronds
- 2 teaspoons whole-grain mustard
- 1 teaspoon minced fresh marjoram
- ¼ teaspoon pepper
- 1 pound bulk pork sausage

CHICKEN

- 2 celery ribs, halved crosswise
- 8 sprigs plus 1 tablespoon minced fresh parsley
- 6 sprigs fresh marjoram
- 1 bay leaf
- 2 teaspoons vegetable oil
- 2 (12-ounce) bone-in split chicken breasts, trimmed
- 2 (12-ounce) bone-in chicken leg quarters, trimmed
  Salt and pepper
- 1½ pounds small red potatoes, unpeeled
- 2 carrots, peeled and cut into ½-inch lengths
- 1 fennel bulb, stalks trimmed, bulb quartered
- 8 whole peppercorns
- 2 garlic cloves, peeled
- 3–3½ cups chicken broth

1. FOR THE SAUSAGE STUFFING: Adjust oven rack to middle position and heat oven to 300 degrees. Pulse bread in food processor until finely ground, 10 to 15 pulses. Add egg, shallot, garlic, parsley, fennel fronds, mustard, marjoram, and pepper to processor and pulse to combine, 6 to 8 pulses, scraping down sides of bowl as needed. Add sausage and pulse to combine, 3 to 5 pulses, scraping down sides of bowl as needed.

2. Place 18 by 12-inch piece of parchment paper on counter, with longer edge parallel to edge of counter. Place half of stuffing on lower third of parchment, shaping it into rough 8 by 2-inch rectangle. Roll up sausage in parchment; gently but firmly twist both ends to compact mixture into 6- to 7-inch-long cylinder, approximately 2 inches in diameter. Repeat with second piece of parchment and remaining stuffing.

3. FOR THE CHICKEN: Using kitchen twine, tie together celery, parsley sprigs, marjoram, and bay leaf. Heat oil in large Dutch oven over medium-high heat until just smoking. Pat chicken breasts and leg quarters dry with paper towels, sprinkle with ½ teaspoon salt, and season with pepper. Add chicken, skin side down, and cook without moving it until browned, 4 to 7 minutes. Transfer chicken to large plate. Pour off and discard any fat in pot.

4. Remove Dutch oven from heat and carefully arrange celery bundle, potatoes, carrots, and fennel in even layer over bottom of pot. Sprinkle peppercorns, garlic, and ¼ teaspoon salt over vegetables. Add enough broth so that top ½ inch of vegetables is above surface of liquid. Place leg quarters on top of vegetables in center of pot. Place stuffing cylinders on either side of leg quarters. Arrange breasts on top of leg quarters. Place pot over high heat

and bring to simmer. Cover, transfer to oven, and cook until breasts register 160 degrees, 60 to 75 minutes.

5. Transfer chicken and stuffing cylinders to carving board. Using slotted spoon, transfer vegetables to serving platter, discarding celery bundle. Pour broth through fine-mesh strainer into fat separator; discard solids. Let stand for 5 minutes.

6. Unwrap stuffing cylinders and slice into ½-inch-thick disks; transfer slices to platter with vegetables. Remove skin from chicken pieces and discard. Carve breasts from bone and slice into ½-inch-thick pieces. Separate thigh from leg by cutting through joint. Transfer chicken to platter with stuffing and vegetables. Pour ½ cup defatted broth over chicken and stuffing to moisten. Sprinkle with minced parsley. Serve, ladling remaining broth over individual servings.

Herb Sauce

MAKES ABOUT ½ CUP

- ⅓ cup extra-virgin olive oil
- 6 cornichons, minced
- 2 tablespoons minced fresh parsley
- 1 tablespoon minced fennel fronds
- 2 teaspoons minced shallot
- 2 teaspoons whole-grain mustard
- 1 teaspoon minced fresh marjoram
- ½ teaspoon finely grated lemon zest plus 2 tablespoons juice
- ¼ teaspoon pepper

Whisk all ingredients together in bowl. Let stand for 15 minutes before serving.

NOTES FROM THE TEST KITCHEN

SLICEABLE STUFFING

Traditional *poule au pot* recipes call for cooking a bread-sausage stuffing inside a whole chicken; we took a simpler route by rolling the stuffing in parchment paper. The sausage-shaped logs cook right alongside the chicken pieces and vegetables.

SKILLET-ROASTED CHICKEN AND STUFFING

✅ **WHY THIS RECIPE WORKS** To translate Sunday-style stuffed chicken into a one-pan weeknight meal, we sped things up by taking the stuffing out of the chicken and making the entire dish in just one skillet. First we sautéed the aromatics for the stuffing on the stovetop, then we placed the chicken—brushed with a flavorful herb butter— right on top. We scattered the bread cubes around the bird and moved the skillet to the oven to simultaneously roast the chicken and toast the bread. As the chicken cooked, the bread soaked up its flavorful juices. Finally, while the chicken rested, it took just a quick stir and a splash of broth to mix in the aromatics and moisten the stuffing before dinner was on the table.

A plain roast chicken is fairly simple to make, but add stuffing (or "dressing") on the side, and suddenly dinner gets a lot more complicated. And don't get me started on all the pots and pans required to prepare it: a baking sheet (to toast or stale the cubed bread), a skillet (to sauté the onion, celery, and herbs), a bowl and wooden spoon (to mix everything together), and a roasting pan (for the chicken itself). Chicken with stuffing is doable as a weekend project, but what if you want it on a Tuesday? I vowed to streamline the recipe.

First, why cook the stuffing on the side and not inside the bird? In the test kitchen, we're not fans of stuffed chickens: By the time the stuffing reaches a safe 165 degrees inside the bird, the breast meat is seriously overcooked, stringy, and dry. On top of that, the cavity of a chicken can't hold enough stuffing to feed four diners. But there's a drawback to cooking the stuffing separately, too: It can't absorb the delicious chicken juices. We've learned to live with that, but only reluctantly.

I didn't have to look too far for great recipes for roast chicken or tasty stuffing; the test kitchen has developed plenty of each. For my starting point, I chose a stovetop stuffing recipe (I'd still have to toast the bread in advance) and a recipe for chicken that called for brushing the bird with herb butter, which I thought would echo the flavors in the stuffing nicely, then roasting it at 325 degrees in a roasting pan, starting it breast side down and flipping it partway through. Since the oven was already on, I could toast the bread cubes on a baking sheet underneath the chicken. As bread and bird cooked, I sautéed onions, celery, thyme, and sage for the stuffing. Ninety minutes

later, the chicken was ready, but in this comparatively slow oven, the bread had staled (good) but not browned (bad, since color translates into flavor). While the chicken rested so the juices could redistribute, I combined the toasted bread cubes, sautéed aromatics, and some chicken broth that I'd warmed up (another pot) and let the mixture sit, covered, for several minutes to moisten.

This chicken was moist, nicely flavored, and buttery, but 90 minutes was a long wait. Also, the stuffing was merely fine; unsurprisingly, it lacked good toasty flavor. I didn't need to be a rocket scientist to solve these problems. I increased the oven temperature to 375 degrees. Now the bread browned properly and the chicken was ready in just 1 hour.

But my kitchen sink was still full of dishes. What if I tried cooking the vegetables with the chicken? This time, I roasted the chicken on a bed of raw onions, celery, and herbs. The vegetables picked up extra flavor from the chicken juices, but that gain was negated by their failure to brown. Since cooking the aromatics in the roasting pan hadn't worked out, how about roasting the chicken in the skillet? After sautéing the vegetables in the skillet, I plopped the raw bird on top and moved the entire setup to the oven, where . . . the delicate breast meat overcooked by the time the thighs were done (white meat is done at 160 degrees, dark meat at 175).

Why? I'd followed normal test kitchen procedure, roasting the chicken breast side down to shield it and slow its cooking. But the skillet was hot before it ever entered the oven, so the breast meat, in direct contact with the hot skillet, actually cooked more quickly—the last thing it needed. The next time, I cooked the chicken breast side up for the entire time, letting the hot pan jump-start the cooking of the thighs; finally the chicken emerged perfectly moist.

I still hoped to cut back on my dirty dishes, and it suddenly occurred to me to scatter the bread cubes in the skillet around the raw chicken instead of toasting them in a separate pan. This way, I would be able to cook my entire meal together in one dish (plus, now the stuffing could absorb the chicken juices after all). The chicken baked, the bread cubes browned, and the kitchen smelled fantastic. When the bird was done, I let it rest on a plate, added a splash of chicken broth to the vegetables and bread cubes still in the skillet, and warmed the stuffing through. Now I can eat my favorite Sunday supper any night of the week.

—CAROLYNN PURPURA MACKAY, *Cook's Country*

SKILLET-ROASTED CHICKEN AND STUFFING

CHOPPING ONIONS FINELY

1. Halve onion pole to pole and cut off top of each half. Peel onion, then make several horizontal cuts from one end of onion almost to other, but don't cut all the way through root end.

2. Make several vertical cuts, pole to pole. Using your knuckles as guide while holding onion with your fingertips, slice onion across cuts to make fine, even dice.

THE BEST INEXPENSIVE SKILLET

A 12-inch skillet is a kitchen workhorse, and a well-made one should last a lifetime. Still, our longtime favorite sells for $155. Do you really need to spend so much to guarantee great performance and durability?

To find out, we bought seven traditional 12-inch skillets, all for less than $100. We seared steaks, made pan sauces, pan-roasted chicken parts, and sautéed onions, tracking the pans' heating patterns with an infrared camera. A few gave steaks a nice sear and cooked them to a perfect medium, and others ran hot. We got similar uneven results when we browned onions. These pans required adjusting the heat more often or extra stirring. We appreciated pans that were lighter, thus easier to handle, and had helper handles. After putting the skillets through their paces on the stovetop, we tested their sturdiness by heating each one to 550 degrees and then plunging it into an ice bath; we then banged it with moderate force against the sidewalk three times. While no disk or rivets came loose, some of the pans got dinged up, and thermal shock caused one to warp. The top performers came out virtually unscathed.

In the end, none of these pans matched the performance of our favorite traditional skillet, but one came remarkably close. The **Tramontina 12-Inch Tri-Ply Clad Sauté Pan**, $39.97, provided steady, controlled heat thanks to its fully clad, tri-ply construction (though it browned steak slightly unevenly) and survived our abuse testing. It weighs over a pound more than our favorite traditional skillet, so it's somewhat harder to maneuver. Still, its performance, design, sturdy construction, and price make it an excellent choice. It's our new Best Buy. (See page 306 for more information on our testing results.)

Skillet-Roasted Chicken and Stuffing
SERVES 4

You can find Italian bread in the bakery section of your grocery store. Take care when stirring the contents of the skillet in steps 4 and 5, as the skillet handle will be very hot.

- 1 (4-pound) whole chicken, giblets discarded
- 6 tablespoons unsalted butter
- 2 tablespoons minced fresh sage
- 2 tablespoons minced fresh thyme
   Salt and pepper
- 2 onions, chopped fine
- 2 celery ribs, minced
- 7 ounces Italian bread, cut into ½-inch cubes (6 cups)
- ⅓ cup chicken broth

1. Adjust oven rack to lower-middle position and heat oven to 375 degrees. Pat chicken dry with paper towels. Melt 4 tablespoons butter in small bowl in microwave, about 45 seconds. Stir in 1 tablespoon sage, 1 tablespoon thyme, 1 teaspoon salt, and ½ teaspoon pepper. Brush chicken with herb butter.

2. Melt remaining 2 tablespoons butter in 12-inch ovensafe skillet over medium heat. Add onions, celery, ½ teaspoon salt, and ½ teaspoon pepper and cook until softened, about 5 minutes. Add remaining 1 tablespoon sage and remaining 1 tablespoon thyme and cook until fragrant, about 1 minute. Off heat, place chicken, breast side up, on top of vegetables. Arrange bread cubes around chicken in bottom of skillet.

3. Transfer skillet to oven and roast until breasts register 160 degrees and thighs register 175 degrees, about 1 hour, rotating skillet halfway through roasting.

4. Carefully transfer chicken to plate and tent loosely with aluminum foil. Holding skillet handle with potholder (handle will be hot), stir bread and vegetables to combine, cover, and let stand for 10 minutes.

5. Add broth and any accumulated chicken juices from plate and cavity to skillet and stir to combine. Warm stuffing, uncovered, over low heat until heated through, about 3 minutes. Remove from heat, cover, and let sit while carving chicken. Transfer chicken to carving board and carve. Serve with stuffing.

GRILLED LEMON CHICKEN

WHY THIS RECIPE WORKS Grilling a whole chicken can be a recipe for disaster thanks to flare-ups caused by the fatty skin. Usually recipes address this problem with a two-stage grilling process: low heat to gently render the fat, then high heat to char the meat and crisp the skin. We found a much faster way to solve the problem: We skipped the rendering step by removing the skin before grilling. To ensure that our chicken got plenty of color and char without overcooking, we butterflied it so it was an even thickness, then we brined it in a sugar and salt solution for juicy meat. For flavor that penetrated all the way to the bone, we cut deep channels in the meat and rubbed it with lemon and herb seasoning. Basting the chicken with a flavorful butter sauce and tenting it with aluminum foil partway through cooking kept the surface moist and tender as it cooked. We quickly charred lemon wedges to squeeze over each portion before serving for even more moisture and flavor.

The embarrassing truth is that I'm not the most confident of grill cooks. For most of my career I've worked with sophisticated restaurant stoves and ovens, so the primitive unresponsiveness of a backyard charcoal grill feels daunting. I can handle low-and-slow projects like barbecued ribs, and quickly searing a steak is no big deal. But grilling a whole chicken brings out my insecurities.

The problem is that you can't simply throw a chicken over a blazing fire. The fat in the skin will melt and drip onto the coals, sending up flames that burn the exterior. For this reason, most grilled chicken recipes call for variable heat: low and slow first—to gently render fat and initiate cooking—and then high heat to finish cooking, crisp the skin, and get that enticing char.

Determined to produce moist, well-flavored, pleasantly charred birds—without the intervention of the local fire department—I headed for the grill. I would start with a half fire, where all the lit coals are poured on one side of the grill for intense heat and the other side is left empty for indirect cooking—in other words, a prime whole-chicken-cooking environment.

I started simply: one whole chicken and a grill. I knew that cooking a 3½-pounder would take a while, but this was positively tedious: I placed the chicken breast side down over low heat to cook off some of the fat and then flipped it. By the time I got to the hotter side, the coals no longer had enough oomph to brown the skin. Yes, it was simple, and there were no flare-ups; but with no high-temperature char, the meat looked and tasted more roasted than grilled, and the white meat was as dry as one might expect after 90 minutes on the grill.

Brining the next chicken in a saltwater solution kept it more moist, but it still required a lot of time on the grill. In an attempt to shorten the cooking time, I employed a technique I've used when roasting chickens: butterflying. I removed the backbone with a pair of kitchen shears and pressed on the breastbone to flatten the bird to a more-or-less uniform thickness. This would speed up cooking by increasing the meat's exposure to heat. I also rubbed some lemon zest, mustard, rosemary, and seasoning on the skin of the chicken for added flavor.

I placed the wide, flat chicken breast side down over the cooler side of the grill and waited for the fat to render, flipping the chicken partway through. Just 30 minutes later, I moved it over to the hotter side to get grill marks on each side. This chicken had promise—evenly cooked meat, a bit of char, and no scary flare-ups—but it still took almost an hour, and tasters thought that the meat was a bit dry. The good news was that they liked the lemon-herb rub; the bad news was that its flavor was only skin-deep.

Brainstorming dishes that combine poultry and high heat, I remembered tandoori chicken, which traditionally cooks in a 900-degree clay oven—without bursting into flames. Why does it work? Because the skin has been removed before cooking. The three separate problems I was trying to fix—flare-ups, long cooking time, and lack of flavor penetration—were all caused by the skin. Yes, the skin protects the meat from overcooking—but remove it and you remove most of the fat, so you can put the chicken directly over high heat, and the chicken cooks so quickly that it has less time to dry out.

A whole chicken with no skin seemed odd at first, but I've witnessed many a guest discreetly set it aside before eating. Maybe a naked chicken was worth a try.

Turns out that taking the skin off a butterflied chicken is pretty easy; using just my hands, a paper towel to improve my grip, and the kitchen shears, it took just a couple of minutes, and I was able to remove the small pockets of fat that lay on the surface of the meat. However, I had underestimated the structural service provided by the skin, and the legs dangled precariously. I strategically threaded a couple of skewers through the thighs and breast to fix that. Then I patted the bird dry, applied the rub, and placed the chicken breast side down over the hotter side of the grill and closed the lid to modify the flow of oxygen and discourage flare-ups.

There was smoke, the smell of charring, and a lot of sizzling noises, too. When I peeked, I did see some flames, but they were weak. After a mere 10 minutes, I flipped the chicken, and after another 10 minutes, I moved it over to the cooler side of the grill to finish cooking. When it reached the target temperature (160 in the breast, 175 in the thigh) in just 8 more minutes, I knew I was onto something. This chicken was the juiciest yet, and who can find fault with a whole chicken that cooks in just 28 minutes?

I can, of course. It was good, but it wasn't perfect. The brief time over intense heat (necessary to prevent overcooking) meant that the surface of the meat was a bit pale and, while not exactly dry, had a tight, cauterized feel to it. And the flavor of the rub was still a bit superficial.

To address the paleness problem, I spiked my brine with sugar, which I hoped would be absorbed into the

bird and aid browning. To solve the flavor penetration issue, I turned once again to tandoori chicken for inspiration. Tandoori cooks cut deep slits in meat before it goes into the oven, so I did the same before brining my bird. When it came out of the brine, I massaged the rub deep into the knife cuts. I reserved a bit of the flavoring agents from the rub—lemon juice, rosemary, mustard, and pepper—and mixed them into a small amount of melted butter to use as a basting sauce. Thinking ahead, I cut an additional lemon into quarters and brought it out to the grill with my chicken and sauce.

Once again, I laid the chicken skinned side down over the hotter side, and this time I also placed the lemon quarters on the grate to char. With the sugar in the brine, this bird achieved a beautiful brown color after just 8 minutes. When I flipped it, I brushed the cooked surface with the flavored butter to prevent it from tightening up, and I tented it with foil as extra insurance. The lemons went into a bowl to cool. After another 8 minutes, I moved the chicken to the cooler side and basted it again, and in 8 more minutes it was done. I took it off the grill and basted it with the last of the butter.

The moist brown exterior of this chicken was accented with hints of tasty black char, and carving it revealed a juiciness that went all the way to the bone and took the flavorful rub along for the ride. A spritz of charred lemon over the top completed the dish. I had met the enemy and emerged victorious.

—ANDREA GEARY, *Cook's Illustrated*

NOTES FROM THE TEST KITCHEN

THE BEST WHOLE CHICKENS

Chicken may be the most popular meat in America, but that doesn't make shopping for it simple. There are a multitude of brands and a wide range of prices, and you need a degree in agribusiness to decode most of the packaging lingo: What's the difference between "all natural," "free range," and "organic"? What does "vegetarian fed" mean? And most important, what tastes best when you strip away the sales pitches?

To find some answers, we rounded up eight national and large regional brands of whole fresh chicken and got to tasting. Some birds boasted "chicken-y" meat that was pleasantly moist; others tasted utterly bland or, worse, faintly metallic, bitter, or liver-y. Chalky, dry meat was a common complaint, but surprisingly, so was too much moisture. To make some sense of this, we looked into the way that chickens are processed. Most companies chill their chickens in a cold water bath; this makes chickens plump up, absorbing up to 14 percent of their body weight in water (which, of course, you're paying for). This helped explain why tasters found the meat in several of these birds to be unnaturally spongy, with washed-out flavor.

That left us with just two birds that weren't water-chilled. Instead, they were air-chilled—circulated on a conveyor belt along the ceiling of a cold room. Air chilling also breaks down the muscle tissue and gives a better texture. With their exceptionally clean chicken-y flavor and moist, tender meat, we declared both **Mary's Free Range Air-Chilled Chicken** and **Bell & Evans Air Chilled Premium Fresh Chicken** our winners. (See page 300 for more information on our testing results.)

Grilled Lemon Chicken with Rosemary

SERVES 4

For a better grip, use a paper towel to grasp the skin when removing it from the chicken.

- 1 (3½- to 4-pound) whole chicken, giblets discarded
- ¾ cup sugar
  Salt and pepper
- 2 lemons
- 1 tablespoon vegetable oil
- 2 teaspoons minced fresh rosemary
- 1½ teaspoons Dijon mustard
- 2 tablespoons unsalted butter

1. With chicken breast side down, using kitchen shears, cut through bones on either side of backbone; discard backbone. Flip chicken over and press on breastbone to flatten. Using fingers and shears, peel skin off chicken, leaving skin on wings.

2. Tuck wings behind back. Turn legs so drumsticks face inward toward breasts. Using chef's knife, cut ½-inch-deep slits, spaced ½ inch apart, in breasts and legs. Insert skewer through thigh of 1 leg, into bottom of breast, and through thigh of second leg. Insert second skewer, about 1 inch lower, through thigh and drumstick of 1 leg and then through thigh and drumstick of second leg.

3. Dissolve sugar and ¾ cup salt in 3 quarts cold water in large, wide container. Submerge chicken in brine, cover, and refrigerate for at least 30 minutes or up to 1 hour.

4. Zest lemons (you should have 2 tablespoons grated zest). Juice 1 lemon (you should have 3 tablespoons juice) and quarter remaining lemon lengthwise. Combine zest, oil, 1½ teaspoons rosemary, 1 teaspoon mustard, and ½ teaspoon pepper in small bowl; set aside. Heat butter, remaining ½ teaspoon rosemary, remaining ½ teaspoon mustard, and ½ teaspoon pepper in small saucepan over low heat, stirring occasionally, until butter is melted and ingredients are combined. Remove pan from heat and stir in lemon juice; leave mixture in saucepan.

5. Remove chicken from brine and pat dry with paper towels. With chicken skinned side down, rub ½ teaspoon zest mixture over surface of legs. Flip chicken over and rub remaining zest mixture evenly over entire surface, making sure to work mixture into slits.

6A. FOR A CHARCOAL GRILL: Open bottom vent completely. Light large chimney starter mounded with charcoal briquettes (7 quarts). When top coals are partially covered with ash, pour evenly over half of grill. Set cooking grate in place, cover, and open lid vent completely. Heat grill until hot, about 5 minutes.

6B. FOR A GAS GRILL: Turn all burners to high, cover, and heat grill until hot, about 15 minutes. Leave primary burner on high and turn off other burner(s).

7. Clean and oil cooking grate. Place chicken, skinned side down, and lemon quarters over hotter part of grill. Cover and cook until chicken and lemon quarters are well browned, 8 to 10 minutes. Transfer lemon quarters to bowl and set aside. Flip chicken over and brush with one-third of butter mixture (place saucepan over cooler side of grill if mixture has solidified). Cover chicken loosely with aluminum foil. Continue to cook, covered, until chicken is well browned on second side, 8 to 10 minutes.

8. Remove foil and slide chicken to cooler side of grill. Brush with half of remaining butter mixture and re-cover with foil. Continue to cook, covered,

PREPPING A WHOLE CHICKEN FOR EVEN, RAPID COOKING ON THE GRILL

1. Cut through bones on either side of backbone; discard.

2. Flip chicken and crack and flatten its breastbone for fast, even grilling.

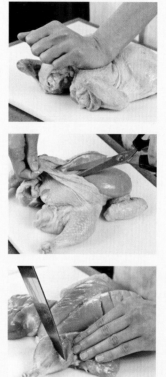

3. Remove skin to avoid flare-ups from rendering fat (leave skin on wings).

4. Make deep cuts in meat to allow seasonings to penetrate to bone.

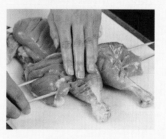

5. Insert skewers through thighs and legs to provide stability.

until breasts register 160 degrees and thighs/drumsticks register 175 degrees, 8 to 10 minutes longer.

9. Transfer chicken to carving board, brush with remaining butter mixture, tent loosely with foil, and let rest for 5 to 10 minutes. Carve into pieces and serve.

SLOW-COOKER PULLED CHICKEN

SLOW-COOKER PULLED CHICKEN

✓ **WHY THIS RECIPE WORKS** For tender, smoky barbecued pulled chicken that's made in the slow cooker but tastes like it's straight off the grill, we ditched the bottled sauce that most recipes call for and made our own quick and easy sauce. Rather than sautéing onions on the stove for the base of our sauce, we found that microwaving them with some oil both softened and caramelized them in one shot. Along with the onions, we microwaved tomato paste, chili powder, garlic, and cayenne to bloom and deepen their flavors, then we added the flavorful mixture to a simple mix of ketchup, molasses, cider vinegar, hot sauce, and mustard. Liquid smoke added great grilled flavor. For the chicken, two cuts were better than one: bone-in, skin-on chicken breasts stayed juicy in the slow cooker and shredded nicely, and chicken thighs added extra meaty flavor.

If you're stuck on pork and have never tried barbecued pulled chicken, you should: The mild chicken soaks up a ton of smoky grill flavor, and the shredded strands of meat hold lots of tangy sauce. While the work is mostly hands-off, preparing this dish does require spending some quality time with your grill. So I wondered, Could I make pulled chicken inside in the slow cooker instead?

It would seem so, as I found lots of recipes for slow-cooker pulled chicken. I selected five representative ones and started cooking. All used either breasts or thighs—with bones and skin or without. Most recipes called for tossing the raw chicken into the cooker with barbecue sauce, letting it cook for several hours, taking out the chicken, discarding the skin and bones, and "pulling" the chicken into shreds before tossing it back into the sauce. The big problems were overcooked meat, a "chopped" (not pulled) texture, and lousy-tasting bottled sauce. I learned that breast meat pulls into nice long strands but dark meat doesn't "pull" as well; I'd go with bone-in, skin-on breasts, because the skin and bones help insulate the white meat from overcooking, and supplement them with a few boneless thighs for their deeper flavor and moister texture.

Moving on to the sauce, I knew I'd make my own. But from-scratch sauces usually start with sautéed onion and require simmering to thicken and concentrate the flavors. I hoped to shortcut the sautéing and simmering. I whisked together a simple "dump-and-stir" sauce

from ketchup, molasses, cider vinegar, hot sauce, and a dash of liquid smoke. While this sauce was agreeably simple, it was too thin and lacked big barbecue flavor.

Using tomato paste in place of some of the ketchup helped thicken and enrich the sauce. For more "barbecue" flavor, I added brown mustard, chili powder, and cayenne pepper and tripled the amount of liquid smoke to make up for the absent grill flavor.

There was one final missing piece: the oniony, aromatic sauce base. Since I wanted to avoid a stovetop sauté, I tried the microwave. After some fiddling, I found microwaving a cup of finely chopped onion for 3 minutes provided a solid oniony foundation for the sauce. Microwaving the chili powder, cayenne, garlic, and tomato paste with the onion bloomed their flavors, giving my sauce even more depth.

I gathered tasters, spooned the saucy shredded chicken onto rolls, doled out the sandwiches, and waited. After a few moments, I broke the silence by asking if the chicken needed anything. "A cold beer on the side," said one. "And some coleslaw," said another. I took that as a sign of success.

—SARAH GABRIEL, *Cook's Country*

Slow-Cooker Pulled Chicken

SERVES 10

Use a relatively mild hot sauce, like Frank's, or the sauce will be too hot.

  5 (10- to 12-ounce) bone-in split
     chicken breasts, trimmed
  7 (3-ounce) boneless, skinless chicken
     thighs, trimmed
     Salt and pepper
  1 onion, chopped fine
  ½ cup tomato paste
  2 tablespoons vegetable oil
  5 teaspoons chili powder
  3 garlic cloves, minced
  ¼ teaspoon cayenne pepper
  1 cup ketchup
  ⅓ cup molasses
  2 tablespoons brown mustard
  4 teaspoons cider vinegar
  4 teaspoons hot sauce
  ¾ teaspoon liquid smoke
 10 sandwich rolls

1. Pat chicken dry with paper towels and season with salt and pepper. Combine onion, tomato paste, oil, chili powder, garlic, and cayenne in bowl and microwave until onion softens slightly, about 3 minutes, stirring halfway through microwaving. Transfer mixture to slow cooker and whisk in ketchup, molasses, mustard, and vinegar. Add chicken to slow cooker and toss to combine with sauce. Cover and cook on low until chicken shreds easily with fork, about 5 hours.

2. Transfer cooked chicken to carving board, tent loosely with aluminum foil, and let rest for 15 minutes. Using large spoon, remove any fat from surface of sauce. Whisk hot sauce and liquid smoke into sauce and cover to keep warm. Remove and discard chicken skin and bones. Roughly chop thigh meat into ½-inch pieces. Shred breast meat into thin strands using 2 forks. Return meat to slow cooker and toss to coat with sauce. Season with salt and pepper to taste. Serve on sandwich rolls.

JUICY GRILLED TURKEY BURGERS

✔ **WHY THIS RECIPE WORKS** To create juicy, flavorful turkey burgers, we ditched store-bought ground turkey in favor of home-ground turkey thighs, which boasted more fat and flavor. To ensure that our turkey burgers delivered maximum juiciness, we used a portion of the ground turkey plus gelatin, soy sauce, and baking soda to make a paste that trapped juices within the burgers and helped tenderize the meat. We also added chopped raw white mushrooms, which amped up the meaty flavor of the burgers and prevented the meat's texture from turning dense once grilled.

The assignment was to create turkey burgers that tasted every bit as meaty, tender, and juicy as the beef kind—and the judges would be my colleagues, all of them hardcore hamburger devotees. It was a tall order for a couple of reasons: For one thing, to ensure that it is safe to eat, the test kitchen brings all poultry to a much higher temperature (160 degrees) than beef (which we often cook medium-rare, or 125 degrees), which squeezes far more moisture out of the meat during cooking. What's more, turkey lacks beef's high percentage of lubricating fat. That accounts for its appeal as a healthier alternative to beef in a burger, but it also explains why these lean patties usually cook up dry, chalky, and bland.

Plenty of recipes try to compensate for those shortcomings by packing ground turkey with a slew of spices and binders that provide flavor and lock in moisture, but my tasters deemed every version that I tried a failure—and I tried many. Most burgers were still dry, and those that did offer some flavor tasted more like overdressed turkey meatloaf than burgers. The recipes all ignored the real problem at heart: the meat itself.

The meat sounded like the right starting point to me, so I shelved my cynicism for the time being and decided to work toward a turkey burger that delivered everything I look for in a beef version—tender, juicy, and flavorful meat—without the distraction of my spice cabinet or other superficial fixes. And if I could throw it over a hot grill to give the meat some smoky char, all the better.

Supermarket ground meat may be a timesaver, but when we want to make the meatiest, juiciest, most tender burgers we can, we grind our own—and if my test recipes were any indication, avoiding the preground stuff would be even more important when it came to turkey burgers. The vast majority of commercial ground meat is processed so finely that it turns pasty and dense, and poultry tends to be the worst offender. And supermarket ground turkey is typically ultralean—an immediate setback when you're going for flavor and juiciness. Grinding my own meat would allow me to control both the cut of meat and the size of the grind.

The obvious starting point was thigh meat, as this cut boasts a decent amount of fat and flavor. I bought a large turkey thigh (about 2 pounds), removed the skin and bone, trimmed it of excess sinew, then followed our grinding procedure: Cut the meat into ½-inch pieces, freeze them for about 40 minutes to firm them up, then process the meat in three batches in a food processor.

About 20 pulses gave me coarsely chopped meat that produced tender, nicely loose-textured burgers, and the flavor of these dark-meat patties was significantly richer than that of any turkey burger I'd had to date. But I still had plenty of work to do to get the juiciness and rich meatiness of a beef burger. By the time they reached 160 degrees, my all-thigh patties were still parched.

Mixing the turkey with a panade (a liquid-and-breadcrumb paste that traps moisture and prevents the meat proteins from binding together too tightly) was the most common moisture-enhancing solution I came across. But it was also universally unsuccessful. While the paste did add juiciness, it also dulled the already mild flavor of the turkey and made the patties meatloaf-like—precisely the consistency I was trying to avoid by grinding my own meat. Other recipes took a more drastic approach, "fattening up" the ground turkey with butter and bacon fat. One even mixed in turkey sausage—and, not surprisingly, the result tasted like a sausage burger. I'll admit, adding fat to the burgers did make them taste juicier (and richer), but it also felt like cheating; at that point, why not just make a beef burger?

Thinking about those two goals, however, triggered an important reminder. While developing a recent stir-fry recipe, we discovered an unlikely technique for improving tenderness and juiciness in lean pork: lightly coating it with baking soda before cooking. When applied to meat, this alkali raises the meat's pH, which tenderizes its muscle fibers and gives it a looser structure that's more capable of retaining water. The quick pretreatment had made all the difference with the pork loin; no reason it shouldn't work for turkey, too, right?

I gave it a shot, mixing up one batch of burgers with a pinch of baking soda and leaving another untreated, then quickly searing the burgers over a hot fire. My tasters gave me approving nods and declared the burgers made with baking soda noticeably juicier and more tender. I knew I was getting somewhere. But I wasn't done yet.

Another of our favorite pantry staples for improving dry meat is gelatin, which can absorb up to 10 times its weight in water. I tried hydrating varying amounts of the unflavored powder in chicken broth and adding the mixture to the turkey when grinding it. This proved to be another good move—just 1 tablespoon of gelatin in 3 tablespoons of broth further compensated for some of the moisture lost during cooking.

Spurred on by these successes, I challenged myself to push the moisture factor a little further and was reminded of the recipe I'd tried with turkey sausage. It had failed for tasting too sausage-y, but it was remarkably juicy, thanks to the finely processed meat, which causes the proteins to stretch out and link up into a stronger network that traps fat and moisture. I got to thinking: If I was already grinding the turkey in the food processor, why not try making my own sausage-like mixture by grinding a portion of the meat even further? I added ½ cup of coarsely ground meat back to the processor along with salt (which activates the meat's sticky proteins), the baking soda, and the softened gelatin and processed it until the mixture turned sticky and smooth; then, with the processor still running, I drizzled in 2 tablespoons of vegetable oil until incorporated.

It worked like gangbusters. When mixed into the remaining ground turkey, this emulsion trapped copious amounts of moisture and fat, resulting in the juiciest turkey burger I'd ever had. There was just one caveat, and it was predictable: My homemade turkey sausage was binding the meat together too firmly, giving it a dense texture.

To get my burgers to loosen up, I needed to add something to the ground turkey to keep its sticky proteins from embracing too tightly. I experimented with various cooked grains and starches—even beans. But while most of them did produce more tender patties, none left me with the loose burger texture I was after, and most of them muted the turkey's flavor.

That's when I switched to mixing vegetables into the meat until I finally hit upon the winner: raw white mushrooms. Chopped in the food processor and mixed into my turkey emulsion, the mushrooms provided three benefits: They interrupted some of the protein binding to increase tenderness, provided extra moisture as their water-filled cells broke down during cooking, and helped boost meatiness, thanks to their high level of glutamates. The mushrooms also inspired me to swap in soy sauce for the salt, bumping up savoriness even more. Just 5 minutes per side over a hot fire was enough to char and cook my mouthwatering turkey burgers—now every bit as enticing as their beefy brothers.

—DAN SOUZA, *Cook's Illustrated*

Juicy Grilled Turkey Burgers

SERVES 6

If you are able to purchase boneless, skinless turkey thighs, substitute 1½ pounds for the bone-in thigh. To ensure the best texture, don't let the burgers stand for more than an hour before cooking. Serve the burgers with one of our burger sauces (recipes follow) or your favorite toppings.

- 1 **(2-pound) bone-in turkey thigh, skinned, boned, trimmed, and cut into ½-inch pieces**
- 1 **tablespoon unflavored gelatin**
- 3 **tablespoons chicken broth**
- 6 **ounces white mushrooms, trimmed**
- 1 **tablespoon soy sauce**
   Pinch baking soda
- 2 **tablespoons vegetable oil, plus extra for brushing**
   Kosher salt and pepper
- 6 **large hamburger buns**

HOW WE BUILT A BETTER BURGER

Typical turkey burgers are dense, dry, and flavorless. To make ours juicy, meaty, and rich, we came up with a few tricks.

GRIND DARK MEAT

Turkey thighs contain more fat and flavor than lean white meat.

ADD BAKING SODA

Just a pinch tenderizes the meat by raising its pH.

MIX IN MUSHROOMS

They add moisture and flavor and lighten the texture of the meat.

ADD GELATIN

Gelatin acts like a sponge, holding up to 10 times its own weight in water.

THE BEST GRILL PAN

When you can't fire up the grill, it's handy to have a stovetop grill pan. Though it can't replicate the flavor of the open flame, a ridged grill pan does make tasty char-grill marks on meat, fish, or vegetables. Some even come with presses for panini and grilled cheese sandwiches. We gathered eight pans in stainless steel, nonstick-coated aluminum, and enameled and plain cast iron with prices ranging from $19 to nearly $200.

Every pan left grill marks on zucchini planks and strip steaks, but some were more crisply defined than others. Pans with broad, shallow ridges left partial, indistinct marks. Cast-iron pans, with ridges ranging from 4 millimeters to 5.5 millimeters high, made the best, most flavorful grill marks—all the food looked grilled, with char lines that went all the way across. By contrast, the ridges on the nonstick pans were just 1.88 millimeters to 3 millimeters and left little impression. Taller ridges also raise the meat away from the rendered fat.

Our favorite grill pan, the **Staub 12-Inch American Square Grill Pan and Press**, turned in a stellar performance, with tall ridges, the largest cooking surface, great cast-iron heat retention, and an enamel coating that's easy to clean and dishwasher-safe. But at $159.90, it's an investment. Our Best Buy, the Lodge Logic Pre-Seasoned Square Grill Pan and Ribbed Panini Press, had tall, cast-iron ridges that made great grill marks. While it's smaller and lacks the enamel coating, its $33.55 combined price (pan and press) makes it a real bargain. (See page 307 for more information on our testing results.)

1. Place turkey pieces on large plate in single layer. Freeze meat until very firm and hardened around edges, 35 to 45 minutes. Meanwhile, sprinkle gelatin over broth in small bowl and let sit until gelatin softens, about 5 minutes. Pulse mushrooms in food processor until coarsely chopped, about 7 pulses, stopping and redistributing mushrooms around bowl as needed to ensure even grinding. Set mushrooms aside; do not wash food processor.

2. Pulse one-third of turkey in food processor until coarsely chopped into ⅛-inch pieces, 18 to 22 pulses, stopping and redistributing turkey around bowl as needed to ensure even grinding. Transfer meat to large bowl and repeat 2 more times with remaining turkey.

3. Return ½ cup (about 3 ounces) ground turkey to bowl of food processor along with softened gelatin, soy sauce, and baking soda. Process until smooth, about 2 minutes, scraping down bowl as needed. With processor running, slowly drizzle in oil, about 10 seconds; leave paste in food processor. Return mushrooms to food processor with paste and pulse to combine, 3 to 5 pulses, stopping and redistributing mixture as needed to ensure even mixing. Transfer mushroom mixture to bowl with ground turkey and use hands to evenly combine.

4. With lightly greased hands, divide meat mixture into 6 balls. Flatten into ¾-inch-thick patties about 4 inches in diameter; press shallow indentation into center of each burger to ensure even cooking. (Shaped patties can be frozen for up to 1 month. Frozen patties can be cooked straight from freezer.)

5A. FOR A CHARCOAL GRILL: Open bottom vent completely. Light large chimney starter filled with charcoal briquettes (6 quarts). When top coals are partially covered with ash, pour evenly over half of grill. Set cooking grate in place, cover, and open lid vent completely. Heat grill until hot, about 5 minutes.

5B. FOR A GAS GRILL: Turn all burners to high, cover, and heat grill until hot, about 15 minutes. Leave primary burner on high and turn off other burner(s).

6. Clean and oil cooking grate. Brush 1 side of patties with oil and season with salt and pepper. Using spatula, flip patties, brush with oil, and season second side. Place burgers over hot part of grill and cook until burgers are well browned on both sides and register 160 degrees, 4 to 7 minutes per side. (If cooking frozen burgers: After burgers are browned on both sides, transfer to cool

side of grill, cover, and continue to cook until burgers register 160 degrees.)

7. Transfer burgers to plate and let rest for 5 minutes. While burgers rest, grill buns over hot side of grill. Transfer burgers to buns and add desired toppings. Serve.

Classic Burger Sauce
MAKES ABOUT ¼ CUP

- 2 tablespoons mayonnaise
- 1 tablespoon ketchup
- ½ teaspoon sweet pickle relish
- ½ teaspoon sugar
- ½ teaspoon white vinegar
- ¼ teaspoon pepper

Whisk all ingredients together in bowl.

Malt Vinegar–Molasses Burger Sauce
MAKES ABOUT 1 CUP

- ¾ cup mayonnaise
- 4 teaspoons malt vinegar
- ½ teaspoon molasses
- ¼ teaspoon Worcestershire sauce
- ¼ teaspoon salt
- ¼ teaspoon pepper

Whisk all ingredients together in bowl.

Chile-Lime Burger Sauce
MAKES ABOUT 1 CUP

- ¾ cup mayonnaise
- 2 teaspoons chile-garlic paste
- 2 teaspoons lime juice
- 1 scallion, sliced thin
- ¼ teaspoon fish sauce
- ⅛ teaspoon sugar

Whisk all ingredients together in bowl.

Apricot-Mustard Burger Sauce
MAKES ABOUT 1 CUP

- ¾ cup mayonnaise
- 5 teaspoons apricot preserves
- 1 tablespoon lemon juice
- 1 tablespoon Dijon mustard
- 1 tablespoon whole-grain mustard
- ¼ teaspoon salt

Whisk all ingredients together in bowl.

SUPER-MOIST ROAST TURKEY

WHY THIS RECIPE WORKS Roast turkey basted with mayonnaise may sound like an odd idea, but it promises exceptionally moist, deeply seasoned meat. To help the mayonnaise cling to the turkey, we first made a spice mixture, rubbed it over the turkey, and let it sit until it formed a paste. The seasoned mayonnaise lent its flavor to the turkey without melting off, and it helped prevent moisture from evaporating from the turkey. To ensure that the white meat and dark meat cooked at the same rate, we skewered the legs to the breasts to lift them up, exposing them to more heat, and we covered the breast with aluminum foil to insulate it. Roasting the turkey on a cooling rack set in a rimmed baking sheet, rather than in a V-rack in a roasting pan, made it easy to baste the entire surface.

Recently, we heard about a recipe that calls for slathering a raw turkey with mayonnaise and roasting it. It may sound strange, but the technique promises an incredibly moist and very nicely seasoned bird. We were skeptical, to say the least, until we heard something else about the technique that made us sit up and take notice: Thomas Keller, arguably the best chef in America, is said to make his turkey this way, just as his mother did. In the test kitchen, eyebrows were raised. But since the idea had the backing of Keller himself, I ordered a few turkeys and a few jars of mayonnaise and prepared to be amazed.

Before heading into the kitchen, I looked for Keller's recipe and others. It turns out that Keller, of The French Laundry in California and Per Se in New York, uses mayonnaise when cooking just a turkey breast, not

SUPER-MOIST ROAST TURKEY

the whole bird, as I wanted to do. (We made Keller's recipe, but his techniques didn't carry over to cooking a whole bird, which is a very different challenge.) But the recipe for the whole bird has taken on a life of its own on the Internet, so I printed out several versions and turned on the ovens. Most recipes worked like this: First, you set the turkey on a V-rack inside a roasting pan. Then you mix mayonnaise with herbs and, depending on the recipe, you smear the flavored mayonnaise over the bird, under its skin, inside the cavity, or some combination of the three. Various recipes call for varying amounts of mayonnaise—sometimes as much as 2 cups.

I followed several recipes to the letter. About 3 hours later, I had mixed results. The turkeys that were coated under the skin and in the cavity were the least successful: The mayonnaise had separated into what looked like cottage cheese. On the positive side, the mayonnaise had turned the skin an especially nice dark golden brown—but only in the patches where the coating hadn't slid off. I sliced into the turkeys. The dark meat was as moist and juicy as I'd hoped, plus the flavored mayonnaise lent tangy herbal flavor. But despite the coating, the breast meat ran toward dry. My mission: to capture the advantages of mayonnaise-rubbed turkey and overcome its drawbacks.

We've solved the slower-cooking dark meat/faster-cooking light meat turkey problem many times in the test kitchen (dark meat is done at 175 degrees, white meat at 160 degrees). Usually, we even out their cooking by starting a turkey breast side down and flipping it halfway through cooking. That method was out of the question with a turkey slicked with mayonnaise. So to get them to cook on one timetable, it occurred to me to lift the (dark meat) legs, thus exposing them to more oven heat (ovens are hottest at the top) and ideally speeding up their cooking. I tried tying the legs together with twine, but that raised them no higher. I tried trussing the turkey, an annoying system of tucking wings, crossing drumsticks, and looping and tying string. It was too much hassle, plus the mayonnaise got in the way. What about a skewer? It easily pierced the thighs, pulling the legs up and forward; this not only exposed them to more heat but also insulated the breast

meat slightly. To insulate the breast even more, I loosely draped it with foil for extra protection from the heat. I cooked the skewered turkey at a gentle 325 degrees, cranking the heat to 450 degrees to brown it in the last 30 minutes. This method worked beautifully.

Now I turned my attention to the mayonnaise. I flavored ½ cup with thyme, rosemary, sage, garlic powder, and paprika and brightened it with vinegar. Since using it in the cavity and under the skin was clearly a nonstarter, I simply brushed it on the skin. The coating still wouldn't stick consistently. I tried drying the turkey skin with paper towels first. Alone, this did little. I changed course and thickened the mayo by, counterintuitively, slowly whisking in a few tablespoons of olive oil to tighten the emulsification. Better, but not good enough. Take three: I let the turkey air-dry for an hour with a heavy dusting of the herbs before painting it with the mayo. As the hour passed, the seasonings formed a paste that stuck to the bird and (finally!) gave the mayonnaise coating something to grip. The herbs also boosted the turkey's flavor.

One problem remained: The V-rack and the deep roasting pan I was using—the test kitchen's standard roast turkey setup—didn't suit this recipe. Because the turkey touched the rack in so many places, it was awkward to brush on the mayonnaise and impossible to get full coverage, especially on the sides. Fortunately, a switch to a rimmed baking sheet fitted with a cooling rack let me brush the mayonnaise all over. Pouring a bit of water into the baking sheet kept the turkey juices from burning.

I roasted another turkey, incorporating all my changes. As I was removing the foil shield, it occurred to me to give the breast a second coat of flavored mayonnaise, which helped the turkey roast to a pretty mottled brown. As the bird was cooking, I got a head start on the gravy: I let a mix of sautéed vegetables, herbs, broth, water, and flour simmer and thicken on the stovetop. Later, I poured the drippings from the turkey into this gravy base, strained the gravy, carved the handsome bird, and asked for feedback. The compliments poured in: so moist, so rustic in look, so tasty. Mayonnaise—who (besides Thomas Keller and his mother) knew?

—DIANE UNGER, *Cook's Country*

Super-Moist Roast Turkey

SERVES 10 TO 12

We like Butterball Frozen Turkeys for this recipe. If you prefer natural, unenhanced turkey, we recommend brining. You will need a 12-inch skewer for this recipe.

TURKEY

- 1 (12- to 14-pound) turkey, neck and giblets removed and reserved for another use
- 1 tablespoon minced fresh thyme
- 1 tablespoon minced fresh rosemary
- 2 teaspoons dried sage
- 1½ teaspoons salt
- 1 teaspoon pepper
- 1 teaspoon garlic powder
- 1 teaspoon paprika
- ½ cup mayonnaise
- 3 tablespoons olive oil
- 2 tablespoons cider vinegar
- 2 cups water

GRAVY

- 4 tablespoons unsalted butter
- 1 onion, chopped
- 1 carrot, peeled and chopped
- 1 celery rib, chopped
- 6 tablespoons all-purpose flour
- 3½ cups water
- 3 cups chicken broth
- 1 bay leaf
- ½ teaspoon minced fresh thyme
- Salt and pepper

1. FOR THE TURKEY: Set wire rack inside rimmed baking sheet. Dry turkey thoroughly inside and out with paper towels. Tuck wings under turkey and transfer to prepared wire rack. Pull legs upward and slide 12-inch skewer under bone of fattest part of drumstick across to other drumstick so skewer connects both and legs cover small point of breast.

2. Combine thyme, rosemary, sage, salt, pepper, garlic powder, and paprika in bowl. Rub 2 tablespoons spice mixture evenly over surface of turkey and let sit at room temperature for 1 hour. Add mayonnaise, oil, and vinegar to remaining spice mixture and whisk to combine. Divide mayonnaise mixture in half.

3. Adjust oven rack to lowest position and heat oven to 325 degrees. Brush half of mayonnaise mixture evenly

HOW TO MAKE SUPER-MOIST ROAST TURKEY
We swapped our usual roasting pan and V-rack for a rimmed baking sheet and wire rack and combined a few techniques to even out the cooking of light and dark meat and produce a moist, well-seasoned bird.

1. Tuck wings underneath turkey; place on wire rack set inside rimmed baking sheet. Lift legs upward and slide 12-inch skewer under bones of fattest part of drumsticks so skewer connects drumsticks and legs cover part of breast.

2. Brush mayonnaise mixture evenly over surface of turkey to add flavor and encourage browning.

3. Place 18-inch square piece of aluminum foil diagonally over breast, tucking point of foil inside cavity and over tops of legs to protect delicate breast meat from drying out.

4. Transfer turkey to oven and pour 2 cups water into bottom of baking sheet to prevent drippings from scorching. Roast until thighs register 165 degrees, 2½ to 3 hours.

over surface of turkey. Place 18 by 18-inch sheet of heavy-duty aluminum foil diagonally over breast, tucking point of foil inside cavity and over tops of legs. Transfer turkey to oven and pour water into bottom of baking sheet. Roast until thighs/drumsticks register 165 degrees, 2½ to 3 hours. Remove turkey from oven and increase oven temperature to 450 degrees.

4. FOR THE GRAVY: While turkey cooks, melt butter in large saucepan over medium heat. Add onion, carrot, and celery and cook until well browned, 7 to 9 minutes. Stir in flour and cook for 1 minute. Slowly whisk in 2 cups water, broth, bay leaf, and thyme. Bring to simmer, reduce heat to low, and cook, covered, stirring occasionally, until mixture has thickened, about 20 minutes (gravy will be very thick). Remove from heat and set aside.

5. Once oven has come to temperature, remove foil and brush remaining half of mayonnaise mixture evenly over turkey. Return turkey to oven and roast until breasts register 160 degrees and thighs/drumsticks register 175 degrees, 25 to 35 minutes. Tip juices from turkey cavity into baking sheet and transfer turkey to carving board. Let rest, uncovered, for 30 minutes.

6. Remove wire rack from baking sheet. Pour remaining 1½ cups water into baking sheet and scrape up any browned bits. Carefully pour pan juices into fat separator and let sit for 5 minutes. Pour defatted pan juices into gravy and bring to simmer over medium heat. Simmer until gravy is thickened and reduced to 3 cups, 15 to 20 minutes. Strain gravy through fine-mesh strainer into clean saucepan; discard solids. Rewarm gravy gently over medium-low heat. Season with salt and pepper to taste. Carve turkey and serve with gravy.

HERB-CRUSTED SALMON

✔ **WHY THIS RECIPE WORKS** Herb-crusted salmon rarely lives up to its name; it most often sports a dusty, bland sprinkling of bread crumbs and hardly any herb flavor. To make this dish the best it could be, we first brined the salmon to keep it moist (brining also inhibits the formation of the white protein albumin that forms on the fish when heated). To protect the delicate flavor of the tarragon in the oven, we mixed the herb with mustard and mayonnaise, layered it on the fish, then sprinkled on the bread-crumb crust seasoned with thyme. A little beaten egg mixed with the bread crumbs helped the crust adhere, and a low oven kept it from scorching while the salmon cooked through.

Herb-crusted salmon always sounds like a good idea. Its very name suggests so much: fresh herb flavor and a crunchy coating that contrasts nicely with the silky salmon. It also sounds simple: Just sprinkle bread crumbs mixed with chopped herbs on a fish fillet and stick the whole thing under the broiler. An easy weeknight meal, served. But as soon as I began my testing, I knew I was

in for a challenge. My first attempts were neither herby nor well crusted. The fresh herb flavor vanished under the intense heat of the broiler, and the oily, overcharred smattering of bread crumbs fell off with the touch of a feather. I set out to make a quick herb-crusted salmon with fresh herb flavor and a crust that stayed in place and delivered a substantial crunch.

I decided to focus first on the crust and worry about incorporating herb flavor later. My earlier tests proved that coarse, Japanese-style panko bread crumbs were a must. I seasoned them with salt and pepper; then, to moisten the mix and increase its cohesion, I tried adding small amounts of mayonnaise, mustard, melted butter, and olive oil, respectively, to four different batches. I applied the mixture to the fish and cooked the fillets on a rack in a 325-degree oven. (I dismissed the char-inducing broiler from the get-go.) Though the added fats helped the crumbs brown evenly and the mustard increased the crust's flavor, none of the binders did much to hold it all together.

I would need something stickier. I tried 2 tablespoons of beaten egg along with some mayo and mustard. This simple combination yielded a crispy crust that held together without being tough and could easily be cut with a fork. On to the crust's flavor.

One of my favorite herbs to pair with salmon is tarragon, so I started with that. The tarragon certainly smelled delicious as it baked on the fish, but by the time the crust was browned and the salmon had cooked, its delicate leaves had lost all their fragrance and flavor. It turns out that herbs can be divided into two categories: The major aromatic compounds in hardy herbs like thyme and rosemary are chemically stable and do not dissipate when heated. Delicate herbs like tarragon, basil, and dill, however, contain unstable aromatic compounds that do not fare well at high temperatures. To protect the tarragon from the heat of the oven, I would need a shield.

What about a bread-crumb shield? I combined tarragon, mayo, and mustard, which I then spread over the top of each salmon fillet. I mixed the egg and panko separately before pressing them on top of the herb spread and baking my fish. The first time I opened the oven door, I smelled success. Instead of the familiar waft of tarragon, I simply smelled cooked salmon; the potent herb flavor was still contained beneath its crusty shield. Happily, when I took a bite, the tarragon flavor was clear and fresh.

But since it didn't contain fat, the bread-crumb crust was pale blond in color and a bit bland. I didn't want to lose my fresh tarragon flavor by upping the oven temperature. Instead, I browned the panko in a pan with some butter, then added just a bit of thyme to the mix. I knew that this hardy herb's flavor compounds could handle the heat.

The last issue to fix was the splotchy white layer of albumin, a protein in fish and other foods that congeals when heated. We've previously found that brining helps prevent some of the albumin formation: The salt in the brine keeps the surface proteins from contracting as they cook and therefore prevents the albumin from being squeezed out of the fish. A quick 15-minute brine worked wonders. This batch had very little of the unsightly white film; plus, it was perfectly seasoned and far moister. It turns out that brining fish works in a similar fashion to brining proteins like chicken and pork. The salt is drawn into the flesh, followed by water, leading to juicier fish. And because muscles in fish are shorter and looser than those in meat, the salt penetrates more rapidly, requiring shorter brining times. Now I could celebrate success: My redesigned herb-crusted salmon was silky, well seasoned, and both herby and crusty.

—LAN LAM, *Cook's Illustrated*

Herb-Crusted Salmon

SERVES 4

For the fillets to cook at the same rate, they must be the same size and shape. To ensure uniformity, we prefer to purchase a 1½- to 2-pound center-cut salmon fillet and cut it into four pieces. Dill or basil can be substituted for tarragon.

Salt and pepper
4 (6- to 8-ounce) skin-on salmon fillets
2 tablespoons unsalted butter
½ cup panko bread crumbs
2 tablespoons beaten egg
2 teaspoons minced fresh thyme
¼ cup chopped fresh tarragon
1 tablespoon whole-grain mustard
1½ teaspoons mayonnaise
Lemon wedges

1. Adjust oven rack to middle position and heat oven to 325 degrees. Dissolve 5 tablespoons salt in 2 quarts water in large container. Submerge salmon in brine and let stand at room temperature for 15 minutes. Remove salmon from brine, pat dry, and set aside.

2. Meanwhile, melt butter in 10-inch skillet over medium heat. Add panko and ⅛ teaspoon salt and season with pepper; cook, stirring frequently, until panko is golden brown, 4 to 5 minutes. Transfer to bowl and let cool completely. Stir in egg and thyme until thoroughly combined. Stir tarragon, mustard, and mayonnaise together in second bowl.

3. Set wire rack in rimmed baking sheet. Place 12 by 8-inch piece of aluminum foil on wire rack and lightly coat with vegetable oil spray. Evenly space fillets, skin side down, on foil. Using spoon, spread tarragon mixture evenly over top of each fillet. Sprinkle panko mixture evenly over top of each fillet, pressing with your fingers to adhere. Bake until center of thickest part of fillets reaches 125 degrees and is still translucent when cut into with paring knife, 18 to 25 minutes. Transfer salmon to serving platter and let rest for 5 minutes. Serve with lemon wedges.

NOTES FROM THE TEST KITCHEN

WHY YOU SHOULD BRINE FISH

In the test kitchen, we brine meats like turkey, chicken, pork, and lamb to improve both flavor and texture. But brining fish can be beneficial, too. We set up a series of tests using different brine concentrations (3, 6, and 9 percent salt-to-water solutions by weight) and types of fish (tuna, salmon, swordfish, and halibut). We found that, for up to six 1-inch-thick steaks or fillets, the optimum concentration was a 6 percent brine (5 tablespoons of salt dissolved in 2 quarts of water) and the ideal time was 15 minutes. It worked no matter the species, improving the texture of the fish without overseasoning.

As it does with meat, brining fish serves two purposes: One, it helps season the flesh, which improves flavor; and two, by partially dissolving muscle fibers to form a water-retaining gel, it helps prevent the protein from drying out. And brining works a lot faster on fish because the structure of muscle in fish is different from that in meat: Instead of long, thin fibers (as long as 10 centimeters in meat), fish is constructed of very short (up to 10 times shorter) bundles of fibers.

In addition, we seared each species of fish to see if using a wet brine would inhibit browning. Luckily, it did not, so long as the fish was dried well with paper towels just before cooking. Finally, we've found that brining helps reduce the presence of albumin, a protein that can congeal into an unappealing white mass on the surface of the fish when heated.

GRILL-SMOKED SALMON

✔ **WHY THIS RECIPE WORKS** We wanted to capture the intense, smoky flavor of hot-smoked fish and the firm but silky texture of the cold-smoked type, without relying on specialized equipment or turning the dish into a day-long project. To prepare the salmon for smoking, we quick-cured the fish with a mixture of salt and sugar, which draws moisture from the flesh and seasons it throughout. We then cooked the fish indirectly over a gentle fire with ample smoke to produce salmon that was sweet, smoky, and tender. We also cut our large fillet into individual serving-size portions. This small step delivered big: First, it ensured more thorough smoke exposure (without increasing the time) by creating more surface area. Second, the smaller pieces of delicate salmon were far easier to get off the grill intact than one large fillet.

The process of smoking fish over hardwood to preserve its delicate flesh has a long tradition, and rich, fatty salmon is well suited to the technique. But smoked salmon's unique taste and texture don't come easy: The translucent, mildly smoky slices piled on bagels are produced by slowly smoking (but not fully cooking) salt-cured fillets at roughly 60 to 90 degrees, a project that requires specialized equipment and lots of time (at least 24 hours and as long as five days). Then there is hot smoking, a procedure in which cured fillets are fully cooked at higher temperatures (100 to 250 degrees) for 1 to 8 hours. The higher heat results in a drier texture and a more potent smokiness, so the fish is often flaked and mixed into dips and spreads.

Both approaches deliver terrific results—but are impractical (if not impossible) for a home cook to pull off. Sure, you can impart a touch of smokiness by tossing wood chips onto hot charcoal and quickly grilling fish, but I had also heard of a lesser-known, more intriguing option that captures both the intense, smoky flavor of hot-smoked fish and the firm but silky texture of the cold-smoked type. The fish is cooked via indirect heat on a grill—a familiar and uncomplicated technique—and although the resulting fillets have a distinctive taste, they are not overpoweringly salty or smoky, so they can be enjoyed either warm from the grill or at room temperature.

To try out these smoky, succulent fillets, I scoured cookbooks for recipes. The typical first step in smoking fish is to cure the flesh with salt; some authors recommended brining, others directly salting the fillet. To keep the preparation time in check, I steered away from recommendations for curing the fish for longer than an hour or two.

The other criteria, smoking temperature and length of exposure—both crucial to the final result—were all over the map. One recipe called for smoking the fish at 350 degrees for a modest 20 minutes; another let it go twice as long at only 275 degrees.

With so many factors at play, I decided to try a simple brine first, soaking a center-cut, skin-on fillet (retaining the skin would make it easier to remove the fillet from the grill) in the test kitchen's usual 6 percent solution of salt and water for 2 hours. For the time being, I dumped a moderate 4 quarts of lit charcoal on one side of the grill, along with a few soaked wood chunks to provide the smoke. I placed the fish on the cooking grate opposite the coals, popped the cover on the grill, and smoked the fish until it was still a little translucent at the center, about 25 minutes.

The result was illuminating if not exactly spectacular. The brine had the unfortunate effect of making the salmon terribly bloated, plus it seemed to highlight the fish's natural oiliness in an unpleasant way—a far cry from the supple but firm texture I was after. When I thought about it, it made sense: Unlike lean, dry proteins such as turkey breast and pork tenderloin, salmon contains so much fat and moisture that the lengthy brine required for salt curing only makes it seem waterlogged.

For my next try, I covered the salmon with a generous blanket of kosher salt (its coarse texture makes it cling to food better than table salt) and refrigerated it, uncovered, on a wire rack in a baking sheet. After an hour, a considerable amount of liquid had been drawn to the surface of the flesh. I knew that if I waited any longer, the fluid would start to migrate back into the salmon through the process of osmosis, leading to the same bloated texture, so I promptly removed it from the refrigerator, blotted the moisture with a paper towel, and took it out to the grill for smoking. This sample was considerably better than the brined fish: incredibly moist yet still firm—and not at all soggy. It wasn't perfect, though; most tasters found it too salty to be enjoyed as a main dish. I tried dialing down the amount of salt as well as salting for a shorter amount of time, but alas, the fish didn't achieve the proper texture.

Back at my desk, I looked for a solution in the recipes that I'd collected and came across a few that called for adding sugar to the cure. I knew that, like salt, sugar is hygroscopic, meaning it attracts water. Could sugar pull moisture from the salmon as effectively as salt? Not quite: Because individual molecules of sucrose are much larger than sodium and chloride ions, sugar is, pound for pound, about 12 times less effective than salt at attracting moisture. Still, it was a workable option; I just had to do some tinkering. Eventually, I determined that a ratio of 2 parts sugar to 1 part salt produced well-balanced taste and texture in the finished salmon. This fish firmed up nicely and it was far less salty, plus the sugar counterbalanced its richness.

With a reliable curing method in hand, I could finally fine-tune my smoking technique. My current setup was far from ideal: By the time the fish was sufficiently smoky, it was dry and flaky. Conversely, when it was cooked perfectly—still silky and slightly pink in the interior, or about 125 degrees—the smoke flavor was faint. Adding more wood chunks only gave the fillet a sooty flavor. Instead, I tried to cool down the temperature of the grill by reducing the amount of charcoal from 4 quarts to 3. This helped somewhat. The fish cooked more slowly (for a full 30 to 40 minutes) and had more time to absorb smoke.

But the smoke flavor still wasn't as bold as I wanted. Rather than manipulating the cooking time any further, I turned to the salmon itself, cutting the large fillet into individual serving-size portions. This seemingly minor tweak resulted in big payoffs: First, it ensured more smoke exposure in the same amount of time by creating more surface area. Second, the delicate pieces were far easier to get off the grill in one piece than a single bulky fillet. (To that end, I also started placing the fillets on a piece of foil.) Finally, I found that I could now use an even cooler fire (produced with a mere 2 quarts of charcoal): The smaller fillets reached their ideal serving temperature in the same amount of time that the single, larger fillet had taken. Plus, the gentler fire rendered the fillets incomparably tender.

With a smoky, rich taste and a silky, supple texture, my quickie smoked salmon recipe was complete. To provide some contrasting flavors, I devised a homemade mayonnaise that incorporated many of the garnishes that are commonly served on a smoked salmon platter—hard-cooked egg, capers, and dill. With this flavorful sauce and a reliable method, I had a recipe that was, to put it plainly, smoking hot.

—ANDREW JANJIGIAN, *Cook's Illustrated*

Grill-Smoked Salmon

SERVES 6

Use salmon fillets of similar thickness so that they cook at the same rate. The best way to ensure uniformity is to buy a 2½- to 3-pound whole center-cut fillet and cut it into six pieces. Serve the salmon with lemon wedges or with our "Smoked Salmon Platter" Sauce (recipe follows).

- **2 tablespoons sugar**
- **1 tablespoon kosher salt**
- **6 (6- to 8-ounce) center-cut skin-on salmon fillets**
- **2 wood chunks soaked in water for 30 minutes and drained (if using charcoal) or 2 cups wood chips, half of chips soaked in water for 15 minutes and drained (if using gas)**

1. Combine sugar and salt in bowl. Set salmon on wire rack set in rimmed baking sheet and sprinkle flesh side evenly with sugar mixture. Refrigerate, uncovered, for 1 hour. With paper towels, brush any excess salt and sugar from salmon and blot dry. Return fish on wire rack to refrigerator, uncovered, while preparing grill.

2A. FOR A CHARCOAL GRILL: Open bottom vent halfway. Light large chimney starter one-third filled with charcoal briquettes (2 quarts). When top coals are partially covered with ash, pour into steeply banked pile against side of grill. Place wood chunks on top of coals. Set cooking grate in place, cover, and open lid vent halfway. Heat grill until hot and wood chunks begin to smoke, about 5 minutes.

2B. FOR A GAS GRILL: Combine soaked and unsoaked chips. Use large piece of heavy-duty aluminum foil to wrap chips into foil packet and cut several vent holes in top. Place wood chip packet directly on primary burner. Turn primary burner to high (leave other burners off), cover, and heat grill until hot and wood chips begin to smoke, 15 to 25 minutes. Turn primary burner to medium. (Adjust primary burner as needed to maintain grill temperature of 275 to 300 degrees.)

3. Clean and oil cooking grate. Fold piece of heavy-duty foil into 18 by 6-inch rectangle. Place foil rectangle over cool side of grill and place salmon pieces on foil, spaced at least ½ inch apart. Cover grill (positioning lid vent over fish if using charcoal) and cook until center of thickest part of fillet registers 125 degrees and is still translucent when checked with tip of paring knife, 30 to 40 minutes. Transfer to platter and serve, or allow to cool to room temperature.

GRILL-SMOKED SALMON

"Smoked Salmon Platter" Sauce

MAKES 1½ CUPS

- 1 large egg yolk
- 2 teaspoons Dijon mustard
- 2 teaspoons sherry vinegar
- ½ cup vegetable oil
- 2 tablespoons capers, rinsed, plus 1 teaspoon caper brine
- 1 large hard-cooked egg, chopped fine
- 2 tablespoons minced shallot
- 2 tablespoons minced fresh dill

Whisk egg yolk, mustard, and vinegar together in medium bowl. Whisking constantly, slowly drizzle in oil until emulsified, about 1 minute. Gently fold in capers, brine, hard-cooked egg, shallot, and dill.

NOTES FROM THE TEST KITCHEN

NOW WE'RE SMOKIN'

The two most common methods for smoking fish are cold and hot smoking. Both approaches require special equipment and a serious time investment and result in a product that is more of an ingredient than a main dish. Our unique hybrid recipe produces an entrée that captures the uniquely smooth and lush texture of cold-smoked salmon and the forward smokiness of hot-smoked salmon. The best part? It cooks in only 30 to 40 minutes on a regular charcoal or gas grill.

COLD-SMOKED
Slick and silky; mild smoke.

HOT-SMOKED
Dry and firm; potent smoke.

HYBRID GRILL-SMOKED
Ultramoist; rich, balanced smoke.

GARLICKY ROASTED SHRIMP

✓ WHY THIS RECIPE WORKS We loved the idea of an easy weeknight meal of juicy roasted shrimp, but getting the lean, quick-cooking shrimp to develop color and roasted flavor before they turned rubbery required a few tricks. First we chose jumbo-size shrimp, which were the least likely to dry out and overcook. Butterflying the shrimp increased their surface area, giving us more room to add flavor. After brining the shrimp briefly to help them hold on to more moisture, we tossed them with a potent mixture of aromatic spices, garlic, herbs, butter, and olive oil. Then we roasted them under the broiler to get lots of color as quickly as possible, elevating them on a wire rack so they'd brown all over. To further protect them as they cooked and to produce a more deeply roasted flavor, we left their shells on; the sugar- and protein–rich shells browned quickly in the heat of the oven and transferred flavor to the shrimp itself.

When I set out to find the best way to make roasted shrimp, I thought I would hit the jackpot. Quick-cooking shrimp make an easy weeknight dinner, and the idea of roasting them until they develop deep, flavorful browning seemed so natural that I figured there were plenty of good recipes out there to learn from.

Imagine my surprise, then, when the handful I tried produced pale, insipid shrimp that looked as though they'd been baked, not roasted. Some of the missteps seemed obvious, such as crowding lots of small shrimp (tossed with oil and aromatics) on a sheet pan or in a baking dish, where their exuded moisture caused them to steam and prevented browning. Some of the oven temperatures were also strangely low—around 300 degrees. I was sure I could do better, while keeping the technique simple enough for an easy weeknight meal.

My challenge was clear from the start. The goals of roasting—a juicy interior and a thoroughly browned exterior—were impeded by the fact that lean shrimp cook through very quickly. Knowing that, I made two immediate decisions: First, I would crank the oven temperature very high to get good browning on the exterior of the shrimp—500 degrees seemed like a fine place to start. Second, I would use the biggest shrimp I could get. That meant skipping past even the extra-large size and reaching for the jumbo shrimp (16 to 20 per pound), which would be the least likely to dry out in the heat. Using larger shrimp would also mean that there would be fewer pieces crowding the pan, and their smaller total surface area would mean that less steam would be created—therefore making browning possible. As a test run, I oiled and seasoned 2 pounds of peeled shrimp with nothing more than a little salt and pepper (I'd explore flavorings once I'd nailed down a cooking method) and slid them into the oven in a sheet pan.

I thought the 500-degree blast would get the shrimp good and brown in a hurry, so I hovered around the oven and checked on their color every couple of minutes. Trouble was, the color never came—and while I waited and waited for the browning to kick in, the shrimp turned from tender and slightly translucent to fully opaque. I knew before I plunged a fork into them that they were overcooked. Clearly, high heat alone wasn't going to cut it, so I started experimenting. "Searing" them by preheating the baking sheet in the 500-degree oven helped, but only a little, since the pan's temperature plummeted as soon as the shrimp hit. Blasting the next batch under the broiler finally delivered some decent browning to the tops of the shrimp, but their undersides were still damp and utterly pale.

Part of the problem was air circulation. When we roast beef or pork, we often elevate it on a rack so that hot air can surround it, drying out and browning even the underside of the meat. I tried broiling my next batch of shrimp on a wire rack set in the baking sheet—and finally started to see some real progress.

But the approach wasn't perfect. Like all broilers, the heat of my broiler was uneven, so I had to rotate the baking sheet halfway through cooking to prevent the shrimp from scorching under the element's hot spots, and even then I got a few desiccated pieces. In addition to using jumbo shrimp, the situation demanded a foolproof buffer against the heat, and the obvious answer was to brine the shrimp. The extra moisture that gets pulled into the lean flesh with the salt helps it stay moist even in a hot oven. Thanks to the shrimp's relatively small size, just a 15-minute soak in brine ensured that inside they stayed nice and plump—not to mention well seasoned throughout. Outside, however, they still shriveled under the broiler's heat before they had a chance to develop deep, "roasted" color and flavor.

I hoped that a more thorough coat of olive oil than the light glossing I'd been giving the shrimp might stave off evaporation, but while the extra fat did keep the shrimp a bit more moist, it did nothing to even out browning. The idea of giving the shrimp a protective layer inspired another idea, though: What if I took advantage of the shrimp's natural protective coating and roasted them in their shells? Surely their "jackets" would prevent the surface of the meat from shriveling and, being drier than the meat, would probably brown quickly, too. Shell-on shrimp are messier to eat, but if the results were good, having to peel them at the table would be worth it.

To make deveining and (later) peeling the shrimp easier, I used a pair of kitchen shears to split their shells from end to end without removing them from the flesh, then I proceeded with my brine-and-broil technique. The results were stunning: shrimp that were moist and plump inside and evenly browned outside. In fact, the depth of the shrimp's "roasted" flavor exceeded my expectations and prompted me to mention the results to our science editor, who replied with some surprising information. Turns out that the shells were doing much more than protecting the crustaceans' flesh: They are loaded with sugars, proteins, and other flavor-boosting compounds that amplify the rich seafood flavor.

Juicy, deeply browned shrimp complete, I moved on to tackle flavorings. I was already splitting the shells across the back and deveining the shrimp, so I took the technique one step further and butterflied the exposed flesh, cutting through the meat just short of severing it into two pieces. This increased the shrimp's surface area, giving me more room to add flavor. Then, to jazz up the oil-salt-pepper base, I added spices (anise seeds and red pepper flakes), six cloves of garlic, parsley, and melted butter (a natural pairing with briny seafood) and worked the flavorful mixture deep into the meat before broiling. Just as brining had seasoned the shrimp throughout, butterflying the pieces and thoroughly coating them with the oil-spice mixture made for seriously bold flavor. And since my tasters instantly gobbled up the shrimp—some of them shell and all—I developed two equally quick, flavorful variations: a Peruvian-style version with cilantro and lime and an Asian-inspired one with cumin, ginger, and sesame.

A great-tasting dish that requires almost no prep work and goes from the oven to the table in fewer than 10 minutes? I knew I'd be making this one year-round.

—ANDREW JANJIGIAN, *Cook's Illustrated*

KEYS TO SHRIMP THAT BROWN DEEPLY—BUT DON'T DRY OUT

USE JUMBOS

Bigger shrimp are less likely to dry out in the heat. Plus, fewer pieces won't crowd the baking sheet and thwart browning.

LEAVE SHELLS ON

Cooking the shrimp shell-on helps protect their lean, delicate flesh from dehydrating before the exterior develops good browning.

BRINE BRIEFLY

Plumping up the shrimp with a quick saltwater soak further buffers them from the oven's heat and also seasons them throughout.

BROIL ON RACK

Broiling the shrimp on a wire rack set in a baking sheet allows the hot air to circulate around them for deep, even color.

THE SURPRISING POWER OF SHRIMP SHELLS

We weren't surprised that cooking shrimp in their shells kept them juicier, but our shell-on roasted shrimp boasted such savory depth that we wondered if there wasn't more to the shell than we thought. Our science editor confirmed our suspicions. First, shrimp shells contain water-soluble flavor compounds that will get absorbed by the shrimp flesh during cooking. Second, the shells are loaded with proteins and sugars—almost as much as the flesh itself. When they brown, they undergo the flavor-enhancing Maillard reaction just as roasted meats do, which gives the shells even more flavor to pass along. Third, like the flesh, the shells contain healthy amounts of glutamates and nucleotides, compounds that dramatically enhance savory umami flavor. These compounds also get transferred to the meat during cooking, amplifying the effect of its own glutamates and nucleotides. Bottom line: Shrimp shells not only protect the meat during cooking but also significantly enhance its flavor. This also proves that those of us who enjoy eating the roasted shell along with the meat are onto something.

SHOPPING FOR SHRIMP 101

Ensuring tender, briny-tasting shrimp starts at the seafood counter. First, just because shrimp is raw doesn't mean it's fresh. Unless you live near a coastal area, chances are the "fresh" shrimp has been previously frozen and later defrosted. Once the shrimp are defrosted, the quality declines with each passing day. If truly fresh shrimp are unavailable, we prefer "individually quick frozen" (IQF) shrimp. These shrimp are frozen right on the boat, and you can thaw them easily right before cooking. But if you must buy defrosted, look for unblemished and firm shrimp that fill their shells and smell of the sea. Finally, make sure that "shrimp" is the only ingredient listed on the package; avoid salt-treated shrimp, which have an unpleasant texture.

Garlicky Roasted Shrimp with Parsley and Anise
SERVES 4 TO 6

Don't be tempted to use smaller shrimp with this cooking technique; they will be overseasoned and prone to overcooking. For more information on deveining the shrimp, see page 6.

- ¼ cup salt
- 2 pounds shell-on jumbo shrimp (16 to 20 per pound)
- 4 tablespoons unsalted butter, melted
- ¼ cup vegetable oil
- 6 garlic cloves, minced
- 1 teaspoon anise seeds
- ½ teaspoon red pepper flakes
- ¼ teaspoon pepper
- 2 tablespoons minced fresh parsley
  Lemon wedges

1. Dissolve salt in 1 quart cold water in large container. Using kitchen shears or sharp paring knife, cut through shell of shrimp and devein but do not remove shell. Using paring knife, continue to cut shrimp ½ inch deep, taking care not to cut in half completely. Submerge shrimp in brine, cover, and refrigerate for 15 minutes.

2. Adjust oven rack 4 inches from broiler element and heat broiler. Combine melted butter, oil, garlic, anise seeds, pepper flakes, and pepper in large bowl. Remove shrimp from brine and pat dry with paper towels. Add shrimp and parsley to butter mixture; toss well, making sure butter mixture gets into interior of shrimp. Arrange shrimp in single layer on wire rack set in rimmed baking sheet.

3. Broil shrimp until opaque and shells are beginning to brown, 2 to 4 minutes, rotating sheet halfway through broiling. Flip shrimp and continue to broil until second side is opaque and shells are beginning to brown, 2 to 4 minutes longer, rotating sheet halfway through broiling. Transfer shrimp to serving platter. Serve immediately, passing lemon wedges separately.

VARIATIONS

Garlicky Roasted Shrimp with Cilantro and Lime

Annatto powder, also called achiote, can be found with the Latin American foods at your supermarket. An equal amount of paprika can be substituted.

Omit butter and increase vegetable oil to ½ cup. Omit anise seeds and pepper. Add 2 teaspoons lightly crushed coriander seeds, 2 teaspoons grated lime zest, and 1 teaspoon annatto powder to oil mixture in step 2. Substitute ¼ cup minced fresh cilantro for parsley and lime wedges for lemon wedges.

Garlicky Roasted Shrimp with Cumin, Ginger, and Sesame

Omit butter and increase vegetable oil to ½ cup. Decrease garlic to 2 cloves and omit anise seeds and pepper. Add 2 teaspoons toasted sesame oil, 1½ teaspoons grated fresh ginger, and 1 teaspoon cumin seeds to oil mixture in step 2. Substitute 2 thinly sliced scallion greens for parsley and omit lemon wedges.

GRILLED BACON-WRAPPED SCALLOPS

✔ **WHY THIS RECIPE WORKS** To recast this cocktail-party favorite as a grilled entrée, we had to find a way to get sturdy, fatty bacon and lean, delicate scallops to come together without compromising either. Parcooking the bacon in the microwave rendered some of the fat, preventing flare-ups when it hit the grill. We built a fire with medium and hot zones, wrapped the bacon around the scallops, skewered them, and placed them over the medium fire to finish cooking the bacon. When the bacon was crisp, we moved the skewers to the hot side of the grill to sear the scallops on just one side (to prevent overcooking). Wrapping each bacon slice around two scallops made for the best ratio. A sprinkling of chopped chives and grilled lemon halves squeezed over the top added a bright final touch.

Anyone who's ever worked in a catering kitchen knows a thing or two about bacon-wrapped scallops; they've been a passed appetizer for at least half of the wedding receptions and cocktail parties I've attended. It's no secret why they're so popular. The smoky, salty bacon beautifully accents the sweet, succulent scallops. Surely taking it to the grill would make a great thing even better.

Grilling scallops is a straightforward matter. Start with "dry" scallops (which have no chemical additives or excess moisture), toss them with oil or melted butter to keep them from sticking to the grate, skewer them, and sear them over high heat for a minute or two on each side until they're just cooked through. But you can't grill bacon like that. The fat will cause flare-ups

that will cover the scallops in soot, and the bacon needs longer, gentler cooking to render and crisp.

I knew that parcooking the bacon before skewering and grilling was a must. I was hoping that I could make my life easier by doing it in the microwave. I started by microwaving the bacon on a plate between layers of paper towels (to absorb the grease). To keep the bacon from curling, I weighed it down with a second plate. After testing various durations, I landed on 4 minutes for bacon that had rendered a good bit of its fat and would finish crisping up after a few minutes on the grill.

Now I needed to find the best way to wrap and skewer the scallops. In the test kitchen, we've grilled scallops on a single skewer as well as on double skewers (that is, with two parallel skewers running through each scallop). The benefit of double skewers is that the scallops can't spin, making them easier to flip and ensuring that they cook evenly. The downside is the amount of work that it takes to double-skewer scallops while keeping the bacon in position. (Once the bacon is cut to length and wrapped around the scallop, the skewer needs to go through the overlapped bacon ends to hold it in place.) For the sake of ease, I decided on a single skewer, taking care to firmly press each bacon-wrapped scallop into its neighbor on the skewer to minimize spinning. I found that tossing the scallops with melted butter not only helped prevent sticking to the grill and added richness but also made the scallops a little sticky and thus easier to handle and skewer.

After several grilling attempts, though, I still had one problem: the fire. I'd been struggling with dripping bacon fat and the resulting flare-ups. It was time to lower the flame and slow down the cooking. Medium heat worked fine on the bacon—it mitigated the flare-ups—but it wasn't hot enough to mark the scallops with a tasty sear. So I created a fire with both medium and hot zones and cooked the bacon sides of the skewers over medium heat, then finished cooking just one of the nonbacon sides over high heat. (There was no need to cook the other side, as the scallops were now cooked just right.)

Both my scallops and bacon were perfectly cooked, but as I pulled the skewers off the grill, I realized I still had one problem. Though a few scallops wrapped in bacon are perfect as an appetizer, six scallops wrapped in bacon means you're eating six slices of bacon for dinner—too much, even for me. I decided to double up the scallops and wrap a single slice of bacon around two of them. Three two-scallop bundles were a perfect dinner portion. Plus, this meant I didn't have to cut the

GRILLED BACON-WRAPPED SCALLOPS

bacon into shorter lengths to comfortably fit around just one scallop—one slice of bacon fit almost perfectly around two scallops.

As final flourishes, I grilled lemon halves and squeezed the juice over the skewers and scattered chopped chives over the platter. With perfectly cooked scallops and bacon spritzed with the smoky juice of grilled lemons, I had given new life to an old favorite. And I could have this party dish whenever I wanted—without having to stand in line to kiss the bride.

—SARAH WILSON WITH CHRIS DUDLEY,
Cook's Country

Grilled Bacon-Wrapped Scallops

SERVES 4

Use ordinary bacon, as thick-cut bacon will take too long to crisp on the grill. When wrapping the scallops, the bacon slice should fit around both scallops, overlapping just enough to be skewered through both ends. We recommend buying "dry" scallops, which don't have chemical additives and taste better than "wet." Dry scallops will look ivory or pinkish; wet scallops are bright white. This recipe was developed with large sea scallops (sold 10 to 20 per pound).

- 12 **slices bacon**
- 24 **large sea scallops, tendons removed**
- 3 **tablespoons unsalted butter, melted**
- ½ **teaspoon salt**
- ⅛ **teaspoon pepper**
- 2 **lemons, halved**
- ¼ **cup chopped fresh chives**

1. Place 4 layers of paper towels on large plate and arrange 6 slices bacon over towels in single layer. Top with 4 more paper towels and remaining 6 slices bacon. Cover with 2 layers of paper towels; place second large plate on top and press gently to flatten. Microwave until fat begins to render but bacon is still pliable, about 4 minutes. Toss scallops, butter, salt, and pepper together in bowl until scallops are thoroughly coated with butter.

2. Press 2 scallops together, side to side, and wrap with 1 slice bacon, trimming excess as necessary. Thread onto skewer through bacon. Repeat with remaining scallops and bacon, threading 3 bundles onto each of 4 skewers.

3A. FOR A CHARCOAL GRILL: Open bottom vent completely. Light large chimney starter filled with

charcoal briquettes (6 quarts). When top coals are partially covered with ash, pour two-thirds evenly over half of grill, then pour remaining coals over other half of grill. Set cooking grate in place, cover, and open lid vent completely. Heat grill until hot, about 5 minutes.

3B. FOR A GAS GRILL: Turn all burners to high, cover, and heat grill until hot, about 15 minutes. Leave primary burner on high and turn other burner(s) to medium.

4. Clean and oil cooking grate. Place skewers, bacon side down, and lemon halves, cut side down, on cooler side of grill. Cook (covered if using gas) until bacon is crisp on first side, about 4 minutes. Flip skewers onto other bacon side and cook until crisp, about 4 minutes longer. Flip skewers scallop side down and move to hot side of grill. Grill until sides of scallops are firm and centers are opaque, about 4 minutes on 1 side only. Transfer skewers to platter, squeeze lemon over, and sprinkle with chives. Serve.

NOTES FROM THE TEST KITCHEN

WRAP AND GRILL
Here's how we ensure that our Grilled Bacon-Wrapped Scallops are properly cooked.

1. Wrap 1 strip parcooked bacon around 2 scallops and run skewer through overlapped bacon. Place three 2-scallop bundles on each skewer.

2. Grill on 2 bacon sides over medium heat for 4 minutes each.

3. Finish by grilling 1 scallop side over high heat for 4 minutes.

CHAPTER 8

DESSERTS

PECAN SANDIES

✓ **WHY THIS RECIPE WORKS** Pecan sandies run the gamut from greasy and bland to dry and crumbly. We wanted a pecan sandy with a tender but crisp texture and a sandy melt-in-the-mouth character. Light brown sugar gave the cookies a subtle caramel flavor that complemented the nuttiness of the pecans and the richness of the butter. To tenderize our cookies, we also included a little confectioners' sugar. For lots of nutty flavor but a delicate sandy texture, we ground the pecans in a food processor. A whole egg made for a too-sticky dough, so we settled on just a yolk for richness and structure. After processing all the ingredients together, we briefly kneaded the dough, then shaped it into logs and chilled it for easy slice-and-bake pecan sandies with clean, crisp edges.

Take shortbread, a Scottish cookie, and give it a dose of Americana—namely, pecans and brown sugar—and it is transformed into a nutty, buttery cookie with a hint of caramel flavor. The texture: tender but crisp and sandy with a melt-in-your-mouth character. Called "pecan sandies," after their noteworthy texture, these cookies are rich in butter like shortbread. And because a crisp, sandy texture—not a puffy or cakey crumb—is the goal, they do not contain chemical leaveners for lift (also like shortbread). Best of all, they are easy to make at home.

To start developing my recipe, I made a variety of published recipes. I made cookies similar to simple sugar cookies that are dropped onto a baking sheet; I baked basic roll-and-cut cookies made with cake flour; I sampled cookies made with vegetable oil and a duo of ground nuts and chopped nuts; I sliced cookies from a refrigerator cookie log. I concluded quickly that cake flour is unnecessary. A tender cookie could be made with unbleached all-purpose flour. I found that oil makes for a sandy texture, but it falls pitifully short in flavor—the rich, sweet flavor of pure butter is paramount. Last, I learned that a dropped cookie doesn't have the neat, clean edges that I wanted. Rolling and cutting the dough or forming it into a sliceable log would be the best way to create a perfect-looking pecan sandy.

Next I needed to determine the best type and amount of sugar for pecan sandies. I assembled a working recipe, then tried light brown sugar, dark brown sugar, granulated sugar, confectioners' sugar, and different combinations of each. Confectioners' sugar, with its small amount of cornstarch, had a noticeable tenderizing

effect on the cookies. Too much, however, and the cookies turned pasty and gummy; a quarter-cup was all that was needed. Granulated sugar had little to offer in the way of flavor, and dark brown sugar offered too much. Light brown sugar, tinged with molasses, gave the cookies a gentle caramel flavor that complemented, not overwhelmed, the nuttiness of the pecans and the richness of the butter.

Next I made batches of pecan sandies with a whole egg and without. I found that a whole egg was excessive—the dough was sticky and difficult to work with. Without an egg, however, the cookies baked up with a texture more like that of pie pastry, and they lost their attractive sharp edges in the oven. A single yolk was just what the dough needed. By comparison, these cookies were fine-pored and stalwart, keeping their crisp, clean look even after baking.

So far, I had been using a good amount of finely chopped nuts, but I wondered if I could get more nutty flavor. I tried grinding a portion of those nuts, leaving the other portion chopped, and found the cookies made with ground nuts to be finer-textured, more tender, and nuttier than those made exclusively with chopped nuts. The oils in the nuts released during grinding contributed to the tenderness and flavor of the cookies. Tasters liked this version, but they demanded an even finer cookie, one in which chopped nuts didn't mar the delicate sandy texture, so I ground all of the pecans.

To round out the flavor, I added a bit of salt, but vanilla extract, even in the smallest amount, was too perfumed and distracting. Tasters did like a light hint of cinnamon, however; its flavor could not be singled out, but it added nuance and a layer of warmth.

Satisfied with the flavor, I turned to the mechanics of my recipe. So far I was grinding the pecans in a food processor, but I was making the cookie dough using the typical creamed butter method in an electric mixer. It occurred to me that these cookies were not a far cry from French tart pastry, which is made entirely in the food processor. Could I use the same technique here? I gave it a whirl, taking the recipe from start to finish in the processor. I ground the nuts with the sugars to help prevent the nuts from getting greasy and clumpy as they broke down, then I added the flour, cut in the butter, and finally added the egg. To ensure that everything was perfectly combined, I emptied the mixture onto the counter and kneaded it gently until it came together into an even, cohesive dough. This method worked faster and more cleanly than I could have hoped—plus now I didn't have to take out the butter ahead of time to soften it for creaming or haul out my electric mixer.

Next I considered options for shaping the cookies. I could roll out the dough into sheets and stamp out cookies with a cutter, but this technique generates scraps, which I preferred to do without. Instead, I used the method for refrigerator cookies, shaping the dough into a 12-inch log, cutting it in half, wrapping each half in plastic wrap, and putting the logs in the freezer just long enough to firm up their exteriors. Then I took them out, rolled them along the counter surface (to round out the flat side they had rested on while soft), then put them in the refrigerator until thoroughly chilled. After a couple of hours, I sliced the logs into ⅜-inch coins and decorated them simply with a pecan half pressed into each slice.

Pecan sandies should become only modestly brown in the oven—the edges should begin to deepen to golden brown, but the bulk of each cookie should be blond. They need to be thoroughly baked, however, even under the pecan adornment, to obtain their characteristic crisp, sandy texture. After testing several different temperatures, I found that a 325-degree oven was ideal—a cooler oven took longer than necessary, and a hotter one gave the cookies too much color. I also made sure to let the cookies cool completely on a wire rack to ensure that they stayed crisp.

As I savored their delicate, melt-in-your-mouth texture and nutty, buttery flavor, all I was missing was a hot cup of tea.

—DAWN YANAGIHARA, America's Test Kitchen Books

Pecan Sandies

MAKES ABOUT 32 COOKIES

Don't substitute another type of sugar for the confectioners' sugar—it is important for a tender, sandy texture.

- 2 cups (8 ounces) pecans
- ½ cup packed (3½ ounces) light brown sugar
- ¼ cup (1 ounce) confectioners' sugar
- 1½ cups (7½ ounces) all-purpose flour
- ¼ teaspoon salt
- 12 tablespoons unsalted butter, cut into ½-inch pieces and chilled
- 1 large egg yolk

1. Reserve 32 prettiest pecan halves for garnishing. Process remaining pecans with brown sugar and confectioners' sugar in food processor until nuts are finely ground, about 20 seconds. Add flour and salt and process to combine, about 10 seconds.

2. Add butter pieces and process until mixture resembles damp sand and rides up sides of bowl, about 20 seconds. With processor running, add egg yolk and process until dough comes together into rough ball, about 20 seconds.

3. Transfer dough to clean counter, knead briefly, and divide into 2 equal pieces. Roll each piece of dough into 6-inch log, about 2 inches thick. Wrap dough tightly in plastic wrap and refrigerate until firm, about 2 hours.

4. Adjust oven racks to upper-middle and lower-middle positions and heat oven to 325 degrees. Line 2 baking sheets with parchment paper.

5. Working with 1 dough log at a time, remove dough log from plastic and, using chef's knife, slice into ⅜-inch-thick rounds, rotating dough so that it won't become misshapen from weight of knife. Space rounds 1 inch apart on prepared baking sheets. Gently press pecan half into center of each cookie. Bake until edges of cookies are golden brown, 20 to 25 minutes, switching and rotating baking sheets halfway through baking. Let cookies cool on baking sheets for 3 minutes, then transfer to wire rack and let cool completely before serving.

VARIATION

Almond Sandies

Replace pecans with equal amount of whole blanched almonds that have been toasted in 350-degree oven for 8 minutes, cooled, and then chopped. Add ¼ teaspoon almond extract with egg yolk.

MOLASSES SPICE COOKIES

✓ **WHY THIS RECIPE WORKS** Molasses cookies, with their moist, tooth-sinking texture and deep, spicy flavor, belie their humble appearance. For the ultimate molasses spice cookie, we found that butter yielded richer cookies than shortening. Blackstrap molasses made the cookies overly bitter; we preferred light or dark molasses for rich but not overwhelming flavor. A combination of dark brown sugar for caramelized flavor and granulated sugar for structure was ideal. Rolling the balls of dough in white sugar gave the finished cookies a sweet, crunchy coating. A mix of vanilla, ginger, cinnamon, cloves, black pepper, and allspice gave the cookies warm, complex flavor. Pulling the cookies from the oven when they looked slightly underdone allowed residual heat to gently finish baking the cookies so they stayed perfectly chewy and moist.

I've come to appreciate good molasses cookies for their honesty and simplicity. Outside, their cracks and crinkles give them a humble, charming countenance. Inside, an uncommonly moist, soft yet chewy texture is half the appeal; the other half is a warm, tingling spiciness paired with the dark, bittersweet flavor of molasses.

Unfortunately, molasses spice cookies are often no more than flat, tasteless cardboard rounds of gingerbread. Some are dry and cakey without the requisite chew; others are timidly flavored with molasses and are either recklessly or meekly spiced.

I started by testing a half-dozen different recipes, using a variety of fats, flours, and mixing methods. Although these early experiments yielded vastly different cookies in terms of flavor and appearance, a few things were clear. The full, rich flavor of butter was in; flat-tasting shortening was out. The best mixing technique was a standard one: Cream the butter and sugar; add the eggs, then the molasses; and, finally, stir in the dry ingredients.

Molasses is at the core of these cookies. It's important to use to give them a dark, smoky, bittersweet flavor, but I found that too much molasses created a sticky, unworkable dough; ½ cup was the limit. But I still wanted bolder molasses flavor. I had been using mild (also called light) molasses up to this point, but in an attempt to boost flavor, I baked batches with dark and blackstrap molasses. Cookies made with dark molasses had bold flavor and rich color, and they garnered much praise from my tasters. Those made with blackstrap molasses had a few fans, but for most the molasses overtook the spices and made the cookies too bitter.

For the sugar, dark brown sugar reinforced the molasses flavor, but it yielded cookies that were surprisingly puffy and cakey, and they spread too little on the baking sheet. Granulated sugar made cookies that were pale in both color and flavor. A combination of granulated and brown sugars was ideal, providing both rich, caramelized flavor and a good, even thickness in the oven After some fiddling, I found equal amounts of brown and granulated sugar to be ideal.

Most molasses cookie recipes call for a single egg to bind things together. However, the egg white made the dough sticky and hard to handle. The white also caused the baked cookies to have a slightly cakelike crumb and a firmer, drier feel. A lone yolk was all the cookies needed; it bound the dough nicely without detracting from the cookies' moist, chewy texture.

Molasses is a mildly acidic ingredient, so it reacts with alkalis like baking soda to provide lift, making baking soda the logical leavener for these cookies. I found that cookies with too little baking soda came out flat and failed to develop the distinctive fault lines I was after. A full teaspoon of baking soda gave the cookies nice height—a pleasure to sink your teeth into—and a winsome appearance, with large, meandering fissures.

It was time to refine the flavor of the cookies. I started with generous amounts of sharp, spicy ground ginger and warm, soothing cinnamon. I also added small amounts of fragrant cloves and sweet allspice. A teaspoon of vanilla extract complemented the spices. I also found that just ¼ teaspoon of freshly ground black pepper added some welcome complexity—a hint of heat against the deep, bittersweet flavor of the molasses.

To shape the molasses cookies, I rolled heaping tablespoons of dough into balls and coated them with granulated sugar, which, after baking, gave the cookies a frosted sparkle. A 375-degree oven baked the cookies to perfection—the edges were slightly crisped and the interiors soft and chewy. I determined that it was essential to bake the cookies one sheet at a time since cookies baked on the lower rack inevitably puffed and turned out smooth rather than craggy and cracked.

Most important, I noted that the cookies must come out of the oven when they appear substantially underdone; otherwise their soft, moist, chewy texture will harden upon cooling. Whisk them out when the edges are hardly set, the centers are still soft and puffy, and the dough looks shiny and raw between the cracks.

These cookies were everything a humble molasses cookie should be—sweet and spicy and complex, with lightly crisp edges and a satisfyingly chewy center.

—DAWN YANAGIHARA, America's Test Kitchen Books

Molasses Spice Cookies

MAKES ABOUT 22 COOKIES

For the best flavor, make sure that your spices are fresh. Light or mild molasses gives the cookies a milder flavor; for a stronger flavor, use dark molasses.

⅓ cup (2⅓ ounces) granulated sugar, plus
    ½ cup for rolling
2¼ cups (11¼ ounces) all-purpose flour
1 teaspoon baking soda
1½ teaspoons ground cinnamon
1½ teaspoons ground ginger
½ teaspoon ground cloves
¼ teaspoon ground allspice
¼ teaspoon pepper
¼ teaspoon salt

12 tablespoons unsalted butter, softened
⅓ cup packed (2⅓ ounces) dark brown sugar
1 large egg yolk
1 teaspoon vanilla extract
½ cup light or dark molasses

1. Adjust oven rack to middle position and heat oven to 375 degrees. Line 2 baking sheets with parchment paper. Place ½ cup granulated sugar in shallow dish; set aside.

2. Whisk flour, baking soda, cinnamon, ginger, cloves, allspice, pepper, and salt together in medium bowl; set aside.

3. Using stand mixer fitted with paddle, beat butter, brown sugar, and remaining ⅓ cup granulated sugar on medium-high speed until light and fluffy, about 3 minutes. Reduce speed to medium-low and add egg yolk and vanilla; increase speed to medium and beat until incorporated, about 20 seconds. Reduce speed to medium-low and add molasses; beat until fully incorporated, about 20 seconds, scraping down bowl as needed. Reduce speed to low and add flour mixture; beat until just incorporated, about 30 seconds, scraping down bowl as needed. Give dough final stir to ensure that no flour pockets remain. Dough will be soft.

4. Working with 1 tablespoon of dough at a time, roll into balls. Roll half of dough balls in sugar and toss to coat. Space dough balls 2 inches apart on prepared baking sheet. Repeat with remaining dough.

5. Bake 1 sheet at a time until cookies are browned, still puffy, and edges have begun to set but centers are still soft (cookies will look raw between cracks and seem underdone), about 11 minutes, rotating baking sheet halfway through baking. Do not overbake.

6. Let cookies cool on baking sheet for 5 minutes; transfer cookies to wire rack and let cool to room temperature before serving.

VARIATIONS

Molasses Spice Cookies with Dark Rum Glaze
If the glaze is too thick to drizzle, whisk in up to an additional ½ tablespoon of rum.

Whisk 1 cup confectioners' sugar and 2½ tablespoons dark rum together in medium bowl until smooth. Drizzle or spread glaze using back of spoon on cooled cookies. Allow glazed cookies to dry for at least 15 minutes.

CHOCOLATE SUGAR COOKIES

Molasses Spice Cookies with Orange Essence
Process ⅔ cup granulated sugar and 2 teaspoons grated orange zest until pale orange, about 10 seconds; transfer sugar to shallow baking dish or pie plate and set aside. Add 1 teaspoon grated orange zest to dough along with molasses and substitute orange sugar for granulated sugar when coating dough balls in step 4.

CHOCOLATE SUGAR COOKIES

✔ **WHY THIS RECIPE WORKS** Making a rich, chocolaty version of our favorite crispy, chewy sugar cookie wasn't as easy as simply stirring in some chocolate. When we tried adding melted chocolate to the dough, the cookies lost their signature chew. Instead, we turned to unsweetened cocoa powder; just ¾ cup provided intense chocolate flavor without changing the cookies' texture. To compensate for the added cocoa powder, we reduced the amount of flour until we found just the right balance—too much and the cookies were cakey; too little and the cookies crumbled. Finally, we made our cookies foolproof by melting most of the butter, then stirring in a portion of cold butter to cool it to just the right temperature for adding to the dough.

I have a thing for sugar cookies, especially the kind with crisp edges, chewy centers, and crunchy, crackled, sugary tops. The ones I'm talking about require no laborious rolling out—just shape the dough into balls, dip in sugar, flatten, and bake. I hoped to take that simple template and find a way to add rich chocolate flavor to create a chocolate sugar cookie.

I decided to adapt my recipe from the test kitchen's recipe for chewy brown sugar cookies. It's an unusual recipe: It calls for melted, browned butter, whereas most recipes use ordinary chilled butter. The browning adds flavor, and the melting adds chew. This recipe also uses lots of dark brown sugar and vanilla for extra flavor.

I'd start by simply adding some melted chocolate. I mixed the brown sugar, vanilla, and salt into 14 tablespoons of melted browned butter; stirred in 1 ounce of cooled, melted chocolate and the eggs; then added leavener and 2¼ cups of flour. I repeated this test several times, increasing the amount of chocolate each time, but by the time the cookies tasted chocolaty (which took 4 ounces), they were no longer chewy. What about cocoa powder? After several tests, I found that I could

use 2¼ ounces of cocoa to replace some of the flour (if I used more cocoa, the cookies crumbled). Fortunately, since cocoa is more intense than bar chocolate, the flavor was just as good—and the cookies retained their chew.

But browning the butter was bothersome. I had to watch it constantly; it could go from brown to burnt in an instant. With so much chocolate in the mix, was it worth adding? I made two new batches of cookies, one with browned butter, the other with unbrowned. As it turned out, few of us could tell the difference.

Just one problem remained: The cookies were good, but the results were inconsistent from batch to batch. Blame the butter. If it was too hot when I added it to the dough, the cookies spread too much. To foolproof my recipe, I melted most (but not all) of the butter, then stirred in the remaining cold butter to cool it down.

Using this technique, I was able to produce round, even cookies with deep chocolate flavor; nice chew; and fissured, sugary tops—every time. Now all I needed was a glass of milk.

—CAROLYNN PURPURA MACKAY, *Cook's Country*

Chocolate Sugar Cookies
MAKES 24 COOKIES

Use a good brand of cocoa powder in this recipe; the test kitchen's favorite brand is Hershey's Natural.

- ⅓ cup (2⅓ ounces) granulated sugar
- 1½ cups (7½ ounces) plus 2 tablespoons all-purpose flour
- ¾ cup (2¼ ounces) unsweetened cocoa powder
- ½ teaspoon baking soda
- ¼ teaspoon baking powder
- 14 tablespoons unsalted butter
- 1¾ cups packed (12¼ ounces) dark brown sugar
- 1 tablespoon vanilla extract
- ½ teaspoon salt
- 1 large egg plus 1 large yolk

1. Adjust oven rack to middle position and heat oven to 350 degrees. Line 2 baking sheets with parchment paper. Place granulated sugar in shallow dish; set aside. Combine flour, cocoa, baking soda, and baking powder in bowl.

2. Microwave 10 tablespoons butter, covered, in large bowl until melted, about 1 minute. Remove from microwave and stir in remaining 4 tablespoons butter until melted. Allow butter to cool to 90 to 95 degrees, about 5 minutes.

3. Whisk brown sugar, vanilla, and salt into butter until no lumps remain, scraping down bowl as needed. Whisk in egg and yolk until smooth. Stir in flour mixture until just combined.

4. Working with 2 tablespoons of dough at a time, roll into balls. Working in batches, roll balls in granulated sugar and divide between baking sheets. Using bottom of drinking glass, flatten cookies to 2 inches in diameter. Sprinkle each sheet of cookies with 1½ teaspoons remaining granulated sugar.

5. Bake 1 sheet at a time until cookies are slightly puffy and edges have begun to set, about 15 minutes, rotating sheet halfway through baking (cookies will look slightly underdone between cracks). Let cookies cool on sheets for 5 minutes, then transfer to wire rack. Let cookies cool completely before serving.

NOTES FROM THE TEST KITCHEN

THE BEST COCOA POWDER

Cocoa powder is a chocolate powerhouse, packing in more flavor ounce for ounce than any other form of chocolate. We reach for it constantly when making cookies, cake, pudding, and hot chocolate, which is why we're picky about what brand we keep around. To find our favorite, we incorporated eight widely available brands of cocoa into chocolate butter cookies, chocolate cake, and hot cocoa.

As tasters evaluated the samples on the intensity and complexity of the chocolate flavor, they noted that lesser powders produced "wan" cakes and hot cocoa that tasted like "dust dissolved in water"; good versions delivered "profound" chocolate flavor and made cookies seem downright "luxurious."

Figuring that the roasting phase of the process might shed some light on the differences, we contacted the manufacturers to inquire about their methods and uncovered a pattern: In the top brands in our lineup the nibs—the dark, meaty flesh that is ground then refined to make chocolate—are separated before roasting, while in lower-ranking brands the whole bean is roasted and shelled afterward. Outside the shell, the nibs roast more evenly, making under or overroasting less probable. We also found that the size of the grind made a big difference. Our top brands had small, distinct particles, while weaker-tasting powders had much larger particles. This finding made sense: The smaller the particle the more surface area that's exposed, hence the more flavor that's released.

Our top pick shared these two key features. In cookies, cake, and hot cocoa, tasters repeatedly singled out **Hershey's Natural Cocoa Unsweetened** for its rich chocolate flavor and particularly deep complexity. (See page 303 for more information on our testing results.)

ALMOND BISCOTTI

✅ **WHY THIS RECIPE WORKS** Italians like these cookies dry and hard, while American versions are more buttery and tender. We wanted something in between—crisp but not tooth-shattering. A judicious 4 tablespoons of butter gave us a dough that was neither too hard nor too lean. Since the small amount of butter was impossible to cream with the sugar, we whipped the eggs first, added the sugar, then folded in the butter and the dry ingredients. The whipped eggs lightened the dough but made the finished cookies too crunchy. Swapping out some of the flour for finely ground nuts gave us a more crumbly, easy-to-bite cookie. A generous amount of almond extract ensured that its nutty flavor didn't dissipate in the oven. Finally, for biscotti with even crunch, we baked the slices on a wire rack inside a baking sheet for even air circulation.

Biscotti literally means "twice-baked." These classic Italian cookies are baked once as a single, oblong loaf. The loaf is then sliced into thin planks, which are returned to the oven to fully dry and crisp. The result: crunchy, nutty (almond is a popular flavor), finger-shaped cookies that are perfect alongside a cup of coffee—or, as in Italy, a glass of sweet *vin santo*.

What separates one style from another mostly boils down to texture—specifically, just how crunchy or soft the cookies are. The most traditional biscotti, known as *cantuccini*, or *biscotti di Prato*, are extremely hard; they are meant to be dunked into a liquid to soften them before taking a bite (which is where the vin santo comes in). Then there are American biscotti—the big, buttery, much softer kind sold in coffeehouse chains, which are more like sugar cookies masquerading as biscotti. Both styles have their supporters, but for my own recipe, I wanted a hybrid of the two: a cookie with big flavor and even bigger crunch but not one so hard that it would jeopardize my dental work—a cookie that would taste as good on its own as it did dipped in coffee.

A review of a handful of recipes suggested—and a subsequent biscotti bake-off confirmed—that the cookies' crunch or lack thereof corresponded with the amount of butter in the dough. Not surprisingly, batches made with little (or even no) fat were rock-hard, while doughs enriched with a full stick of butter baked up much softer, thanks to the fat's tenderizing effect. With that in mind, I began experimenting with a basic creating formula—beat together the butter and sugar; alternately fold in the dry ingredients (flour, baking powder, coarsely chopped almonds, salt, and spices) with the wet (eggs and vanilla or almond extract)—while varying the amount of butter in each batch.

Half a stick turned out to be the ideal compromise: Any less and the dough was too lean; any more and the cookies were too soft. The only problem was that a mere 4 tablespoons of butter (plus 1 cup of sugar) didn't give the stand mixer enough to work with. Instead of beating air into the butter to lighten it, all the mixer could do was soften the fat, and the resulting biscotti were dense and squat. My other idea for giving the dough some lift was to up the baking powder, but this was effective only to a point; any more than 2 teaspoons and the biscotti baked up crumbly. (Baking powder is more effective at expanding existing air bubbles than it is at creating its own.)

It was time to brainstorm: What other ingredients could be aerated in the stand mixer? I scanned my list and landed on a solution so obvious I was surprised I hadn't thought of it sooner: eggs. My recipe already included two eggs; I simply needed to add them earlier. Reversing the order of operations, I whipped the eggs until they were light in color, then added the sugar and continued to beat the mixture. Finally, I folded in the butter (melted and cooled), followed by the dry ingredients. When it came time to shape the dough, I portioned it into two relatively short, wide logs; that way, the cut cookies would span 4 inches from end to end—perfect for repeat dunking. To give the finished cookies a nice sheen, I brushed the logs with a beaten egg white. Then I baked the logs for about a half-hour, sliced them on the bias into ½-inch-thick cookies, and returned the cookies to the oven for round two.

The good news was that my unorthodox mixing technique was a major breakthrough; the whipped eggs gave the dough the lightness and lift it had been lacking. But despite their lighter, more open crumb, the biscotti were still jawbreakers. Also, I'd added a judicious amount of almond extract to bring out the nuts' flavor, but its distinct taste was surprisingly faint.

I'd already maxed out the amount of fat I could add to the dough, but could other factors be responsible for the overly hard cookies? That's when the bread baker in me began to wonder if the dough had developed too much gluten (the network of proteins that gives baked goods their structure). In the moist environment of a bread dough, lots of gluten produces chewiness as the gluten strands resist being pulled apart; in a dry cookie, the result is hardness, as the gluten resists breaking.

My first thought was to try using lower-protein cake flour in place of the all-purpose, since its reduced gluten content would result in weaker gluten structure. The swap did make the biscotti easier to eat but not in a good way: The cake flour made the biscotti less hard, but it also made them more fragile. Even combining all-purpose and cake flours was a bust.

It seemed that less gluten was not the answer. What I really needed was a way to modify the texture of the biscotti so that the gluten it contained had less impact on the overall hardness of the cookie, while still providing the crumb itself with plenty of structure.

That's when I remembered that one of the early recipes I tried had called for finely ground (rather than coarsely chopped) almonds. The flavor of the nuts had gotten lost in the biscotti, but they'd also made the cookies much more crumbly—and a little bit of crumbliness might be just what these cookies needed. I swapped out ½ cup of flour for an equal amount of almonds that I had ground to a fine powder in the food processor. Since I was now using the processor to grind the nuts, I also used it to whip the eggs, and it worked just as well as the stand mixer. One bite and I knew I was onto something. These biscotti were still plenty hard, but the almond meal made them far easier to bite into. In fact, they were breaking apart too easily, so I tried again, scaling back the almond meal to ¼ cup. This time I hit the nail on the head. The cookies' texture was perfect: crunchy but easy to bite.

What was it about the nut meal that produced a more breakable cookie? According to our science editor, the ground nuts broke up the gluten structure so that there were smaller pockets of gluten networks rather than one large one. As a result, the cookies gave way more easily when bitten, but the crumb itself didn't lose its hard crunch. And to appease those who missed the bursts of nuttiness from whole pieces, I added back 1 cup of coarsely chopped almonds when it came time to fold in the dry ingredients.

All that remained was to beef up the weak almond flavor. The curious thing was that the almond extract aroma was strong during the first baking but had all but vanished by the time the cookies had baked twice.

A little research explained that benzaldehyde, the main compound responsible for the flavor and aroma of almonds, is highly volatile and had evaporated during the cookies' long exposure to heat. To compensate, I would need to start with a higher dose. I experimented until I found that 1½ teaspoons—triple the amount that I had started with—did the trick. Similarly, when I developed my anise, hazelnut-orange, hazelnut-lavender, and pistachio-spice variations, I found that I had to load up on other ingredients with volatile compounds like aromatic herbs, spices, and citrus zest.

At last, I had a biscotti recipe I could be proud of: Boldly flavored and crunchy, these biscotti were hard but not hard to eat, given the line of tasters asking for more.

—ANDREW JANJIGIAN, *Cook's Illustrated*

Almond Biscotti

MAKES 30 COOKIES

The almonds will continue to toast while the biscotti bake, so toast the nuts only until they are just fragrant.

1¼ cups (6¼ ounces) whole almonds,
      lightly toasted
1¾ cups (8¾ ounces) all-purpose flour
  2 teaspoons baking powder
  ¼ teaspoon salt
  2 large eggs, plus 1 large white beaten
      with pinch salt
  1 cup (7 ounces) sugar
  4 tablespoons unsalted butter, melted
      and cooled
1½ teaspoons almond extract
  ½ teaspoon vanilla extract
      Vegetable oil spray

1. Adjust oven rack to middle position and heat oven to 325 degrees. Using ruler and pencil, draw two 8 by 3-inch rectangles, spaced 4 inches apart, on piece of parchment paper. Grease baking sheet and place parchment on it, penciled side down.

2. Pulse 1 cup almonds in food processor until coarsely chopped, 8 to 10 pulses; transfer to bowl and set aside. Process remaining ¼ cup almonds in food processor until finely ground, about 45 seconds. Add flour, baking powder, and salt; process to combine, about 15 seconds.

Transfer flour mixture to second bowl. Process 2 eggs in now-empty food processor until lightened in color and almost doubled in volume, about 3 minutes. With processor running, slowly add sugar until thoroughly combined, about 15 seconds. Add melted butter, almond extract, and vanilla and process until combined, about 10 seconds. Transfer egg mixture to medium bowl. Sprinkle half of flour mixture over egg mixture and, using spatula, gently fold until just combined. Add remaining flour mixture and chopped almonds and gently fold until just combined.

3. Divide batter in half. Using floured hands, form each half into 8 by 3-inch rectangle, using lines on parchment as guide. Spray each loaf lightly with oil spray. Using rubber spatula lightly coated with oil spray, smooth tops and sides of rectangles. Gently brush tops of loaves with egg white wash. Bake until loaves are golden and just beginning to crack on top, 25 to 30 minutes, rotating pan halfway through baking.

4. Let loaves cool on baking sheet for 30 minutes. Transfer loaves to cutting board. Using serrated knife, slice each loaf on slight bias into ½-inch-thick slices. Lay slices, cut side down, about ¼ inch apart on wire rack set in rimmed baking sheet. Bake until crisp and golden brown on both sides, about 35 minutes, flipping slices halfway through baking. Let cool completely before serving. Biscotti can be stored in airtight container for up to 1 month.

VARIATIONS

Anise Biscotti
Add 1½ teaspoons anise seeds to flour mixture in step 2. Substitute anise-flavored liqueur for almond extract.

Hazelnut-Orange Biscotti
Substitute lightly toasted and skinned hazelnuts for almonds. Add 2 tablespoons minced fresh rosemary to flour mixture in step 2. Substitute orange-flavored liqueur for almond extract and add 1 tablespoon grated orange zest to egg mixture with butter.

Hazelnut-Lavender Biscotti
Substitute lightly toasted and skinned hazelnuts for almonds. Add 2 teaspoons dried lavender flowers to flour mixture in step 2. Substitute 1½ teaspoons water for almond extract and add 2 tablespoons grated lemon zest to egg mixture with butter.

WHY NUTS TAKE SOME BITE OUT OF BISCOTTI

We wanted our biscotti to pack just as much crunch as the traditional Italian kind but also to break apart easily when you take a bite. Adding extra butter to the dough helped, but our ultimate solution was cutting the flour with finely ground nuts. While butter merely made the cookie more tender, ground nuts actually weakened its structure.

Both ingredients influence the texture because of their effect on gluten, the web of flour proteins that gives baked goods structure. The fat in butter "shortens" the gluten strands by surrounding individual strands and preventing them from linking up into larger networks. Ground nuts interfere with gluten formation in a slightly different way, getting in between pockets of gluten to create microscopic "fault lines" in the biscotti, which allow the hard cookie to break apart easily.

PROPERLY MELTED CHOCOLATE FOR DIPPING

Dipping biscotti in chocolate adds a new spin to the confection. But to avoid a coating that turns streaky or matte instead of staying glossy, it's important to melt the chocolate properly. That's because when melted chocolate resolidifies, the fat can recrystallize into any one of six different forms, only one of which (called the beta crystal) hardens up shiny. The key to preserving the shiny beta crystal is keeping the temperature of the chocolate below 94 degrees. Here's how:

Melt 8 ounces bittersweet chocolate in bowl set over pan of almost-simmering water, stirring once or twice, until barely melted (about 89 degrees). Remove from heat. Stir additional 2 ounces finely chopped bittersweet chocolate into melted chocolate until smooth. Dip cookies into chocolate to coat one side, scrape off excess with finger, and place cookies chocolate side up on parchment paper–lined baking sheet. Refrigerate until set.

Pistachio-Spice Biscotti

Substitute shelled pistachios for almonds. Add 1 teaspoon ground cardamom, ½ teaspoon ground cloves, ½ teaspoon pepper, ¼ teaspoon ground cinnamon, and ¼ teaspoon ground ginger to flour mixture in step 2. Substitute 1 teaspoon water for almond extract and increase vanilla extract to 1 teaspoon.

SUMMER BLUEBERRY BUNDT CAKE

✔ WHY THIS RECIPE WORKS For an elegant Bundt cake boasting lots of sweet, juicy blueberries, we needed to find a way to maximize the flavor of widely available cultivated berries. The large berries refused to stay suspended in the batter and burst into bland, soggy pockets in the oven. Our solution was to puree the fruit so that it could be easily swirled into the batter. To thicken the puree enough that it formed a distinct layer in the cake, we bumped up its natural pectin content with low-sugar pectin. Then we enhanced its flavor with sugar and lemon for a fresh-tasting filling that was beautifully marbled throughout the delicate, tender yellow cake.

Somewhere along the line, blueberries got a reputation for being a casual fruit, best for tossing into pancakes or folding into hearty snack cakes. But my grandmother, a lifetime Mainer and baker, was never one to so pigeonhole them. She'd whip up a batch of rustic blueberry scones at the drop of a hat, but she'd just as often reserve her handpicked berries for grander desserts. My favorite? A delicate yellow Bundt cake speckled with intensely flavored wild Maine blueberries.

I no longer have easy access to fresh, wild Maine blueberries, but that does little to suppress my craving for that cake. I decided that it was time to take on the challenge of baking just such a cake—one that was truly packed with fresh blueberry flavor. I'd use widely available (and more affordable) cultivated blueberries and our years of baking experience to re-create this memorable dessert.

While my intentions were good, my early tests were total failures. In every one of the recipes I tried, the large cultivated blueberries drifted defiantly to the bottom of the pan rather than remaining evenly dispersed through the cake like their compact wild forebears. The few berries that did manage to stay in place burst into big, soggy pockets when subjected to the heat of the oven. To make matters worse, tasters found that these watery cultivated blueberries tasted incredibly bland.

Undeterred by these early setbacks, I regrouped. I restarted my testing using one of the test kitchen's tried-and-true Bundt cake recipes (which uses a base of creamed butter and sugar for a light texture) and focused my efforts on wrangling the berries.

MARBLED BLUEBERRY BUNDT CAKE

Hoping to address both flavor and texture issues in one fell swoop, I tried tossing the blueberries with various combinations of flour, cornstarch, and cornmeal, along with some sugar and lemon zest. My hope was that the dry starches would not only absorb and trap the liquid as the berries burst but also provide some added texture to their smooth exteriors, creating enough drag to help the fruit stay put in the cake. No dice on either front. Most of the dry mixture simply sloughed off the berries as I incorporated them into the batter, leaving gummy streaks throughout. And the fruit still plummeted to the bottom of the pan like little stones.

Next I tried macerating 10 ounces of berries in sugar in a colander set over a bowl, hoping to draw out excess liquid before they reached the cake. But after a full hour, the fruit hadn't exuded even a drop of juice. It turns out that in addition to their generous size, commercial blueberry breeds are selected for the durability of their skins—a boon for transport but a barrier against the hygroscopic pull of sugar. I attempted a second batch for which I first lightly squished the blueberries with a potato masher, but alas, the juice yield barely budged. But this got me thinking: If the berries insisted on bursting inside the cake, why not beat them to the punch and burst them myself before adding them to the batter?

Of course, adding plain crushed berries directly to the batter would be neither tasty nor attractive. But I could puree them and then swirl the thick mix through the batter to produce an elegant marbled cake. Pureeing was simple enough with a quick spin in the blender. And, with the switch to pureed blueberries, I was able to bump up the flavor by adding sugar, lemon juice and zest, and a pinch of salt directly to the fruit. This mixture tasted bright and balanced. But the puree was too thin and liquid to swirl into the cake batter on its own. I had to find a way to thicken it up.

My first thought was the simplest: Just fold a bit of the cake batter into the puree. This would add heft to the puree—no additional ingredients needed. But this method delivered a soggy, purple-blue cake that tasted only weakly of blueberries. I tried cooking down the raw puree to thicken it, but tasters lamented the loss of fresh berry flavor. So I rounded up the usual thickening suspects: flour, cornstarch, and tapioca. I tried cooking a small portion of the puree with various amounts of all three, then stirring that into the remaining raw puree to retain fresh flavor. Unfortunately, in order to produce a mixture that was thick enough to be successfully swirled into the batter without becoming a leaky blue mess, I needed to use a significant amount of each starch. The fallout? Dulled flavor, an artificial texture, or, most often, both. I was at a loss.

Then, after processing another batch of puree, I left my station to brainstorm with a few fellow test cooks. With a healthy dose of suggestions and encouragement I returned to my blueberries. To my astonishment, the puree had slightly gelled and thickened—on its own. The reason? With some research, I learned that blueberries contain a small amount of natural pectin (it's stored in their cell walls, particularly in their skins), which had been released in the blender. My next move was clear: Boost the naturally present pectin with additional store-bought pectin.

Since my filling was quite tart, I opted for pectin for low-sugar recipes. I tried dissolving varying amounts of pectin—along with sugar, lemon zest, and salt—in just ¼ cup of the puree on the stovetop. While it was still warm, I stirred this sticky mixture into the remaining blueberry puree and let it sit until slightly cooled. Just as I'd hoped, the extra pectin (3 tablespoons proved ideal) gelled my blueberry mixture just enough. I could now fold and swirl it into the cake batter, where it maintained a distinct identity and baked into a satisfying texture. And this swirl tasted like fresh fruit—something that couldn't be said for my starch-thickened trials. Finally satisfied with this filling, I focused on putting it all together.

The reengineered filling was so good at staying in place that I couldn't simply swirl it into the top of the cake and let it flow into the rest of the batter during baking—it would remain stuck in place. Instead, I added it in two phases. After spraying my 12-cup nonstick Bundt pan with baking spray, I spooned in half of the batter and formed a shallow channel in the middle of it. I then added half of the filling to this depression and thoroughly swirled and folded it in with a butter knife, ensuring that no large pockets of filling remained. I repeated these steps for the second layer before baking my cake at 325 degrees for about an hour. The cake emerged from the oven lightly bronzed and smooth, with spotty hints of the lacy marbling that lay beneath. Tasters tucked into this cake and were pleased with its hits of blueberry in every bite. I think my grandmother would have been proud.

—DAN SOUZA, *Cook's Illustrated*

LET IT SWIRL

Properly swirling the thickened blueberry puree is key to producing an elegantly marbled cake.

1. After spooning half of batter into Bundt pan, make channel with back of spoon.

2. Using spoon, fill channel with half of blueberry filling in even layer.

3. Using butter knife, swirl filling through batter. Repeat these steps with remaining batter and filling.

OVERCOMING BLUEBERRY BUMMERS

Cultivated blueberries can be problematic in baking, often blowing out and clumping at the bottom of the pan. Plus, these watery berries taste disappointingly bland. Our solution? Puree the berries with sugar, salt, and lemon zest to improve flavor, then thicken the mixture with pectin and swirl it evenly through the batter.

CLUMPY BLOWOUTS

EVEN SUSPENSION

Marbled Blueberry Bundt Cake

SERVES 12

Spray the pan well in step 1 to prevent sticking. If you don't have nonstick baking spray with flour, mix 1 tablespoon of melted butter and 1 tablespoon of flour into a paste and brush it inside the pan. If using frozen berries, thaw them before blending in step 3. This cake can be served plain or with Cinnamon Whipped Cream or Lemon Glaze (recipes follow).

CAKE

- 3 cups (15 ounces) all-purpose flour
- 1½ teaspoons baking powder
- ¾ teaspoon baking soda
- 1 teaspoon salt
- ½ teaspoon ground cinnamon
- ¾ cup buttermilk
- 2 teaspoons grated lemon zest plus 3 tablespoons juice
- 2 teaspoons vanilla extract
- 3 large eggs plus 1 large yolk, room temperature
- 18 tablespoons (2¼ sticks) unsalted butter, softened
- 2 cups (14 ounces) sugar

FILLING

- ¾ cup (5¼ ounces) sugar
- 3 tablespoons low-sugar or no-sugar-needed fruit pectin
  Pinch salt
- 10 ounces (2 cups) fresh or thawed frozen blueberries
- 1 teaspoon grated lemon zest plus 1 tablespoon juice

1. FOR THE CAKE: Adjust oven rack to lower-middle position and heat oven to 325 degrees. Heavily spray 12-cup nonstick Bundt pan with baking spray with flour. Whisk flour, baking powder, baking soda, salt, and cinnamon together in large bowl. Whisk buttermilk, lemon zest and juice, and vanilla together in medium bowl. Gently whisk eggs and yolk to combine in third bowl.

2. Using stand mixer fitted with paddle, beat butter and sugar on medium-high speed until pale and fluffy, about 3 minutes, scraping down bowl as needed. Reduce speed to medium and beat in half of eggs until incorporated, about 15 seconds. Repeat with remaining eggs, scraping down bowl after incorporating. Reduce speed to low and add one-third of flour mixture, followed by half of buttermilk mixture, mixing until just incorporated after each addition, about 5 seconds.

Repeat, using half of remaining flour mixture and all of remaining buttermilk mixture. Scrape down bowl, add remaining flour mixture, and mix at medium-low speed until batter is thoroughly combined, about 15 seconds. Remove bowl from mixer and fold batter once or twice with rubber spatula to incorporate any remaining flour. Cover bowl with plastic wrap and set aside while preparing filling (batter will inflate a bit).

3. FOR THE FILLING: Whisk sugar, pectin, and salt together in small saucepan. Process blueberries in blender until mostly smooth, about 1 minute. Transfer ¼ cup puree and lemon zest to saucepan with sugar mixture and stir to thoroughly combine. Heat sugar-blueberry mixture over medium heat until just simmering, about 3 minutes, stirring frequently to dissolve sugar and pectin. Transfer mixture to medium bowl and let cool for 5 minutes. Add remaining puree and lemon juice to cooled mixture and whisk to combine. Let sit until slightly set, about 8 minutes.

4. Spoon half of batter into prepared pan and smooth top. Using back of spoon, create ½-inch-deep channel in center of batter. Spoon half of filling into channel. Using butter knife or small offset spatula, thoroughly swirl filling into batter (there should be no large pockets of filling remaining). Repeat swirling step with remaining batter and filling.

5. Bake until top is golden brown and skewer inserted in center comes out with no crumbs attached, 60 to 70 minutes. Let cake cool in pan on wire rack for 10 minutes, then invert cake directly onto wire rack. Let cake cool for at least 3 hours before serving.

Cinnamon Whipped Cream
MAKES ABOUT 2 CUPS

For the best texture, whip the cream until soft peaks just form. Do not overwhip.

- 1 cup heavy cream
- 2 tablespoons confectioners' sugar
- ¼ teaspoon ground cinnamon
- Pinch salt

Using stand mixer fitted with whisk, whip all ingredients on medium-low speed until foamy, about 1 minute. Increase speed to high and whip until soft peaks form, 1 to 3 minutes.

Lemon Glaze
MAKES ABOUT 2 CUPS

- 3–4 tablespoons lemon juice (2 lemons)
- 2 cups (8 ounces) confectioners' sugar

1. While cake is baking, whisk together 3 tablespoons lemon juice and sugar until smooth, gradually adding more lemon juice as needed until glaze is thick but still pourable (mixture should leave faint trail across bottom of mixing bowl when drizzled from whisk).

2. After cake has been removed from pan and inverted onto wire rack set in baking sheet, pour half of glaze over warm cake and let cool for 1 hour. Pour remaining glaze evenly over cake and continue to let cool to room temperature, at least 2 hours.

FRENCH APPLE CAKE

✓ WHY THIS RECIPE WORKS For our own version of this classic French dessert, we wanted the best of both worlds: a dessert with a custardy, apple-rich base beneath a light, cakelike topping. To ensure that the apple slices softened fully but didn't fall apart in the cake, we microwaved them briefly—once baked, they were tender, yet retained their structure. And to create two differently textured layers from one easy batter, we divided the batter and added egg yolks to one part to make the custardy base and a few tablespoons of flour to the rest to form the cakey top layer.

"How the heck did they make this?" is what I was asking myself as I sat in a Parisian bistro marveling over a slice of apple cake. I'd tasted plenty of apple cakes before, but none that came anywhere close to this. The custardy base that surrounded the apples was rich, creamy, and dense but not in the least bit heavy. The butter-soft apple slices, simultaneously tart and sweet, were perfectly intact despite their tender texture. And above the rich custard sat a double layer of real cake—light and airy on the inside, with a beautifully golden-brown, crisp top. Together, the contrasting layers made for one amazing dessert.

I appealed to the restaurant owner for a recipe, or at least an explanation of how the cake had been prepared, but she declined. So I returned home with nothing more than a memory—and a desire to sort out the secrets of that cake.

The apple cake recipes I unearthed in my research yielded some useful clues. They all followed a simple approach: Stir eggs, milk, vanilla, and melted butter or oil together; whisk in flour, sugar, salt, and leavening until smooth; add cut-up apples; pour the batter into a springform pan; and bake until the fruit has softened and the cake has set. But the results varied widely: Some produced a crumb that was dry, airy, and cakelike, while others were moist and puddinglike. The consistency of the apples varied as well: Some held on to their shape tenaciously, even to a leathery fault, while others practically dissolved into the cake, leaving it a sodden mess. None of the cakes were particularly attractive when sliced; either they were so soft that the slices sagged, or the apples were too hard and dragged beneath the knife, leaving a ragged edge. But most important, not one of these cakes displayed the stratified layers that my Parisian cake did. To get that, I assumed that I'd have to create two separate batters. But for the time being, it made the most sense to focus on one layer at a time.

I started with the bottom layer, which meant starting with the apples. When I went back and remade the most promising of the cakes I had tested, a problem became immediately apparent. This particular cake got much of its flavor from using a variety of apples, and they cooked quite differently. Some were so soft as to be mushy, and others were dry and leathery. In addition, the different varieties released moisture into the surrounding cake to varying degrees, creating sodden patches here and there. So my first order of business would be to get the apples to cook more consistently.

The simplest way to do that, of course, would be to limit myself to just one type of apple. Since I wanted the apples to hold their shape entirely, I opted for Granny Smiths; among the firmer apples, their tartness stood out most clearly against the sweet, dense background of the cake. To add back some of the complexity lost by using just one kind of apple, I tossed the apples with a tablespoon of Calvados, a French apple brandy, along with a teaspoon of lemon juice, and I substituted neutral-flavored vegetable oil for the butter used in the original batter, since the butter flavor tended to obscure that of the apples.

As for texture, the Granny Smiths held their shape nicely after baking, but they were inclined to be leathery, which made the cake difficult to slice cleanly. I tried macerating the slices in sugar to soften them, but that only made them drier and therefore tougher when baked. In the end, precooking them in the microwave for a few minutes—just to the point where they were pliable—was all the head start they needed. In the finished cake, the apples were tender and easily sliced but still retained their structure.

I could now focus on the texture of the custardy cake layer itself. Even with apples that released less water, the cake remained somewhat soupy at the center. I assumed that the batter itself contained too much liquid, so I tried reducing the amount of milk or increasing the amount of flour it contained, but both adjustments only served to make the cake pasty and grainy. Adding another egg did firm it up a bit, but it also left it a bit tough because of the extra white. I tried adding just another egg yolk. This was a step in the right direction, as it gave the cake more cohesiveness while enhancing its custardlike qualities. Adding a third yolk improved things even further.

But my cake was still wet at the center. After some thought, I wondered whether the problem was not too much moisture in the batter but rather that it wasn't cooking long and low enough. This cake wasn't merely custardlike; it was essentially a real custard, especially with two extra egg yolks in the mix. I'd been cooking it at 375 degrees, but maybe it could stand to be cooked more gently, allowing the eggs to set up before so much moisture was wrung from the apples. So for my next test, I lowered the temperature to 325 degrees and dropped the cake one rack lower in the oven, so that it would cook from the bottom up and brown more slowly on top. After nearly an hour, a toothpick inserted into the center of the cake came out clean, and after it cooled, the cake had the perfect texture: The apples were tender and moist, fully embedded in a custardy matrix that was silky and smooth from center to edge.

Now that I had a perfect custardy base layer, I could focus on creating a cakelike topping for it. I wasn't that happy about having to make two separate batters, but I saw no other option if I wanted distinct layers. Rather than start from scratch completely, though, I returned to my tasting notes from those first trial recipes to find one with a batter that had a more cakelike consistency.

But when I looked more closely at the batter recipes, I noticed something interesting: Minor variations aside, they really differed only in the ratios among a few key ingredients. The drier, more cakelike ones contained more flour and fewer eggs, while the more custardy ones had a far higher ratio of eggs to flour. Was it possible that I didn't need two separate batters after all? Maybe I just needed to get my one batter to behave differently, depending on where it was in the cake.

To test this theory, I began by simply doubling the overall amount of batter and dividing it into two portions. I added the apples to one half, poured this mixture into the pan and then poured the remaining batter over it, and baked the cake as before. The results were promising: Though the batter was identical in both layers, the top half—since it lacked moisture-contributing apples—was already much more open and cakelike. It wasn't perfect yet, though. It was a bit too moist and dense, and it didn't form much of a crisp crust on its top surface.

But what if I simply increased the flour and lost the extra egg yolks in the top batter? The simplest way to do that, I figured, would be to make the batter in two stages: First, combine all of the ingredients except for the extra egg yolks. Then divide the batter in two and add the yolks to one half and a few tablespoons of flour to the other half.

This time around, the cake was near perfection: creamy and custardy below and airy above. True, it wasn't quite crisp enough on top, but sprinkling it with granulated sugar just before it went into the oven solved that, giving my cake a crisp top layer. Finally I had equaled that Paris cake of my memory. But here's the best part: When I served the cake to a baker friend one night, do you know what he said? "How the heck did you do that?"

—ANDREW JANJIGIAN, *Cook's Illustrated*

French Apple Cake
SERVES 8 TO 10

The microwaved apples should be pliable but not completely soft when cooked. To test for doneness, take one apple slice and try to bend it. If it snaps in half, it's too firm; microwave it for an additional 30 seconds and test again. If Calvados is unavailable, 1 tablespoon of apple brandy or white rum can be substituted.

- 1½ **pounds Granny Smith apples, peeled, cored, cut into 8 wedges, and sliced ⅛ inch thick crosswise**
- 1 **tablespoon Calvados**
- 1 **teaspoon lemon juice**
- 1 **cup (5 ounces) plus 2 tablespoons all-purpose flour**
- 1 **cup (7 ounces) plus 1 tablespoon granulated sugar**
- 2 **teaspoons baking powder**
- ½ **teaspoon salt**
- 1 **large egg plus 2 large yolks**
- 1 **cup vegetable oil**
- 1 **cup whole milk**
- 1 **teaspoon vanilla extract**
  Confectioners' sugar

1. Adjust oven rack to lower-middle position and heat oven to 325 degrees. Spray 9-inch springform pan with vegetable oil spray. Place prepared pan in rimmed baking sheet lined with aluminum foil. Place apple slices in microwave-safe pie plate, cover, and microwave until apples are pliable and slightly translucent, about 3 minutes. Toss apple slices with Calvados and lemon juice and let cool for 15 minutes.

NOTES FROM THE TEST KITCHEN

ENSURING TENDER APPLES

Why do apples that go straight into the cake batter bake up too firm, while those same raw apples come out soft and tender if microwaved a bit before heading into the oven? Common sense might suggest that precooking simply hastens the fruit's breakdown. But there's more to the answer than that. As so often happens in cooking, an enzyme is involved, in this case a temperature-sensitive enzyme called pectin methylesterase (PME). As the batter's temperature climbs and lingers between 120 and 160 degrees, the PME sets the pectin in the fruit, so the slices will remain relatively firm no matter how long they are cooked. The catch, though, is that the PME is deactivated at temperatures above 160 degrees. Enter the microwave. A 3-minute zap quickly brings the apples to 180 degrees—high enough to permanently kill any activity of the PME—so the precooked fruit emerges fully soft in the finished cake.

We even double-checked the science with a side test: heating vacuum-sealed batches of both raw and microwaved apples in a *sous vide* machine to the final temperature of the cake (208 degrees) for the same amount of time it bakes (1¼ hours). The microwaved apples were predictably tender, while the slices that we didn't microwave remained firm. Furthermore, these slices never fully softened, even after we continued to cook them for another 40 minutes.

NOT MICROWAVED
Tough, dry apples.

MICROWAVED
Tender yet firm apples.

PEACH MELBA CRISP

2. Whisk 1 cup flour, 1 cup granulated sugar, baking powder, and salt together in bowl. Whisk egg, oil, milk, and vanilla together in second bowl until smooth. Add dry ingredients to wet ingredients and whisk until just combined. Transfer 1 cup batter to separate bowl and set aside.

3. Add egg yolks to remaining batter and whisk to combine. Using spatula, gently fold in cooled apples. Transfer batter to prepared pan; using offset spatula, spread batter evenly to pan edges, gently pressing on apples to create even, compact layer, and smooth surface.

4. Whisk remaining 2 tablespoons flour into reserved batter. Pour over batter in pan, spread batter evenly to pan edges, and smooth surface. Sprinkle remaining 1 tablespoon granulated sugar evenly over cake.

5. Bake until center of cake is set, toothpick inserted in center comes out clean, and top is golden brown, about 1¼ hours. Transfer pan to wire rack; let cool for 5 minutes. Run paring knife around sides of pan and let cool completely, 2 to 3 hours. Dust lightly with confectioners' sugar and cut into wedges. Serve.

PEACH MELBA CRISP

✔ **WHY THIS RECIPE WORKS** For an easy fruit dessert we could enjoy year-round, we wanted to translate the classic flavors of peach Melba (peaches and raspberries) into a warm summer crisp. The juiciness of peaches varies dramatically based on their ripeness and whether they are fresh or frozen, so to ensure that our crisp would come out right every time, we macerated and drained the peaches to avoid runny filling and soggy topping. Then we added back a measured amount of the peach juice, thickened with a little ground tapioca, to create a fruity, flavorful filling. Sprinkling the delicate raspberries on top of the peaches instead of folding them in created a pretty layered effect and prevented them from being crushed. A simple topping of oats, flour, and nuts made a crisp and buttery crown for the sweet fruit filling.

Peach Melba is a classic combination of poached peaches and vanilla ice cream drizzled with raspberry sauce. I wanted to borrow this delicious combination for the quintessential easygoing summer dessert: a crisp.

I soon discovered that I'm not the first person to think of this, so I assembled a few recipes and baked them to assess the territory. While the flavor combo was predictably delicious, these crisps shared several problems: The peaches released so much juice that the fillings were soupy and the toppings soggy. And, just as bad, the raspberries disintegrated with baking.

I threw together a standard topping from butter, flour, oats, pecans, sugar (brown and white), and cinnamon (I later spiced it up with ginger), then set the topping aside as I combined the peach slices and raspberries with more sugar. A few of the recipes I had tried didn't use a thickener in the fruit at all (no wonder those were soupy), but most called for a few tablespoons of either flour or cornstarch. We preferred instant tapioca to either, as it produced a jammy filling with clean, bright fruit flavor. To boost the flavor further, I stirred in vanilla extract and lemon juice. To keep the final dish from being gritty, I ground the tapioca to a fine powder.

As I was working through these thickener tests, I noticed that no matter how carefully I folded the berries in with the peaches, they fell apart in the oven. To avoid smashing them, I scattered the berries on the bottom of the baking dish and gently placed the sweetened peaches and the topping over them. While more berries survived this test than before, it still wasn't a rousing success. But if I put the peaches on the bottom and the raspberries in the middle, the delicate berries were jostled less, protected from the direct heat of the baking dish, and remained intact.

Thinking my work was about done, I made another crisp for good measure. I peeled, sliced, topped, and baked, and a half-hour later I stared at . . . a soupy mess. Had I forgotten the tapioca? I didn't think so. Aggravated, I baked another crisp. The results were just as bad. I rummaged through my folder and studied my recipe, trying to figure out what had gone wrong. Suddenly, it dawned on me: During the week of testing, the firm, slightly underripe peaches I'd started with had softened and become deliciously juicy: perfect for eating, problematic for cooking. I'd need to standardize them so no matter how variable, the recipe would always work.

Clearly, I'd need to get rid of some juice before the crisp ever went into the oven. Macerating fruit draws off liquid, so I combined the peaches with sugar and salt (to season them slightly), let them sit for 30 minutes, and drained them. Then I made the recipe as before, this time with my drained peaches and 2 tablespoons of their juice (during tests the peaches released as much as ½ cup or as little as 2 tablespoons of juice). I also raised the oven temperature from 350 to 400 for extra browning and crispness.

Finally, we had it: The fruit was fresh and bright, the peaches tender but not mushy, the topping crisp, and the balance of sweet, tart, and buttery richness exactly right. In a nod to the classic dessert, we devoured the warm crisp with scoops of vanilla ice cream.

—REBECCAH MARSTERS, *Cook's Country*

Peach Melba Crisp

SERVES 6

Do not use quick or instant oats in this recipe. Measure the tapioca, which may be sold as "Minute Tapioca," before grinding it.

FILLING

- **2** tablespoons instant tapioca
- **2½** pounds fresh peaches, peeled, halved, pitted, and cut into ½-inch wedges, or 1¾ pounds frozen sliced peaches, thawed
- **¼** cup (1¾ ounces) granulated sugar
- **⅛** teaspoon salt
- **1** tablespoon lemon juice
- **1** teaspoon vanilla extract
- **10** ounces (2 cups) raspberries

TOPPING

- **½** cup (2½ ounces) all-purpose flour
- **¼** cup packed (1¾ ounces) brown sugar
- **¼** cup (1¾ ounces) granulated sugar
- **¼** teaspoon ground cinnamon
- **¼** teaspoon ground ginger
- **¼** teaspoon salt
- **6** tablespoons unsalted butter, cut into ½-inch pieces and chilled
- **½** cup (1½ ounces) old-fashioned rolled oats
- **½** cup pecans, chopped

1. FOR THE FILLING: Grind tapioca in spice grinder to fine powder, about 30 seconds. Gently toss peaches with sugar and salt in bowl and let sit, stirring occasionally, for 30 minutes. Drain peaches through colander set inside bowl; reserve peach juice. Return drained peaches to original bowl and toss with 2 tablespoons reserved peach juice, ground tapioca, lemon juice, and vanilla.

Transfer to 8-inch square baking dish and press gently into even layer. Top peaches with raspberries.

2. FOR THE TOPPING: While peaches are macerating, combine flour, brown sugar, granulated sugar, cinnamon, ginger, and salt in food processor and process until combined, about 15 seconds. Add butter and pulse until mixture resembles wet sand, about 8 pulses. Add oats and pecans and pulse until mixture forms marble-size clumps and no loose flour remains, about 15 pulses. Chill mixture for at least 15 minutes. Adjust oven rack to upper-middle position and heat oven to 400 degrees.

3. Distribute topping evenly over fruit. Bake until topping is well browned and fruit is bubbling around edges, about 30 minutes, rotating dish halfway through baking. Cool on wire rack for at least 30 minutes. Serve.

MARLBOROUGH APPLE PIE

WHY THIS RECIPE WORKS This early American pie combines the classic flavors and flaky, buttery crust of traditional apple pie with a rich, silky custard. Combining both sweet and tart apples gave us just the right balance of flavor. Grating the apples allowed them to meld nicely with the custard, but they leached moisture, turning the filling grainy. A quick sauté in melted butter evaporated the apples' excess moisture and concentrated the flavors. We flavored the sweet, rich custard with lemon zest, vanilla, cinnamon, mace, and a good dose of sherry. A gentle 325-degree oven kept the custard from curdling, and parbaking the crust ensured that it stayed flaky and crisp.

Today, apple pie inevitably means sweetened, sliced apples flavored with cinnamon in a double-crust pie. But before the Civil War, the dessert had a lot more latitude: The apples might be precooked and combined with eggs, cream, or rosewater. The pie might not have a bottom crust, or the top "crust" could be meringue. Forget baking—early apple pies were sometimes steamed. And they weren't always called pies: Old cookbooks used "pudding" and "pie" interchangeably. One almost-forgotten version is Marlborough apple pie, a single-crust pie filled with grated or sliced and stewed apples in a spiced, sherry-flavored custard. This sounded much too good to leave to the history books.

The recipe first appeared in the United States in 1796 in Amelia Simmons's *American Cookery*. It shared the table with mincemeat pie and plum pudding at many 18th- and 19th-century New England holiday dinners. The apples were grated or stewed so housewives from a more frugal time could disguise aging, bruised apples. By the 20th century, the pie had mostly vanished. I dug up five recipes and got out a rolling pin and a box grater.

Several hours later, we tasted these Marlborough apple pies. We preferred grated apples, but however the apples were handled, the crusts were soggy, the custards were broken and runny, and the lemon came on too strong. Despite the problems, we spied sweet, apple-y, creamy potential.

The crust was an easy fix. None of these test pies had called for a prebaked crust. (Maybe the colonial housewife prebaked by instinct? The Simmons book merely says, "Lay in paste [an old word for pastry] in a deep dish . . .") But prebaking crusts for custard pies is a time-honored way to avoid soggy bottom crusts, so I followed a favorite test kitchen crust recipe and parbaked it empty. I let the shell cool, then filled and baked a pie. This time, the crust was flaky and delicious.

I turned to apple selection, working from a recipe that combined the best features from my initial test pies. Since few of us have root cellars where we sock away bruised apples, I'd use what I could find in the supermarket. After sampling many pies built from many different apples, we voted for tart Granny Smiths (for apple flavor that didn't fade) balanced by a sweeter type; Fuji, Gala, and Golden Delicious all worked well.

Older recipes use lemon juice with a free hand, and descriptions of Marlborough apple pie paint a picture of a tart, even bracing, dessert. But my pie was downright sour. I backed off, eventually baking a pie with lemon zest but no juice at all. This tasted right, but why? It hit me that when made with bruised (read: sweet) apples, Marlborough apple pie needed sourness for balance. But carefully stored supermarket apples got enough pucker from lemon zest alone. For the other flavors, we preferred sherry to wine and a pinch each of cinnamon and mace—a spice that's almost as rare on contemporary tables as this pie itself.

The continued curdled appearance of these pies indicated that the custard was overcooking. A gentler oven (I dropped the temperature 50 degrees) repaired the broken texture, but the filling remained wet instead of creamy. As the grated apples baked, their juice was watering down the custard. To prevent this, I sautéed the grated apples in melted butter on the stovetop. This step drew moisture from the apples and evaporated it, concentrating the apple flavor. After the apples cooled, I stirred them into the custard and poured this filling into the waiting prebaked crust.

Forty minutes later, this pie emerged from the oven with a tender, flaky crust and an apple-y, sweetly boozy, creamy custard. Marlborough apple pie definitely isn't your grandmother's apple pie—though it may be your great-great-grandmother's apple pie. No matter which generation is baking it, our recipe always turns out delicious.

—REBECCAH MARSTERS, *Cook's Country*

EASY APPLE PREP

Before we mix them with a custard, the apples are shredded and sautéed.

1. Shred apples on large holes of coarse grater, then move to skillet with warm melted butter.

2. Cook apples to evaporate their juice (preventing watery custard) and concentrate their flavor.

THE BEST ROLLING PIN

Nowadays, when choosing a rolling pin, choices abound. To see if innovation could trump the tried and true, we rounded up nine pins in wood, metal, and silicone, tapered and straight, with handles and without.

A good rolling pin should spread pie dough easily, without sticking or tearing. Handle-free French rolling pins gave us a better sense of the dough's thickness. Featherweight pins did almost none of the work for us. Some handled pins simply spun in place instead of rolling. Our go-to pin turned out to be the 19-inch, handle-free **J.K. Adams Plain Maple Rolling Dowel**, $13.95. At 1½ pounds, it was just weighty enough to lend us a hand but light enough to maneuver easily, with a slightly textured surface that prevented slipping and sticking. (See page 309 for more information on our testing results.)

THE BEST SHERRY

In the test kitchen, we use sherry in everything from apple pie to stir-fry sauces and French onion soup. We've found that sweet sherries are fine as an aperitif, but in cooking they overwhelm other flavors. Stick with dry sherry for savory cooking; medium-dry may work in desserts. We don't recommend sherry cooking wine, which is made with salt and preservatives. Most samples we tasted were fine in creamed onions, but in the pie, one stood out: **Lustau Palo Cortado Península Sherry**. Aged for 11 to 12 years, it was the oldest and the most expensive sherry in our lineup. But in this case you get what you pay for.

Marlborough Apple Pie

SERVES 8

Shred the apples on the large holes of a box grater. The pie can be stored in the refrigerator for up to 24 hours.

CRUST

- 1¼ cups (6¼ ounces) all-purpose flour
- 1 tablespoon sugar
- ½ teaspoon salt
- 4 tablespoons vegetable shortening, cut into ¼-inch pieces and chilled
- 6 tablespoons unsalted butter, cut into ¼-inch pieces and chilled
- 3–4 tablespoons ice water

FILLING

- 4 tablespoons unsalted butter
- 2 Granny Smith apples, peeled and shredded (2 cups)
- 2 Fuji, Gala, or Golden Delicious apples, peeled and shredded (2 cups)
- ½ cup (3½ ounces) sugar
- ¼ teaspoon ground cinnamon
- ¼ teaspoon ground mace
- ¼ teaspoon salt
- 3 large eggs, lightly beaten
- ½ cup heavy cream
- 5 tablespoons dry sherry
- 1 teaspoon grated lemon zest
- 1 teaspoon vanilla extract

1. FOR THE CRUST: Process flour, sugar, and salt in food processor until combined. Add chilled shortening and pulse until coarsely ground. Add chilled butter and pulse until mixture resembles coarse crumbs. Transfer to large bowl.

2. Sprinkle 3 tablespoons water over flour mixture. Using rubber spatula, stir mixture until dough forms. If dough remains crumbly, add remaining 1 tablespoon water. Form dough into 4-inch disk, wrap tightly in plastic wrap, and refrigerate for at least 1 hour or up to 2 days. (Dough can be frozen, wrapped tightly in plastic and aluminum foil, for up to 2 months. Thaw completely at room temperature before using.)

3. Let chilled dough soften slightly at room temperature, about 10 minutes. Working on lightly floured counter, roll dough into 12-inch circle. Transfer dough to pie plate. Trim, fold, and crimp edges.

4. Cover unbaked pie shell with plastic wrap and refrigerate for 40 minutes, then freeze for 20 minutes. Adjust oven rack to lower-middle position and heat oven to 375 degrees. Line chilled pie shell with two 12-inch squares of parchment paper, letting parchment lie over edges of dough. Top with pie weights and bake until surface of dough no longer looks wet, 20 to 25 minutes. Transfer pie shell to wire rack and carefully remove parchment and weights. Let cool to room temperature.

5. FOR THE FILLING: Adjust oven rack to lower-middle position and heat oven to 325 degrees. Melt butter in 12-inch skillet over medium heat. Add apples and cook, stirring frequently, until pan is dry and apples have softened, 12 to 14 minutes. Transfer apples to bowl and let cool to room temperature, about 20 minutes.

6. Whisk sugar, cinnamon, mace, and salt together in large bowl. Add eggs, cream, sherry, lemon zest, and vanilla and whisk until smooth. Add cooled apples and stir to combine.

7. Pour mixture into pie shell and bake until center is just set, about 40 minutes. Cool completely on wire rack, about 4 hours. Serve.

LEMON CHIFFON PIE

WHY THIS RECIPE WORKS With a silky, lemony filling and a crisp, buttery crumb crust, lemon chiffon pie is a surprisingly simple yet elegant dessert. A quick cooked lemon curd made with plenty of lemon juice and zest provided the perfect flavor base for the filling. For a double layer of lemon flavor, we spread a portion of the curd on the bottom of the pie, then whipped the rest into the chiffon layer for bright, citrusy flavor and a thick, rich texture. To ensure that the chiffon was perfectly creamy but still sliceable, we thickened it with a combination of cornstarch and gelatin and whipped in some cream cheese for structure and richness. A simple buttery graham cracker crust added a nice contrast to the light, lemony filling.

When it hit the dessert scene in the early 20th century, chiffon pie was a breakthrough idea. Not only was the filling particularly light and silky, but it came together in no time—with nothing more than egg yolks, sugar, fruit juice or puree, and a little cream cooked into a curd and folded with sweetened whipped egg whites.

Many versions didn't even require baking; instead, they were set with gelatin and chilled in the refrigerator. Even the crust was a snap to make: Around the same time that chiffon pies became popular, crumb crusts did, too. They were easier to make than pastry, and their crisp, delicate texture became a common base for the billowy curd. It's no wonder the concept made its way into dozens of American cookbooks and magazines over the years and spawned dozens of flavor variations—strawberry, pumpkin, and my favorite, lemon, among them.

The dessert's popularity has waned somewhat, but to me its combination of ease and elegance is as appealing as ever. And yet I've never managed to produce a version that I'd consider perfect. Some attempts have even been complete failures, either because the filling failed to set properly and gushed like soup when I attempted to remove a slice or, conversely, because it set up too much and turned out springy and chewy like a marshmallow. And the citrus flavor? With all those egg whites and the sugar, it was a little flat. In other words, this retro classic was due for a makeover. I moved ahead with my own ideal in mind: a filling that's creamy, rich, and set but not stiff—and that packs plenty of bright lemon punch.

A classically crisp, buttery graham cracker crust seemed just fine here, so I skipped straight to the filling and sized up a handful of different recipes. For the most part, the formulas were about the same, and all were quite simple: After cooking the lemon curd until it thickens, stir in a couple of teaspoons of unflavored gelatin (dissolved in a little water) and let the mixture cool. Then whip egg whites with sugar until they hold stiff peaks, gently but thoroughly combine the curd and whites, pour the pale yellow filling into a prebaked crumb crust, and chill until set. Given the uniformity of the methods, I wasn't surprised when most of the finished pies shared the same core flaw: a filling so bouncy that the most glaring example drew comparisons to marshmallow Peeps.

I knew that too much gelatin was responsible for the springiness, but I also knew that I couldn't do without at least a small amount of this particular thickener. The outlier recipe I'd tried, an approach from mid-20th-century pie baker Angie Earl, relied on cornstarch (¼ cup dissolved in ½ cup of water), not gelatin, to thicken the filling, and the results had been disastrously soupy. I tried upping the amount of cornstarch that I was adding to the lemon curd and couldn't deny that the sturdiness of the filling improved with every extra tablespoon. But the more cornstarch I added, the duller the lemon flavor became—not surprising, since starch granules are known to absorb flavor molecules.

I tried going back to gelatin and made several more pies with varying amounts but had no consistent luck. The problem, I discovered, was that gelatin is finicky. Even when I used the right amount, if I allowed the gelatin-thickened curd to firm up a bit too long, it wouldn't incorporate evenly and left streaks of curd in the chiffon. I even tried adding more eggs (both whole and just yolks) to the cornstarch curd, hoping that their proteins, fat, and emulsifiers would help the filling gel better. Including two egg whites helped a little; when heated, their proteins form a gel that traps water. But any more egg and the chiffon tasted more like an omelet than a dessert.

I'd exhausted my options when it came to trying each of the thickeners alone, but what about using them together in moderation? Assuming that I could nail the right ratio, the gelatin would supply the chiffon with just enough structure to make it sliceable, and the cornstarch would give it a bit more body. A few days' worth of tests and several pie breaks for my colleagues later, I almost had it: 1 tablespoon of cornstarch plus a mere teaspoon of gelatin—about half as much as most recipes call for—produced a filling that wasn't soupy. However, it still seemed too airy and flimsy. Not wanting to risk dulling the flavor with more cornstarch, I wondered if I could make the filling a little denser with something other than a thickener. That's when I thought of whipping: Most chiffon pie recipes call for gently folding the curd into the whipped whites to preserve the filling's cloudlike consistency. I wanted to pull back on that approach, so I switched to a much more aggressive incorporation method: whipping the two components together in a stand mixer. Just as I'd hoped, this vigorous approach produced a filling that was less foamy and a bit thicker and more dense.

Now that I'd straightened out the structural issues, I could work on brightening up the lemon flavor and ideally make the filling a bit richer, too.

Some of the most lemony pies I'd made early on got their citrus flavor not only from fresh-squeezed juice but also from zest and even lemon extract. Extract gave the filling an unappealing "cooked" lemon flavor, but grating some of the fruit's fragrant peel and adding it to the filling rounded out the acidity of the juice with a fresher, more complex perfume. And yet the big lemon kick that my tasters clamored for still hadn't fully come through. What the pie needed, they said, was another layer of lemon flavor.

Another layer—that wasn't a bad idea, actually. What if, instead of mixing all of the potent lemon curd with the whipped egg white mixture, I reserved a portion of it to line the pie shell? I took 1¼ cups of the curd base (a little more than half of the total), spread it in the bottom of the pie shell, and froze it briefly to help it set. It delivered precisely the extreme tanginess we'd been craving, not to mention an eye-catching pop of color. The only hitch was that now the ratio of curd to whipped egg whites had changed, so the texture of the chiffon was off. Since I was losing some of the gelatin to the curd liner, the chiffon layer now squished under the knife when I sliced it. It also tasted a bit lean, since the curd took some of the yolks and cream with it, too. Fortunately, there was an obvious way to solve the consistency problem: Divide the teaspoon of gelatin between the two layers. This way, both components contained just enough to be creamy yet stable.

Dairy was the obvious go-to for richness, but I could add only so much before the gelatin lost its grip on the chiffon. That ruled out liquids like heavy cream and half-and-half. But what about something more solid, like cream cheese? Four ounces, stirred into the remaining portion of the curd, enriched the chiffon nicely and also thickened it up a bit.

Creamy but sturdy, rich but still lightweight, and full of bright citrus tang, this pie was a showstopper.

—LAN LAM, *Cook's Illustrated*

Lemon Chiffon Pie
SERVES 8 TO 10

Before cooking the curd mixture, be sure to whisk thoroughly so that no clumps of cornstarch or streaks of egg white remain. Pasteurized egg whites can be substituted for the 3 raw egg whites. Serve with lightly sweetened whipped cream.

CRUST
- **9 whole graham crackers**
- **3 tablespoons sugar**
- **⅛ teaspoon salt**
- **5 tablespoons unsalted butter, melted**

FILLING

- 1 teaspoon unflavored gelatin
- 4 tablespoons water
- 5 large eggs (2 whole, 3 separated)
- 1¼ cups (8¾ ounces) sugar
- 1 tablespoon cornstarch
- ⅛ teaspoon salt
- 1 tablespoon grated lemon zest plus ¾ cup juice (4 lemons)
- ¼ cup heavy cream
- 4 ounces cream cheese, cut into ½-inch pieces, softened

1. FOR THE CRUST: Adjust oven rack to lower-middle position and heat oven to 325 degrees. Process graham crackers in food processor until finely ground, about 30 seconds (you should have about 1¼ cups crumbs). Add sugar and salt and pulse to combine. Add melted butter and pulse until mixture resembles wet sand.

2. Transfer crumbs to 9-inch pie plate. Press crumbs evenly into bottom and up sides of plate. Bake until crust is lightly browned, 15 to 18 minutes. Allow crust to cool completely.

3. FOR THE FILLING: Sprinkle ½ teaspoon gelatin over 2 tablespoons water in small bowl and let sit until gelatin softens, about 5 minutes. Repeat with second small bowl, remaining ½ teaspoon gelatin, and remaining 2 tablespoons water.

4. Whisk 2 eggs and 3 yolks together in medium saucepan until thoroughly combined. Whisk in 1 cup sugar, cornstarch, and salt until well combined. Whisk in lemon zest and juice and heavy cream. Cook over medium-low heat, stirring constantly, until thickened and slightly translucent, 4 to 5 minutes (mixture should register 170 degrees). Stir in 1 water-gelatin mixture until dissolved. Remove pan from heat and let stand for 2 minutes.

5. Remove 1¼ cups curd from pan and pour through fine-mesh strainer set in bowl. Transfer strained curd to prepared pie shell (do not wash out strainer or bowl). Place filled pie shell in freezer. Add remaining water-gelatin mixture and cream cheese to remaining curd in pan and whisk to combine. (If cream cheese does not melt, briefly return pan to low heat.) Pour through strainer into now-empty bowl.

6. Using stand mixer, whip 3 egg whites on medium-low speed until foamy, about 2 minutes. Increase speed to medium-high and slowly add remaining ¼ cup sugar. Continue whipping until whites are stiff and glossy,

CRUMB CRUST DONE RIGHT

Using bottom and sides of measuring cup, press crumb mixture firmly and evenly across bottom of pie plate. Then, using measuring cup and your thumb simultaneously, pack crumbs against side of pie plate.

CREATING A SMOOTH LEMON LAYER

After spreading the lemon curd over the crust, we briefly pop the curd-lined crust in the freezer to firm it up; that way, it won't squish when topped with the chiffon.

FOR FLAWLESS CHIFFON, TWO THICKENERS ARE BETTER THAN ONE

Most recipes call for adding either gelatin or cornstarch to the curd before combining it with the whipped egg whites. We made dozens of failed pies (some stiff, some soupy) before we realized that the solution was to use a little of both.

JUST GELATIN: RUBBERY

Gelatin, a pure protein, works by forming a gel network that traps liquid in the filling. But too much can lead to a bouncy texture—and even the ideal amount produces inconsistent results. If it's allowed to firm up a tad too long before being combined with the egg whites, it leaves streaks.

JUST CORNSTARCH: SOUPY

Cornstarch thickens when its starch molecules bond together and trap water, creating a solid, jellylike structure. It's more forgiving than gelatin, but unless you add a glut of it, the filling will be loose. And too much cornstarch will mute the flavor of the filling.

GELATIN + CORNSTARCH: PERFECT

Using both gelatin and cornstarch in moderation produces chiffon that sets up reliably but isn't rubbery. The proteins in just 1 teaspoon of gelatin are enough to form a gel network, and a mere tablespoon of cornstarch acts as a filler that makes the network more stable without dulling the filling's lemony punch.

about 4 minutes. Add curd–cream cheese mixture and whip on medium speed until few streaks remain, about 30 seconds. Remove bowl from mixer and, using spatula, scrape sides of bowl and stir mixture until no streaks remain. Remove pie shell from freezer and carefully pour chiffon over curd, allowing chiffon to mound slightly in center. Refrigerate for at least 4 hours or up to 2 days before serving.

BANANA CREAM PIE

✔ **WHY THIS RECIPE WORKS** This layered diner-style pie of pastry cream and sliced bananas topped with whipped cream is often delicious and sometimes sliceable, but very rarely both. We wanted a banana cream pie that had it all. For our filling, we started with a classic pastry cream made with half-and-half, egg yolks, butter, and cornstarch for a rich, sliceable, but not rubbery, texture. Looking to add banana flavor, we found banana extract tasted artificial and banana liqueur wasn't practical. Instead, we infused the half-and-half for the pastry cream with a few sautéed bananas, which we later strained out. We also layered the pastry cream with fresh banana slices. To keep the banana slices from browning unattractively, we mixed them with a splash of orange juice. Cookie-crumb crusts were too sweet for this pie, so we chose a simple parbaked pie dough shell. Finally, we topped off our pie with a layer of sweetened whipped cream.

Banana cream pie is a staple of slapstick comedy. Unfortunately, our first round of testing was no laughing matter. The soft, creamy quality that makes it perfect for pie-in-the-face gags and such a pleasure to eat is precisely what makes it tricky to get right. My initial tests revealed problems with every aspect of this pie.

The creamiest versions were unsliceable, and the tidiest slices were starchy and gloppy. To reinforce the banana flavor, some recipes use banana extract or banana liqueur in the pastry cream. We liked the idea in theory, but the extract tasted artificial, and buying a bottle of liqueur for the small amount we'd need in the pie seemed crazy. Pies with cookie-crumb crusts were too sweet. And in every last test pie the sliced bananas turned brown by the time the pastry cream set. Clearly I'd need to start my recipe from scratch.

To make pastry cream, you combine egg yolks, flour or cornstarch, and sugar; whisk in hot half-and-half; stir over low heat until thick; then add vanilla and a little butter. (The butter melts in the hot pastry cream but resolidifies and stiffens the cream as it cools.) Hoping to strike a compromise between starchy and runny, I made pastry cream again and again over a series of days, adjusting each component. Eventually, I figured out my ratios and settled on cornstarch (a more foolproof thickener than flour). I assembled a pie—arranging three sliced bananas between two layers of pastry cream in a prebaked pie shell—let it chill for 4 hours, and then nervously cut . . . a perfect slice!

But the bananas were turning brown. To investigate possible solutions, I tossed banana slices with various ingredients alleged to protect them from browning, left them out on the counter, and checked in periodically to see which browned the slowest. Sugar and vodka were a bust. Salt, vinegar, and lemon juice slowed browning but tasted either salty or sour. Orange juice, however, slowed browning without affecting the mellow, fruity banana flavor, so I assembled a pie. Tasters approved.

Next, I turned to bumping up the banana flavor. Since banana extract and liqueur were out, I tried smashing up a banana in the pastry cream. No dice: It turned the pastry cream brown. Someone recommended banana baby food—great idea, I thought. Another failure: It made the pastry cream runny. So I borrowed an idea from our recipe for banana pudding, using pureed roasted bananas to flavor my pastry cream. Delicious. Unfortunately, it was also loose and turned brownish gray. I tried sautéing the bananas in butter, and again I pureed them into the cream. Once more, delicious—and gray.

I was starting to get really frustrated when the solution occurred to me: Maybe I could infuse the half-and-half with banana flavor and then strain out the fruit. Two bananas (sliced) gave my pastry cream a banana-y boost, and straining minimized the unappealing color change. Sacrificing two bananas at $0.49 a pound was a bargain compared with $4 for a bottle of fake-tasting banana extract or $15 for a bottle of banana liqueur that would gather dust in my cabinet.

With a creamy yet sliceable banana-boosted pastry cream, mellow and (finally) yellow sliced bananas, and a light and stable whipped cream (thank you, confectioners' sugar), this pie put a smile on our faces.

—SARAH GABRIEL, *Cook's Country*

Banana Cream Pie

SERVES 8

Peel and slice the bananas just before using to help prevent browning.

CRUST

- 1¼ cups (6¼ ounces) all-purpose flour
- 1 tablespoon sugar
- ½ teaspoon salt
- 4 tablespoons vegetable shortening, cut into ¼-inch pieces and chilled
- 6 tablespoons unsalted butter, cut into ¼-inch pieces and chilled
- 3-4 tablespoons ice water

FILLING

- 5 ripe bananas
- 4 tablespoons unsalted butter
- 2½ cups half-and-half
- ½ cup (3½ ounces) plus 2 tablespoons granulated sugar
- 6 large egg yolks
- ¼ teaspoon salt
- 2 tablespoons cornstarch
- 1½ teaspoons vanilla extract
- 2 tablespoons orange juice
- 1 cup heavy cream
- 2 tablespoons confectioners' sugar

1. FOR THE CRUST: Process flour, sugar, and salt in food processor until combined. Add chilled shortening and pulse until coarsely ground. Add chilled butter and pulse until mixture resembles coarse crumbs. Transfer to large bowl.

2. Sprinkle 3 tablespoons water over flour mixture. Using rubber spatula, stir mixture until dough forms. If dough remains crumbly, add remaining 1 tablespoon water. Form dough into 4-inch disk, wrap tightly in plastic wrap, and refrigerate for at least 1 hour or up to 2 days. (Dough can be frozen, wrapped tightly in plastic and aluminum foil, for up to 2 months. Thaw completely at room temperature before using.)

3. Let chilled dough soften slightly at room temperature, about 10 minutes. Working on lightly floured counter, roll dough into 12-inch circle. Transfer dough to 9-inch pie plate, fold edge of dough under itself so edge of fold is flush with outer rim of plate, and flute edges. Refrigerate for 40 minutes, then freeze for

20 minutes. Adjust oven rack to lower-middle position and heat oven to 375 degrees.

4. Line chilled pie shell with 12-inch square of aluminum foil, folding foil over edges of dough. Fill with pie weights and bake for 20 minutes. Carefully remove foil and weights, rotate plate, and continue baking until crust is golden brown, 7 to 11 minutes. Let cool to room temperature.

5. FOR THE FILLING: Peel 2 bananas and slice into ½-inch-thick pieces. Melt 1 tablespoon butter in medium saucepan over medium-high heat. Add sliced bananas and cook until they begin to soften, about 2 minutes. Add half-and-half, bring to boil, and boil for 30 seconds. Remove from heat, cover, and let sit for 40 minutes.

6. Whisk granulated sugar, egg yolks, and salt together in large bowl until smooth. Whisk in cornstarch. Strain cooled half-and-half mixture through fine-mesh strainer into yolk mixture—do not press on bananas—and whisk until incorporated; discard cooked bananas.

7. Transfer mixture to clean medium saucepan. Cook over medium heat, whisking constantly, until thickened to consistency of warm pudding (180 degrees), 4 to 6 minutes. Remove pan from heat; whisk in remaining 3 tablespoons butter and 1 teaspoon vanilla. Transfer pastry cream to bowl, press greased parchment paper directly against surface, and let cool for about 1 hour.

8. Peel and slice remaining 3 bananas ¼ inch thick and toss with orange juice. Whisk pastry cream briefly, then spread half over bottom of pie shell. Arrange sliced bananas on pastry cream. Top with remaining pastry cream.

NOTES FROM THE TEST KITCHEN

THE BEST PIE SERVER

A gorgeous pie can take hours to make—and be mangled in seconds if you cut it with the wrong tool. A pie server must be sharp enough to cut cleanly and agile enough to neatly slide under a fragile slice to lift and transport it intact. It's been six years since we last tested pie servers, so recently we tried five priced from $6.99 to $21.14, including our previous favorite. After slicing cream pies and fruit pies, pastry and crumb crusts, we confirmed our previous findings. Though the **OXO Steel Pie Server**, $9.99, has a tip that is slightly blunter than ideal, that's a small concession for all-around solid performance.

9. Using stand mixer fitted with whisk, whip cream, confectioners' sugar, and remaining ½ teaspoon vanilla on medium-low speed until foamy, about 1 minute. Increase speed to high and whip until stiff peaks form, 1 to 3 minutes. Spread whipped cream evenly over top of pie. Refrigerate until set, at least 5 hours or up to 24 hours. Serve.

VARIATION

Chocolate-Peanut Butter Banana Cream Pie

Combine 4 ounces chopped milk chocolate and 1½ tablespoons half-and-half in bowl; microwave until melted, about 40 seconds, stirring halfway through. In step 8, spread melted chocolate in bottom of prebaked pie shell. Sprinkle ⅓ cup chopped, salted dry-roasted peanuts over chocolate. Continue with recipe, layering pastry cream and sliced bananas on top. In step 9, reserve ¼ cup heavy cream and whisk with 2 tablespoons creamy peanut butter in bowl until smooth. Stir peanut butter mixture into whipped cream before spreading over top of pie. Sprinkle pie with 2 tablespoons more chopped peanuts. Refrigerate until set, 5 to 24 hours. Serve.

CHOCOLATE ANGEL PIE

✔ **WHY THIS RECIPE WORKS** Chocolate angel pie is a lavish version of chocolate cream pie that combines a rich, creamy chocolate mousse, fluffy whipped cream, and a light, crisp meringue crust. True meringue takes time, and we found that 2½ hours in a low oven was necessary for the lightest, crispest crust. To prevent the crust from sticking to the pan, we relied on cornstarch, both in the egg whites and dusted over the pie plate. The original recipes we found were weak on chocolate flavor. We found we could load nearly a pound of chocolate into the filling by making a cooked custard. Using both milk chocolate and bittersweet chocolate lent depth and complexity. To finish, we topped the pie with lightly sweetened whipped cream and a sprinkling of cocoa powder for a decadent, supremely chocolaty dessert that was definitely worth the wait.

If you think counting angels on the head of a pin is hard, try defining angel pie (also known as heavenly pie). An assortment of recipes going by this name first appeared in print in the 1920s, but it was only after World War II that the name was used for a meringue pie shell filled with creamy mousse and topped with whipped cream. This version was an instant hit—and no wonder. Rationing was at an end, so eggs and sugar were in plentiful supply. A lavish dessert was in order. In my book, it still is. Ideally, chocolate angel pie should have a light, crisp meringue crust; a filling so chocolaty and satiny it could put a truffle to shame; and plenty of whipped cream.

Instead, the recipes I tested produced pies with chewy, brown meringue shells so sticky and brittle that I couldn't cut slices without the crust shattering. The fillings typically called for whipping 1 cup of heavy cream and folding it into 2 to 4 ounces of melted semisweet chocolate (pastry chefs call this a quick mousse). Whipped cream and chocolate are guaranteed to taste pretty good, but that being said, these fillings fell flat, with little chocolate punch.

I'd start with the meringue and work my way up to the pie layers. The meringue is made by whipping egg whites with sugar, vanilla, and cream of tartar (for stability) until stiff. The mixture is spread in a pie plate and baked. Most recipes I found called for relatively high oven temperatures and short baking times (325 degrees for 35 minutes). But this yielded sticky, dark tan meringues, indicating that the sugar was burning. I unearthed a few recipes that called for longer baking times at lower temperatures: 1 hour at 250 degrees, then 3 hours to overnight in the turned-off oven. I liked the results of this technique—pale, crunchy, light meringues—but not the timetable.

To get a crisp meringue more quickly, I'd need to remove excess moisture faster. Adding 1 tablespoon of cornstarch to the egg white mixture sped up the baking time somewhat. Fiddling with times and temperatures eventually produced a crunchy shell on a more reasonable timetable. My solution was to bake the shell at 275 degrees for 1½ hours, then drop the temperature to 200 degrees for an additional hour. Unfortunately, the pie shell still stuck to the pie plate. I greased the pie plate to no avail. Next, I greased the pie plate and dusted it with flour, as though I were baking a cake. The raw flour left a pasty film on our tongues. What if I dusted the pie plate with cornstarch instead? This method worked. Now my meringue shell was delicate and crunchy, and it was easy to remove a slice intact.

I turned my attention to the filling. I'd been using 4 ounces of bittersweet chocolate for the filling, but its normally strong, complex flavor was muted by all the

CHOCOLATE ANGEL PIE

whipped cream. I tried simply using more chocolate, but with just a few extra ounces, the filling's appealing creaminess was ruined. I hit the cookbooks for ideas and found an old recipe that called for a cooked custard. A cooked custard, I realized excitedly, could handle extra chocolate. Following the recipe, I scalded half-and-half on the stovetop, slowly added it to three egg yolks and sugar, and poured this custard mixture over a generous 8 ounces of chocolate. I let the mixture cool a little and folded in whipped cream.

The result spoke for itself: This chocolate filling was bold, smooth, and silky. It wasn't merely extra chocolate that accounted for the extra flavor, our science editor speculated; because of the yolks, the flavor molecules got pulled into the emulsified mixture of fat and water, where receptors in the mouth and nose can detect them more readily. He added that the yolks stabilized the emulsification between cream and chocolate, yielding that silken texture. As a bonus, I wasn't stuck with unused egg yolks.

Having unlocked the secret to great chocolate flavor, I pushed my luck by working my way up to nearly a pound. But now the bittersweet flavor came on too strong. I tested more pies (no complaints from eaters) with various ratios of milk chocolate to bittersweet. The filling achieved depth and balance at 9 ounces milk chocolate to 5 ounces bittersweet—more than three times the amount of chocolate I'd found in any other recipe. The airy, crisp meringue was its perfect counterpoint. To finish, I slathered on lightly sweetened whipped cream. "It's like the chocolate is sitting on a cloud," one taster exclaimed. "Heavenly," sighed another.

—CRISTIN WALSH, *Cook's Country*

NOTES FROM THE TEST KITCHEN

DON'T MAKE THIS MISTAKE—BUSTED CRUST

The egg white crust is part of what distinguishes angel pie. To avoid a sticky, broken meringue shell, we added cornstarch to the whites, and we greased the pie plate and dusted it with more cornstarch. We also figured out the ideal baking time and temperatures to ensure that the interior and exterior of the meringue cooked properly.

Chocolate Angel Pie

SERVES 8 TO 10

Serve the assembled pie within 3 hours of chilling.

FILLING

- **9 ounces milk chocolate, chopped fine**
- **5 ounces bittersweet chocolate, chopped fine**
- **3 large egg yolks**
- **1½ tablespoons granulated sugar**
- **½ teaspoon salt**
- **½ cup half-and-half**
- **1¼ cups heavy cream, chilled**

MERINGUE CRUST

- **1 tablespoon cornstarch, plus extra for pie plate**
- **½ cup (3½ ounces) granulated sugar**
- **3 large egg whites**
- **Pinch cream of tartar**
- **½ teaspoon vanilla extract**

TOPPING

- **1⅓ cups heavy cream, chilled**
- **2 tablespoons confectioners' sugar**
- **Unsweetened cocoa powder**

1. FOR THE FILLING: Microwave milk chocolate and bittersweet chocolate in large bowl at 50 percent power, stirring occasionally, until melted, 2 to 4 minutes. Whisk egg yolks, sugar, and salt together in medium bowl until combined, about 1 minute. Bring half-and-half to simmer in small saucepan over medium heat. Whisking constantly, slowly add hot half-and-half to egg yolk mixture in 2 additions until incorporated. Return half-and-half mixture to now-empty saucepan and cook over low heat, whisking constantly, until thickened slightly, 30 seconds to 1 minute. Stir half-and-half mixture into melted chocolate until combined. Let cool slightly, about 8 minutes.

2. Using stand mixer fitted with whisk, whip cream on medium-low speed until foamy, about 1 minute. Increase speed to high and whip until soft peaks form, 1 to 3 minutes. Gently whisk one-third of whipped cream into cooled chocolate mixture. Fold in remaining whipped cream until no white streaks remain. Cover and refrigerate for at least 3 hours, or until ready to assemble pie. (Filling can be made up to 24 hours in advance.)

3. FOR THE MERINGUE CRUST: Adjust oven rack to lower-middle position and heat oven to 275 degrees. Grease 9-inch pie plate and dust well with extra cornstarch, using pastry brush to distribute evenly. Combine sugar and 1 tablespoon cornstarch in bowl. Using stand mixer fitted with whisk, whip egg whites and cream of tartar on medium-low speed until foamy, about 1 minute. Increase speed to medium-high and whip whites to soft, billowy mounds, 1 to 3 minutes. Gradually add sugar mixture and whip until glossy, stiff peaks form, 3 to 5 minutes. Add vanilla to meringue and whip until incorporated.

4. Spread meringue in prepared pie plate, following contours of plate to cover bottom, sides, and edges. Bake for 1½ hours. Rotate pie plate, reduce oven temperature to 200 degrees, and bake until completely dried out, about 1 hour longer. (Shell will rise above rim of pie plate; some cracking is OK.) Let cool completely, about 30 minutes.

5. FOR THE TOPPING: Spoon cooled chocolate filling into cavity of pie shell, distributing evenly. Using stand mixer fitted with whisk, whip cream and sugar on medium-low speed until foamy, about 1 minute. Increase speed to high and whip until stiff peaks form, 1 to 3 minutes. Spread whipped cream evenly over chocolate. Refrigerate until filling is set, about 1 hour. Dust with cocoa. Slice with sharp knife and serve.

BEST CHOCOLATE TART

✔ **WHY THIS RECIPE WORKS** For us, a great chocolate tart should possess deep chocolate flavor, a rich, lush texture, and a sophisticated presentation. First we made a custardy filling by melting chocolate into hot cream, adding eggs, and baking. Using a dark chocolate with about 60 percent cocoa solids was important; it had intense chocolate flavor taste with enough sweetness that no additional sugar was necessary. To enrich the filling's flavor, we added some butter; just 4 tablespoons amplified the chocolate flavor and gave our custard depth. We avoided added flavorings that would detract from the chocolate but found that a little instant espresso added an echo of bittersweetness that highlighted it. Because custards tend to curdle under high heat, we baked the tart in a very low 250-degree oven for a smooth and silky texture. To make our tart a showstopper, we topped it with a simple glossy glaze of chocolate, cream, and corn syrup. A classic sweet pastry dough flavored with ground almonds made the perfect complement to the filling.

"Outrageously elegant," "ridiculously scrumptious," "intensely and irresistibly chocolaty." Inflated descriptors are de rigueur when it comes to chocolate tarts. For me, though, the real draw of the dessert is its pure, uncomplicated nature: The best versions boast a flawlessly smooth texture, clean chocolate flavor, and a sophisticated look. With the holidays approaching, I wanted to uncover the makings of a chocolate tart par excellence.

As I pored over cookbooks, I noticed that although there is little variation in the filling ingredients—recipes contain only chocolate and cream plus butter or eggs—three unique tart styles exist. The first type involves whipping the egg whites for aeration. Once baked, the tart has a slightly souffléed, brownielike texture—not quite the suave, polished dessert that I had in mind. The second kind is essentially chocolate ganache. Chocolate is melted into hot cream, then butter is whisked in before the filling is poured into a prebaked shell and chilled. It offers an unctuous, über-rich, melt-in-your-mouth quality. The third type also starts with melting chocolate into hot cream, but eggs, rather than butter, are incorporated before baking. Once baked, this custard-style tart boasts an agreeable "set" consistency.

Both the ganache and custard styles seemed worth considering. Since the main flaw of the ganache-style tart was a greasy texture, I tried drastically reducing the butter content. However, the flavor fell flat and the consistency turned waxy. With little else to explore about ganache tarts, I committed to a custard-style tart.

While I perfected the filling, I would use the test kitchen's basic sweet pastry dough (pâte sucrée) as a placeholder crust. And for the deep flavor I sought, the test kitchen's favorite dark chocolate, Callebaut Intense Dark Chocolate, L-60-40NV, which contains about 60 percent cocoa solids, would be just the ticket. It has a pleasantly intense taste and supplies enough sweetness that no additional sugar would be necessary.

First up: Determine the right proportions of chocolate and cream. For a 9-inch tart, chocolate quantities in recipes ranged from 7 ounces to 10 ounces; cream ranged from ¾ cup to 1½ cups. Too much chocolate and the filling was too intense to enjoy more than a bite or two; too much cream and it was too mild and slack in consistency. In the end, 9 ounces of chocolate and 1¼ cups of cream struck an ideal balance.

Recipes for baked chocolate tart typically call for one or two eggs. I tried various combinations of eggs and yolks. The differences were quite subtle, but two eggs added just the right amount of richness. The problem was the consistency: The filling was plagued by a slightly curdled, dense texture. It occurred to me that perhaps the 350-degree oven I'd been using was too hot for the task. Custards, after all, are delicate mixtures because of the eggs; overcooking results in firm, curdy texture. To test my theory, I baked tarts at 350, 325, 300, and 250 degrees. The differences were astounding. The 350-degree tart was stiff and dense; but with each reduction in temperature, the texture improved. The 250-degree tart, baked for 30 minutes, had exactly the silky, ethereal quality that I was hoping for.

I now had the texture I wanted, but the filling was still a little dull and one-dimensional tasting. Custard-style chocolate tarts don't typically call for butter, but I wondered if adding some would help since it had made all the difference in the ganache tarts. I compared fillings made with 2, 4, 6, and 8 tablespoons of butter, and none at all. The ideal amount was right in the middle: 4 tablespoons of butter nicely amplified the chocolate.

Finally, I considered flavorings. It's tempting to pair ingredients like orange zest and Cognac with chocolate, but I found that these only detracted from its taste. The exception was instant espresso, which added an echo of bittersweetness that highlighted the chocolate.

My tart now tasted fantastic—but its appearance was another story. In the heat of the oven, its surface formed tiny fissures and took on a drab, matte finish. I wanted this celebratory dessert to boast a slick, glistening sheen. A simple chocolate glaze would do the trick. I played with a few formulas and settled on one based on chocolate and cream, plus a measure of corn syrup for glossiness.

With the filling now complete, I test drove other pastry options, pitting cocoa and almond pastries against the basic tart dough. The cocoa pastry, with its dark crust and dark filling, made for a dramatic-looking dessert, but chocolate-on-chocolate didn't offer any flavor contrast. The almond pastry swept the tasting—its deep nutty flavor, pleasantly nubby texture, and speckled look were an ideal match for the chocolate filling.

A dollop of lightly sweetened whipped cream plus a dusting of cocoa, a sprinkle of coarse sea salt, or a pile of chocolate curls were easy finishing touches for a stunning presentation. This was an ultraluxe, deliciously lush, supremely succulent chocolate tart, to use a few inflated (but not entirely inapt) descriptors.

—DAWN YANAGIHARA, *Cook's Illustrated*

Best Chocolate Tart
SERVES 12

Toasted and skinned hazelnuts can be substituted for the almonds. Use good-quality dark chocolate containing a cacao percentage between 60 and 65 percent; our favorites are Callebaut Intense Dark Chocolate, L-60-40NV, and Ghirardelli 60% Cacao Bittersweet Chocolate. Let tart sit at room temperature before glazing in step 6. The the finished tart can be garnished with chocolate curls or with a flaky coarse sea salt, such as Maldon. Serve with lightly sweetened whipped cream; if you like, flavor it with cognac or vanilla extract.

CRUST

- 1 **large egg yolk**
- 2 **tablespoons heavy cream**
- ½ **cup sliced almonds, toasted**
- ¼ **cup (1¾ ounces) sugar**
- 1 **cup (5 ounces) all-purpose flour**
- ¼ **teaspoon salt**
- 6 **tablespoons unsalted butter, cut into ½-inch pieces**

FILLING

- 1¼ **cups heavy cream**
- ½ **teaspoon instant espresso powder**
- ¼ **teaspoon salt**
- 9 **ounces bittersweet chocolate, chopped fine**
- 4 **tablespoons unsalted butter, cut into thin slices and softened**
- 2 **large eggs, lightly beaten, room temperature**

GLAZE

- 3 **tablespoons heavy cream**
- 1 **tablespoon light corn syrup**
- 2 **ounces bittersweet chocolate, chopped fine**
- 1 **tablespoon hot water**

1. FOR THE CRUST: Beat egg yolk and cream together in small bowl. Process almonds and sugar in food processor until nuts are finely ground, 15 to 20 seconds. Add flour and salt; pulse to combine, about 10 pulses. Scatter butter over flour mixture; pulse to cut butter into flour until mixture resembles coarse meal, about 15 pulses. With processor running, add egg yolk mixture and process until dough forms ball, about 10 seconds. Transfer dough to large sheet of plastic wrap and press into 6-inch disk; wrap dough in plastic and refrigerate until firm but malleable, about 30 minutes. (Dough can be refrigerated for up to 3 days; before using, let stand at room temperature until malleable but still cool.)

2. Roll out dough between 2 large sheets of plastic into 11-inch round about ⅜ inch thick. (If dough becomes too soft and sticky to work with, slip it onto baking sheet and refrigerate until workable.) Place dough round on baking sheet and refrigerate until firm but pliable, about 15 minutes.

3. Adjust oven rack to middle position and heat oven to 375 degrees. Spray 9-inch tart pan with removable bottom with vegetable oil spray. Keeping dough on sheet, remove top layer of plastic. Invert tart pan (with bottom) on top of dough round. Press on tart pan to cut dough. Using both hands, pick up sheet and tart pan and carefully invert both, setting tart pan right side up. Remove sheet and peel off plastic; reserve plastic. Roll over edges of tart pan with rolling pin to cut dough. Gently ease and press dough into bottom of pan, reserving scraps. Roll dough scraps into ¾-inch rope (various lengths are OK). Line edge of tart pan with rope(s) and gently press into fluted sides. Line tart pan with reserved plastic and, using measuring cup, gently press and smooth dough to even thickness (sides should be about ¼ inch thick). Using paring knife, trim any excess dough above rim of tart; discard scraps. Freeze dough-lined pan until dough is firm, 20 to 30 minutes.

4. Set dough-lined pan on baking sheet. Spray 12-inch square of aluminum foil with oil spray and press foil, sprayed side down, into pan; fill with 2 cups pie weights. Bake until dough is dry and light golden brown, about 25 minutes, rotating pan halfway through baking. Carefully remove foil and weights and continue to bake until pastry is rich golden brown and fragrant, 8 to 10 minutes longer. Let cool completely on baking sheet on wire rack.

5. FOR THE FILLING: Heat oven to 250 degrees. Bring cream, espresso powder, and salt to simmer in small saucepan over medium heat, stirring once or twice to dissolve espresso powder and salt. Meanwhile, place chocolate in large heatproof bowl. Pour simmering cream mixture over chocolate, cover, and let stand for 5 minutes to allow chocolate to soften. Using whisk, stir mixture slowly and gently (so as not to incorporate air) until homogeneous. Add butter and continue to whisk gently until fully incorporated. Pour beaten eggs through fine-mesh strainer into chocolate mixture; whisk slowly until mixture is homogeneous and glossy.

Pour filling into tart crust and shake gently from side to side to distribute and smooth surface; pop any large bubbles with toothpick or skewer. Bake tart, on baking sheet, until outer edge of filling is just set and very faint cracks appear on surface, 30 to 35 minutes; filling will still be very wobbly. Let cool completely on baking sheet on wire rack. Refrigerate, uncovered, until filling is chilled and set, at least 3 hours or up to 18 hours.

6. FOR THE GLAZE: Thirty minutes before glazing, remove tart from refrigerator. Bring cream and corn syrup to simmer in small saucepan over medium heat; stir once or twice to combine. Remove pan from heat, add chocolate, and cover. Let stand for 5 minutes to

NOTES FROM THE TEST KITCHEN

FITTING THE TART DOUGH INTO THE PAN

1. Invert tart pan on top of dough round. (Removable bottom will drop onto dough.) Press on tart pan to cut dough. Pick up baking sheet, carefully invert it, and set tart pan down. Remove sheet and peel off plastic wrap.

2. Roll over dough edges with rolling pin to cut, reserving scraps. Gently ease and press dough into bottom of pan.

3. Roll dough scraps into ¾-inch rope. Line edge of tart pan with rope and gently press into fluted sides.

4. Line tart pan with reserved plastic wrap. Using measuring cup, gently press dough to even thickness. Sides should be ¼ inch thick. Use paring knife to trim excess dough above rim of tart.

allow chocolate to soften. Whisk gently (so as not to incorporate air) until mixture is smooth, then whisk in hot water until glaze is homogeneous, shiny, and pourable. Working quickly, pour glaze onto center of tart. To distribute glaze, tilt tart and allow glaze to run to edge. (Spreading glaze with spatula will leave marks on surface.) Pop any large bubbles with toothpick or skewer. Let cool completely, about 1 hour.

7. TO SERVE: Remove outer ring from tart pan. Insert thin-bladed metal spatula between crust and pan bottom to loosen tart; slide tart onto serving platter. Cut into wedges and serve.

MAGIC CHOCOLATE FLAN CAKE

✔ **WHY THIS RECIPE WORKS** This unique dessert combines a layer of fudgy chocolate cake and a layer of rich, caramel-coated flan that "magically" switch places as they bake. We started with an easy dump-and-stir cake recipe. The cake's flavor was great, but it was soggy due to the moisture from the flan. Cutting some of the buttermilk and sugar from the cake batter did the trick. To help our flan firm up, we swapped some of the egg yolks for whole eggs and added cream cheese. The cream cheese also lent the flan a tanginess that offset its sweetness. Convenient store-bought caramel sauce topped it all off.

Recently, magic chocolate flan cake has generated buzz online and in cooking magazines, and no wonder. Picture a big, showy dessert: a layer of chocolate cake, topped with creamy, vanilla-scented flan, all dripping with caramel. And I haven't even gotten to the magic—to make it, first you line the pan (often a Bundt) with caramel. Then you pour in the cake batter and, last, the flan batter. As the cake bakes, the flan sinks and the cake rises, so when you flip the whole thing out of the pan, the caramel-lined flan sits on top. There's also magic in the amalgam of dense, deep chocolate; smooth, light flan; and sweet, sticky caramel.

Many recipes use cake mix for the base, but I also found a handful that started from scratch, so I lined up pans and got to work on both. The cakes went into the oven (some in water baths to help gently bake the flan), and many hours later we tasted them—or, more accurately, we gobbled them up. Despite their appeal,

though, the mechanics needed refining. The cake mix cakes tasted artificial, but the from-scratch cakes had problems, too: They were soggy and had weak chocolate flavor. Several of the flans curdled. Taken as a whole (cake plus flan plus caramel), the dessert was too sweet. Even chilled, these cakes stuck to their pans, and once I'd coaxed them out, they slumped instead of sliced.

To simplify my testing, I'd start with proven test kitchen recipes for chocolate cake and flan. Since magic chocolate flan cake requires that you make a cake, flan, and, in some cases, caramel, I would streamline, as long as it didn't harm the finished product. I opted for a simple dump-and-stir recipe for the cake—no mixer required. For the flan, I used our classic recipe: Mix sugar, eggs, and milk with sweetened condensed milk and bake in a water bath. For now, I'd use store-bought caramel. I adjusted the amounts to fit in a Bundt pan and worked out the right ratio of cake to flan; we found that we preferred more flan and less cake (it was deep and fudgy, so a little went a long way).

Of course, while the individual recipes had proven track records, once I put them together, all bets were off. The flavor of the chocolate cake was great, but the cake was still wet (it was obviously absorbing moisture from the flan). While the flan hadn't curdled, it was wobbly and didn't slice cleanly. Finally, with caramel, cake, and flan in every slice, the sugar remained in overdrive. I'd start by reducing the amount of sugar called for in the chocolate portion, hoping to kill two birds with one stone: The cake would be both less sweet and less wet, because sugar not only sweetens baked goods but also retains moisture. I cut back gradually, stopping when I'd reduced the sugar by one-third. The cake was still a little soggy, so for my next test, I also reduced the cake's liquid ingredient: buttermilk. This cake was fudgy and luscious, like an especially rich brownie.

I turned to the flan. Our recipe called for both egg yolks and whole eggs. Since I knew that whole eggs provide more structure, I tried fewer yolks and more whole eggs. That helped, but not quite enough. Looking for ideas in the recipes I'd collected, I noticed that some included cream cheese. I tried it out and was thrilled with the sturdiness that 6 ounces of cream cheese added to my flan. And, as a bonus, the tanginess offset the overall sweetness of the dessert nicely. Once it had chilled, I easily cut this cake into neat and clean slices.

I had been using store-bought caramel sauce, but I wondered if I should make it myself. I pitted a

MAGIC CHOCOLATE FLAN CAKE

chocolate flan cake made with homemade caramel against one using store-bought. The homemade caramel was truly delicious. But the jarred was remarkably good, too, and saved so much trouble that, all things considered, I opted to use it. For easier, more even distribution, I warmed the caramel sauce in the microwave before pouring it into the pan.

Speaking of ease, could I also skip the water bath? I baked two cakes side by side, one set in a roasting pan filled with warm water, the other alone in its pan like an ordinary cake. Several hours later, I had the answer: Without a water bath to modulate the heat, the flan cooked unevenly.

Throughout my testing, I'd struggled to get the cake out of the pan without sticking, no matter how well I greased the Bundt pan. Eventually, I found an easy solution: After thoroughly chilling the cake, I stuck the bottom of the pan in hot tap water for about a minute.

NOTES FROM THE TEST KITCHEN

MODULATE THE HEAT

A water bath, or bain-marie, can be created by simply placing your baking vessel in a larger vessel (we use a roasting pan) and filling the latter with water. The water makes for a more even, temperate baking environment.

THE BEST CONDENSED MILK

Although 21st-century Americans have refrigerators and no longer need to rely on canned milk for safety, we still reach for sweetened condensed milk to make such desserts as flan and Key lime pie because it's sweet, thick, smooth, and resistant to curdling. To find out which product is best, we tasted four (all about $3 for 14 ounces), both plain and in flan. Three contained only whole milk and sugar; the fourth was made from nonfat milk "filled" with partially hydrogenated soybean oil. When we tasted the canned milk on its own, our preferences varied. In the flan, though, one whole-milk brand was too thin and produced a looser, grainier flan. To ensure perfect desserts without unnecessary ingredients or extra work, we'll reach for **Borden Eagle Brand** or **Nestlé Carnation**.

The caramel warmed and loosened, in turn releasing the rich, grand, decadent chocolate flan cake—like magic.
—CAROLYNN PURPURA MACKAY, *Cook's Country*

Magic Chocolate Flan Cake

SERVES 16

It's worth using good-quality caramel sauce, such as Fat Toad Farm Goat's Milk Caramel. If your blender doesn't hold 2 quarts, process the flan in two batches. The cake needs to chill for at least 8 hours before you can unmold it.

CAKE

- ½ cup caramel sauce or topping
- ½ cup (2½ ounces) plus 2 tablespoons all-purpose flour
- ⅓ cup (1 ounce) unsweetened cocoa powder
- ½ teaspoon baking soda
- ⅛ teaspoon salt
- 4 ounces bittersweet chocolate, chopped
- 6 tablespoons unsalted butter
- ½ cup buttermilk
- ½ cup (3½ ounces) sugar
- 2 large eggs
- 1 teaspoon vanilla extract

FLAN

- 2 (14-ounce) cans sweetened condensed milk
- 2½ cups whole milk
- 6 ounces cream cheese
- 6 large eggs plus 4 large yolks
- 1 teaspoon vanilla extract

1. FOR THE CAKE: Adjust oven rack to middle position and heat oven to 350 degrees. Grease 12-cup nonstick Bundt pan. Microwave caramel until easily pourable, about 30 seconds. Pour into pan to coat bottom. Combine flour, cocoa, baking soda, and salt in bowl; set aside. Combine chocolate and butter in large bowl and microwave at 50 percent power, stirring occasionally, until melted, 2 to 4 minutes. Whisk buttermilk, sugar, eggs, and vanilla into chocolate mixture until incorporated. Stir in flour mixture until just combined. Pour batter over caramel in prepared pan.

2. FOR THE FLAN: Process all ingredients in blender until smooth, about 1 minute. Gently pour flan over cake batter in Bundt pan and place pan in large roasting pan. Place roasting pan on oven rack and pour warm water into roasting pan until it reaches halfway up side of Bundt pan. Bake until toothpick inserted in cake comes out clean and flan registers 180 degrees, 75 to 90 minutes. Transfer Bundt pan to wire rack. Let cool to room temperature, about 2 hours, then refrigerate until set, at least 8 hours. (Remove roasting pan from oven once water has cooled.)

3. Place bottom third of Bundt pan in bowl of hot tap water for 1 minute. Invert completely flat cake platter, place platter over top of Bundt pan, and gently turn platter and pan upside down. Slowly remove pan, allowing caramel to drizzle over top of cake. Serve.

BUTTERSCOTCH PUDDING

✔ **WHY THIS RECIPE WORKS** With its incredibly rich, nuanced, bittersweet flavor, from-scratch butterscotch pudding is worlds away from the dull, achingly sweet kind you get from an instant mix. But to get that unique toffee flavor, first you have to make the butterscotch caramel, which can be a temperamental process. To ensure that our caramel was foolproof, we boiled it to jump-start the cooking, then reduced the heat to a low simmer to give us a larger window to get it to just the right temperature. The slow simmer also gave the caramel more time to develop its complex flavor. To turn our butterscotch into pudding, we ditched the traditional and time-consuming tempering method in favor of a revolutionary technique that calls for pouring the boiling caramel sauce directly over the thickening agents (egg yolks and cornstarch thinned with a little milk). The result is a flawlessly creamy pudding with the sophisticated bittersweet flavor of traditional butterscotch—with far less fuss.

Butterscotch pudding has become synonymous with a powdered mix or those hermetically sealed plastic cups from the supermarket. Rarely do we take the time to make it from scratch—which is a shame. Real butterscotch gets its rich, nuanced, slightly bitter character from the complex reactions that take place when brown sugar and butter are cooked together into a caramel; when it's combined with custard, the result is miles away from the painfully sweet puddings produced commercially. But it comes with a price of admission: Before you even get to the point of making pudding, you've got to successfully cook the caramel, which isn't easy.

With this in mind, I set myself a high bar: Take the intimidation factor out of making caramel, simplify the pudding-making process, and ultimately bring the flavor of true butterscotch back into the American repertoire.

I started with a recipe that Ruth Wakefield (of Toll House chocolate chip cookie fame) developed in the 1936 edition of *Toll House Tried and True Recipes*. Unfortunately, I found it easy to under- or overcook the butterscotch, resulting in pudding that was either too sweet or unpalatably bitter. The problem revolved around visual cues: I never knew whether I'd reached the critical "dark brown" stage of making butterscotch because the brown sugar–butter mixture is already dark. I needed more precision, and that meant breaking out the thermometer.

I tried again, melting butter with equal amounts of granulated and brown sugars, salt, and a little water. I boiled several batches, aiming for 300 degrees—the peak of flavor development—before adding ¼ cup of cream to halt the cooking process. But I couldn't consistently nail that temperature. The window of doneness, which lasted only a few seconds (somewhere between the 6- and 7-minute mark), was simply too narrow. If it was even a couple of degrees over, the caramel burned.

I needed to slow things down, so I switched gears and tried simmering a couple of batches over a low flame. This afforded me a much wider window (minutes, not seconds) in which to check the temperature of the mixture and add the cream. The trade-off was time: This approach took 30 minutes—triple the amount that I had been spending. But maybe I could have it both ways. In the name of compromise, I tried a hybrid method, boiling the butterscotch hard at first to get the caramelization going, then dropping the heat and gently simmering it to the finish line. Bingo. A 5-minute boil brought the mixture to 240 degrees, at which point I lowered the heat for another 12 to 16 minutes of simmering to allow it to climb the final 60 degrees. This method was foolproof—and surprisingly, it produced a richer-tasting butterscotch than the high-heat method did.

Curious about the improved flavor, I did a little research and discovered that the flavor of butterscotch is largely produced by the Maillard reaction; the milk proteins in the butter react with the sugar to develop hundreds of new flavor compounds. And the longer the pudding cooks and the higher the temperature at which it cooks, the more flavor that develops.

My method allowed the pudding to spend more time at higher temperatures, which translated into deeper flavor. It was a great side effect of my relatively quick, foolproof method.

I wondered if I could use this knowledge to get even deeper flavor. Because the Maillard reaction is fueled by simple sugars like glucose and fructose, I cast about for other sources of these sugars and made two additions to the butterscotch mixture: corn syrup, which is loaded with glucose; and lemon juice, which promotes the breakdown of sucrose, a complex sugar, into simple glucose and fructose molecules. As the butterscotch simmered away, more and more sucrose broke down, providing extra fuel for the flavorful reaction.

With my rich-flavored, foolproof butterscotch in place, I moved on to streamlining my pudding approach. The classic method of cooking an egg- and starch-thickened custard goes as follows: Bring the liquid (the butterscotch caramel thinned with milk and cream) to a simmer; stir a portion of it into a mixture of egg yolks, cornstarch, and a little liquid such as milk to temper the mixture; return everything to the pot; and bring it up to a full boil. Finally, strain the mixture into a separate bowl to remove the inevitable bits of overcooked egg, cover, and chill until set. Looking for a less fussy alternative, I paged through a number of cookbooks and stumbled upon a technique in which the liquid is brought to a full boil, immediately poured over the thickening mixture (egg yolks, cornstarch, and milk), and simply whisked until combined.

Intrigued, I cooked another batch of butterscotch; whisked together my yolks, cornstarch, and milk in a separate bowl; and poured the hot butterscotch mixture over the yolk mixture and whisked vigorously. The result shocked me: Rather than a lumpy mess of curdled yolks, the pudding was smooth and glossy. Why did the mixture thicken properly—and why didn't it curdle?

It turns out that I'd misunderstood pudding making—and tempering—all along. Boiling pudding guarantees that it will thicken, but because the two components that thicken pudding—cornstarch and egg yolks—do so at temperatures well below the boiling point of 212 degrees, it's far more heat than necessary.

As for why the pour-over method didn't cause the eggs to curdle, the explanation was twofold: First, the yolks were protected by the cornstarch, which absorbs water, swells, and slows down the binding of the egg proteins. Second, the pour-over approach removes the custard from direct heat, thereby eliminating any risk of curdling.

Pleased with my revamped caramel and pudding methods, I had one last tweak to make: I added 2 teaspoons of vanilla extract and 1 teaspoon of dark rum to mirror the deep caramel notes of the butterscotch. With a dollop of lightly sweetened whipped cream on top, my butterscotch pudding was the ultimate version—simple to make, yet with a flavor so complex and sophisticated that I wouldn't hesitate to serve it to company.

—DAN SOUZA, *Cook's Illustrated*

Best Butterscotch Pudding

SERVES 8

When taking the temperature of the caramel in step 1, tilt the pan and move the thermometer back and forth to equalize hot and cool spots. Work quickly when pouring the caramel mixture over the egg mixture in step 4 to ensure proper thickening. Serve the pudding with lightly sweetened whipped cream.

- 12 tablespoons unsalted butter, cut into ½-inch pieces
- ½ cup (3½ ounces) granulated sugar
- ½ cup packed (3½ ounces) dark brown sugar
- ¼ cup water
- 2 tablespoons light corn syrup
- 1 teaspoon lemon juice
- ¾ teaspoon salt
- 1 cup heavy cream
- 2¼ cups whole milk
- 4 large egg yolks
- ¼ cup cornstarch
- 2 teaspoons vanilla extract
- 1 teaspoon dark rum

1. Bring butter, granulated sugar, brown sugar, water, corn syrup, lemon juice, and salt to boil in large saucepan over medium heat, stirring occasionally to dissolve sugar and melt butter. Once mixture is at full rolling boil, cook, stirring occasionally, for 5 minutes (caramel will register about 240 degrees). Immediately reduce heat to medium-low and gently simmer (caramel should maintain steady stream of lazy bubbles—if not, adjust

A NEW WAY TO CONSISTENTLY PERFECT CARAMEL

The rich flavor of our butterscotch pudding depends on cooking the caramel mixture to exactly 300 degrees before adding the cream, but it's easy to over- or undercook the mixture when it's boiled from start to finish (the usual approach). Our more forgiving method: Boil the caramel over medium heat until it reaches 240 degrees, then reduce the heat to medium-low and gently simmer it until it reaches 300 degrees. The simmer phase takes about 12 to 16 minutes—plenty of time in which to grab a thermometer and the cream.

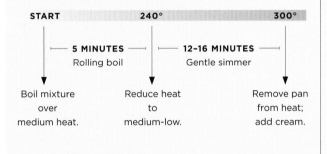

START	240°	300°
5 MINUTES	12–16 MINUTES	
Rolling boil	Gentle simmer	
Boil mixture over medium heat.	Reduce heat to medium-low.	Remove pan from heat; add cream.

SMOOTHER ROUTE TO PUDDING?

Pudding recipes almost always have you temper the yolks and cornstarch (i.e., add some hot dairy to the mixture to gradually raise its temperature), add everything to the remaining dairy in the pot, and stir constantly as the mixture slowly comes to a boil and thickens. Inevitably, bits of egg still overcook and need to be strained. We wondered if there was a better way.

We made one batch of pudding the conventional way and a second batch in which the yolks never saw the heat of the stove: We added a little warm milk to the yolks and cornstarch, brought the remaining "dairy" (in our recipe, the butterscotch mixture) to a boil, and then dumped this hot liquid over the egg mixture and whisked briefly as the pudding thickened almost instantly. The conventional pudding needed straining, while the "no-cook" custard was utterly smooth and perfectly thickened.

The reason? Boiling pudding is overkill. When cornstarch is combined with liquid, it thickens between 144 and 180 degrees, while the diluted yolks coagulate between 180 and 185 degrees—both significantly lower temperatures than the boiling point of 212 degrees. Whisking the hot butterscotch mixture into the yolk mixture heated the pudding to about 185 degrees—plenty hot to properly thicken it but not so hot that the yolks overcooked.

heat accordingly), stirring frequently, until mixture is color of dark peanut butter, 12 to 16 minutes longer (caramel will register about 300 degrees and should have slight burnt smell).

2. Remove pan from heat; carefully pour ¼ cup cream into caramel mixture and swirl to incorporate (mixture will bubble and steam); let bubbling subside. Whisk vigorously and scrape corners of pan until mixture is completely smooth, at least 30 seconds. Return pan to medium heat and gradually whisk in remaining ¾ cup cream until smooth. Whisk in 2 cups milk until mixture is smooth, making sure to scrape corners and edges of pan to remove any remaining bits of caramel.

3. Meanwhile, microwave remaining ¼ cup milk until simmering, 30 to 45 seconds. Whisk egg yolks and cornstarch together in large bowl until smooth. Gradually whisk in hot milk until smooth; set aside (do not refrigerate).

4. Return saucepan to medium-high heat and bring mixture to full rolling boil, whisking frequently. Once mixture is boiling rapidly and beginning to climb toward top of pan, immediately pour into bowl with yolk mixture in 1 motion (do not add gradually). Whisk thoroughly for 10 to 15 seconds (mixture will thicken after a few seconds). Whisk in vanilla and rum.

Spray piece of parchment paper with vegetable oil spray and press on surface of pudding. Refrigerate until cold and set, at least 3 hours. Whisk pudding until smooth before serving.

RASPBERRY SORBET

WHY THIS RECIPE WORKS For a raspberry sorbet with a delicately icy yet smooth texture, we came up with a few tricks. First we super-chilled the base and used just the right ratio of sweeteners to water to ensure the finest-textured ice crystals possible. Swapping corn syrup for some of the sugar gave the sorbet a creamy texture without making it overly sweet. We also supplemented the berries' natural pectin to give the sorbet stability both in the freezer and out. Paying attention to visual cues ensured that we were churning the mixture just long enough to allow it to form ice crystals without incorporating too much air, which made it crumbly and dulled its flavor.

Sorbet has always been the neglected stepchild of homemade frozen desserts. This is a shame, because good sorbet can hold its own against ice cream any day.

RASPBERRY SORBET

A well-made batch is almost as creamy and smooth as its dairy-based relative, but rather than finishing with mouth-coating richness, it should be delicately icy and dissolve on the tongue, leaving behind an echo of clean, concentrated fruit flavor.

But delicacy is where most recipes get hung up. The majority of homemade sorbets have big, jagged ice crystals rather than super-fine ones and are so hard they're impossible to get out of the carton. I've also scooped plenty of versions that are crumbly, coarse, and dull and have watched seemingly stable sorbets melt into syrupy puddles within minutes of leaving the freezer.

Despite this long list of hazards, I was determined to figure out a way to pull off the perfect batch. For flavor, I was set on raspberry; not only is it a quintessential summer fruit, but the berries also freeze well, meaning I could make it any time of year.

Before I got to churning, I reviewed what I knew about sorbet. Regardless of how ripe, sweet, and juicy the fruit, freezing a puree of straight berries doesn't work. The relatively small amount of moisture in the fruit will freeze completely, and its crystals will be separated only by the berries' fibers. The result—a solid, impenetrable block—wouldn't be pretty.

To get sorbet with the ideal consistency—delicately icy, velvety smooth, and easily scoopable—adding both water and sugar is crucial. The two work in tandem. Some of the water freezes, which creates ice crystals. But because sugar depresses the freezing point of water, some of it will also remain liquid. This so-called "free" water lubricates the ice crystals, producing a smooth, scoopable texture. My challenge, then, would be to achieve just the right balance of water and sugar in the base.

With that in mind, I mixed up my first batch of the base in a blender using 4 cups of berries, ½ cup of water, and ¾ cup of sugar—which I hoped could sweeten the mixture just enough and provide exactly the right ratio of sugar to water. Once the mixture was smooth, I strained it and poured it into my ice cream machine; churned it for 30 minutes, until it froze to a soft-serve consistency; transferred it to a container; and put it in the freezer overnight. The next morning I summoned my colleagues for a taste. I wasn't expecting perfection on the first go-round, but from their frowns I could tell I was far from my goal. It wasn't the flavor that needed help. Though not rock hard, the sorbet was still too solid to scoop (even when thawed at room temperature for a while). Worse, it was as grainy as a granita.

To solve the hardness problem, I added more water to the mixture to create more free water. By the time I'd doubled the liquid, the sorbet was perfectly scoopable. But by solving the first problem I'd exaggerated the second, as the ice crystals were now larger and coarser than ever.

Fortunately, I had an idea to help minimize the size of the crystals: separating out a small amount of the base and freezing it separately, then adding it back into the rest. Our science editor explained to me that because the small portion would freeze much more rapidly than the whole batch, there wouldn't be enough time for large ice crystals to grow, and instead very small ice crystals would be formed. Then, when I added this frozen mix back to the rest of the base (which would have been chilled in the meantime), the tiny crystals would act as a catalyst, triggering a chain reaction that would very rapidly form equally small crystals in the bigger mix. I gave this a whirl here, freezing a small amount of the base before churning it together with the rest of the base. The difference was significant; everyone agreed that this latest batch was noticeably smoother. But it still hadn't achieved the velvety texture of professionally made sorbet.

One thing I hadn't yet tried was playing with the amount of sugar. Sugar reduces the tendency of ice crystals to grow large, thus contributing to smoother texture. The only problem was that, flavor-wise, I had the sugar right where I wanted it. Increasing it to 1 cup smoothed out the texture but made an achingly sweet dessert. That got me thinking of another trick we used in our ice cream recipe: swapping some of the sugar for corn syrup. Because corn syrup tastes less sweet than sugar, I could use more of it without oversweetening the sorbet.

I tried swapping in varying amounts of corn syrup for sugar. The more sugar I replaced with syrup, the softer and smoother the texture became. The winning batch contained ½ cup plus 2 tablespoons of sugar and ¼ cup of corn syrup and offered an ideal balance of sweetness, smoothness, and scoopability.

At last, the texture of the sorbet was ideal—at least, it was ideal straight out of the freezer. But once it sat at room temperature for even a few minutes, it began to melt into a soupy mess. The downside to depressing the freezing point of a frozen dessert is that the unfrozen water is free to move about and quickly leaks from the mixture, leaving the ice surrounded by syrupy puddles. Professional sorbet manufacturers get around this problem with stabilizers like guar gum and locust bean gum. These additives act like sponges, corralling the free water within a loose matrix so that it can remain unfrozen while still not flowing freely. I couldn't get my hands on either of those products, but I did have access to pectin, which can also act as a stabilizer. After testing with varying amounts of the powder, I learned that a mere teaspoon (bloomed first in the water) was enough to keep the sorbet from immediately puddling.

My sorbet was finally starting to come together, save for one nagging problem: The quality of the churned base was inconsistent. Every few batches, the mixture came out of the canister not with a soft-serve consistency but with a crumbly, fluffy texture and a noticeably duller berry flavor. Since some batches were coming out perfectly smooth and brightly flavored, I suspected that the problem was the result of my churning method and not the base itself. Was I under- or overchurning the sorbet?

I hadn't paid much attention to the churning time. Most ice cream and sorbet recipes I've made end with the same directive: "Churn according to manufacturer's instructions." But the more I thought about it, the more I realized that this vague set of instructions made no sense. Just as mixing times will vary for different types of cake batter, so, too, should the churning times be specific for different types of frozen desserts. I also thought some visual cues would be helpful.

With a timer and a thermometer at the ready, I poured several identical batches of my sorbet base into canisters and let the mixtures churn for increasing lengths of time, noting their temperatures and how their consistencies varied based on churning time.

The results were surprising: The longest-churned batch was the thickest coming out of the canister but also the most granular and snowlike after freezing. I'd assumed that, just as with ice cream, the longest possible stay in the machine would result in a smoother sorbet because the constant agitation would help prevent large ice crystals from forming after the move to the freezer, but this test proved me wrong. Instead, longer churning times seemed to give the free-water and ice crystal mixture more time to grow ever-larger ice crystals. In fact, the best batch came from a base that I stopped churning almost as soon as the mixture started to thicken up, right around 18 degrees and the 20-minute mark.

To look at this batch, you wouldn't have expected it to turn into a nicely dense, stable sorbet; at the point at which I stopped the machine, it had a loose, pourable consistency, like a milkshake, because less water was frozen. But after an overnight stint in the freezer, it set up perfectly. A little research explained the difference between the two frozen desserts: During churning, air gets incorporated in the mixture. However, unlike with ice cream, in which a certain amount of incorporated air contributes a pleasing lightness, that air renders sorbets loose and crumbly and dulls their flavor. This is because ice cream contains fat and protein, both of which act to stabilize the air bubbles. Sorbet, on the other hand, contains no cream. The upshot: a loose and crumbly, duller-tasting dessert that easily falls apart after overnight freezing.

To guarantee good results, I came away with a visual cue, which ensured that the sorbet would turn out dense and smooth no matter what ice cream machine was used: The color of the mixture began to lighten up considerably soon after it started to thicken, a sure sign that it was beginning to take on air and was in need of a transfer to the freezer.

My only remaining tasks were to punch up the berries' intensity—a pinch of salt did the trick—and dream up a few flavor variations. Fruity ruby port made for a natural pairing, as did bracing ginger and mint, and a healthy shot of lime juice made a tasty "rickey" version. With four recipes on file, I knew this sorbet formula would get me through a summer's worth of entertaining—and that this frozen dessert would no longer play second fiddle to a quart of ice cream.

—ANDREW JANJIGIAN, *Cook's Illustrated*

Raspberry Sorbet

MAKES 1 QUART

Super-chilling part of the sorbet base before transferring it to the ice cream machine will keep ice crystals to a minimum. If using a canister-style ice cream machine, be sure to freeze the empty canister for at least 24 hours and preferably 48 hours before churning. For self-refrigerating machines, prechill the canister by running the machine for 5 to 10 minutes before pouring in the sorbet mixture. Allow the sorbet to sit at room temperature for 5 minutes to soften before serving. Fresh or frozen berries may be used. If using frozen berries, thaw them before proceeding. Make certain that you use Sure-Jell engineered for low- or no-sugar recipes (packaged in a pink box) and not regular Sure-Jell (in a yellow box).

1 cup water

1 teaspoon Sure-Jell for Less or No Sugar
Needed Recipes

⅛ teaspoon salt

1¼ pounds (4 cups) raspberries

½ cup (3½ ounces) plus 2 tablespoons sugar

¼ cup light corn syrup

1. Combine water, Sure-Jell, and salt in medium saucepan. Heat over medium-high heat, stirring occasionally, until Sure-Jell is fully dissolved, about 5 minutes. Remove saucepan from heat and allow mixture to cool slightly, about 10 minutes.

2. Process raspberries, sugar, corn syrup, and water mixture in blender or food processor until smooth, about 30 seconds. Strain mixture through fine-mesh strainer, pressing on solids to extract as much liquid as possible. Transfer 1 cup of mixture to small bowl and place remaining mixture in large bowl. Cover both bowls with plastic wrap. Place large bowl in refrigerator and small bowl in freezer and cool completely, at least 4 hours or up to 24 hours. (Small bowl of base will freeze solid.)

3. Remove mixtures from refrigerator and freezer. Scrape frozen base from small bowl into large bowl of base. Stir occasionally until frozen base has fully dissolved. Transfer mixture to ice cream machine and churn until mixture has consistency of thick milkshake and color lightens, 15 to 25 minutes.

4. Transfer sorbet to airtight container, pressing firmly to remove any air pockets, and freeze until firm, at least 2 hours. Serve. (Sorbet can be frozen for up to 5 days.)

VARIATIONS

Raspberry-Port Sorbet

Substitute ruby port for water in step 1.

Raspberry Sorbet with Ginger and Mint

Substitute ginger beer for water in step 1. Add 2-inch piece peeled and thinly sliced ginger and ¼ cup mint leaves to blender with raspberries. Decrease amount of sugar to ½ cup.

Raspberry–Lime Rickey Sorbet

Reduce water to ¾ cup. Add 2 teaspoons grated lime zest and ¼ cup lime juice to blender with raspberries.

NOTES FROM THE TEST KITCHEN

THE ROAD TO PERFECT SORBET
We had to solve four problems before we arrived at a smooth, dense, scoopable, and stable sorbet.

PROBLEM 1: TOO HARD TO SCOOP
For sorbet that's soft enough to scoop, some water should freeze but some should remain liquid and "free" to flow between the ice crystals, providing the sensation of creaminess. Added water and sugar are critical. Water ensures that there's enough of it in the mix to remain free. Sugar aids the process by getting in the way of the water freezing.

PROBLEM 2: ICY, GRAINY TEXTURE
Big ice crystals turn sorbet grainy. Freezing the base as fast as possible is the antidote. First, it doesn't give the base time to form large crystals. Second, once small "seed" crystals get started, they trigger a chain reaction, continuously turning more unfrozen water into equally tiny crystals.

PROBLEM 3: CRUMBLY TEXTURE, DULL TASTE
Too much churning has a negative effect on the final texture of sorbet: Because the dessert has no fat or protein to stabilize the air bubbles incorporated during churning, longer churning times produce sorbets that are loose, crumbly, and dull-tasting. Churning just until the mixture reaches the consistency of a thick milkshake produces dense, flavorful sorbet.

PROBLEM 4: RAPID MELTING
Sorbet is prone to rapid melting once it is scooped and served. Commercial manufacturers stave off melting by incorporating ingredients like guar gum that trap some of the free water so it won't readily leak out at room temperature. Instead of those additives, we used gelatin and pectin.

THE BEST CHINOIS SIEVE
For straining stocks and sauces, we usually reach for a bowl-shaped fine-mesh strainer, but would a chinois, a conical French sieve with ultra-finely woven mesh, give smoother results? We pitted three chinois priced from $33.78 to $118 against our favorite fine-mesh strainer, straining pureed raspberries for sorbet and chicken stock. We learned that the difference in mesh gauge didn't matter. What the best conical sieves offered were capacity and stability.

Though it performed well, the round strainer was too shallow to strain all of the stock at once. The larger chinois could filter the entire batch in one pour and were stabilized by sturdy L-shaped hooks. Our pick, the **Winco Reinforced Extra Fine Mesh Bouillon Strainer**, $33.78, is comfortable, stable, and reasonably priced. Round strainers are still more versatile, but if you prepare large amounts of stock, jam, or sorbet, a roomy chinois makes the work much easier.

TEST KITCHEN RESOURCES

Every product tested may not be listed in these pages. Please visit CooksIllustrated.com to find complete listings and information on all products tested and reviewed.

BEST KITCHEN QUICK TIPS

QUICKER CHILLING

When you need to quickly chill a liquid—whether it's an ice cream base or a soup—recipes often instruct you to pour it into a metal bowl set in a larger bowl filled with ice water. Jennifer Hadley of Madison, Wis., has found a way to speed up the process: She pours the liquid into a metal Bundt pan and then places the Bundt pan in an ice bath. More of the liquid comes in contact with cold metal in a Bundt pan than in a bowl, so the temperature nosedives faster.

DIGITAL SHOPPING LIST

Instead of writing down the ingredients he needs for a particular magazine or cookbook recipe, Justin Keith of Boston, Mass., has a high-tech solution: He snaps a picture of the ingredient list with his smartphone. He can easily reference it at the market and is sure to grab exactly what he needs.

KEEPING OVEN MITTS WITHIN REACH

Shaneitra Johnson of Columbus, Ohio, could never find her oven mitt or dish towel when she needed it, so she devised a simple way to keep it in sight: Hang the mitt or towel from a shower curtain hook placed on the oven door's handle.

FLATTENING OUT PARCHMENT PAPER

Parchment paper is a kitchen workhorse, but it comes with one drawback: It curls into a scroll the second it is cut from the roll. Lloyd Lehn of Annandale, Va., has a simple solution.

1. Lightly crumple the sheet of parchment paper.

2. Unfold the parchment and smooth it flat. The folds will help keep it from curling.

NO MORE SOOTY HANDS

Filling a chimney starter with a precise amount of charcoal can be a messy enterprise, but David Detlef of Alexandria, Va., has a handy solution: He repurposes the long plastic bags in which his newspapers are delivered, using them as mitts. The bags keep his hands clean as he reaches into the sack to grab handfuls of coal.

INSTANT WINE BUCKET

When he needed a way to quickly chill a bottle of white wine at a picnic, Tim Farrell of Bayside, N.Y., improvised by cutting the top off an empty plastic 2-liter soda bottle, filling it about one-third of the way with ice and water, and placing the wine bottle inside. The wine was crisp and cool in minutes.

PRESERVING LEFTOVER WINE

Allowing red wine to "breathe," or briefly exposing it to air, can enhance its flavor. But prolonged exposure causes it to overoxidize and take on an unpleasant, vinegar-like taste. Gadgets like vacuum pumps minimize air exposure to preserve the flavor of leftovers, but Andrea Pepicelli of Cumberland, R.I., gets the job done with this homemade solution: Completely fill an airtight container, like a small Mason jar or an empty water bottle, with leftover wine (the wine must reach the very top of the container to eliminate all air). Screw on the top and refrigerate for up to one week.

A GRATE IDEA FOR HARD BROWN SUGAR

When Gloria Lynch of Colorado Springs, Colo., finds that her brown sugar has turned from granular into a solid brick, she pulls out her grater. Running the block along the tool's sharp holes quickly breaks down the hard sugar into a measurable state.

LABEL MAKER

Lauren Threadgill of Augusta, Ga., is an avid baker and stocks multiple kinds of flour in clear plastic storage containers. To keep track of what's inside, she came up with a crafty solution: She cuts the labels out of the flour bags and tapes them to the outsides of the containers.

SMARTER STRAWBERRY HULLING

Natalie Burks of Elkhart, Tex., found that the serrated tip of a grapefruit spoon is a better tool than a paring knife for removing the green crown from strawberries. It's faster, easier to maneuver, and wastes less fruit.

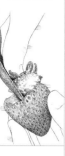

LESS PAIN, BETTER STRAIN

Laurel Damashek of Belmont, Mass., has learned that pushing any type of food through a fine-mesh strainer goes much faster—and requires less elbow grease—when the round bottom of a ladle is used instead of a spatula or wooden spoon. Simply press the bowl of the ladle, which follows the curve of the strainer, against the solids in a circular motion.

SAVING CAKE

Noreen Awan of Seattle, Wash., uses this method to prevent leftover layer cake from staling: She arranges a folded piece of parchment paper to fit over the exposed edges. Pressing the parchment onto the cake lessens air exposure and keeps the next slices as good as the first.

PREMARKED BUTTER MEASUREMENTS

It's a pain when the butter wrapper or box with measurement markings gets discarded before a stick of butter is used up, leaving you guessing just how to measure a tablespoon of solid butter. Erica Wilson of Mount Holly, N.J., avoids this quandary by lightly marking all 8 tablespoons with a knife before unwrapping each stick of butter, so she's always able to easily measure out the amount that she needs.

A COOL TRICK FOR ROLLING OUT PIE DOUGH

Temperamental pie and tart doughs can't take the heat: In order to bake up flaky, the fat in the dough must stay cool, which is problematic, since working the dough warms it up. Rebecca Webber of Cambridge, Mass., uses this method to keep it cool.

1. While the dough is chilling in the refrigerator, fill 2 gallon-size zipper-lock bags halfway with ice and lay them on the rolling surface for 20 minutes.

2. When ready to roll out the dough, remove the ice bags and wipe any condensation from the surface. Work quickly with the dough in a cold space as directed in the recipe.

CONTAINING LIDS

Kathleen Sayce of Nahcotta, Wash., borrowed from her office to organize the disarray of plastic lids in her kitchen cabinet. A magazine box keeps reusable container lids in one place for easy retrieval. (Depending on the height of your cabinet, you may have to lay the box flat on its long side.)

A STOVETOP KETTLE GRILL

A grill pan is a good alternative when outdoor grilling is not an option, but it tends to create messy grease splatters and imparts minimal smoke to the food. Casey Grant of Covington, Ky., inverts a disposable aluminum roasting pan over the top of his grill pan to catch splatters. The technique also concentrates smoky flavor in whatever food he is grilling, much like the closed lid of a kettle grill.

BEST KITCHEN QUICK TIPS

FRIDGE TRIAGE BOX

Yuka Yoneda of Flushing, N.Y., hated throwing away expired food that had been pushed to the back of her refrigerator and forgotten. Her solution: Put anything in danger of going bad into a container on the top shelf. Now every time she opens the door, she's reminded of what should be consumed first.

CREATING PERFECT CHOCOLATE CURLS

After producing nothing but a pile of broken shards when she tried to create perfectly spiraled chocolate curls, Joann Sherman of Garrison, N.Y., used to think that the decoration could be created only by pastry chefs. Then she learned the secret: warming the chocolate.

1. Wrap a chocolate bar in plastic wrap and then rub the palm of your hand against the edge of the bar until it is warm.

2. To make curls, remove the plastic and run a vegetable peeler along the chocolate bar toward you. Repeat the warming process as needed.

COOLING MELTED BUTTER MORE QUICKLY

When Jen Chandler-Ward of Somerville, Mass., is preparing a recipe that calls for melted butter cooled to room temperature, she speeds up the process with this method: Melt three-quarters of the desired amount of butter on the stovetop or in the microwave. Off the heat, whisk the remaining one-quarter of the cold butter into the melted butter. The unmelted portion will help lower the warm butter's temperature in less time than it takes to heat and then cool the full amount.

A PIE-MEASURING METHOD

For Iva Palacios Konieczka of Charlestown, Mass., the holidays mean lots of pie making. Rather than pulling out a ruler every time she rolls out a crust, she uses masking tape to create a 12-inch square on her countertop to use as a guide for rolling out a 12-inch crust.

GETTING A GRIP ON MINI MUFFIN TINS

Miniature muffin tins are usually fitted with a rim that is too tiny to grasp with bulky oven mitts. Jennifer Chou of Berkeley, Calif., no longer struggles because she leaves one corner cup empty. Now she has a place to insert her thumb, allowing her to remove the tin without getting burned.

SOG-FREE SALAD ON THE GO

Bringing a salad for lunch usually means packing a separate container of dressing, as even the hardiest pre-dressed greens quickly turn soggy. Joanne Kramer of Cleveland, Ill., takes a multilayered approach to fitting everything in one container: She adds the dressing to the bottom of the container; covers it with chopped vegetables, fruit, beans, and cheese; and places the greens on top. To dress the salad, she simply shakes the container.

THUMBS-UP COOKIE SHAPING

While thumbprint cookies get their name from the digit that's used to make the jam-filled indentation, Linda George of Twain Harte, Calif., prefers to use a clean rubber wine cork. It creates a perfect circle every time and keeps her hands clean.

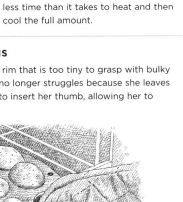

SPRING CLEANING

Kitchen and household spray cleaners can take up valuable cabinet space under your kitchen sink. Rachel Paris-Lambert of East Seattle, Wash., takes her organization to the next level by installing a spring-tension curtain rod near the top of her cabinet. Spray bottles can then hang by their trigger levers, leaving plenty of room underneath for other supplies.

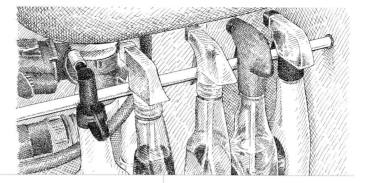

TIDY BREAKFAST SANDWICHES

Metal egg rings confine fried eggs to a circular shape—perfect for breakfast sandwiches served on an English muffin or a bagel. Looking for a no-gadget solution that delivered the same neat results, Elizabeth Fallon of Coventry, R.I., turned to her crisper drawer.

1. Slice a ring from a cored, seeded bell pepper. (Alternatively, an onion also works well.)

2. Melt a pat of butter in a nonstick skillet and then place a pepper ring in the pan. Crack an egg inside the ring and cook to the desired doneness.

A MOUSE (PAD) IN THE KITCHEN

When Mike Meyers of Macclenny, Fla., is having a difficult time grasping a hard-to-open jar lid, he grabs his computer mouse pad. Its rubber bottom—engineered to anchor it to a desk—creates a good grip that helps budge stubborn lids.

POP SECRET SEASONING

Sprinkling popcorn with table salt usually results in a pile of salt at the bottom of the bowl—and a bland snack. Clingy superfine popcorn salt is available for purchase, but Pam Sansbury of Midwest City, Okla., has found that it's easy to make your own.

1. Process salt in a spice grinder for about 30 seconds (its texture should be very fine). Pour the salt into an empty spice jar fitted with a perforated shaker lid.

2. Season the popcorn in a very large bowl, carefully stirring to evenly distribute the salt.

USING YOUR NOODLE

Rather than purchase the special scalloped-edge square cookie cutter called for in a recipe, Stephanie Keller of Glen Rock, N.J., used the curved edge of a dry lasagna noodle to cut her rolled-out cookie dough. In fact, it was better than a cookie cutter because the long noodle could cut more dough at once, and without the wasted in-between scraps left by a stamp-style cutter.

A SLICK SOLUTION FOR STICKY DOUGH

Working with high-hydration bread doughs that are extremely wet can be messy, especially when it comes to prying the sticky mass from the mixing bowl or food processor. Brenda Rodman of Springfield, Mass., has found that spraying both sides of a spatula with vegetable oil spray allows her to effortlessly scrape the dough from the container.

ALL ABOUT TOMATOES

Here's our guide to making the most of those luscious in-season tomatoes, as well as what the supermarket has to offer the rest of the year.

BUYING THE BEST

Even buying tomatoes at the height of summer won't guarantee that you're getting juicy, flavorful fruit, but keeping these guidelines in mind will help.

CHOOSE LOCALLY GROWN

The most important way to help ensure a flavorful tomato is to buy a locally grown one. Why? First, the less distance the tomato has to travel, the riper it can be when it's picked. Second, commercial high-yield production can strain the tomato plant, resulting in tomatoes without enough sugars and other flavor compounds. Third, to withstand machine harvesting and long-distance transport, commercial varieties are engineered to be sturdier with thicker walls and less of the flavorful jelly.

SUPERMARKET STANDOUTS

When we can't get tomatoes at our local farm market, we look for the following varieties at the grocery store.

KUMATO: These startlingly green-brown European imports have more fructose than conventional tomatoes, which makes them taste sweeter. Tasters also found their texture meatier.

UGLYRIPE: These knobby-looking fruits are left on the living vine longer than most other commercial varieties, which explains why our tasters found them sweeter and juicier. Because of their delicateness, each fruit is individually packed in protective foam netting.

TRY AN HEIRLOOM

Grown for decades from naturally pollinated plants and seeds that haven't been hybridized (unlike commercial varieties), heirlooms are some of the best local tomatoes you'll find.

LOOKS AREN'T EVERYTHING

Oddly shaped tomatoes are fine; only commercial tomatoes are bred to be symmetrical. Even cracked skin is OK, but avoid tomatoes that are overly soft or leaking juice. Choose tomatoes that smell fruity and feel heavy.

IN THE CAN

Canned tomatoes are better stand-ins than bland, off-season fresh options. For a chunkier texture in your finished dish, choose diced tomatoes—they contain more calcium chloride (which maintains firmness) than whole tomatoes. Whole and crushed give a smoother texture when cooked.

TEST KITCHEN FAVORITES

Whole	Muir Glen Organic
Crushed	Tuttorosso
Diced	Hunt's
Puree	Muir Glen Organic
Juice	Campbell's
Paste	Goya

STORAGE SMARTS

DON'T REFRIGERATE

Cold damages enzymes that produce flavor compounds and ruins texture by rupturing tomato cells, turning the flesh mealy. Even cut tomatoes should be kept at room temperature, tightly wrapped in plastic wrap, and used within a few days.

FREEZE FOR THE OFF-SEASON

If you have a glut of end-of-summer tomatoes, core them and freeze them whole in freezer storage bags for later use in sauces. Freezing preserves their flavor better than canning. (That method's high temperature destroys tomato flavor even more than cold does.)

STORE STEM END DOWN

Place unwashed tomatoes stem end down at room temperature. We've found that this prevents moisture from escaping and bacteria from entering through the scar, prolonging shelf life. If the vine is still attached, though, leave it on and store tomatoes stem end up.

BAG 'EM WITH A BANANA

If you have underripe tomatoes, store them in a paper bag with a banana or an apple, both of which naturally emit the ethylene gas that hastens ripening.

DON'T BE FOOLED BY "VINE RIPENED"

The term only indicates that the tomatoes were picked when 10 percent of the skin started to turn from green to red. Since most of their maturation happens off the vine, they'll never taste as good as naturally ripened fruit. That said, we prefer them to regular supermarket tomatoes, which are picked when fully green and treated with ethylene gas to develop texture and color.

ANATOMY OF A FLAVORFUL TOMATO

The best-tasting tomatoes tend to have thin walls, which leaves more room for the most flavorful part of the tomato: the jelly that surrounds the seeds, which is three times richer in savory glutamates than the flesh is. Some sources recommend removing the seeds to avoid their bitter taste, but we haven't found that they negatively affect flavor. If you do choose to remove the seeds for aesthetic reasons, strain them and reserve the jelly.

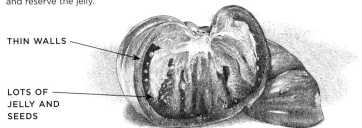

THIN WALLS

LOTS OF JELLY AND SEEDS

PREPPING TECHNIQUES

BLANCHING AND PEELING

If you don't own a serrated peeler, blanching is the easiest way to remove tomato skins. Scoring an X into the bottom of the tomato (core it first) causes the skin to curl back in the boiling water, giving you an easy place to begin peeling after blanching.

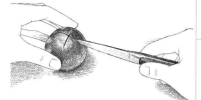

1. Using paring knife, score X in bottom of tomato.

2. Blanch in boiling water for 15 to 30 seconds (riper tomatoes will need less time). Transfer tomatoes to ice-water bath.

3. Grab curled skin from bottom and strip off.

CORING

Inserting the tip of a sharp paring knife at an angle about 1 inch into the tomato just outside of the core allows you to free the tough stem and minimize the flesh that's cut away.

GRATING

When you need to crush only a couple of tomatoes, grate halved, unpeeled tomatoes on the large holes of a grater rather than opening a whole can.

CHOPPING

Place round tomatoes cored side down to create a stable surface. (For a plum tomato, first slice off one long side to make a stable surface.) Slice, stack slices in pairs, and cut into strips. Turn the stack and slice crosswise.

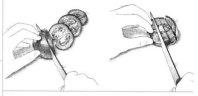

EASY PEELING

We found that the Messermeister Pro-Touch Serrated Peeler ($10) cleanly pulls skin off tomatoes, with no need for blanching.

QUICK FRESH TOMATO SAUCE

Makes 2 cups; enough for 1 pound pasta

In-season, locally grown tomatoes are essential for this recipe. To keep the garlic from burning, start the olive oil and garlic in a cold pan.

- **3 tablespoons extra-virgin olive oil**
- **4 garlic cloves, minced**
- **2 pounds tomatoes, cored, peeled, and cut into ¾-inch chunks**
  Salt and pepper
- **¼ cup chopped fresh basil**

Stir oil and garlic together in large skillet. Turn heat to medium and cook until garlic is sizzling and fragrant, about 2 minutes. Stir in tomatoes and ½ teaspoon salt. Bring to rapid simmer and cook, stirring occasionally, reducing heat if sauce begins to stick to bottom of pan, until thickened and chunky, 15 to 20 minutes. Remove from heat. Stir in basil and season with salt and pepper to taste.

COOKING TIPS

CHOOSE PLUMS

Meaty plum (or Roma) tomatoes contain less moisture than other varieties so are best for sauces, stews, and canning.

SALT TOMATOES FOR UNCOOKED RECIPES

For raw-tomato applications like salsa, it's best to salt the chopped tomatoes, let them stand for 30 to 60 minutes, and pat them dry before using. The salt not only forces flavor compounds to separate from proteins, making them accessible to our tastebuds for a fuller and more complex flavor, but also rids the fruit of excess moisture.

DON'T COOK TOMATOES IN REACTIVE METAL

Tomato acid reacts with cast iron, uncoated copper, and aluminum, leaving food tasting harsh and metallic and damaging the surface of the cookware.

DON'T ADD TOMATOES TOO EARLY

The acid that tomatoes release during cooking can prevent other foods from breaking down. To ensure that all the elements achieve the proper texture, ingredients like onions and beans should be fully softened before the tomatoes are introduced.

TAME TARTNESS WITH SUGAR

Tomatoes vary in sweetness, so it's important to taste dishes during cooking and adjust the seasoning as necessary. Adding a pinch of sugar can tone down acidity and enhance flavor from proteins.

BEYOND RICE: A GUIDE TO OTHER GRAINS

These days, supermarkets offer an entire universe of grains—and with the right method they're as easy to cook, and as versatile, as rice. Here are six of our favorites.

BARLEY

Best known in this country as a staple used in soups, this high-fiber grain's nutty, subtly sweet flavor makes it an ideal accompaniment to meat, chicken, and fish. Both hulled and pearl barley (the most widely available varieties) are stripped of their tough outer covering, but we prefer quicker-cooking pearl barley, which has been polished to remove the bran layer as well.

KNOWING WHEN IT'S DONE: The grains will be softened and plump but still somewhat firm in the center.

TIP: For a hearty alternative to risotto, substitute pearl barley for the Arborio rice typically used. Like rice, the barley will release starches when stirred, creating a creamy consistency. Be sure to add extra liquid since barley takes a bit longer to cook.

BULGUR

Bulgur is made from wheat berries that have been steamed or boiled and ground into fine, medium, coarse, or very coarse grain. Don't confuse it with cracked wheat, which is not parcooked.

KNOWING WHEN IT'S DONE: The grains will be somewhat tender but still firm.

TIP: Instead of simmering it in water, we often reconstitute fine- or medium-grain bulgur by soaking it in water flavored with lemon, lime, or tomato juice (use ⅔ cup of liquid for 1 cup of bulgur and soak for 60 to 90 minutes).

FARRO

A favorite ingredient in Tuscan cuisine, these hulled whole-wheat kernels boast a sweet, nutty flavor and a chewy bite. In Italy, the grain is available in three sizes—*farro piccolo*, *farro medio*, and *farro grande*—but the midsize type is most common in the United States.

KNOWING WHEN IT'S DONE: The grains will be tender but have a slight chew, similar to al dente pasta.

TIP: Although we usually turn to the absorption method for quicker-cooking grains, farro takes better to the pasta method because the abundance of water cooks the grains more evenly.

MILLET

The mellow corn flavor and fine texture of these tiny seeds make them extremely versatile in both savory and sweet applications, including flatbreads, polenta-like puddings, and pan-fried cakes. We particularly like them in pilafs or even just mixed with a pat of butter.

KNOWING WHEN IT'S DONE: All of the cooking liquid will be absorbed and the grains will be fully tender.

TIP: Slightly overcooking millet causes the seeds to burst and release starch, creating a creamy consistency that makes this grain ideal for breakfast porridge.

QUINOA

Though actually a seed, quinoa is often referred to as a "supergrain" because it's a nutritionally complete protein. We love the pinhead-size seeds (which can be white, red, black, or purple) for their faint crunch and mineral taste.

KNOWING WHEN IT'S DONE: The grains will unfurl and expand to about three times their size.

TIP: Toast quinoa in a dry (no oil or butter) pot before adding water; we've found that toasting it in fat gives the grain a slightly bitter flavor.

WHEAT BERRIES

These are not berries at all but whole, husked wheat kernels with a rich, earthy flavor and firm chew. Because they're unprocessed, they remain firm, smooth, and distinct when cooked, which makes them great for salads.

KNOWING WHEN IT'S DONE: The grains will be softened but still quite chewy, smooth, and separate.

TIP: Though not typically done when boiling grains, we toast wheat berries in oil before adding them to the water, which brings out their nutty flavor.

MIND THE STORAGE

To prevent open boxes and bags of grains from spoiling in the pantry, store them in airtight containers and, if you have space, in the freezer. This is especially important for whole grains like wheat berries that turn rancid with oxidation.

TIMES, METHODS, AND MEASUREMENTS

1 CUP RAW	BARLEY	BULGUR	FARRO	MILLET	QUINOA	WHEAT BERRIES
Method(s)	Pasta	Absorption	Pasta	Absorption/Pilaf	Absorption/Pilaf	Pasta
Water	4 quarts	1 cup	4 quarts	2¼ cups	1 cup	4 quarts
Time	20–25 min	13–18 min	15–20 min	25–30 min	16–18 min	1 hour
Yield	3½–4 cups	2¼ cups	3 cups	2¼ cups	2¾ cups	3 cups

THREE COOKING METHODS

Most grains not only follow the same familiar cooking methods as rice but are actually more forgiving because they don't break down and turn mushy as easily. Most grains should be rinsed and spread out on a towel-lined baking sheet to dry before cooking to remove excess starch, detritus, or bitter coatings.

ABSORPTION

The grains are simmered slowly in a measured quantity of liquid until tender.

BEST FOR: Tender grains like bulgur, millet, and quinoa

1. Combine 1 cup grains, water, and ½ teaspoon salt in saucepan.

2. Bring mixture to simmer, then reduce heat to low, cover, and simmer until grains are tender and liquid is absorbed. Off heat, let sit, covered, for 10 minutes. Fluff with fork and serve.

TIP: A clean dish towel, placed between the pot and the lid while the cooked grains rest off the heat, will absorb excess moisture and prevent the grains from turning gummy.

PILAF

In this variation on the absorption method, the grains are toasted first to impart a nutty flavor.

BEST FOR: Tender grains like millet and quinoa

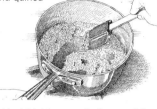

1. Heat 1 tablespoon butter or oil in saucepan over medium-high heat until shimmering. Add 1 cup grains and toast until lightly golden and fragrant, about 3 minutes. Add ½ teaspoon salt and water.

2. Bring mixture to simmer, then reduce heat to low, cover, and simmer until grains are tender and liquid is absorbed. Off heat, let sit, covered, for 10 minutes. Fluff with fork and serve.

TIP: For a more complex-tasting pilaf, sauté spices and aromatics like onions and garlic before adding the grains, swap in chicken broth for the water, and stir in fresh chopped herbs before serving.

PASTA

The grains are cooked like pasta in an abundant quantity of boiling water.

BEST FOR: Firm grains like barley, farro, and wheat berries

1. Bring 4 quarts water to boil in Dutch oven. Stir in 1 cup grains and 1 tablespoon salt. Return to boil, reduce heat, and simmer until grains are tender.

2. Drain in strainer set in sink. Let sit in strainer for 5 minutes before using (or pat dry with paper towel) to remove any excess moisture.

TIP: To quickly cool down boiled grains for a cold salad, rinse them with cold water while they are in the strainer.

SPEEDING UP THE PROCESS

The earthy flavor and chew of firm grains like wheat berries (and others like rye berries, spelt, and kamut) make them ideal for side dishes, but their cooking time (at least 1 hour) is an obstacle. Soaking overnight or adding baking soda to the cooking water will cut down the cooking time. (We don't recommend soaking or adding baking soda to grains cooked according to the absorption or the pilaf method; these shortcuts will throw off the amount of measured water the grains absorb.)

SOAK OVERNIGHT

Covering the grains with water for 8 hours (for safety, store them in the refrigerator) will shave 10 to 20 minutes off their cooking times—and ensure that they cook more evenly. Drain the grains before adding the cooking water.

ADD BAKING SODA

Adding ½ teaspoon of baking soda to 4 quarts of water will speed the grains' cooking time by 5 to 10 minutes.

MAKE AHEAD AND FREEZE

All types of cooked grains freeze well for at least three months, so making a large batch to freeze in smaller portions is a timesaver.

1. Place 2 cups cooled grains in zipper-lock bag. Lay bag flat and press out air. (To save space, freeze bags flat and stack once frozen.)

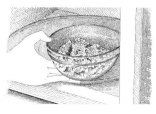

2. To warm, transfer frozen grains to bowl and microwave until grains are hot, 2 to 3 minutes.

COMPLETE GUIDE TO GRILL ROASTING

The oven isn't your only option for roasting meat. For cuts that cook over moderate heat, the grill works just as well—if not better. Here's how to do it right.

TURN YOUR GRILL INTO AN OVEN

Building a moderate, indirect fire and covering the grill turns it into an outdoor oven best for large, tender cuts like prime rib, whole chicken, and pork loin.

VENTING HELPS

Adjusting the vents on the lid and bottom of a charcoal grill helps regulate the heat. We leave the vents partially closed, which prevents the coals from burning too fast and helps the grill retain heat.

CATCHALL FOR DRIPS

When grill-roasting fatty cuts, we place a disposable aluminum roasting pan beneath the meat to catch drippings.

BRIQUETTES DO IT BETTER

We like natural hardwood charcoal for grilling, but it's not the best choice for grill roasting. Though both hardwood charcoal and briquettes burn fast and hot for the first 30 minutes, we've found that hardwood then abruptly turns to ash while the briquettes keep going, taking hours to fall below 250 degrees.

SMOKING PERMITTED—AND ENCOURAGED

If you'd like, add a couple of soaked wood chunks or a packet of aluminum foil–wrapped chips to the fire to infuse the meat with smoke flavor.

BUILDING THE FIRE

To create indirect heat on a charcoal or gas grill, we use one of two fire setups: banked or split. Both setups create a hot zone and a cool zone.

BANKED CHARCOAL FIRE

All of the coals are piled on one side of the grill, creating a long-lasting fire with a hotter side and a cooler side. Cuts with more intramuscular fat (like prime rib) or those that benefit from a deeply browned crust (like beef tenderloin) can be quickly seared over the heat to create flavorful browning and then transferred to the cooler side to finish cooking.

GAS GRILL SETUP

Preheat the grill and then leave the primary burner on high, or as directed in the recipe; turn off the other burners and place the food on the cooler side of the grill.

TIP: Rotate the food during cooking so the side that starts out closest to the fire doesn't cook too quickly.

SPLIT CHARCOAL FIRE

Coals are piled on either side of the kettle, creating a cool, evenly heated area in the middle; there's no need for rotating the food. Since the two hot areas have fewer coals that burn out faster than coals banked to one side, the setup is ideal for quicker-cooking items, such as whole chickens, that don't need to be seared.

TIP: The coals should be piled high against the side of the grill to form tall but narrow piles; with wider piles, the cool spot in the middle won't be large enough to protect the food from direct heat.

GAS GRILL SETUP

A split fire only works on gas grills with at least three burners, so we typically don't call for this setup in recipes tailored for gas. If your grill does have the requisite burners and configuration, after preheating, turn the center burner off and leave the end burners on. Cook the food over the turned-off burner.

FAVORITE CUTS AND HOW TO HANDLE THEM

For the most well-seasoned, juicy results, we recommend salting or brining these grill-roasting go-tos. Salting is best for cuts that are already relatively moist and well marbled; because it introduces moisture to the meat, brining provides added insurance against drying out for leaner cuts. When salting, use 1 teaspoon of kosher salt per pound of meat; for brining, use ¼ cup of table salt per 2 quarts of water (for a whole chicken, use ½ cup of table salt).

CUT	BRINE/SALT TIME	TYPICAL FIRE	COMMENTS
Top Sirloin Roast (3 to 4 pounds)	Salt 6 to 24 hours	Banked	A lengthy exposure to salt helps tenderize this inexpensive, exceptionally beefy roast.
Beef Tenderloin (6 pounds)	Salt 6 to 24 hours	Banked	Adding a little smoke to the fire will give this mild-tasting roast a flavor boost.
Prime Rib (7 pounds)	Salt 6 to 24 hours	Banked	When trimming, leave about a ¼-inch-thick layer of fat to baste the meat and prevent it from drying out.
Whole Chicken (3½ to 4 pounds)	Salt 6 to 24 hours or brine ½ to 1 hour	Split	Start the bird breast side down to allow the grill marks to fade and the skin to brown more evenly.
Whole Turkey (12 to 14 pounds)	Salt 24 to 48 hours or brine 6 to 12 hours	Split	Birds larger than 14 pounds risk burning before the interior is cooked through. Propping up the bird on a V-rack helps prevent scorching.
Turkey Breast (5 to 7 pounds)	Salt 6 to 24 hours or brine 3 to 6 hours	Banked	Look for breasts smaller than 7 pounds, which will cook through by the time the fire burns out.
Boneless Pork Loin (2½ to 3 pounds)	Salt 6 to 24 hours or brine 1½ to 2 hours	Split	To prevent drying out, look for roasts with at least a ⅛-inch-thick layer of fat on one side.
Bone-In Pork Roast (4 to 5 pounds)	Salt 6 to 24 hours	Banked	Ask your butcher to remove the tip of the chine bone and cut the remainder between the ribs for easy carving.

THREE KEYS TO THE BEST RESULTS

USE A THERMOMETER

Since the type of grill and even the weather can affect cooking times, the only way to ensure proper doneness is to take the meat's temperature. We highly recommend the instant-read Thermoworks Splash-Proof Super-Fast Thermapen ($89) and the Taylor Instruments Wireless Remote Thermometer ($21.95).

RACK IT UP

To protect the bottom crust from turning soggy as the meat rests, set the roast on a wire rack as it cools.

DON'T RUSH THE REST

Resting meat for at least 20 minutes (or as long as 40 minutes for very large roasts) after cooking helps it hold on to precious juices. Want proof? Four-pound pork roasts cooked at 400 degrees that we sliced immediately after cooking shed an average of 10 tablespoons of liquid, while meat rested for 40 minutes lost an average of just 2 teaspoons.

IF YOU WANT SMOKE

While charcoal will infuse a little smokiness into grill-roasted meat (gas adds none), adding wood chunks or chips to the fire is the only way to get a real boost of smoke.

CHIPS OR CHUNKS?

Chips work on charcoal and gas grills, but use chunks only on a charcoal grill. They must sit on a pile of lit coals to smoke.

WRAP CHIPS IN FOIL

Sealing chips in a foil packet with slits prevents them from igniting while allowing smoke to escape. On a gas grill, place the packet directly on top of the primary burner; on a kettle, put it directly on the lit charcoal.

PICK A GOOD WOOD

Widely available hickory is our standard. For food that isn't heavily spiced, we also like apple and cherry wood. Avoid mesquite, which can impart an acrid flavor.

GOOD SOAK = MORE SMOKE

Soaking chunks in cold water for 1 hour before use prevents them from igniting over the coals and allows them to smolder slowly. (Wood chips are sometimes soaked, sometimes not, depending on how quickly they're meant to ignite.)

TIP: For instant soaked chunks, soak wood chunks ahead of time for 1 hour, drain, seal in a zipper-lock bag, and freeze. When ready to cook, place the frozen chunks on the grill, where they'll defrost quickly.

THE ESSENTIAL GUIDE TO KNIFE CARE

Knives are vital kitchen workhorses, and it's important to keep them sharp. But what does that mean? How do you accomplish it? What should you *not* believe?

OUR FAVORITE KNIVES

VICTORINOX FIBROX 8-INCH CHEF'S KNIFE ($24.95)

This lightweight, easily maneuverable knife can outperform heavier, more expensive blades.

WÜSTHOF CLASSIC 10-INCH BREAD KNIFE ($109.95)

The uniform, moderately sized pointed serrations on this knife excelled at slicing through food quickly and easily.

WÜSTHOF CLASSIC WITH PETEC 3½-INCH PARING KNIFE ($39.95)

This knife is nimble and precise with its thin, slightly curved blade, pointed tip, and comfortable grip.

VICTORINOX FIBROX 12-INCH GRANTON EDGE SLICING KNIFE ($39.95)

This knife's tapered, scalloped 12-inch blade helps prevent sticking. It's perfect for slicing large cuts of meat.

MASAMOTO VG-10 GYUTOU ($180)

This hybrid knife has a slim, sharp tip and an acutely tapered blade, which makes it feel especially light as well as slightly flexible.

KEEPING KNIVES CLEAN

We recommend cleaning knives with a sponge, hot water, and soap. Scrub pads can eventually damage the blade's finish. Avoid the dishwasher: The knocking around can damage the edges, as can the corrosive nature of dishwasher detergent. If you have a carbon steel knife, be sure to dry it carefully or it will rust and blacken.

UNDERSTANDING DEGREES OF DULLNESS

It doesn't take months or weeks for a knife to lose its sharpness. Even a few minutes of cutting can cause the blade to feel slightly dull. That said, a knife that feels only a little dull probably does not need to be sharpened. The edge of a slightly dull knife is usually just misaligned and merely needs to be repositioned with a honing steel. A truly dull knife has an edge that is rounded and worn down and needs a sharpener to restore the edge.

SHARP
A sharp knife holds a 20-degree angle on each side of the edge.

SLIGHTLY DULL
The misaligned edge of a slightly dull knife is easily fixed with a steel.

VERY DULL
A very dull, worn-down knife needs a sharpener to restore the edge.

HOW TO TELL IF YOUR KNIFE IS SHARP

In the test kitchen, we use a very simple test to see if knives need to be honed or sharpened: the paper test. Hold a sheet of paper by one end and drag your knife, from heel to tip, across it. If the knife snags or fails to cut the paper, it needs to be honed or sharpened. Try honing first. If the knife still fails the test, run it through a sharpener.

GOOD OPTIONS FOR KNIFE STORAGE

If you store your knives loose in a drawer, you're putting the sharp edge of your blades—not to mention your fingers—in danger.

KNIFE GUARD

The **Victorinox 8- to 10-Inch BladeSafe Knife Guard** ($5.95) is a wide polypropylene case that securely covers a variety of chef's, slicing, and paring knives.

UNIVERSAL KNIFE BLOCK

The **Bodum Bistro Universal Knife Block** ($49.95) boasts a "slotless" frame filled with a nest of plastic rods to accommodate any arsenal of cutlery and holds knives in a compact footprint.

MAGNETIC KNIFE STRIP

The **Messermeister Bamboo Knife Magnet** ($69.99) is a wall-mounted magnetic knife strip that offers ample room to store knives without demanding drawer or counter space. It can accommodate even the longest knives.

DON'T BELIEVE THESE COMMON SHARPENING MYTHS

MYTH: Honing steels sharpen your knives.

TRUTH: These rods merely straighten the cutting edge. As a knife is used, the cutting edge tends to bend and fold over slightly, giving the perception of a less sharp knife. Running the edge of a knife across a steel straightens the edge, making the knife perform better. A knife sharpener, on the other hand, actually removes metal from the blade's edge, creating a new surface for cutting.

MYTH: For a truly sharp knife, you need to use a whetstone.

TRUTH: A whetstone is just one way to return a factory edge to a knife. A sharpening stone, or whetstone, is an abrasive block that removes metal from a knife's blade to re-create its sharp edge. If you know how to use it, a whetstone can be a very effective tool. However, using one is a specialized skill that takes a good deal of time and practice to do properly. And so if you don't know how to use a whetstone, it can do more harm than good.

MYTH: Electric sharpeners are better than manual ones.

TRUTH: A good manual sharpener can be as effective as an electric model. When we pitted our favorite electric sharpener against our top manual model, we found that the manual sharpener was every bit as good as the electric one when it came to restoring a worn blade. Nicked or badly damaged knives were another story. Manual sharpeners take off less metal than electric ones and simply can't remove enough to restore a proper edge to really damaged blades. In such cases, an electric sharpener is the better choice.

MYTH: You can't sharpen a serrated knife at home.

TRUTH: You can—but only with a manual sharpener. Though serrated-specific sharpeners do exist, we've found them to be disappointing. And electric sharpeners don't do enough: Their spinning wheels sharpen merely the edges and tips of the serrations, not the valleys between these tips. But our favorite manual sharpener uses a V-shaped tungsten carbide blade that can ride up and down the serrations, sharpening not only the edges and tips but also the deep valleys. (Serrated edges don't need to be sharpened nearly as often as smooth blades: Their pointed teeth do most of the work.)

MYTH: You can't sharpen an Asian knife in a Western sharpener.

TRUTH: It's not ideal, but you can sharpen an Asian knife in a Western sharpener. Asian knives have a 15-degree cutting angle on one or both sides of the blade, while European knives use a 20-degree angle. But this doesn't mean that you can't use your regular sharpener on them. We dulled one of our favorite Japanese chef's knives and then sharpened it in our favorite electric sharpener, which creates a 20-degree angle, and compared it with the same type of knife dulled and then sharpened in an Asian sharpener. The good news: Both the 15- and 20-degree edges were sharp enough to slice a tomato effortlessly. Only a few testers noticed some drag with the 20-degree angle that wasn't there with the 15-degree blade. So in a pinch, you could just use a good Western knife sharpener—it's always better than a dull knife.

MYTH: And you can't sharpen a Western knife in an Asian sharpener.

TRUTH: You can—but we don't recommend it. The geometry and metal of a 20-degree Western knife are not designed to be at 15 degrees. Sharpening a 20-degree angle to 15 degrees will likely require frequent resharpening, which will rapidly wear down your blade. It's best to maintain the original edge.

MYTH: Electric sharpeners take off too much metal.

TRUTH: With the right brand of electric sharpener, there's no need to worry about excessive metal loss. Electric sharpeners do take off a small amount of metal each time you grind your knife. But our favorite electric sharpener has three options for sharpening: coarse, fine, and a nonmotorized steel. The fine slot is the one you will use most often just to polish up a barely dull knife. Because you will be maintaining the sharpness of your knife with the lightest of the sharpening options rather than giving it an intense regrinding with the coarse slot, you shouldn't worry about metal loss.

MYTH: For that matter, honing steels can take off too much metal.

TRUTH: Again, with the right tool, metal loss is nothing to worry about. The three types of steels—regular, fine, and polished cut—all accomplish the same task to a lesser or greater degree. The rough, filed lines of the regular-cut steel are best for home cooks who only occasionally steel the edge of a knife. For professional chefs and meat cutters who steel their knives daily, the fine and polished cuts are a better choice.

OUR RECOMMENDED SHARPENERS

ELECTRIC

The Chef's Choice Model 130 ($139.99) gives knives a sharp, polished edge. Its spring-loaded blade guides hold the blade against the sharpening wheels at the proper angle. One slot acts like a honing steel but removes the guesswork.

MANUAL

The AccuSharp Knife and Tool Sharpener ($7.99) makes admirably quick and thorough work of basic sharpening tasks at a fraction of the price of an electric sharpener.

BOLSTER BLUES

If you have a knife with a full bolster, we don't recommend an electric sharpener: The thick end of the blade can't be run all the way through. Instead, use a manual sharpener.

THE SMART KITCHEN

Having a few specialized techniques up your sleeve will make you a better, more efficient cook. Here are the tricks we turn to every day to make our kitchen work faster and easier.

TIPS TO SAVE MINUTES, HOURS, OR EVEN DAYS

RIPENING ROCK-HARD FRUIT

Climacteric fruits (including apples, apricots, avocados, bananas, mangos, nectarines, peaches, pears, plums, and tomatoes) ripen off the plant once their ethylene gas content reaches a certain level. Hasten ripening by storing unripe fruit in a brown paper bag with ripe fruit already producing copious amounts of ethylene, such as bananas.

CHILLING WHITE WINE

Wrap the bottle in a wet kitchen towel and place it in the freezer. Since cooling occurs when heat is transferred away from an item, the water in the towel will quickly freeze, dropping the temperature of the wine to 50 degrees in only 30 minutes. To release the towel, place it briefly under warm running water.

PROOFING BREAD DOUGH

Jury-rigging a proofing box in your oven is faster than waiting for dough to rise at room temperature. Adjust an oven rack to the middle position and place a loaf or cake pan in the bottom of the oven. Place the dough on the middle rack and pour 3 cups of boiling water into the pan. Close the oven door and allow the dough to rise as instructed. If you limit the time that the oven door is open, the proof box can be used for both the first and second rises without need to refresh the water.

SOFTENING BUTTER

Cutting butter into cubes is one way to hasten softening, but this trick is even faster: Place the cold butter in a plastic bag and use a rolling pin to pound it to the desired consistency in a matter of seconds.

BOILING WATER

Speed the tedious process of boiling water by dividing the water into two pots, one large enough to hold the total amount of water. When the water in both vessels is boiling, carefully pour the water from the smaller pot into the larger and proceed as directed.

A QUICK DIP TO WARM UP

Thawing frozen meat and taking the chill off of refrigerator-cold food can require hours—even days. Here's how a water bath can help.

FOOD	METHOD	TIME
Eggs	Place whole eggs in 125-degree water to cover.	5 minutes
Cream cheese	Submerge foil-wrapped package in 80-degree water to cover.	10 minutes
Soft, creamy cheeses (such as Brie and Camembert)	Place cheese in a zipper-lock bag in 4 quarts of 80-degree water.	About 1 hour, or until cheese reaches 72 degrees
Thin cuts of frozen meat (such as chicken breasts, steaks, and chops)	Seal frozen meat in a zipper-lock bag and submerge it in very hot (140-degree) water.	Chicken thaws in less than 8 minutes, other cuts in roughly 12 minutes
Frozen turkey	Place turkey in a bucket of cold water, changing the water every 30 minutes.	30 minutes per pound

AERATING RED WINE

Decanting a wine for several hours exposes much of its surface area to oxygen, which breaks down tannins and sulfur compounds, softening harsh flavors. Pouring the wine from one pitcher to another 15 times achieves the same effect in seconds.

CLEANING A SPICE GRINDER

Add several table-spoons of raw white rice to the grinder and pulverize to a fine powder. This will absorb residue and oils.

CHOPPING CELERY

Rather than breaking off one or more ribs for a small amount of chopped celery, chop the entire stalk across the top. It is easier to get just the amount you need, and storing the celery is more convenient, since the whole stalk gets shorter as you use it.

SCRUBBING A BLENDER

Fill the dirty blender bowl halfway with hot water and add a couple of drops of liquid dish soap. With the top firmly in place, turn the blender on high for 30 seconds. Most of the debris pours right out with the soapy water, and the blender jar need only be rinsed or washed lightly by hand.

MINCING GARLIC

Not even professional chefs can match the speedy, precise work of a good garlic press. Our favorite from Kuhn Rikon ($20) breaks down cloves more finely and evenly than a knife can, which means better distribution of garlic flavor throughout a dish.

WIPING DOWN A MICROWAVE

Fill a microwave-safe bowl with water and microwave for 10 minutes. The steam loosens dried food particles so they can be wiped off with ease.

PREPPING FOR CAKE BAKING

While measuring the dry ingredients for the cake you're baking at the moment, also measure ingredients for future cakes into two or three zipper-lock bags. Label each with the date, the name of the cake, and the location of the recipe and pop them into the freezer for future use.

SEEDING TOMATOES

When seeding tomatoes, your salad spinner is a speedy alternative to scooping the guts out by hand. Core and cut the tomatoes into small pieces and spin them until most of the seeds are released. Repeat the spinning process as necessary to remove excess seeds.

PEELING HARD-COOKED EGGS

After draining the hot water from the pot used to cook the eggs, shake the pot back and forth to crack the shells. Add enough ice water to cover the eggs and let cool. The water seeps under the broken shells, allowing them to be slipped off without a struggle.

ZAP TIME FROM RECIPES

The microwave isn't just for reheating leftovers. For some applications, it's the most efficient appliance in the kitchen.

INSTANT DRIED HERBS: Why wait days for herbs to air-dry when the microwave can dehydrate them in minutes? Place hearty herbs (such as sage, rosemary, thyme, oregano, mint, and marjoram) in a single layer between two paper towels and microwave for 1 to 3 minutes.

HANDS-OFF CARAMEL: Boiling sugar to make caramel on the stove without burning it can be tricky, but it's a snap in the microwave. Place 1 cup of sugar, 2 tablespoons of corn syrup, 2 tablespoons of water, and ⅛ teaspoon of lemon juice in a microwave-safe measuring cup or glass bowl. Microwave until the mixture is just beginning to brown, 5 to 8 minutes. Remove the caramel from the microwave and let it sit on a dry surface for 5 minutes or until it darkens to a rich honey brown.

EASY-PEEL GARLIC: Rather than tediously stripping away their papery exterior, microwave skin-on garlic cloves for 15 seconds. Their skin will peel right off.

BAKED POTATOES IN A HURRY: The microwave can cut a russet potato's hour-long baking time in half. Poke a few holes in each potato with a fork and microwave them for 6 to 12 minutes, turning halfway through cooking (the potatoes should be slightly soft to the touch). Transfer the potatoes to the middle rack of a preheated 450-degree oven and bake until a skewer easily glides through the flesh, about 20 minutes.

THE FRUGAL KITCHEN

No cook likes needless waste in the kitchen. And why spend money on expensive equipment if you don't have to?

BE SCRAPPY WITH YOUR INGREDIENTS

Here are some of our favorite ways to repurpose scraps and leftovers.

CHEESE RINDS

Save your Parmesan rinds and do as the Italians do: Toss one into a soup or stew. It's an age-old trick for adding savory depth. Stored in a zipper-lock freezer bag in the freezer, the rinds will keep indefinitely (no need to thaw them before using).

STALE BREAD

Bread that is two to three days old is ideal for making bread crumbs: It has become quite firm but still retains some moisture. Pulse leftover slices in a food processor until crumbs are formed and then use them right away or freeze them in a zipper-lock freezer bag. (In recipes, ⅔ cup of finely processed frozen crumbs or 1 cup of coarsely processed frozen crumbs equals one large 1.5-ounce slice of sandwich bread.) Stale bread can also be a great thickener for soups and stews.

FRY OIL

Unless you have used it to fry fish, don't throw away your leftover fry oil—you can use it three or four more times. Once the oil has cooled, we filter it through a strainer lined with two or three layers of cheesecloth or paper coffee filters. For short-term storage, store oils (leftover or new) in a cool, dark spot, since exposure to air and light makes oil turn rancid faster. But for long-term storage (beyond one month), the cooler the storage temperature, the better—we recommend the freezer.

CURED MEAT SCRAPS

Instead of tossing out scraps of cured meat such as dry sausage and prosciutto, place leftovers in a zipper-lock freezer bag and store them in the freezer. When making tomato sauce, soups, or stews, add the meat to the simmering pot for extra flavor.

PICKLE JUICE

Instead of tossing out a jar of pickle juice after finishing the last spear, use the tangy liquid to make a new condiment. Add thinly sliced onions to the juice and let them marinate in the refrigerator for a few days. The drained pickled onions can be used as a topping for hot dogs and hamburgers or in salads. This method also works well with the spicy packing juice from pickled peppers.

CILANTRO STEMS

While some herb stems (like parsley) can taste bitter, cilantro is different. Sure, the leaves are tasty, but the great flavor found in the stems caught us off guard. Sweet, fresh, and potent, the flavor intensified as we traveled down the stem but never became bitter. If a recipe calls for cilantro and a slightly crunchy texture isn't an issue, use the stems as well as the leaves—you'll get more for your money.

DON'T THROW AWAY

Expired doesn't always mean retired.

CANNED GOODS

The "best by" date printed on some canned foods is not an "expiration" date: It refers strictly to the manufacturer's recommendation for peak quality, not safety concerns. As long as cans look good and have been stored well (in a dry place between 40 and 70 degrees), their contents should remain safe to use indefinitely. Be sure to discard cans with a compromised seal or cans that are bulging or that spurt liquid when opened.

"EXPIRED" PAM

Nonstick vegetable oil spray likewise lasts past its "best by" date. We tested this by making two sheet cakes. For one, we sprayed the pan with a can of PAM that was a year past its "best by" date, and for the other, we used a new can of the same product. The results? Both cakes tasted exactly the same. The reason is that fats are most likely to spoil by exposure to oxygen, which makes them turn rancid. But the fats in cans of vegetable oil spray are contained under pressure with a gas, preventing oxygen from coming in contact with the fat, so it doesn't turn rancid. (The makers of PAM do not advise using products past their "best by" dates—but we feel comfortable using our slightly "vintage" spray.)

FREEZE FOR LATER USE

When it's not possible to use leftover ingredients immediately, we turn to the freezer for longer-term storage. You'll be surprised at what keeps.

FOOD	PREP FOR FREEZER	STORAGE AND USE
Bacon	Roll up bacon in tight cylinders, with two to four slices of bacon in each; place in zipper-lock freezer bag and freeze.	When ready to use, simply pull out desired number of slices.
Bananas	Peel bananas and freeze in zipper-lock freezer bag.	Use to make banana bread or muffins, or drop into blender while still frozen for fruit smoothies.
Buttermilk	Place some small paper cups on tray and fill each with ½ cup buttermilk; place tray in freezer.	Once buttermilk is frozen, wrap each cup in plastic wrap and store in large zipper-lock freezer bag. Defrost amount needed in refrigerator before use.
Canned chipotle chiles in adobo	Spoon chiles, each with a couple of teaspoons of adobo sauce, onto different areas of baking sheet lined with parchment paper and freeze.	Transfer frozen chiles to zipper-lock freezer bag for long-term storage.
Citrus zest	Remove zest from entire fruit. Deposit grated zest in ½-teaspoon increments on plate and transfer plate to freezer.	Once piles are frozen, place them in zipper-lock freezer bag and return them to freezer.
Herbs	Chop leftover fresh parsley, sage, rosemary, or thyme by hand or in food processor; transfer by spoonfuls into ice cube trays; and top with water to cover. For standard ice cube tray, place 2 tablespoons chopped herbs and 1 tablespoon water in each cube. Freeze tray.	Once cubes are frozen, transfer to zipper-lock freezer bag. Store until you want to add herbs to sauces, soups, or stews.
Nuts	Freeze nuts in zipper-lock freezer bag.	Frozen nuts stay fresh for months. No need to defrost before using; frozen nuts can be chopped just as easily as fresh.
Stock	Pour stock into coffee mug lined with quart-size zipper-lock freezer bag. Place bag on baking sheet and freeze.	Once stock is frozen, remove bag from sheet and return to freezer.
Tomato paste	Open both ends of tomato paste can. Remove lid from one end and use lid at other end to push out paste onto sheet of plastic wrap. Wrap paste in plastic and place in freezer.	When paste has frozen, cut off only as much as needed for particular recipe and return frozen log to freezer.
Wine	Measure 1 tablespoon wine into each well of ice cube tray and freeze.	Use paring knife or small spatula to remove each frozen wine cube and add as desired to pan sauces.

QUALITY ON THE CHEAP

You don't always have to pay top dollar to get high-performing pots, pans, and knives. Here are some of our favorite best buys.

TRAMONTINA 6.5-QT. CAST IRON DUTCH OVEN, $49.97

Crafted from enameled cast iron, this pot produced glossy, deeply flavored beef stew; fluffy white rice; and crispy French fries in the test kitchen—in other words, it works as well as pots costing more than five times as much.

VICTORINOX FIBROX 8-INCH CHEF'S KNIFE, $24.95

This chef's knife is one of the cheapest we've ever tested. Nonetheless, it is also a longtime favorite among test cooks who fancy lighter knives. The grippy material, shape, and overall comfort of the handle drew testers' praise.

CUISINART MULTICLAD UNLIMITED 4-QUART SAUCEPAN, $69.99

At about a third of the price of the top saucepan we tested, this lightweight saucepan performed virtually identically. It boasts a well-balanced handle and a rolled lip, ensuring a spill-free pour.

T-FAL PROFESSIONAL NON-STICK FRY PAN, 12.5 INCHES, $34.99

Outperforming competing models at a fraction of the price, this pan had the slickest, most durable nonstick coating; it released perfectly. It is well proportioned, with a comfy handle and a generous cooking surface.

CHILI POWDER

Chili powder is a seasoning blend made from ground dried chiles and an assortment of other ingredients. There is no single recipe, but cumin, garlic, and oregano are traditional additions. Chili powder is not to be confused with the lesser-known chile powder (also often spelled chili powder), which is made solely from chiles without additional seasonings. We use the blend to season batches of chili and add it to spice rubs and marinades. But which brand is best? In search of a bold, complex powder with a warm but not scorching heat, we chose seven widely available chili powders and tasted them sprinkled over potatoes—to assess each uncooked on a neutral base—and cooked in beef-and-bean chili. Top picks won praise for bold heat; those we liked less we faulted as "meek." Our top two products also used a combination of peppers to achieve more complex flavor. When it came to supporting spices, our favorites stuck with the classics: cumin, oregano, and garlic, with minor deviations, such as black pepper and parsley—and they did not include salt. Chili powders are listed in order of preference.

RECOMMENDED

MORTON & BASSETT Chili Powder
PRICE: $5.19 for 1.9 oz ($2.73 per oz)
INGREDIENTS: Paprika, cumin, cayenne pepper, garlic, parsley, oregano, black pepper
COMMENTS: This "smoky, sizzling, full-flavored" chili powder was "much more dimensional than others." "The flavor I've been waiting for!" one taster wrote. The "hot, smoky, herbaceous" powder was "balanced," "bright," and "lively," with "raisiny fruitiness" and a "nice building heat."

PENZEYS SPICES Medium Hot Chili Powder
PRICE: $6.85 for 2.4 oz ($2.85 per oz)
INGREDIENTS: Sweet ancho chili pepper, cayenne red pepper, paprika, cumin, garlic, Mexican oregano
COMMENTS: Our second-place powder, Penzeys' best-selling chili powder, was similar to our winner, with "rich, round, balanced, roasted chili flavor [and] mild but perceptible heat." "Smokiness is tempered by sweetness," with "savory and bright" notes. The "nice kick" of heat was "low-lying."

RECOMMENDED WITH RESERVATIONS

SIMPLY ORGANIC Chili Powder
PRICE: $5.08 for 2.89 oz ($1.76 per oz)
INGREDIENTS: Organic chili powder, organic cumin, organic oregano, organic coriander, organic garlic, silicon dioxide (an anticaking ingredient), organic allspice, organic cloves
COMMENTS: This "sweet" powder was "perfumy," "earthy," and "woodsy and fragrant," with "Indian flavors" (coriander, allspice, and cloves are included). Tasters found it "nice but not super-complex," with a "lingering sweetness" and "mild" heat: "I could go for something livelier," one taster wrote. "Frankly, it's kind of boring."

NOT RECOMMENDED

FRONTIER Chili Powder
PRICE: $4.59 for 2.08 oz ($2.21 per oz)
INGREDIENTS: Chili peppers (may contain silicon dioxide), cumin, garlic, oregano, coriander, cloves, allspice
COMMENTS: This dark-hued powder had strong "roasted," "earthy" chili flavor, "like I ate a bag of anchos," one taster wrote. Some thought it less versatile than other products in our lineup: "Overt smokiness would prevent my using this as all-purpose." A common complaint was a "lack of heat" that made it "wimpy."

SPICE ISLANDS Chili Powder
PRICE: $4.99 for 2.4 oz ($2.08 per oz)
INGREDIENTS: Chili pepper, spices, salt, garlic powder, silicon dioxide
COMMENTS: This powder was "so mild it was hard to taste," "super-boring and a little sweet, with no heat," said one taster. "Tastes like curry, cinnamon, or any of those warm spices," "not distinct chili." It had a "subtle" heat that was "bland and boring." "Doesn't taste of much."

MCCORMICK Hot Mexican-Style Chili Powder
PRICE: $3.29 for 2.5 oz ($1.32 per oz)
INGREDIENTS: Chili peppers, cumin, salt, oregano, silicon dioxide, garlic
COMMENTS: Marketed as "hot," this product was hotter than the standard powder made by the same manufacturer but still "very mild" compared with others in our lineup. "Really one-dimensional" and "straight-up sweet," with "virtually no heat" and "little oomph." "Why bother?"

MCCORMICK Chili Powder
PRICE: $2.99 for 2.5 oz ($1.20 per oz)
INGREDIENTS: Chili pepper, spices, salt, silicon dioxide, garlic
COMMENTS: This last-place powder was weak all around, making for "school-cafeteria chili, wan and bland, lacking complexity and heat." "Am I even eating chili?" asked one taster. At best it was "weak" and "oddly sweet." It was also "dusty," with a "metallic twang at the end."

STEAK SAUCE

A.1. Steak Sauce reigns supreme in the United States, accounting for the majority of steak sauce sold, but it's not the only brand on the market. We gathered seven brands to see if A.1. deserved its de facto popularity. Steak sauce ingredients tend toward the eclectic and the pungent: raisin paste, turmeric, tamarind, grapefruit puree, malt vinegar, and salty anchovies all appeared on various ingredient lists. We like a steak sauce that can slice through rich, meaty beef with a jolt of flavor that's at once sweet, sour, and salty. But we don't want it to overwhelm the steak's own flavor. Some sauces were excruciatingly salty; others were overly sour or vinegary. And textures varied almost as much as flavor—from too thin to too thick. Tasters preferred a sauce with a mellow, balanced flavor, a smooth texture, and enough body to cling to the steak without being stiff and gluey. Steak sauces are listed in order of preference.

RECOMMENDED

HEINZ 57 Sauce
PRICE: $3.59 for 10 oz (36 cents per oz)
SODIUM: 200 mg per tablespoon
FLAVOR PROFILE: Earthy, tangy tomato
COMMENTS: Our top-rated brand provided "a nice counterpart that let the meat shine through without overwhelming." It's "tomatoey, spicy, and earthy," with a "sweetness [that] is rich and fruity," and it has a "peppery tang." A hint of smoke was kept in check: "Not exactly smoky but has a woodsy, campfire feel." Finally, the "smooth" texture was spot-on: "Coats the steak but isn't gloppy."

LEA & PERRINS Traditional Steak Sauce
PRICE: $7.24 for 15 oz (48 cents per oz)
SODIUM: 330 mg per tablespoon
FLAVOR PROFILE: Vinegary tang with a peppery kick
COMMENTS: This flavorful sauce had hints of "prune," "tamarind," and "molasses." It was bolder than our winner, a quality that some tasters liked. The sweetness was balanced by a "nice bit of heat" and lots of black pepper. A "kick of vinegar" added a zippy "tartness" that wasn't "metallic, like others," and "complemented the steak."

RECOMMENDED WITH RESERVATIONS

A.1. Steak Sauce
PRICE: $4.99 for 10 oz (50 cents per oz)
SODIUM: 280 mg per tablespoon
FLAW: Sharp and overpowering
COMMENTS: This brand won points for nostalgia, with more than half of tasters recognizing its flavor in our blind tasting: "I'm a little biased because I grew up on A.1. and London broil"; "Boy, A.1. is distinct"; "Tastes like good old A.1., part nostalgia, part sweet, salty, tangy, tamarind." An equal number found this ubiquitous sauce too sharp: "It totally overpowers the meat; very acidic"; "Tastes like a lime freeze pop"; "Super-tangy, big anchovy, and too bold."

NOT RECOMMENDED

SMITH & WOLLENSKY Steak Sauce
PRICE: $9.99 for 12 oz (83 cents per oz)
SODIUM: 120 mg per tablespoon
FATAL FLAW: Chunky texture, burnt flavor
COMMENTS: Tasters disliked the "chunky," overabundant "oniony lumps. UGH." "Like burnt rubber with stringy bits in it, both unexpected and unpleasant." Almost half of our tasters picked up on a smoky, burnt flavor ("natural smoke flavor" is among the ingredients): "I could burn my own food, thank you very much!" Plus, it costs more than twice what our winner does.

JACK DANIEL'S Steak Sauce Original
PRICE: $6.95 for 10 oz (70 cents per oz)
SODIUM: 210 mg per tablespoon
FATAL FLAW: Cloves, nutmeg, cloying
COMMENTS: Only one taster noticed the booze (whiskey flavoring is added). For the rest, the sauce was simply "syrupy sweet," tasting "like pancake syrup with molasses" and turning the steak into "meat candy." Tasters weren't crazy about the aggressive cloves either: "Weird; here we go again with nutmeg and cloves. Flavors like a pie"; "Too much warm spice."

HP SAUCE
PRICE: $3.65 for 9 oz (41 cents per oz)
SODIUM: 190 mg per tablespoon
FATAL FLAW: Sharp vinegar taste and sweetness
COMMENTS: Tasters were "zapped" by this jolting sauce (vinegars are the first and fifth ingredients), noting its "overly tart," "crazy tang." "My lips are puckering" with its "medicinal sharpness," said one. This aggressive acidity was paired with a "super molasses-y, syrupy" sweetness that was "like hoisin sauce." The combination was described as "sour honey" and "syrupy mouthwash." Many also noted that the sauce gave the beef "metallic" flavor.

ZIP SAUCE
PRICE: $7.95 for 12 oz (66 cents per oz)
SODIUM: 585 mg per tablespoon, with unsalted butter
FATAL FLAW: Inedibly salty
COMMENTS: This unconventional steak sauce is heated in a saucepan with butter (a 4-ounce stick combined with the 12-ounce bottle). Even made with unsalted butter, it was a "salt lick" and "crazy salty," our tasters said. We also found it too thin, like a "watery beef bouillon" that "separated in the cup"; even after vigorous whisking, the butter stayed in an "oil slick" on top.

HUMMUS

With just five ingredients—chickpeas, tahini, garlic, olive oil, and lemon juice—plus a smattering of spices, hummus should be nearly impossible to get wrong. The ideal spread is appealingly smooth and creamy, with the fresh, clean flavor of buttery chickpeas in balance with the earthy toasted-sesame taste of tahini, set off by a lemon-garlic bite. But some store-bought hummus doesn't even come close, with funky off-flavors and a stodgy, grainy consistency. We tasted eight nationally available samples of plain hummus, including a shelf-stable hummus that contains no oil, a soy-chickpea-blend hummus, and a box mix that requires stirring in hot water and olive oil. We found that many weren't worth buying, but a few hit the mark with nutty, earthy flavor and a wonderfully thick, creamy texture. Hummuses are listed in order of preference.

RECOMMENDED

SABRA Classic Hummus
PRICE: $4.49 for 10 oz (45 cents per oz)
FAT: 18.8%   **SODIUM:** 420 mg in 100 g
PROTEIN: 7.4%
WATER/MOISTURE: 55.4%
COMMENTS: This "hearty but not dense" hummus had a "very clean flavor of tahini" that was also "earthy" and had tasters praising it as "tahini heaven." Its richness made it taste "like good homemade: real buttery, almost sweet." One taster confessed, "I'd eat this with a spoon."

CEDAR'S All Natural Hommus, Classic Original
PRICE: $3.49 for 8 oz (44 cents per oz)
FAT: 12.1%   **SODIUM:** 370 mg in 100 g
PROTEIN: 6.8%
WATER/MOISTURE: 67.2%
COMMENTS: This less tahini-forward, "lemony" hummus had a "super-soft and silky," "smooth" texture. With its high degree of moisture, it struck some tasters as "watered down" and "lacking substance." But most found it "good all around." "Now this is a hummus I can get with," one taster raved.

TRIBE Classic Hummus
PRICE: $3.49 for 8 oz (44 cents per oz)
FAT: 15.4%   **SODIUM:** 430 mg in 100 g
PROTEIN: 7%
WATER/MOISTURE: 59.9%
COMMENTS: "Creamy," with a "thick and smooth," "very likable texture," this "clean-tasting" hummus had "deep savory notes." A few tasters acknowledged its "strong tahini flavor," which was "almost like peanut butter." For some, it was too much tahini.

NOT RECOMMENDED

ATHENOS Original Hummus
PRICE: $3.75 for 7 oz (54 cents per oz)
FAT: 8.9%   **SODIUM:** 580 mg in 100 g
PROTEIN: 6.3%
WATER/MOISTURE: 65.2%
COMMENTS: "Tastes like taco night," and not in a good way, with "too much cumin." Tasters also complained that it was "too tangy." Its "creamy" texture was undermined by "random grains of chunky chickpeas." For others it was "a touch bitter."

NOT RECOMMENDED *(continued)*

WILD GARDEN Traditional Hummus Dip
PRICE: $1.90 for 1.76 oz ($1.08 per oz)
FAT: 7.4%   **SODIUM:** 580 mg in 100 g
PROTEIN: 5.4%
WATER/MOISTURE: 71.3%
COMMENTS: With the highest amount of water and the lowest amount of protein and fat among the products in our lineup, this shelf-stable hummus was "like mustard," with a "runny" texture "reminiscent of baby food." Some tasters found its "citrusy," "garlicky" flavors "almost abrasive."

FANTASTIC WORLD FOODS Original Hummus
PRICE: $3.65 for 12 oz prepared from 6-oz box (30 cents per oz)
FAT: 10.4%   **SODIUM:** 410 mg in 100 g
PROTEIN: 6.6%
WATER/MOISTURE: 64.1%
COMMENTS: Reconstituted from chickpea flour and dried tahini and seasonings, this box-mix hummus had a "dry" and "sandy" texture. It was also "bland" and "stale," with "lots of raw spice in there," and most of us "could barely taste any tahini."

ATHENOS Greek-Style Hummus
PRICE: $3.75 for 7 oz (54 cents per oz)
FAT: 10.2%   **SODIUM:** 490 mg in 100 g
PROTEIN: 5.7%
WATER/MOISTURE: 67.1%
COMMENTS: If this was hummus, some tasters didn't believe it. With "very little chickpea," it "tastes like sandwich spread" or "like an Italian seasoning packet." Several tasters found it "sour" and "quite salty."

NASOYA Classic Original Super Hummus
PRICE: $2.99 for 10 oz (30 cents per oz)
FAT: 10.1%   **SODIUM:** 350 mg in 100 g
PROTEIN: 12.9%
WATER/MOISTURE: 65.7%
COMMENTS: With a "very creamy," "mousselike" texture, this soybean-chickpea hummus had "maple-like undertones." No wonder: It was the only product in our lineup with added sugar. Though it was high in protein, the soybeans made this hybrid hummus taste strange; some tasters speculated that it was "fermented."

MULTIGRAIN BREAD

"Multigrain" is a vague term in the bread industry. A grain is defined merely as wheat or any other cultivated cereal crop used as food, such as barley, triticale, buckwheat, amaranth, and brown rice. We set off to define what we expect from multigrain bread and which brand offers the best flavor and texture. We bought seven top-selling multigrain breads, each containing from 10 to 15 different types of grains, and tasted them plain and toasted with butter. A strong preference for heartier loaves emerged. We praised substantial slices with naturally sweet, wheaty flavor. In general, we liked brands with more whole-wheat and less white flour; if white flour was high on the ingredient list (listed by weight), other grains had to be, too, to achieve the wholesome texture tasters preferred. And the more nuts and seeds in a loaf, the better. Breads are listed in order of preference.

RECOMMENDED

NATURE'S PRIDE 12 Grain
PRICE: $2.99 for 24 oz (12 cents per oz)
WEIGHT PER SLICE: 42.53 g
GRAINS: Wheat, oats, barley, rye, triticale, buckwheat, millet, corn, sorghum, brown rice, amaranth, quinoa
COMMENTS: This "hearty" and "wholesome" loaf lists whole-wheat flour first and white flour third, closely followed by a mix of whole grains. It had "substantial" and "chewy" slices that "felt homemade." Tasters praised the "nutty," "crunchy" seeds flecked throughout and a "wheaty, not-in-your-face sweetness."

NATURE'S OWN Specialty 12 Grain
PRICE: $2.99 for 24 oz (12 cents per oz)
WEIGHT PER SLICE: 44.65 g
GRAINS: Wheat, rye, oats, barley, triticale, millet, amaranth, brown rice, buckwheat, khorasan, corn, spelt
COMMENTS: The darkest loaf we tested, this rolled oat–topped loaf contains no white flour whatsoever. Slices were "nutty, hearty with seeds and nuts," with a "pleasant chewiness" and a "substantial," "moist, not spongy" texture.

ARNOLD 12 Grain
(sold as Oroweat 12 Grain Bread in the western United States and Brownberry 12 Grain Bread in the Midwest)
PRICE: $4.49 for 24 oz (19 cents per oz)
WEIGHT PER SLICE: 43.03 g
GRAINS: Wheat, rye, oats, corn, buckwheat, brown rice, triticale, barley, millet
COMMENTS: This cushiony loaf lists white flour second (after whole wheat), which creates "fluffy" slices that seemed more "delicate" than others we tasted. "Closer to what I expect of a white bread," said a taster, adding, "sweet and buttery." Though described as 12-grain on the label, wheat was counted twice and flaxseeds and sunflower seeds were counted as grains.

PEPPERIDGE FARM 15 Grain
PRICE: $4.29 for 24 oz (18 cents per oz)
WEIGHT PER SLICE: 42.52 g
GRAINS: Wheat, wheat berries, oats, barley, rye, triticale, millet, corn, brown rice, buckwheat, amaranth, quinoa, sorghum, spelt
COMMENTS: This bread lists whole-wheat flour first and less than 2 percent white flour, for "earthy, crunchy," "very nutty" slices full of wheat berries and seeds. Tasters noted a sour aftertaste, and while some liked the "tangy" flavor, others found it too bold, even bitter.

RECOMMENDED WITH RESERVATIONS

ARNOLD Health-full 10 Grain
(sold as Oroweat Health-full 10 Grain in the western United States and Brownberry Health-full 10 Grain in the Midwest)
PRICE: $4.59 for 24 oz (19 cents per oz)
WEIGHT PER SLICE: 36.83 g
GRAINS: Wheat, rye, corn, buckwheat, brown rice, oats, triticale, barley, millet
COMMENTS: This loaf starts with whole-wheat flour, followed directly by white flour. It had an airy texture and the lightest and slimmest slices, which led a number of tasters to find it "unsubstantial." Others, however, approved, praising it as "soft and fresh, [with] nice texture"; "light and airy"; and "springy."

PEPPERIDGE FARM Farmhouse 12 Grain
PRICE: $5.15 for 24 oz (21 cents per oz)
WEIGHT PER SLICE: 40 g
GRAINS: Wheat, wheat berries, oats, barley, rye, triticale, corn, millet, brown rice, buckwheat, amaranth
COMMENTS: This loaf starts with white flour, with whole-wheat flour third, and has less than 2 percent of the remaining 11 grains; it was topped with a nice mixture of wheat berries and flaxseeds: "Seeds/nuts on crust add a lot of flavor." But many found the loaf dry (even though it was well within its sell-by date).

SARA LEE 12 Grain
PRICE: $2.99 for 24 oz (12 cents per oz)
WEIGHT PER SLICE: 41 g
GRAINS: Wheat, rye, oats, barley, corn, millet, triticale, brown rice, buckwheat, amaranth, spelt, sorghum
COMMENTS: This brown, tight-crumbed loaf lists whole-wheat flour first, followed by wheat and the rest of its added grains. Many tasters liked the texture, finding it chewy, dense, and hearty. But they were bothered by the amount of sugar—the most by weight among the seven products. "Sweet taste won't leave my mouth!" complained one taster. Also, the seeds were few and far between, only "occasionally visible."

SUPERMARKET MEDIUM-ROAST COFFEE

Medium-roast coffee boasts a broader spectrum of flavors than darker roasts, with floral, fruity notes and bright, lively acidity. To find our favorite brand, we selected medium-roast blends from seven popular brands and started brewing. As we sampled the coffees (without milk or sweeteners), it appeared that most of us weren't ready to switch our allegiance to the lighter side of flavor. Our favorite brew was the darkest roast of the bunch by far. Tasters lauded this coffee's "toasty" earthiness and hints of "chocolate." By and large, super-bright, acidic flavors—hallmarks of lighter roasts—didn't rate well. The lightest roast in our lineup was panned for having the most markedly acidic taste and fell to second-to-last place. Our research showed that these brands get their beans from less reliable sources—where the beans are often stored improperly or for too long—and use faster, more economical roasting processes that compromise the beans' quality and flavor. Our favorite brands source their beans more selectively and roast them carefully for optimal results, paying particular attention to the moisture level in the beans (if the roasted beans are too dry, their flavors won't extract properly when they're brewed). Coffees are listed in order of preference.

RECOMMENDED

PEET'S COFFEE Café Domingo
PRICE: $13.95 for 1-pound bag ($0.87 per oz)
AGTRON: 39   QUAKERS: 1
pH: 5.33   MOISTURE: 1.2%
COMMENTS: By far the darkest roast in the lineup, this sample came across as "extremely smooth" and "bold-tasting," with a "stronger finish" than other samples. It tied for the smallest number of defective beans and had low acidity and optimal moisture. Its "rich," "chocolate," and "toast" flavors make it the perfect brew for those who want a break—but not too much of one—from ultradark French roasts.

MILLSTONE Breakfast Blend
PRICE: $9.17 for 12-ounce bag ($0.76 per oz)
AGTRON: 47   QUAKERS: 2
pH: 5.22   MOISTURE: 1.6%
COMMENTS: This "satiny" coffee was "lemony" and "very enjoyable," with a "slightly nutty aftertaste." It "hit the middle of the road" for "acidity, earthiness, and complexity." As with our winner, lab results showed low acidity, few defective beans, and ideal moisture. It's a good choice for those who enjoy brighter, livelier medium-roast flavors.

RECOMMENDED WITH RESERVATIONS

CARIBOU COFFEE Daybreak
PRICE: $12.54 for 12-ounce bag ($1.05 per oz)
AGTRON: 46   QUAKERS: 1
pH: 5.19   MOISTURE: 0.06%
COMMENTS: Some tasters were able to detect a "slight berry taste" with "black tea–like" undertones in this coffee. For others, it was "flat," "bland," and "not very distinctive." "Smells nutty but no taste" is how one taster put it. The lab results indicated extremely low moisture in the beans, which almost certainly weakened the brew.

STARBUCKS BLONDE Veranda Blend
PRICE: $11.95 for 1-pound bag ($0.75 per oz)
AGTRON: 46   QUAKERS: 5
pH: 5.25   MOISTURE: 0.14%
COMMENTS: The "approachable" taste of this offering from the dark-roast giant of coffee companies "goes down pretty smooth," though some thought it "one-dimensional," like "cardboard." Said one taster: "It doesn't have that weight-on-your-tongue feeling that I like in coffee." Lab tests confirmed the problems, finding low moisture and some defective beans.

RECOMMENDED WITH RESERVATIONS *(continued)*

GREEN MOUNTAIN COFFEE Our Blend
PRICE: $9.36 for 12-ounce bag ($0.78 per oz)
AGTRON: 46   QUAKERS: 3
pH: 5.09   MOISTURE: 0.14%
COMMENTS: This sample had "a little dried fruit toward the finish but that's it," as one taster put it. Though "robust upfront," it finished with an overly "flat, lemony" taste. Lab results supported these impressions, showing relatively high acidity and not much moisture, which limited its extraction.

NOT RECOMMENDED

DUNKIN' DONUTS Original
PRICE: $11.99 for 12-ounce bag ($1 per oz)
AGTRON: 57   QUAKERS: 7
pH: 4.94   MOISTURE: 0.68%
COMMENTS: This medium-roast stalwart, the lightest roast in our tasting, was so "sharp and bright and very acidic" that it had one taster pleading, "I need milk!" Another deemed it an "acid bomb"; lab tests confirmed that this was the most acidic coffee we tasted. A high number of defective beans gave it weird "cherry/almond" off-tastes.

EIGHT O'CLOCK COFFEE Original
PRICE: $6.95 for 12-ounce bag ($0.58 per oz)
AGTRON: 47   QUAKERS: 14
pH: 5.06   MOISTURE: 3.85%
COMMENTS: Our least favorite coffee was "sour" and "dirty-tasting—like socks," with a "fermented taste." This brew was also "slightly metallic," "like coffee you'd get at a diner." With the highest number of defective beans of all the coffees we sampled, it tasted "sweetly acidic"; the fermented flavor likely came from its high level of moisture.

GOAT CHEESE

It's not hard to see why fresh goat cheese is so popular: With its unmistakable tang, it can be eaten straight on crackers, enliven the simplest salad or pasta dish, enhance pizza toppings, and add creamy richness to sautéed greens. With so many new domestic choices available on top of the many imported options, which one comes out on top? We gathered nine widely available samples (seven of them stateside products), ranging from $0.82 to $1.63 per ounce, and set to work finding out. We first tasted the cheese straight out of the package on plain crackers. Then, to see if heat changed its character, we rolled it in bread crumbs and baked it. The good news: Sampled straight from the fridge, the majority of our nine selections were smooth and creamy, with a tangy, grassy taste—just what we want in goat cheese. Only a few had issues, including a chalky, Spackle-like texture; a too-neutral flavor; or an overly gamy taste. Products that were chalky straight out of the package didn't improve with baking—and several that were creamy sampled plain surprised us by baking into crumbly, grainy blobs. When we investigated further, we found that much of this difference was due to the cheeses' salt content. The ions in salt help the proteins in cheese bind and retain water, which means that more moisture is retained during cooking and that the cheese melts more smoothly; the products with more salt stayed smooth and cohesive when baked. Cheeses are listed in order of preference.

RECOMMENDED

LAURA CHENEL'S CHÈVRE Fresh Chèvre Log
PRICE: $6.99 for 8 oz ($0.87 per oz)
MADE IN: California
SALT: 1,053 mg in 100 g **pH:** 4.05
FAT: 21.20 g in 100 g (6 g in 1-oz serving)
COMMENTS: "Rich-tasting," "grassy," and "tangy," our favorite goat cheese was "smooth" and "creamy" both unheated and

baked, and it kept its "lemony, bright flavor" in both iterations. A high salt content helped: Salt not only enhances flavor but also contributes to keeping the cheese creamy when heated.

VERMONT CREAMERY Fresh Goat Cheese, Classic Chèvre
PRICE: $4.99 for 4 oz ($1.25 per oz)
MADE IN: Vermont
SALT: 784 mg in 100 g **pH:** 3.95
FAT: 20.96 g in 100 g (5.9 g in 1-oz serving)
COMMENTS: "Smooth and creamy" and with a "slightly citrusy," "clean, lactic" taste, this was one of our favorite goat cheeses for

sampling straight from the package. Its moderate salt content allowed it to turn slightly "mealy" when baked, but its "grassy," "citruslike" flavors continued to earn raves from tasters.

CHEVRION Plain Goat Cheese
PRICE: $4.29 for 4 oz ($1.07 per oz)
MADE IN: France
SALT: 1,200 mg in 100 g **pH:** 3.91

FAT: 16.89 g in 100 g (4.8 g in 1-oz serving)
COMMENTS: This "tangy," "creamy" sample was "very strong" and "goaty" eaten unheated, but it mellowed to "bright, tangy, and sweet" when baked, when it also retained a "luscious" texture, thanks to its high salt content.

CYPRESS GROVE CHÈVRE Ms. Natural Goat Milk Cheese
PRICE: $6.50 for 4 oz ($1.63 per oz)
MADE IN: California
SALT: 955 mg in 100 g **pH:** 4.04

FAT: 21.55 g in 100 g (6.1 g in 1-oz serving)
COMMENTS: Unheated, this cheese wowed us with "lemony," "grassy" flavors and a "smooth," "melts-in-your-mouth" texture. Though baking dried out its texture a bit, tasters still gave it an enthusiastic thumbs-up.

RECOMMENDED (continued)

SIERRA NEVADA CHEESE CO. Bella Capra Chèvre
PRICE: $7.99 for 8 oz ($1.00 per oz)
MADE IN: California
SALT: 882 mg in 100 g **pH:** 3.86

FAT: 25.56 g in 100 g (7.2 g in 1-oz serving)
COMMENTS: "Fresh" and "tangy" and with a "creamy" texture when sampled unheated, this cheese with a moderate salt content turned a little "crumbly" when baked but still offered "tang" and "good goat flavor."

CHAVRIE Fresh Goat Cheese
PRICE: $8.99 for 11 oz ($0.82 per oz)
MADE IN: Pennsylvania
SALT: 1,078 mg in 100 g **pH:** 4.66
FAT: 22.86 g in 100 g (6.5 g in 1-oz serving)
COMMENTS: Though it had some fans, the "barnyard" and "gamy" flavor of this cheese reminded some tasters of "lamb fat." These

flavors dissipated in baking, when this sample shone with a "tasty tang and milky flavor" and a "nice creamy texture."

RECOMMENDED WITH RESERVATIONS

MONTCHÈVRE Fresh Goat Cheese
PRICE: $3.99 for 4 oz ($1.00 per oz)
MADE IN: Wisconsin
SALT: 686 mg in 100 g **pH:** 4.27

FAT: 24.49 g in 100 g (6.9 g in 1-oz serving)
COMMENTS: Though "very creamy" and with a "nice smooth consistency" when unheated, without much salt, it was "neutral" to many and just "mildly tangy." Too little salt also left it "watery and crumbly" when baked.

NOT RECOMMENDED

COACH FARM Natural Goat's Milk Cheese
PRICE: $4.50 for 4 oz ($1.13 per oz)
MADE IN: New York
SALT: 441 mg in 100 g **pH:** 3.93
FAT: 23.59 g in 100 g (6.7 g in 1-oz serving)
COMMENTS: Its very low salt content didn't do this cheese any

favors. Unheated, it had a "chalky," "puttylike" texture and "weak" taste. Baking didn't redeem it: Most tasters found it "chalky" again, with "not enough goat" flavor.

ARTISANAL CHEDDAR

Your average block of American cheddar doesn't resemble the complex-tasting farmhouse-style wheels that have been produced in England for centuries, but American cheddar is poised to climb out of this rut. Many companies now offer "artisanal" domestic cheddars that claim to rival the English stuff and fetch prices just as high. We held a tasting, sampling nine artisanal cheddars from both small and large producers straight from the package. (Fine cheeses like these aren't intended for cooking.) One thing was clear: The best cheddars were worth every penny. Several wowed us with "intensely nutty," "buttery" tang and creamy-textured crumbliness. Cheddars are listed in order of preference.

HIGHLY RECOMMENDED

MILTON CREAMERY Prairie Breeze
PRICE: $15.98 per lb   AGED: 9 to 12 months
CHEDDARING: Traditional   AGING MATERIAL: Plastic
COMMENTS: This cheese was one of the youngest in the lineup, but thanks to an extra cocktail of bacterial cultures, it wowed tasters with "deeply rich," "buttery" flavors and a "sweet" finish that reminded some of "pineapple." It boasted a "crumbly" yet "creamy" texture reminiscent of "young Parmesan."

CABOT Cellars at Jasper Hill Clothbound Cheddar
PRICE: $23.98 per lb   AGED: 10 to 14 months
CHEDDARING: Modern   AGING MATERIAL: Cloth
COMMENTS: Cabot's high-end line (it was one of the priciest American cheese we tasted) is also inoculated twice and won raves from tasters for its "mature sharpness" and "rich dairy flavor" that they likened to Gruyère. But the bigger draw: its "craggy" texture that broke into addictively "jagged," "crystalline" shards.

RECOMMENDED

TILLAMOOK Vintage White Extra Sharp Cheddar Cheese
PRICE: $9.50 per lb   AGED: At least 2 years
CHEDDARING: Modern   AGING MATERIAL: Plastic
COMMENTS: Compared with the company's other cheddars, this two-plus-year-old cheese is "vintage," but unlike some other long-aged samples, its sharpness was "appropriately bold" and "balanced." Fans of smoother cheddars will appreciate its "extremely creamy" texture—not to mention its affordable price tag.

BEECHER'S Flagship Reserve Handmade Cheese
PRICE: $25 per lb   AGED: 12 months
CHEDDARING: Traditional   AGING MATERIAL: Cloth
COMMENTS: Besides conventional cheddar descriptors like "nutty" and "sharp," this "firm," "grainy" clothbound cheese earned compliments for more complex flavors like "buttery walnuts" and a "gamy," "Parmesan-like" tang. No wonder: Like our two favorites, it received a second shot of nontraditional cultures.

GRAFTON VILLAGE Vermont Clothbound Cheddar
PRICE: $15.99 per lb   AGED: At least 6 months
CHEDDARING: Traditional   AGING MATERIAL: Cloth
 COMMENTS: A classic example of clothbound cheddar, this sample was wrapped in a butter-dipped cloth and soaked up a "fruity and nutty" flavor hinting of "caramel." It breaks into "firm" shards, which makes it a bit tricky to slice but a pleasure to eat out of hand.

RECOMMENDED (continued)

FISCALINI FARMSTEAD Bandage-Wrapped Raw Milk Cheddar
PRICE: $24 per lb   AGED: 18 months
CHEDDARING: Traditional   AGING MATERIAL: Cloth
 COMMENTS: As artisanal cheddars go, this cheese was well liked but unremarkable. Its "complex," "fruity" aroma prompted the same pineapple analogy as our winner, but its texture was softer and creamier—even "waxy" and "squeezable," according to some.

CABOT PRIVATE STOCK Classic Vermont Cheddar Cheese
PRICE: $8.49 per lb   AGED: Up to 16 months
CHEDDARING: Modern   AGING MATERIAL: Plastic
COMMENTS: The flavor of this "no-frills" crowd-pleaser—also our favorite supermarket cheddar—was "straight-up sharp" but "not distinctive," with a "firm and creamy"  texture that reminded us of "what you'd find on the end of a toothpick at a cocktail party."

SHELBURNE FARMS 2-Year-Old Farmhouse Cheddar Cheese
PRICE: $19 per lb   AGED: 2 years
CHEDDARING: Traditional   AGING MATERIAL: Plastic
COMMENTS: After two years of aging in plastic, this cheddar tasted like "wet wool" and "barnyard funk"—a trait that some thought made it a "serious cheddar,"  while others weren't convinced. But all were agreed: The plastic's moisture-locking seal ensured a "moist, creamy," "mouth-coating" texture.

RECOMMENDED WITH RESERVATIONS

WIDMER'S CHEESE CELLARS Two Year Old Cheddar Cheese
PRICE: $7.90 per lb   AGED: 2 years
CHEDDARING: Traditional   AGING MATERIAL: Plastic
COMMENTS: Neon orange and shrink-wrapped, this cheddar looked the most like a supermarket block and tasted like it, too.  Though deemed an "all-around good snacking cheddar," its "mild" profile was "lackluster" in comparison with others in the lineup, and we're not sure we'd go out of our way to mail-order it.

GRAFTON VILLAGE Classic Reserve 2-Year Aged Vermont Raw Milk Cheddar Cheese
PRICE: $17.99 per lb   AGED: 2 years
CHEDDARING: Traditional   AGING MATERIAL: Plastic
COMMENTS: Thanks to a combination of aging, moisture content, and bacteria cultures, this cheddar was so "sulfurous" that it elicited comparisons to "rotten eggs." Only  those who wanted a really "funky" cheddar found this one palatable, though many appreciated its "rich and creamy texture."

PEPPER JACK CHEESE

Add hot pickled peppers to Monterey Jack, a mild California cow's-milk cheese, and you've got pepper Jack. We like pepper Jack for its creamy melting properties, and we've used it in enchiladas, biscuits, nachos, seven-layer dip, Tex-Mex meatloaf, and much more. To select a favorite product, we tasted seven nationally available cheeses: six in block form and one preshredded from a prominent brand that doesn't sell blocks. We tried the cheeses on their own and melted in quesadillas. Although every product uses jalapeños (with one adding habanero), the heat levels ranged. We preferred the spicier cheeses. Peppers aside, the cheeses themselves ranged from "bland" and "kid-friendly" to pleasingly "sharp," "grassy," "buttery," and "tangy." Tasters liked those with more "bite and sharpness" to balance the hot peppers. Fat played a role in our rankings, too, providing buttery, creamy, rounded background to the tang, saltiness, and heat of pepper Jack, as well as helping the cheese melt smoothly. Pepper Jacks are listed in order of preference.

RECOMMENDED

BOAR'S HEAD Monterey Jack Cheese with Jalapeño
PRICE: $6.99 for 8 oz (87 cents per oz)
STYLE: Block
PEPPERS: Jalapeño
FAT: 9 g per oz
HEAT: 3
COMMENTS: This "buttery" cheese had a "tangy," "cheddarlike" flavor that was "clean" and "nicely balanced," and the jalapeños gave it a "bright," "assertive" kick. The texture was "even and firm" yet "creamy."

TILLAMOOK Pepper Jack Cheese
PRICE: $16 for 2 lb (50 cents per oz)
STYLE: Block
PEPPERS: Jalapeño
FAT: 9 g per oz
HEAT: 2
COMMENTS: This cheese's "very strong, sharp flavor" was "more tangy than milky," "fairly acidic," and "complex." The heat was "moderate" and the texture "soft."

RECOMMENDED WITH RESERVATIONS

VELLA Jalapeño Jack
PRICE: $24 for 2.5 lb (60 cents per oz)
STYLE: Block
PEPPERS: Jalapeño
FAT: 9 g per oz
HEAT: 1.5
COMMENTS: Vella's "full milky flavor" was "creamy" and "rich," while the spice level was "mild but consistent"; some tasters preferred hotter products. The cheese was "soft," "smooth," and "nearly gooey."

CABOT Pepper Jack
PRICE: $3.59 for 8 oz (45 cents per oz)
STYLE: Block
PEPPERS: Jalapeño
FAT: 9 g per oz
HEAT: 2
COMMENTS: This pepper Jack reminded us of "mild cheddar." The large chunks of jalapeño gave it a "vegetal," "fruity" pepper flavor. Good, but alas, the texture was "waxy" and "rubbery."

RECOMMENDED WITH RESERVATIONS (continued)

LAND O'LAKES Hot Pepper Jack
PRICE: $6.99 per lb (44 cents per oz)
STYLE: Block
PEPPERS: Jalapeño
FAT: 9 g per oz
HEAT: 2
COMMENTS: Tasters wished for "more sharpness" in this "bland" cheese, although at least the pepper flavor was "pronounced" and "lingering." The texture was "weirdly soft, like bad American cheese," said one taster; another compared it to Cheez Whiz.

NOT RECOMMENDED

ORGANIC VALLEY Pepper Jack Cheese
PRICE: $7.99 for 8 oz ($1 per oz)
STYLE: Block
PEPPERS: Jalapeño
FAT: 8 g per oz
HEAT: 1
COMMENTS: The flavor was "subtle" in this "very mild," "kid-friendly" cheese, which had "almost no heat," with "sweet," "not at all spicy" peppers. We found the texture "mushy" and "sticky."

SARGENTO OFF THE BLOCK Pepper Jack Traditional Cut
PRICE: $3.59 for 8 oz (45 cents per oz)
STYLE: Shredded
PEPPERS: Jalapeño and habanero
FAT: 8 g per oz
HEAT: 3
COMMENTS: We liked the definite pepper heat in this preshredded cheese (it includes habanero as well as jalapeño). But the ingredients added to prevent caking (potato starch and powdered cellulose) made the cheese chalky and powdery when eaten plain and "stiff" and "grainy" when melted.

WHOLE CHICKENS

To find the best-tasting whole chicken on the market, we rounded up eight national and large regional brands. Some birds boasted moist, "chicken-y" meat; others tasted bland, faintly metallic, bitter, or liver-y. Chalky, dry meat was a common complaint, but surprisingly, so was too much moisture. Our research revealed that most companies chill their chickens in a cold-water bath where they can absorb a significant amount of water, which translated to diluted flavor and a spongy texture. We preferred air-chilled birds for their superior texture. Chickens are listed in order of preference.

HIGHLY RECOMMENDED

MARY'S Free Range Air Chilled Chicken
(also sold as Pitman's)
PRICE: $1.99 per lb
DISTRIBUTION: California, Oregon, Washington, Hawaii, Arizona, and Nevada
ANTIBIOTIC USE: "No antibiotics ever"
VEGETARIAN FEED: Yes
CHILLING METHOD: Air
FAT: 14.2%   SODIUM: 85 mg per 4-oz serving
COMMENTS: Air chilling plus a higher percentage of fat (compared with the more diluted water-chilled chicken) added up to a bird that tasters raved was "clean," "sweet," "buttery," "savory," "chicken-y," and "juicy," with "richly flavored" dark meat that was "so moist" and "tender." In sum: "Really perfect."

BELL & EVANS Air Chilled Premium Fresh Chicken
PRICE: $3.29 per lb
DISTRIBUTION: East of the Rockies
ANTIBIOTIC USE: "No antibiotics ever"
VEGETARIAN FEED: Yes
CHILLING METHOD: Air
FAT: 15.6%   SODIUM: 75 mg per 4-oz serving
COMMENTS: Thanks to almost 3 hours of air chilling, this bird's white meat was "perfectly moist," "rich and nutty," and "concentrated and chicken-y," and its dark meat "silky-tender" yet "firm." Several tasters remarked that it seemed "really fresh" and "clean-tasting." Also helpful to flavor: It had the highest fat percentage of any bird in the tasting.

RECOMMENDED

SPRINGER MOUNTAIN FARMS Fresh Chicken
PRICE: $1.89 per lb
DISTRIBUTION: National, with concentration east of Mississippi
ANTIBIOTIC USE: "No antibiotics ever"
VEGETARIAN FEED: Yes
CHILLING METHOD: Water
FAT: 6.3%   SODIUM: 80 mg per 4-oz serving
COMMENTS: Compared with that of our air-chilled winners, this water-chilled bird's meat was "extremely mild-tasting." It also contained the least amount of fat. Even so, tasters thought both the white and dark meat boasted "nice chew." It bears the seal "American Humane Certified"—which mainly guarantees standard industry practices.

RECOMMENDED *(continued)*

COLEMAN ORGANIC Whole Chicken
(also sold as Rosie Organic Whole Chicken)
PRICE: $2.29 per lb
DISTRIBUTION: National
ANTIBIOTIC USE: "No antibiotics"
VEGETARIAN FEED: Yes
CHILLING METHOD: Water (some birds are air-chilled; package will specify)
FAT: 12%   SODIUM: 80 mg per 4-oz serving
COMMENTS: Its "super-moist meat" came across as "tender" but "not mushy" in both white and dark samples. However, tasters ranked its flavor as only "moderately chicken-y."

EMPIRE KOSHER Broiler Chicken
PRICE: $3.89 per lb
DISTRIBUTION: National
ANTIBIOTIC USE: "Never ever administered antibiotics"
VEGETARIAN FEED: Yes
CHILLING METHOD: Water, koshered (salted, soaked, and rinsed)
FAT: 9.2%   SODIUM: 290 mg per 4-oz serving
COMMENTS: Reactions to this kosher chicken's high sodium level were mixed: Some tasters found its white meat "rich" and its dark meat "roasty"; others found it "salty" and "gamy."

RECOMMENDED WITH RESERVATIONS

PERDUE Fresh Whole Chicken
PRICE: $1.99 per lb
DISTRIBUTION: National
ANTIBIOTIC USE: "Perdue does not use antibiotics for growth promotion"
VEGETARIAN FEED: Yes
CHILLING METHOD: Water
FAT: 9.8%   SODIUM: 80 mg per 4-oz serving
COMMENTS: Your "basic," "bland" chicken that some found "super-tender" but others deemed "dry." Perdue uses antibiotics "only when necessary" and boasts that the birds are vegetarian fed (which can mean a diet of bakery scraps) and are not kept caged within the chicken houses—which is standard practice.

TYSON Young Chicken
PRICE: $1.69 per lb
DISTRIBUTION: National
INGREDIENTS: Contains up to 12 percent chicken broth, sea salt, natural flavorings
ANTIBIOTIC USE: Yes
VEGETARIAN FEED: No
CHILLING METHOD: Water
FAT: 9.4%   SODIUM: 150 mg per 4-oz serving
COMMENTS: You know something's fishy when your chicken has an ingredient list. Tasters found this broth-injected bird "spongy," "wet," and "bland beyond description."

COUNTRY HAMS

Country ham is a strong, salty, dry-cured product produced primarily in Virginia, North Carolina, Tennessee, Kentucky, and Missouri. Country hams cure for anywhere from three months to years in a warm environment; the heat accelerates enzymatic activity, giving the ham unique robust, pungent flavors. We selected hams that were aged from three to six months because these are the most widely sold. When we tallied the results, we learned that of the seven products, we disliked just one. The top five, all recommended, were in a virtual tie. They were porky and complex with robust flavors. Hams are listed in order of preference.

RECOMMENDED

HARPER'S Grand Champion Whole Country Ham
PRICE: $61.21 for a 14- to 15-lb ham (shipping included)
ORIGIN: Kentucky
SODIUM: 1,980 mg per 3-oz serving
CURE AND AGE TIME: 3-month minimum
COMMENTS: Our top country ham pick was "delicious and savory"; "bacony"; "rich and deeply flavored"; "quietly smoky," with an "interesting mineral taste"; "well balanced"; and "not overwhelmed by salt." It was on the "tender" side of the spectrum with "moist," "juicy" meat.

BURGERS' SMOKEHOUSE Ready to Cook Country Ham
PRICE: $69.95 for a 13- to 15-lb ham (shipping included)
ORIGIN: Missouri
SODIUM: 1,490 mg per 3-oz serving
CURE AND AGE TIME: 4 to 6 months
COMMENTS: This "balanced" ham had a "nuanced," "rich, fatty" ham flavor that was "very deep" and spoke of "awesome bacon" with "a nice amount of fat to balance flavor." Slices were "silky," tender, and "slightly dry."

EDWARDS VIRGINIA TRADITIONS Uncooked Virginia Ham
PRICE: $97.53 for a 13- to 14-lb ham (shipping included)
ORIGIN: Virginia
SODIUM: 2,272 mg per 3-oz serving
CURE AND AGE TIME: 4 to 6 months
COMMENTS: The smoke flavor was stronger here, in this "very meaty"; "porky, nutty, and complex"; and "very deep, bacony" ham. It was drier than some other samples, with a "firm, good chew" that was "dense" and "compact" yet remained "tender" with "marbled fat." With all these winning characteristics, the relatively high salt level didn't bother us.

TRIPP COUNTRY HAMS Whole Country Ham
PRICE: $66.20 for a 13- to 14-lb ham (shipping included)
ORIGIN: Tennessee
SODIUM: 1,620 mg per 3-oz serving
CURE AND AGE TIME: 4 to 5 months
COMMENTS: This "super-concentrated" ham was "meaty," with a "slightly gamy" aftertaste and "intense pig flavor" combined with "some sweetness." Salt levels were balanced by the porky complexity. Slices were "moist," "plump, and juicy."

RECOMMENDED (continued)

GOODNIGHT BROTHERS Whole Country Ham
PRICE: $61.78 for a 12- to 15-lb ham (shipping included)
ORIGIN: North Carolina
SODIUM: 1,618 mg per 3-oz serving
CURE AND AGE TIME: 3 to 4 months
COMMENTS: This ham was salt-forward with "wild, funky" flavors balanced by a "strong *umami* flavor." This was the only unsmoked ham in our lineup, and a few tasters missed the smoke. It was on the dry side, with a "fatty" and "dense" bite.

RECOMMENDED WITH RESERVATIONS

JOHNSTON COUNTY HAMS INC. Whole Uncooked Country Ham
PRICE: $75.95 for a 13-lb ham (shipping included)
ORIGIN: North Carolina
SODIUM: 1,620 mg per 3-oz serving
CURE AND AGE TIME: 4 months
COMMENTS: This ham was "intense," with "hints of sweetness" and a "slightly funky, gamy" flavor. Tasters found its robust, complex taste "good in small amounts" but wished for more ham flavor beyond "funk." The texture was "lean" and "drier" than most.

NOT RECOMMENDED

SMITHFIELD HAMS Country Whole Ham (Uncooked)
PRICE: $79.99 for a 14- to 17-lb ham (shipping included)
ORIGIN: Virginia
SODIUM: 2,500 mg per 3-oz serving
CURE AND AGE TIME: 3 months
COMMENTS: This ham was nearly "inedible" due to a "mouth-puckering" saltiness combined with a funky, smoky flavor that was "like licking a smokehouse." "Lots going on here covering up the pork flavor," said one taster. The texture was "tough" and "leathery."

READY-MADE PIE CRUSTS

Homemade pie crust is worth the effort, but we don't always have the time. Enter premade crust—it may not be Grandma's, but it's fast and easy. Could we find one that is delicious as well? We put eight products to the test, choosing a mix of frozen and refrigerated doughs, including three sold in sheets and five in aluminum pie plates. We ate the shells baked plain, in single-crust pumpkin pies, and in double-crust apple pies, evaluating them on flavor, texture, capacity, and handling. Our benchmark was homemade crust: buttery, tender, and flaky. Many were too small for a standard 9-inch pie plate, and making a double-crust pie with preshaped crusts proved awkward. And thanks to the flimsy aluminum plates, the crusts burned in spots. We preferred the doughs sold in more versatile sheets. Some products were dense and tasted "processed" or included too much sugar or salt. The crusts we liked best used palm oil for a tender, flaky texture; they were neither too savory nor too sweet, and they didn't taste artificial. Pie crusts are listed in order of preference.

RECOMMENDED

WHOLLY WHOLESOME 9" Certified Organic Traditional Bake at Home Rolled Pie Dough
PRICE: $5.99
STYLE: Roll
FAT: Palm oil
COMMENTS: Slightly less flaky than the pan version from the same maker, this dough was "subtly sweet, rich," and "tender." It fluted well but takes a little care to unroll (sold frozen, it requires 3 hours of defrosting). It's an acceptable substitute if you don't have time to make a homemade crust.

RECOMMENDED WITH RESERVATIONS

WHOLLY WHOLESOME Organic Traditional 9" Pie Shells
PRICE: $3.59
STYLE: Pan
FAT: Palm oil
COMMENTS: In texture and taste, this crust was our favorite—"light and flaky," "crispy but yielding," with a "toasty," "buttery" flavor. But the shell was too small to hold fillings for standard 9-inch pie crust recipes. It was also slightly too dry to flute when we made a double-crust pie.

PILLSBURY Pie Crusts
PRICE: $3.49
STYLE: Roll
FAT: Partially hydrogenated lard
COMMENTS: Our previous favorite, formerly known as Pillsbury Just Unroll!, excelled at handling, producing perfect-looking pies that were dead easy to shape but baked up "thin," "brittle," and "crackerlike." Some found the dough "too salty" and disliked the "oily" finish.

MARIE CALLENDER'S 2 Deep Dish Pie Shells
PRICE: $2.99
STYLE: Pan
FAT: Vegetable shortening
COMMENTS: These crusts were "delightfully light" but were "devoid of flavor." Said one taster: "Tastes like shortening," which was, in fact, the second ingredient. They handled the best of all pan-style crusts during our double-crust pie testing.

RECOMMENDED WITH RESERVATIONS *(continued)*

PET-RITZ Pie Crusts by Pillsbury
PRICE: $3.69
STYLE: Pan
FAT: Partially hydrogenated lard
COMMENTS: These "light" yet "firm" crusts had the "sandy," "crisp" crumble of "shortbread," with a "sweet, cookielike flavor." Yet they became "mushy" when filled with pumpkin pie filling.

MRS. SMITH'S Deep Dish Pie Crusts
PRICE: $2.99
STYLE: Pan
FAT: Vegetable shortening, margarine
COMMENTS: These tightly packed crusts were "dense" and "short," with a "nice fatty crumble," but they turned mushy under pumpkin pie filling. The flavor was lackluster: "inoffensive" but "neutral." They baked without shrinking or tearing.

ORONOQUE ORCHARDS 9" Deep Dish Pie Crusts
PRICE: $3.59
STYLE: Pan
FAT: Vegetable shortening, margarine
COMMENTS: Tasters found this crust virtually indistinguishable from Mrs. Smith's, which makes both products (the company said there are slight ingredient differences), with similarly "short" and "dense" crusts that were "basic," if somewhat "bland." Pumpkin pie filling turned the crust soggy.

NOT RECOMMENDED

IMMACULATE BAKING CO. Ready-to-Bake Pie Crusts
PRICE: $3.99
STYLE: Roll
FAT: Palm fruit and canola oils
COMMENTS: This dough handled well but had a strong "sour" flavor: One taster called it a "deadly aftertaste"; another wrote "rancid." Cultured whey is added, which could produce a sour, fermented flavor.

SUPERMARKET COCOA POWDER

Cocoa powder is a chocolate powerhouse, packing in more flavor ounce for ounce than any other form of chocolate. In the test kitchen, we reach for it constantly when making cookies, cake, pudding, hot chocolate—even chili—which is why we're picky about what brand we keep around. Our top-rated cocoa powder from a 2005 tasting is available only by mail-order. Could we find a more convenient option that still boasted great flavor? We incorporated eight widely available brands of cocoa into chocolate butter cookies, chocolate cake, and hot cocoa, evaluating the samples on the intensity and complexity of the chocolate flavor. Lesser powders produced "wan" cakes and hot cocoa that tasted like "dust dissolved in water"; good versions delivered "profound" chocolate flavor and made cookies seem downright "luxurious." Brands that roast their cacao beans whole ended up with weaker flavor, while brands that shelled their beans first and roasted just the nibs—the dark, meaty flesh that is ground and later refined to make chocolate—had superior flavor. How finely the beans were ground also made a difference; the smaller the particle, the more surface area that's exposed, hence the more flavor that's released. Cocoa powders are listed in order of preference.

RECOMMENDED

HERSHEY'S Natural Cocoa Unsweetened
PRICE: $3.49 for 8 oz (44 cents per oz)
ROASTING STYLE: Nib
FAT: 11.46%
COMMENTS: Our winner is proof that you needn't look beyond the supermarket baking aisle for great cocoa. Hershey shells the nibs before roasting them and then grinds them very fine for cocoa boasting "assertive" chocolate flavor underlined by hints of "coffee," "orange," and "cinnamon."

DROSTE Cocoa
PRICE: $10.50 for 8.8 oz ($1.19 per oz)
ROASTING STYLE: Nib
FAT: 21.80%
COMMENTS: This Dutch-processed import impressed tasters with "round," "bold" flavor and "lots of depth." If it didn't cost nearly three times as much as our winner, it would be an appealing alternative. We'll splurge on it for recipes calling for Dutched cocoa.

HERSHEY'S Special Dark Cocoa
PRICE: $3.49 for 8 oz (44 cents per oz)
ROASTING STYLE: Nib
FAT: 12.61%
COMMENTS: A sibling of our winner, this blend of natural and Dutched cocoa tinted cakes and cookies such a deep color that one taster dubbed it "chocolate with a vengeance." But its "pleasant," "fruity" flavor didn't quite live up to the hue.

VALRHONA COCOA POWDER
PRICE: $11.99 for 8.82 oz ($1.36 per oz)
ROASTING STYLE: Proprietary
FAT: 21.94%
COMMENTS: This "grown-up" Dutched powder was "dynamite" in cookies, in which lots of butter rounded its "smoky" notes into "pronounced" chocolate flavor. But its smokiness made leaner cake taste as though it was "cooked over wood chips."

RECOMMENDED WITH RESERVATIONS

GHIRARDELLI Natural Unsweetened Cocoa
PRICE: $5.59 for 10 oz (56 cents per oz)
ROASTING STYLE: Nib
FAT: 12.56%
COMMENTS: Despite being nib-roasted, which gave other brands depth and richness, this "mild" powder tasted merely "respectable," with "smooth but undistinguished" flavor.

SCHARFFEN BERGER Unsweetened Natural Cocoa Powder
PRICE: $8.79 for 6 oz ($1.47 per oz)
ROASTING STYLE: Whole bean
FAT: 22.30%
COMMENTS: Tasters who appreciated a lighter-bodied natural cocoa praised this brand for tasting "more milky than bittersweet." But for most of us, it was simply "lacking in rich flavor." Its sky-high price also knocked it down a notch.

NESTLÉ Toll House Cocoa
PRICE: $2.69 for 8 oz (34 cents per oz)
ROASTING STYLE: Whole bean
FAT: 12.31%
COMMENTS: With "weak" chocolate flavor, this "kid-friendly" natural powder was described as "mild" and "one-dimensional."

EQUAL EXCHANGE Baking Cocoa
PRICE: $7.84 for 8 oz (98 cents per oz)
ROASTING STYLE: Whole bean
FAT: 11.54%
COMMENTS: Some tasters picked up on "malty" and "caramel" notes in this Dutched cocoa, but most agreed that its chocolate flavor "lacked intensity" and was "almost an afterthought." Other tasters found it a little "sour" or even "acidic."

VEGETABLE PEELERS

Dull, inefficient peelers make a mountain of tiresome work out of a simple task. A good peeler should be fast and smooth, cleanly removing the skin or peel without wasting food. We put 10 peelers through their paces, from lightweight tasks like potatoes, carrots, and apples to tough-skinned butternut squash, knobby ginger, delicate ripe tomatoes, and elegant chocolate curls. Vegetable peelers are listed in order of preference.

HIGHLY RECOMMENDED	PERFORMANCE	TESTERS' COMMENTS
KUHN RIKON Original Swiss Peeler MODEL: 2212 PRICE: $3.50 BLADE: Carbon steel WEIGHT: ⅜ oz AVG. PEEL THICKNESS: 0.90 mm	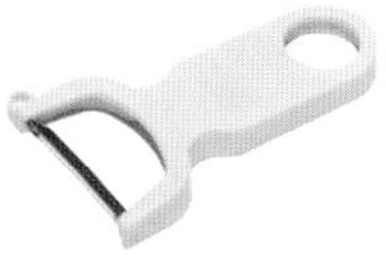 PERFORMANCE: ★★★ EASE OF USE: ★★★ DESIGN: ★★★	Don't be fooled by its featherweight design and cheap price tag. This Y-shaped peeler easily tackled every task, thanks to a razor-sharp blade and a ridged guide, which ensured a smooth ride with minimal surface drag.
MESSERMEISTER Pro-Touch Fine Edge Swivel Peeler MODEL: 800-58 PRICE: $10 BLADE: Stainless steel WEIGHT: 1½ oz AVG. PEEL THICKNESS: 0.82 mm	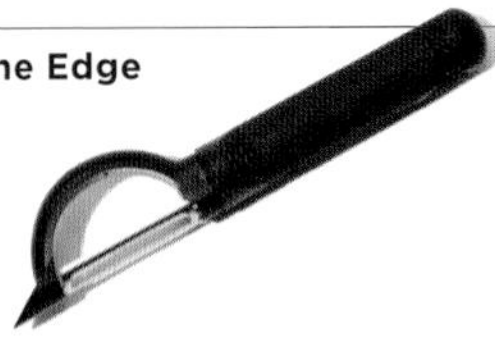 PERFORMANCE: ★★★ EASE OF USE: ★★★ DESIGN: ★★★	A stellar choice for those who prefer a straight peeler. Lightweight, sharp, and comfortable, this model rivaled the winner, gliding over fruits and vegetables and producing almost transparent peels. Its high arch meant no clogging.

RECOMMENDED		
WMF Profi Plus Horizontal Vegetable Peeler MODEL: 1872616030 PRICE: $18 BLADE: Stainless steel WEIGHT: 3¼ oz AVG. PEEL THICKNESS: 1.08 mm	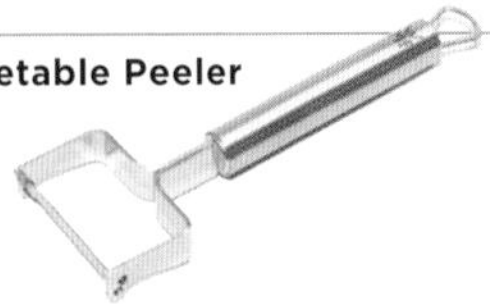 PERFORMANCE: ★★½ EASE OF USE: ★★★ DESIGN: ★★★	The other model with a ridged guide, this sturdy, sharp—and most expensive—peeler glided over everything from carrots to rough-textured celery root, though its peels were thicker than some.
MESSERMEISTER Culinary Instruments Swivel Peeler, Y Shape MODEL: 900-189 PRICE: $7.50 BLADE: Stainless steel WEIGHT: 1 oz AVG. PEEL THICKNESS: 1.11 mm	 PERFORMANCE: ★★½ EASE OF USE: ★★ DESIGN: ★★	Though it quickly removed wide swaths of peel and off-loaded waste easily, this Y peeler was outshone by its sibling when it skinned a little too deep. Its broad blade was a bit tricky to maneuver around smaller potatoes and curvy, bumpy celery root.
SWISSMAR Swiss Classic Peeler, Scalpel Blade MODEL: 00447 PRICE: $10.17 BLADE: Stainless steel WEIGHT: ⅝ oz AVG. PEEL THICKNESS: 1.05 mm	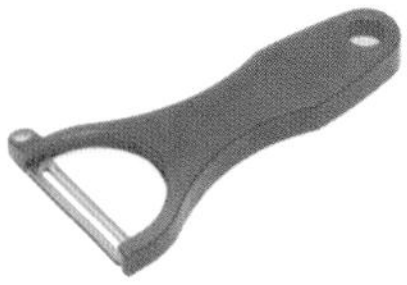 PERFORMANCE: ★★½ EASE OF USE: ★★ DESIGN: ★★	Sharp and maneuverable, this lightweight peeler bit through the toughest peels with ease but also stripped away a good bit of flesh. A closer look revealed why: Its blade has a curved belly that bites deeply, creating more waste.

RECOMMENDED WITH RESERVATIONS		
RACHAEL RAY TOOLS 3-in-1 Veg-A-Peel Vegetable Peeler/Brush MODEL: 55250 PRICE: $9.06 BLADE: Stainless steel WEIGHT: 1⅜ oz AVG. PEEL THICKNESS: 1.05 mm	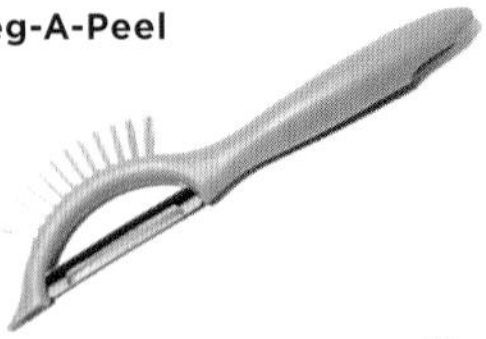 PERFORMANCE: ★★½ EASE OF USE: ★★ DESIGN: ★½	Peels were thin and waste was minimal; in fact, this model often required a few extra strokes. We might have liked this peeler's attached vegetable brush if it didn't mean that our thumb was prone to gripping the blade on the other side as we scrubbed—ouch.
OXO Good Grips Swivel Peeler MODEL: 20081 PRICE: $7.99 BLADE: Stainless steel WEIGHT: 2⅜ oz AVG. PEEL THICKNESS: 0.71 mm	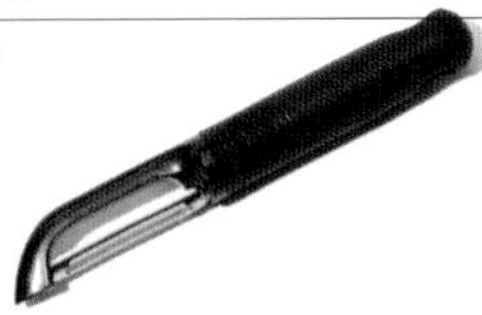 PERFORMANCE: ★★ EASE OF USE: ★½ DESIGN: ★★	This model produced the thinnest peels and the least amount of waste, but we often needed to go over patches again to finish the job. Many testers found the thick handle fatiguing and clunky. Its low bridge clogged frequently.

NOT RECOMMENDED		
KYOCERA Ceramic Y Peeler MODEL: CP-10N PRICE: $8.12 BLADE: Ceramic WEIGHT: 1 oz AVG. PEEL THICKNESS: 1.05 mm	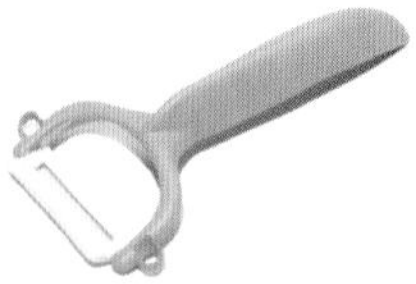 PERFORMANCE: ★½ EASE OF USE: ★ DESIGN: ★★	Potatoes and carrots were no problem, but the high bridge provided less leverage and control. This peeler struggled with celery root and utterly failed to skin butternut squash. Its ceramic blade was noticeably duller after testing.

SALAD SPINNERS

All salad spinners share a basic design: a perforated basket that balances on a point in the center of a larger bowl and spins to propel water off of greens. But the spinning mechanisms and other differences in design affect how well salad spinners work. Our favorite spinning mechanism was a pump: The simple up-and-down motion takes little effort, and since it's set in the center, the spinner won't dance around on the counter. We disliked conical spinners with smaller bases, which wobbled at high speeds. To test drying ability, we weighed batches of greens before and after washing to see which spinner threw off the most water. Baskets with large capacities let us dry the greens in fewer batches. When it was time to clean up, we found that white or clear baskets were the easiest to clean; green baskets made it difficult to see trapped greens. Salad spinners are listed in order of preference.

HIGHLY RECOMMENDED	PERFORMANCE	TESTERS' COMMENTS
OXO GOOD GRIPS Salad Spinner MODEL: 32480V2 PRICE: $29.99 SPIN MECHANISM: Pump CAPACITY: 4½ qt WATER LEFT BEHIND AFTER SPINNING: 44 g	EASE OF USE: ★★★ CLEANUP: ★★★ STURDINESS: ★★★	Our redesigned favorite is better than ever. Its pump mechanism was the easiest to use among the models we tested, and its performance remained superb, holding plenty of greens and getting them driest. The new, wider base provides more stability, the smaller pump increases the spinner's capacity, and the flat lid comes apart for easy cleaning and storage.

RECOMMENDED

ZYLISS Smart Touch Salad Spinner MODEL: 15912 PRICE: $29.95 SPIN MECHANISM: Lever CAPACITY: 5 qt WATER LEFT BEHIND AFTER SPINNING: 59 g	EASE OF USE: ★★½ CLEANUP: ★★★ STURDINESS: ★★½	We liked the large capacity, which let us wash and dry 2 pounds of greens in two batches. The lever was easy to use and worked similarly to the pump on the OXO model, and it locked down for easy storage. However, because the lever pushes slightly to one side, this spinner did hop about a bit. It comes in green or white; the white is easier to clean, as you can see any trapped herbs.

RECOMMENDED WITH RESERVATIONS

CHEF'N Large Salad Spinner MODEL: 83845018216 PRICE: $19.95 SPIN MECHANISM: Lever CAPACITY: 3½ qt WATER LEFT BEHIND AFTER SPINNING: 63 g	EASE OF USE: ★★ CLEANUP: ★★ STURDINESS: ★★	This spinner got the job done, but its combined flaws lowered its rank. It took three batches to clean 2 pounds of greens, and while the spinner did an adequate job of drying them, its lever made disconcerting clicking noises, making us worry that it might wear out quickly. Its lid does not collapse for storage, and its green basket made trapped particles difficult to see.
PROGRESSIVE Ratchet Salad Spinner MODEL: SAL-100 PRICE: $37.71 SPIN MECHANISM: Ratchet handle CAPACITY: 5 qt WATER LEFT BEHIND AFTER SPINNING: 64 g	EASE OF USE: ★★ CLEANUP: ★★ STURDINESS: ★★	We have few complaints about this model's performance. It has a large capacity, and the ratchet mechanism is effortless to use (though slightly uncomfortable if you are left-handed). Unfortunately, the basket's conical shape reduced its usable capacity, and it is harder to store because it's taller than other models, with a lid that makes stacking impossible.
ZYLISS Easy Spin Salad Spinner MODEL: 15103 PRICE: $24.99 SPIN MECHANISM: Self-retracting cord CAPACITY: 5 qt WATER LEFT BEHIND AFTER SPINNING: 49 g	EASE OF USE: ★½ CLEANUP: ★½ STURDINESS: ★½	This model placed just behind our winner when it came to drying ability, and it spun 2 pounds of greens in a respectable three batches. However, the spinning mechanism (a pull cord) makes you pull away from the spinner, so you have to apply significant pressure to hold down the lid, occasionally causing it to go askew and partially fall into the spinner.

NOT RECOMMENDED

KITCHENAID Professional Salad Spinner MODEL: KG308ER PRICE: $34.99 SPIN MECHANISM: Pump CAPACITY: 5 qt WATER LEFT BEHIND AFTER SPINNING: 63 g	EASE OF USE: ½ CLEANUP: ★½ STURDINESS: ★	This model had a fatal flaw: Push the pump too far down and the spinning basket locks, requiring you to stop, remove the lid, turn the pump until it unlocks, and rethread the pump through the lid before you can (finally) continue spinning. Also, the pump runs down the center of the basket, taking up space, and the bowl's narrow base reduces stability.

INEXPENSIVE TRADITIONAL SKILLETS

A 12-inch skillet is a kitchen workhorse, and a well-made one should last a lifetime. But we wondered how much we really needed to spend to guarantee great performance and durability. We bought seven skillets, all for less than $100, and put them to the test. We seared steaks, made pan sauces, pan-roasted chicken parts, and sautéed onions, tracking the pans' heating patterns with an infrared camera. We also tested their durability by heating each pan to 550 degrees, plunging it into an ice bath, then banging it against the sidewalk. One skillet stood out for its performance, design, and sturdy construction. Skillets are listed in order of preference.

RECOMMENDED

	PERFORMANCE	TESTERS' COMMENTS
TRAMONTINA 12-Inch Tri-Ply Clad Sauté Pan `BEST BUY` **MODEL:** 80116/509 **PRICE:** $39.97 **WEIGHT:** 3.9 lb **COOKING SURFACE DIAMETER:** 9½ in **HANDLE LENGTH:** 8½ in **MATERIAL:** Fully clad, stainless with aluminum core	COOKING: ★★★ HANDLING: ★★ DURABILITY: ★★★	In performance, design, and construction, this skillet resembled our favorite high-end All-Clad skillet. It's big enough to pan-roast eight pieces of chicken without crowding and offers steady heat for good browning; a long handle for good leverage; and low, flaring sides to encourage evaporation. Our abuse testing left barely visible dents. Our only gripe: its weight—it's considerably heavier than the All-Clad pan.
EMERIL Pro-Clad Stainless Steel Tri-Ply 12-Inch Fry Pan **MODEL:** E9830764 **PRICE:** $59.99 **WEIGHT:** 2.75 lb **COOKING SURFACE DIAMETER:** 9 in **HANDLE LENGTH:** 7½ in **MATERIAL:** Fully clad, stainless with aluminum core	COOKING: ★★½ HANDLING: ★★ DURABILITY: ★★	This pan weighed 2.75 pounds, the same as our high-end favorite pan by All-Clad. It cooked fairly well, heating just slightly faster than our winner, with food getting darker more quickly. The pan was mostly comfortable to use, but the short handle made it awkward to move a loaded pan into the oven. The pan suffered a few dings during durability testing.
CUISINART 12-Inch MultiClad Pro Skillet **MODEL:** MCP22-30H **PRICE:** $69.95 **WEIGHT:** 3.7 lb **COOKING SURFACE DIAMETER:** 10½ in **HANDLE LENGTH:** 8½ in **MATERIAL:** Fully clad, stainless with aluminum core	COOKING: ★★½ HANDLING: ★★ DURABILITY: ★★	Fitting eight pieces of chicken in this spacious skillet was no problem, and the helper handle eased moving this somewhat hefty pan in and out of the oven. Inconsistent heating was a minor problem: Onions cooked slowly and evenly at the start, but later on hot spots appeared. Still, overall, the pan performed adequately in all of our tests.

RECOMMENDED WITH RESERVATIONS

	PERFORMANCE	TESTERS' COMMENTS
COOL KITCHEN Integral 3 by Josef Strauss **MODEL:** CKZ30SK **PRICE:** $99 **WEIGHT:** 4.15 lb **COOKING SURFACE DIAMETER:** 9¾ in **HANDLE LENGTH:** 9¾ in **MATERIAL:** Fully clad, stainless with aluminum core	COOKING: ★★ HANDLING: ★ DURABILITY: ★★★	At more than 4 pounds, this was the heaviest skillet we tested. Its helper handle made it easier—but still not easy—to maneuver. It heated a little slower than other skillets we tested and slightly unevenly. The pan sailed through the durability tests unscathed.
CALPHALON Tri-Ply Stainless Steel 12-Inch Omelette Pan **MODEL:** 1767730 **PRICE:** $94.95 **WEIGHT:** 3.2 lb **COOKING SURFACE DIAMETER:** 9¾ in **HANDLE LENGTH:** 8¼ in **MATERIAL:** Fully clad, stainless with aluminum core	COOKING: ★★ HANDLING: ★★ DURABILITY: ★★	This pan was acceptable in every test but never impressive. It heats a little fast, requiring extra vigilance to avoid overbrowning or burning. In the durability testing it got a little dinged up. (Although the manufacturer labels it an "omelette pan," it's meant to be used as an ordinary skillet, not merely for omelets.)
T-FAL Ultimate Stainless Steel Copper Skillet **MODEL:** C8360764 **PRICE:** $36.52 **WEIGHT:** 3.3 lb **COOKING SURFACE DIAMETER:** 10 in **HANDLE LENGTH:** 6¼ in **MATERIAL:** Disk bottom; stainless steel pan with copper and stainless steel disk	COOKING: ★ HANDLING: ★ DURABILITY: ★	We hoped the copper disk would make this pan a star performer. Oh, well. While it heated slowly and for the most part evenly, there were hot spots where the disk ended. Also, grease that splashed onto the thin, stainless steel sides scorched on in an instant. The short handle flexed and was too hot to hold.

GRILL PANS

When you can't fire up the grill, it's handy to have a stovetop grill pan. Though it can't replicate the flavor of the open flame, a ridged grill pan does make crusty, tasty char-grill marks on meat, fish, and vegetables. We gathered eight pans in stainless steel, nonstick-coated aluminum, and enameled and plain cast iron. The price range was dramatic—from about $19 to nearly $200. Nonstick pans were easy to clean but left partial, indistinct grill marks on the food. The nonstick pans also had shallower ridges. The low ridges let food fry in its own rendered fat, giving us greasy results. Cast-iron pans made the best grill marks and did better at retaining heat. Grill pans are listed in order of preference.

	PERFORMANCE	TESTERS' COMMENTS

HIGHLY RECOMMENDED

STAUB 12-Inch American Square Grill Pan and Press
PRICE: $159.90, including press
MODEL: 120 28 23
MATERIAL: Enameled cast iron
RIDGE HEIGHT: 5.5 mm
COOKING AREA: 110 sq in

GRILL MARKS: ★★★
CLEANUP: ★★★
CAPACITY: ★★★

This handsome pan consistently produced crisp, distinct grill marks. It had the highest ridges of the pans tested, keeping food well above rendered fat. It weighs a hefty 10 pounds (without the press), but it's the solid cast-iron construction that accounts for flawless heat retention. It has ample room and a scrubbable enamel coating.

RECOMMENDED

LE CREUSET Panini Press Skillet Grill Set
PRICE: $199.95, including press
MODEL: L2021-26
MATERIAL: Enameled cast iron
RIDGE HEIGHT: 4 mm
COOKING AREA: 64 sq in

GRILL MARKS: ★★★
CLEANUP: ★★★
CAPACITY: ★★

This pricey enameled cast-iron pan grilled nearly as well as our winner and made crisp, distinct char marks with comparatively high grill ridges. But it barely fit three burgers or two strip steaks. The enamel coating aided cleanup.

LODGE LOGIC Pre-Seasoned Square Grill Pan and Ribbed Panini Press (LPP3) `BEST BUY`
PRICE: $18.97 (press sold separately for $14.58)
MODEL: L8SGP3
MATERIAL: Cast iron
RIDGE HEIGHT: 4.8 mm
COOKING AREA: 76.5 sq in

GRILL MARKS: ★★★
CLEANUP: ★★
CAPACITY: ★★

Perfect grilling at a low price made this a solid Best Buy. But its smaller surface fits just three burgers or two strip steaks and can't be cleaned with soap. As with our favorite cast-iron skillet, it scrubs clean with hot water and a stiff brush. (Also like that skillet, it will become more nonstick with use.)

RECOMMENDED WITH RESERVATIONS

CALPHALON Contemporary Nonstick Square Grill Pan
PRICE: $39.95
MODEL: JR1111P
MATERIAL: Hard anodized aluminum, nonstick coating
RIDGE HEIGHT: 1.88 mm
COOKING AREA: 100 sq in

GRILL MARKS: ★
CLEANUP: ★★★
CAPACITY: ★★★

This large nonstick-coated pan easily fit four burgers, released glazed salmon, and cleaned up with a few swipes. Grill marks were its downfall: The round, low ridges of this pan did nothing to burgers on the second side (except fry them).

ANOLON NOUVELLE Copper Hard Anodized Nonstick Deep Grill Pan, Round
PRICE: $49.99
MODEL: 82742
MATERIAL: Hard anodized aluminum, nonstick coating
RIDGE HEIGHT: 2.6 mm
COOKING AREA: 85 sq in

GRILL MARKS: ½
CLEANUP: ★★★
CAPACITY: ★★★

The broken circular pattern of this pan's low ridges made grill marks that looked like a nuclear fallout symbol on one side of the burgers (and fried the other side). But it was roomy, easily fitting four burgers, and it released glazed salmon flawlessly.

NOT RECOMMENDED

ALL-CLAD d-5 Stainless Steel Square Grill Pan
PRICE: $149.95
MODEL: 2974517
MATERIAL: 18/10 stainless steel
RIDGE HEIGHT: 3.1 mm
COOKING AREA: 81 sq in

GRILL MARKS: ★
CLEANUP: ½
CAPACITY: ★★★

The wide, broken grill marks from the shallow ridges on this pan impressed no one. Glazed salmon stuck stubbornly. Although decently roomy, this not inexpensive pan fried burgers instead of grilling them—and its surface blackened after a few uses.

COOKIE SHEETS

It's just a flat piece of metal, so you'd think a cookie sheet couldn't fail. In fact, we've seen them bake unevenly and warp, not to mention let cookies burn, stick, or spread into blobs. Cookie sheets also come in many materials, sizes, thicknesses, and finishes, insulated or not, with rims or not. So what works best? We gathered eight, priced from $12 to $24, testing both single sheets and insulated versions. To test them, we baked three types of cookies on both unlined and parchment paper–lined sheets. We looked at how evenly the sheets baked, how well the cookies released from the sheets, whether or not the sheets warped, and how well the sheets were designed. Cookie sheets are listed in order of preference.

	PERFORMANCE	TESTERS' COMMENTS
HIGHLY RECOMMENDED		
VOLLRATH Wear-Ever Cookie Sheet (Natural Finish) MODEL: 68085 PRICE: $15.99 BAKING SURFACE: 17 by 14 (238 sq in) THICKNESS: 2.46 mm MATERIAL: 10-gauge 3004 aluminum	PERFORMANCE: ★★★ DESIGN: ★★½ DURABILITY: ★★★	This solid sheet pan is roomy, and raised edges on two sides make it easy to maneuver (though it's a bit heavy). Cookies baked evenly, both across the sheet and from top to bottom, and its thick aluminum resists warping. Even without parchment, this sheet released cookies easily.
RECOMMENDED		
FAT DADDIO'S Cookie Sheet, Commercial Weight MODEL: CSHD-12516 PRICE: $24.12 BAKING SURFACE: 16 by 12½ in (200 sq in) THICKNESS: 2.37 mm MATERIAL: 10-gauge anodized aluminum	PERFORMANCE: ★★ DESIGN: ★★★ DURABILITY: ★★★	Similar to our winner in shape and construction, this sheet was slightly smaller and weighed less, making it easier to maneuver. Also, it baked faster. Though the pan heated evenly, cookie bottoms browned far more than their tops.
RECOMMENDED WITH RESERVATIONS		
AIRBAKE BY T-FAL Natural Insulated Large Cooking Sheet MODEL: 08603PA PRICE: $12.10 BAKING SURFACE: 15½ by 14 in (217 sq in) THICKNESS: 4.34 mm MATERIAL: Aluminum	PERFORMANCE: ★★ DESIGN: ★★ DURABILITY: ★★	The best of the insulated models, this roomy sheet baked evenly and released well, even without parchment. The single raised rim made it slightly more difficult to maneuver, and it warped a little, distorting our lace cookies.
NOT RECOMMENDED		
USA PANS Cookie Sheet, 18" x 14" MODEL: 1030LC PRICE: $18.99 BAKING SURFACE: 17 by 12¼ in (208.25 sq in) THICKNESS: 0.83 mm MATERIAL: Silicone-coated aluminized steel	PERFORMANCE: ★ DESIGN: ★½ DURABILITY: ★	This thin sheet baked so fast that it nearly burned every batch. Moreover, it baked unevenly and was prone to warp. Its super-slick silicone-coated surface could easily send parchment and cookies flying.
FARBERWARE Insulated Bakeware 14 x 16 Inch Cookie Sheet MODEL: 52151 PRICE: $14.95 BAKING SURFACE: 16½ by 13 in (214.5 sq in) THICKNESS: 4.35 mm MATERIAL: Nonstick-coated carbon steel	PERFORMANCE: ★ DESIGN: ★★ DURABILITY: ½	This dual-layer sheet warped each and every time we used it. It also ran hot, baking nearly a third faster than times indicated by the recipes in several cases and turning cookie bottoms very dark.
NORPRO S/S Cookie Baking Sheet MODEL: 3862 PRICE: $15.66 BAKING SURFACE: 16 by 11½ in (184 sq in) THICKNESS: 0.65 mm MATERIAL: Stainless steel	PERFORMANCE: ★ DESIGN: ★ DURABILITY: ★	Thin, cramped, and flimsy, this sheet warped almost immediately. If the limited baking surface was not problem enough, the raised edges on each side made it even harder to navigate our spatula around the cookies.
WILTON EXCELLE ELITE Air Insulated Sheet Pan MODEL: 2105-422 PRICE: $23.89 BAKING SURFACE: 18 by 14 in (252 sq in) THICKNESS: 6.4 mm MATERIAL: Nonstick-coated steel	PERFORMANCE: ★ DESIGN: ★ DURABILITY: ★	This pan was oversize, cumbersome, and pricey. It also baked unevenly, with dark cookies around the perimeter of the pan and underdone cookies in the center. Its nonstick surface scratched and looked beat-up by the end of testing.

ROLLING PINS

Choosing a rolling pin used to be simple: Almost all were made from wood, and the only question was whether to go with handles or without. Nowadays, the choices for materials and designs could take hours to consider. To see if innovation could trump the tried and true, we rounded up nine pins in wood, metal, and silicone, tapered and straight, with handles and without, priced from $9.99 to $45. We wanted an all-purpose pin, so we set to work rolling out pie crust, yeasted rolls, cookies, and pizza. We found that we preferred simple wooden pins with enough flat surface area for efficient rolling, a moderate weight, and a slightly textured surface to move dough without slipping or sticking. Rolling pins are listed in order of preference.

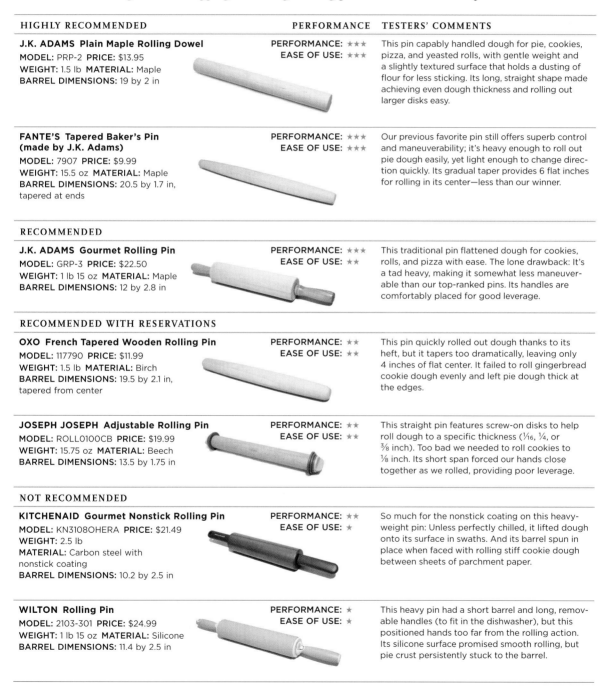

HIGHLY RECOMMENDED	PERFORMANCE	TESTERS' COMMENTS
J.K. ADAMS Plain Maple Rolling Dowel MODEL: PRP-2 PRICE: $13.95 WEIGHT: 1.5 lb MATERIAL: Maple BARREL DIMENSIONS: 19 by 2 in	PERFORMANCE: ★★★ EASE OF USE: ★★★	This pin capably handled dough for pie, cookies, pizza, and yeasted rolls, with gentle weight and a slightly textured surface that holds a dusting of flour for less sticking. Its long, straight shape made achieving even dough thickness and rolling out larger disks easy.
FANTE'S Tapered Baker's Pin (made by J.K. Adams) MODEL: 7907 PRICE: $9.99 WEIGHT: 15.5 oz MATERIAL: Maple BARREL DIMENSIONS: 20.5 by 1.7 in, tapered at ends	PERFORMANCE: ★★★ EASE OF USE: ★★★	Our previous favorite pin still offers superb control and maneuverability; it's heavy enough to roll out pie dough easily, yet light enough to change direction quickly. Its gradual taper provides 6 flat inches for rolling in its center—less than our winner.

RECOMMENDED		
J.K. ADAMS Gourmet Rolling Pin MODEL: GRP-3 PRICE: $22.50 WEIGHT: 1 lb 15 oz MATERIAL: Maple BARREL DIMENSIONS: 12 by 2.8 in	PERFORMANCE: ★★★ EASE OF USE: ★★	This traditional pin flattened dough for cookies, rolls, and pizza with ease. The lone drawback: It's a tad heavy, making it somewhat less maneuverable than our top-ranked pins. Its handles are comfortably placed for good leverage.

RECOMMENDED WITH RESERVATIONS		
OXO French Tapered Wooden Rolling Pin MODEL: 117790 PRICE: $11.99 WEIGHT: 1.5 lb MATERIAL: Birch BARREL DIMENSIONS: 19.5 by 2.1 in, tapered from center	PERFORMANCE: ★★ EASE OF USE: ★★	This pin quickly rolled out dough thanks to its heft, but it tapers too dramatically, leaving only 4 inches of flat center. It failed to roll gingerbread cookie dough evenly and left pie dough thick at the edges.
JOSEPH JOSEPH Adjustable Rolling Pin MODEL: ROLL0100CB PRICE: $19.99 WEIGHT: 15.75 oz MATERIAL: Beech BARREL DIMENSIONS: 13.5 by 1.75 in	PERFORMANCE: ★★ EASE OF USE: ★★	This straight pin features screw-on disks to help roll dough to a specific thickness ($\frac{1}{16}$, $\frac{1}{4}$, or $\frac{3}{8}$ inch). Too bad we needed to roll cookies to $\frac{1}{8}$ inch. Its short span forced our hands close together as we rolled, providing poor leverage.

NOT RECOMMENDED		
KITCHENAID Gourmet Nonstick Rolling Pin MODEL: KN3108OHERA PRICE: $21.49 WEIGHT: 2.5 lb MATERIAL: Carbon steel with nonstick coating BARREL DIMENSIONS: 10.2 by 2.5 in	PERFORMANCE: ★★ EASE OF USE: ★	So much for the nonstick coating on this heavy-weight pin: Unless perfectly chilled, it lifted dough onto its surface in swaths. And its barrel spun in place when faced with rolling stiff cookie dough between sheets of parchment paper.
WILTON Rolling Pin MODEL: 2103-301 PRICE: $24.99 WEIGHT: 1 lb 15 oz MATERIAL: Silicone BARREL DIMENSIONS: 11.4 by 2.5 in	PERFORMANCE: ★ EASE OF USE: ★	This heavy pin had a short barrel and long, removable handles (to fit in the dishwasher), but this positioned hands too far from the rolling action. Its silicone surface promised smooth rolling, but pie crust persistently stuck to the barrel.

PEPPER MILLS

For our money, a pepper mill has one purpose: to swiftly crank out the desired size and amount of fresh ground pepper, without any guesswork in grind selection or extra strain on our wrists. Simple criteria, and yet many models fail to measure up. To find one that would, we rounded up nine contenders, both manual and battery-powered, priced from $27 to nearly $100, and got grinding. We tested each mill by timing how long it took to produce the equivalent of 2 tablespoons of finely ground pepper. We also looked at how easily each mill allowed us to control the grind size and whether the mills could produce a range of sizes from fine to coarsely ground. Pepper mills are listed in order of preference.

HIGHLY RECOMMENDED	PERFORMANCE	TESTERS' COMMENTS
COLE & MASON Derwent Gourmet Precision Pepper Mill MODEL: H59401G PM PRICE: $40 GRIND MECHANISM: Carbon steel CAPACITY: Scant ½ cup	GRIND QUALITY: ★★★ EASE OF USE: ★★★ FINE-GRIND SPEED: ★★	When it comes to grind quality, this mill is tops. It made grind selection a snap, with clear markings corresponding to grind size, and every one of its six fixed settings performed well. Its transparent acrylic body proved easy to load and grasp.

RECOMMENDED

PEUGEOT DAMAN u'Select Shaftless Pepper Mill MODEL: PM25441 PRICE: $75 GRIND MECHANISM: Carbon steel CAPACITY: ½ cup	GRIND QUALITY: ★★½ EASE OF USE: ★★ FINE-GRIND SPEED: ★★★	This high-performing mill was fast and consistent, but if its peppercorn supply fell below 1 inch, output slowed. However, with no center shaft and a clever magnetized lid, this mill is a snap to refill. We would prefer that the grind-size adjuster click firmly into place: It can slip if you grab it during grinding.
TRUDEAU Easy Grind 6½-Inch Pepper Mill MODEL: 0716027 PRICE: $33.99 GRIND MECHANISM: Carbon steel CAPACITY: ⅔ cup	GRIND QUALITY: ★★½ EASE OF USE: ★★ FINE-GRIND SPEED: ★★★	This inexpensive crank-style mill lived up to its name with an easy-to-grip handle that had us cranking out pepper at a rapid clip. A downside: The grind adjustment dial has no fixed grind sizes, making it hard to get just the right pepper size.
UNICORN Magnum Plus Pepper Mill MODEL: 61695 PRICE: $45 GRIND MECHANISM: Stainless steel CAPACITY: 1⅛ cups	GRIND QUALITY: ★★ EASE OF USE: ★★ FINE-GRIND SPEED: ★★★	Our old favorite remains fast and efficient, with a generous capacity and a smooth operation, but its "fine" grind looked more like medium. There are no fixed grind settings, requiring trial and error to get the right grind size, and the loading ring twisted open during grinding, spilling out peppercorns.

RECOMMENDED WITH RESERVATIONS

VIC FIRTH 8-Inch Federal Pepper Mill MODEL: FED08PM21 PRICE: $45.95 GRIND MECHANISM: Stainless steel CAPACITY: ¼ cup	GRIND QUALITY: ★★★ EASE OF USE: ★★ FINE-GRIND SPEED: ★½	Comfortable to hold and twist, this wood mill produced uniform grinds in each setting. Its major flaws were a very small capacity to hold peppercorns, which were difficult to load, and poor output: It finely ground pepper at a very slow pace, even when we loosened the setting a few notches.
UNICORN KeyTop Professional Pepper Mill MODEL: 91597 PRICE: $27 GRIND MECHANISM: Stainless steel CAPACITY: Scant ½ cup	GRIND QUALITY: ★★½ EASE OF USE: ★★ FINE-GRIND SPEED: ★★	The grind mechanism on this mill from Unicorn is smaller than that of its predecessor, and its key top was hard to grasp, slowing our efforts. It made a better fine grind than did the Magnum Plus but didn't produce uniformly coarse pepper.

NOT RECOMMENDED

PEUGEOT Saint Malo 5.7 Inch Pepper Mill MODEL: PM27483 PRICE: $49.95 GRIND MECHANISM: Carbon steel CAPACITY: Scant ¼ cup	GRIND QUALITY: ★½ EASE OF USE: ★ FINE-GRIND SPEED: ★★★	This small crank-style mill ground pepper in a flash, but it was uncomfortable to hold and crank and fussy to load. Its fine grind produced too many large pieces—most likely because its crank handle loosened the finial that controls the grind setting.
WILLIAM BOUNDS HM 11-Inch Proview Pepper Mill MODEL: 04817 PRICE: $70 GRIND MECHANISM: Ceramic CAPACITY: ⅔ cup	GRIND QUALITY: ★½ EASE OF USE: ★½ FINE-GRIND SPEED: ★	This tall, heavy mill grinds pepper by twisting in both directions, but that didn't make it more efficient—its shallow-grooved ceramic grinder took far longer than carbon steel to crack peppercorns.

DRIP COFFEE MAKERS

In the past, we've found that few automatic drip coffee makers achieve research-based standards for brew cycle time and water temperature, two factors necessary for bringing out the fullest flavor in coffee without bitter notes. With a number of new, high-end coffee makers on the market, we wondered if any were up to par. To find out, we bought seven coffee makers with thermal carafes (the hot plates beneath most glass carafes scorch coffee in minutes) and got brewing. Coffee makers are listed in order of preference.

HIGHLY RECOMMENDED	PERFORMANCE	TESTERS' COMMENTS
TECHNIVORM Moccamaster 10-Cup Coffee Maker with Thermal Carafe MODEL: KBGT 741 PRICE: $299 AVERAGE BREW TIME: 6 min, 11 sec BREW TEMPERATURE IN IDEAL RANGE: 87% WATER CAPACITY: 40 oz	BREW FLAVOR: ★★★ DESIGN: ★★★ CARAFE: ★	Certified by the Specialty Coffee Association of American (SCAA), the updated version of our old favorite (the KBT 741) meets time and temperature guidelines with utter consistency. As a result, it produces a "smooth," "velvety" brew. It's also intuitive to use. The carafe lost some heat after 2 hours but still kept the coffee above 150 degrees.
BONAVITA 8-Cup Coffee Maker with Thermal Carafe [BEST BUY] MODEL: BV 1800 TH PRICE: $149 AVERAGE BREW TIME: 6 min, 43 sec BREW TEMPERATURE IN IDEAL RANGE: 78% WATER CAPACITY: 40 oz	BREW FLAVOR: ★★★ DESIGN: ★★½ CARAFE: ★	Simple to use and SCAA-certified, this brewer spends most of the cycle in the ideal temperature range. Its coffee had "bright," "full" flavor that was a bit more "acidic" than the Technivorm's. The widemouthed carafe is easy to clean, but there's no brew-through lid; you must remove the brew basket and screw on a separate lid to keep coffee hot.

RECOMMENDED		
BUNN HT Phase Brew 8-Cup Thermal Carafe Coffee Maker MODEL: HT PRICE: $139.99 AVERAGE BREW TIME: 4 min, 49 sec BREW TEMPERATURE IN IDEAL RANGE: 87% WATER CAPACITY: 40 oz	BREW FLAVOR: ★★½ DESIGN: ★★★ CARAFE: ★★	This SCAA-certified pot heats the water completely before releasing it over the grounds. That explained its impressive temperature accuracy, though the coffee was somewhat "acidic." (Note: Early versions of this model shorted out when home voltage fluctuated; Bunn states that it has solved this problem, and our machine worked fine.)

NOT RECOMMENDED		
CAPRESSO MT600 PLUS 10-Cup Programmable Coffee Maker with Thermal Carafe MODEL: 485 PRICE: $129.99 AVERAGE BREW TIME: 10 min, 26 sec BREW TEMPERATURE IN IDEAL RANGE: 35% WATER CAPACITY: 40 oz	BREW FLAVOR: ★½ DESIGN: ★½ CARAFE: ★★	This model's water temperature climbed above the ideal zone for most of the cycle—hence the "burnt" complaints. Its cycle also ran too long. The design wasn't great: Controls were confusing, loading the reservoir was awkward (you must peer around the side to see the water level), and the carafe dribbles.
BODUM BISTRO b. over Coffee Machine MODEL: 11001-565US PRICE: $250 AVERAGE BREW TIME: 5 min, 54 sec BREW TEMPERATURE IN IDEAL RANGE: 35% WATER CAPACITY: 40 oz	BREW FLAVOR: ★½ DESIGN: ★ CARAFE: ★★★	This machine's brew cycle was erratic (running first cool and then hot); its design was flimsy; and, most damning, its small brew basket overflowed, pouring coffee and grounds onto its power button, which stuck "on." The carafe was the best heat retainer of the lineup and was easy to pour from.
BREVILLE YouBrew Drip Coffee Maker with Built-In Grinder MODEL: BDC600XL PRICE: $279.95 AVERAGE BREW TIME: 10 min, 57 sec BREW TEMPERATURE IN IDEAL RANGE: 16% WATER CAPACITY: 60 oz	BREW FLAVOR: ★½ DESIGN: ★ CARAFE: ★★	This is a pricey grind-and-brew machine that does the thinking for you—after you fuss with the endless customizable options. It spent a measly 16 percent of its long brew cycle in the ideal temperature zone—no wonder the coffee tasted "weak" and "bitter." Most important, the brew basket is too small to hold the SCAA-recommended amount of coffee when brewing a full pot.
MR. COFFEE Optimal Brew Thermal Coffeemaker, 10 Cup MODEL: BVMC-PSTX91 PRICE: $69.99 AVERAGE BREW TIME: 7 min, 41 sec BREW TEMPERATURE IN IDEAL RANGE: 63% WATER CAPACITY: 50 oz	BREW FLAVOR: ½ DESIGN: ★ CARAFE: ★★★	By calling for far less than the SCAA-recommended amount of grounds, this machine made "dishwater." With the right amount of coffee for a full pot, the grounds overflowed the filter. Also, the basket's side drawer must be pulled out completely to fill—annoying if your counter is small—and its reservoir acquired a musty smell we couldn't eradicate.

PRESSURE COOKERS

To find our favorite pressure cooker, we tested eight stovetop and four electric models, comparing size, shape, weight, ease of use, evenness of browning, cooking temperature, and evaporation levels. Overall, we preferred stovetop models; although electric models offer the convenience of being able to walk away, we found them to be smaller and less durable, and browning was a challenge. We liked models with thicker bottoms for even cooking, generous cooking surfaces, and simple, intuitive controls and pressure indicators. A size of at least 8 quarts was optimal for large batches of stocks and soups. Pressure cookers are listed in order of preference.

Stovetop Models

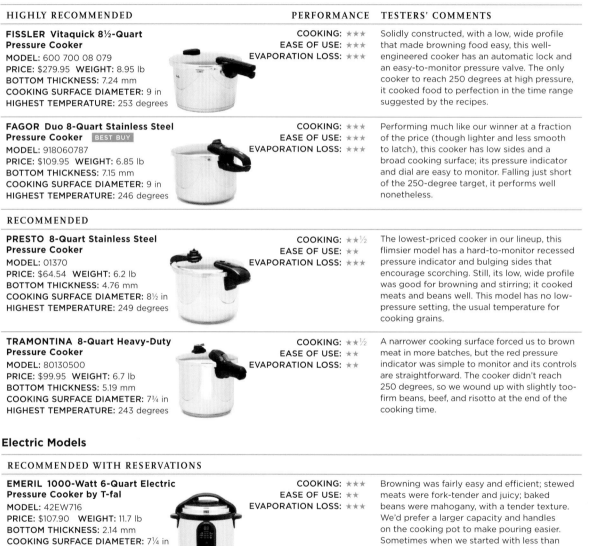

HIGHLY RECOMMENDED	PERFORMANCE	TESTERS' COMMENTS
FISSLER Vitaquick 8½-Quart **Pressure Cooker** MODEL: 600 700 08 079 PRICE: $279.95 WEIGHT: 8.95 lb BOTTOM THICKNESS: 7.24 mm COOKING SURFACE DIAMETER: 9 in HIGHEST TEMPERATURE: 253 degrees	COOKING: ★★★ EASE OF USE: ★★★ EVAPORATION LOSS: ★★★	Solidly constructed, with a low, wide profile that made browning food easy, this well-engineered cooker has an automatic lock and an easy-to-monitor pressure valve. The only cooker to reach 250 degrees at high pressure, it cooked food to perfection in the time range suggested by the recipes.
FAGOR Duo 8-Quart Stainless Steel **Pressure Cooker** `BEST BUY` MODEL: 918060787 PRICE: $109.95 WEIGHT: 6.85 lb BOTTOM THICKNESS: 7.15 mm COOKING SURFACE DIAMETER: 9 in HIGHEST TEMPERATURE: 246 degrees	COOKING: ★★★ EASE OF USE: ★★★ EVAPORATION LOSS: ★★★	Performing much like our winner at a fraction of the price (though lighter and less smooth to latch), this cooker has low sides and a broad cooking surface; its pressure indicator and dial are easy to monitor. Falling just short of the 250-degree target, it performs well nonetheless.

RECOMMENDED	PERFORMANCE	TESTERS' COMMENTS
PRESTO 8-Quart Stainless Steel **Pressure Cooker** MODEL: 01370 PRICE: $64.54 WEIGHT: 6.2 lb BOTTOM THICKNESS: 4.76 mm COOKING SURFACE DIAMETER: 8½ in HIGHEST TEMPERATURE: 249 degrees	COOKING: ★★½ EASE OF USE: ★★ EVAPORATION LOSS: ★★★	The lowest-priced cooker in our lineup, this flimsier model has a hard-to-monitor recessed pressure indicator and bulging sides that encourage scorching. Still, its low, wide profile was good for browning and stirring; it cooked meats and beans well. This model has no low-pressure setting, the usual temperature for cooking grains.
TRAMONTINA 8-Quart Heavy-Duty **Pressure Cooker** MODEL: 80130500 PRICE: $99.95 WEIGHT: 6.7 lb BOTTOM THICKNESS: 5.19 mm COOKING SURFACE DIAMETER: 7¾ in HIGHEST TEMPERATURE: 243 degrees	COOKING: ★★½ EASE OF USE: ★★ EVAPORATION LOSS: ★★	A narrower cooking surface forced us to brown meat in more batches, but the red pressure indicator was simple to monitor and its controls are straightforward. The cooker didn't reach 250 degrees, so we wound up with slightly too-firm beans, beef, and risotto at the end of the cooking time.

Electric Models

RECOMMENDED WITH RESERVATIONS	PERFORMANCE	TESTERS' COMMENTS
EMERIL 1000-Watt 6-Quart Electric **Pressure Cooker by T-fal** MODEL: 42EW716 PRICE: $107.90 WEIGHT: 11.7 lb BOTTOM THICKNESS: 2.14 mm COOKING SURFACE DIAMETER: 7¼ in HEIGHT OF SIDES: 6¼ in HIGHEST TEMPERATURE: 245 degrees	COOKING: ★★★ EASE OF USE: ★★ EVAPORATION LOSS: ★★★	Browning was fairly easy and efficient; stewed meats were fork-tender and juicy; baked beans were mahogany, with a tender texture. We'd prefer a larger capacity and handles on the cooking pot to make pouring easier. Sometimes when we started with less than 2 cups of liquid, the pot switched to "keep warm" mode.
CUISINART 1000-Watt 6-Quart **Electric Pressure Cooker** MODEL: CPC-600 PRICE: $96 WEIGHT: 12.15 lb BOTTOM THICKNESS: 2.5 mm COOKING SURFACE DIAMETER: 7¼ in HEIGHT OF SIDES: 6¼ in HIGHEST TEMPERATURE: 241 degrees	COOKING: ★★★ EASE OF USE: ★★ EVAPORATION LOSS: ★★½	This model is very similar to the Emeril model in design and cooking (food was slightly less stellar but still quite good). It allowed more evaporation, and we would prefer a larger capacity and less-slippery liner. Sometimes when we started with less than 2 cups of liquid, the pot switched to "keep warm" mode.

BLENDERS

When you come right down to it, a blender has one job—to blend food into a uniform consistency, whether it's crushing ice or producing perfect purees for soups, smoothies, or hummus. To find the best blender for any task, we corralled nine models and put them to the test. Some flat-out failed at ice crushing. Others barely sputtered their way through milkshakes. Fibrous frozen pineapple and mango and stringy raw kale bested several machines. But two models plowed through every task without flinching. Blenders are listed in order of preference.

HIGHLY RECOMMENDED

VITAMIX 5200
MODEL: 5200
PRICE: $449

PERFORMANCE

DURABILITY: ★★★
SPEED: ★★½
NOISE: ★★½

HUMMUS: ★★½
FRUIT SMOOTHIE: ★★★
KALE SMOOTHIE: ★★★
MILKSHAKE: ★★½
MARGARITA: ★★★
ICE CRUSHING: ★★★

TESTERS' COMMENTS

Years of hard-core test kitchen use have not compromised this blender's superior performance. Its hummus and milkshakes weren't as silky-smooth as others, but its 1,380-watt motor propelled it through most tasks with ease.

RECOMMENDED

BREVILLE The Hemisphere Control `BEST BUY`
MODEL: BBL605XL
PRICE: $199.99

DURABILITY: ★★½
SPEED: ★★½
NOISE: ★★★

HUMMUS: ★★★
FRUIT SMOOTHIE: ★★★
KALE SMOOTHIE: ★★½
MILKSHAKE: ★★
MARGARITA: ★★★
ICE CRUSHING: ★★★

With a curved jar, six well-configured blades, and a relatively powerful (750-watt) motor, this blender excelled at almost every task—and it's less than half the cost of our winner.

RECOMMENDED WITH RESERVATIONS

NINJA Professional Blender
MODEL: NJ600
PRICE: $99.99

DURABILITY: ★★
SPEED: ★★★
NOISE: ★½

HUMMUS: ★★★
FRUIT SMOOTHIE: ★★½
KALE SMOOTHIE: ★
MILKSHAKE: ★★½
MARGARITA: ★★
ICE CRUSHING: ★★★

This 1,000-watt blender, with a central shaft bearing three sets of food processor-like blades, crushed ice in 7 seconds. Unfortunately, it left margaritas crunchy and couldn't fully break down tough, fibrous kale.

HAMILTON BEACH Rio Commercial Bar Blender
MODEL: HBB250R
PRICE: $109.99

DURABILITY: ★★★
SPEED: ★★
NOISE: ★

HUMMUS: ★★★
FRUIT SMOOTHIE: ★★★
KALE SMOOTHIE: ★★
MILKSHAKE: ★
MARGARITA: ★★½
ICE CRUSHING: ★

This low-cost, moderately powered (480-watt) blender was a whiz with hummus and fruit smoothies. But its fluted jar trapped ice cubes, and its four short, poorly positioned blades couldn't reach kale without a good spatula push.

NOT RECOMMENDED

CUISINART Blend and Cook Soup Maker
MODEL: SBC-1000
PRICE: $199

DURABILITY: ★★
SPEED: ★½
NOISE: ★★

HUMMUS: ★★★
FRUIT SMOOTHIE: ★★
KALE SMOOTHIE: ★★
MILKSHAKE: ★
MARGARITA: ★★
ICE CRUSHING: ★★

While it had six blades and plenty of power (900 watts), the large, flat bottom of the jar didn't do this machine any favors. It made excellent hummus but failed to blend a shake, emitting a burning smell as it tried.

HAMILTON BEACH Wave Maker 2-Speed Blender
MODEL: 53205
PRICE: $39.99

DURABILITY: ★★
SPEED: ★½
NOISE: ★★★

HUMMUS: ★★
FRUIT SMOOTHIE: ★★
KALE SMOOTHIE: ★
MILKSHAKE: ★
MARGARITA: ★½
ICE CRUSHING: ★

Thanks to its flat-bottomed jar and four very short blades that were not only symmetrical but also set directly atop one another, this 360-watt blender either struggled or flat-out failed to perform most tasks.

OSTER 7-SPEED Reversing Motor Blender
MODEL: BVCB07-Z
PRICE: $59.99

DURABILITY: ★
SPEED: ★
NOISE: ★

HUMMUS: ★
FRUIT SMOOTHIE: ★★★
KALE SMOOTHIE: ★½
MILKSHAKE: ★
MARGARITA: ★★★
ICE CRUSHING: ★½

This model had six blades and a pretty strong motor (600 watts), but the jar tapered so dramatically that large chunks and thick food couldn't reach the blades. Its performance declined during testing.

TWO-SLOT TOASTERS

To find a dependable toaster, we lined up 10 toasters from major brands and toasted more than 1,000 slices of sandwich bread. Then we tackled bagels, toaster pastries, English muffins, and frozen waffles. Overall, the results were disappointing. At the very least, toasters should pop out nicely browned bread in the shade that you select. But that's just where most fail. Set to "light," every toaster in our lineup produced pale, slightly warm slices. A few made medium toast only when they were set on "dark." And on "dark" settings, the toast often burned. Others rendered all three shades across a single slice or toasted only one side properly. Just one toaster out of seven earned perfect marks. Toasters are listed in order of preference.

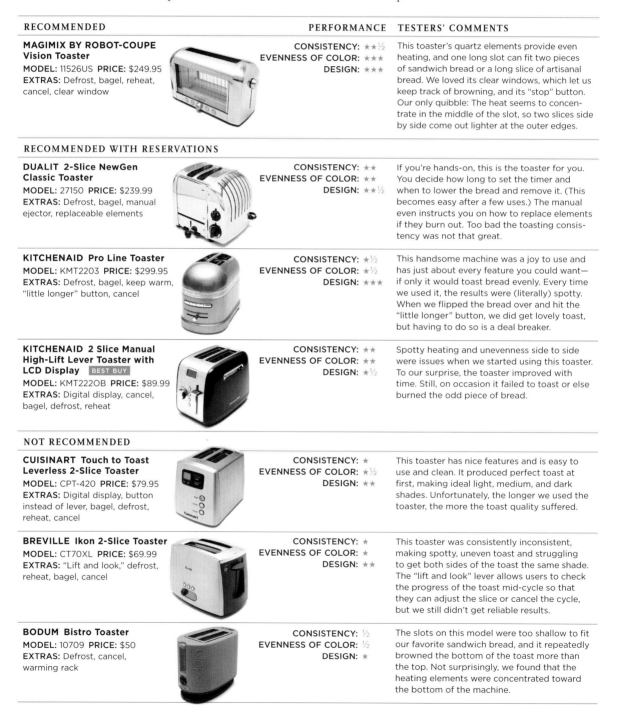

RECOMMENDED

	PERFORMANCE	TESTERS' COMMENTS
MAGIMIX BY ROBOT-COUPE Vision Toaster **MODEL:** 11526US **PRICE:** $249.95 **EXTRAS:** Defrost, bagel, reheat, cancel, clear window	CONSISTENCY: ★★½ EVENNESS OF COLOR: ★★★ DESIGN: ★★★	This toaster's quartz elements provide even heating, and one long slot can fit two pieces of sandwich bread or a long slice of artisanal bread. We loved its clear windows, which let us keep track of browning, and its "stop" button. Our only quibble: The heat seems to concentrate in the middle of the slot, so two slices side by side come out lighter at the outer edges.

RECOMMENDED WITH RESERVATIONS

	PERFORMANCE	TESTERS' COMMENTS
DUALIT 2-Slice NewGen Classic Toaster **MODEL:** 27150 **PRICE:** $239.99 **EXTRAS:** Defrost, bagel, manual ejector, replaceable elements	CONSISTENCY: ★★ EVENNESS OF COLOR: ★★ DESIGN: ★★½	If you're hands-on, this is the toaster for you. You decide how long to set the timer and when to lower the bread and remove it. (This becomes easy after a few uses.) The manual even instructs you on how to replace elements if they burn out. Too bad the toasting consistency was not that great.
KITCHENAID Pro Line Toaster **MODEL:** KMT2203 **PRICE:** $299.95 **EXTRAS:** Defrost, bagel, keep warm, "little longer" button, cancel	CONSISTENCY: ★½ EVENNESS OF COLOR: ★½ DESIGN: ★★★	This handsome machine was a joy to use and has just about every feature you could want— if only it would toast bread evenly. Every time we used it, the results were (literally) spotty. When we flipped the bread over and hit the "little longer" button, we did get lovely toast, but having to do so is a deal breaker.
KITCHENAID 2 Slice Manual High-Lift Lever Toaster with LCD Display `BEST BUY` **MODEL:** KMT222OB **PRICE:** $89.99 **EXTRAS:** Digital display, cancel, bagel, defrost, reheat	CONSISTENCY: ★★ EVENNESS OF COLOR: ★★ DESIGN: ★½	Spotty heating and unevenness side to side were issues when we started using this toaster. To our surprise, the toaster improved with time. Still, on occasion it failed to toast or else burned the odd piece of bread.

NOT RECOMMENDED

	PERFORMANCE	TESTERS' COMMENTS
CUISINART Touch to Toast Leverless 2-Slice Toaster **MODEL:** CPT-420 **PRICE:** $79.95 **EXTRAS:** Digital display, button instead of lever, bagel, defrost, reheat, cancel	CONSISTENCY: ★ EVENNESS OF COLOR: ★½ DESIGN: ★★	This toaster has nice features and is easy to use and clean. It produced perfect toast at first, making ideal light, medium, and dark shades. Unfortunately, the longer we used the toaster, the more the toast quality suffered.
BREVILLE Ikon 2-Slice Toaster **MODEL:** CT70XL **PRICE:** $69.99 **EXTRAS:** "Lift and look," defrost, reheat, bagel, cancel	CONSISTENCY: ★ EVENNESS OF COLOR: ★ DESIGN: ★★	This toaster was consistently inconsistent, making spotty, uneven toast and struggling to get both sides of the toast the same shade. The "lift and look" lever allows users to check the progress of the toast mid-cycle so that they can adjust the slice or cancel the cycle, but we still didn't get reliable results.
BODUM Bistro Toaster **MODEL:** 10709 **PRICE:** $50 **EXTRAS:** Defrost, cancel, warming rack	CONSISTENCY: ½ EVENNESS OF COLOR: ½ DESIGN: ★	The slots on this model were too shallow to fit our favorite sandwich bread, and it repeatedly browned the bottom of the toast more than the top. Not surprisingly, we found that the heating elements were concentrated toward the bottom of the machine.

CHARCOAL GRILLS

In search of a well-engineered, user-friendly charcoal grill that's up to any outdoor cooking task, we lined up seven models. Our battery of tests included burgers, sticky glazed beef satay, thick salmon fillets, and barbecued ribs. To check their height, we shut each grill's lid over a whole turkey; we monitored temperature retention; and we kept track of how easy the grills were to set up and to clean up. Grills are listed in order of preference.

HIGHLY RECOMMENDED	PERFORMANCE	TESTERS' COMMENTS
WEBER Performer Platinum 22.5-Inch Charcoal Grill with Touch-n-Go Gas Ignition MODEL: 1481001 PRICE: $349 GRATE: Steel, 363 sq in FAVORITE FEATURES: Push-button gas ignition, rolling cart, charcoal storage bin, Tuck-Away lid holder, ash catcher, thermometer	GRILLING: ★★★ BBQ/HEAT RETENTION: ★★★ DESIGN: ★★★ ASSEMBLY: ★★★ CLEANUP: ★★★ CAPACITY: ★★★ CONSTRUCTION QUALITY: ★★★	The convenience of gas plus the flavor of charcoal makes this grill a worthwhile (albeit pricey) upgrade from the basic model. Built around our favorite 22.5-inch Weber kettle is a roomy, easy-to-roll cart (much sturdier than the kettle's legs) with a pullout charcoal storage bin; a lid holder; and, most significant, a gas ignition system that lights coals with the push of a button—no chimney starter needed.
WEBER One-Touch Gold 22.5-Inch Charcoal Grill BEST BUY MODEL: 1351001 PRICE: $149 GRATE: Steel, 363 sq in FAVORITE FEATURES: Ash catcher, thermometer (on newest model), hinged grate	GRILLING: ★★★ BBQ/HEAT RETENTION: ★★★ DESIGN: ★★½ ASSEMBLY: ★★★ CLEANUP: ★★★ CAPACITY: ★★★ CONSTRUCTION QUALITY: ★★½	Weber's versatile, well-designed classic kettle was an expert griller and maintained heat well, and its well-positioned vents allowed for excellent air control. The sturdy ash catcher makes cleanup a breeze, and it was the fastest and easiest model to assemble and move. We wish its tripod legs were sturdier and that the hinged portions of its grate were slightly larger.

RECOMMENDED		
RÖSLE 24-Inch Charcoal Grill MODEL: 25004 PRICE: $400 GRATE: Steel, 416 sq in FAVORITE FEATURES: Ash catcher, lever that marks vent position, hinged lid, thermometer	GRILLING: ★★★ BBQ/HEAT RETENTION: ★★ DESIGN: ★★½ ASSEMBLY: ★★★ CLEANUP: ★★★ CAPACITY: ★★★ CONSTRUCTION QUALITY: ★★★	This pricey kettle is sturdier than the Weber One-Touch and offers more cooking space, plus a few perks: a lever that marks vent positions and a hinged lid. But while it grilled well, its roomy interior lost heat relatively quickly. Its top vent sits in the center of the lid—a disadvantage for indirect cooking.
STOK Tower Charcoal Grill MODEL: SCC0140 PRICE: $122 GRATE: Cast iron, 363 sq in FAVORITE FEATURES: Cast-iron grate, built-in chimney starter, thermometer	GRILLING: ★★★ BBQ/HEAT RETENTION: ★★½ DESIGN: ★★ ASSEMBLY: ★★ CLEANUP: ★★ CAPACITY: ★★ CONSTRUCTION QUALITY: ★★	Its cast-iron grate is just as big as the Weber's (and seared beautifully), but everything else about this inexpensive kettle is small—from its footprint to the space above and below the grates. Consequently, it holds heat well but struggles with indirect cooking since there is little room for a cooler zone. We appreciated its built-in chimney starter.

RECOMMENDED WITH RESERVATIONS		
BRINKMANN Trailmaster Limited Edition Grill and Smoker MODEL: 855-6305-S PRICE: $299 GRATE: Steel, 938 sq in FAVORITE FEATURE: Small firebox for smoking, thermometer	GRILLING: ★★ BBQ/HEAT RETENTION: ★★ DESIGN: ★½ ASSEMBLY: ★★ CLEANUP: ★ CAPACITY: ★ CONSTRUCTION QUALITY: ★★★	This grill-smoker combo boasts plenty of cooking surface (including a separate firebox for smoking), but since opening the lid uncovered only part of that space, visibility was limited and smoke blew into our eyes. Without an ash catcher, shoveling is the only option. Also, it's a big, heavy beast: Moving it was a chore, and storing it was a challenge.

NOT RECOMMENDED		
CHAR-BROIL 30-Inch Charcoal Grill MODEL: 12301672 PRICE: $199 GRATE: Cast iron, 504 sq in FAVORITE FEATURES: Crank for adjusting coal height, rolling cart, cast-iron grate, flip-up side shelves, thermometer, warming shelf	GRILLING: ★★½ BBQ/HEAT RETENTION: ½ DESIGN: ★★ ASSEMBLY: ½ CLEANUP: ★★ CAPACITY: ★★★ CONSTRUCTION QUALITY: ★	This grill was a heartbreaker. Though outfitted with great features—a crank that adjusts coal height, a high lid, cast-iron cooking grates, a "keep-warm" shelf, and flip-up side tables—its cheap construction defeated it at every turn. Paper-thin walls and an ill-fitting lid leaked heat (barbecued ribs were not quite finished after 4 hours). Assembly took hours. When it rolled, it rattled horribly.

CONVERSIONS & EQUIVALENCIES

SOME SAY COOKING IS A SCIENCE AND AN ART. We would say that geography has a hand in it, too. Flour milled in the United Kingdom and elsewhere will feel and taste different from flour milled in the United States. So, while we cannot promise that the loaf of bread you bake in Canada or England will taste the same as a loaf baked in the States, we can offer guidelines for converting weights and measures. We also recommend that you rely on your instincts when making our recipes. Refer to the visual cues provided. If the bread dough hasn't "come together in a ball," as described, you may need to add more flour—even if the recipe doesn't tell you so. You be the judge.

The recipes in this book were developed using standard U.S. measures following U.S. government guidelines. The charts below offer equivalents for U.S., metric, and imperial (U.K.) measures. All conversions are approximate and have been rounded up or down to the nearest whole number. For example:

1 teaspoon = 4.929 milliliters, rounded up to 5 milliliters
1 ounce = 28.349 grams, rounded down to 28 grams

VOLUME CONVERSIONS

U.S.	METRIC
1 teaspoon	5 milliliters
2 teaspoons	10 milliliters
1 tablespoon	15 milliliters
2 tablespoons	30 milliliters
¼ cup	59 milliliters
⅓ cup	79 milliliters
½ cup	118 milliliters
¾ cup	177 milliliters
1 cup	237 milliliters
1¼ cups	296 milliliters
1½ cups	355 milliliters
2 cups	473 milliliters
2½ cups	591 milliliters
3 cups	710 milliliters
4 cups (1 quart)	0.946 liter
1.06 quarts	1 liter
4 quarts (1 gallon)	3.8 liters

WEIGHT CONVERSIONS

OUNCES	GRAMS
½	14
¾	21
1	28
1½	43
2	57
2½	71
3	85
3½	99
4	113
4½	128
5	142
6	170
7	198
8	227
9	255
10	283
12	340
16 (1 pound)	454

CONVERSIONS FOR INGREDIENTS COMMONLY USED IN BAKING

Baking is an exacting science. Because measuring by weight is far more accurate than measuring by volume, and thus more likely to achieve reliable results, in our recipes we provide ounce measures in addition to cup measures for many ingredients. Refer to the chart below to convert these measures into grams.

INGREDIENT	OUNCES	GRAMS
Flour		
1 cup all-purpose flour*	5	142
1 cup cake flour	4	113
1 cup whole wheat flour	5½	156
Sugar		
1 cup granulated (white) sugar	7	198
1 cup packed brown sugar (light or dark)	7	198
1 cup confectioners' sugar	4	113
Cocoa Powder		
1 cup cocoa powder	3	85
Butter†		
4 tablespoons (½ stick, or ¼ cup)	2	57
8 tablespoons (1 stick, or ½ cup)	4	113
16 tablespoons (2 sticks, or 1 cup)	8	227

* U.S. all-purpose flour, the most frequently used flour in this book, does not contain leaveners, as some European flours do. These leavened flours are called self-rising or self-raising. If you are using self-rising flour, take this into consideration before adding leavening to a recipe.

† In the United States, butter is sold both salted and unsalted. We generally recommend unsalted butter. If you are using salted butter, take this into consideration before adding salt to a recipe.

OVEN TEMPERATURES

FAHRENHEIT	CELSIUS	GAS MARK (imperial)
225	105	¼
250	120	½
275	135	1
300	150	2
325	165	3
350	180	4
375	190	5
400	200	6
425	220	7
450	230	8
475	245	9

CONVERTING TEMPERATURES FROM AN INSTANT-READ THERMOMETER

We include doneness temperatures in many of our recipes, such as those for poultry, meat, and bread. We recommend an instant-read thermometer for the job. Refer to the table above to convert Fahrenheit degrees to Celsius. Or, for temperatures not represented in the chart, use this simple formula:

Subtract 32 degrees from the Fahrenheit reading, then divide the result by 1.8 to find the Celsius reading.

EXAMPLE:

"Roast chicken until thighs register 175 degrees."
To convert:

175° F − 32 = 143°
143° ÷ 1.8 = 79.44°C, rounded down to 79°C

INDEX

J

K

L

M